POLICY, REGULATION, AND INNOVATION IN CHINA'S ELECTRICITY AND TELECOM INDUSTRIES

The scale of China's innovation ambitions inspires worldwide commentary, much of it poorly informed. Focusing on electricity, telecommunication, and semiconductors, this book offers a focused and detailed account of China's effort to promote innovation. Massive application of human, policy, and financial resources shows great promise, but institutional obstacles, conflicting objectives, ill-advised policies, and Soviet-era legacies inject inefficiencies, resulting in a complex mosaic of success and failure in both technical and commercial dimensions. Thus, State Grid leads the world in high-voltage power transmission, while domestic semiconductors remain far behind the international frontier. China's electricity and telecom providers record impressive technical advances, but excess investment and inefficient operation contribute to high costs and prices. Nuclear power displays an unexpected combination of technical excellence and commercial weakness. Cost reduction rather than technical advance underpins commercial success in solar materials. These granular studies look beyond specific technologies to incorporate the policy matrix, regulatory structures, and global technical developments into the appraisal of China's innovation prospects.

Loren Brandt, a China specialist, is the Noranda Chair Professor of Economics and International Trade at the University of Toronto. His current research focuses on issues of industrial upgrading and development, China's long- run economic growth, and inequality dynamics.

Thomas G. Rawski is Emeritus Professor of Economics and History at the University of Pittsburgh. His research focuses on the development and modern history of China's economy. His publications include a 2008 volume, *China's Great Economic Transformation*, co-edited with Loren Brandt.

Policy, Regulation, and Innovation in China's Electricity and Telecom Industries

Edited by

LOREN BRANDT

University of Toronto

THOMAS G. RAWSKI

University of Pittsburgh

CAMBRIDGE
UNIVERSITY PRESS

CAMBRIDGE
UNIVERSITY PRESS

University Printing House, Cambridge CB2 8BS, United Kingdom

One Liberty Plaza, 20th Floor, New York, NY 10006, USA

477 Williamstown Road, Port Melbourne, VIC 3207, Australia

314–321, 3rd Floor, Plot 3, Splendor Forum, Jasola District Centre,
New Delhi – 110025, India

79 Anson Road, #06–04/06, Singapore 079906

Cambridge University Press is part of the University of Cambridge.

It furthers the University's mission by disseminating knowledge in the pursuit of
education, learning, and research at the highest international levels of excellence.

www.cambridge.org
Information on this title: www.cambridge.org/9781108480994
DOI: 10.1017/9781108645997

© Cambridge University Press 2019

First published 2019

Printed in the United Kingdom by TJ International Ltd, Padstow Cornwall

A catalogue record for this publication is available from the British Library.

Library of Congress Cataloging-in-Publication Data
Names: Brandt, Loren, editor. | Rawski, Thomas G., 1943– editor.
Title: Policy, regulation and innovation in China's electricity and telecom industries / edited
by Loren Brandt, University of Toronto, Thomas G. Rawski, University of Pittsburgh.
Description: Cambridge, United Kingdom ; New York, NY : Cambridge University Press,
2019.
Identifiers: LCCN 2018055388 | ISBN 9781108480994 (hardback)
Subjects: LCSH: Electric utilities – China. | Telecommunication – China.
Classification: LCC HD9685.C62 P65 2019 | DDC 333.793/20951–dc23
LC record available at https://lccn.loc.gov/2018055388

ISBN 978-1-108-48099-4 Hardback
ISBN 978-1-108-70369-7 Paperback

Contents

Figures

Tables

ix

Contributors

Loren Brandt is the Noranda Chair Professor of Economics and International Trade at the University of Toronto. With Thomas Rawski, he was co-editor and major contributor to *China's Great Economic Transformation* (Cambridge University Press, 2008), which provides an integrated analysis of China's unexpected economic boom. His current research focuses on issues of industrial upgrading and development, China's long-run economic growth, and inequality dynamics.

Michael Davidson is a post-doctoral fellow in the Harvard Kennedy School's Belfer Center for Science and International Affairs. Michael studies the engineering implications and political conflicts of building electricity market institutions and deploying renewable energy at scale, with a focus on China and India. His modeling work has appeared in various publications including *Nature Energy*, and he was a contributor to *The Political Economy of Clean Energy Transitions* (2017). He holds a PhD in engineering systems from the Massachusetts Institute of Technology.

Douglas B. Fuller is an associate professor at City University of Hong Kong. He is the author of *Paper Tigers, Hidden Dragons: Firms and the Political Economy of China's Technological Development* (2016) among other works, and his main research interests are China, technology policy, and the political economy of development.

Ravi Madhavan is Professor of Business Administration, Alcoa Foundation International Faculty Fellow, and Director of the International Business Center at the Joseph M. Katz Graduate School of Business, University of Pittsburgh. Ravi studies how networks drive complex capabilities, with current field work focused on Chinese investments in two systems integration industries, nuclear power, and commercial aircraft. Ravi has published papers in premier Management journals such as *Academy of Management Review, Journal of International Business Studies, Strategic Management Journal*, and *Academy of Management Journal*, and has received research grants from the National Science Foundation and the Alfred P. Sloan Foundation.

Margaret M. Pearson is Professor and Distinguished Scholar-Teacher in the Department of Government and Politics, University of Maryland. She is author (with Scott Kastner and Chad Rector) of *China's Strategic Multilateralism: Investing in Global Governance* (Cambridge University Press, 2018).

Thomas G. Rawski is Emeritus Professor of Economics and History at the University of Pittsburgh. His research focuses on the development and modern history of China's economy, including studies of China's reform mechanism and achievements, as well as analyses focused on productivity, investment, industry, trade, energy, labor markets, environment, and economic measurement. Recent publications include (with Hinh Dinh, Ali Zafar, Lihong Wang, and Eleonora Mavroeidi) *Tales from the Development Frontier* (2013) and, with Loren Brandt (co-editor and contributor), *China's Great Economic Transformation* (Cambridge University Press, 2008).

Timothy Sturgeon is senior researcher at the at the Massachusetts Institute of Technology's Industrial Performance Center (IPC). His research focuses on the processes of global economic integration, with an emphasis on offshoring and outsourcing practices in the electronics, automotive, and services industries. His work explores how evolving technologies and business models are altering linkages between industrialized and developing economies. His work appears in international peer-reviewed journals including *Studies in Comparative International Development, Industrial and Corporate Change, Review of International Political Economy, Journal of East Asian Studies*, and *Journal of Economic Geography*.

Eric Thun is the Peter Moores Associate Professor in Chinese Business at Oxford's Saïd Business School and a Fellow of Brasenose College, Oxford. His areas of expertise include business in China, industrial development and upgrading in China, and the Chinese political economy, as well as global strategy and global value chains. He is the author of *Changing Lanes in China: Foreign Direct Investment, Local Governments and Auto Sector Development* (Cambridge University Press, 2005).

Qingfeng Tian is Associate Professor of Business Administration in the School of Management at Northwestern Polytechnical University, Xi'an, China. He also works at China's National Center for Science and Technology Evaluation. His research focuses on Chinese case studies of large commercial aircraft manufacture and civil nuclear power, including complex capability formation, business model innovation, knowledge management, and management systems. His current work includes studies of internationalization of business models among China's high-end equipment manufacturers, China's civil-military integration strategy, and innovation models and mechanisms within China's comprehensive innovation reform.

Luhang Wang is Assistant Professor of Economics in the School of Economics and Wang Yanan Institute for Studies in Economics at Xiamen University, China. She received her PhD in economics from the University of Toronto in 2013. She specializes in studies of international trade and the Chinese economy. She co-authored "WTO and the Effect of Trade Liberalization on Productivity in Chinese Manufacturing," which appeared in the *American Economic Review* (2017).

Irene S. Wu is a senior analyst in the International Section of the US Federal Communications Commission and teaches at Georgetown University's Communications, Culture, and Technology Program. Recently, she was a fellow at the Woodrow Wilson Center for International Scholars researching how to measure soft power resources in the international system. She is author of *Forging Trust Communities: How Technology Changes Politics* (2015) and *From Iron Fist to Invisible Hand: The Uneven Path of Telecommunications Reform in China* (2009). She holds degrees from Harvard and Johns Hopkins School of Advanced International Studies.

XU Yi-chong is a professor in the School of Government and International Relations at Griffith University in Brisbane, Australia. Her recent books include *Sinews of Power: the Politics of the State Grid Corporation of China* (2017) and (with Patrick Weller), *The Working World of International Organisations* (2018).

Acknowledgments

This volume reflects a long process that benefited from the contributions of many individuals and organizations whose names do not appear in the List of Contributors. Our greatest obligation is to the Smith Richardson Foundation, which provided generous and patient support that permitted project members to conduct unusually intensive fieldwork. The University of Pittsburgh and the University of Toronto contributed both financially and administratively. Zhang Wenkui and Liu Qilin provided indispensable advice and introductions. Regina Abrami, Scott Kennedy, Qiang Zhi, and Richard P. Suttmeier joined in the project's initial stages. As the project approached completion, extensive comments from several anonymous reviewers and advice from many individuals at Cambridge University Press, especially Karen Maloney and Rachel Blaifeder, enabled us to improve the final product. Rebecca Collins, Jim Diggins and Gayathri Tamilselvan provided expert editorial support.

L. B. and T. G. R.
September 2018

Abbreviations

3GPP	Third Generation Partnership Project
A&T	assembly and testing
AC	alternating current
AI	artificial intelligence
ARM	a UK-based semiconductor design house
ARPU	average revenue per use
ASME	American Society of Mechanical Engineers
AUSC	advanced ultra super-critical
BTU	British thermal unit
CATT	China Academy of Telecommunications Technology
CCTV	China Central Television
CDB	China Development Bank
CDM	(United Nations) Clean Development Mechanism
CDMA	one of several technical interconnect standards for 2G wireless telecom networks
CEC	China Electricity Council
CFIUS	Committee on Foreign Investment in the United States
CGN	China General Nuclear Corporation, formerly China Guangdong Nuclear
CHFI	China First Heavy Industries
CIC	China industrial classification
CIGRE	International Council on Large Electric Systems
CMOS	complementary metal oxide semiconductor
CNNC	China National Nuclear Corporation
CPI	China Power Investment Corporation
CPU	central processing unit
CSMC	Central Semiconductor Manufacturing Corporation

DC	direct current
DRAM	dynamic random-access memory
DRC	Development Research Center of the State Council
EDA	electronic design automation
EDF	Électricité de France
EED	energy-efficiency dispatch
EIA	US Energy Information Administration
EPRI	Electric Power Research Institute
ERCOT	Electricity Reliability Council of Texas
EV	electric vehicle
FCC	Federal Communications Commission (United States)
FDD	Frequency Division Duplexing
FDI	foreign direct investment
FIT	feed-in tariff
FYP	Five-Year Plan
GCE	grams of coal equivalent
GDP	Gross Domestic Product
GDSII	Gerber Data Stream Information Interchange
GEI	Global Energy Interconnection
GEIDCO	Global Energy Interconnection Development and Cooperation Organization
GMS	Google mobile services
GNI	Gross National Income
GPU	graphics processing unit
GSM	one of two technical standards for China's 2G telecom networks
GVC	global value chain
GW	gigawatt
GWe	gigawatt electrical
GWh	gigawatt hour
HHNEC	Huahong-NEC, a Sino–Japanese joint venture firm
HS	Harmonized Commodity Code and Classification System
HTDZ	high technology development zone
HTGR	High Temperature Gas-cooled Reactor
HVAC	high-voltage alternating current
HVDC	high-voltage direct current
IAEA	International Atomic Energy Agency
IC	integrated circuit
ICT	information and communications technology

IDM	integrated device manufacturer
IEA	International Energy Agency
IEEE	Institute of Electrical and Electronics Engineers
IGCC	integrated gasification combined cycle
IP	intellectual property
IPO	initial public offering
IPTV	Internet Protocol television
IRENA	International Renewable Energy Agency
ISC	Internet Society of China
ITRS	International Technology Roadmap of Semiconductors
ITU	International Telecommunications Union
JV	joint venture
KM	kilometers
KV	kilovolt
KW	kilowatt
KWh	kilowatt hour
LED	light-emitting diode
LTE	Long-Term Evolution (standard for high-speed wireless communication)
LTE-FDD	Long-Term Evolution – Frequency Division Duplexing: 4G standard evolved from Chinese 3G standard (TDCDMA)
LTE-TDD	Long-Term Evolution – Time Division Duplexing: 4G standard evolved from global 3G standard (CDMA)
MCI	Microwave Communications Inc.
MEP	Ministry of Electric Power
MIC 2025	Made in China 2025
MII	(former) Ministry of Information Industry
MIIT	Ministry of Industry and Information Technology
MITI	Ministry of International Trade and Industry (Japan)
MLP	2006 Medium- and Long-Term Plan for the Development of Science and Technology
MNC	multinational corporation
MOST	Ministry of Science and Technology
MOU	memorandum of understanding
MOX	mixed oxide fuel
MPT	Ministry of Post and Telecommunications
MSS	Ministry of State Security
MTK	MediaTek, a Taiwan-based chip design company
MVNO	mobile virtual network operators

MW	megawatt
MWh	megawatt hour
NAND	not-AND memory
NARI	Nanjing Automation Research Institute
NBS	National Bureau of Statistics
NDRC	National Development and Reform Commission
NEA	National Energy Agency
NEC	Nippon Electric Corporation (Japan)
NELG	National Energy Leading Group
NEV	new energy vehicles
NNSA	National Nuclear Safety Agency
NPP	nuclear power plant
NTT	Nippon Telephone and Telegraph Corporation (Japan)
OECD	Organization for Economic Cooperation and Development
PCT	Patent Cooperation Treaty
PHS	Personal Handy-phone Service
PLA	People's Liberation Army
PPP	purchasing-power parity
PRC	People's Republic of China
PV	photovoltaic
R&D	research and development
RDA	RDA Microelectronics, a fabless semiconductor company
RF	radio frequency
RFID	radio-frequency identification
RMB	Renminbi
ROA	return on assets
S&T	science and technology
SAIL	Shanghai Alliance Investment Limited
SAPPFRT	State Administration of Press, Publication, Radio, Film and Television
SARFT	State Administration of Radio, Film and Television
SASAC	State-owned Assets Supervisory and Administration Commission
SAT	State Administration of Taxation
SC	super-critical
SCDMA	Synchronous Code-Division Multiple Access
SEI	strategic emerging industry

SEMI	a global electronics manufacturing supply chain industry association
SERC	State Electricity Regulatory Commission
SGCC	State Grid Corporation of China
SGCET	China Electric Power Equipment and Technology Co. Ltd.
SIH	Shanghai Industrial Holdings
SMIC	Semiconductor Manufacturing International Corporation
SMIT	English name for Chinese firm, Guowei Jishu
SNPTC	State Nuclear Power Technology Corporation
SO$_2$	sulfur dioxide
SOC	system-on-chip
SOE	state-owned enterprise
SPC	State Power Corporation
SPI	State Power Investment Corporation
Sub	sub-critical
T&D	transmission and distribution (of electricity)
TDD	Time Division Duplexing
TD-LTE	4G iteration of time division technology
TD-SCDMA	Time Division Synchronous Code Division Multiple Access
TFP	total factor productivity
TRIMs	trade-related investment measures
TSMC	Taiwan Semiconductor Manufacturing Co. Ltd.
UF6	uranium hexafluoride
UHV	ultra-high voltage
UMC	United Microelectronics Corporation, a Taiwanese semiconductor company
USC	ultra super-critical
VAT	value-added tax
VC	venture capital
WANO	World Association of Nuclear Operators
WCDMA	Wide Band Code Division Multiple Access
WTO	World Trade Organization
XD	Xidian Group
XMC	Wuhan Xinxin Semiconductor Manufacturing Corporation
YMTC	Yangtze Memory Technology Corporation

Map of China

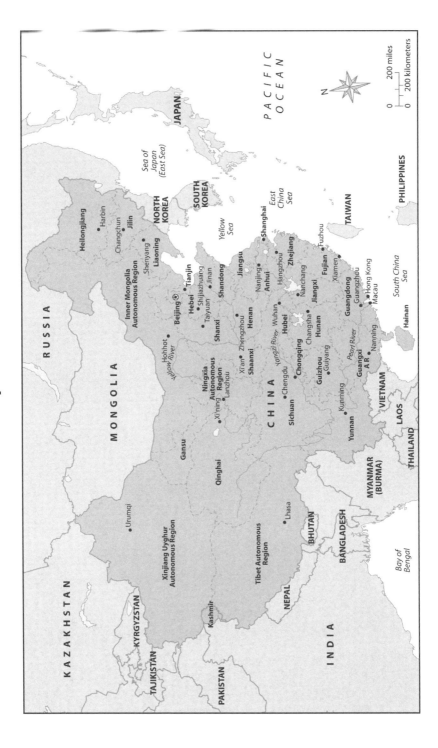

Policy, Regulation, and Innovation in China's Electricity and Telecom Industries

Loren Brandt and Thomas G. Rawski

Britain's industrial revolution spawned efforts by "followers" to match and surpass the achievements of leading firms and industries in advanced nations.[*] Two centuries later, the drive for industrial upgrading, which Nelson and Rosenberg (1993) define as "the processes by which firms master and get into practice product designs and manufacturing processes that are new to them, if not to the universe or even the nation," continues. There is a parallel history of governmental efforts to accelerate the progress of national firms and industries toward global best practice and, upon approaching the frontier, to enter the realm of original innovation.

China's unprecedented economic surge, now entering its fifth decade, adds a new dimension to the history of industrial upgrading and to ongoing debate over the effectiveness of supportive official actions. Growing evidence of Chinese technical prowess has inspired a jumble of observations, ranging from fears that shifting corporate research and development (R&D) activity to China "could destabilize the interaction of all the other parts of the [US] innovation ecosystem" (Segal 2011) or "destroy ... entire business models" (Kennedy 2017) to skeptics who "don't believe that China will lead in innovation anytime soon" (Sass 2014) and explain "why China can't innovate" (Abrami, Kirby, and McFarlan 2014). Comment on this vital dimension of China's economy bristles with stereotypes and unwarranted generalizations. China's industrial policy is routinely viewed as both ineffectual and threatening, sometimes on the same page![1]

[*] We gratefully acknowledge generous financial support from the Smith Richardson Foundation and from our home institutions.
[1] "Soviet planning cannot replicate the Silicon Valley. Ming Dynasty mindsets can't create microchips. Megaprojects ... are likely to end in a trail of tears. As more details of indigenous innovation plans emerge, American and European politicians are seeing an assault on their core national economic strengths" (McGregor 2010, p. 37).

Such wide disagreement reflects a knowledge gap that surrounds the fulcrum of official efforts to lever China's economy onto a new innovation-based growth trajectory. It signals that outside observers lack a nuanced understanding of China's regulatory structures and industrial policies, which range from general measures that encourage startup firms and raise university enrollment to sharply focused efforts that channel resources to help priority sectors and favored firms master specific technologies.

The chapters that follow are the outcome of a group effort to remedy this disturbing and, from a foreign policy perspective, dangerous lacuna. To pursue this subject, we convened a multidisciplinary group of researchers to investigate Chinese efforts to energize upgrading and innovation. Inclusion of multiple specialties facilitates work that follows policy initiatives from start to finish, avoiding the incompleteness of studies that focus on policy and neglect outcomes (common among political scientists) or examine outcomes without links to policies (widespread among economists).

To achieve depth in a field beset by facile generalizations, our work combines documentary research with extensive field study, and focuses on electricity and telecommunications, along with semiconductors – a core component in telecommunications systems. With recent developments, notably the cessation of labor force growth and the declining growth rate of investment, enhancing the centrality of innovation and upgrading as determinants of future growth, the following chapters address four inter-related sets of questions arising from recent Chinese experience:

- How does the Chinese state promote industrial upgrading and inno-vation? To what extent can we identify direct links, positive or nega-tive, between policy objectives and innovative outcomes?
- How do Chinese regulatory and institutional structures influence business behavior? Do regulations encourage firms to make cost-effective investment choices – for example in building new facilities or purchasing production equipment? Or do official actions distort enterprise-level incentives in directions that incline enterprise man-agers toward unproductive or wasteful decisions?
- What is the trajectory of Chinese improvements in quality, cost, and productivity? When and, if so, how do Chinese producers approach global best practice? When and where can we observe evidence of cutting-edge advances that extend global production possibilities?
- How can the development of specific industries illuminate future prospects for China's national innovation system?

We preface our review of these issues with a brief description of the sectors under review here and a summary of ongoing controversy over the practicality of state intervention to accelerate industrial upgrading and innovation.

CHARACTERISTICS OF ELECTRICITY AND TELECOMMUNICATIONS

Electricity and telecommunications fall into the category of "network industries." These sectors display somewhat unusual features (Shy 2001). Network industries have high fixed costs – expenses that arise regardless of the level of output. High fixed costs open the door to scale economies – meaning that unit costs decline as output rises. Scale economies undermine market competition – because small entrants cannot match the low costs attained by well-established incumbents. Consumers of network products purchase systems (e.g. smart phones with operating systems that provide access to multiple software options) rather than individual products (e.g. a haircut or a shirt). The benefit available to individual purchasers of such systems increases with their popularity. Unlike buyers of haircuts or shirts, buyers of network products may find that switching from one system to another (e.g. from IOS to Android) imposes considerable financial and start-up costs. The resulting "lock-in" effect adds to the market power of incumbent firms. Extensive market power, especially for items seen as necessities, invites government intervention, which may take the form of regulation, public ownership, or, as in China, both.

The difficulty of melding the peculiarities of network industries, the benefits of business competition, and the need to limit the power of entrenched suppliers has defeated efforts to delineate preferred market structures. Global reform efforts intended to inject competition into industries formerly treated as "natural monopolies" have delivered mixed results. There is no clear model of success. Reform remains a work in progress. Efforts to deregulate US electricity markets, for example, have stumbled over episodic price spikes, opportunistic supplier behavior and shortages.

These industries deploy a mix of old and new technologies. Semiconductor technology has evolved through the commercialization and upgrading of mid-twentieth century innovations. Telecoms combine the popularization of old (fax, landline) and the rapid development of new (3G, 4G, 5G, mobile phone miniaturization) technologies. The combined

impact of hardware and software innovations has revolutionized the conduct of daily affairs for individuals in China and across the world.
Advances in electric power depend on the refinement of well-known,
widely disseminated technologies. Larger plants (reflecting scale economies), fine-tuning of controls, and combustion at higher temperatures and
pressures have raised the efficiency of coal-fired thermal plants. Solar
technology is not new – massive cost reduction is the chief innovation.
Wind turbines also employ familiar technology – a wide array of engineering firms can easily enter this market. Nuclear technology, like semiconductors, emerged from mid-twentieth century innovations. Potentially
significant innovations, including smart meters, automated grid systems,
distributed power generation and new techniques for large-scale storage of
electricity, hold great promise, but lack sufficient traction to influence the
analysis offered in this volume.

HISTORIC DEBATE OVER INTERVENTIONIST POLICY

Controversies over the efficacy of interventionist policy in accelerating
technological change date from nineteenth-century clashes between free
traders, among them David Ricardo and Frederic Bastiat, and early advocates of state developmentalism, including Alexander Hamilton and
Friedrich List. Recent debate has swirled around the dynamic East Asian
region, with the share of opinion highlighting or disparaging the contribution of interventionist policies fluctuating with the economic fortunes of
the region's high-growth economies.[2] China's explosive growth provides
fresh ammunition for controversy, with some analysts portraying Chinese
industry as a frightening colossus marching to the dictates of a central plan,
while others insist that institutional shortcomings and epidemic levels of
fraud and corruption must hobble efforts to progress from imitation and
cost reduction to cutting-edge innovation.

Proponents of activist policies justify their stance with appeals to market
failure and externalities. Without forceful governmental intervention,
capital market imperfections may limit funding to start-up firms.
Protection for "infant industries" shelters nascent sectors from ruinous
competition while they traverse learning curves and build competitive

---

[2] Johnson (1982), Kim (1987), Wade (2004), and World Bank (1993), among others,
emphasize the benefits of state intervention; recent setbacks in Japan and Korea have
stimulated critical approaches, for example by Miwa (2004) and Miwa and Ramseyer
(2010).

strength. Without subsidies or protection, individual firms may limit spending on research or labor training because they cannot capture benefits that diffuse across the economy. Coordinated expansion of manufacturing and infrastructure "can help foster a mutually profitable big push even when ... investment in any one sector appears unprofitable" (Murphy, Schleifer, and Vishny 1989, p. 1024). In China (and elsewhere), such thinking is often reinforced by the perception that foreign-dominated global value chains may choke domestic upgrading opportunities – for example by refusing to transfer or license proprietary technologies.

The perennial issue concerns the state's *most effective* levers for accelerating an economy's progress toward global technological frontiers. There are two competing policy designs. The *private initiative approach* sees government's key function as "setting the table" for private endeavor by creating a business environment conducive to entrepreneurship. Relevant policies include promoting universal education, expanding universities, creating courts and other regulatory mechanisms, establishing export zones or industrial parks, and financing basic research. Supporters oppose prioritizing specific industries, firms or technologies, fearing that ill-advised official efforts to "pick winners" among potentially dynamic sectors or firms stand little chance of success and, worse yet, may open the door to "crony capitalism," with corrupt officials ladling out subsidies, protection and monopoly rights to well-connected insiders.

Interventionists believe that, in addition to creating attractive conditions for commercial ventures, states can beneficially deploy a range of policy tools such as grants, tax concessions, risk-sharing arrangements, officially inspired consortia, and trade protection to accelerate advances in carefully selected segments of manufacturing. Japan's post-war development of steel and autos (Johnson 1982; Okimoto 1989) and Taiwan's push into electronics and chips (Hsueh, Hsu, and Perkins 2001; Amsden and Chu 2003, Wade 2004) demonstrate the potential gains from policy activism.

China's strongly interventionist stance is congruent with recent research highlighting the contribution of activist governments to accelerating innovation and technological catchup in both advanced (Block and Keller 2011; Mazzucato 2013) and developing (Rodrik 2004; Cimoli, Dosi, and Stiglitz 2009) nations. China's approach reflects Beijing's reading of international best practice as well as its skepticism toward Anglo-American "invisible hand" perspectives that extol the innovative capacity of private firms and free markets.

New work that re-evaluates the links among basic science, applied research, and commercial development of new or improved products casts further doubt on the independent innovative capacity of private business. Conventional thinking partitions R&D space into "basic" science, which produces new concepts, theories, and materials that provide the foundation for commercial innovation, and "applied" research, which moves such discoveries toward commercial fruition. The "public good" nature of basic research (meaning that, unlike products that confer benefits only upon individual buyers, scientific advances – for example calculus or plastics – benefit entire societies), and the consequent benefit of direct public support, is not in dispute. Applied research, by contrast, promises immediate financial returns that obviate the need for public support, as when developers of techniques that extend battery life for mobile phones can obtain patents and collect royalties.

Gregory Tassey (2014) presents a more complex picture of the path from basic discovery to commercial sale. He divides applied research into three stages, namely:

- Proof-of-concept technology research, for example "Bell Labs' demonstration ... that semiconductor materials can be organized to perform the functions of an electronic switch or amplifier" (2014, p. 37);
- Infratechnologies – essential technical tools "often embodied in the standards that are ubiquitous in high-tech industries" (2014, p. 38); and
- Commercial product development.

Only the last of these stages involves activity that is mainly "private" in the sense that operators can expect to capture most of the financial payoff arising from their effort. Tassey doubts that private businesses can justify paying the full cost of efforts associated with proof-of-technology or infratechnology development. Survey evidence shows major American corporations increasingly focusing R&D activity on projects that promise short-term payoffs. Globalization-inspired competitive pressures deter firms from supporting the "luxury" of basic and mid-stream research that generates more prestige than profit.

Tassey observes that strenuous opposition[3] to modifying the traditional reliance on private sector initiative to conduct the entire gamut of "applied" research places the US national innovation system at a disadvantage in competing with rival systems, including China's, where

---

[3] Thus the "Heritage Foundation ... argues that the federal government should fund only very basic scientific research and get out of the business of helping companies commercialize new energy technologies" (Plumer and Davenport 2017).

government business-university partnerships routinely support activities that occupy Tassey's proof-of-concept and infratechnology categories.

TASK OF THIS BOOK

Electricity and telecoms, like many other segments of China's economy, represent epic success stories. During the early days of reform, we toured factories by flashlight and watched Chinese colleagues send cyclists across Beijing to deliver lunch invitations rather than attempt to communicate by telephone. All this has changed. Chinese systems now provide nationwide access to electricity, phone and internet services. Leading Chinese firms sell telecom equipment in the United Kingdom and Australia and operate grid systems on several continents. China is a major exporter of power plant equipment and a nascent supplier in the global market for nuclear power plants.

The following chapters investigate the contribution of official policies and regulatory actions to these impressive advances. The issue is complex. If innovation and upgrading occur – as in telecom and nuclear power – are these advances a product of official initiatives? Of unrelated accumulation of technical and managerial capabilities? Of some combination of the two? Can we see specific instances in which government initiatives accelerate (or obstruct) innovation? What of high priority sectors – semiconductors offer an obvious example – that fail to gain competitiveness despite determined (and expensive) official support?

We adopt a broad definition of innovation, which extends beyond completely new developments to encompass upgrading of products and services that falls short of the global frontier. Once commercialized, innovations of both types – world-leading Chinese voice recognition software or improvements that reduce unit coal consumption in thermal power plants – raise product value, reduce input requirements, or both. The result is higher productivity (or lower cost, its mirror image).

Innovation of either variety increases demand. Rising demand encourages higher output, which promotes scale economies and experience-based learning, both likely to reduce costs and thus refresh the cycle of fruitful interaction between productivity and growth. Rising productivity is the central feature of long-term economic expansion in every society. Looking ahead, China's shrinking labor force, diminishing returns to investment, and the declining growth rate for capital formation arising from economic rebalancing toward consumption all ensure the continued dominance of productivity increase as the key determinant of future growth.

Focusing on electricity, telecommunications, and semiconductors, we find a wide dispersion of innovative outcomes that includes instances of impressive achievement, numerous areas of solid advance, and occasional failure. We can summarize our findings regarding innovation outcomes by looking successively at technology, services, and market penetration.

INNOVATION OUTCOMES

Technology

Our studies find a mix of success and failure. We observe many instances of successful absorption and operation of advanced technologies developed outside China. Examples include supercritical and ultra-supercritical thermal power generation technology as well as Westinghouse's Generation III nuclear reactor design.

Examples from telecom and power sectors illustrate an intermediate outcome in which Chinese firms absorb overseas technology but also contribute to technical advance. Eric Thun and Timothy Sturgeon in Chapter 5, for example, document Chinese participation in joint efforts to develop standards for 4G and 5G networking. Telecom equipment specialist ZTE's 2016 agreement "to sell a patent portfolio – including, significantly, a number of China-only patent families" to a US firm provides clear evidence of growing Chinese presence at the global knowledge frontier (Ellis 2017). The decision by Huawei, another leading producer of telecom equipment, to launch patent infringement lawsuits against T-Mobile and Samsung in US courts points in the same direction (Pressman 2016). Xu Yi-chong in Chapter 6, examines State Grid Corporation's success in extending global distance and voltage standards for long-distance transmission of electricity. Her findings illustrate China's emergent capacity to achieve frontier innovation.

Douglas Fuller in Chapter 7 shows that sustained and costly effort has done little to reduce the distance between Chinese semiconductor producers and global leaders. Fuller finds that leading Chinese firms have attained "intermediate" levels of technological capability in two major industry segments, foundry and complementary metal oxide semiconductor (CMOS) image sensors; elsewhere, available information indicates that Chinese firms achieve no more than "relatively low technology capability."

Services

Chinese telecom customers enjoy inexpensive, high-quality voice service. Operators like Alibaba and TenCent provide convenient and highly innovative online services that enjoy huge popularity. Electrical service, although expensive – except for subsidized residential and agricultural users – is reliable, especially in urban centers. Both power and telecom networks provide nationwide coverage – an impressive achievement for a continental nation. Broadband service, although widely available, is slow[4] and relatively expensive. Despite the ubiquity of online consumer activity, the poor quality of broadband service contributes to the hesitancy of many Chinese businesses to explore internet-related opportunities (Woetzel et al. 2014, pp. 18, 28, 41).

Market Penetration

Trends in market shares captured by various producers provide a valuable metric for the progress or absence of innovation and upgrading, especially in the presence of open competition that obliges enterprises to meet customer requirements without official support. The success of unheralded producers of telecom and construction equipment in capturing domestic market share, scaling industry quality ladders, and breaking into global markets formerly dominated by powerful multinationals illustrates the link between openness and innovative success (Brandt and Thun 2010, 2016).

International competition generates particularly valuable information about the extent of innovative advance. The news may be unwelcome, as when a German auto club labeled a Chinese-made SUV as "the worst performer in its 20-year testing history," or when the Massachusetts Department of Transportation rejected a bid from a major Chinese rail-car manufacturer "in three categories: technology, manufacturing and quality assurances" (Spinelli 2005; Mouawad 2015). Brandt and Wang find that quality issues have prevented Chinese wind turbines, unlike other types of power generating equipment, from attaining substantial overseas sales. Fuller's study of semiconductors provides another instance in which substantial growth of domestic output has brought little overseas market penetration.

Successful outcomes, however, convey an equally clear message. China's substantial exports of solar panels, telecom equipment, and rail cars to

---

[4] "Global ranking of China in terms of broadband speed: 91st"; see www.chinadaily.com.cn/china/2016even/ (accessed August 19, 2018).

advanced nations demonstrate international competitiveness, as does the growing capacity of Chinese firms to wrest domestic market share from leading multinational vendors of construction equipment. In hydropower equipment, China has become "the dominant global force in manufacturing and exporting." (Chellaney 2011, p. 65). Exports of thermal power generation equipment, telephone handsets and, looking forward, nuclear power equipment, most directed toward low- and middle-income economies, indicate competitive strength that suffices for some markets but cannot satisfy the demands of high-end customers.

CHINA'S PROMOTION OF UPGRADING AND INNOVATION

China's efforts to accelerate industrial upgrading and innovation fall into two categories. One is the accumulation of resources and development of institutions that can support innovation. The second is the implementation of policies that channel resources in directions that reflect the state's strategic ambitions. We discuss each in turn.

Accumulating Resources and Building Institutions

Systematic development of innovation-related resource pools and institutional arrangements dates from the 1950s, when China pushed to expand mass education, initially emphasizing universal primary attendance, dispatched students to study technical subjects in the Soviet Union and Eastern Europe, and created a thick web of science and technology related schools, research establishments and professional associations. Despite politically inspired disruptions arising from the Hundred Flowers campaign, the Great Leap Forward, China's split with the Soviet Union, and the Cultural Revolution, these efforts increased literacy and school attendance. Of particular relevance to our sectoral focus, the 1950s witnessed the emergence of at least ten universities focused on electricity or telecommunications.

Following the start of reform in the late 1970s, the push to expand innovation-linked resources became more intense and more consistent. Further expansion of the education system multiplied middle school, high school, college, and university enrollments. Changing employment patterns in state-owned enterprises (SOEs) and institutions reflect a shift of official priorities toward technology-intensive industries. While SOE employment dropped by nearly half between 1997 and 2015, falling from 97.2 to 49.6 million, the number of employees classified as technical personnel (专业技术人员 *zhuanye jishu renyuan*) rose from 28.6 to 30.9 million, raising the share of such workers from 29 to 62 percent of the total.[5]

Steep increases pushed research and development outlays beyond 2 percent of GDP, exceeding comparable totals for all low-income nations and a handful of advanced economies. R&D activity has shifted toward industry, whose share of R&D financing (74.7 percent in 2015) and spending (76.8 percent in 2015) exceeds comparable figures for all OECD nations other than Japan and South Korea (OECD 2016, p. 14). Chinese R&D focuses on development, which accounts for 84.2 percent of recent R&D outlays, rather than basic (5 percent) or applied (10.8 percent) research (Kennedy 2017, p. 20).

The reform era wrought sweeping changes in the organization of economic activity, of which the transitions from plan to market and from isolation to economic openness are particularly relevant for this study. The shift from plan to market, while gradual and incomplete, has put enterprise leaders in charge of a growing array of decisions about business strategy, product mix, price-setting, sales effort, hiring, input purchases, investment, and many other matters. Reform has spawned a succession of institutional innovations to meet the needs of an economy that now displays extensive decentralization of authority. These include commercial legislation and courts tasked with adjudicating commercial disputes, markets for the exchange of commodities and the issuance and exchange of corporate shares and bonds, a patent system, venture capital agencies, industrial parks, incubators for nurturing start-up firms, and many other novel arrangements.

Gradual transfer of authority from state organs to firms compels the state to develop regulatory systems in place of the command structures that formerly moved enterprises and resources in directions desired by policymakers. As Irene Wu, in Chapter 2, demonstrates, building regulatory mechanisms that address multiple objectives – efficiency, wide access, and providing a "level playing field" for an increasingly heterogeneous population of actors – is no easy task, particularly in a society renowned for the ability of individuals and groups to "game the system" using networks of informal relationships. Regulation is particularly important in network industries like telecommunication and electricity, where the presence of large incumbents and the expectation that unit costs decline with rising firm size creates opportunities for abusive behavior.[6]

---

[5] S&T Yearbook 2016, p. 16. The data for 2015 include collective as well as SOEs and institutions.

[6] Chen (2012) blames telecom monopolies for "expensive and slow" internet service. In 2015, "at least forty-eight cities in fourteen provinces and regions have enacted … rules" specifying that "only transmission company-hired crews can install power lines and

Openness to the movement of commodities, people, information, ideas, technology, and investment across both national and domestic borders is another central feature of China's post-1978 reforms. What began as hesitant experimentation mushroomed into a sea change that has vaulted China into global prominence as the world's largest trading nation, its second largest recipient of incoming direct investment, a leading destination for international travel, and, most recently, a major source of international travelers, overseas students and outbound foreign investment.

Discussion of China's "open door" policy focuses on flows of trade, investment, and technology, most to and from a handful of coastal provinces. Equally important, however, are exchanges of people and information. Explosive growth of Chinese translations and adaptations of materials ranging from scientific papers to popular entertainment, overseas study and work experience, and participation in supply chains leading to production facilities of Toyota, Siemens, General Electric, Doosan, and other global leaders have extended the knowledge and understanding available to thousands of Chinese enterprises and millions of Chinese citizens.

Shaanxi province illustrates the profound impact of globalization on economic activity even in China's interior. Notwithstanding its limited involvement in global trade – 2009 data place the province's trade ratio (combined exports and imports as a percentage of GDP) at 7 percent – one-sixth of the national average for the same year (Yearbook 2010, pp. 38, 51, 230, 247) – fallout from the autumn 2008 global financial crisis hit Shaanxi immediately. Electricity consumption by large industrial users began to fall in October; incremental growth resumed only in June 2009 (Shaanxi Electricity 2009). Early 2009 brought the first reduction in Shaanxi's industrial output since 1949 (Shaanxi Output 2009).

Interventionist Policies and Programs

The measures described above are consistent with a private initiative strategy that leaves the direction and intensity of innovative effort to the discretion of decentralized operators. China's government, however, combines this approach with interventionist policies that assign special priority and channel substantial resources to expedite the development of selected industries, the acquisition, absorption, and mastery of specific technologies, and the expansion and market share of favored companies or enterprise groups.

related equipment," a measure that in some instances doubled connection costs and prompted some property developers to cancel building plans (Huang 2015).

Interventionist policies date buck to Japanese-led efforts to develop a heavy industry complex in China's northeast (Manchurian) region at the time of World War I. The Guomindang administration established an array of SOEs during the 1930s to promote defense-related manufacturing. Beginning in the mid-1950s, the newly established People's Republic initiated a sequence of Five Year Plans, a tradition that has continued despite the post-1978 expansion of the market. At this writing, China is in the midst of its 13th Five-Year Plan (FYP) covering the years 2016–20.

FYPs provide a point of departure for additional programs that target specific industries, activities, or segments of the economy. The list includes Spark, which promotes rural innovation; Torch and 863, both aimed at high technology industries; 973, which boosts basic science capabilities in certain strategic areas; the National Medium- and Long-Term Plan for the Development of Science and Technology 2006–20; the 2007 Medium–Long Term Plan for nuclear development; the 2007 Medium–Long Term Plan for renewable energy development; and the 2014 National Integrated Circuit Industry Guidelines.

Government agencies deploy a long-standing and extensive menu of interventions to assist entities tasked with pursuing strategic priorities. Beneficiaries often receive direct financial transfers in the form of cash grants or tax reductions. "Access to assets and resources" – including land, bank loans, essential commodities, and technical expertise or intellectual property housed in government research agencies – "at below-market prices" represents another class of benefits (Zeng and Williamson 2007, p. 19). Interest-rate subsidies to state firms, which Gatley (2018) places at a minimum of RMB 250–330 billion per year, illustrate the scale of such measures. The state's long reach, enhanced by ubiquitous Party influence, extends the impact of official preferences beyond state budgets and official actions.

Sub-national governments achieve unusual prominence in Chinese economic policy implementation: Bardhan and Mookherjee (2006) point to China as the lone example among low-income nations in which local government contributes substantially to economic growth. Innovation efforts are no exception: during the decade ending in 2016, the share of provincial and local governments in China's steeply rising overall fiscal outlays on science and technology rose from 47–9 percent during 2007–11 to 58–9 percent in 2015–16[7]. Local governments actively promote

---

[7] www.stats.gov.cn (accessed July 23, 2018).

advanced products, including majority investments in four of five plants established by BOE Technology Group, "the only Chinese display company that supplies Apple, which is notoriously finicky in its demands for top-quality components" (Kubota 2018). In Chapter 3, Margaret Pearson focuses on the efforts of sub-national governments to promote the manufacture of solar cells and electric vehicles; Dinh et al. (2013) provide further illustrations.

Along with policy tools routinely deployed in many nations, China's large and rapidly growing domestic market has enabled officials to demand that global multinationals share proprietary technology in return for (often limited) market access. In addition, there is credible evidence that China's government condones, organizes and in some instances conducts what specialists describe as an unprecedented campaign of cyber-espionage aimed at "compromising organizations across a broad range of industries" (Mandiant 2013, p. 4), with targets extending far beyond defense-linked producers (Brenner 2014). Cybersecurity specialist James Lewis states that "Chinese companies used to be able to direct the PLA or MSS [referring to Chinese military and security agencies] to hack into Western competitors." More recently, presumably following a 2013 US-China agreement to curtail economic espionage, "companies can still put in a request for a target to be hacked but no longer can assign tasks to the teams directly" (Wilkes 2017).

Official support routinely encompasses segments of the innovation process that Tassey, discussed above, views as involving high "public good" content and thus likely to lack commercial viability. Government-funded researchers "completely dominate" China's push into third-generation technology for solar power generation while "private sector actors are still waiting to see if there is a realistic chance of commercializing" novel methods that are "not considered as market-ready yet" (Sun 2016, p. 31). The origin of China's Time Division Synchronous Code Division Multiple Access (TD-SCDMA) standard for 3G telecom discussed in Chapter 5 by Thun and Sturgeon, in a "research institute under the Ministry of Information" (Zeng and Williamson 2007, p. 157), illustrates public sector involvement in "proof of concept" research. Another example comes from Davidson's description of the National Energy Agency's lead role in the "700°C Coalition," a group that considers prospects for advanced supercritical thermal power generation. Speeches by representatives of three major government agencies at an event hailing the emergence of COSINE, "China's first set of nuclear power design and safety analysis software" following a five-year effort that included official approval for building a "key laboratory of national energy nuclear power software" highlight state involvement in creating tools and standards – part of Tassey's infratechnology category.

Three Decades of Innovation: Good but Not Good Enough

Several decades of market-leaning reform gradually built an environment powerfully supportive of innovation and upgrading, with domestic sectors mastering technologies and processes unknown in China's pre-reform economy, and in many cases supplying the resulting products to overseas as well as domestic markets. The remarkable expansion and modernization of China's electric power and telecommunications networks illustrates this process. Chinese utility customers, formerly faced with primitive and often unreliable service, now benefit from systems that often approach and sometimes surpass comparable arrangements in advanced nations. The operations of China's utility networks rest squarely on domestic equipment, much of which finds ready overseas markets, including substantial sales of telecom equipment to advanced nations like the United Kingdom and Australia.

The extension of economic openness, which created substantial domestic opportunities for foreign firms and their products, also permitted well-endowed coastal regions to pursue somewhat independent economic strategies and multiple upgrading paths (e.g. Vogel 1989; Segal 2003; Thun 2006; Breznitz and Murphree 2011). Manufacturers of power generating equipment thrived on joint ventures – more than fifty for Shanghai Electric alone (https://en.wikipedia.org/wiki/Shanghai_Electric). Huawei honed its now-formidable capabilities first by selling in third and fourth tier Chinese cities and then by marketing its telecom equipment in Africa. China's emergence as a major force in the global market for nuclear electricity rests on a complex combination of domestic development (China National Nuclear), deep ties with French partners (China General Nuclear), and licensing agreements that include a complete transfer of Westinghouse Electric's Generation III AP1000 technology (State Power Investment).

Building on the successes of this market-oriented, globalist approach, the World Bank and the Development Research Center (发展研究中心), a prominent government think tank operating under China's State Council, issued a joint report, *China 2030*, that enunciates a development strategy for pushing China's economy toward new levels of productivity, prosperity, and innovative achievement. The report, completed in 2012 and formally released in 2013, proposes major policy adjustments to facilitate China's emergence as global leader increasingly focused on advanced technology and frontier innovation rather than the past emphasis on "catching up" with advanced nations. The authors repeatedly emphasize the centrality of openness and competition for successful completion of this transition.

The report advocates "increased competition in all sectors, including in strategic and pillar industries" (WB and DRC 2013, p. xxii). The authors insist that "A competitive market environment is a necessary condition for steady improvement in productivity" (p. 173). Emphasizing that "the role of the private sector is critical because innovation at the technology frontier is quite different in nature from simply catching up" (p. 17), the report advises immediate removal of formal and informal entry barriers that "convey the clear policy message – competition from private firms is not welcome" (p. 26). Looking ahead, the authors advise that success "will require further integration with the global economy and increased specialization" and that "The benefits of openness will be central to increasing efficiency, stimulating innovation, and promoting international competitiveness" (pp. 19, 22).

The joint report also specifies policies that, in the view of the World Bank-DRC team, are unlikely to deliver strong results. Continuation of entry restrictions and regulatory approaches tilted toward state-linked enterprises threatens to "dampen innovation and creativity, and slow productivity growth" because state-owned firms "are indifferently managed ... less receptive to strategies that give primacy to growth through innovation ... [and their investment in R&D] tends to be unproductive and poorly integrated with the rest of their operations" (pp. 36, 170). "Direct government intervention may actually retard growth, not help it ... [because] Innovation is not something that can be achieved through government planning" (p. 17). Therefore, "the government needs to withdraw from direct involvement in production, distribution, and resource allocation" because "the government's continued dominance in key sectors of the economy, while earlier an advantage, is in the future likely to act as a constraint on productivity improvements, innovation, and creativity" (pp. 18, 25).

Shortly thereafter, the November 2013 Decision of the Communist Party's Central Committee on "Major Issues Concerning Comprehensively Deepening the Reform" appeared to set the stage for implementing the policy agenda recommended in the joint Bank-DRC report. The Decision announces the Party's determination "to deepen economic system reform by centering on the decisive role of the market in allocating resources" (Decision 2014, Item 3). The Party will "promote market-oriented reform in width and in depth [by] greatly reducing the government's role in the direct allocation of resources" (Item 3). Openness – both domestic and international – is another prominent theme: "... we must ... overcome the barriers of solidified interests" (Item 4), "continue to break up all forms of administrative monopoly" (Item 7), and, aside from a "negative list" of specific areas that are off-limits to some would-be investors, welcome "all kinds of market players ... on an equal basis ... [and] strictly ban and punish all unlawful acts extending preferential policies" (Item 9). The Decision envisions a growing role for private business, pledging to "persist in equality of rights, opportunities and rules, abolish all forms of irrational regulations for the non-public economy, remove all hidden barriers ... encourage non-public enterprises to participate in SOE reform, foster mixed enterprises with non-public capital as the controlling shareholder, and encourage qualified private enterprises to establish the modern corporate system" (Item 8).

This seeming victory for proponents of openness, competition, and market dominance, however, soon revealed itself as a short-lived episode in an ongoing tug-of-war with a rival economic strategy emphasizing a different route toward the common goal of promoting innovation and raising productivity and living standards toward advanced-country levels.

The alternative strategy emphasizes central leadership in prioritizing innovations, concentrates innovation resources in large SOEs and promotes self-reliant paths to innovation and technical development. Heilmann and Shih (2013) identify its proponents as "a 'centrist' or 'statist' advocacy coalition" – in opposition to *China 2030* supporters, who promote "market liberalization."[8] "Statist" thinking, which dominated Chinese policy prior to the onset of economic reform, maintained a strong presence throughout the reform era. Its influence is readily apparent, for example, in the 2006 "National Medium- to Long-Term Plan for the Development of Science and Technology" (Cao, Suttmeier, and Simon 2006) and the 2010 "Decision of the State Council on Accelerating the Fostering and Development of Strategic Emerging Industries" (Strategic 2010). The same thinking motivates "Made in China 2025," a program announced in 2015 that forms the centerpiece of China's present industrial policy.

Before investigating the nature and consequences of Made in China 2015, we speculate on the cause of the sudden about-face from the 2013

---

[8] At a deeper level, this debate reflects an intense internal ideological struggle in the Chinese leadership over Western influence in economic policy-making and the push for a self-reliant China under a "home-grown" system of socialism with Chinese characteristics. On this point, see Gewirtz, 2017, p. 13.

"market dominance" strategy and its emphasis on domestic and international openness. The 2008 global financial crisis and ensuing recession necessitated forceful government action to limit the short-term damage, a circumstance that inevitably strengthened the leverage of interventionist ideas. And, like the Great Depression of the 1930s, the global recession weakened advocates of openness and internationalism and strengthened economic nationalists everywhere.

In addition, completely distinct domestic circumstances contributed to the rapid unraveling of the apparent 2013 convergence of expert policy advice and Communist Party economic strategy supporting market liberalization.[9]

Several decades of enviable progress may have left incoming President Xi and other Chinese leaders far from satisfied. Frustration with limited innovative capacity has become a common theme. A 2016 review of machinery manufacture, China's largest industry, is typical: while "some segments have reached the international level of advanced technology . . . autonomous innovative capacity is weak" (自主创新能力不强 *zizhu chuangxin nengli buqiang*: Equipment Report 2016, p. 2). This observation echoes numerous accounts of large gaps between the capabilities of Chinese firms and leading overseas companies in technical level, product quality and many other areas (e.g. Equipment Report 2016, pp. 71, 165–6, 273).

Several features of China's innovation landscape appear to strike Chinese leaders as particularly galling. Chinese innovations, often concealed within the anonymous mechanisms of global supply chains, lack visibility. Additionally, governance of these supply chains, especially for advanced products with the brightest future prospects, remains concentrated among overseas multinationals. Distinctively Chinese innovations are rare. Where are the instantly recognizable Chinese brands? Why are there no Chinese contributions to rival the Ford assembly line or the Toyota production system? Peter Nolan captures this mood:

The areas in which indigenous Chinese firms do have significant market share in the high-income countries are few, most notably telecommunications equipment (Huawei) and PCs (Lenovo). After three decades of evolutionary industrial policy based mainly around state-owned enterprises, China still faces an immense challenge if it is to achieve its long-stated goal of nurturing a substantial group of indigenous firms that can compete in international markets.

---

[9] Cox notes that "Liu He, an influential economic adviser to Xi Jinping, was one of the driving forces behind" the joint Bank-DRC report (Cox 2017, p. 8).

At the same time that China's SOEs have failed to build globally competitive businesses, global high-technology and branded-goods producers have rapidly expanded their investment and market share within China in the many sectors that are relatively open to international competition. Large swathes of the domestic market are dominated by global oligopolies. (2014, pp. 133–4)

No longer content with innovation outcomes resulting from a structure that, despite significant state intervention, rested heavily on a market economy substantially influenced by foreign firms and foreign-led supply chains, China's leaders have opted for a major expansion of state intervention. The objective is not simply to accelerate the pace of innovation, but to steer the "commanding heights" of China's economy toward a carefully crafted array of specific sectors, technologies, and outcomes.

"Made in China 2025" [中国制造2025], announced in 2015, is the centerpiece of this new innovation strategy. This program offers a detailed, ten-year agenda for innovation and upgrading in ten industries, including power plant equipment, telecommunications and semiconductors, complete with timetables for achieving precise technical benchmarks. Thus, China aims to produce complete sets of equipment for Generation III+ nuclear plants of 1000 and 1500 MW capacity by 2020 and of 2000 MW capacity by 2025, all capable of operating at ninety-three percent of capacity for sixty years (Roadmap 2015, p. 123). Documents surrounding this program (many listed in Wübbeke et al. 2016, p. 66 and US Chamber of Commerce 2017, p. 42ff) advance a multitude of quantitative targets for 2020 and 2025 covering a wide array of indicators. For example:

- *output value* for railway, power transmission and farm equipment (Roadmap 2015, pp. 85, 132, 134)
- *output quantity* for power generation equipment (ibid., p. 117)
- *unit production costs* for electric batteries (ibid., p. 95)
- *export proportion* for railway and power generating equipment (ibid., pp. 85, 117)
- *export composition* for power transmission equipment (ibid., p. 132)
- *market share* "hundreds of market share targets for 2020 and 2025, both domestic and international" (EU Chamber 2017, p. 11)
- *domestic market composition* sales share of new energy vehicles (Roadmap 2015, pp. 82, 103)
- *global market share* for Chinese-made high-end computers, mobile phone chips and equipment (ibid., p. 8)

Echoing officially sponsored consolidation efforts in coal, steel, railway equipment, and shipbuilding, the new policy aims to establish concentrated industry structures. Planned outcomes include two of the top ten global producers of new energy vehicles as well as three globally competitive enterprise groups capable of providing complete sets of large scale, technologically advanced equipment for thermal, hydro, nuclear, and renewable power generation and storage, all backed by independent intellectual property rights (Roadmap 2015, pp. 101, 117).

In addition to budgetary appropriations and policy support, resources for implementing this agenda come from government guidance funds (政府引导基金 *zhengfu yindao jijin*), hybrid entities that have mushroomed in recent years and now exist at multiple administrative levels. Provinces direct the largest funds, with smaller operations housed at "over 300 city-level governments." Initial funding from official budgets attracts private capital, which is "fighting to get a piece of the action" because "partnering with state funds can lower the cost of capital and obtain support from the government" (Xiang 2017).

The combined scale of these funds, RMB 1.5–2 trillion at year-end 2015 (Xiang 2017; Blair 2017) and RMB 5.3 trillion in early 2017 (*Economist* 2017, p. 65), towers above 2015 government appropriations for science and technology (RMB 700 billion) and nationwide expenditure on R&D projects (RMB 1.22 trillion; see S&T Yearbook 2016, pp. 14–15). Guidance funds invest some of their assets in joint or private venture capital funds, further extending the reach of official preferences (Millward 2016). Both guidance and venture funds enjoy wide latitude in choosing avenues to support target industries, which may include equity investments, loans, reimbursing firms for qualified expenditures, and participation in funding for domestic or overseas mergers.

While encouraging favored technologies and firms, Chinese governments appear to have stepped up efforts to undermine the competitive position of "outsider" firms. Official efforts to promote import replacement increasingly target foreign firms and foreign-linked joint ventures. Policy-makers may steer official agencies, state-controlled enterprises, and even non-state firms toward domestic products rather than imported alternatives.

Numerous examples illustrate the application of regulatory tools – product specifications, tender qualifications, product catalogs, or requirements to share technology or disclose software codes – to obstruct entry or restrict sales of unwelcome products or vendors even as low tariffs maintain a façade of market openness. A 2016 list of thirty-one officially approved suppliers for electric vehicle batteries excluded two prominent Korean firms on the grounds "that their Chinese factories had been in operation for less than a year, a requirement" not previously announced

(EU Chamber 2017, p. 40). Entry into the cloud computing market requires a license from the Internet Data Center, which refuses licenses to foreign firms (US Chamber 2017, p. 28). U.S. researchers report that China has "issued licenses for value-added [telecom] services to 29,000 domestic suppliers" but only forty-one to foreign suppliers (US Chamber 2017, p. 28).

What are the characteristics of this new policy and regulatory environment? How will this initiative shape the evolution of innovative effort within and beyond China's power, telecom and semiconductor industries beyond?

China's New Industrial Policy and Regulatory Environment – Characteristics

The new policy agenda partially reverses major elements of China's reform-era economic landscape.

Made in China 2025 and related programs greatly expand the scope and the resources devoted to top-down pursuit of big innovations. This approach is the polar opposite of the decentralized, increasingly market-driven processes that have powered four decades of spectacular growth. Most Chinese firms "pursue incremental rather than radical innovation . . . [they] seldom go for 'moonshot' innovations – not for them 'iPhone envy'. They prefer pragmatic and predictable innovations" (Yip and McKern 2016, pp. 82–3). But "moonshots" are exactly what MIC 2025 proposes.

In sharp contrast to the Bank-DRC report and the 2013 Party Decision, Made in China 2025, developed by the Chinese Academy of Engineering (中国工程院; Interveiw, June 2018, and MIC 2025), relegates market forces to the background as officially imposed targets and quotas pre-empt commercial competition in an enlarged universe of strategic priorities. The new agenda rarely mentions cost and ignores returns on investment. Instead of openness, the new approach revives the Maoist vision of self-reliance. Emphasis on "autonomous" (自主*zizhu* i.e. without foreign involvement) innovation adds a further non-market dimension. The new agenda seems to overlook, or perhaps devalue, what economic researchers see as the immense, and immensely valuable, knowledge transfer arising from the Chinese operations of foreign firms and the rich harvest of often invisible, but commercially significant innovations by Chinese participants in global supply chains (Zeng and Williamson 2007; Breznitz and Murphree 2011).

Growing prominence of mercantilist views that equate foreign profit with Chinese loss and implicitly deny the possibility of mutually beneficial commercial trade underpins strident demands to replace imports with domestic goods, especially in technology-intensive sectors like semiconductors, IT, and nuclear power. Royalty payments to foreign vendors of technology and other intellectual property, which amount to an economically trivial 1 percent of annual exports, draw particular ire.[10]

To implement a big push for breakthrough innovations beyond the reach of market pressures and foreign involvement, strategic plans inevitably concentrate expectations and resources in the hands of state enterprises, especially the giant firms operating under the aegis of State-owned Assets Supervision and Administration Commission (SASAC) – a group that includes major operators in the sectors examined in this book. Recent steps elevate the position of Party structures within these firms, for example by mandating that the Board of China Railway Group "shall first listen to the opinions of the party committee of the company" before it "decides on material issues" (Hughes 2017).

China's New Industrial Policy and Regulatory Environment – Consequences

Following in the footsteps of China's initial Five Year Plans and the early post-war programs of Japan's fabled Ministry of Trade and Industry (MITI), China's leaders have crafted a massively funded, top-down, non-market, SOE-centered strategy intended to accelerate the development of highly visible innovations resting on a foundation of Chinese intellectual property. How will this affect the prospects for innovation within and beyond electricity, telecommunications, and semiconductors? What is the likely impact on the wider economy?

China's new approach to innovation bifurcates the economy along lines reminiscent of the 1980s policy of "Planned economy as the mainstay, market allocation as supplementary" (计划经济为主，市场调节为辅 *jihua jingji weizhu, shichang tiaojie weifu*) as well as the "big push" industrialization strategy intended to graft a self-contained network of advanced

---

[10] China's 2016 international payments for the use of intellectual property amounted to US$24 billion or just above 1% of China's 2016 exports, which totaled US$2,120 billion in the same year. Ireland ($76 billion), the Netherlands ($48 billion) and the United States ($43 billion) surpassed China's total in 2016; Japan (($20 billion) and Singapore ($19 billion) followed close behind. Data from World Bank's World Development Indicators.

producers atop an economy populated by firms with lesser capabilities (Rosenstein-Rodan 1943; Murphy, Schleifer, and Vishny 1989).

The difficulty is that, as both Chinese and external commentators (e.g. Chen 2012; Tse 2015, p. 47) observe and as recent Chinese experience copiously demonstrates, expansion of market forces promotes innovation and productivity growth, while concentration of resources in the state sector has the opposite effect. Market regimes sharpen incentives. Success brings extraordinary rewards, while laggards experience Joseph Berliner's "invisible foot," which market systems apply "vigorously to the backsides of enterprises that would otherwise have been quite content to go on producing the same products in the same ways, and at a reasonable profit, if they could only be protected from the intrusion of competition" (1976, p. 529).

Opening China's economy to international trade and investment attracted a torrent of new technologies and advanced products into the domestic market, creating both risk and opportunity:

> Chinese companies have gained a great deal of knowledge from multinationals in China through acting as their suppliers and customers, and as staff trained by foreign investors have hopped across to jobs with Chinese organizations … The scale of inward foreign investment and trade has meant that Chinese companies have been forced to learn how to compete with multinationals from day one in order to survive in their home market. Compared to their Japanese and Korean cousins, Chinese companies have had to face the cold winds of international competition almost from infancy (Zeng and Williamson 2007, p. 17).

Case studies show how Chinese producers of telecom and construction equipment used the accumulation of technical knowledge and market experience as a springboard to claw their way into fiercely competitive global markets, eventually wresting market share from long-entrenched multinational rivals (Brandt and Thun 2010, 2016). Mandel (2013) finds rapid quality improvement of Chinese exports (measured by rising unit values and growing penetration of high-income markets), demonstrating the breadth and strength of links between openness and upgrading. Brandt, Van Biesebroeck, Wang, and Zhang (2017) find a causal relation between reduced tariffs on both outputs and inputs, signals of growing economic openness, and sector-level productivity growth.[11] These effects extend into the state sector, with the likelihood of dismissal for leaders of poorly performing SOEs rising in sectors experiencing lower tariffs.

---

[11] In addition, falling tariffs push firms to lower markups (the ratio of sales price to marginal cost), indicating reduced market power.

Extending domestic openness to include "all kinds of market players" (Decision 2014, Item 9) seems equally beneficial. While SOE dominance coincides with strong productivity outcomes in some instances, enterprise-level data for 1998–2007 reveal a strong association between state sector influence and poor results. Total factor productivity (TFP, discussed below) *rose* by an average of 20.8 percent in sectors where the output share of SOEs was below 50 percent and *declined* by 11.7 percent in sectors where SOEs provided the majority of output value. Perhaps more important than this yawning gap is the observation that, in SOE-dominated sectors, new entrants on average *reduced* TFP outcomes regardless of ownership, "suggesting an entry process that is highly politicized and distorted," with connections, rather than competence, in the driver's seat (Brandt 2016, p. 289).

Bifurcation signals a partial reversal of the gradual and uneven, but cumulatively massive shift in the direction of greater market discipline that has accompanied four decades of reform. Official assignment of innovation targets rolls back past efforts to commercialize state enterprises, for example under the rubric of "separating government from enterprises" (政企分开 *zhengqi fenkai* see Decision 2014, Item 7). It is the antithesis of Chen Qingtai's (2012) vision of a renewed state sector in which "the government no longer controls and manages, firms become independent market entities oriented to financial outcomes, led by boards of directors, that gain strength and expand through market competition."

Partial retreat from the spread of market forces follows a period of rapid expansion and consolidation among giant state-sector firms in coal, steel, railway equipment, and shipbuilding, among others. Between 2004 and 2015, the number of subsidiaries under centrally led enterprise groups that existed in both years jumped from 6,830 to 14,227; in 2014, these groups also held minority stakes in over 5,000 non-subsidiary firms (Brandt, Dai, and Zhang 2017).

The sheer size of the now-enlarged priority sector, the continuing inflow of innovation-linked resources, and the prospect of expanded official protection for firms that already enjoy a regime of "limited competition . . . and . . . virtually insurmountable barriers to new firm entry" (Naughton 2015, p. 52) means that the rollback of market discipline accompanying the shift toward plan fulfillment is likely to spill beyond the boundaries of the priority sector.

Relaxation of competitive pressures arising from priority status and from the growing market power of SOE giants imposes unwelcome costs. State Grid Corporation's 2009 acquisition of Pinggao (平高电气) and Xuji (许继电气), two prominent manufacturers of electrical machinery, illustrates the problem. An industry source reports that these mergers triggered abrupt declines in (formerly excellent) quality and service (Interview, June 2013), apparently because the two firms viewed their new association with State Grid, the world's largest public utility, as guaranteeing ample sales.[12]

Bifurcation means exclusion. Priority status for some firms relegates multiple enterprise categories to the periphery of China's new innovation efforts. Official preference for scale excludes small firms, which the joint Bank-DRC report lauds as "the big firms of the future" (WB & DRC 2013, p. 36), including all but the largest private operators. Strategic planners tilt toward vertical integration, as Brandt and Wang note for wind turbines. They favor multi-purpose manufacturers, insisting, for example, that applicants seeking recognition as manufacturers of new energy vehicles (NEV) "demonstrate that they have mastered the . . . technology for the complete NEV, not just for one of three core technologies" (EU Chamber 2017, p. 39). Such measures exclude specialist firms that contribute substantially to innovative structures both within and outside China.[13] Nationalist objection to imports of technology-related commodities and services erects barriers to the involvement of imported goods or foreign-linked domestic firms in priority innovation projects.[14]

Innovation outcomes are highly uncertain. New ideas appear in unexpected places. Unheralded firms or even individuals – think of Microsoft's Bill Gates, Apple's Steve Jobs, Alibaba's Jack Ma, Huawei's Ren Zhengfei, Baidu's Li Yanhong, TenCent's Pony Ma, State Grid's Liu Zhenya, or Haier's Zhang Ruimin – can build hugely influential operations from scratch. Experts can easily misjudge the potential of would-be innovators, as when Japan's legendary Ministry of Trade and Industry "attempted to

---

[12] Xu 2017 notes that these particular acquisitions prompted "strong criticism" that "accused SGCC of using its economic muscle to . . . squeeze out competitors, and make it difficult for other manufacturers to get fair deals from the giant consumer" (2017, p. 258). More generally, "Many small and medium companies complain that . . . large SOEs . . . are abusing their market power by favoring their own connected companies and excluding" others (WB & DRC 2013, p. 170).

[13] Excluded firms seeking to sell into priority sectors may find themselves forced into costly and unwanted alliances with insider firms. As Breznitz and Murphree note, "virtually all high-technology enterprises seek what Adam Segal (2003) terms 'a bureaucratic mother-in-law' by becoming an affiliate of a state agent" (2011, p. 44). Private wind farm operators complain that even with official approval of their projects, they cannot avoid selling out to state-sector rivals (Zhang 2016).

[14] The term 自主 (*zihu*) meaning "autonomous" or "acting for oneself," as in autonomous research, intellectual property, brands, innovation, design, etc. appears 123 times in Roadmap 2015.

deny a fledgling Sony the $25,000 . . . to license transistor technology from Western Electric" (Johnstone 1999, p. xv).

Channeling large-scale innovation support to administratively selected insider firms is unwise in any context. China's strategy of concentrating resources and responsibilities in the hands of state enterprises, a problematic group with a collective history of "weak cost, profit and productivity performance" seems particularly dangerous (Brandt, Ma, and Rawski 2017, p. 223). Unpleasant surprises await, as "companies with innovative ideas find themselves out of the loop" (Breznitz and Murphree 2011, p. 32), while state-run champions equipped with "the capacity for innovation" but saddled with "defective incentive systems" (Fu 2013, p. 54) expend valuable resources on poorly chosen projects.

While four decades of reform have wrought remarkable changes in China's economy, it is easy to overlook the distinctive legacies of Soviet-inspired institutional structures, especially in SOE-dominated segments of the economy. Consider the following observations by Peter Wiles, all written long before the start of China's economic reform:

- There is something 'socialist' and 'progressive' about mere size, even if unaccompanied by lower costs (1962, pp. 304–5).
- Perpetual loss-makers are either subsidized . . . forcibly amalgamated with profit-makers, or kept alive by bank loans (1968, p. 48).

And, particularly relevant to innovation, what Wiles dubs:

- Technological snobbery . . . the notion that the most modern way of producing the most fashionable product is the best way to employ our resources (1968, p. 178).

Announcement of competition-stifling mega-mergers, complaints that soft budget constraints prolong the existence of uneconomic "zombie" enterprises (僵尸企业 *jiangshi qiye*), and a report that "By mid-2016, 28 provinces and provincial-level cities had designated robotics as a priority sector" (EU Chamber 2017, p. 35), confirm the uncanny relevance of Wiles' half-century-old observations about the former Soviet Union.

An official innovation strategy that promises a partial revival of Soviet-style planning can only increase the already considerable costs that Soviet-era legacies impose on China's economy.[15] Several areas seem particularly relevant.

---

[15] To cite a single example: during the recent financial crisis, the worst in living memory, quarter-to-quarter fluctuations in US nominal investment spending fell short of 10%. In

Innovation without Economic Benefit

Accounts of Chinese innovation often focus on inputs – rising numbers of research personnel, growing R&D outlays, or expanding ranks of engineering graduates – factors that elevate innovative potential rather than results. Common measures of innovation output – numbers of publications, share of output designated as "new" or "high tech" products[16] – are easy to manipulate and may therefore have little connection with innovation outcomes.

Studying patents, which researchers view as "a leading indicator of emerging technological prowess" offers a more promising link to innovation, one that is particularly relevant for this volume because electrical engineering accounts for 57 percent of Chinese applications under the Patent Cooperation Treaty (PCT; see Boeing and Mueller 2016, p. 145; 2018, p. 17). A steep rise in patent submissions has vaulted China past the United States as the leading source of worldwide patent applications beginning in 2011 (Boeing and Mueller 2016, p. 145). China climbed into second place for PCT submissions during 2017, trailing only the United States (WIPO 2018).

Focusing on international search reports associated with PCT applications to avoid biases arising from the nationalistic inclinations of individual patent offices, Boeing and Mueller analyze trends in the quality of Chinese patent submissions and compare them with similar results for the United States, Germany, Japan, and Korea. To measure quality, they calculate the frequency with which specific patents receive citations in subsequent submissions originating in other countries, in the patent-holder's home country and/or in self-citations by the initial patent-holder.

Basing their quality measure solely on overseas citations leads Boeing and Mueller to conclude that, relative to submissions from other leading sources of patent submissions, the quality of Chinese patents is low and declining. Including domestic and self-citations produces results that approach or surpass outcomes for the international comparison group (2018, p. 16).

Boeing and Mueller attribute the latter outcomes to measurement bias. Noting economists' long-standing concern that "indicators fail as reliable measures if they become the target of policy," they find that China "has incentivized increases in the quantity of applications to the detriment of

China, the legacy of giant plan-inspired seasonal fluctuations persists: periodic reports issued by the National Bureau of Statistics show first-quarter investment spending routinely dropping more than 40% from the figure for the previous year's fourth quarter.

[16] The authors have visited "high tech" production facilities that resemble garment factories, except that workers use screwdrivers and other manual tools rather than sewing machines and assemble electrical components rather than pieces of fabric.

quality." Their conclusion: current policy "rewards low quality patents with no economic benefit," transforming "Chinese patent applications and citations thereof" into "questionable measures of innovation levels" (2018, p. 29).

Episodes of innovation with little benefit and prioritizing quantity or scale over quality reverberate across the landscape surveyed in the chapters that follow.

Michael Davidson in Chapter 4 finds that low utilization saps the expected benefits of advanced thermal power units.

A Chinese specialist offered the view that developing ultra-supercritical thermal power equipment would require massive expenditure to obtain "marginal" performance improvements (Interview, June 7, 2013).

Beijing plans a massive expansion of China's electric vehicle fleet even though researchers at Tsinghua University find that the "life cycle energy consumption and greenhouse gas emissions of ... battery electric ... vehicles in Chinese context ... are about 50% higher than those of an internal combustion engine vehicle" (Qiao et al. 2017).

Developing advanced technology for its own sake – Wiles' "technological snobbery" – creates benefits that may fall short of the "opportunity cost" of deploying resources elsewhere.

In 2017, following eight years of experimentation, Dongfang Electric completed factory testing of a prototype 5 KW offshore wind turbine designed for service in typhoon-prone waters off Fujian province (Dongfang 2017). The prototype builds on autonomous (自主 *zizhu*) intellectual property, electronic controls and core technology and achieves a "high degree of localization." Data compiled by Brandt and Wang show that, as of 2012, Chinese firms put far greater effort into large wind turbines than foreign manufacturers: their Table 9.10 shows five international firms offering two models rated at 5KW or more, whereas ten Chinese firms offer ten models in the same category, with an additional five prototypes in preparation. With equipment rated at or below 2KW consistently accounting for more than 80 percent of new Chinese installations, concentrating R&D efforts on improving the (currently low) quality of their main products would in all likelihood have generated far greater economic benefits than developing prototypes of prestigious (and far more complex) but little-used large-scale devices.[17]

While Xu shows in Chapter 6 how State Grid has become a world leader in ultra-high voltage long distance power transmission, Thomas G. Rawski

---

[17] Yang (2015) gives annual market shares for turbines of various sizes for 2012–14. For 2015, see www.researchandmarkets.com/research/p4pwbh/global_and_china (accessed August 15, 2018).

in Chapter 8 notes that domestic critics assail the costs associated with this undoubted technical advance: they complain that transmission lines incorporating the new technology suffer from higher costs and lower utilization rates than conventional alternatives. Widespread comment on the costs associated with China's inadequate facilities for cross-regional power transmission[18] encourages the view that State Grid's successful pursuit of global technology leadership has come at the expense of much-needed expansion of conventional power transmission facilities.

Observing that the slogan *zizhu chuangxin* 自主创新, officially translated as "indigenous innovation," could also be fairly translated as "autonomous innovation," Arthur Kroeber notes that the objectives of Made in China 2025 "and other Chinese innovation policies often seem less about creativity per se, and more about reducing reliance on imported products, services and ideas" (2016, p. 65).

As the world's largest producer and consumer of many commodities, domestic production often makes good economic sense. But since exchange of similar commodities – for example machine tools, automotive components, and patent licenses – occupies a huge share of international trade among advanced nations, the *economic* benefit of pursuing wide-ranging replacement of imported products, components, software and technology is far from clear.

Market Segmentation and Market Power

Chinese governments at all levels routinely place a premium on building large-scale enterprises. They also promote industrial concentration – i.e. raising the market share of the largest producers. Market segmentation, which creates barriers that exclude outsiders to benefit favored participants, magnifies the consequences of policies that promote scale and concentration.

Chen Qingtai (2012) eloquently explains the caste system that governs Chinese business. State enterprises are "insiders" (体制内 *tizhinei*) with privileged access to natural resources, finance, administrative approvals, and entry conditions that are often "made to measure" (量身定制 *liang-shen dingzhi*) for large firms. Centrally directed firms like State Grid, China Telecom and the big power generation and nuclear firms, "have the highest social status and the right to speak up." Locally supervised state enterprises

---

[18] For example, the provincial NDRC head in Gansu, a leading producer of wind and solar power, attributes the province's massive spillage of renewable power to weak demand and to "limited capacity for outbound transmission" (Zhang Zirui 2017a).

occupy the second rank. Then come foreign invested firms with "consider-able strength and voice." Finally, private firms, which are "blocked by glass barriers," seen as uncreditworthy by banks, and "often forced to merge with money-losing state firms," occupy "the least favorable status." Chen concludes that segmentation of firms according to ownership status, along with unresolved issues of local protectionism, which imposes its own entry barriers, creates "two powerful anti-competitive forces that reduce effi-ciency and limit our development potential."

With growing emphasis on autonomy, import replacement and self-reliance, China's current innovation strategy raises the prospect of new entry barriers aimed at imported products, foreign-invested enterprises and foreign-owned intellectual property. Wübbeke et al. (2016, p. 7) summarize potential difficulties facing foreign businesses and high priority sectors:

While Chinese high-tech companies enjoy massive state backing, their foreign competitors in China face a whole set of barriers to market access and obstacles to their business activities: the closing of the market for information technology, the exclusion from local subsidy schemes, the low level of data security and the intensive collection of digital data by the Chinese state.

Access depends on fine-grained official actions that often allow extensive local discretion:[19]

As more industries implement Internet-enabled products and services, standards have the potential to create trade barriers in industries nominally open to foreign investment (US Chamber 2017, p. 30).

Implementation at the local level is often a major barrier ... obtaining [High- and New-Technology Enterprise status] ... depends on local authorities' inter-pretation of the requirements, as well as their political and industrial strategies. This discretionary approach creates uncertainty ... (EU Chamber 2017, p. 60).

Reference to the "political and industrial strategies" of sub-national governments serves as a reminder of their tendency to replicate the center's effort to nurture "champion" firms in "strategic" industries and to protect these clients from unwelcome rivals. Although the proliferation of trucks and expressways has eroded historic barriers to domestic trade, we now find provinces and localities blocking electricity "imports" from elsewhere. As Beijing moves to limit firms with partial or full foreign ownership from

---

[19] Official discretion is commonplace. A manager in the electrical equipment sector notes "high ranking officials of grade 6 or 7" make purchasing decisions; in doing so, "they may award contracts to familiar firms without even looking at the bid documents" (Interview, October 2012).

participating in priority industries, we can expect local officials to apply their own brand of mercantilism to domestic as well as foreign outsiders. Requiring wind farms to install locally manufactured turbines (Zhang Zirui 2017b) or ordering taxi companies to replace conventional cars with electric vehicles whose manufacturer promises local production (Taiyuan 2016) illustrates a wider protectionist agenda:

Local protectionism creates regional entry barriers ... for example by forbidding or restricting sales of outside products, implementing special approval procedures ... or tax and fee standards for outside enterprises and products, or implementing different standards for quality and technical inspections or different price restrictions for local and outside firms (Fu 2013, p. 54).

Poor Investment Decisions

Kornai (1980) noted that universal shortages of goods stoked an unlimited appetite for investment in the former Soviet Union and its European socialist allies because new production could always find buyers. In China, this "investment hunger" persists even in the absence of excess demand. Prominent Marxian economist Liu Guoguang is among many authors who deplore China's "long history of deep-rooted investment hunger and impulse for blind expansion" (根深蒂固的投资饥饿 和盲目扩张冲动 *genshen digu de touzi ji'e he mangmu kuozhang chongdong*; 2000, p. 6).

The incentives underlying widespread investment excesses include the benefit that building new facilities confers on leaders' career prospects, widespread preference for local self-sufficiency, and the informal income opportunities surrounding every stage of project planning, approval, and implementation. Weak financial controls surrounding innovation outlays – Xiang (2017) notes that government guidance funds "often operate in utmost secrecy," that "most ... do not conduct performance assessment" and that "no one is named to be accountable for performance" – encourage the worst features of past investment behavior.

Despite four decades of market-leaning reform, demand prospects, price-cost comparisons and other standard market metrics often have little place in the calculus underlying investment decisions, especially within the state sector. In January 2018, for example, a news report announced that a newly completed hydropower plant along Sichuan's Yalong River faced immediate closure because protracted wrangling over a proposed transmission line left the new facility without links to potential markets (Su 2018). Continued pursuit of new power generation projects in the face of declining utilization rates highlights the non-commercial nature of many investment decisions. Generating companies view these investment excesses as "staking a claim" (跑马圈地 *paoma quandi*) to future delivery quotas, which are typically distributed among all available producers (He 2015; see also Excess Capacity 2016).

In a 2017 interview, power specialist Yuan Jiahai (袁家海) offers the prospect that yet another tranche of reforms may inject (previously absent) economic calculation into electricity investors' decision-making:

Reformed arrangements in which newly approved power plants no longer receive delivery quotas and government no longer sets prices will lead investors to make rational decisions [合理决策 *heli juece*], so that the market mechanism will curb the enthusiasm for investing in new thermal power plants (Yu 2017).

While Yuan's observations focus on thermal power, planned economy thinking pervades every segment of the power sector, with producers first building new facilities and then looking to government to arrange outlets for enlarged power production.

Electricity is not unique. Enhanced entry and diminished exit, both documented in Margaret Pearson's exploration of local government behavior, breed overinvestment and excess capacity. Announcements of strategic priorities spark widespread investment excesses, as companies, localities, universities, and research institutes scramble to share in the bonanza of cash and recognition lavished on robotics, new energy and other "hot" sectors. The result: repeated criticism of "blind expansion" and "Great Leap-style" overinvestment not just in thermal power, but also in renewable energy, electric vehicles, semiconductors, and elsewhere.[20]

Electric power illustrates the scale of excess investment. Power systems maintain a cushion of reserve generating capacity that enables them to respond effectively to unforeseen equipment failure or demand spikes. US industry specialists recommend a back-up capacity amounting to 15 percent of a power system's peak load (Lin, Liu, and Kahrl 2016, p. 10). In 2015, the average and median back-up capacity among China's provinces exceeded 90 percent of peak load. No less than twenty-four province-level jurisdictions reported 2015 back-up capacity exceeding 50 percent of peak load, with Inner Mongolia, which houses the largest generating capacity, maintaining reserve capacity amounting to 278 percent of its peak load. Yet investment rolls on. Provinces with capacity cushions exceeding 50 percent

---

[20] For recent criticism of "blind expansion," see Jia 2017 (thermal power), He 2017 (batteries), Zhang Zirui 2016 (wind power), Bie 2017 (clean coal); for "Great Leap," see Thermal Leap 2015 (thermal power). Critiques referring to both include Blind Leap 2012 (new energy vehicles) and Green Energy Leap 2015 (wind and solar power).

accounted for 83 percent of nationwide growth in generating capacity during 2015/16 (Power Compendium 2016).

Excess capacity erodes the payoff to new technologies. Brandt and Wang show how low utilization rates and grid connection issues – another consequence of excess capacity – drive up the cost of wind and solar electricity (see also Lam, Branstetter and Azevedo 2016). Utilization rates for thermal power plants have declined sharply amid a recent burst of expansion: the 2016 average of 4,165 hours, the lowest since 1964, is far short of the 5,000–5,500 hours needed to cover costs. Madhavan, Rawski, and Tian report that average 2016 operating hours for nuclear plants may have fallen below 7,000 (sources disagree on the exact figure), the benchmark allowing timely repayment of loans. With analysts predicting further declines in operating hours, generation companies will face escalating financial pressures.

Overcapacity limits environmental as well as financial benefits from technical upgrades. Michael Davidson shows how China's long-standing system of equally distributing operating hours among incumbent generating plants translates into low utilization rates for the newest and most efficient facilities. This arrangement limits production from cleaner plants to preserve market share for lesser facilities, a common outcome of Chinese industrial and regulatory policy. The result: higher costs and excess burdens on China's already overloaded air resources.

Quality Lapses

Neglect of quality is a long-standing weakness among Chinese manufacturers that dates from the initial years of socialist planning. A 1957 commentary advocated "creating an atmosphere in which importance is attached to quality." Two decades later, Deng Xiaoping demanded that products falling "below the quality standard should not be allowed to leave the plant" (quoted in Rawski 1980, pp. 119, 125). A 1982 account castigated "the existing erroneous tendency to . . . neglect product quality" (FBIS 1982).

Despite vast reform-era improvements and occasional pockets of excellence, the legacy of socialism, along with pressure from cost-conscious customers, has left quality issues to fester in many segments of manufacturing. The machinery industry, China's largest and also the centerpiece among the ambitious targets written into Made in China 2025, has not overcome its history of limited attention to quality. In 2015, an American energy company's personnel discovered that their Chinese licensee had skipped some segments of a quality control protocol; when confronted with this lapse, the Chinese supplier responded that it had to meet its production schedule (Interview, September 2017). Neglect of quality is widespread. In 2016, former Deputy Machinery Minister Shen Liechu (沈 烈初) summarized the reputation of Chinese-made equipment among both domestic and foreign buyers as "usable but not too reliable" (能用, 不太可靠 *nengyong butai kekao*) – particularly because "small defects continue" (小毛病不断 *xiaomaobing buduan;* Hu 2016). Echoing earlier discussions of quality issues in the manufacture of nuclear equipment, an enterprise-based author writes that "procedural violations (违章现象) are very common" and that "reversing the habit of violating procedures is difficult" (Shao Yong 2016, p. 55; see also Li Xiushan 2012 and Tan Gan 2012).

Quality problems extend beyond machine building. A brief September 2017 document issued by China's highest authorities – the Communist Party's Central Committee and the State Council – lamented the "inadequate effective supply of mid-level and high end products and services." Summoning language that echoes pleas of earlier decades, China's leaders urge "across the board effort to push economic development into an era of quality" (Central Committee 2017).

With its emphasis on large firms and "big innovation," China's latest innovation push may overlook the humdrum bits and pieces that underpin the precision and durability of advanced systems. A 2016 survey noted that "production technology for parts and components lags behind the advances of major equipment" manufacture, illustrating the problem with reference to the limited reliability and durability of hydraulic pneumatic seals (Equipment report 2016, p. 261).

Current stress on import replacement threatens to undermine product quality in the technically advanced sectors that dominate official innovation plans by encouraging premature adoption of inadequate domestic components. After presenting a litany of shortcomings, noting, for example, that "the reliability of domestic sensors lags 1–2 orders of magnitude behind comparable foreign products," a review of instrument manufacture proposes that trade policy should "adjust procurement of meters and instruments to give a certain policy preference to domestic products" (Equipment Report 2016, pp. 249, 254).

USING PRODUCTIVITY TO RECONCILE
CONFLICTING EVIDENCE

Faced with substantial reason to anticipate both acceleration and slowdown of innovation and upgrading we turn to productivity trends, which combine a multitude of factors into a single measure of an economy's trajectory. While no one can foretell the future, we know that continued rapid growth depends on what Gordon Redding calls "the crucial test of productivity" expansion (2016, p. 58).

Brandt, Van Biesebroeck, and Zhang (2012) and Brandt, Van Biesebroeck, Wang, and Zhang (2017) document impressive productivity growth in Chinese manufacturing through 2007 that matches or exceeds achievements in other Asian economies during similar periods in their development. The metric is total factor productivity (TFP), the economist's yardstick for measuring the pace of innovation and upgrading in any economy.[21] Underlying these gains are highly complementary domestic market reforms, including initiatives that lowered entry barriers for new firms, and trade liberalization.

Table 1.1[22] provides related information for 1998–2013 at the three-digit level[23] for industry as a whole (manufacturing, mining, and utilities) and for several sectors analyzed in the following chapters.[24] Annual TFP growth for the entire industrial sector averages 1.44 percent – a substantial figure – over the entire period, but well below the result for 1998–2003 and especially 2003–8. Beginning in 2008, the figures show a sharp downturn in overall productivity advance, which averages only 0.38 percent for the period between 2008 and 2013.

Among the specific sectors highlighted in Table 1.1, telecom equipment – sector 405 in the Chinese industrial classification (CIC) – displays the best performance, with substantial growth of TFP in all sub-periods, including exceptional annual growth in excess of 5 percent during 2003–8.

Subdivisions linked to the production and transmission of electricity deliver mixed results. Generation and transmission equipment (CIC 381

---

[21] TFP is the ratio of deflated gross output (roughly equivalent to sales revenue in constant prices) to an index of combined inputs (labor, capital and intermediates like the coal used to generate electricity). TFP rises if average output per combined unit of labor, capital and materials is increasing; its rise reflects both cost reductions and improvement in product quality.

[22] Quantitative results presented in the tables and figures below are the product of joint work involving Brandt, Luhang Wang, Johannes Van Biesebroek, and Yifan Zhang.

[23] A one-digit breakdown of manufacturing separates firms into broad categories such as textiles, chemicals, and machinery. A two-digit breakdown distinguishes segments within each broad category, e.g. electrical equipment and transport equipment within the machinery category. Table 1.1 employs a three-digit classification that provides a further breakdown, e.g. showing separate figures for power generation (category 381) and power transmission equipment (382) within the broader electrical machinery category.

[24] We restrict the comparison to 1998–2013 to avoid issues of comparability arising from periodic revisions to China's industrial classification system. We are unable to isolate data for semiconductor firms.

Table 1.1 *Total Factor Productivity Growth for Manufacturing and Electricity-Related Subsectors, 1998–2013*

		Average Annual Percent Change			
CIC Code		1998–2013	1998–2003	2003–8	2008–13
	All Industry	1.44%	1.64%	2.25%	0.38%
	Subtotal for Electricity and Telecom-Related Sectors	1.66%	1.36%	3.27%	0.42%
381	Generation Equipment	1.51%	2.10%	3.83%	**−1.37%**
382	Transmission Equipment	0.82%	1.31%	2.84%	**−1.67%**
383	Wires and Cables	0.54%	1.41%	0.14%	0.08%
392	Telecom Equipment	2.88%	1.21%	5.05%	2.32%
	Solar Materials and Equipment	1.35%	0.84%	2.79%	**−1.65%**
	Wind Turbines	n.a.	n.a.	0.38%	**−4.54%**

Note: For wind turbines, sufficient data to develop sector-wide TFP data become available only from 2003.
China Industrial Classification (CIC) codes are those implemented in 2013. We classified firms as producers of wind turbines or solar (silicon, panels, and modules) based on descriptions of their main products.
Source: Analysis of firm-level data compiled by China's National Bureau of Statistics.

and 382) show positive and increasing levels of TFP growth up to 2008, but suffer declining TFP (shown in boldface) thereafter. TFP for producers of solar panels and materials such silicon, wafers and cells rises to 2008, but declines thereafter. Wind turbines experience negligible growth between 2003 and 2008, followed by sharply negative TFP change during 2008–13.

The sources of these changes deserve close attention. Table 1.2 presents decompositions of TFP growth in each of three sub-periods – 1998–2003, 2003–8, 2008–13 – into four components, which jointly account for overall TFP growth. The components include "Incumbents," which measures the contribution to TFP change from improvements in *incumbent* firms that operated throughout the period of analysis. "Entrants" captures TFP changes attributable to the activities of *new firms*. "Exit" measures changes in TFP due to the disappearance of firms – presumably poor performers – that leave the industry. "Reallocation" measures TFP change arising from the redistribution of resources *between* firms; the contribution is positive if high-productivity firms enlarge their share of available resources, and thus market share. The four components' share in overall TFP change add to 100 percent when TFP rises, and to –100 percent when TFP declines.

Table 1.2 *Decomposition of Total Factor Productivity Change in Six Subsectors during Each of Three Periods, 1998–2013*

Panel A: TFP Changes during 1998–2003

	Average Annual TFP Growth	Percent Share of TFP Change in This Sub-period Due to			
		Incumbent	Reallocation	Entrant	Exit
Generation Equipment	2.10%	54%	−5%	48%	3%
Transmission Equipment	1.31%	39%	−7%	54%	13%
Wires and Cables	1.41%	36%	18%	39%	7%
Telecom Equipment	1.21%	29%	−28%	97%	2%
Solar Materials and Equipment	0.84%	**−101%**	**−82%**	145%	138%

Panel B: TFP Changes during 2003–2008

	Average Annual TFP Growth	Percent Share of TFP Change in This Sub-period Due to			
		Incumbent	Reallocation	Entrant	Exit
Generation Equipment	3.83%	66%	−22%	56%	1%
Transmission Equipment	2.84%	61%	−20%	57%	1%
Wires and Cables	0.14%	238%	**−168%**	184%	**−154%**
Telecom Equipment	5.05%	79%	−16%	29%	7%
Solar Materials and Equipment	2.79%	**−11%**	**−12%**	90%	33%
Wind Turbines	0.39%	375%	**−340%**	**−136%**	0%

Panel C: TFP Changes during 2008–13

	Average Annual TFP Growth	Percent Share of TFP Change in This Sub-period Due to			
		Incumbent	Reallocation	Entrant	Exit
Generation Equipment	**−1.38%**	30%	**−46%**	**−75%**	**−9%**
Transmission Equipment	**−1.67%**	**−3%**	**−20%**	**−79%**	2%
Wires and Cables	0.08%	3%	126%	82%	**−110%**
Telecom Equipment	2.32%	30%	10%	38%	22%
Solar Materials and Equipment	**−1.65%**	**−54%**	**−8%**	**−66%**	28%
Wind Turbines	**−4.54%**	6%	**−20%**	**−84%**	**−2%**

Note: For wind turbines, sufficient data to develop sector-wide TFP data become available only from 2003.
Source: Analysis of firm-level data compiled by China's National Bureau of Statistics

Prior to 2008, the leading sources of productivity growth are entry of new firms with above-average productivity, followed by improvements among incumbents. Solar is the exception, with incumbents exerting consistently negative effects on TFP outcomes – meaning that TFP among incumbent producers of solar panels and materials and declined during each sub-period.

During 2008–13, however, only telecom equipment maintains TFP momentum amid a general collapse of productivity improvement. The matrix of components bristles with negative components (shown in bold-face), previously confined mainly to the column headed "Reallocation."

Two features stand out. In a dramatic change highlighted in Figure 1.1, the impact of new firms on TFP turns negative: generation equipment, transmission equipment, solar, and wind turbines all show entry exerting a negative impact on sector-wide TFP.[25] This means that, on average, new firms have lower productivity than incumbents – stunning evidence of poor investment choices.

Equally striking is the consistently negative TFP impact of "Reallocation" throughout the entire period covered in Table 1.2. These negative entries indicate that shifts of labor, capital, and other resources among incumbent firms have, on average, elevated the market share of poor performers at the expense of firms achieving higher levels of TFP – again signaling substantial inefficiency.

Recent productivity outcomes for the electricity and telecom-related sectors included in Table 1.1 and in Figures 1.1 and 1.2 seem representative of industry-wide trends. The top row of figures in Table 1.1 shows that the TFP trajectory described above – substantial advance during 1998–2008 followed by a steep drop-off in TFP growth thereafter – characterizes the recent evolution of China's entire industrial sector.

Further similarities emerge from Figure 1.2, which displays the contribution (rather than percentage shares) of the previously discussed components to industry-wide TFP change during the periods shown in Table 1.1. Two observations stand out. The positive impetus to TFP arising from the appearance of new enterprises virtually disappears after 2008. And for the entire industrial sector, as for the electricity and telecom-related segments described in Table 1.2, the TFP impact of Reallocation is generally negative – meaning that market share gravitates from higher to lower productivity firms, an inherently wasteful and debilitating outcome.

---

[25] Figures 1.1 and 1.2 draw on the same data used to compile Tables 1.1 and 1.2.

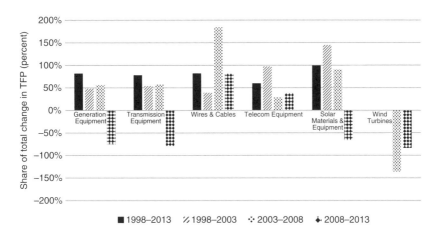

Figure 1.1 Contribution from Entry of New Firms to Total Factor Productivity Change by Period in Six Subsectors, 1998–2013

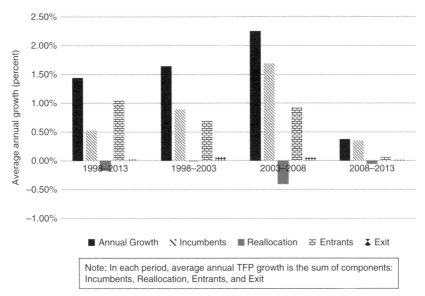

Note: In each period, average annual TFP growth is the sum of components: Incumbents, Reallocation, Entrants, and Exit

Figure 1.2 Average Annual Total Factor Productivity Growth and Components for China Industry, 1998–2013

These productivity outcomes encourage a skeptical appraisal of the likely impact of recent policy trends on future prospects for innovation and upgrading. One puzzling aspect: how can productivity decline in industries like power generation and transmission equipment when, as the chapters by Michael Davidson, Xu Yi-chong, and Thomas Rawski amply demonstrate, these very sectors have demonstrated the capacity to master new product varieties that embody advanced, and in some cases, world-class technologies?

One possibility is a slowdown in demand growth for electricity that reduces sales prospects, and thus productivity growth, for electrical equipment. However, the recent decline in electricity demand growth cannot explain the weak productivity outcomes for 2008–13 shown in Table 1.1.

More plausible explanations cluster on the supply side. Decision-makers who are partially or entirely divorced from market discipline may pursue innovations that, while technically feasible, fail to generate enough revenue to drive productivity growth. Consistently negative "reallocation effects" in Table 1.2 and Figure 1.2, indicate flows of resources *toward low-productivity firms*, and signal the presence of incentives and/or institutional arrangements that systematically promote productivity *decline*. Finally, high system costs of the sort observed in electricity generation and distribution (Chapter 8) may undercut potential productivity advances.

Looking beyond the sectors covered in Table 1.1, trends in the generation and distribution of electricity illustrate the potential for simultaneous appearance of technical advance and weak productivity outcomes. Electricity consumption per unit of generating capacity (1,000KWh per KW of installed capacity) rose from 3.54 in 1957 and 4.11 in 1976 to a peak of 4.97 in 2004, and then languished below the 1986 level throughout 2008–17. The average for 2008–17, 4.09, is 10.2 percent below the comparable figure for 1998–2007.[26] Such a decline surely erodes, and perhaps overwhelms simultaneous improvements in combustion efficiency and output per worker, pointing toward an unlikely coincidence of widespread upgrading and weak productivity results.

The total factor productivity metric employed in the foregoing discussion is best suited to gauging an economy's long-term success in absorbing and diffusing new and improved technologies. The influence of cyclical factors can push short-term results, such as those discussed here, above or below longer-term trends. In addition, productivity calculations are complex; uncertainties surrounding the underlying Chinese data, which include enterprise-level figures for output value, employment, and capital stock as well as sectoral and economy-wide measures of price change, necessitate substantial error margins.

---

[26] See authors' file Electric Power Use & Generating Capacity Data Summary.072518, available upon request.

Because of their short time span and lack of precision, the productivity results in Figure 1.1 and Table 1.1 cannot support definitive projections of future productivity trends. Evidence of the recent productivity slowdown, however, continues to accumulate. Unpublished materials that classify China's exports to Germany during 2000–15 according to varying levels of technological sophistication show the share of exports in the topmost category declining since 2010, with the 2015 level falling below the 2005 figure. Furthermore, the share of products in the lowest category has risen steadily; beginning in 2011, it exceeds the share from the top category. These data show China's exports to Europe's leading economy evolving in a direction that differs widely from what Chinese upgrading plans envision.

Many sources observe weak productivity outcomes. Ross Garnaut (2016) finds a "bleak story" with no "sign of a lift in the low rates of productivity growth that emerged in the aftermath of the fiscal and monetary expansions of 2008 and 2009." Economy-wide studies by Dollar (2016), by Wei, Xie, and Zhang (2017), and by Bai and Zhang (2017), all employing different data, find little evidence of productivity growth since the global financial crisis.

Convergence of results pointing to a steep decline in the most comprehensive measure of economically relevant innovation makes it difficult to avoid the conclusion that the economic impact of innovation and upgrading appears to have slowed or even stalled in major segments of Chinese manufacturing, in the entire industrial sector, and in the whole economy.

CHINA'S INNOVATION PROSPECTS BEYOND ELECTRICITY AND TELECOM

China represents the most recent and largest proving ground for competing visions of innovation dynamics. Building on extensive field study as well as detailed documentary research, this volume offers a series of case studies focused on the development and operation of three sectors: electricity, telecom, and semiconductors. Our findings include observations that will encourage proponents of both decentralized and interventionist approaches to promoting innovation and upgrading.

China's success in building modern and widely accessible infrastructure systems, including high-speed rail, expressways, civil aviation, and ports as well as the electricity and telecom networks analyzed in the chapters that follow, demonstrates the potential of interventionist policies to deliver stunning success. Despite the inevitable costs associated with features that critics of interventionism fiercely denounce – top-down planning, state enterprises and heavily restricted market access – China's semi-market environment has nurtured a dynamic process of innovation and upgrading that has produced innovative and entrepreneurial firms, improved "soft skills" as well as technical capabilities, and produced instances of world class achievement.

Douglas Fuller's study in Chapter 7 documenting the failure of protracted and expensive official efforts to establish a competitive beachhead in semiconductors leads a parade of difficulties, many self-inflicted, that bedevil innovation efforts in the industries studied in this volume. Excess costs, idle facilities, wasted investments, local protectionism, and ill-advised nativism, all conducted against a backdrop of large-scale diversion of public resources into private pockets, cumulate into a powerful indictment of Chinese-style interventionism.

But innovation, like economic growth, is an inherently wasteful process. While cataloging large and persistent inefficiencies and tabulating the likely magnitude of avoidable costs, we must recall the wisdom of Joseph Schumpeter, who famously wrote that a system:

that at *every* given point in time fully utilizes its possibilities to the best advantage may yet in the long run be inferior to a system that does so at *no* given point in time, because the latter's failure to do so may be a condition for the level or speed of long-run performance" (1942, p. 83, with emphasis in the original).

The Schumpeterian disconnect between efficiency and growth summarizes the post-World War II experience of East Asian economic dynamism, which combines unprecedented growth with massive inefficiency, a pairing much in evidence in the recent history of Japan, South Korea, and, above all, of China itself. In the same vein, Thun and Sturgeon highlight the possibility of "successful failure," meaning that failed attempts to master specific technologies or products may create capabilities that allow the economy to navigate formerly unattainable innovative paths.

Mounting evidence of weakening productivity performance warns that continuing along the trajectory of the recent past may produce outcomes weighted toward inefficiency rather than innovation. Episodic efforts to enlarge the orbit of market forces, most notably in segments of the energy sector, cannot conceal the absence of major reform initiatives of the sort that removed major barriers to entry, competition and through them, innovation during the 1980s and again in the 1990s.

Reflecting the protracted struggle between supporters and opponents of greater market opening, reduced top-down economic control, and expanded opportunity for private enterprise – prominent features of reform efforts during both the 1980s and 1990s, recent policy initiatives, with Made in China 2025 in the forefront, move in the opposite direction, emphasizing top-down technological choice, relying on state-run firms, and insulating priority sectors from potential rivals. Current policy trends magnify plan-era weaknesses that four decades of reform have never squarely confronted. Worse yet, China's leaders seem intent on reviving Mao Zedong's economically counterproductive veneration of self-reliance and suppression of criticism. Beijing's mercantilism, amplified by exclusionary echoes among China's provinces and localities, threatens to undermine product quality, a central component of success in the advanced industries that dominate China's ambitious innovation agenda.

China's new ten-year plan aims to inject Chinese technology and Chinese producers into the forefront of multiple high-end industries. The scale and breadth of this initiative has no parallel; it extends far beyond historical predecessors in Stalin's Soviet Union, Mao's China, and Kennedy's America. China's unique combination of momentum, confidence, scale, determined leadership, and vast financial and human resources creates massive potential for innovation – a frightening prospect for would-be competitors.

Yet the mechanics of China's new innovation drive – substituting official directives for market logic, elevating bureaucratic entities over commercial businesses, spurning established products and technologies in favor of untested Chinese alternatives – add new dangers into the unavoidably risky pursuit of cutting-edge innovation.

Looking forward, we expect China's innovation drive to deliver a mixture of headline-making successes and failures. The scale of Chinese demand, the size of individual Chinese industries and the magnitude of official support leads us to anticipate that, whatever the degree of success, Chinese efforts to target specific technologies and products will exert deep and protracted influence over a wide swathe of global markets during the coming decades.

While Chinese leaders and outside observers focus on iconic products of advanced technology, the outcome of China's innovation agenda will rest on the less visible results of myriad upgrading efforts affecting the millions of bits and bytes that collectively fill out the architecture of modern industry. For these operations, implementation of policy and regulation is far more important than plan announcements. If China's leaders allow regional governments and entrepreneurial managers to bend policies to suit ground-level economic realities, if private business dynamism can survive growing Party oversight, if official paeans to self-reliance can coexist with extensive Chinese participation in global supply networks, innovation may thrive both within the industries we have studied and throughout China's economy. Doctrinaire enforcement of policies that extend recent limitations on competition and openness, the key drivers of China's post-1978 economic gains, has the potential to hobble or even stall China's remarkable economic trajectory.

References

Abrami, Regina M., William C. Kirby, and F. Warren McFarlan. 2014. "Why China Can't Innovate." *Harvard Business Review*. 92(3).

Amsden, Alice H. and Wan-wen Chu. 2003. *Beyond Late Development: Taiwan's Upgrading Policies*. Cambridge, MA: MIT Press.

Bai, Chong-en and Qiong Zhang. 2017. "Is the People's Republic of China's Current Slowdown a Cyclical Downturn or a Long-term Trend? A Productivity-based Analysis." Manila: Asian Development Bank Institute Working Paper No. 635.

Bardhan, Pranab and Dilip Mookherjee. 2006. *Decentralization and Local Governance in Developing Countries: a Comparative Perspective*. Cambridge, MA: MIT Press.

Berliner, Joseph S. 1976. *The Innovation Decision in Soviet Industry*. Cambridge, MA: MIT Press.

Bie Fan 别凡. 2017. 清洁取暖, 煤炭仍可发力 [Clean and warm, coal still has room to grow]. 中国能源报 [China Energy Report]. April 24, 2017. p. 15.

Blair, David. 2017. "Growing Future Money Trees." *China Daily*. April 14, 2017. http://usa. chinadaily.com.cn/epaper/2017–04/14/content_28930514.htm (accessed September 16, 2017).

Blind Leap. 2012. 新能源汽车"大跃进" 盲目发展后患无穷 [Great Leap in new energy vehicles – blind development, endless trouble]. August 13, 2012. www.douban .com/note/230835650/ (accessed July 31, 2017).

Block, Fred and Matthew R. Keller, eds. 2011. *State of Innovation: The U.S. Government's Role in Technology Development*. Boulder, CO: Paradigm.

Boeing, Philipp and Elisabeth Mueller. 2016. "Measuring patent quality in cross-country comparison." *Economics Letters*. 149. pp. 145–7.

2018. "Measuring patent quality based on ISR citations: Development of indices and application to Chinese firm-level data." China Center for Economic Research Working Paper Series E2018007. February 26.

Brandt, Loren. 2016. "Policy Perspectives from the Bottom Up: What Do Firm Level Data Tell Us China Needs to Do." In Reuven Glick and Mark M. Spiegel eds., *Policy Challenges in a Diverging Global Economy*. San Francisco, CA: Federal Bank of San Francisco. pp. 281–302.

Brandt, Loren, Ruochen Dai, and Xiaobo Zhang. 2017. "The Anatomy of Chinese Business Groups: A Hierarchical Network Analysis." Working Paper.

Brandt, Loren, Debin Ma, and Thomas G. Rawski. 2017. "Industrialization in China." In Kevin O'Rourke and Jeffrey Williamson eds., *The Spread of Modern Industry to the Global Periphery Since 1871*. Oxford: Oxford University Press. pp. 197–228.

Brandt, Loren and Eric Thun, 2010. "The Fight for the Middle: Upgrading, Competition, and Industrial Development in China." *World Development*. 38 (11). pp. 1555–74.

2016. "Constructing a Ladder for Growth: Policy, Markets, and Industrial Upgrading in China." *World Development*. 80. pp. 78–95.

Brandt, Loren, Johannes Van Biesebroeck, Luhang Wang, and Yifan Zhang. 2017. "WTO Accession and Performance of Chinese Manufacturing Firms." *American Economic Review*. 107(9). pp. 2784–820.

Brandt, Loren, Johannes Van Biesebroeck, and Yifan Zhang. 2012. "Creative accounting or creative destruction? Firm-level productivity growth in Chinese manufacturing." *Journal of Development Economics* 97.2, pp. 339–51.

Brandt, Loren, Luhang Wang, and Yifan Zhang. 2017. "Productivity in Chinese Industry: 1998–2013." Background report prepared for Development Research Centre-World Bank project on "China's New Drivers of Economic Growth."

Brenner, Joel. 2014. "The New Industrial Espionage." *The American Interest*. 10 (1).

Breznitz, D. and M. Murphree. 2011. *Run of the Red Queen: Government, Innovation, Globalization and Economic Growth in China*. New Haven, CT: Yale University Press.

Cao, Cong, Richard P. Suttmeier, and Denis Fred Simon. 2006. "China's 15-year science and technology plan." *Physics Today*. 59 (12).

Central Committee. 2017. 我国提升国产核电质量竞争力 创新用能服务 [China elevates the competitive quality of nuclear equipment and innovative services for energy users]. September 14, 2017. www.china5e.com/news/news-1002445–1 .html (accessed September 14, 2017).

Chellaney, Brahma. 2011. *Water: Asia's New Battleground*. Washington, DC: Georgetown University Press.

Chen Qingtai 陈清泰. 2012. 陈清泰：国企改革转入国资改革 [Chen Qingtai on transforming Reform of state enterprises into reform of state assets]. May 9, 2017. http://naes.org.cn/article/31909 (accessed September 24, 2017).

Cimoli, Mario, Giovanni Dosi, and Joseph E. Stiglitz, eds. 2009. *Industrial Policy and Development: the Political Economy of Capabilities Accumulation*. Oxford: Oxford University Press.

Cox, Simon. 2017. "Emerging Markets: Out of the Traps." *Economist* special report. October 7, 2017.

Decision. 2014. "Decision of the Central Committee of the Communist Party of China on Some Major Issues Concerning Comprehensively Deepening the

Reform." Posted January 16, 2014. www.china.org.cn/china/third_plenary_session/2014–01/16/content_31212602.htm (accessed October 10, 2017).

Dinh, Hinh, Thomas G. Rawski, Ali Zafar, Lihong Wang, and Eleonora Mavroeidi. 2013. *Tales From the Development Frontier: How China and Other Countries Harness Light Manufacturing to Create Jobs and Prosperity*. Washington, DC: The World Bank.

Dollar, David. 2016. "China's New Macroeconomic Normal." Paper presented at the East West Center – Korea Development Institute conference on China's New Normal and Korea's Growth Challenge Honolulu, HI 3–4 November 2016.

Dongfang. 2017. 东方电气5 MW 抗台风海上风机下线 [Dongfang Electric's 5 MW typhoon-resistant offshore wind turbine rolls off the assembly line]. 中国能源报 [China Energy Report]. September 11, 2017. p. 18.

Economist. 2017. "Biting the Bullet: China Sets Its Sights on Dominating Sunrise Industries." September 23, 2017. p. 65.

Ellis, Jack. 2017. "ZTE revealed as vendor of Chinese patents sold to NPE set up by ex-Acacia executives." May 12, 2017. www.iam-media.com/blog/Detail.aspx?g=f4bf83e8-07c2-48a1-9ac9-12bb7213f31d (accessed October 8, 2017).

Equipment Report. 2016. 中国装备制造业发展报告2016 [2016 Development Report on Equipment Manufacturing]. Beijing: Shehui kexue wenxian chubanshe.

European Union Chamber of Commerce in China. 2017. *China Manufacturing 2025: Putting Industrial Policy Ahead of Market Forces*. Beijing: European Union Chamber of Commerce in China.

FBIS 1982. US Foreign Broadcast Information Service. July 8, 1982.

Excess Capacity. 2016. 电力产能过剩创纪录难抑投资冲动 电企大面积亏损 [Excess power capacity new record, investment impulse hard to control, losses mount for electricity companies]. August 15, 2016. http://www.china5e.com/news/news-956079–1.html (accessed September 1, 2016).

Fu Baozong 付保宗. 2013. 当前我国装备制造业竞争力现实特征及影响因素 [Current circumstances and influences on the competitive strength of China's equipment manufacturers]. 中国经贸导刊 [China economic and trade leader] no 7, pp. 51–4.

Gatley, Thomas. 2018. "The True Value of SOE Interest Rate Subsidies." Gavekal Dragonomics Ideas, August 30.3333.

Garnaut, Ross. 2016. "China's new normal inches on." East Asia Forum. Posted July 10 at http://www.eastasiaforum.org/2016/07/10/chinas-new-normal-inches-on/ (accessed July 25, 2018).

Gewirtz, Julian. 2017. *Unlikely Partners: Chinese Reformers, Western Economists, and the Making of Global China*. Cambridge, MA: Harvard University Press.

Green Energy Leap. 2015. 绿色能源大跃进：谨防高价买破坏 [Great Leap Forward in green energy: beware of paying high prices to purchase damage]. February 11, 2015. http://view.news.qq.com/original/intouchtoday/n3067.html (accessed July 31, 2017).

He Ying. 何英. 2017. 不能盲目追求电池能量密度 -访银隆新能源董事长魏银仓 [Do not blindly pursue battery energy density – interview with Yinlong New

Energy Board Chairman Wei Yincang]. 中国能源报 [China Energy Report]. June 12, 2017. p. 9.

He Yongjian 何勇健. 2015. 十三五电力规划应强调系统优化 [Power planning for the 13th Five Year Plan should emphasize system optimization]. 中国能源报 [China Energy Report]. August 3, 2015. p. 3.

Heilmann, Sebastian and Lea Shih. 2013. "The Rise of Industrial Policy in China, 1978–2012." Harvard-Yenching Institute Working Paper Series.

Hsieh, Li-min, Chen-kuo Hsu, and Dwight H. Perkins, eds. 2001. *Industrialization and the State: the Changing Role of the Taiwan Government in the Economy, 1945–1998*. Cambridge, MA: HIID.

Hu Qing 胡清. 2016. 国产装备如何杜绝质量瑕疵 [How to eliminate quality defects in Chinese-made equipment]. 中国能源报 [China Energy Report]. July 11, 2016. p. 20.

Huang, Kaixi. 2015. "Power Hook-up Policy a Live Wire in Guangxi." March 4, 2015. http://english.caixin.com/2015-03-04/100787992.html?utm_source=The+Sinocism+China+Newsletter&utm_campaign=11f7c7e5a7-Sinocism03_05_15&utm_medium=email&utm_term=0_171f237867-11f7c7e5a7-29602929&mc_cid=11f7c7e5a7&mc_eid=05464ef5ec (accessed March 8, 2015).

Hughes, Jennifer, 2017. "China's Communist party writes itself into company law." *Financial Times*. August 14. www.ft.com/content/a4b28218-80db-11e7-94e2-c5b903247afd (accessed October 10, 2017).

Jia Kehua 贾科华. 2017. 重组:解煤电矛盾的有效方式—专访电力行业专家陈宗法 [Reorganization: an effective way to alleviate contradictions between coal and electricity – interview with electricity expert Chen Zongfa]. 中国能源报 [China Energy Report]. September 18, 2017. p. 4.

Johnson, Chalmers. 1982. *MITI and the Japanese Miracle: the Growth of Industrial Policy, 1925–1975*. Stanford, CA: Stanford University Press.

Johnstone, Bob. 1999. *We Were Burning: Japanese Entrepreneurs and the Forging of the Electronic Age*. Boulder, CO: Westview Press.

Kennedy, Scott. 2017. *The Fat Tech Dragon: Benchmarking China's Innovation Drive*. Washington, DC: Center for Strategic & International Studies.

Kim, Linsu. 1997. *Imitation to Innovation: the Dynamics of Korea's Technological Learning*. Boston, MA: Harvard Business School Press.

Kornai, Janos. 1980. *The Economics of Shortage*. Amsterdam and New York: North Holland.

Kroeber, Arthur R. 2016. *China's Economy: What Everyone Needs to Know*. Oxford and New York: Oxford University Press.

Kubota, Yoko. 2018. "China Focuses on Apple Ambitions." *Wall Street Journal*. July 23, 2018.

Lam, Long T., Lee Branstetter, and Ines M. L. Azevedo. 2016. "China's wind electricity and cost of carbon mitigation are more expensive than anticipated." *Environmental Research Letters*. 11.

Li Xiushan 李秀山. 2012. 国内核电设备制造企业质量管理分析与对策 [Analysis and policy toward quality control in domestic manufacture of nuclear power equipment]. 质量管理 [Quality Management]. No. 1. pp. 24–31.

Lin, Jiang, Xu Liu, and Fredrich Kahrl. 2016. "Excess Capacity in China's Power Systems: A Regional Analysis." Ernest Orlando Lawrence Berkeley National Laboratory LBNL-1006638.

Liu Guoguang 刘国光. 2000. 中国经济增长形势分析 [Analysis of China's growth situation]. 经济研究 [Economic Research] No. 6. pp. 3–10, 76.

McGregor, James. 2010. *China's Drive for 'Indigenous Innovation': a Web of Industrial Policies.* Washington, DC: Global Regulatory Cooperation Project, US Chamber of Commerce.

Mandel, Benjamin. 2013. "Chinese exports and U.S. import prices." Federal Reserve Bank of New York Staff Reports No. 591.

Mandiant. 2013. "APT1. Exposing one of China's Cyber Espionage Units." Internet document. www.nationalcyberwatch.org/resource/apt1-exposing-one-of-chinas-cyber-espionage-units-2/(accessed September 25, 2017).

Mazzucato, Marianna. 2013. *The Entrepreneurial State: Debunking Public vs. Private Sector Myth.* London: Anthem Press.

MIC 2025. 2015. '中国制造2025'不是德国工业4.0翻版 [Made in China 2025 is not a replica of Germany's Industrialization 4]. May 15, 2015. www.miit.gov.cn/n973401/n1234620/n1234630/n1234633/c3793484/content.html (accessed July 18, 2018).

Millward, Steven. 2016. "China's state VC fund now has $336b to throw at startups." March 11, 2016. www.techinasia.com/china-state-vc-fund-over-330-billion-dollars (accessed September 16, 2017).

Miwa, Yoshiro. 2004. *State Competence and Economic Growth in Japan.* London and New York: Routledge Curzon.

Miwa, Yoshiro and J. Mark Ramseyer. 2010. *The Fable of the Keiretsu: Urban Legends of the Japanese Economy.* Chicago, IL: University of Chicago Press.

Mouawad, Jad. 2015. "Chinese Rail Firm Makes Inroads with U.S. Factory and Boston Transit Deal." *New York Times.* September 3 2015.

Murphy, Kevin M, Andrei Shleifer, and Robert W Vishny. 1989. "Industrialization and the *Big Push.*" *Journal of Political Economy.* 97 (5). pp. 1003–26.

Naughton, Barry. 2015. "The Transformation of the State Sector: SASAC, the Market Economy, and the New National Champions." In Barry Naughton and Kellee Tsai eds., *State Capitalism, Institutional Adaptation, and the Chinese Miracle.* New York: Cambridge University Press. pp. 46–71.

Nelson, Richard R. and Nathan Rosenberg. 1993. "Technical Innovation and National Systems." In Richard R. Nelson ed. *National Innovation Systems: A Comparative Analysis.* New York and Oxford: Oxford University Press. pp. 3–21.

Nolan, Peter. 2014. *Re-balancing China.* London and New York: Anthem Press.

OECD. 2016. *Main Science and Technology Indicators.* Issue 2.

Okimoto, Daniel I. 1989. *Between MITI and the Market: Japanese Industrial Policy for High Technology.* Stanford, CA: Stanford University Press.

Plumer, Brad and Coral Davenport. 2017. "Trump's Plan on Energy Calls for Deep Cuts to Innovation Program." *New York Times.* May 24, 2017.

Power Compendium. 2016. 二0一五年电力工业统计资料汇编 [Compendium of Electricity Industry Statistical Materials for 2015]. Beijing: 中国电力企业联合会 规划发展部.

Pressman, Aaron. 2016. "Chinese telecom giant brings lawsuits ahead of phones to U.S. market." July 8, 2016. http://fortune.com/2016/07/08/huawei-lawsuits-phones-u-s-market/ (accessed October 8, 2017).

Qiao, Qinyu et al. 2017. "Cradle-to-gate greenhouse gas emissions of battery electric and internal combustion engine vehicles in China." *Applied Energy*. Vol. 204. October 15, 2017. pp. 1399–411.

Rawski, Thomas G. 1980. *China's Transition to Industrialism*. Ann Arbor, MI: University of Michigan Press.

Redding, Gordon. 2016. "Impact of China's invisible social forces on its intended evolution." In Arie Y. Lewin, Martin Kenney, and Johann Peter Murmann eds., *China's Innovation Challenge: Overcoming the Middle-income Trap*. Cambridge: Cambridge University Press. pp. 56–86.

Roadmap. 2015. 《中国制造2025》重点领域技术路线图 [Key area technology road-map for Made in China 2025]. Beijing: 国家制造强国建设战略咨询委员会.

Rodrik, Dani. 2004. *Industrial Policy for the Twenty-First Century*. Cambridge, MA: Kennedy School of Government.

Rosenstein-Rodan, P. N. 1943. "Problems of Industrialisation of Eastern and South-Eastern Europe." *The Economic Journal*. 53 (210/211). pp. 202–11.

S&T Yearbook. 2016. 中国科技统计年鉴2016 [China Yearbook of Science and Technology Statistics 2016]. Beijing: China Statistics Press.

Sass, Stephen L. 2014. "Can China Innovate Without Dissent?" *New York Times*. January 22, 2014.

Schumpeter, Joseph A. 1942. *Capitalism, Socialism and Democracy*. New York: Harper.

Segal, Adam. 2003. *Digital Dragon: High-Technology Enterprises in China*. Ithaca, NY: Cornell University Press.

Segal, Adam. 2011. Statement on "Chinese Technology Policy and American Innovation," delivered to the US–China Economic and Security Review Commission, June 15, 2011.

Shaanxi Electricity. 2009. 陕西前五月电量逆势增长1.44% [Shaanxi first five months – contrarian electricity consumption growth of 1.44%]. June 8, 2009. http://ceppc.chinapower.com.cn/newsarticle/1094/new1094936.asp (accessed July 6, 2016).

Shaanxi Output. 2009. 上半年全省经济运行情况分析 [Analysis of Provincial economic activity in the first six months]. August 13, 2009. www.sn.stats.gov.cn/news/tjxx/200981384252.htm (accessed November 10, 200)9.

Shao Yong. 邵勇. 2016. 国内核电设备制造企业质量管理分析与对策 [Analysis and policy toward quality control in domestic manufacture of nuclear power equipment]. 质量探索 [Quality Forum]. No. 3. pp. 55–56.

Shy, Oz. 2001. *The Economics of Network Industries*. Cambridge and New York: Cambridge University Press.

Spinelli, Mike. 2005. "Chinese SUV Scores Zero in European Safety Test." *Jalopnik.* September 19, 2005. https://jalopnik.com/126200/chinese-suv-scores-zero-in-eur open-safety-test (accessed October 10, 2017).

Strategic. 2010. "Strategic emerging industries likely to contribute 8% of China's GDP by 2015." People's Daily Online October 19, 2010. http://en.people.cn/90001/ 90778/90862/7170816.html (accessed September 3, 2018).

Su Nan 苏南. 2018. 300亿度四川水电面临"投产即遭弃"[300 MW Sichuan hydro plant begins production and suddenly faces shutdown]. 中国能源报 [China Energy Report]. January 8, 2018. p. 1.

Sun, Xiaojing. 2016. The Role of Policy and Markets in the Development of the Solar Photovoltaic Industry: Evidence From China. PhD Dissertation. School of Public Policy, Georgia Institute of Technology.

Tan Gan 覃乾. 2012. 国产核电安全几何? [How safe is made-in-China nuclear power?]. 中国新时代 [China's new era]. August 16, 2012.

Taiyuan. 2016. "China's Coal Capital is Spending Millions to Go Green." October 16, 2016. www.bloomberg.com/news/articles/2016-10-16/china-s-poisonous-coal-capital-is-spending-millions-to-go-green (accessed September 27, 2017).

Tassey, Gregory. 2014. "Competing in Advanced Manufacturing: The Need for Improved Growth Models and Policies." *Journal of Economic Perspectives.* 28 (1). pp. 27–48.

Thermal Leap. 2015. 【报告】火电项目跃进将造成7000亿投资浪费 [Report: Great Leap in thermal power projects will produce RMB 700 billion of wasted investment]. Posted November 19, 2015. www.yicai.com/news/4714336.html (accessed October 17, 2017).

Thun, Eric, 2006. *Changing Lanes in China: Foreign Direct Investment, Local Governments and Auto Sector Development.* Cambridge and New York: Cambridge University Press.

Tse, Edward. 2015. *China's Disruptors: How Alibaba, Xiaomi, Tencent, and Other Companies Are Changing the Rules of Business.* New York: Penguin.

US Chamber of Commerce. 2017. US Chamber of Commerce. *Made in China 2025: Global Ambitions Built on Local Protections.* Washington, DC.

Vogel, Ezra. 1989. *One Step Ahead in China: Guangdong under Reform.* Cambridge, MA: Harvard University Press.

Wade, Robert. 2004. *Governing the Market: Economic Theory and the Role of Government in East Asian Industrialization.* Princeton, NJ: Princeton University Press.

Wei, Shang-jin, Zhuan Xie, and Xiaobo Zhang. 2017. "From 'Made in China' to 'Innovated in China': Necessity, Prospect, and Challenges." *Journal of Economic Perspectives*, 31(1). pp. 49–70.

Wiles, P. J. D. 1962. *The Political Economy of Communism.* Cambridge, MA: Harvard University Press.

  1968. *Communist International Economics.* New York: Praeger.

Wilkes, William. 2017. "Germany Combats Hackers from China." *Wall Street Journal.* September 25, 2017.

WIPO. 2018. World Intellectual Property Organization. "China Drives International Patent Applications to Record Heights." Posted March 21, 2018. www.wipo.int/pressroom/en/articles/2018/article_0002.html (accessed July 24, 2018).

Woetzel, Jonathan et al. 2014. *China's Digital Transformation: The Internet's Impact on Productivity and Growth*. NP: McKinsey Global Institute.

World Bank. 1993. *The East Asian Miracle: Economic Growth and Public Policy*. New York: Oxford University Press.

World Bank and Development Research Center of the State Council, People's Republic of China. 2013. *China 2030: Building a Modern, Harmonious, and Creative Society*. Washington, DC: World Bank

Wübbecke, Jost et al. 2016. *Made in China 2025: the Making of a High-Tech Superpower and Consequences for Industrial Countries*. Berlin: Mercator Institute for China Studies.

Xiang, Nina. 2017. "Rise Of Trillion-RMB Government Funds Reshapes China's Investment Landscape." January 13, 2017. www.chinamoneynetwork.com/2017/01/13/rise-of-trillion-rmb-government-funds-reshapes-chinas-investment-landscape (accessed September 11, 2017).

Xu, Yi-chong. 2017. *Sinews of Power: The Politics of the State Grid Corporation of China*. New York: Oxford University Press.

Yang, Hua. 2015. "State of the Art and Outlook of Chinese Wind Power Industry." May. Internet document. www.hh.se/download/18.22f781e714df33c44a0ccfb3/1435318137713/State+of+the+Art+and+Outlook+of+Chinese+Wind+Power+Industry+.pdf (accessed September 27, 2017).

Yearbook. 2010. 中国统计年鉴 2010 [China Statistical Yearbook 2010]. Beijing: Zhongguo tongji chubanshe.

Yip, George S. and Bruce McKern. 2016. *China's Next Strategic Advantage: from imitation to innovation*. Cambridge, MA: MIT Press.

Yu Xuehua 于学华. 2017. 袁家海：放开发电计划需关注煤电资产搁浅 [Yuan Jiahai: pay attention to stranded thermal power assets while releasing power generation from planning]. Posted August 21, 2017. http://news.bjx.com.cn/html/20170821/844538.shtml (accessed October 17, 2017).

Zeng, Ming and Peter J. Williamson. 2007. *Dragons at your Door: How Chinese Cost Innovation is Disrupting Global Competition*. Cambridge, MA: Harvard Business School Press.

Zhang Zirui 张子瑞 2016. 2016中国风电迈上新高度 [China's wind power reaches new heights in 2016]. 中国能源报 [China Energy Report]. December 26, 2016. p. 18.

2017a. 问计清洁能源消纳难 [Questions about the difficulty of absorbing clean energy]. 中国能源报 [China Energy Report]. March 13, 2017. p. 2.

2017b. 十三五风电如何破茧重生 [Rebirth of wind power under the 13th Five Year Plan]. 中国能源报 [China Energy Report]. June 19, 2017. p. 18.

2

China's Electricity and Communications Regulation in Global Context

Irene S. Wu[*]

INTRODUCTION

Twenty years ago, hotel reservations by fax were the cutting edge and you were lucky to have an electric fan during the summer heat.[**] Air-conditioned restaurants and online shopping are commonplace in today's Beijing. Most chapters in this volume are about tangible, physical products made in China that could be exported abroad. In contrast, this chapter is about the intangible – electricity and communications services – that to date are not generally exportable.

Essentials of modern life like reading after dark and talking to friends far away are only possible when all the relevant parts of the physical network connect with each other properly through a series of standards and interfaces set by governing authorities. What use is an unconnected generator or disconnected phone? The characteristics of the service mold the equipment, and the quality of the network gives value to the infrastructure, not the other way around. Furthermore, in electricity and communications, the more people are connected, the greater the network's value (Brennan 2009).

Electricity and communications are special in that they are network industries. Whereas clothing manufacturers can source, create, and deliver

[*] This work represents the view of the author only, not of the Federal Communications Commission or its Commissioners.

[**] In addition to the volume editors, I wish to thank for their insights: Regina Abrami, Tim Brennan, Michael Davidson, Max Dupuy, Mike Gaw, Terry Graham, Colette Hodes, Fredrich Kahrl, Guenther Lomas, Peter Lovelock, Daphne Mah, Jenny May, Joseph Mok, Brian O'Hanlon, Margaret Pearson, Russell Pittman, Paroma Sanyal, Len Tao, Nate Taplin, Sandra Waldstein, Heidi Werntz, Rick Weston, and C.K. Woo. All errors remain my responsibility.

products directly to customers largely on their own, a phone company can only deliver its client's message to a competitor's client by connecting to the competitor's network. Likewise, for electricity, generators need to connect with the grid in order to reach their end users. In both cases, that interface is a fraught space, the locale of the hardest, dragged-out fights in regulation. Behind the polite language and business suits, there are champion wrestling matches in the guise of administrative declarations and legal filings. A fraction of a cent change in an interconnection fee can send millions of dollars from one company to another. By modernizing its electricity and communications services, China's regulators leave the calm of the monopoly country club and join this regulatory fight league.

While communications and electricity regulation share many traits, they differ in two important respects. First, while communications can easily be stored and conveyed later, electricity cannot at a reasonable cost. When electricity is in demand is when electricity has to be generated. Therefore, while managing congestion on a communications network affects service quality, managing congestion on an electricity network is the difference between success and failure. Consequently, while price, terms, and conditions governing interconnection among operators are important for both sectors, they are especially important in electricity. Second, in communications, there is often more than one infrastructure over which a message can be sent, reducing the relative importance of any single interconnection. In contrast, in electricity, since most countries have just one transmission grid, properly functioning rules for transmission prices, terms, and conditions, are the difference between a working market and a blackout.

This chapter highlights five regulatory challenges China faces today and puts them in an international context. First, China has established regulators separate from network operators in both electricity and communications. Regulators are like referees in sports, in this case in a game with multiple teams of different sizes and strengths. Each team needs an independent and fair referee, but some teams have more influence than others. This is as true in China as elsewhere. However, unique to China is the national government's broader goals of promoting state-owned enterprises (SOEs) over private and foreign firms, and national companies over local ones.

Second, firms in China enter and exit the market under significant government guidance. Many of the other chapters highlight this phenomenon. In Chapter 4 Michael Davidson and in Chapter 3 Margaret M. Pearson track the struggles of local and provincial government to champion their own power generators and electric vehicle manufacturers contrary to central government priorities. Eric Thun and Timothy Sturgeon in Chapter 5 and

Table 2.1 *Electricity and Communications Services Market Segments*

Service Generation	Core Transmission Network	Local Distribution Network	Retail Service

Douglas B. Fuller in Chapter 7 discuss the central government's preferences for SOEs over hybrid companies with foreign investment and technology. All note the difficulty companies face in trying to exit the market. Loren Brandt and Thomas G. Rawski particularly highlight how blocking market exit decreases total factor productivity (TFP). To explore these problems more clearly, this section breaks down the electricity and communications sectors into four segments, as shown in Table 2.1, and discusses the entry and exit regulations for each that apply in China.

Third, a major issue in network regulation is how generators and retailers attach to the network and how competing network operators connect with each other. In communications, this is called interconnection. In electricity, these are issues around transmission and distribution (T&D). China's regulatory strategy is consistent with international practice – where barriers to entry are lower, allowing new companies to enter market segments, and where barriers to entry are higher, dividing large monopolies into smaller ones and benchmarking their costs and prices against each other. However, in the general literature on interconnection and T&D, the goal of regulation is promoting market efficiency to achieve greater economic growth. As is evident in the following chapters, the Chinese government additionally has ambitions that SOEs achieve international prestige. These goals compete for priority.

Fourth, there are intersecting issues that compete with economic regulation goals of market efficiency and overall economic growth. In electricity, this intersection is with environmental regulatory goals in China. China has achieved universal electricity service, but its environmental impact takes a toll on everyday quality of life in some regions. In communications, this intersection is with media regulation. The government's ideological concerns about foreign and subversive content pervade media regulation and directly impact internet industries.

Finally, the last section discusses safety regulation, especially how international safety standards support innovation in China. Two chapters in this volume note China's innovation successes – Ravi Madhavan, Thomas G. Rawski, and Qingfeng Tian's chapter 10 on nuclear power generators and Xu Yi-Chong's chapter 6 on ultra-high voltage transmission. Both are extremely dangerous to life and property and, therefore, the international safety standards are high. Foreign clients are only willing to purchase infrastructure that is certified safe. Chinese companies' success under these international regulatory regimes demonstrates the value of independent regulation to innovation. This suggests conforming China's regulatory regime for the environment and internet content to global norms could also enhance how industries perform in foreign markets.

SEPARATING INDUSTRY REGULATORS FROM OPERATORS

Today leading scholars and practitioners agree that establishing an independent regulator and introducing competition in the communications and electricity markets are essential for innovation and growth. In communications, in most major markets, independent regulators and privatized former monopolies are the norm (Wu 2008). In electricity, independent regulators are common but state-owned utilities are still common (Kessides 2012).

In China, regulatory authorities are separate from operators in both communications and electricity. The government took the first steps in 1997. In communications, the Ministry of Post and Telecommunications (MPT) was separated from China Telecom in 1997. At the same time, MPT merged with the Ministry of Electronics Industry that owned Unicom, a small competitor to China Telecom. Also in 1997, in the electricity industry the Ministry of Electric Power was separated from the operator the State Power Corporation of China. After several organizational shuffles, a new State Electricity Regulatory Commission (SERC) was created in 2002 as an autonomous regulator reporting directly to the State Council, China's cabinet level body.

Both regulators were kept weak by the assignment of key powers to higher government bodies. In electricity, National Development and Reform Commission's (NDRC) Energy Bureau had responsibility for planning policy and development. NDRC also held approval authority over major investments in generation and transmission. The NDRC pricing department retained the authority to set electricity prices. In communications, various State Council Leading Groups took leadership in major areas like internet policy (Wu 2009). For both sectors, the State-owned Asset Supervision and Administration Commission (SASAC), in its role as owner of state enterprises, held responsibility for personnel decisions, public listing of enterprises, and their merger and acquisition.

In 2008, there was another round of re-organizations. In communications, the ministry gained responsibility for additional technology sectors and became the Ministry of Industry and Information Technology (MIIT). By comparison, in electricity there has been more reshuffling: the Energy Bureau, the State Energy Office, and the nuclear power administration were combined into the National Energy Administration (NEA), which became part of NRDC. Electricity pricing was not assigned to NEA, but remained with the pricing unit of NRDC (OECD 2009). In March 2012, National Energy Administration (NEA) absorbed SERC (Xinhua October 2, 2013 and March 26, 2013). In early 2018, news reports suggested that a new ministry may take NEA's functions away from NDRC (Mason and Lim 2018).

Independent Regulators: the International Context

In electricity and communications, the number of countries that created independent regulatory authorities has skyrocketed over the last several decades. In a dataset of forty-eight countries, the number of independent regulatory agencies grew from 14 to 148 from 1990 to 2007 (Jordana, Levi-Faur, and Fernandez 2011). Consequently, several studies show that an independent regulator and competitive market structure are more important to realizing economic benefits than privatization.

In communications, Wallsten's World Bank study of 200 countries from 1987 to 1999 shows that establishing a regulatory authority before privatization increased telecom investment and enhanced the development of both fixed and mobile phone networks. Further, he found telecom firms in markets with a regulatory authority attracted more investment (Wallsten 2002). Also, in communications, Edwards and Waverman's study of fifteen European regulators from 1997 to 2003 shows that markets with an independent regulator and a privatized telecom operator had the lowest interconnection rates – the price that telecom networks pay each other to complete their calls. Next best interconnection rates were those observed in markets with independent regulators and state-owned incumbents (Edwards and Waverman 2006). In electricity in a study of thirty-six developing and transition countries from 1985 to 2003, Zhang, Parker, and Kirkpatrick (2008) show while privatization may improve performance, competition, and independent regulation have a greater impact.

Further studies discuss what factors can enhance a regulator's independence. In my study of communications regulators, I identify other strategies to enhance regulatory independence. For example, the Hong Kong regulator is funded through fees, rather than from government budget allocations. In the United States, administrative procedures require the publication of all proposed rules and comments in advance, during, and after regulatory decisions. In Japan, the culture of government officials separates those working for government from those in industry, dampening the lobbyist "revolving door" effect, which can bias regulation. "Independence" in this context is not only the separation of regulator and operator, but also separation of regulator from other parts of the government that may have competing policy goals like the promotion of national champions. In the case of China, the former is still a challenge (Wu 2008).

In electricity, Haney and Pollitt (2011) in their survey of forty regulators in forty countries in 2008 found regulators in competitive markets were more likely to use benchmarking, a widely accepted best practice when regulating formerly monopoly markets. Regulators benchmark by collecting cost data from several firms, comparing them with each other, and setting tariffs or regulated prices, based on these comparisons. The presence of multiple firms makes it easier for regulators to apply this practice. Also, they found regulators with more experience and greater insulation from political intervention performed better. Finally, they found regional clusters of good regulatory practice; countries learn from their neighbors. Such regional clustering is also evident in communications regulation (Wu 2014).

China's Regulators in Global Context

Over the last twenty years, the Chinese government has repeatedly reorganized the electricity and communications regulatory authorities. However, few observers would describe these regulators as independent. For example, the corporate and government sectors operate within a single administrative hierarchy, within which corporate executives often outrank regulatory officials (Kahrl 2015). In practice, large SOE operators routinely flout official regulations, such as setting telecom service prices below the official government rate or illegally operating Personal Handy-phone Service without a license (Wu 2009). Similarly, in electricity, big generating firms build power plants without required permits and environmental clearance. In the case of Inner Mongolia, the local authorities supported the construction of the Xinfeng power plant without the proper certificates, perhaps contributing to the accidental death of construction workers (Ni 2007).

In an ideal world, regulators look to market forces to discipline competition, but in China, the regulator relies on the SOEs to execute regulatory decisions (Mah 2015). Furthermore, many observers note that regulatory agencies in China are understaffed or short of technical skills and, therefore, must rely on companies for expertise. A key example is that regulators responsible for setting communications interconnection fees and electricity T&D fees are hamstrung by their inability to extract detailed cost data from the operators, leading to high charges imposed on users in both sectors. These problems contributed to the government dividing the electricity grid and the communications wireline phone systems into two large companies, one north and one south, insuring that in any situation the government has at least two sets of accounts to compare. This makes benchmarking somewhat easier (Wu 2009).

China's Powerful Local and Provincial Authorities

In China, another challenge is competing authorities at different levels of government. In communications, in the 2000s, China Telecom surreptitiously rolled out a low quality, but affordable Personal Handy-phone System called "Little Smart" in cities across the country, repeatedly ignoring central government orders to shut it down. Local and provincial authorities recognized their communities benefited from the cheap Little Smart service and allowed it to grow (Wu 2006) Pearson in Chapter 3 discusses the popularity of affordable, low-speed electric vehicles that meet a practical need in many parts of China. Again, with local government support the vehicles persist despite central government calling them "junk technology." In both cases, local and provincial authorities' priorities were able to override the central government's ambition to invest only in internationally prestigious technology.

Davidson in Chapter 4 demonstrates local and provincial authorities' commitment to offer a reliable electricity service to investors and to the population in general. They have the strongest incentive to see that sufficient power generation projects are in place and the willingness to absorb the costs of overcapacity. Mah and Hills' studies of wind energy policy in Guangdong, Beijing, and Xinjiang demonstrate the significant influence of provincial authorities within the larger context of national policy directives. Guangdong was able to replace a central government policy requiring competitive bidding with a fixed price approach that gave investors a better incentive to install wind projects. A few years later, the central government abandoned competitive bidding for a fixed-price approach (Mah and Hills 2008, 2014b). In research and development (R&D), Shanghai's well-developed civil society organizations for science and technology enabled local companies like Sewind to close the technology gap with sector leaders.

Instead of backing a few winners, Guangdong's contrasting approach was to level the playing field for several players (Mah and Hills 2014a).

In electricity, the competing goals of central, provincial, and local authorities crystallize in conflicts over approving projects. In many countries, there is a regulatory process periodically to evaluate demand for electricity, resources for power generation, capital for investment, and plan future projects accordingly. In China, the provincial and local governments are strongly motivated to support reliable electricity suppliers. On the other hand, if all projects are approved at the central level in Beijing (Mah 2008; Kahrl 2015), then local authorities pour their efforts into getting central level approval for proposed projects instead of proper forecasting and planning, a condition that incentivizes rent-seeking and corruption. On the other hand, in 2015 when a new policy regime shifted project approval to the local level, designed to ameliorate the disconnect between needs and investment spending, it had the opposite effect. Local governments rushed to approve and then build thermal power projects despite the emergence of large-scale excess generating capacity. In response, the center retook control over project approval amidst efforts to rescind approvals and terminate projects already in progress (Kahrl 2015). The later chapters in this volume illuminate this continuing tug of war.

Privatization as a Step toward Strengthening the Regulator

The literature on establishing industry regulators agrees that privatization strengthens a regulator's independence. Privatization is selling a SOE to a few large private investors or listing the company on the stock exchange. Privatization fully separates the entity that regulates from the entity that provides service to the public. When the government plays both roles there can be internal conflicts between the goals of regulation, which promote the interests of the broader public, and the financial objective of maximizing revenue for the government treasury. Privatizing a government enterprise is a major step toward ensuring it will no longer receive favored regulatory treatment compared to its competitors and is free it to respond to market incentives.

In communications, many countries have privatized their national telecom monopoly. In the 1990s a wave of OECD countries privatized their utilities, among them telecommunications and energy (Nestor and Mahboobi 1999). Among developing countries, by 1999, one-quarter of Sub-Saharan countries, one-half of Asian countries, and two-thirds of

Latin American countries had partially privatized their telecom operator. In electricity, however, government ownership is common. State-owned electricity utilities in South Korea, Taiwan, and Singapore illustrate the capacity of public sector firms to achieve excellent levels of efficiency and service (Besant Jones 2006).

In China, all the telecommunications operators and electricity grid companies are state-owned. In communications, this covers network operators and local loop; in electricity, this covers T&D. The government is both owner and regulator of the SOEs. Its ownership interest is represented by the State-owned Assets Supervision and Administration Committee (SASAC) and its regulatory interest by the Ministry of Industry and Information Technology (MIIT) and NEA within the NDRC. In both sectors, there are private companies in other segments of the market.

DEFINING MARKETS FOR COMPETITION POLICY

Some segments of the communications and electricity sector have lower technical and investment barriers to entry than others that makes it easier for new entrants to compete with a former monopoly. This section outlines these diverse market segments and discusses in each the level of competition and private participation in China.

Communications Service Market Segments

For most countries, communications started as a government monopoly service. However, early adopter countries like Sweden and the United States in the early twentieth century began with several competing telephone companies that were later consolidated into national monopolies (Wallsten 2005; Brock 2002). In the 1990s, mobile telecommunications networks began direct competition with traditional wireline operators. Their profitable success underscored the economic gains from a competitive market structure and the old beliefs in the benefits of a national monopoly evaporated. Today, the communications services market can be defined in four basic segments, as shown in Table 2.2.

For the core backbone networks, technology change in the 1970s lowered the investment cost to build competing networks. In the United States, Microwave Communications, Inc. (MCI) used microwave technology to compete with AT&T's wireline long distance network. The local loop that connects the core network to the customers' premises is the costliest to

Table 2.2 *Communications Market Segments*

Content (media, internet, other users)	Backbone, Core Network	Network's Local Loop (last mile, last kilometer)	Retail

Table 2.3 *Electricity Market Segments*

Generation	Transmission (large volume)	Distribution (delivery to customer)	Retail

build out of all four market segments. Mobile phone technology enables customers to connect directly with the core network, bypassing local loops. Cable television technology connects households to the internet, also bypassing the local loop.

Content used to be divided between phone calls for telecommunications and radio and television over the airwaves, but the advent of the internet has blurred that distinction. In some countries, online video and audio programming has unsettled the control of traditional television and radio monopolies. In the retail segment, regulations vary as to whether third parties can act as intermediaries by renting network services, repackaging them with some special services that add value, and selling them on to the customer. In short, in communications, technical developments spurred competition in each segment of the market.

Electricity Service Market Segments

In electricity, again most countries began with a vertically integrated, state-owned electricity system. In this sector, the impetus for market structure reform is often the failure of the monopoly to provide quality service necessary to support economic growth and improve public welfare. Between 1990 and 2006, about half the 150 developing countries started electricity reforms (Besant Jones 2006). Electricity markets comprise several segments: generation, T&D, and retail, as shown in Table 2.3.

In contrast with communications, where competition in every segment is normal, in electricity just taking the basic steps to separate a vertically integrated monopoly into segments is considered a major structural reform. Separating electricity generation from the rest of the utility sector and allowing more companies in the generation market makes it possible for the regulator to establish incentives for efficient generation. Generators can sell electricity to a purchasing agent at prices that include a capacity charge to cover fixed costs and an energy charge to cover variable costs. Power from generators can be dispatched (i.e. distributed to users) based on variable cost, beginning with the cheapest sources (Hunt and Shuttleworth 1996; OECD 2009). In electricity, T&D today are usually combined and are still often monopolies. However, power generation is often a competitive market. In the retail segment, like in communications, competition means allowing third parties to repackage electricity services, add value, and sell them directly to customers.

Breaking the Network Monopoly

In both communications and electricity, the two center market segments are the most difficult ones to introduce competition into. In communications, this is the core network and, especially, the local loop. In electricity, this is T&D. In communications, even the powerful mobile telecom companies need to interconnect with the rest of the network to reach their customers. In every country, the terms and conditions of interconnection are contentious issues. In electricity, T&D are still monopoly services and the on-grid tariffs faced by power generators define the nature of a country's electricity service. A separate section of this chapter is devoted to communications interconnection and electricity T&D.

In addition to allowing new companies to enter a market, there are two other ways of breaking a monopoly: dividing it into several parts that compete or prohibiting monopolies from entering new, related markets. In communications, the United States divided AT&T into a long-distance company and a collection of local companies. Local companies were prohibited for a time from entering new markets, like long-distance and mobile communications. Japan has structurally separated long-distance communications from local, and separated local into two regional companies. New entrants were able to go into the mobile phone and internet markets (Anchordoguy 2001).

In the 1980s, China's rapid economic growth increased demand for electricity and telecommunications services. For the first two decades, the government's main concern was boosting supply to meet demand.

In communications, the Ministry of Post and Telecommunications converted large internal government networks into public networks and China Telecom built a nationwide wireline network. In electricity, faced with crippling power shortages, China broke the power monopoly, allowing local governments and private firms, including foreign owners, to invest in power generation. In addition to changing the market structure, the government implemented policies to reduce costs, reduce coal use per KWh, reduce in-plant power consumption, and transmission losses.

After the Asian financial crisis in 1997, due to declining demand, electricity under capacity became overcapacity. Independent power producers occupied more than 50 percent of the market. Local protectionism hurt the nationally funded power generators. These companies were consolidated into State Power Corporation in 1997. In 2003, the government split State Power Corporation into five generating companies, two grid companies, and several service companies. State Grid and Southern China Power Grid, the new grid companies, both sold their generating capacity. Crucially, for competition, grid companies retained responsibility for dispatch, which controls which generators send electricity to which customers.

In the communications industry, in 1994 Unicom entered as a competitor to the wireline monopoly China Telecom. Both Unicom and China Telecom had mobile networks as well, and China Telecom favored its own network to the detriment of Unicom's mobile network. In 1999, China Telecom's mobile operation spun off to become China Mobile. In the wireline network, China Telecom remained the de facto monopoly nationwide. In 2002, the government split China Telecom in two. The north became China Unicom, and the south retained the China Telecom brand. Subsequently, the mobile operators have been reorganized several times (Wu 2009). At the time of writing, in 2018, there are three large network operators: China Unicom, wireline and mobile; China Telecom, wireline and mobile; and China Mobile, with no wireline network.

In short, the market structure in the core networks of electricity and communications services look similar – two companies, each a monopoly in its respective region, one north and the second south. In communications, China Unicom has the wireline monopoly in the north and China Telecom in the south. They each have a mobile operation which competes with the primarily mobile China Mobile. All three companies are state-owned. In electricity, State Grid has the transmission monopoly in the north and Southern Grid has the transmission monopoly in the south. Both are state-owned. China's approach to breaking up a national monopoly to create regional monopolies is similar to the approach in countries like the United States and Japan; however, in the United States all the companies are commercially owned, and in Japan there is majority private investment.

Exit and Entry: Competition in the Market

One of the regulator's major responsibilities is to set rules for entry and exit of the market for companies. In some countries, these decisions are so important they are elevated above the regulator to higher bodies. Typically, rules on entry and exit are implemented through issuing or cancelling licenses to operate. Sometimes, licenses can be transferred from one company to another, if one company acquires another or if there is a merger.

The previous section of this chapter discussed divestiture of the incumbent monopoly network operator in both electricity and communications. This section discusses the new entry of companies into each of the market segments. First, the core service segments (a) in communications – backbone and local loop, see Table 2.2 and (b) in electricity – T&D, see Table 2.3. Second, the edge market segments (a) in communications – content and retail and (b) in electricity – generation and retail.

Competition in the Core Network Segments
Mobile phone subscribers in China exceed the number of wireline subscribers, in keeping with global trends (World Bank). Mobile operators are significant competitors to wireline monopolies, unlike in electricity where grids typically are still monopolies. Government decisions on which firms receive mobile licenses fundamentally shape the market structure.

In mobile, the technology for transmitting communications signals over the airwaves has evolved through several generations, colloquially known as 2G, 3G, and 4G. Each generation includes multiple technical standards which reflect different approaches to solving how a signal is transmitted. However, most consumers are unaware of these intricacies and distinguish one generation from another principally by communication speed.

In 2009, the MIIT issued three 3G licenses, each in a different technical standard, to the country's three mobile operators. China Mobile, the strongest operator, received TD-SCDMA, the standard with weakest commercial potential; the weakest operator received the standard with the rosiest commercial potential (Qin 2011). In contrast, in a free market, operators choose their own standards and the strongest player would be expected to be able to access the most commercially profitable technology.

The major distinction that 4G mobile service has over a 3G system is that it allows faster internet service. In December 2013, MIIT issued 4G licenses for TD-SCDMA, one each to China Mobile, China Telecom, and Unicom. China Mobile was eager to move to 4G because its 3G standard was not as popular with subscribers as those of Unicom and Telecom. In contrast, when the 4G licenses were issued, China Telecom and Unicom continued trying to recoup investment from their 3G networks (Tan 2013). In late 2016, China's 4G user base surpassed 700 million, led by China Mobile, with over 500 million 4G subscribers (4G Users 2016).

Cable television networks, if they could carry an internet service, in principle were able to compete with China's wireline networks. In China, the central government pursued a market-led strategy for the digitalization of cable including offering a subsidy program to cable operators to purchase set-top boxes and give them free to households (Starks 2010). Since this program launched, more than 200 cities have joined, and 100 have finished their digital transition (Zhou 2010). The current goal is the complete digitalization of the cable network by 2018 – pushed back from an initial 2015 target (Starks 2010).

In electricity, there are no major competitors to State Grid and Southern Grid in the areas of T&D. However, in principle, distributed generation offers a modest opportunity for introducing some competition into China's T&D markets (Kessides 2012). Following the US imposition of tariffs on imported Chinese solar panels in 2013, China implemented distributed generation policies, including construction and operation subsidies for small solar projects from 6 to 20MW (Kahrl 2015). Distributed generation projects generate power for use in the immediate vicinity; they require no additional transmission lines (Zhang, Deng, Margolis, and Su 2015). Industrial parks, suburban agricultural land development, and property developers who have to build their own utility infrastructure offer potential sites for distributed generation (Dupuy 2015; Mah 2015). While large solar projects are concentrated in western China, with more land and space but less demand, distributed generation solar projects cluster in the east. Zhang, Hao, and Margolis (2015) note difficulties with distributed generation projects, including weak roof supports, complicated building ownership arrangements, low prices for residential electricity from the grid, and complex permitting procedures. Despite these difficulties, growth has accelerated, with National Energy Administration figures reporting a 200 percent growth of new installations during 2015 to 2016 (Clover 2017).

Competition in Service Generation

In electricity, there is competition in generation. Like many other developing countries, the early stages of China's power sector reform encouraged private investment in power generation. In some cases, private owners benefited from special arrangements, including guaranteed operating hours and permission to engage in direct sales to large power users. The 2003 reforms refocused on central government-owned power companies. The five big generating firms control slightly over half of China's generating capacity and produce a comparable share of overall electricity output (Pollitt, Yang, and Chen 2017). The rest are owned by primarily by consortia at the local government level (OECD 2009).

In this volume, both Davidson in Chapter 4 and Loren Brandt and Luhang Wang in Chapter 9 note that exit is a particular problem. Davidson discusses how in a context of myriad central government goals, local governments use their limited autonomy to prioritize their own objectives which include generating enough electricity to spur local economic growth and increase employment. In electricity generation, while national initiatives retired inefficient provincial generators, there was a massive inflow of other kinds of poorly performing generators. In an environment where companies exited only by government fiat, there are few efficiency gains. Brandt and Wang observe a similar dynamic with wind and solar generation. Regulations limit who can bid on wind and solar projects. Companies in the market face soft budget constraints, which weaken incentives to exit if the business is not profitable. This makes it difficult to realize productivity gains and inhibits the efficient reallocation of resources.

In communications, generating the content to send over communications networks naturally has many sources including users, companies affiliated with the network operators, and independent companies. In the internet market, private, not state-owned companies dominate applications and services. WeChat, a mobile app that allows subscribers to leave audio voice chat messages, is a prominent example. WeChat's success shrank the telecom companies' texting revenue. Initially, the telecom companies demanded payment, but the government refused to take what would have been an unpopular action (Bloomberg News 2003). Similar conflicts have occurred with Voice-Over-Internet Protocol in the past (Wu 2009). Overshadowing these innovations is the government's interest in controlling internet content. For example, Thun and Sturgeon in Chapter 5 discuss the regulation of internet through organizations like the Internet Society of China, which contributes to licensing to control market entry, and setting censorship rules. Thun and Sturgeon argue that the Great Firewall that keeps foreign content out of China's internet created a shielded space for Chinese app developers to thrive. A separate section of this chapter discusses the intersection between economic and ideological regulation of the communications market.

Competition in the Retail Segment

In electricity, the 2015 reforms open the door to possible expansion of retail competition in two respects – directing sales from generators to large users at discounted prices and retail companies that package value-added services along with electricity and sell them to households and businesses. Industrial consumers comprise about 70 percent of demand in China; commerce, government, schools, hospitals, and residential consumers occupy the remaining 30 percent (Dupuy 2015). As Rawski discusses in Chapter 8, many industrial consumers face relatively high prices for electricity compared to other countries, while residential users face lower prices compared to other countries.

For large users of electricity, direct sales first began in 2002 (Dupuy 2015). More recently, widespread excess generating capacity, which reduced 2016 utilization rates for thermal power plants to levels last seen in the mid-1960s, gave power producers ample incentive to reduce prices in exchange for guaranteed sales. The expanded direct sales policies led to them accounting for 19 percent of overall power consumption in 2016 (Gu 2017).[1]

For smaller commercial electricity users as well as households, who previously had no option other than to purchase power from regional grid monopolies, the 2015 reform allows competition in retail electricity. Policy announcements opened electricity retailing to a wide range of entrants – grid companies, firms in other industries, and private start-ups. As of July 2017, there were 1859 registered electricity retail firms (Gu 2017).

In the communications sector, private companies can enter the mobile market as mobile virtual network operators (MVNO). These companies may lease services from the big three network operators, but cannot own their own facilities. The challenge for MVNOs is to develop value-added services that can attract customers away from their current providers. One of the larger MVNOs, Snail, for example, is primarily a video game company. The first MVNOs went live in May 2014 (Telegeography

---

[1] For clarification on retail competition reforms, I am grateful to Thomas G. Rawski.

June 5, 2014), but with poor interconnection terms from the large operators, they find it hard to compete. Nonetheless, China's MVNO subscriber
base has grown rapidly, reaching 43 million by the end of 2016
(Telegeography 23 January, 2017, China MVNOs 2016). In addition to
MVNOs, there are many private internet service providers in China. For
connectivity to the internet, these retail internet service providers must rely
on the backbone providers, China Mobile, China Telecom, and China
Unicom (Hu 2011).

CORE ISSUES IN ELECTRICITY AND COMMUNICATIONS

In both sectors, the heart of regulatory disputes center on competitors'
access to the network. In electricity there are conflicts over the on-grid fees
that State Grid charges generators for T&D. At the other end of service
delivery, retail companies face tariffs for the electricity they package for end
users. In communications, the conflicts are over interconnection, which
every service provider needs to reach the customers of competing
companies. There are the interconnection rates that operators face to
connect to a competitor's network. Also, there are the tariffs that resellers
face when repackaging services for retail customers.

Core Issues: Electricity Transmission and Distribution

Electricity is expensive to store, therefore, delivering power from where it is
generated to where it is needed in the proper time is a key function of the
system. This is a characteristic unique to electricity, different from other
utilities, for example telecom or water. In electricity, the grid's transmission (high voltage) and distribution (low voltage) networks are the segments where introducing competition is most complicated and these often
remain as monopoly. Leautier and Thelen's work on reformed markets
identifies approaches for managing structures ranging from complete
vertical integration to systems with independently owned and operated
transmission mechanisms. Most countries have something in between,
such as legal unbundling, which forces an incumbent to transfer power
transmission to a completely separate organization, while retaining ownership (Joskow 2008). Leautier and Thelen suggest that in systems with
congestion, vertical separation of generation and transmission combined
with regulatory incentives are necessary to improve performance. They
find vertical separation alone is insufficient.

In China, the two state-owned grid companies each have a monopoly in their respective regions. In the market reform of 2003, when State Power Corporation was split up, distribution, transmission, and dispatch remained under the ownership of the grid operators (OECD 2009). In general, dispatch manages the power generators' access to the grid; transmission is the high voltage, large volume transport of electricity; distribution is the low voltage, low volume delivery of electricity to the customer. There are seven regional networks (Northeast, Northwest, East, Central, South, and Guangdong) and five provincial networks (Shandong, Fujian, Xinjiang, Hainan, and Tibet) (OECD 2009). The South China Power Grid controls South and Guangdong. The much larger State Power Grid controls all the others, except for rural areas in which separate companies operate smaller distribution networks (Pittman and Zhang 2010).

Dispatch as Policy Instrument for Favored Generators
State Grid manages interregional dispatch, while each regional grid subsidiary has its own dispatch center (OECD 2009). China's electricity grid is not yet integrated, which complicates the development of regional wholesale markets and the transmission of electricity from the resource rich West to the power-hungry East. To integrate this fragmented system, the big grid companies have built major interregional transmission corridors in the north, central, and south (Pittman and Zhang 2010; Yi, Xu, and Fan 2016).

The dispatch system is designed for a system long dominated by coal-powered generation. Since the 1980s, China has allocated operating hours equally among generators, an approach known as "equal shares dispatch," or average dispatch. Regulators managed the assignment of wholesale prices and operating hours to allow each plant to achieve a regulated rate of return (Kahrl 2013). There was no systematic effort to increase the assigned quota of operating hours for more efficient plants. Beginning in 2007, pilot programs sought to increase power generation efficiency and reduce environmental impact. Instead of every generator receiving equal hours, if safety and reliability were not compromised, dispatch priority would to go renewables and hydropower first, followed by nuclear, coal, natural gas, and oil. In December 2010, the China Southern Grid Corporation began applying this dispatch regime throughout its five provinces (Kahrl 2013). Despite recent expansion of renewables, coal-fired generators delivered 65.2 percent of overall electricity production in 2016 (Power Overview 2016).

Favorable On-Grid Prices for Preferred Generators

The government sets "on-grid" prices for electricity sold by power generators to the grid companies. These prices directly influence investment in generation and reflect the policy priorities of the time. Prior to 1984, power generation prices were internal transfers within a vertically integrated system. In 1985, the government started pricing based on the financial lifetime of the generator. Plants with better repayment terms received higher, more favorable prices (Kahrl 2013). The policy goal was to increase investment in generation without committing government funds (OECD 2009). Beginning in 2001, prices were set based on the operational lifetime of the generator (Kahrl 2013). Furthermore, plants built before 1985 were given prices that covered only operational, not fixed costs. In short, new power plants received favorable prices compared to older ones (Pittman and Zhang 2010).

In 2004, the government planned to begin setting prices based on coal prices, but these were not fully implemented. Subsequent changes in international coal price were not reflected in prices. This was likely due to government concern about inflation when prices rose and resistance from power generators when prices fell. Coal-fired generators face two prices for coal. Generators can purchase limited quantities of coal at below-market rates. Beyond that, generators buy coal at a rate determined by the international market (Kahrl 2013). Maintaining a below-market rate for a limited amount of coal reflects the government's concern with minimizing upward price fluctuations. This allowing of market-rate coal purchases reflects the government's concern about shortages.

In 2007, the government lowered on-grid prices for small, inefficient coal-powered generators. Most of these units have now been taken out of service (Ma 2011). As China's government makes environmental goals a higher priority, one regulatory reform to watch are moves to increase on-grid prices that favor renewables relative to coal.

Using On-Grid Prices as Incentives for Grid Efficiency

Prior to reforms initiated in 2015, the major grid companies bought and sold at regulated prices; their revenues came from the difference between retail power prices and the on-grid fees at which they purchased electricity from generation companies. Although the grid companies report only modest profits, industry specialists believe that revenues have increased dramatically in the last twenty years, while costs have risen more slowly. They became targets for reform (Kahrl 2015).

The grid firms' refusal to provide detailed cost information – State Grid classified nearly one third of its costs as "other" – left government regulators without the means to implement a cost-based approach to determine the grid companies' share of electricity sales revenue (Kahrl 2015). The 2015 reforms introduced the cost-plus approach typical of many other countries' regulatory regimes.

Chinese regulators moved to assert control over grid company revenues beginning with a 2014 audit of Southern Grid's Shenzhen operations. After removing disallowed cost items, which amounted to nearly one-quarter of reported cost in the initial Shenzhen audit, regulators applied a standard mark-up, in the range of 8 percent, and determined annual grid charges for three years beginning in 2015. The National Development and Reform Commission soon expanded these reviews to eighteen provinces, with audits rejecting an average of 14.5 percent of proposed costs (Gu 2017; Li Zhiyong 2017).

The long-hidden grid charges were replaced with a standard rate-of-return model. Usually with the rate-of-return approach, the regulated entity continues to collect revenue at the tariffed rate even if its efficiency improves. At the next review, the tariff is revised, taking into account the new efficiency, and passing on the savings to users. The reverse is true if the grid's costs rise (Dupuy 2015; Weston 2015; Huang, Xi, and Lu 2015). The underlying goal is to transform the grid from a monopoly with market power to an access carrier, wholesale utility that offers reliable and affordable access to every generator and retailer.

Another approach to unmasking grid costs is to create alternatives to the state grid companies' T&D service. Direct sales, whereby large electricity users buy electricity directly from generation firms, and efforts to encourage microgrids, make an alternate set of retail prices transparent to the market. The regulator can compare these alternate price sets, each reflecting where supply and demand clear in their respective markets, with conventional tariffed rates. When the alternatives are higher, the conventional tariff may be favoring buyers. When alternatives are lower, the conventional tariff may be favoring sellers.

Rawski in Chapter 8 notes that for industry, Chinese electricity prices are higher than in the United States. This may be in part due to China's greater cross-subsidization of household electricity, or the grid companies' extraction of monopoly rents from the market. Rawski also notes that reforms may have saved electricity users RMB 700 million between 2015–17 in Shenzhen and RMB 5.6 billion in 2016–18, in Southern Grid's other five provinces. In the north, users saved RMB 56 billion in the first half of 2017.

While these are gains, they are small in light of total grid revenues of RMB 3653 billion in 2015.

Madhavan, Rawski, and Tian in Chapter 10 present evidence that the State Grid's prices are too high. In 2016, after regulatory reform allowed large electricity buyers to contract directly with power generators, these contract prices were about 20 percent less than regulated rates. In 2016, such contracts covered about 20 percent of all power sales. For 2017 such contracts covered 30–50 percent of all power sales, according to estimates, with further price reductions later. Davidson in Chapter 4 also observes that direct sales have resulted in price reductions.

The State Grid responsible for electricity distribution in China is a character with two faces in this volume. Xu Yi-chong in Chapter 6 lauds the company's innovative and entrepreneurial spirit. State Grid has succeeded where other foreign companies have not, by developing, testing, installing, and now exporting a technology that enables the transmission of ultra large volumes of electricity over long distances. By contrast, in every other chapter where State Grid is discussed, the authors reflect only complaints and criticisms from every other corner of the electricity market. Brandt and Wang in Chapter 9 note that many solar and wind generation plants cannot get connected to the grid – so all the power they generate is wasted – or they are curtailed in their connection to the grid – so that only some of their generated power is used.

The innovation and international industry leadership demonstrated by State Grid in Chapter 6 is funded by monopoly rents the grid extracts from every corner of the electricity market. In the communications sector, Mexico followed a similar path with Telmex, with the main difference being that Telmex was privately owned, making its owner Carlos Slim one of the richest men in the world. In addition, Telmex maintained its domestic wireline phone monopoly and became the dominant mobile operator in Mexico. The revenue generated enabled Telmex to be one of the major foreign investors in the Americas and other parts of the world on par with major US and European telecommunications companies. However, an analysis of Mexico's telecommunications service market put prices higher and service quality lower than Brazil, which in the same period had implemented policies to enable competition in several segments of the market. With several Brazilian telecommunications companies in competition with each other in the domestic market, none was an international leader (Mariscal and Rivera). State Grid's significant international and technical accomplishments may be at the expense of other aspects of domestic electricity development and growth.

Core Issues: Communications Interconnection

Making interconnection work among operators is key to the establishment of a modern competitive telecom market. Consumers expect to be able to call anyone they choose from one telephone to another, even if the party they are calling is on a different operator's network. This is possible only because operators, even those that compete with one another, interconnect their networks. Monopolies do not have interconnection issues. However, in a multi-operator environment, interconnection is important. Because an incumbent operator is unlikely to interconnect voluntarily, explicit rules that govern interconnection are necessary.

Interconnection rules typically include several kinds of conditions. For example, there is often a set of legal obligations that identify what kind of operator is required to provide interconnection, the procedures an operator must follow to request interconnection, and a dispute resolution mechanism to manage conflicts among operators. Also, there are often technical rules that identify the minimum points in the network where interconnection should take place; furthermore, operators with market power are often obligated to lease essential elements of their network to other operators, and time frames are often indicated for delivering these technical services. Finally, there are usually rules that establish a pricing standard for interconnection. These can be specific prices, price ceilings, or prices based on economic cost models (Wu 2002).

In the communications sector, most large economies in the world have competitive markets in the communications backbone, the large volume trunks that carry data across country; in terminal equipment, like phone handsets, personal computers, and other consumer products at the edge of the network; and in applications, services like Netflix, Skype, or general internet services that ride capacity on the network. The least amount or no competition exists, even in advanced large economies, in the last mile or last kilometer of the wireline telecommunications network that connects from the central network to the customer's premises. The investment required to build out this last kilometer to every small office and household in the country is enormous. The companies who were able to carry out this role are the old historical monopolies – AT&T in the United States, NTT in Japan, BT in the United Kingdom, Deutsche Telekom in Germany, and Telstra in Australia. In their day, these companies were among the largest companies in their respective economies, often the largest employers, and frequently, among the leading firms listed on the national stock market. In contrast, in many developing countries, the historical telecommunications company never completed this task of reaching every household with a wireline phone, as mobile phone technology, cable modem, and wireless technologies substituted for the wireline last kilometer.

Interconnection in China

The story of interconnection in China is a string of disputes and their resolution, an ever-evolving series of government-issued rules and procedures, and a mix of government institutions with varying capacity to handle the disputes in line with the rules that have been issued. The state has not yet succeeded in establishing a regulatory framework for interconnection that operators are willing to use, which creates market uncertainty that favors the most powerful operators. MIIT needs the cost data from firms in order to make good interconnection pricing decisions. Further, it may lack the technical skill to process the data in order to strengthen the interconnection regime. In short, the interconnection regime in China is weak, leaving a vacuum that is filled by the most powerful operators moderated only by occasional State Council fiats (Wu 2009).

In 1995, MPT issued a number of initial technical specifications for interconnection. In 1999, MII issued provisional interconnection rules, which are still in effect today. The Telecommunications Decree of 2000 contains some language on interconnection, largely focusing on dispute resolution procedures. In the meantime, the government's successive decisions to divide China Telecom, once in 1999 and a second time in 2002, can be interpreted as the use of structural separation as a tool to prevent anti-competitive conduct in recognition of the failure of the rules-based interconnection regime (Wu 2009).

The most recent major upset was a 2010 Chinese Academy of Social Sciences report that linked the national firewall directly to slow domestic Internet connections. To maintain the firewall, the government allows only China Telecom and Unicom to connect to the global internet backbone. Limiting international access allows these two companies to charge high prices for poor broadband speed (Cao 2011). In early 2011, the China Internet Network Information Center (CNNIC) released its first study of broadband speed, conducted by testing twenty major websites in thirty-one provinces and municipalities, once an hour for twenty-four hours. Guangzhou, Shanghai, and Beijing were congested, so the top provinces turned out to be Henan, Hunan, and Hebei (CNNIC 2011).

Amid a general sense that broadband development in China had stalled, the NDRC announced an anti-monopoly investigation against

Table 2.4 *Affordability of Fixed Broadband Services*, Selected Markets 2015

Country	Rank	Cost in US$	Cost as % of GNI per Capita
US	3	16.32 for 1.5 mbps	0.35
Japan	9	22.43 for 5 mbps	0.51
Korea	51	29.17 for 50 mbps	1.29
Hong Kong	60	64.20 for 100 mbps	1.53
China	89	31.81 for 2 mbps	3.12

Source: ITU

China Unicom and China Telecom for abusing market power in the internet market (Cao 2011). Caixin reported that the NDRC action was backed by other government entities such as State Administration of Radio, Film, and Television (SARFT), with an interest in making it easier for broadcasters and cable television companies to enter the internet market. Not only were broadband speeds slow, but broadband prices in China were three times higher than in Vietnam, four times higher than the United States, and twenty-nine times higher than South Korea (*Caixin* December 26, 2011). Table 2.4 shows China's relatively high broadband prices in 2015.

The Chinese government's internet content filtering policy requires all Chinese internet traffic to traverse a limited number of points controlled by the state-owned telecom operators. The government can direct traffic over the network to comply with internet content filtering objectives. Control over these bottlenecks enables facility owners to charge monopoly rates for their services. In addition, limited competition allows major telecom providers to maintain high interconnection fees. This in turn limits the decline in retail rates for internet users (Hu 2011).

Communications Tariffs Abandoned

For years, prices were held high by government-set tariffs; periodic price wars would break out among operators in contravention of regulations. Prior to 2014, the ministry submitted major tariff changes to the National Development and Reform Commission for approval. Other government players include the local telecommunications authorities who have a key role in setting some retail rates. By the 2000s, the government tariff was often higher than the prices consumers found in the market. As various new technologies emerged like Personal Handy-phone System and Voice-Over Internet Protocol (VOIP), operators flouted the tariffs, apparently

Table 2.5 *China's Mobile Communications Service Prices, 2013–2015*

Year	Mobile-cellular Sub-basket Cost, US$	Mobile-cellular Sub-basket Cost as % of GNI per Capita
2013	4.04	0.74
2014	4.07	0.75
2015	4.01	0.65

Source: ITU

chasing new subscribers instead of looking for higher profits (Wu 2009). In May 2014, China's Ministry of Industry and Information Technology stopped regulating retail tariffs in the telecoms sector (Telegeography, May 12, 2014), in keeping with regulatory practice in many other competitive major markets.

After de-tariffing, however, the government continued to interfere in the setting of prices. In May 2015 Premier Li Keqiang demanded that telecom providers "raise speed, drop prices." The three big service providers agreed to drop interconnection charges for small- and medium-sized enterprise internet services, reduce retail international call prices, and eliminate international and long-distance surcharges on mobile calls (China Telecom 2017). As shown in Table 2.5, price survey data collected by the International Telecommunication Union show a rise in both price for mobile service and for mobile service as a fraction of Gross National Income (GNI) per capita between 2013 and 2014, followed by a decline in 2015 (ITU 2014; ITU 2015; ITU 2016).

An analysis of tariff reform in China's telecom market illustrates the futility of the government's effort to contain the market under state control. In those areas of telecom policy where actors are few – such as in decisions on how many operators should be licensed in the market or interconnection, where the only actors are the limited number of operators – the government has many tools available to guide the market. In tariffs, where dozens of local branch operators have surreptitiously offered many varieties of service packages to millions of consumers, the state lacks leverage to enforce regulations in the market. Consumers and producers of communications services are forced toward a shift from command economy pricing to market pricing. The abolition of retail telecom tariffs in 2014 is the culmination of this trend.

INTERSECTING ISSUES THAT COMPETE WITH MARKET EFFICIENCY AND ECONOMIC GROWTH

Each preceding section of this chapter has centered on issues common to electricity and communications. This section now explores a set of competing policy goals for each sector that challenge the usual regulatory objectives of improving efficiency and contributing to overall economic growth. In communications, media censorship's goal is to preserve the rule of China's Communist party, a goal that competes with normal regulatory objectives. In electricity, the drive to improve the environment also can be at odds with normal market regulation objectives.

Telecom: Intersection with Media

While the focus of this study is telecommunications, the distinction between telecom and media is rapidly disappearing. Voice as a fraction of communications traffic is now less than 1 percent in the United States; the remaining traffic is all data (Hurpy 2014). In China, in 2015, 79 percent of all internet traffic derived from video (Cisco). Internet video traffic is driving growth in overall internet traffic and investment. In response, many countries have merged their telecom and media regulators. Merged regulators include Hong Kong's Office of Communications Authority (2012), the Australian Communications and Media Authority (2005), Taiwan's National Communications Commission (2006), and the UK's Office of Communications (2003). However, in China this issue remains unresolved. In early 2014, the government announced President Xi Jinping would head a new State Council central Internet Security and Informatization Leading Group. The group's goal is to direct and coordinate internet security and informatization policy, especially to balance the priorities of expanding internet use in China and "maintaining proper guidance of online opinions in terms of timing, intensity and impact" (Xinhua February 27, 2014). One observer, Willy Wo-Lop Lam, interpreted the creation of this leading group as a sign of further crackdowns to come on internet content (Lam 2015). Others view the creation of the leading group as an acknowledgment that the growth of the internet cannot be left in the hands of the propaganda system, but did have to be balanced against the need for growth and development (Graham 2015).

The State Administration of Press, Publications, Film, Radio, and Television (SAPPFRT) regulates Chinese media, including internet content. SAPPFRFT reports directly to the cabinet-level State Council. SAPPFRT officials are also in the Propaganda Bureau of the Chinese Communist Party The linkage between state and party is closer in the field of media than it is in the broader information technology and communications policy areas. In 2013, SAPPFRT was created out of the State Administration for Film, Radio, and Television (SARFT) and the General Administration for Press and Publications. In early 2018, news reports suggest SAPPFRT will become the State Administration for Radio and Television (Frater 2018).

Internet Protocol Television

The history of Internet Protocol Television (IPTV) licensing in China illustrates the tension between the media regulator and communications regulator. In China Internet Protocol Television generally refers to a package of video channels offered by an Internet Service Provider as a pay television service. In 1999, during the very early days for IPTV, only SARFT (and not the telecom ministry), could issue licenses. In 2003, SARFT issued over eighty licenses to organizations to provide audiovisual content over the internet. However, in 2004, SARFT reversed its position, awarding such licenses only to television stations and other media organizations previously licensed by SARFT. According to Liu and Jayakar (2012), SARFT's reversal was driven by propaganda policy requirements to maintain better control over the content. In 2008, when there was a government wide reshuffle, SARFT's position was strengthened relative the telecom authorities and the State Council reiterated SARFT's leadership over digital television.

Currently, a company offering IPTV services in China requires four licenses: one for IPTV from SARFT, another for content from the Ministry of Culture; and two from the Ministry of Industry and Information Technology (MIIT) – one for internet content provision and, for mobile providers, and another for mobile value-added service. At the end of 2011, there were about 14 million IPTV users in China. Most users were on the unlicensed China Telecom trial network. Others were on the Unicom network, also without a license (Wu and Leung 2012). While licenses are required, some seem to operate without them. By end 2017, there were 120 million subscribers, 92 million with China Telecom and 28 million with China Unicom (Feng 2018).

Three Network Convergence

For many years, the central government has sought to unify the telecom, broadcast, and internet networks. The most recent effort began in 2010 (Wu and Leung 2012). Telecom operators were encouraged to produce and transmit television and radio shows; television and radio companies were encouraged to partner with telecom companies (Bao 2010). In June 2010, the government launched a pilot project to converge the three networks in twelve cities. This convergence of the three networks was identified in 2011 as a development of national strategic significance. The pilot project was expanded to forty-two cities in 2012 (Wu and Leung 2012).

The convergence program envisioned two stages: 2010–12, for trials connecting broadcast and telecom networks, and 2013–14, for network architecture integration (Bao 2010), with full integration proposed for 2015. News reports pointed to difficulties arising from clashes between broadcast and telecom regulators (Wu and Leung 2012).

The upgrading of cable networks to carry digital signals were also part of the convergence plan (Wu and Leung 2012). In 2014, the China Broadcasting Network (CBN) launched as the country's fourth national operator, to compete with China Mobile, China Telecom, and China Unicom, by building a nationwide digital cable network. CBN is also state-owned (Telegeography June 5, 2016).

With progress held up by bureaucratic infighting, audiences began to shift from conventional to online programming. One internet entrepreneur suggested in late 2011 that 60 percent of Chinese television programming had already migrated online, in part because of lighter online content censorship (Zhao 2011). Relief from censorship was only temporary, however, as regulators ordered license-holders to remove third-party applications that were not officially approved, including those that enabled live-streaming. Users suddenly found their installed apps broken and their histories erased (Zhao 2017).

Internet Content Filtering Regime
Internet filtering takes place at two levels, firstly, the national internet service providers, and, secondly, local internet service providers. The latter interact directly with internet users. There are seven backbone providers: four smaller ones which are run by the government directly, such as for scientific research or education, and the three large telecom operators, China Mobile, China Telecom, and China Unicom. Backbone providers filter content at via international gateways in Beijing, Guangzhou, and Shanghai; this prevents foreigners from seeing certain domestic sites and people in China from seeing unwelcome foreign sites. Local internet service providers censor content under the supervision of the local telecom authorities. They regularly carry out "strikes" against specific content (Hu 2011).

Reportedly, local authorities also try to escape the firewall. A 2015 study of Chongqing documents the local government's frustration with MIIT's restrictions on internet content. The Chongqing government tried to build a data center in its free trade zone that sat outside the firewall to attract international customers (Graham 2015).

In the communications arena, the government is now interested in promoting the success of globally competitive Chinese internet and technology companies. If content policy creates a special Chinese environment, the question remains: Will firms grown in this ecosystem be able to compete in the global market? A related question is whether foreign markets will accept technology that conforms to China's rather than international standards of content censorship and personal surveillance.

Electricity: Intersection with the Environment

In China, as in many other countries, electricity generation is a major source of environmental pollutants. 2016 figures for China show that coal plants account for 64 percent of generating capacity and 71.6 percent of power output (Power Overview 2016). Today's system was designed to raise capital for investment to meet technology and growth targets. There are limited incentives for efficiency in the use of capital, natural resources, or electricity itself. The operation of power generators is decentralized, while planning and price setting are centralized, and investment decisions are caught in a central–provincial tug-of-war. The whole structure of China's power sector reflects the long-standing predominance of coal-fueled power generation. Under such circumstances, changing gears cannot be easy (Kahrl 2015).

Moving away from thermal generation will require a combination of reducing effluents from coal-fired power plants and replacing coal generation with electricity from cleaner alternatives – hydro, wind, nuclear, and solar. Growing environmental awareness has inspired a succession of measures aimed at limiting the growth of power-related environmental costs. These included the closure of inefficient thermal generation facilities, high feed-in tariffs for wind and solar installations, growing pressure on power plants to retrofit devices to capture sulfur dioxide and other noxious effluents, and the imposition of penalty rates on firms running obsolete equipment in steel and other energy-intensive sectors.

In March 2015, State Council adopted a new framework that prioritizes environmental goals for power sector reform (State Council 2015).

Unusually, the new policy emerged as a joint announcement by the State Council and the Communist Party Central Committee, sending a powerful political signal (Dupuy 2015; Mah 2015). Recent reforms begin equipping the traditionally weak regulatory system with the tools essential for effective environmental remediation (Kahrl, Williams, Ding, and Hu 2011). In short, power sector reform, a major aspect of environmental policy, will be difficult to execute until market and regulatory reforms, especially price reform, gain traction.

Subsidies

China's policy arsenal includes subsidies intended to promote environmentally beneficial activities and suppress harmful ones. For example, NDRC assigned low on-grid prices for small, polluting coal generators in 2007 (closing many of them before 2011). Similarly, NDRC assigned high on-grid prices for wind and solar projects in excess of the amounts paid out to producers of hydro, thermal, or nuclear power. Now, after the investors have flooded into wind and solar, the government is shrinking the premiums.[2]

China's electricity regulators face the same pricing dilemma found in many other economies: how to incorporate a fast-growing renewable segment into dispatch arrangements without undermining incentives for non-renewable generators and thus endangering the responsiveness and stability of the entire power system (Dupuy 2015; Kahrl 2015). One possible approach to a more efficient operation of the grid is to separate dispatch from fixed cost recovery. Renewables generally have lower variable costs; and basing dispatch on variable costs will favor them. Fixed costs can be covered with a supplemental capacity fee. While this two-pronged structure is common in other countries, it is not used China (Kahrl 2015).

Technical Retrofitting

The policy of closing small, inefficient, and high polluting generators had has the dual effect of increasing the average efficiency of generators and reducing pollution. Regulators forced remaining thermal power plants to install scrubbers and other emissions-reducing devices. The plants were rewarded with small price increases. However, they

---

[2] See, for example Price Competition 2016, which reports falling on-grid prices for renewables in multiple provinces. For insight on price levels, I am grateful to Tom Rawski.

complained that the revenue did not cover compliance costs and payments were delayed. However flawed, these technological retrofitting
programs are a major factor in increasing efficiency (Ma and Zhao
2015).

Transmission

In China, while electricity demand is in the east, wind resources are in
the north and significant hydropower lies in the central and southwest
regions. It is difficult to transmit renewable resources like wind and
hydro outside their regions, and this severely curtails the usefulness of
any investment in their development (Kahrl et al. 2011).
The underinvestment in transmission results in inefficiency both at
the generation and the user end. First, some generation facilities
stand idle because there is no way to transmit their power to regions
where demand exceeds local supply. Second, some of the installed long-
distance transmission facilities are under-utilized. This is likely due to
poor demand forecasting or poor coordination between the grid company and economic planners. The State Grid's innovations in high
voltage capacity address this issue, but regulatory challenges remain
in establishing intra-regional markets.

Demand Side Management

Demand side policies address how people use electricity. Dupuy suggests that if electric vehicles become widely popular in China, time-of-
use pricing may shift household demand to off-peak hours with lower
prices (2015). However, for this to be effective, many challenges
remain. First, this would require "smart meters" that measure both
the amount and the timing of power use. While Chinese cities are
gradually installing smart meters (Mah 2015), the impact of demand
management remains small (Mah 2015). A 2012 survey of residential
energy consumption covering 1,450 households in twenty-six provinces found that when time-of-use pricing policy was available,
only 38 percent of surveyed were aware of it and only 14 percent
had applied to participate. Tellingly, only 13 percent of the surveyed
had heard about it from the grid company (Zheng et al. 2014). Finally,
households occupy a small share of overall electricity use in China, at
only 13.6 percent in 2016 (Power Overview 2016). Nevertheless, China
is the largest market for smart meters in the world, with 469 million
installed as of September 2017 (Metering and Smart Energy
International 2017).

DANGER. HOW INTERNATIONAL SAFETY REGULATION
PROMOTES INNOVATION IN CHINA

For two of the products discussed in this volume – nuclear power generators and ultra-high voltage transmission projects – equipment failure could lead to catastrophic loss of life and property. Therefore, safety standards are high, strict, and required, as compared to other arenas where standards are progressive, relaxed, and voluntary. Also, since both of these products are for the international market, there are international safety standards on top of domestic, national safety standards.

In sectors like communications and electricity, the typical process for any new piece of equipment would for be for manufacturers to take their products before safety standards bodies for evaluation. These safety standards bodies can be national, regional, or international organizations, usually run by a combination of government, corporate, and science professionals. Once a product is accepted for evaluation, the organization forms a committee to handle the review. The committee draws up a list of potential safety and standard issues, and then oversees testing the product to identify what technical parameters must be met. Once there is agreement, that committee will issue its findings. Depending on how seriously a standard is needed, the findings can be voluntary or eventually become a required industry standard.[3]

After the standards are established, manufacturers that subsequently produce these products submit them to conformity assessment. In practice, this means that sample products are sent to laboratories and tested to see whether the products conform to the established standards. Once the lab completes a conformity assessment, the product is approved for market release.[4] Usually, the product then bears the seal of the lab. In the United States, for example, many electrical products carry a distinctive "UL" seal reflecting that Underwriters Labs assessed product for conformity with US safety standards. Other labs also conduct these assessments. In most countries the labs that conduct these tests are themselves subject to standards of technical competence and, depending on the gravity of the standard, independence from manufacturing corporations. The labs can be privately run for profit, or in other cases, they are not-for-profit organizations.

---

[3] For more information see http://standards.ieee.org/develop/index.html?utm_source =mm_link&utm_campaign=faw&utm_medium=std&utm_term=develop%20standards %2C%20find%20working%20group (accessed December 12, 2018).

[4] For more information see www.iso.org/conformity-assessment.html (accessed December 12, 2018).

Several chapters in this book dwell on how China is not an innovator in manufacturing electricity and telecom related products, but there are two major exceptions, both in the electricity sector. China is today a world leader in the construction of nuclear power generators and ultra-high voltage transmission lines, as detailed in by Xu in Chapter 6 and Madhavan, Rawski, and Tian in Chapter 10. In both arenas, safety failures can be catastrophic. China's nuclear power industry made safety a high priority after Japan's Fukushima nuclear disaster in 2011. Ultra-high voltage transmission lines that transport large volumes of electricity over long distances, are also potentially dangerous.

Also, in both arenas there are robust international regimes that govern safety standards. China participates in safety discussions, including taking leadership roles in setting safety and other standards. Because nuclear power and high voltage transmission are dangerous technologies, the barriers to entering the international market are clear and they are set high. Madhavan, Rawski, and Tian discuss how Chinese companies have responded positively to very strict safety nuclear regulations, particularly after Fukushima. They identify 2015 as the first year that China implemented these newly strict regulatory requirements. Xu in Chapter 6 notes with pride the achievements of State Grid in manufacturing and installing high voltage transmission lines in China and other countries. In her book *Sinews of Power*, Xu also describes how Chinese executives took leadership roles in organizations like the International Electric Commission by identifying potential safety and other standards issues, overseeing testing, and participating in standard setting. Future high voltage transmission projects will need to conform to these standards, whether built by Chinese or other companies from other countries (Xu 2016).

Once Chinese company products are certified safe by international standards, other countries are more likely to accept them in comparison to other sectors where quality barriers to entry are low and relatively relaxed, such as equipment for wind and solar generation or even handsets and semiconductors. The presence of international standards and Chinese companies' participation and compliance with international standards enables Chinese companies to overcome a lingering reputation for poor quality and unsafe products.

CONCLUSION: CHINA'S REGULATION IN CONTEXT

Everywhere in China, there are phones and electricity. Compared to other countries at comparable levels of development, this is a remarkable achievement and a great boon to the quality of life for ordinary Chinese. Now that electricity and communications service are widely available nationwide, the next level goal is to maximize these services' contribution to economic growth. This chapter has focused on five major regulatory issues: establishing a regulator, defining markets for competition policy, core network regulation, intersecting issues like media regulation and the environment, and implementing safety standards.

Establishing a regulator independent from the operators and creating conditions for market competition are the two most important factors that maximize electricity and communications' contributions to economic growth. Starting in the 1990s, the government repeatedly took steps to separate regulators from operators. Every step incrementally increased the regulator's scope and depth of authority. Nevertheless, the objectives of SOEs, such as becoming global leaders in specialized export products, often appear to be higher priorities than growing the domestic services market through competition. SOE executives often outrank regulatory officials. Companies routinely fail to comply with regulations that, for example, ban cheap communications services or affordable electric vehicles in favor of more expensive and prestigious technologies the government likes to promote. This culture of non-compliance undermines regulators in China.

In both electricity and communications, there is more competition in market segments with lower barriers to entry and incentive regulations in place than in market segments with higher barriers to entry. Tables 2.6 and 2.7 summarize competition in each of these segments.

In communications, there is some level of competition in nearly every market segment. In addition, there is technological innovation in internet applications in the retail segment, as discussed by Thun and Sturgeon in Chapter 5, within the constraints of content regulation. In electricity, there is competition in generation and retail. In power generation, there is technical innovation in nuclear reactors, as discussed by Madhavan, Rawski, and Tian in Chapter 10. In addition, State Grid has successfully developed the high technology ultra-high voltage transmission, an investment that draws on the monopoly rents it gains from its market monopoly.

In terms of regulating the core network, in communications, the public consensus in China is that poor interconnection among operators results in high prices and inferior service including broadband. Government statements suggest resolving interconnection problems is a priority, but the problem has dragged on for nearly two decades. In addition, internet regulation requires routing all traffic through specific network points in order to filter out content the government thinks unsuitable, which

Table 2.6 *Competition in Communications Services*

Market Segments	State of Competition
Content Generation	Competitive under ideologically driven content. Internet applications are mostly private companies. Television programming is carried out by both central and provincial authorities.
Backbone, Core Network	Wireline: two state-owned companies, China Unicom and China Telecom, each is a monopoly in its own region. Mobile: three state-owned companies, China Mobile, China Unicom, and China Telecom.
Local Loop	Wireline: two state-owned companies, China Unicom and China Telecom, each is a monopoly in its own region. Mobile: three state-owned companies, China Mobile, China Unicom, and China Telecom.
Retail	Recent entry of private companies as mobile virtual network operators.

Table 2.7 *Competition in Electricity Services*

Market Segments	State of Competition
Generation	Competitive. SOEs are favored over local and provincial enterprises.
Transmission (high capacity, high voltage)	Two state-owned companies: State Grid and Southern Grid, each is a monopoly in its own region.
Distribution (low voltage, transport to customer)	Two state-owned companies: State Grid and Southern Grid, each is a monopoly in its own region.
Retail	Newly competitive. Mostly private companies as resale entrants for small customers. Direct sales from generators to large customers.

contributes to congestion. In electricity, the reform wave initiated in 2015 with a regulatory audit of Southern Grid Corporation's Shenzhen branch, has spread to other regions and promises to shrink the Grid companies' monopoly rents to the benefit of generators, retailers, and ultimntcly. u…r … However, international experience shows that such reforms are difficult in the best of political circumstances and will take some time to show results.

Regulatory decisions directly affect markets for manufacturing equipment and infrastructure. In mobile communications, the government's 3G and 4G licensing decisions shaped the market demand for 3G and 4G handsets in China, which redounded to the global market. Broadband speeds are slow in China, seventy-fourth in the world after Vietnam and Malaysia, due to interconnection disputes and conflicts, which inhibits the otherwise vibrant internet apps market. In renewable electricity generation, on-grid prices and dispatch practices that favor coal result in curtailment of wind and solar power – electricity generated but never sent to the grid for distribution (Akamai 2017; Unplugged 2014; Chen, Seong, and Woetzel 2015).

International safety regulation also affects technological innovation in China. In electricity, high voltage transmission and nuclear power generation are two technologies that if they fail threaten life and property. Consequently, Chinese companies and international safety standards organizations have a history of working closely together. Now accepted into international standards organizations, Chinese companies' technologies comply with international safety standards. Foreign markets trust Chinese technology in these highly risky areas, whereas in other industries, Chinese products have a reputation more for affordability compared to reliability or quality.

So far, this chapter has treated electricity and communications service as primarily domestic services that are not exported across international borders. However, this is a moment in time when technology change may shift our view. If instead of categorizing industries as goods (shoes) and services (haircuts), we think of them as tradables (financial services) and non-tradables (concrete), new vistas open (Corden 1986). On the horizon are innovations that possibly challenge communications and electricity service as non-tradables. In electricity, China's development of ultra-high voltage transmission systems may mean large volumes of electricity are more transportable across large geographic regions. As the physical barriers to electricity trade come down, the main challenges to electricity trade across borders – sometimes international, sometimes across provinces or states – may be political and regulatory. In communications, one possible application of 5G technology is to divorce service delivery from geographic location. For example, 5G

Table 2.8 *Government Agencies and Major State-Owned Enterprises: Chinese and English Names*

English Name	English Abbreviation	Chinese Name
China Broadcasting Network	CBN	中国广播网
China Mobile		中国移动
China Telecom		中国电信
China Unicom		中国联通
General Administration of Press and Publication	GAPP	国家新闻出版总署
Ministry of Electric Power	MEP	电力部
Ministry of Industry and Information Technology	MIIT	中华人民共和国工业和信息化部
Ministry of Post and Telecommunications	MPT	邮电部
National Development and Reform Commission	NDRC	国家发展和改革委员会
National Energy Administration	NEA	国家能源管理局
Southern Grid		中国南方电网
State Administration of Press, Publication, Radio, Film and Television	SAPPRFT	国家新闻出版广电管总局
State Administration of Radio, Film and Television	SARFT	国家广播电视总局
State Council		国务院
State Electricity Regulatory Commission	SERC	国家电力监管委员会
State Grid		国家电网
State Power Corporation		国家电力公司
State-owned Asset Supervision and Administration Commission	SASAC	国务院国有资产监督管理委员会

technology may allow a construction worker in one location to operate a bulldozer at a construction site in a second location. That second location can be across state or national borders.

With ultra-high voltage transmission infrastructure, China's adherence to strict safety standards has opened up new foreign export markets. However, for 5G technology, foreign markets' lack of confidence in China's intrusive regulation of internet content has shaken potential customers' interest. Foreigners have similar concerns about the quality, safety, and environmental impact of Chinese products in other electricity and communications markets. While the role of service regulation is first to improve overall public welfare and economic gains for the domestic market, its implications extend to how welcome China's manufactures and infrastructure will be in foreign markets.

References

4G Users. 2016. "China's 4G User Base Surpasses 700 M." November 30, 2016. www .mobileworldlive.com/featured-content/top-three/chinas-4g-user-base-surpasses-700 (accessed June 13, 2017).

Akamai 2017. "State of the Internet Q1 2017 Report."www.akamai.com/us/en/multi media/documents/state-of-the-internet/q1-2017-state-of-the-internet-connectivity-report.pdf (accessed August 10, 2017).

Anchordoguy, Marie. 2001. "Nippon Telegraph and Telephone Company (NTT) and the Building of a Telecommunications Industry in Japan." *The Business History Review*. 75(3). pp. 507–41.

Bao, Youbin. 2010. "China to Consolidate Media Networks." January 15. *Caixin*.

Bloomberg News. 2013. "How a free chat app ate into profits of China's Communist Party." April 24, 2013. www.bloomberg.com/news/2013–04-24/how-a-free-chat-app-ate-into-profits-of-china-s-communist-party.html (accessed December 12, 2018).

Besant-Jones, John E. 2006. "Reforming Power Markets in Developing Countries: What Have We Learned?" Energy and Mining Sector Board Discussion Paper, No. 19. World Bank Group, Washington, DC.

Brennan, Timothy. 2009. "Network Effects in Infrastructure Regulation: Principles and Paradoxes." *Review of Network Economics*. 8(4). pp. 279–301.

Brock, Gerald. 2002. "Historical Overview." In Martin Cave, Sumit Majumdar, and Ingo Vogelsgang eds., *Handbook of Telecommunications Economics, Vol. 1: Structure, Regulation, and Competition*. Elsevier: Amsterdam. pp. 44–74.

Caixin. 2011. "Survey: Chinese Broadband Users Underserved." December 26, 2011. *Caixin*.

Cao, Haili, Doudou Ye, and Hejuan Zhao. 2011. "Telecoms Pressured to Widen Broadband Access." November 29, 2011. *Caixin*.

Chen, Yougang, Jeongmin Seong, and Jonathan Woetzel. 2015. "China's Rising Internet Wave: Wired Companies." *McKinsey Quarterly*. January.

China Internet Network Information Center (CNNIC). 2011. *Statistical Report on Internet Development in China*. https://cnnic.com.cn/IDR/ReportDownloads/ (accessed December 12, 2012).

China MVNOs. 2016. "How MVNOs are Performing in China." February 19, 2016. www.telecomlead.com/telecom-services/mvnos-performing-china-67467 (accessed June 13, 2017).

China Telecom. 2017. "China Telecom Eyes Revenue Growth amid further Tartiff Reductions." March 21, 2017. www.scmp.com/tech/china-tech/article/ 2080759/china-telecom-posts-10pc-decline-2016-net-profit (accessed June 13, 2017).

Cisco Visual Networking Index. 2016. China, 2016–2021. www.cisco.com/c/dam/m/ en_us/solutions/service-provider/vni-forecast-highlights/pdf/ China_2021_Forecast_Highlights.pdf (accessed June 19, 2018).

Clover, Ian. 2017. "China's 200% DG solar growth rooted in agriculture sector, finds AECEA." *PV Magazine*. February 7. \www.pv-magazine.com/2017/02/07/chinas-200-dg-solar-growth-rooted-in-agriculture-sector-finds-aecea/ (accessed June 7, 2017).

Corden, Max. 1986. *Inflation, Exchange Rates, and the World Economy*. Chicago, IL: University of Chicago.

Downs, Erica S. 2008. "China's 'New' Energy Administration." *China Business Review*. November. www.frankhaugwitz.eu/doks/policy/2008_11_China_NEA_Brookings .pdf (accessed December 12, 2018).

Du, Limin, Yanan He, and Jianye Yan. 2013. "The Effects of Electricity Reforms on Productivity and Efficiency of China's Fossil-Fired Power Plants: an Empirical Analysis." *Energy Economics* 40. pp. 804–12.

Dupuy, Max. 2015. Interview. Dupuy is Senior Associate, The Regulatory Assistance Project.

Edwards, Geoff and Leonard Waverman. 2006. "The Effects of Public Ownership and Regulatory Independence on Regulatory Outcomes." *Journal of Regulatory Economics*. 29 (1). pp. 23–67.

Feng, Dong. 2018. "China Mobile's new IPTV license could herald end of traditional cable TV." *People's Daily*. June 20, 2018. https://variety.com/2018/film/asia/china-media-under-cabinet-level-control-abolish-sapprft-1202725104/ (accessed December 12, 2018).

Frater, Patrick. 2018. "China to put media under cabinet-level control, abolish SAPPRFT." March 13, 2018. https://variety.com/2018/film/asia/china-media-under-cabinet-level-control-abolish-sapprft-1202725104/ (accessed December 12, 2018).

Graham, Terence. 2015. Interview. Graham is Researcher, Telecommunications Research Project, Hong Kong University.

Gu Yang 顾阳. 2017. 电力体制改革步入"下半场"深化改革仍须爬坡迈坎 [Electricity reform enters the second stage – more effort needed to deepen reform]. www.china5e.com/news/news-996482–1.html (accessed July 29, 2017).

Haney, A. B. and Michael Pollitt. 2011. "Exploring the Determinants of 'Best Practice' Benchmarking in Electricity Network Regulation." *Energy Policy* 39(12). pp. 7739–46.

Hu, Henry. 2011. "The Political Economy of Governing ISP's in China: Perspectives on Net Neutrality and Vertical Integration." *China Quarterly*. pp 523–40.

Huang, Kaixi, Xuena Xi, and Xiaoxi Lu. 2015. "Shenzhen Businesses Set to Save Money on Electricity Bills, Government Says." April 16, 2015. *Caixin*.

Hunt, Sally and Graham Shuttleworth. 1996. *Competition and Choice in Electricity* Chichester, England: John Wiley & Sons.

Hurpy, Charles. 2014. "The New Reality of Telecommunications in the US: a Drop of Voice in an Ocean of Data." Analysys Mason. October 13. www .analysysmason.com/PageFiles/43966/The-new-reality-of-telecommunications-in-the-US-a-drop-of-voice-in-an-ocean-of-data-AnalysysMason-Oct2013.pdf (accessed June 23, 2015).

iResearch. 2016. "IPTV is Popular With Hard Core of the Society in China in 2016." May 11, 2016www.iresearchchina.com/content/details7_22333.html (accessed June 13, 2017).

Industry Statistics. 2016. *2016* 中国工业统计年鉴 [China Industry Statistical Yearbook]. 2 vols. Beijing: China Statistics Press.

ITU 2014. Measuring the information society. International Telecommunication Union. Geneva. www.itu.int (accessed August 10, 2017).

2015. Measuring the information society. International Telecommunication Union. Geneva. www.itu.int (accessed August 10, 2017).

2016. Measuring the information society. International Telecommunication Union. Geneva. www.itu.int (accessed August 10, 2017).

Jayakar, Krishna and Chun Liu. 2014. "Universal Service in China and India, Legitimating the State?" *Telecommunications Policy*. 38. pp. 186–99

Joskow, Paul, 2008. "Lessons learned from electricity market liberalization." In "The future of electricity," Special Issue 2. *The Energy Journal*. 29. pp. 9–42.

Kahrl, Fredrich. 2013. "The Political Economy of Electricity Dispatch Reform in China." *Energy Policy*. 53. pp. 361–69.

2015. Interview. Kahrl is Senior Consultant, E3.

Kahrl, Fredrich, Jim Williams, Jianhua Ding, and Junfeng Hu. 2011. "Challenges to China's Transition to a Low Carbon Electricity System. *Energy Policy*. 39. pp. 4032–41.

Kessides, Ioannis. 2012. "Electricity Reforms: What Some Countries Did Right and Others Can Do Better." *Viewpoint: Public Policy for the Private Sector*. World Bank, Washington, DC Note No. 322. October. www.esmap.org/sites/esmap.org/files/DocumentLibrary/VP332-Electricity-Reforms.pdf (accessed December 12, 2018).

Jordana, Jacint, David Levi-Faur, and Xavier Fernández i Marín. 2011 "The global diffusion of regulatory agencies: channels of transfer and stages of diffusion. *Comparative Political Studies*. 44(1). pp. 1343–69.

Lam, Willy Wo-Lop. 2015. *Chinese Politics in the Era of Xi Jinping: Renaissance, Reform, or Retrogression*. New York and Abingdon: Routledge.

Le'eautier, Thomas-Olivier and Ve'ronique Thelen. 2009. "Optimal Expansion of the Power Transmission Grid: Why Not?" *Journal of Regulatory Economics*. 36. pp. 127–53.

Li Zhiyong 李志勇. 2017. 发改委：未来价格改革将进入"深水区" [National Development and Reform Commission Reports that Power Price Reform Will

Soon Deepen]. www.china5e.com/news/news-996915-1.html (accessed July 31, 2017).

Liu, Chun and Krishna Jayakar. 2012. "The Evolution of Telecommunications Policy-making: Comparative Analysis of China and India." *Telecommunications Policy*. 36. pp. 13–28.

Liu, Wei and Hong Li. 2011. "Improving Energy Consumption Structure: a Comprehensive Assessment of Fossil Energy Subsidies Reform in China." *Energy Policy*. 39. pp. 4134–43.

Ma, Chunbo and Xiaoli Zhao. 2015. "China's electricity market restructuring and technology mandates: Plant-level evidence for changing operational efficiency." *Energy Economics*. 47. pp. 227–37.

Ma, Jinlong. 2011. On-grid electricity tariffs in China: development, reform and prospects. *Energy Policy*. 39. pp. 2633–45.

Mah, Daphne Ngar-yin. 2015. Interview. Mah is Assistant Professor, Department of Geography, and Director, Asian Energy Studies Centre, Hong Kong Baptist University.

Mah, Daphne Ngar-yin and Peter Hills. 2008. "Central-Local Relations and Pricing Policies for Wind Energy in China." *China Review*. 8(2). pp. 261–93.

2014a. "Collaborative Governance for Technological Innovation: a Comparative Case Study of Wind Energy in Xinjiang, Shanghai, and Guangdong." *Environment and Planning C: Government and Policy*. 32. pp. 509–29.

2014b. "Policy Learning and Central-Local Relations: a Case Study of the Pricing Policies for Wind Energy in China (from 1994 to 2009)" *Environmental Policy and Governance*. 24(3).

Mariscal, Judith and Eugenio Rivera. 2005. "New Trends in Latin American Telecommunications market: Telefonica and Telmex." *Telecommunications Policy*. 29. pp. 757–77.

Mason, Josephine and Benjamin Kang Lim. 2018. "China plans to create energy ministry in government shake-up." Reuters. March 8, 2018. https://ca.reuters.com/article/topNews/idCAKCN1GK179-OCATP (accessed December 12, 2018).

Metering and Smart Energy International. 2018. "China leads smart electric meter market." January 11, 2018. www.metering.com/industry-sectors/smart-energy/china-smart-electric-meter-market/ (accessed December 12, 2018).

Nepal, Rabindra and Tooraj Jamasb. 2012. "Reforming the power sector in transition: do institutions matter? *Energy Economics*. 34. pp. 1675–82.

Newsdoug. 2013. "Unicom sides with Tencent WeChat." Young's China Business Blog. April 3, 2013. www.youngchinabiz.com/en/unicom-sides-with-tencent-wechat/ (accessed December 12, 2018).

Ni, Chun Chun. 2007. "The Xinfeng power plant and challenges for China's electric power industry." Institute of Energy Economics Japan. https://eneken.ieej.or.jp/en/data/pdf/382.pdf (accessed December 12, 2018).

Organisation of Economic Cooperation and Development (OECD). 2009. *China: Review of Regulatory Reform*. Paris: OECD.

Pittman, Russell and Vanessa Yanhua Zhang. 2010. "Electricity Restructuring in China: How Competitive Will Generation Markets Be?" *The Singapore Economic Review.* 55(2). pp. 377–400.

Pollitt, Michael, Chung-Han Yang, and Hao Chen. 2017. "Reforming the Chinese Electricity Supply: Lessons from International Experience." Cambridge Working Paper Economics: 1713. www.energy.cam.ac.uk/news-and-events/news/reform ing-the-chinese-electricity-supply-sector-lessons-from-international-experience (accessed December 12, 2018).

Power Overview. 2016. 2016年全国电力工业统计快报一览表 [2016 National Electricity Sector Statistical Bulletin]. www.cec.org.cn/guihuayutongji/tongj xinxi/niandushuju/2017–01-20/164007.html (accessed July 23, 2017).

Price Competition 2016. 全国电价大比拼系列2 [National Price Competition Series 2]. Posted November 24, 2016. http://shoudian.bjx.com.cn/news/20161124/ 791369.shtml (accessed June 1, 2017).

PwC. 2016. *China Entertainment and Media Outlook 2016–2020.* www.pwccn.com/en/ industries/telecommunications-media-and-technology/publications/china-entertainment-and-media-outlook-2016-2020.html (accessed December 12, 2018).

Qin Min. 2011. "China Mobile Sees Slow Growth in 3G Users." November 22, 2011. *Caixin.*

Shanxi Anti-monopoly. 2017. 电力反垄断第一案浮出水面 山西发电企业几乎全卷入 [First electricity anti-monopoly case surfaces – nearly all Shanxi power firms are involved] www.china5e.com/news/news-990260–1.html (accessed June 7, 2017).

Starks, Michael. 2010. "China's Digital Switchover: International Context." *International Journal of Digital Television.* 1. pp 89–93.

State Council of China. 2015. "Deepening Reform of the Power Sector." 2015: Document 9 (《关于进一步深化电力体制改革的若干意见（中发〔2015〕9号）文》全文) www.ne21.com/news/show-64828.html (accessed June 29, 2015).

Stilpon, Nestor and Ladan Mahboobi. 1999. "Privatisation of public utilities: the OECD experience." www.oecd.org/daf/ca/corporategovernanceofstate-ownedenter prises/1929700.pdf (accessed December12, 2018).

Tan, Min. 2013. "Competitors Try Curbing China Mobile's 4G Urge." May 7, 2013. *Caixin.* www.caixinglobal.com/2013–05-07/101014460.html (accessed December12, 2018).

Telegeography.com. 2014. "Chinese Operators Now Free to Set Their Own Tariffs." May 12, 2014. www.telegeography.com/products/commsupdate/articles/2014/05/ 12/chinese-operators-now-free-to-set-their-own-tariffs/ (accessed August 19, 2014).

2014. "China's First MVNO Goes Live." May 6, 2014. www.telegeography.com/ products/commsupdate/articles/2014/05/06/chinas-first-mvno-goes-live/ (accessed December12, 2018).

2014. "700 MHz Ban Off Limits Until 2020; Telecom Handed Trial FD-LTE License." June 26, 2014. www.telegeography.com/products/commsupdate/articles/2014/06/ 26/700mhz-band-off-limits-until-2020-telecom-handed-trial-fd-lte-licence/ (accessed December12, 2018).

2014. "Strong 3G Performance Fends Off Decline as Competition Hits Telecom's Customer Base." August 27, 2014. www.telegeography.com/products/commsup

date/articles/2014/08/27/strong-3g-performance-tends-off-decline-as-competition-hits-telecoms-customer-base/ (accessed December12, 2018).

2015. "Cellcos to Renew Handset Subsidy, China Nears 100 m LTE Users." January 20, 2015. www.telegeography.com/products/commsupdate/articles/ 2015/01/20/cellcos-to-renew-handset-subsidy-push-china-nears-100m-lte-users/ (accessed December 12, 2018).

2015. "MIIT looking to improve competition in 'unbalanced' market." November 10, 2015. www.telegeography.com/products/commsupdate/articles/2015/11/10/miit-looking-to-improve-competition-in-unbalanced-market/ (accessed June 11, 2017).

2016. "China Issues National Telecom License to CBN." May 6, 2016. www .telegeography.com/products/commsupdate/articles/2016/05/06/china-issues-national-telecom-licence-to-cbn/ (accessed June 11, 2017).

2017. "MVNO Monday: a guide to the week's virtual operator developments." January 23, 2017. www.telegeography.com/products/commsupdate/articles/ 2017/01/23/mvno-monday-a-guide-to-the-weeks-virtual-operator-developments/ (accessed December 12, 2018).

Unplugged 2014. "Unplugged and Unproductive." *Economist*. July 26. p. 57.

Wallsten, Scott. 2002. "Does Sequencing Matter? Regulation and Privatization in Telecommunications Reforms." World Bank. February 2002. http://info .worldbank.org/etools/docs/voddocs/152/334/sequencing.pdf (accessed June 12, 2015).

2005. "Returning to Victorian competition, ownership, and regulation: an empirical study of European telecommunications at the turn of the twentieth century." *The Journal of Economic History*. 65(3). pp. 693–722.

Weston, Frederick. 2015. Interview. Weston is Principal and Director, China Program, The Regulatory Assistance Project.

World Bank. World Development Indicators. World Bank. http://data.worldbank.org (accessed June 12, 2015).

Wu, Irene. 2002. US Federal Communications Commission. "Setting Up Interconnection Regimes: References for Regulators." November 2002. https:// apps.fcc.gov/edocspublic/attachmatch/DOC-229565A1.pdf (accessed June 17, 2015).

2008. "Who Regulates Phones, Television and the Internet? What Makes a Communications Regulator Independent and Why It Matters." *Perspectives on Politics*. 6(4). pp. 769–83.

2009. *From Iron Fist to Invisible Hand: the Uneven Path of Telecommunications Reform in China*. Stanford: Stanford University Press.

2014. "Diffusion of Regulatory Policy across Nations: The Example of Number Portability." *Digiworld Economic Journal*. 95.

Wu, Richard W. S. and Grace L. K. Leung. 2012. "Implementation of Three Network Convergence in China: a New Institutional Analysis." *Telecommunications Policy*. 36. pp. 955–65.

Xinhua 2013. "China to restructure National Energy Administration." March 10, 2013. http://news.xinhuanet.com/english/china/2013-03/10/c_132221775.htm (accessed June 1, 2018).

———. 2013. "Former electricity regulator leads national energy watchdog." March 26, 2013. http://news.xinhuanet.com/english/china/2013-03/26/c_132262648.htm (accessed June 1, 2018).

———. 2014. "Xi Jinping Leads Internet Security Group." Beijing. February 27, 2014. http://news.xinhuanet.com/english/china/2014-02/27/c_133148273.htm (accessed June 1, 2018).

Xu Yi-chong. 2016. *Sinews of Power: the Politics of the State Grid Corporation of China.* Oxford: Oxford University Press.

Zhang, Fang; Hao Deng, Robert Margolis, and Jun Su. 2015. "Analysis of Distributed-Generation Photovoltaic Deployment, Installation Time and Cost, Market Barriers and Policies in China." *Energy Policy.* 81. pp. 45–55.

Zhang, Yin-Fang, David Parker, and Colin Kirkpatrick. 2008. "Electricity Reform in Developing Countries: an Econometric Assessment of the Effects of Privatization, Competition, and Regulation." *Journal of Regulatory Economics.* 33. pp. 159–78.

Zhao, Elaine Jing. 2017. "The Bumpy Road towards Network Convergence in China: The Case of Over-the-top Streaming Services." *Global Media and China.* 2 (1). pp. 28–42.

Zhao, Hejuan. 2011. Disputes sound media integration death knell. April 12, 2011. *Caixin.* http://english.caxin.com/2011-04-12/100247201.html (accessed June 26, 2014).

Zhao, Xiaoli and Chunbo Ma. 2013. "Deregulation, Vertical Unbundling, and the Performance of China's Large Coal-fired Power Plants." *Energy Economics* 40. pp. 474–83.

Zheng, Xinye et al. 2014. "Characteristics of Residential Energy Consumption in China." *Energy Policy.* 75. pp. 125–35.

Zhou, Yan. 2010. "The Positioning and Current Situation of China's Digital TV." *International Journal of Digital Television.* 1. pp. 95–104.

3

Local Government and Firm Innovation in China's Clean Energy Sector

Margaret M. Pearson

INTRODUCTION

What role do local governments play in promoting innovation by Chinese firms? [*] Much scholarship on Chinese political economy has argued that local governments have played a highly beneficial role in promoting China's explosive growth over the past decades.[1] This picture is undoubtedly accurate in the export-oriented manufacturing sectors that were the engine of Chinese growth during this period. Local governments fostered the growth of firms that benefited, too, from newly available labor, falling transport costs, easily obtainable low-end but completely adequate technology (including technology obtained through global supply chains), and global consumers interested in paying low prices for products sourced from China. Yet as the low-hanging fruit from simple manufacturing exports has to a large degree been picked, and as People's Republic of China (PRC) government policies have focused on innovation-led intensive growth, often in advanced-technology industries, can local governments continue to provide a favorable ecosystem? Chinese local governments face a double-edged challenge: fostering the commercial integration of new technologies and responding to central government directives encouraging innovation. Despite the political and economic emphasis the Chinese government has placed on upgrading, the impact of local officials on the ecosystem for firm innovation is curiously under-examined in the growing literature on innovation in China. A major study

[*] Thanks to Liu Wei for research assistance, and to Loren Brandt, Jennifer Hadden, Jennifer Lewis, Jonas Nahm, and Tom Rawski for helpful comments on early drafts of this chapter.
[1] On the developmental role of local government see, for example, Bardhan and Mookherjee (2006); Chen (2012); Dinh et al. (2013); Huang (2002); Heilmann (2008); Heilmann et al. (2013); Montinola et al. (1995); Oi (1992, 1999); and Xu (2011).

of China's innovation capacity by the OECD, for example, only briefly mentions the role of local governments (OECD 2007).[2]

This chapter's empirical focus is on local government influence on the development of clean energy manufacturing industries, specifically solar cells (photovoltaic (PVs)) and electric vehicles (EVs).[3] Innovative manufacturing in the clean energy sector is a key theme in discussions on China's response to environmental degradation and climate change. Yet clean energy manufacturing is not just an energy or environmental policy; it also is treated in China as, and is perhaps foremost, an industrial policy. As a result, the emergence of China's clean energy industry – as a part of China's push for innovation as well as sustainable development – has followed in the well-trod footsteps of Chinese industrial policies. Clean energy has been designated as a strategic emerging industry (SEI) and fully incorporated into the Five-Year Plan process.[4] While not unexpected in the Chinese policy context, the envelopment of the sector by industrial policy processes has left a distinctive mark on the trajectory of China's clean energy industry.

This chapter considers the various ways in which local governments in China, operating in the context of the PRC political and industrial policy systems do and do not foster an innovative ecosystem for firms.[5] Local governments are important economic actors in China's efforts at upgrading. Two core roles of local officials – promoting growth and

---

[2] Industry-specific studies also often fail to highlight the role of local governments except in passing, e.g., Bär (2013). Exceptions include OECD 2008 (ch. 7); Dai 2015; Helveston et al. (2016); and Liu and Chen 2012.

[3] Note that these cases are manufacturing industries related to electric power, as distinct from some of the other chapters in this book that analyze network industries of electric power generation (from traditional and clean sources) and transmission. However, the roles of local governments in upgrading network industries can be informed by many of the dynamics described in this chapter.

[4] The SEI initiative was introduced in 2006, but only gained momentum with the 2008 financial crisis. Beijing emphasizes domestic self-reliance in order to avoid royalty payments to foreign firms and overdependence upon foreign sources of technology (Kennedy, Suttmeier, and Su 2008). Government policy explicitly mandates that these "strategic" industries should be "innovative," and in addition to the SEI policy has set forth multiple other initiatives to this end. This is especially true in the EV industry, in which foreign technology barriers to entry (particularly for hybrid vehicles) have been high.

[5] While the chapter focuses on the impact of local government on upgrading, it should not be construed to imply that other factors are unimportant. Many of those other factors, including the level of technology available to PRC firms and the role of global value chains, are described elsewhere in this volume and later in this chapter. On the importance of global value chains in innovation, see Humphrey and Schmitz 2002; Gereffi, Humphrey, and Sturgeon 2005; Berger 2006.

development in their jurisdictions, and responding to policy initiatives from Beijing – guarantee they are important actors. Sometimes these two roles align, and sometimes they conflict. Outcomes of alignment or conflict between local imperatives and central pressures are sometimes favorable for firm innovation (as exemplified by the case of low-speed EVs), but some sometimes they are unfavorable (exemplified below in the case of solar panels).

As other chapters in this volume illustrate, it is clear that in some respects new energy industries in China have successfully upgraded, in terms of both cost and process, and perhaps product.[6] Yet new energy industries also exhibit substantial variation across the sector. This chapter illustrates the path by which upgrading has occurred, most notably in the niche sector of low-speed EVs. Development of this sector, interestingly, occurred with the strong support of subnational governments, but in contravention to explicit central government preferences. At the same time, the discussion illustrates that even when local officials foster upgrading, this effort can involve considerable waste. Waste is seen in the excessive entry of new firms (over-investment) in which firms gain government-delivered benefits, and local cadres hope to be rewarded for quick results. It is also seen in inadequate exit when firms fail and yet remain protected by local governments. These dynamics are illustrated in this chapter by the solar PV case. Waste occurs in all innovating systems, including advanced industrial economies (e.g. Lerner 2009), and in significant ways China is not unique. The underlying point is that problems – and prospects – for upgrading and innovation in China are in important ways a function of the deeply rooted systemic incentives local officials face in the context set by China's industrial policy system.

The next section of this chapter reviews how the literature on the government's role in innovation suggests local governments might ideally establish an environment favorable to firm innovation. The third section discusses the important role of Chinese local officials in economic development, and how industrial policy processes shape this role. The fourth section presents a series of mini-case studies in the solar PV and EVs industries that illustrate how local governments have served, variously, to enable firms in innovation-related industries but also to hinder the local

---

[6] Scholars identify several basic categories of innovation, often distinguishing between product and process innovation. On categories of innovation, see Fagerberg, Mowery and Nelson (2005). Relevant studies on innovation in clean energy include Nahm and Steinfeld (2014); Nahm (2017); and Lewis (2013).

innovation ecosystem. The cases highlight wasted local government investment, local protectionism, fragmentation of efforts, problematic firm responses to subsidies, and lack of adequate private financing. The concluding section summarizes.

HOW LOCAL GOVERNMENTS CAN PROMOTE INNOVATIVE INDUSTRIES

Debates about the relationship between local governments and firm innovation are set squarely in the two dominant literatures on the state and innovation: those emphasizing market-driven upgrading, on the one hand, and those emphasizing the need for state support in fostering innovation, on the other. Market-based theories on successful innovation depict the upgrading process primarily as bottom-up, originating with non-state entrepreneurs, and often pivoting off firms' access to and position in global or regional value chains.[7] In this model, entrepreneurs – sometimes with the aid of venture capital – endeavor to provide a response to (potential) market demand. They may misjudge, or wastefully duplicate efforts of others. They succeed or fail mainly based on their own merits. The role of local governments is depicted as secondary, at best. The competing statist approach places government policy at the center. One sub-approach of state-supported innovation models, the developmental state literature, draws inspiration from Gershenkron's (1962) argument that state institutions and a capable bureaucracy can work with industrial firms to leapfrog developmental stages that had been followed in advanced Western economies.[8] A second sub-approach focuses on the state's role in ameliorating market failure, i.e., governments intervene when markets do not adequately incentivize the flow of resources into knowledge creation and innovation.[9] Governments can play a positive role not just by establishing proper institutions (rights to intellectual property, etc., that are also favored in market-based approaches) but also by directing public financing

---

[7] The classic work on market-driven disruption is Christensen (1997).

[8] Gershenkron's argument underpins the East Asian developmental state literature. See Johnson (1982); Amsden (1989); and Wade (1990). On how China has retained elements of this statist approach, including the use of industrial policy, see Chen and Naughton (2016).

[9] Arrow (1962) identifies how the market fails to invest when innovative knowledge is imperfectly excludable. Hall (2005) theorizes that funding for new untried ideas cannot ex ante identify successful ideas from failures.

to firms, reducing the risk firms face from failed innovation efforts (Hall and van Reenen 2000). Similarly, governments may help create a market for products through demand-side subsidies or purchases. A third sub-approach focusing on "national innovation systems" goes even further to suggest the benefit of extensive government contributions including funding public research and development, and expansive funding for public education. Taken as a whole, the literature emphasizing state-driven innovation does not assume the absence of markets but, rather, the extensive and purposive efforts by governments to shape market incentives and outcomes, and ameliorate market failure. The statist literature pays less attention to the problem of political failure, when political concerns of government officials produce other incentives that may hinder innovation. Such political failure is important in the cases analyzed below. Both of these broad literatures suggest clear policy prescriptions, few of which are mutually exclusive. Given externalities inherent in environmental technologies, it is unsurprising that many attempts at innovation in the clean energy sector are policy-driven.

How might *local* governments foster innovative industries? The "regional innovation systems" approach (a subset of Nelson's [1993] classic "national innovation systems" approach) emphasizes that innovation – as a collective enterprise – is best served when collaboration is promoted between subnational governments, firms, and research organizations such as universities and institutes. Much as occurs with industrial production clusters, the co-location of these actors may create synergies (Asheim and Gertler 2005; Sagar and Zwaan 2006). In theory, proximity can open the door for local governments to help coordinate the circulation of knowledge as well as the promotion of strong systemic relationships between firms and a given region's knowledge infrastructure.

Local governments also often channel economic resources from the national government to the cluster or firm (Asheim and Gertler 2005). Yet the vision of local-government-as-coordinator is not limited to implementing policy from the national level. Local coordination can help overcome lack of trust that may be inherent between actors – actors in competing firms, institutes, and funding organizations (Powell and Grodal 2005). Coordination can direct resources to where they are most effectively used, and prevent wasteful duplication. Local governments also may set a proper local policy environment, particularly for market entrance and exit of firms, but also for tax policy (e.g. tax incentives related to technology zones), designing effective allocation schemes for funds (including public and private lending) and land, among other standard policy instruments.[10]

THE ROLE OF CHINESE LOCAL GOVERNMENTS IN PROMOTING INNOVATION

Turning to China, the central government's innovation-related policies contain elements of each set of policy prescriptions found in the broader literature, as well as a role for local government. Innovation-promotion policies in China are quite diverse, relying on both top-down industrial policy and attempts to spur bottom-up market driven factors. The government's emphasis during the past decade on commercialization of technology and the core role of technology firms in innovation recognizes the importance of market-based forces, including firms already deeply engaged in global value chains. At the same time, the role of the Chinese state in innovation promotion remains vast, and places industrial policy instruments implemented primarily via local governments at center stage.[11] As in other economies, firms operate within market structures and regulatory environments that sets parameters for their growth and upgrading. But in China, especially in sectors targeted by Beijing to lead its continued economic rise, industrial policy remains particularly important. It influences the distribution of state resources (grants, loans, subsidies, research funds), sets terms for international protection, and clearly signals priorities. All of these factors in turn influence market structure. In addition to broad policies such as the SEI initiative, industrial policy continues to govern specific industries.[12] This section discusses the general role local officials in China have played in innovation, and then focuses on the impact of Beijing's industrial policy on this role.

---

[10] On sub-national governments' roles in provision of these public goods in Europe, see OECD (2007), p. 48. With regard to China, Breznitz, and Murphree (2011) compare the models employed in three Chinese regions – Beijing, Shanghai, and the Pearl River Delta – and how each succeeded in promoting process innovation. Works that demonstrate regional differences in a single sector include, for IT, Chen (2012) and Segal (2003) and, for the automobile industry, Thun (2006).

[11] Beijing also has increased its emphasis on providing support for innovation with *domestic* origins, so-called "indigenous innovation." In contrast, the upgrading policy implicit to Deng Xiaoping's "opening to the outside world" actively sought foreign technology via foreign investment and purchases of technology on international markets (Ernst 2009). See also OECD (2008), ch. 10.

[12] A good summary of the industrial policy for automobiles and EVs is Helveston et al. (2016).

Local governments throughout China have played roles highlighted in the regional innovation systems literature. Local government coordination is especially evident in the proliferation of high technology development zones (HTDZs), science parks, and other "incubators." The rapid development of small, technology firms in the past decade is in part a reflection of the huge investment made by local governments in science parks, often in conjunction with local universities and research institutes (Zhou 2008; OECD 2008). These parks were to be developed under the auspices of the Torch program (under the Ministry of Science and Technology (MOST)), and yet control over their establishment and management (as well as funding) was given to local governments, which also have donated land and other resources.[13] When successful, local governments have spurred on anchor firms that then attract complementary industries to the region, creating an "innovation cluster." For example, in the solar sector, Yingli Solar (a private firm) was given a prominent anchor location in the HTDZ in Baoding.

Linked closely to the coordination function of local governments is the provision of significant local funding for potentially innovative firms. Indeed, it is difficult to overstate how important local funding has been for innovation programs in China. According to OECD (2007, p. 56), "For programmes to support the commercialization of research, such as Torch and Spark, the [central] government accounts for no more than 2 to 5 percent of total funding, while local governments and enterprises typically provide large shares of funding for programs related to innovation and dissemination of technologies."[14] Liu and Chen (2012) report similarly that the total amount of research and development (R&D) investment by regional governments is larger than that of the central government. The bulk of this local investment is in wealthy provinces and municipalities such as Jiangsu, Shanghai, Guangdong, Shandong, and Zhejiang. Support occurs in the form of direct grants, low-interest bank loans, and state-backed venture capital.

Local governments also commonly provide subsidies, on both the producer and the demand sides (see examples in the case studies below), but

---

[13] HTDZs – and the Torch program projects – were not intended to support basic research but, rather, innovation that could rapidly be commercialized and therefore produce jobs. Breznitz and Murphree (2011), p. 81, point to the Shenzhen HTDZ as a successful example of local (provincial in this case) governmental coordination by streamlining procedures and ensuring access for firms to a complete value chain. Heilmann et al. (2013) have argued that the Torch program for high technology zones has had a very positive feedback effect on central policy.

[14] See also Nahm (2017).

especially the former. In recent years, local governments, particularly in wealthy regions, have not only given direct grants but also have coordinated local venture capital (VC) to invest in tech start-ups. Although the source of some VC investment is international firms, outside of major metropolitan areas such as Beijing and Shanghai, more of the VC funds have come from local sources. Liu and Chen (2012) point to the emergence of government-coordinated VC firms in Jiangsu in which officials do not directly manage the capital but instead hire a professional commercial organization to do so. Wuxi in particular, in the mid-2000s, began a high-risk-high return government VC fund to help fund innovative firms (He 2006b). This may be a creative way to mobilize local funds where private institutional capital is not readily available.

Municipal and county level governments also possess *China-specific* resources they can supply to facilitate firm innovation in a manner consistent with what is envisioned in the regional innovation system perspective. First, local governments contain institutionalized pockets of expertise that facilitate and support innovative enterprises. Many of these are a legacy of the massive expansion carried out by institutions and the resources used to support training and research during the central planning era (Brandt, Ma, and Rawski 2017). Thus, at present local offices of provincial and municipal-level institutes of the Chinese Academy of Sciences, local Science and Technology bureaus of MOST, and local offices of the National Development and Reform Commission (NDRC) are available to provide appropriate knowledge-input. Many cadres in sub-national bureaus in provinces and large municipalities have provided input into the formulation of innovation policies at the national level, such as the SEIs (interviews; and OECD 2008, p. 363). Since the mid-1990s, locally-funded research institutes (or branches of national institutes) have contributed to the technology and social and human capital needed for the commercialization of innovation. They have, often for a licensing fee, provided key technology to firms. Local offices of industrial, commerce, and trade bureaus also have proved valuable in connecting local firms with international market actors, linking local firms with global value chains.

Moreover, local discretion in implementation of – and experimentation with – policy has long been an integral part of the Chinese political system. A well-established tradition of local policy experimentation in China lends itself to the promotion of innovation by local political actors, or to their support of firm innovation efforts that could benefit the local jurisdiction (Oi 1992; Heilmann 2008; Xu 2011). And, as noted previously, despite much waste and corruption, local governments are widely seen to have been a key factor in promoting firm entrepreneurship and China's remark able post-Mao growth. OECD (2008, ch. 7) shows for the regional systems of Shanghai, Liaoning, and Sichuan each region has its own plan for how to meet innovation goals, with each plan to some degree reflecting the local context and comparative advantage.[15]

It is important to emphasize that most of these tools of local governments are not evenly distributed across China.[16] Governments in poorer counties and cities cannot often afford to provide high sub-sidies to firms – though many can contribute land. Despite the generally notable level of expertise throughout China's bureaucracy, technical capacity may be more concentrated in areas such as Beijing and Shanghai. The shortage of resources in some areas, as we shall see, may create incentives for local officials to create "innovations" that are less effective than in other areas.

While unevenly distributed, subsidies, funds, technical expertise, and other resources can help local governments foster innovative activities from the bottom up, and as a result help respond to local developmental needs and conditions. But this job of local cadres exists in tandem (and sometimes in tension) with the other role of local governments: to imple-ment central policy. The central government has a number of tools with which to influence local governments to produce innovation of the pre-ferred types. Note that China has a unitary (as opposed to federal) system of government, i.e., local officials are conduits of central government policy, including industrial policy and other directives such as Five-Year Plans. Despite the shift from directive planning to "guidance" planning in which central statements serve more as a guide than a mandate, local officials are still expected to respond to the center, including to both broad Five-Year Plans and sector-specific policies. First and foremost, the central guidance, such as in the SEI initiative in general, and new energy industry promotion specifically, are signals of the center's policy preferences, to which local officials must show some degree of responsive-ness, if not full compliance (Zhi and Pearson 2017). The promotion system for local officials also requires responsiveness to central signals. The top-down cadre management system produces career incentives for local officials wishing to be promoted to show responsiveness. This occurs

---

[15] A similar study is by Sigurdson (2004).
[16] On significant regional disparities in R&D expenditures (from all sources, including local governments) and R&D intensity (expenditures as a percentage of GDP) see OECD (2008), p. 43.

through regular performance evaluation, rotation, and turnover.[17] Furthermore, the cadre management system – in addition to and supportive of a norm of local "experimentation" – helps protect local cadres' promotion ambitions as they creatively experiment with how to align their concrete governance interests with the signals of the center.[18]

If we accept, as most scholars of Chinese political economy do, that local cadres are much concerned with how their performance affects their prospects for promotion, and understand the local flexibility to develop specific plans for innovation, then it becomes clear how well-known cracks in the alignment between central guidance and local interests might affect local governments' innovation incentives. Local officials in the state's *nomenklatura* system typically have quite short time horizons.[19] As their terms in office often are shorter than the official five years, their promotion prospects – the ability to show results from their leadership –are quite short. The incentive to make an impression on immediate superiors in the short-term (two or three years) is strong. This short time horizon is a problem when technological innovations may require a longer term to come to fruition, especially when commitments to innovation projects are used to demonstrate political results.[20] Officials are incentivized to produce "quick" results at the expense of genuinely innovative ones that may take more time to realize.

One further observation about the policy environment for local officials is warranted. The matrix of centrally designed policies to which

---

[17] On the relationship between cadres' performance and the criteria for career advancement, see Mei (2009), Landry (2008), and Li and Zhou (2005).

[18] The implication is that local officials can feel more emboldened in carrying out localized interests as long as they can plausibly argue to be aligned with central interests.

[19] Chinese local officials are not the only local officials with short time horizons, of course. Two-year election cycles for the US Congress shorten representatives' time horizons as well. However, Chinese style industrial policy, a mainstay of the PRC's policy instruments for investment in key policies, is intended to work over a much longer time horizon than is practical for most local officials.

[20] According to Landry (2008), while the formal term of mayors is five years, the average duration of Chinese mayors' terms in 2000 was 2.2 years. Heads of SOEs, themselves subject to the *nomenklatura* system, also have a short time horizon that may be contrary to investment in innovation activities. Not all local officials are subject to promotion, and some remain in the same locale for long periods. In this situation, two other, complementary, views on how local interests may de-align with the center are: Kostka and Hobbs (2012) on "interest bundling"; and Ahlers and Schubert (2009) on "strategic groups." Similarly, Chen Jinjin (2011, p. 5082) argues that "some local governments believe that only through deviations from the central directives can economic growth be achieved. . ." On payoffs for deviations from central directives, see Mei and Pearson (2014).

local officials must attend, even for an area seemingly as narrow as clean energy, is multi-layered and complex. Clean energy manufacturing is affected by overlapping policies in the realms of manufacturing promotion (traditional sector industrial policy, especially relevant to EVs), overall planning (Five-Year Plans), national champion policy (such as the SEI initiative), innovation policy (such as the Medium- and Long-term Plan for Science and Technology or the 863 National High-Tech Research and Development Program), climate policy, and energy reform policy. The promulgation of industrial policies under Xi Jinping continued. For example, the Made in China 2025 policy announced in May 2015 attempts to promote industrial upgrading, particularly in the advanced-technology sectors. In automobiles, in addition to efforts by MOST to promote EVs, the Ministry of Industry and Information Technology and National Development and Reform Commission (NDRC) together in April 2017 released the "Automotive Industry Medium-Long Term Development Plan," outlining the main goals for the auto industry for the next ten years, and published blueprints for New Energy Vehicles (NEVs), including efforts to create "smart" cars with advanced electronics equipment.[21] Unsurprisingly, policies are frequently produced by a small groups of experts seconded from multiple industries, and reflect compromises among them.[22] Industrial policies are not only multiple and overlapping, but are often are quite general in nature, with subsequent implementing regulations – which may appear many months later – providing greater specificity. For example, the 2012 NEV Development Plan (State Council 2012) was issued a decade after EVs became a "key project" in science and technology innovation, and while it detailed targets for production, sales, and fuel efficiency, it did not lay out technical plans or standards beyond saying they should achieve an advanced international level. Presumably, some of these technical advances were to take place through experimentation, as through the "10 Cities 10,000 Vehicles" program discussed below. Initially vague policies can leave local officials both uncertain about, but also with flexibility (understood as policy experimentation) about, how best to respond.[23] An important question is the degree to which top down industrial policy initiatives actually facilitate or crowd out genuinely local initiatives.

---

[21] *USITO Newsletter*, 2 May 2017.   [22] Interviews, June 2015 and March 2016.
[23] Zhi and Pearson (2017); Heilmann (2013).

LOCAL GOVERNMENT INVOLVEMENT IN CHINA'S SOLAR AND ELECTRIC VEHICLES SECTORS: A BALANCE SHEET

As the previous discussion has shown, local state involvement in China's clean energy sector revolves around two sets of goals. First, local officials need to respond to conditions they face on the ground. Their responses may include market-conforming efforts directed at helping firms build on their existing capabilities. Furthermore, local officials are keen to have development of these industries serve other economic needs, particularly employment and taxes.[24] At the same time, however, local officials must engage with the institutional infrastructure of industrial policy that reflects the massive role the state plays in China's economy. Thus, local cadres' efforts may be directed at the political benefits (especially promotion) they stand to gain from showing a loyal response to the center's signals for "innovation." While the consequence of local officials' desire to meet both top-down political and local development goals need not always be negative, this dynamic often provides a breeding ground for political failure, i.e., officials taking actions that could in principle create net benefits but fail to deliver in reality because political concerns push implementation in unfortunate directions.[25] The following discussion on solar PV and EV industries illustrates both the positive and negative impacts of the local political ecosystem for green energy firms.

Helpful Local Government Participation

It is not difficult to find evidence of local government efforts to create a positive ecosystem for potentially innovative firms in solar and EVs, and one that thus appears to bolster firm innovation. As we shall see, such efforts do not exclude the fact that in some of these same cases, the local government role simultaneously was – or became – problematic. Moreover, local officials have particular goals with which they expect local firms to align. Primary among these goals are the creation of jobs, revenues, and a positive reputation for both the jurisdiction and the

---

[24] Dai's (2015) interviews in the solar and wind sectors demonstrate that employment and tax concerns were paramount in local officials' attitudes toward creating an ecosystem for firms.

[25] Actions of Chinese local governments are not completely unique in this regard. The US government, for example, has dozens of overlapping conflicting, duplicative programs to encourage policy goals, including for green energy.

official(s) involved.[26] The possibility of such economic and political pay-offs leads local officials to advocate and negotiate on behalf of local firms.

In the solar industry, the photovoltaic solar cell producer Suntech (无锡尚德), in part due to support by the Wuxi government, has often been held up as a model of business and innovation success (He 2006a). These successes –including in innovation[27] – were most notable before 2006, prior to the firm's financial problems and the 2012 international trade disputes that affected the solar PV industry as a whole. Wuxi municipal and Jiangsu provincial officials helped attract the firm and its entrepreneurial founder, Shi Zhengrong, an overseas Chinese engineer living in Australia. The Wuxi government provided sizable initial start-up grants and subsidies, and took a 75 percent equity stake in the firm in return for US$ 6 million. City officials later helped Suntech obtain funding from national and local sources, such as from the provincial department of MOST. Some of these "loans" did not need to be repaid. Wuxi officials further helped organize a sizable package of loans from banks and local venture capital groups; notably, former official turned Suntech board chair Li Yanren helped arrange for 5 billion yuan in low-interest loans. Subsequently, and in anticipation of Suntech's 2006 listing on the New York Stock Exchange, the Wuxi government offloaded its shares to other investors – including local state backed "venture capital" (Ahrens 2013). In addition, the government was instrumental in setting up a regional cluster for the PV industry in Jiangsu, establishing a relatively complete value chain in a few years. Suntech also set up an R&D center that led to manufacturing and efficiency improvements, though the commoditization of solar cells in recent years has rendered its products more price and quality-driven than innovation-driven. Nevertheless, presumably in part because of large-scale support, upgraded silicon slicing technology was developed and commercialized in the region (Liu and Chen 2012). Wuxi government officials also sought to bolster demand by identifying building projects for which Suntech could supply solar panels. In short, the "Wuxi Model" of financial support from the city government has been touted as a major reason for Suntech's success, with the implication that it helped Suntech thrive as an innovative firm. Suntech was, furthermore, the

---

[26] See Dai (2015).

[27] Suntech made efficiency improvements in low-cost solar cells, improved wafer technology, and obtained fifty-five patents (He 2006a; Ahrens 2013). Subsequently, it moved into thin-film technology, allowing further diversification of its business to higher margin areas. Suntech also made some favorable strategic moves, including securing long-term upstream contracts for silicon supplies.

prototype for Wuxi's 2006 "530 Plan," designed to supply between 1 and 3 million RMB per approved project, the major criterion for approval being that a project is technologically promising.

Similarly, Baoding municipal officials (Hebei Province) played an important part in the emergence of the private Yingli Solar (英利太阳能). Key supports were the provision of land, tax reductions, and help obtaining building permits. Local officials also have supported Yingli's applications for funding from Beijing. Local government contributions are generally required in order to be awarded central funds. Local government approval of bank loans remains necessary, and also is considered a de facto government guarantee for the repayment of loans. Baoding has not been the only local government to help Yingli. As the firm began to diversify away from PV production toward downstream power generation, it relied on a provincial government-based organizational strategy. Yingli planned to decentralize operations away from its Baoding headquarters by building independent solar generating stations, especially in western and southwestern provinces (e.g. Xinjiang, Yunnan, Guangxi, and Shaanxi).[28] Building new branches in other provinces meant courting close ties with those provincial governments, as Yingli needed substantial funds for these generating stations from local governments. The firm requested these governments to contribute land and facilitate loans from other sources including provincial branches of the China Development Bank and Bank of Transportation.[29] Yingli also expanded to Hainan; firm representatives attribute the ability to build the production facility within three months to positive coordination between the firm's CEO and the Hainan provincial government.

In a similar fashion, the founder of LDK Solar (江西赛维), Peng Xiaofeng, shopped around to find the most favorable city government, one that would provide financial support and generally mobilize around the industry. Peng found his answer in the city of Xinyu (Jiangxi Province) (Wang 2007). Although LDK gained the support of the Xinyu city government, and despite LDK's ability to claim itself part of a strategic emerging

---

[28] Yingli pursued this strategy vigorously in the wake of the collapse of international markets for solar panels and the US–China trade war, as well as the PRC central government's subsequent efforts to limit bank loans for producers of solar panels. On this strategy, see http://guangfu.bjx.com.cn/news/20140220/492008.shtml (accessed August 8, 2014).

[29] On China Development Bank (CDB) loans, see www.china5e.com/news/news-336467–1.html (accessed December 15, 2016).

industry, there is little apparent innovation involved in the company a
problem discussed below.

The willingness of wealthy localities to invest more broadly rather than
in a single firm is also important. This was evident in Wuxi (Jiangsu),
where the ability of entrepreneurial officials to attract and support Suntech
was linked to the creation of a local value chain, and as noted earlier
ultimately led the city to promote the "Wuxi" model. The multiplier effect
of a solar industry value chain centered on Suntech held tremendous value
not only for Wuxi but also for Jiangsu province as a whole. According to
Suntech's founder Shi Zhengrong, the Jiangsu PV industry can be valued at
200 billion RMB, and employs 170,000 local workers. Such enticements
would be attractive to any local leader in any country. In addition, the
Wuxi mayor, prior to the collapse of the PV export market, was able to
leverage this and other "pro-innovation" activities into his promotion to
Jiangsu party secretary.

Even short of achieving the notoriety of Wuxi, this dynamic is repeated
in localities across China. A local government increases its prospects for
gaining coveted central governmental "support" by showing support for an
innovation project – as in the case of Shenzhen's (BYD) and Hangzhou
(Kandi), noted below – or gaining favorable national attention as an
experimental site (*shidian*). Being designated a model city by the center
is itself a signal used to encourage other firms to invest in its jurisdiction –
the designation helps the city to create an innovation "brand." Baoding
City (Hebei) leveraged early successes in promoting solar technology firms
into its label as a "Green City," despite having notoriously horrendous air
quality. Indeed, these green energy successes were likely a result of earlier
efforts by leaders in Baoding, including the mayor, to leverage central
funds as well as local capital to build "Baoding Electronics Valley."[30] And
Baoding has in fact become home to successful "green" industries, notably
Yingli Solar. Model status can further allow local leaders to gain access to
additional central government resources (such as from NDRC and the
Ministry of Finance, or for low interest loans from the China Development
Bank), as well as foreign investment.

Turning to the EV sector, note that China's auto industry structure has
been characterized by the emergence of a few national firms (many a mix of
state-owned enterprises (SOEs) and private-foreign joint ventures).
Beijing's EV policy seems to have assumed these large firms would lead

---

[30] Similarly, Baoding government responded quickly to the central government's signals to
promote rapid expansion of wind power firms.

the foray into EV sedans. At the same time, many provinces have home-grown local auto industries, many of which have been beneficiaries of barriers to entry via local (provincial) protectionism. These local firms often produce cheap, low-quality vehicles.

In the EV sector, Shenzhen's BYD Auto (比亚迪), has been at the forefront of China's EVs industry, becoming a national firm. BYD exemplifies how local government support facilitated the emergence of this sector. Subsidies on the supply and demand sides alike have been important.[31] BYD's income statements show government grants (by all levels of government) of 400–500 million RMB. The firm also enjoys large revolving lines of bank credit, for example, a 10 billion RMB line of credit from the China Development Bank. The 2011 interim financial report by the Shenzhen Development and Reform Commission shows total subsidies of 1 billion RMB.[32] The Shenzhen municipal government provided coordination between the firm, banks and other SOEs, while the Guangdong provincial government issued official documents expressing support for BYD electric car projects (Chen Zhijie 2008). Perhaps most importantly, the Shenzhen municipal government agreed to purchase BYD EVs for its municipal taxi and public security bureau fleets. So did governments in other jurisdictions where BYD agreed to invest, including Tianjin, Xi'an, Kunming, and Chengdu. This "demand pull" support became a central pillar of BYD's business plan. Shenzhen municipality also subsidized the purchase of BYD EVs for individual consumers,[33] and facilitated the

---

[31] Central subsidies to consumers for EV passenger vehicles on the approved list of the Ministry of Industry and Information Technology, which oversees industrial policy for the sector, have been between 35,000 and 60,000 yuan, though these were scaled back starting in 2014. In addition, substantial reductions or exemptions from purchase taxes are also applied to EVs. For example, in 2014 rebates on a BAIC EV200 sedan, which was listed at CNY296,900 (approximately US$32,500) were CNY90,000 (approximately US $12,900), or 40% of the list price. See http://chinaautoweb.com/car-models/baic-ev200/ (accessed December 19, 2016). Local subsidies in some places as much as double this one-time purchase subsidy. See Mock and Yang (2014) and "China Offers Billions to Subsidize Electric Cars on Gas," *Bloomberg News*, December 10, 2014. China is far from alone in subsidizing EVs, as the European Union and United States also maintain sizable subsidy programs and other advantages at both the national and subnational levels, with total rates of subsidization generally exceeding those of China. On comparisons, see Yang (2014) and McKinsey (2015, p. 16).

[32] For these figures, see: http://business.sohu.com/20111024/n323217435.shtml (accessed October 11, 2013) and http://money.163.com/11/1025/16/7H7P6V4T00253G87.html (accessed October 11, 2013).

[33] "BYD Leverages the 'Power' of the Shenzhen Government" [借力深圳政府 比亚迪来 "电"了] *Auto World* [汽车大世界] January 4, 2010. http://news.mycar168.com/2010/01/ 151898.html (accessed October 11, 2013).

establishment of a number of charging stations for electric cars, though as we shall see these have been insufficient. A similar story of local government demand support can be told for Xiangfan New Energy Vehicles in Xiangfan, Hubei (Li 2010).

Local government initiatives were bolstered by central government industrial policy programs. MOST and the Ministry of Finance in 2009 tried to spur local experimentation in EVs through the 2009 "10 Cities, 1000 Vehicles" program.[34] Cities such as Guangzhou, Shanghai, and Hangzhou were given leeway to decide how to best promote the expansion of EV usage in their cities, and tended to develop strategies that centered on their "local" industry (for example, BYD in Shenzhen).[35] Hangzhou municipality (Zhejiang province), for example, built on its past positive experiences with bicycle rentals to build electric battery rental and mini-bus rental models, and to promote "battery switching" as a remedy for the lack of a charging infrastructure. Kandi Automotive (康迪汽车), traditionally a manufacturer of lightweight vehicles such as ATVs, go-karts, and golf carts, was at the forefront of these efforts. Kandi worked closely with the Hangzhou and Zhejiang governments[36] and, subsequently, the Shanghai government. The municipal governments provided land for rental locations and charging stations operated by a Kandi JV, ZZY (左中右).[37] Kandi also was greatly benefited by forming a joint venture with the large private Shanghai firm Geely (吉利), which allowed Kandi to switch from the use of lead acid batteries to lithium iron phosphate batteries. Geely also helped Kandi gain approval in 2013 from the central NDRC for Kandi's its low-speed models, resulting in these models being listed in the Ministry of Industry and Information Technology (MIIT) directory as approved and qualifying for

---

[34] The June 2009 plan for the industry was to have 500,000 EVs deployed by 2015, and 5 million by 2020. The number of cities was subsequently expanded from ten in 2009 to twenty-five in 2011. A 2013 report notes that "by the end of 2012, only about 17,400 EVs were deployed nationwide." Official figures put the number of Energy Saving and New Energy Vehicles (which include but are not limited to EVs) combined at 27,400; only 16% were sold to private buyers, underscoring public sector dominance in this developing market (China Greentech Report 2013). See also Gallagher (2014).

[35] Guangzhou municipality promoted the adoption of EVs for taxis by providing charging locations for taxicabs.

[36] Jinhua, Zhejiang, the home city of Kandi, was named a provincial pilot city for new energy by the Zhejiang government.

[37] Rentals were not profitable as of late 2014; the company was only renting half of the six hours per day needed to break even: 华泰证券研究报告 [Huatai Securities research report], 新能源汽车产业链调研之康迪车业:微公交模式点燃市场 [New energy automotive industry survey of Kandi Auto: Micro-bus mode ignites the market] http://finance.qq.com/a/20140827/054110.htm (accessed January 14, 2015).

consumer EV subsidies from the central government, not just from provinces. The combination of business model innovation, cooperation with other major market actors, and positive support from local governments allowed Kandi to lead sales of all EVs in China in the 2012–14 period, and facilitated the firm's entrance to major markets outside of Zhejiang Province, such as Shanghai and Nanjing.[38] These sorts of experiments, when aligned with Beijing's intentions, therefore can be seen as a positive part of China's policy process (Marquis et al. 2013). As will be discussed below, however, there is a significant downside to these local experiments insofar as they can promote protectionism and hinder the adoption of nationwide standards that might better facilitate EV adoption.

A particularly instructive case of local government support for upgrading in EVs is the promotion of low-speed EVs in Shandong Province. Local economic development agents and auto firms in Shandong – notably the Shifeng Automotive Group (山东时风汽车集团), traditionally a producer of trucks and tractors – lobbied hard beginning in 2009 for the provincial government to approve a pilot for producing low-speed, light weight vehicles particularly suited for rural areas.[39] The low-speed vehicles were to be modified from existing product lines of light trucks, and could offer customers upgrades from bicycles, electric scooters, and three wheel motorcycles to a larger lightweight vehicle. They would be affordable to rural businesses and families.[40] Part of the low cost of these was due to the use of lead acid batteries as opposed to the lithium batteries preferred in Beijing. Low-speed EVs were even more affordable for a time because the vehicles were not classified as "automobiles," so owners required no license and therefore could avoid costly licensing fees. This is not an insignificant matter; in Shanghai, for example, the fees to obtain a license plate in 2015 exceeded US$10,000, more than the cost of purchasing a low-end internal combustion vehicle.[41] County and municipal government support for a

---

[38] Kandi's success at topping sales is reported in http://cleantechnica.com/2014/10/27/china-electric-car-sales-reach-record-high-charts/ (accessed January 14, 2015).

[39] Shandong provincial officials viewed low-speed vehicles as part of broader plan for the province's EV industry sales to reach 100 billion yuan, with 300,000 vehicles, by 2014. NetEase Auto 网易汽车, http://auto.163.com/13/1024/16/9BVE5VFD00084TV1.html (accessed October 24, 2013).

[40] As Brandt and Thun (2010) argue, domestic firms that cannot compete with large SOEs or foreign firms often innovate by targeting low quality, low price-points segments. Thus, the success of these EV firms may be due more to market position and strategy than their special treatment by the provincial government.

[41] "Shanghai $10,000 License Plates Drive Car-Hire Company Financing," *Bloomberg News*, August 6, 2015, online at: www.bloomberg.com/news/articles/2015-08-06/shanghai-10-000-license-plates-drive-car-hire-company-financing (accessed December 21, 2016).

nascent low-speed EV industry included lobbying Beijing on behalf of firms and providing investment funds and land for industrial parks.

The example of the development and commercialization of low-speed EVs is interesting, because the development of low-speed vehicles was fostered by local governments, but opposed by Beijing. In a sense, it shows an effort by Beijing to snuff out come commercially successful local "winners" when central officials deemed their innovation not up to par. Beijing argued that, akin to driving golf carts on city roads, the vehicles' low speed could disrupt regular traffic, which together with their light weight, created safety concerns. NDRC officials in Beijing publicly called such vehicles "junk technology" (垃圾技术), saying they failed to meet national standards.[42] Despite the absence of central approval, the backing of the provincial government helped the local pilot to put affordable EVs on the roads, especially in rural areas. Whereas Beijing's target aimed to put 500,000 hybrids and EVs into use by the end of 2015, in 2012 Shifeng delivered about 30,000 low speed vehicles to dealers.[43] Beijing eventually relented in its opposition, and in the fall of 2014 allowed subsidies to be applied to these vehicles, making such innovation is no longer "illegal."[44]

Distortive Influences of Local Government

Local governments clearly have substantial opportunities to take on coordination roles in support of the development of clean energy technology as a public good. Beyond the cases highlighted above, there are myriad examples in which local governments have pursued coordination and financing mechanisms to support prospective innovators. Yet despite successes, local government participation often has failed to create a truly innovative ecosystem for new energy firms, or has engaged in highly

---

[42] NDRC Department of Industry Director Li Gang's declaration that EVs are "junk technology": 耿慧丽: "低速电动车争议再起 发改委官员公开否定," 2011年07月29日, 经济观察网。 [Geng Huili: "Controversy Over Low-Speed Electric Vehicles has Arisen Again, as NDRC Officials Publicly Reject," July 29, 2011, Economic Observer Online] http://auto.qq.com/a/20110729/000199.htm (accessed January 14, 2015). Protectionism for major incumbent auto-makers was also likely involved in the efforts of both NDRC (responsible for setting Strategic Emerging Industries (SEI) policy) and MIIT (responsible for setting standards in the EV sector) to squelch low-speed EV manufacturing.

[43] "Rural Chinese Flock to Tiny Electric Cars," *New York Times*, April 19, 2012.

[44] In 2014 Guangdong and Hebei provinces followed suit, with provincial pilot programs to support low-speed lead acid battery vehicles.

wasteful endeavors in pursuit of upgrading. Several patterns of local government behavior hinder and at times even overshadow what otherwise might be a positive catalytic function.

The Interplay Between Central "Signals" and Tangible Local Results

As discussed previously, the incentive structure for local officials gives them reason to demonstrate quick responsiveness to central leaders. This incentive affects how local officials demonstrate "innovation results" to political superiors. For officials hoping to convert local results into attractive job promotions, the establishment of a High technology development zone (HTDZ) or the launch (with quick demonstrable success) of an innovative industry – particularly one that is the focus of national level policy, such as an SEI – can bring positive attention to officials who can claim responsibility. For example, snagging a label as a "national" high-tech zone is a coup. A second marker is the ability for local firms to gain the designation of a "National Key Lab," showing it had been singled out by the center for its innovation. Third, the potential to create jobs and local growth through the attraction of industries that can be labeled "innovative" is a powerful incentive for local officials (Dai 2015). Using central initiatives to create jobs and other benefits that stay in the locality also will be powerful for local officials below the top echelon who may not be part of the *nomenklatura* promotion system.

Local government officials are well versed in how to jump onto this bandwagon, and even be seen as "ahead of the curve" in competition with other provinces. Jiangsu provincial officials, for example, attempted to get a head start in the inter-provincial competition for reputation as an innovative region. Whereas the central government set the goal that China should be an "innovative country" by 2020, wealthy Jiangsu set the provincial goal at 2015. Similarly, in response to the central government's emphasis in 2009 on SEIs, governments from some cities proposed they would carry out "100 major projects" related to SEIs during each year of the 12th Five-Year Plan (FYP) (Liu and Chen 2012). Such goal setting compels governments to meet the numeric goal regardless of the quality of projects.

This dynamic is accentuated outside of major cities, where officials strive to compete with more developed locales. In pursuit of a chunk of the low-speed EV industry, officials in small cities with access to rural markets have set up many "new energy automotive industry parks," and contributed many acres of land and millions of yuan in funds. For example, in 2014 the Linfen government (Shanxi) agreed with the Mei Year Group to invest 14.8

billion yuan (US\$2.3 billion) to build a new energy automotive industrial park (Linfen has the informal designation of China's most polluted city). Similar investments in such parks also have also been planned in Inner Mongolia, Luoyang, Ningbo, Changde, and Guizhou, many of which are relatively poor.[45]

At the same time, leaders' needs for quick payoffs from a supported firm can lead to the construction of financing mechanisms that pressure firms to pay the local government back quickly. Jiangxi's LDK Solar was caught by the local government's pressure to show quick results using the financial support it received from the city government: if the firm did not pay out profits and reimburse the government within a short period, then the cost of the capital would be substantially increased.[46] A related criticism has been made of the implementation of the Torch program and the establishment of HTDZs by local governments; funding went to mature technologies that could be rolled out to market quickly, but often did not include advanced technology or were not notably "innovative" (Breznitz and Murphree 2011, pp. 77–8).

Such behaviors by local cadres often have created political failures, including wasted and duplicative investment (with attendant opportunity costs of capital), shady land deals, corruption, and other ills. The desirability of being seen as responsive to central signals, and to help build the local brand too, often leads to a shallow or even a "false" response. The competition to gain the "doorplate" label of, e.g., "Green City," has led some local officials to act with great alacrity. This is especially true with the contributions of land, which has been a major investment resource for local governments to use for promoting industry. Central funds designed to address a potential downturn from the 2008 global financial crisis provided a major boost in favor of SEIs. Localities that suddenly had access to a flood of central funds had to quickly spend them. Pursuit of SEI-related industries that unlocked these funds, such as the "internet of things," incentivized the opening of development parks that supposedly focused on such high-tech industries. Instead, however, the result was too often new, often empty, office parks and other industrial real estate projects. This problem was frequently observed in Wuxi; one example is the "Internet of Things

---

[45] "Low-speed electric vehicles heavily gamble new energy automotive industry park" [低俗电动车巨资豪赌新能源汽车产业园] *21st Century Business Herald [21世纪经济报道]* October 15, 2014, http://auto.cnr.cn/qczcjj/201410/t20141015_516598395.shtml (accessed May 25, 2015).

[46] "PV Impulse."

Office Park," which was simply a real estate development project, sponsored by Wuxi government.[47]

BYD provides a firm-specific example of political "support" that resulted in inefficient outcomes. Setting up charging stations has been a major challenge for EV firms, especially in space-deprived first-tier cities. Local governments can ease this problem by providing land for stations.[48] BYD built charging stations in jurisdictions outside Shenzhen in order to create favorable conditions for sales of its EVs. However, once a few stations had been set up – enough to demonstrate political support of EVs but not enough to spur meaningful consumer demand – local leaders reportedly lost interest and moved on to other projects.[49] Local government efforts often have appeared to be for show only. A similar dynamic surrounds "National Key Labs." In firm visits, managers touted they had received the designation, but there was no evidence of significant activity in the lab. This was the case, for example, in a wind turbine factory. A tour of the key lab – well advertised on plates but kept behind locked doors – revealed broken equipment, and virtually no activity. Similarly, Yingli Solar showed that it had designations for a "State Key Lab of Photovoltaic Materials and Technology" (2010) and "State Key Lab of National Energy Photovoltaic Technology" (2011), yet offered little obvious evidence of outputs from these labs.[50]

The dynamic in which local officials are incentivized to respond to central signals and the resulting effort to create a "brand" for a locality that would be useful to attract cognate industries has not always created a negative environment for firms. However, evidence of wasted efforts and the establishment of firms that are not successful, much less innovative, is problematic. Hence, the longstanding criticism (within China) that the Chinese system's propensity to incentivize wasteful investment is repeated

---

[47] The son of a high-ranking official who runs a radio-frequency identification (RFID) consortium was likely instrumental in bringing these funds to Wuxi.

[48] Consumers are reluctant to buy EV sedans if they do not have convenient mechanisms for charging them. Provision of charging stations has been taken on as a public good in other economies, including in the United States as market actors have been unsure of the economics of this service beyond at-home plug in connection. Without out-of-home stations, consumers are often reluctant to invest in pure EVs, especially given the price premium, and government efforts to prop up demand have not worked well as of yet. This dynamic is one reason e-taxis have been an obvious industry for local governments to support (despite problems surrounding the need for daytime charging).

[49] Compounding the likelihood that the establishment of charging stations would be mostly a "political task" was the fact that there was no clear business model for them, such that the business sector was unlikely to take on the problem ("BYD Leverages" 2010).

[50] This does not mean Yingli has not shown innovative capacity overall; rather, the point is that the key labs designation may not be very relevant, hence "wasteful."

in the clean energy sector. Moreover, it is clear that local governments are keen for market entry of new firms, as symbols of and perhaps the reality of growth. Yet, as examples below will further illustrate, local governments are not keen to allow market exit of local firms, especially those firms they have supported with funds in the past.

Protectionism, Fragmentation, and Stovepiping

While we can observe successful examples of local government-generated coordination (e.g. Suntech in its heyday), local politics in China is often characterized by three interrelated behaviors that run counter to coordination: protectionism, fragmentation, and stovepiping.[51] Through the reform era, competition between regions to attract firms for local development has been intense.[52] Moreover, China's nascent post-Mao market economy was marked by significant local protectionism (Wedeman 2003; Cai 2004; Bai et al. 2004). To this day, local government officials try to sustain a local advantage. Despite much progress in the development of national markets, and central government efforts to rein in local protectionism, local officials often continue to erect internal market barriers. Firms are often complicit.

BYD's reliance on local government jurisdictions to purchase EVs provides a good illustration of the impact of local protectionism. Local governments can often be relied upon to provide a demand pull for new technologies. To this end, several subnational governments, including Shenzhen (the BYD headquarters), Tianjin, Xian, Yunnan, Changsha, and Chengdu, agreed to buy BYD vehicles for their municipal fleets. But these local officials would only purchase if the vehicles came from a "local" company. BYD therefore had to invest in local factories in order to make these sales – a political rather than a business strategy decision. Local officials could then claim these investments as their own "pro-innovation" industries.

More broadly, governments in the "10 Cities" EV pilot often have endeavored to protect their own local auto companies. Most of these cities allowed just two auto companies to sell EVs, with one of these firms being a local company.[53] Even when the NDRC directed that these cities needed to

---

[51] These factors are not unique to China, but appear more severe, and are overcome with greater difficulty, in the Chinese context.

[52] Many scholars attribute this competition, and efforts to gain advantages through protectionism, as a function (at least in part) of the aforementioned cadre promotion system. On inter-jurisdictional competition, see Lü and Landry (2014).

[53] MOST often selected cities with strong auto firms – such as Shenzhen and Shanghai – as pilot cities. This choice has the obvious advantage of placing resources where infrastructure already exists (a hallmark of China's experimentation policy).

allow 30 percent of inlen from other provinces, provinces seeking protection would strike an agreement with another province that the whole of that outside 30 percent would come only from that partner locality. Local governments often subsidize more generously purchases of EVs from local auto firms.

Fragmentation between actors within a jurisdiction also can harm coordination. Multiple funding sources at the central and provincial levels may be used for local innovation projects – such as central and local branches of NDRC, Ministry of Finance, Chinese Academy of Sciences, and MOST– yet these sources often are poorly coordinated. Thus, local efforts to snag resources and then show results from the investment often mean not just competition between local projects, but also wasteful duplicative investment sponsored by different agencies within a location. Particularly in an environment where market exit is seen as a sign of political failure, duplicative investment can be presumed to be especially wasteful. Beijing's recent efforts to curb the overexpansion of technology parks, particularly those related to the SEI industry of cloud computing, reflect recognition of this problem.[54] Yet as long as local bureaus of national ministries are more likely to serve horizontal interests than their vertical masters, the problem will remain (OECD 2008, pp. 363–4).

Related to the stovepiping of the local bureaucracy is that *each* bureaucracy within a local jurisdiction may feel compelled to respond to Beijing's initiatives, exacerbating wasteful duplication. Duplication of efforts is not the only problem to grow out of fragmentation and stovepiping; such a structure creates barriers to diffusion of technology that is seen as crucial to creating effective innovative "clusters" (OECD 2007, p. 41). Also detrimental is the stifling of development of national standards for new industries. Local governments focus on developing standards that benefit their own specific location, and local companies, rather than working toward national (or even international) standards. Similarly, while the development of locally oriented technologies is rational from one perspective, it can hinder the development of a more robust national market. Chongqing municipality's deployment of a fast-charging battery model is a prime example. This model was based on the unique characteristics of proximity to the Three Gorges dam and relatively reliable power grid. A battery-

---

[54] Beijing has carried out multiple campaigns to avoid wasteful investment by local governments and firms, such as in iron and steel, and real estate development. Yet these campaigns often are in a "macro-retrenchment" environment. Projects tied to the "innovation" silo may be protected from such campaigns.

swapping model à la Hangzhou and Shenzhen relies on relatively flat geography, and hence is not feasible in hilly Chongqing, whereas the energy supply intensity and reliability needed to make a fast-charge model succeed is not available elsewhere (Marquis et al. 2013).

Local Governments as a Source of Sustainable Demand?

Local firms have relied heavily on governments at all levels to help create or stimulate demand for new energy industries.[55] Local governments often have been channels to promote central tax breaks and subsidies for consumer purchases in the solar, wind, and EV sectors.[56] Local governments also have responded to Beijing's directive to promote EVs in government procurement; in late 2013, Beijing issued regulations stating that new government procurement (sedans and buses) were to reach at least 30 percent (Economy 2014). Local governments have made supplemental efforts to develop local markets, and foster public demand as a major stimulus for EV sales. BYD's aforementioned experience with various local government deals to purchase their EVs illustrates local protectionism, but also exemplifies how firms often rely on local governments to create demand. Shenzhen municipality offered further support to BYD to overcome the huge market-diffusion hurdle posed by the establishment of charging stations (discussed above), and this has become a core program of support for all major municipalities. Local government efforts to promote charging stations have run up against the power of electric grid monopolies. The provision of plug in electric stations is decided primarily by provincial offices of the State Grid, and until recently the grid company was reluctant to make this investment.[57]

While government supports for the EV industry have led some companies to jump on the bandwagon, others cite the industry's reliance on government support rather than market demand as reason to wait to enter the sector. Representatives of the private firm Chang Cheng (长城)

---

[55] On public sector demand creation in the United States, see Mazzucato (2013) and Weiss (2014).

[56] On tax supports in wind, see Lewis (2013, pp. 56–7) and Gallagher (2014, ch. 4). Many central subsidies to consumers for the purchase of EVs were eliminated in 2014.

[57] The three main aspects of the provision of electric power – generation, dispatch, and grid interconnection – are all controlled in significant ways at the local level in China. For example, there are myriad local independent power producers (IPPs) that generate electricity, and dispatch is heavily localized. The 2002 breakup of State Power Corporation's monopoly led to the regionalization of the grid. See Huang and Taplin (2012). By 2018, grid companies planned to increase their provision of charging stations, and enhance connectivity, significantly. Babones (2018).

Motor (Baoding) indicated that while they had explored entering the market, they at least temporarily decided to hold back. They indicate that the market is not mature, that the push is completely led by the government, but with insufficient and unreliable financial supports. They also reiterated problems with grid interconnection and insufficient charging stations.

Problems with grid interconnection have also hindered China's solar industry.[58] Solar cell manufacturers large and small have been frustrated by efforts to sell electricity on the domestic grid. Local governments have contributed land and housing to huge solar farms projects, many of which sit idle for reasons already discussed. In addition, local governments have been unable to guarantee grid connectivity. Consumers have faced similar frustrations. Some consumers have invested in solar cells, partly spurred by the national "Golden Sun" and "Golden Rooftop" program subsides for installation of solar cells, and partly spurred by prospects of not only providing a source of power for their own use but also of selling the electricity they generate at home to the grid. Yet grid companies have been unwilling, despite directives from the former regulator (State Electricity Regulatory Commission), to facilitate interconnection for households or solar farms without burdensome forecasts of generation and at a reasonable price.[59]

Local Governments as Savvy Financiers?

Successful entrepreneurs in solar and EV industries often cite the importance of local government financing. Yet two main questions about local government support arise: can local governments make wise investments in the absence of complementary market-based mechanisms to guide market entry and exit, and does local financing encourage undue firm dependence on government funding? Criticism of local governments' failure to effectively "pick winners" is common in the Chinese press. Local government is on the front line of choosing which firms to reward, and yet there often is a structural expertise gap. Or, where expertise does exist, such as in local S&T bureaus, expert opinions must compete with other considerations, such as the search for quick returns by local officials demonstrating a political response to Beijing, as discussed previously.

---

[58] See the related discussions in chapters by Davidson (Chapter 4), Brandt and Wang (Chapter 9), and Rawski (Chapter 8).

[59] Beijing has largely ended subsidies for solar installation, in part in response to wasted investment (Interview, December 6, 2014, Beijing).

Well-functioning venture capital institutions could act as a funnel, with-drawing funding from ventures that have failed to show promise (or live up to promise), while continuing funding for viable ventures. But there remains a gap in such market-based institutions in China. As noted, there has been a push to establish local venture capital firms to (help) fund innovative ideas. Some local VCs have come under scrutiny for making poor decisions, being too closely tied to the government, or encouraging excessive government risk when they gain implicit govern-ment guarantees. Wuxi Venture Capital Fund, an integral part of the Wuxi "Model" has met criticism for failing to assemble a "professional team to carry out project selection, due diligence, post-monitoring, intellectual property investigations, business partner surveys, communications plat-form, and other procedures" (He 2006b).

Local government financing has been criticized on other grounds too. One example is the "gamble" loan scheme between solar firm LDK and "state-background" lenders, in which the loans had to be repaid very quickly or else face extremely high interest rates ("PV Impulse" 2012[60]). At the same time, when local governments are faced with the prospect of failure by a firm around which they have tried to create a "brand," particularly when substantial resources have been invested in not just the firm but also supportive supply industries, they may be tempted to throw good money after bad. Such is the case with Xinyu government in Jiangxi Province, the backer of LDK Solar. As with Wuxi's Suntech adventure (though for different reasons), local officials have felt compelled to use government funds and help ensure the availability of funds from other sources (such as local banks) in order to bail out the firms.[61] Thus, in light of this gap in expertise and institutions to pick worthy "winners," it is not surprising that local officials' choices might then be made based on other considerations, such as political connections. Altogether, there remains a host of moral hazard problems. And, as with LDK and Suntech, local governments have been compelled to bail out firms so as not to bring a black mark to its "brand."

A second problem with the model of financial support is its impact on industry. Rather than spurring innovative industries, such support seems to promote waste. The solar panel industry is perhaps the best-known example. Many local governments, responding to international market

[60] See also http://money.163.com/12/0723/15/874080K5002540O2B.html (accessed October 11, 2013).
[61] Ibid.

demand and drawing un national policy incentives, saw export of solar panels as a lucrative business. Too many localities invested in solar cell production, creating a glut on the international market, and helping precipitate a collapse of that market.[62] In other situations, extensive government supports have also created a tendency for firms to depend on those government supports, and to use this support to go in business directions they might better have avoided. LDK Solar, given extensive support from the entrepreneurial Xinyu government, made aggressive forays into ancillary businesses, though as a family-run company it lacked expertise to do so. Similarly, BYD Auto expanded into the solar industry largely based on government supports. In the EV industry, two of the "10 Cities" pilot cities with little existing infrastructure in the auto industry (Xiangfan and Nantong) have been accused of strategies that focus on "receiving preferential policies and financial resources, as opposed to developing their EV adoption capability" (Marquis et al. 2013). Even the more successful of the "10 Cities" – Hangzhou, Shenzhen, and Hefei – proclaimed higher goals than requested by the center, and failed to meet them (Bär 2013). Reports of similar dynamics have appeared for clean energy sectors of wind, LEDs, and biomass ("PV Industry Incubators"). Interviewees have also suggested there is a class of smaller firms that have been established and remain in existence due solely to government support.

CONCLUSION

Scholarship on industrial upgrading suggests that local governments have a lot of potential to create a favorable ecosystem for innovative firms, through mechanisms such as provision of resources and coordination. That expectation is perhaps even stronger for China, given the ample role for the state in economic upgrading, and the dual role of local officials – as both a conduit for the center's "pro-innovation" policies and attendant resources, and as an overseer of local experimentation. We can expect such a role to apply in clean energy industries related to the electricity sector. Some previous studies describe how local governments have successfully supported innovation in clean energy industries (e.g. Helveston et al. 2016; Nahm 2017). The case evidence presented in this

---

[62] As is well-known, other problems have beset the Chinese PV industry, including the global financial crisis and declines in PV prices, collapse of key international markets (notably Spain), and the 2012 international trade dispute surrounding allegations of "dumping" of Chinese solar cells in Western markets.

chapter concurs, but only in part; along with promoting and supporting innovation in some arenas, the behaviors of local cadres in pursuit of innovation can be highly wasteful, can hinder market exit by under-performing firms, and may divert resources from more genuinely inno-vative pursuits.

In what ways have local cadres fostered a positive environment for upgrading? The discussion above illustrates how upgrading by new energy firms has occurred in several ways. In the solar panel sector, cost and process innovation has resulted from deep competition among solar panel producers that survived the export industry shakeout. Local govern-ments contributed to these successes, at least initially, through use of traditional industrial policy tools. Subsidies (direct funds, tax breaks, pre-ferential access to loans from state banks, contributions of land, etc.) provided by local officials helped some successful solar producers, such as Suntech and Yingli, get off the ground and expand. More interestingly, in other cases local governments have advocated for firms that have chosen to innovate in ways to which Beijing has been unfriendly. This occurred in the low-speed end of the EV market. Firms attempting to enter – or, really, *create* – the low end of the consumer EV market have been successful at leveraging local government cooperation and even political protection to upgrade existing product lines in order fill a "green" niche, though some-times not using cutting edge "green" technology (such as using lead acid rather than lithium batteries). Shifeng low speed autos benefited massively from advocacy on its behalf by the Shandong provincial government. As a result, energy efficient electricity-driven transport was brought to consumers in rural areas and in many fourth and fifth tier cities overlooked by govern-ment initiatives involving higher end EV sedans. This low-end segment is the most successful portion of China's entire EV market, and success has continued even as the rest of the EV market has taken off since 2015.[63] One reason for the generally slow takeoff of new energy sedans was Beijing's insistence on pure EVs over hybrids (due to difficulty obtaining foreign intellectual property) (Tillemann 2015). By 2014, however, some EV firms had gone their own way on this issue as well; similar to the situation with low-speed vehicles, local governments have supported the development and sale of hybrids, particularly in Shanghai (Wang 2015).

On the negative side of the ledger, however, there is cause for skepticism that local governments can be counted on to foster a vibrant innovative ecosystem. The incentives for local officials to respond to central signals,

---

[63] www.eeo.com.cn/2017/0210/297815.shtml (accessed November 7, 2017).

but to do so creatively in a way to support their political needs for quick payoffs in terms of branding and employment, has been a major contributor to wasted, duplicative, and sometimes "false" investment. The tendency for waste is exacerbated by incentives for local governments to prevent exit of unsuccessful firms when such market exit could harm employment. More mundane, local governments face difficulty providing effective coordination due to longstanding problems of protectionism, stovepiping and fragmentation. Central industrial policies shoulder responsibility for some of these problems. The "10 Cities" EV pilots, in incentivizing local government support for firms within their jurisdiction, harmed or delayed the establishment of standards for a national market, and exacerbated longstanding problems of provincial protectionism.[64] Reliance on government demand for EV sedans has not ameliorated the basic problem of market failure that these government interventions were intended to address. On the financial side, reliance on local governments to make sound investment decisions when private financing does not exist means officials have often lacked adequate signals about the quality of projects. This criticism has frequently been leveled at investments in solar panel firms, such as LDK. All told, behaviors of local officials – reflecting a mixture of incentives to align with the center and cultivate an image as innovative leaders – can nurture weeds in the innovation environment. Waste and the intolerance of firm failure are particularly pernicious.

From a firm-level perspective, failure is sometimes in part due to expectations that government supports would continue as long as quick results are achieved. This was a prominent dynamic for some solar panel manufacturing companies. In the EV sector, despite obvious innovation at the low end of the market, and facing many of the same technical barriers the industry confronts around the world, all the supports and subsidies have not prevented the widespread view – including within China – of industry underperformance, at least until 2015. Beijing acknowledged that, as of September 2014, China had met only 12 percent of its target for alternative-energy vehicles to be introduced by 2015.[65] One study calculates that of all the cars produced in China in 2013, only 0.008 percent were highway-

---

[64] This has not been a problem in the solar panel sector, where technology is relatively standardized.

[65] "China Offers Billions to Subsidize Electric Cars on Gas," *Bloomberg News*, December 10, 2014. On China facing the same barriers as those encountered worldwide, such as high battery costs and generally high costs relative to combustion engines, see Bernstein Research (2013).

ready electric passenger vehicles (Altenberg et al. 2015). Most of these sales reflected government-driven demand; before 2015, 80 percent of new energy vehicles sales were to public fleets, indicating an early failure in transformation from state to consumer demand (Howell et al. 2014). In the first decade of EV industrial policy China was unable to move the market for EVs forward on a par with many European countries and California (Mock and Yang 2014). That picture began to change around 2015. Xi Jinping doubled down on the country's commitment to NEV industrial policy with the announcement in 2017 of a plan to phase out internal combustion engines and convert to an all-electric industry – to be led by Chinese auto companies and battery makers.[66] Under this top-down pressure, it will be interesting to see how local governments will respond and contribute.

Several further concluding observations can be made about the role of local government in upgrading. It must be acknowledged, of course, that both international and domestic factors out of reach of local government control have influenced outcomes in the two industries considered in this chapter. Reliance on international markets, which then collapsed, harmed the solar panel industry, as have problems of connectivity and inconsistent central policies. The EV sedan sector has been slow to take off in China, as elsewhere. This is due, arguably, to industrial policy choices made by the center, choices to develop an "indigenous" format and avoid going the route of Sino-foreign joint ventures (JVs) that were used for internal combustion engines (Tillemann 2015; Helveston et al. 2016; Yang 2014). Beyond international partnerships and technology choices, the interaction of two other variables – which are related to the behavior of local governments – appear to have affected the development of the EV and the solar panel industry. The first relates to industry characteristics: the inter-related factors of barriers to entry, fragmentation of the market, and presence of large incumbents. For example, the solar panel industry has been characterized by low technological barriers to entry, deep ties to global value chains, and despite the presence of some large firms (such as Suntech, Trina, and Yingli), also contained many small and local firms with strong ties to local officials. Similarly, the low-speed and e-bicycle segment of the EV market are quite different from EV sedans, and have more in common with the solar cell market (although unlike the PV sector EVs from the start

---

[66] *Economist*, 14 September, 2017. Online at www.economist.com/business/2017/09/14/china-moves-towards-banning-the-internal-combustion-engine (accessed November 7, 2017).

were produced mainly for the domestic market). Firms (such as Shifeng) have built on manufacturing and cost advantages in their regions, and lack of foreign competition, to supply the low end of the market. Neither technology nor cost barriers to entry are as high as in the sedan sector. Low barriers to entry may open space for local governments to be more creative, though not always in a way that benefits upgrading. In the solar case, support sometimes was wasteful and led to overexpansion. In contrast, the market for large EVs (sedans and buses) has depended heavily on large domestic auto companies (e.g. Geely, BYD). Technological barriers to entry are significant, and the cost of the key components – especially lithium-based batteries – remains high (Bernstein Research 2013).

The second dimension is the strength of the center's industrial policy signals. As noted, Beijing has pressed a "green energy" agenda, implemented primarily through various industrial policies, and as well as an "indigenous innovation" agenda. Local officials can benefit from showing responsiveness to Beijing's SEI agenda, but the parameters of that support have been set mostly from the outside and through formal industrial policy programs. Strong central signals for EV sedan development led to local experiments and pilots, but have not guaranteed success in innovation or creation of a national market adequate to fulfilling Beijing's vision. Indeed, local experiments have hindered standardization. Under the "10 Cities" pilot program, a total of 343 models, made by seventy-six automakers, were approved to receive subsidies (Zheng et al. 2012). In contrast, weak or negative central signals provide a different context for local government behavior. Beijing's treatment of the solar industry started out more supportive than for low-end EVs, and for example made comparatively limited subsidies for solar available. Later, however, and particularly after export markets collapsed in 2012, central bureaucrats signaled displeasure with the industry over runaway investment by local governments.[67] Still, local governments have been far keener than the center to subsidize the establishment of new solar panel firms, as they have in mind the purpose of local industrial development more than upgrading. NDRC's negative statements about low-speed EVs – actively trying to squelch that segment of the EV industry – catalyzed local government support. For solar panels and low-speed EVs, then, weak central industry policy signals gave local governments leeway to respond to local interest, even if this was wasteful.

---

[67] In particular, with the collapse of international export markets as a result of the 2012 international trade dispute over solar panels, NDRC officials were not supportive of bailouts for ailing Chinese solar panel firms.

In sum, as a result of these varying dynamics, at least in part, key differences in the local ecosystems emerge. Local governments do not create innovation, but can play important roles based on their place in China's political economy and policy processes. It is important to reiterate that it remains incumbent on local officials in China to play a role in potential economic development schemes, such as in SEI industries. Especially when the signals emanating from Beijing's industrial policy are strong, local officials cannot sit idly by and allow markets to work things out. Yet the ability of local governments to respond to Beijing's signals in a positive and market-conforming way has been shown here to be variable. Local governments can be conduits for central pressures to innovate and build innovative industries, facilitators of new ideas or responses to market opportunities, or deploy resources wastefully. Many factors determine the precise impact of local government, but the relevance of their role at this stage of China's development cannot be disputed.

References

Ahlers, Anna L. and Gunter Schubert. 2009. "'Building a New Socialist Countryside': Only a Political Slogan?" *Journal of Current Chinese Affairs.* 38 (4). pp. 35–62.

Ahrens, Nathaniel. 2013. "Case Study: Suntech." In *China's Competitiveness: Myth, Reality, and Lessons for the United States and Japan.* Washington, DC: CSIS.

Altenburg, Tilman, Eike W. Schamp, and Ankur Chaudhary. 2015. "The emergence of electromobility: Comparing technological pathways in France, Germany, China and India." *Science and Public Policy.* 43(4). pp. 464–75. doi:10.1093/scipol/scv054.

Amsden, Alice H. 1989. *Asia's Next Giant: South Korea and Late Industrialization.* New York: Oxford University Press.

Arrow, Kenneth J. 1962. "Economic Welfare and the Allocation of Resources for Invention." In National Bureau of Economic Research ed., *The Rate and Direction of Inventive Activity: Economic and Social Factors.* Princeton: Princeton University Press. pp. 609–26.

Asheim, Bjorn T. and Meric S. Gertler. 2005. "The Geography of Innovation." In Fagerberg Jan, David C. Mowery, and Richard R. Nelson eds., *The Oxford Handbook of Innovation.* Oxford: Oxford University Press. pp. 291–317.

Babones, Salvatore. 2018. "China Could be the World's First All Electric Vehicle Ecosystem." Forbes online. March 6, 2018. www.forbes.com/sites/salvatorebabones/2018/03/06/china-could-be-the-worlds-first-all-electric-vehicle-ecosystem/#6b1edd41130f (accessed April 2, 2018).

Bai, Chong-En, Yingjuan Du, Zhigang Tao, and Sarah Y. Tong. 2004. "Local protectionism and regional specialization: evidence from China's industries." *Journal of International Economics* 62(2), pp. 397–417.

Bär, Holger. 2013. *Lead Markets for electric vehicles – China's and Germany's strategies compared.* Lead Markets Working Paper No. 12. http://kooperationen.zew.de/fileadmin/user_upload/Redaktion/Lead_Markets/Werkstattberichte/WB_12_Baer_2013_Electric_vehicles.pdf (accessed February 27, 2014).

Bardhan, Pranab K. 2010. *Awakening Giants, Feet of Clay: Assessing the Economic Rise of China and India.* Princeton, NJ: Princeton University Press.

Bardhan, Pranab and Dilip Mookherjee, eds. 2006. *Decentralization and Local Governance in Developing Countries: A Comparative Perspective.* Cambridge, MA: MIT Press.

Berger, Suzanne. 2006. *How We Compete: What Companies Around the World Are Doing to Make It in Today's Global Economy.* New York: Doubleday.

Bernstein Research. 2013. *Chinese Autos, Part 1: The Quest for Global Competitiveness – Technology, Competence, Ambition and Politics.* New York: Stanford L. Berstein and Co. LLC.

Brandt, Loren, Debin Ma, and Thomas G. Rawski. 2017. "Industrialization in China." In Kevin O'Rourke and Jeffrey Williamson eds., *The Spread of Modern Industry to the Global Periphery Since 1871.* Oxford: Oxford University Press. pp. 197–228.

Brandt, Loren and Eric Thun. 2010. "The Fight for the Middle: Upgrading, Competition, and Industrial Development in China." *World Development.* 38(11). pp. 1555–74.

Breznitz, Dan and Michael Murphree. 2011. *The Run of the Red Queen: Government, Innovation, Globalization and Economic Growth in China.* New Haven, CT: Yale University Press.

Cai, Yongshun. 2004. "Irresponsible State: Local Cadres and Image-building in China." *Journal of Communist Studies and Transition Politics* 20.4. pp. 20–41

Chen Jinjin. 2011. "China's Experiment on the Differential Electricity Pricing Policy and the Struggle for Energy Conservation." *Energy Policy* 39. pp. 5076–85.

Chen, Ling. 2012. "National Policy Paradigms and Local Government Initiatives: The Campaign of Industrial Upgrading in China's Electronics Industry." Paper presented at the annual meetings of the Association for Asian Studies, Toronto.

Chen, Ling and Barry Naughton. 2016. "An Institutionalized Policy-Making Mechanism: China's Return to Techno-Industrial Policy." *Research Policy.* 45. pp. 2138–52. http://dx.doi.org/10.1016/j.respol.2016.09.014.

Chen Zhijie. 陈志杰. 2008. "Bank and Government Support for BYD Electric Cars" [比亚迪电动车获银行与政府支持] 南方日报 [Nanfang Daily]. December 15, 2008. www.qqddc.com/html/news/news_11325_1.html (accessed October 11, 2013).

China Greentech Report 2013: *China at a Crossroads.* 2013. Hong Kong: Greentech 2013). http://284582c4ec799f36cf68-3958fb6e2144223e03d1fa1c325551a2.r86.cf1.rackcdn.com/The%20China%20Greentech%20Report%202013%20(English%20version).pdf (accessed February 27, 2014).

Christensen, Clayton M. 1997. *The Innovator's Dilemma: When New Technologies Cause Great Firms to Fail.* Boston: Harvard Business School Press.

Dai, Yixin. 2015. *Who Drives Climate-relevant Policy Implementation in China?* IDS Evidence Report #134. London: IDS, and Beijing: Tsinghua University.

Dinh, Hinh, Thomas G. Rawski, Ali Zafar, Lihong Wang, and Eleonora Mavroeidi 2013. *Tales From the Development Frontier: How China and Other Countries Harness Light Manufacturing to Create Jobs and Prosperity.* Washington, DC: The World Bank.

Economy, Elizabeth. 2014. "China Round Two on Electric Cars: Will It Work?" *Asia Unbound.* New York: Council on Foreign Relations. www.forbes.com/sites/ elizabetheconomy/2014/04/18/chinas-round-two-on-electric-cars-will-it-work/ (accessed July 17, 2014).

Ernst, Dieter. 2009. *A New Geography of Knowledge in the Electronics Industry?: Asia's Role in Global Innovation Networks.* Honolulu: East-West Center.

Fagerberg, Jan. 2005 "Innovation: A Guide to the Literature." In Jan Fagerberg, David C. Mowery, and Richard R. Nelson eds., *The Oxford Handbook of Innovation*, Oxford: Oxford University Press. pp. 1–26.

Fagerberg, Jan, David C. Mowery, and Richard R. Nelson, eds. 2005. *The Oxford Handbook of Innovation.* Oxford: Oxford University Press.

Gallagher, Kelly Sims. 2014. *The Globalization of Clean Energy Technology: Lessons from China.* Cambridge, MA: MIT Press.

Gereffi, Gary, John Humphrey, and Timothy Sturgeon. 2005. "The Governance of Global Value Chains," *Review of International Political Economy.* 12(1). pp. 78–104.

Gershenkron, Alexander. 1962. *Economic Backwardness in Historical Perspective: A Book of Essays.* Cambridge, MA: Harvard University Press.

Hall, Bronwyn H. 2005. "The Financing of Innovation." In Scott Shane ed., *Blackwell Handbook of Technology and Innovation Management.* Oxford: Blackwell Publishers. pp. 409–31.

Hall, Bronwyn H. and John van Reenen. 2000. "How Effective are Fiscal Incentives for R&D? A Review of the Evidence." *Research Policy.* 29. pp. 449–69.

He, Yifan 何伊凡. 2006a. "The richest man, the government made," ["首富,政府造"] *China Entrepreneur* [中国企业家], 6: 6. www.iceo.com.cn/renwu2013/2013/0321/ 265279.shtml (accessed October 11, 2013).

He, Yifan 何伊凡. 2006b, "From Shi Zhengrong to Shi Zhenrong ["从施正荣到施振 荣"], China *Entrepreneur* [中国企业家], 6. http://finance.sina.com.cn/leadership/ crz/20060324/19162446376.shtml (accessed October 11, 2013).

Heilmann, Sebastian. 2008. "Policy Experimentation in China's Economic Rise." *Studies in Comparative International Development.* 43(1). pp. 1–26.

Heilmann, Sebastian, Lea Shih, and Andreas Hofem. 2013. "National Planning and Local Technology Zones: Experimental Governance in China's Torch Programme." *The China Quarterly.* 216. pp. 896–919.

Helveston, John Paul, Yanming Wang, Valerie Karplus, and Erica R. H. Fuchs. 2016. "Up, Down, and Sideways: Innovation in China and the Case of Plug-In Electric Vehicles." August 1, 2016. SSRN. http://ssrn.com/abstract=2817052 (accessed August 11, 2017).

Howell, Sabrina, Henry Lee, and Adam Heel. 2014. "Leapfrogging or Stalling Out? Electric Vehicles in China," *Harvard Kennedy School Research Working Paper Series* (RWP 14–035).

Huang, Andrew and Nate Taplin. 2012. *Electricity: Lost in Transmission.* Beijing: GK Dragonomics (April).

Huang, Yasheng. 2002. "Managing Chinese Bureaucrats: An Institutional Economics Perspective." *Political Studies.* 50. pp. 61–79.

Humphrey John and Hubert Schmitz. 2002. "How Does Insertion in Global Value Chains Affect Upgrading in Industrial Clusters?" *Regional Studies.* 36(9). pp. 1017–27.

Johnson, Chalmers. 1982. *MITI and the Japanese Miracle: The Growth of Industrial Policy, 1925–1975.* Stanford, CA: Stanford University Press.

Kennedy, Scott, Richard P. Suttmeier, and SU Jun. 2008. *Standards, Stakeholders, and Innovation: China's Evolving Role in the Global Knowledge Economy.* Washington, DC: National Bureau of Asian Research.

Kostka, Genia and William Hobbs. 2012. "Local Energy Efficiency Policy Implementation in China: Bridging the Gap between National Priorities and Local Interests." *The China Quarterly.* 211. pp 765–85

Landry, Pierre F. 2008. *Decentralized Authoritarianism in China: The Communist Party's Control of Local Elites in the Post-Mao Era.* New York: Cambridge University Press.

Lerner, Josh. 2009. *Boulevard of Broken Dreams: Why Public Efforts to Boost Entrepreneurship and Venture Capital Have Failed–and What to Do About It.* Princeton, NJ: Princeton University Press.

Lewis, Joanna I. 2013. *Green Innovation in China: China's Wind Power Industry and the Global Transition to a Low-Carbon Economy.* New York: Columbia University Press.

Li, Hongbin and Li-An Zhou. 2005. "Political Turnover and Economic Performance: The Incentive Role of Personnel Control in China." *Journal of Public Economics.* 89.9/10. pp. 1743–62. /doi.org/10.1016/j.jpubeco.2004.06.009.

Li Ling 李玲. 2010. 新能源汽车展上的三大现象 [Three phenomena at the new energy auto show]. *Commercial Vehicle News*, August 2, 2010.

Liu, Xielin and Ao Chen. 2012. "Lesson from Jiangsu: The Transition from Manufacturing Region to Innovative Region." Paper presented at Conference on the Structure, Process, and Leadership of the Chinese Science and Technology System, University of California San Diego.

Lü, X. and P. F. Landry. (2014). "Show Me the Money: Interjurisdiction Political Competition and Fiscal Extraction in China." *American Political Science Review.* 108(03). pp. 706–22. https://doi.org/10.1017/S0003055414000252.

McKinsey & Company. (2015). Supercharging the Development of Electric Vehicles in China. www.mckinseychina.com/wp-content/uploads/2015/04/McKinsey-China_Electric-Vehicle-Report_April-2015-EN.pdf?5c8e08 (accessed July 23, 2016).

Marquis, Christopher, Hongyu Zhang, and Lixuan Zhou. 2013. "China's Quest to Adopt Electric Vehicles." In *Stanford Innovation Review* (Spring), pp. 52–7.

Mazzucato, Mariana. 2013. *The Entrepreneurial State: debunking public vs. private sector myths.* London: Anthem Press.

Mei, Ciqi. 2009. *Bring the Politics Back in: Political Incentive and Policy Distortion in China*. PhD Dissertation, University of Maryland, College Park.

Mei, Ciqi and Margaret Pearson. 2014. "Killing the Chicken to Scare the Monkeys: Deterrence Failure and Local Defiance in China." *The China Journal*. 72. pp. 75–97. https://doi.org/10.1086/677058.

Mock, Peter and Zefei Yang. 2014. *Driving Electrification: A Global Comparison of Fiscal Incentive Policy for Electric Vehicles*. Washington, DC: International Council on Clean Transportation.

Montinola, Gabriella, Yingyi Qian, and Barry R. Weingast. 1995. "Federalism, Chinese Style: The Political Basis for Economic Success in China." *World Politics*. 48.1. pp. 50–81.

Nahm, Jonas. 2017. "Exploiting the Implementation Gap: Policy Divergence and Industrial Upgrading in China's Wind and Solar Sectors." *The China Quarterly*. 231. pp. 705–27. https://doi.org/10.1017/S030574101700090X.

Nahm, Jonas and Edward Steinfeld. 2014. "Scale Up Nation: China's Specialization in Innovative Manufacturing." *World Development*. 54. pp. 288–300. https://doi.org/10.1016/j.worlddev.2013.09.003.

Nelson, Richard, ed. 1993. *National Innovation Systems: A Comparative Analysis*. New York: Oxford University Press.

OECD. 2007. *Reviews of Innovation Policy: China, Synthesis Report*. Paris: OECD.

2008. *Reviews of Innovation Policy: China*. Paris: OECD.

2009. *Measuring China's Innovation System: National Specificities and International Comparisons* Paris: OECD Directorate for Science, Technology and Industry.

Oi, Jean Chun. 1992. "Fiscal Reform and the Economic Foundations of Local State Corporatism in China." *World Politics*. 45.1. pp. 99–126.

1999. *Rural China Takes Off: Institutional Foundations of Economic Reform*. Berkeley, CA: University of California Press.

Powell, Walter W. and Stine Grodal. 2005. "Networks of Innovators." In Jan Fagerberg, David C. Mowery, and Richard R. Nelson eds., *The Oxford Handbook of Innovation*. Oxford: Oxford University Press.

"PV "impulse" behind the LDK and the kidnapped government." [光伏冲动背后 LDK 与被绑架的政府"], *China Economic Weekly* [中国经济周刊].July 31, 2012. http://news.xinhuanet.com/energy/2012–07/31/c_123498731.htm (accessed October 11, 2013).

"PV Industry Incubators Premature Decline" [光伏兴业双雄早"], *China Entrepreneurs* [中国企业家]. October 22, 2012. http://tech.sina.com.cn/it/2012–10-22/10567726065.shtml (accessed October 11, 2013).

Ru, Peng, Qiang Zhi, Fang Zhang, Xiaotian Zhong, Jianqiang Li, and Jun Su. 2012. "Behind the Development of Technology: The Transition of Innovation Modes in China's Wind Turbine Manufacturing Industry." *Energy Policy*. 43. pp. 58–69.

Sagar, Ambuj D. and Bob van der Zwaan. 2006. "Technological innovation in the energy sector: R&D, deployment, and learning-by-doing." *Energy Policy* 34(17). pp. 2601–8.

Segal, Adam. 2003. *Digital Dragon: High-Technology Enterprise in China*. Ithaca, NY: Cornell University Press.

Suryon, Sylvia G. and Magnus Breidne. 2007. "China's Fifteen-Year Plan for Science and Technology: An Assessment." *Asia Policy*. 4. pp. 135–64.

Sigurdson, Jon. 2004. Regional Innovation Systems (RIS) in China, *Working Paper No. 19*. European Institute of Japanese Studies, Stockholm School of Economics. http://swopec.hhs.se/eijswp/papers/eijswp0195.pdf

State Council. [2012] Notice on the State Council Energy-saving and New Energy Automotive Industry Development Plan (2012–2020) [国务院关于印发节能与新能源汽车产业发展规划（2012—2020年）的通知]. No. 22, issued 6-28-2012. www.gov.cn/zwgk/2012–07/09/content_2179032.htm (accessed October 11, 2013).

Thun, Eric. 2006. *Changing Lanes in China: Foreign Direct Investment, Local Government, and Auto Sector Development*. Cambridge: Cambridge University Press.

Tillemann, Levi. 2015. *The Great Race: The Global Quest for the Car of the Future*. New York: Simon and Schuster.

USCBC. 2013. *China's Strategic Emerging Industries: Policy, Implementation, Challenges, and Recommendations*. Washington, DC: US-China Business Council.

Wade, Robert. 1990. *Governing the Market: Economic Theory and the Role of Government in East Asian Industrialization*. Princeton, NJ: Princeton University Press.

Wang, Dehe. 2007. "LDK Solar to build support for the development of wafers" [支持 LDK 发展打造太阳能 硅片制度] China Jiangxi News (2007–6-14). www.jxcn.cn/161/2007–6-14/30079@314781.htm (accessed October 11, 2013).

Wang, Tao. 2015. "China's New Energy Vehicles Depend on Policy." [中国新能源汽车要走出政策以来]. Beijing: FTChinese.com. www.ftchinese.com/story/001062435?full=y (accessed August 15, 2015).

Wedeman, Andrew. 2003. *From Mao to Market: Local Protectionism, Rent-Seeking, and the Marketization of China, 1984–1992*. New York: Cambridge University Press.

Weiss, Linda. 2014. *America, Inc.?: Innovation and Enterprise in the National Security State*. Ithaca, NY: Cornell University Press.

Xu, Chenggang. 2011. "The Fundamental Institutions of China's Reforms and Development." *Journal of Economic Literature*. 49.4. pp. 1076–151.

Yang, Zifei. 2014. If Subsidies are no Panacea, How to Incentivize Electric Vehicles in China? ICCT. www.theicct.org/blogs/staff/if-subsidies-are-no-panacea-how-incentivize-electric-vehicles-china (accessed October 20, 2013).

Zheng, J., S. Mehndiratta, J. Y. Guo, and Z. Liu. 2012. "Strategic Policies and Demonstration Program of Electric Vehicles in China." *Transport Policy*. 19 (1) pp. 17–25.

Zhi, Qiang and Margaret M. Pearson. 2017. "China's Hybrid Adaptive Bureaucracy: the Case of the 863 Program for Science and Technology." *Governance*. 30(3). pp. 407–24. doi:10.1111/gove.12245.

Zhou, Yu. 2008. *The Inside Story of China's High-Tech Industry: Making Silicon Valley in Beijing*. Lanham, MD: Rowman and Littlefield.

4

Technology Integration in China's Electricity System: Central Targets and Local Challenges

Michael Davidson

INTRODUCTION

China's development and regulation of the electric power sector have been fundamentally determined by shifting government relations between the center and the provinces.[*] Beginning with massive electricity shortages in the 1980s, provincial governments and local enterprises increasingly shared planning roles with the central bureaucracy. Following sector restructuring in 1997–2002, local governments retained an important role in planning and arguably the crucial role in operation – through the annual generation plan allocation – which they have exercised to increase local tax revenues, bolster local economic growth and satisfy other political priorities.

Technological progress of advanced electricity generation technologies over the same time period has primarily occurred in centrally state-owned enterprises (SOEs) under close coordination and funding by central ministries and national research institutions. Five-Year Plans have consistently highlighted the importance of energy efficiency and self-sufficiency, and spearheaded development and deployment programs for ultra-supercritical (USC) boilers, the world's most efficient coal-fired power plant technology. China's coal-fired fleet is now roughly 15 percent more efficient than that of the United States.

These impressive achievements have justifiably attracted significant attention and positive appraisal. At the same time, however, the different levels of electricity sector priorities – at once centralized technology target-

[*] This research benefited from generous financial support from the Smith Richardson Foundation. The author is especially thankful for thoughtful suggestions by Thomas Rawski and Loren Brandt. Any deficiencies remain my own.

setting and localized systems operation and planning – point to several potential weaknesses in the top-down system. First, the potential local benefits of new technologies – in terms of economic outcomes, public health, and others – are difficult to encapsulate in a handful of technological targets. Second, five- or ten-year technology plans may have limited capacity to adjust to changes in macro-economic conditions that make some technology designs less preferred or viable.

Capital misallocations in China's electricity system are potentially abundant: unused wind capacity leading to high curtailment rates of over 40 percent in some regions, underutilization of high-efficiency coal-fired generators relative to older plants, and underutilized or inefficiently utilized transmission capacity. While sweeping changes in operation were envisioned in the 2002 reforms – most notably the creation of wholesale markets that would diminish provincial government influence – these have largely gone nowhere and, in the latest reforms of 2014–15, have even undergone a partial reversal with broader priorities aimed at degrading State Grid's monopoly and a push toward more localization of power sector functions such as approval processes and market design.

Central policy responses to these and other electricity system inefficiencies have been multi-pronged, though largely centering on high-level mandatory directives. Some mandatory directives have been successfully implemented, but the proliferation of many – sometimes conflicting – central goals also presents opportunities for local political leaders to pursue their own interests. As a result, similar to other broad central mandates that require local enforcement, central directives have faced implementation challenges.

This chapter first provides background on the local integration challenges of advanced electricity generation technologies in China. It outlines how technology systems fit into China's characteristic central-local governance structures. It then provides an historical perspective on China's electricity reforms, following the changing decision-making locus. The chapter further highlights three important integration issues observed in China: overcapacity and under-utilization of advanced coal-fired power plants, low and inefficient transmission line utilization, and renewable energy curtailment. Subsequently, it discusses major policy interventions to address inefficiencies in the power sector, highlighting successes and challenges. One case study explores in greater detail the development to deployment of supercritical (SC) and ultra-supercritical (USC) coal-fired power plants, including operational issues. It then concludes with implications for policy.

TECHNOLOGY SYSTEMS INTEGRATION IN A LOCAL CONTEXT

China's impressive achievements in technological development and deployment can be at least partially attributed to central policies that encourage or constrain certain economic activities of local governments. Hence, starting with the durable structure of central and local governance systems in China, this chapter identifies how technological growth is targeted. Integration into the broader technological system – which the chapter defines, generally, as the way in which a particular component affects and is affected by the larger system of linked technologies and institutions – presents some unique differences from more traditional industrial policy, and guides us to the particular case of electricity systems, the focus of the following section.

Central and Local Governance Systems in China

Prior to market reforms in the late 1970s, economic and political activity in China was organized through a network of ministries and coordinating committees or agencies. Conflicts between local and central control over decision-making authority, which extended across virtually the entire economy, revealed significant challenges in growing the economy and, in the energy sector in particular, maintaining adequate supply to fuel growth (Andrews-Speed 2013; Naughton 1995).

Reforms over the 1980s and 1990s sought to further localize control by, e.g., decentralizing fiscal decisions and removing direct control over local appointments to give more autonomy to provincial governments to pursue economic policy in line with local conditions and objectives (Jin, Qian, and Weingast 2005; Mertha 2005). These reforms are largely credited with China's unprecedented economic growth over this period (Oi 1999; Rawski 1995). Incorporating local and specialized knowledge in decision-making has long been considered a valuable aspect of well-functioning bureaucracies, as lower levels with flexible means are free to pursue objectives appropriately (Weber 1947).

When giving more power to local counterparts, central agencies sought to simplify their regulatory tasks by installing targets for local official performance, and by threatening to punish officials for failing to follow through with them. However, despite remarkable economic performance, local implementation gaps on a variety of objectives are commonplace. In one extremely blatant flouting of central directives, officials tasked to curb overcapacity in steel production in 2004 resisted these directions and were cautioned, but were left with few lasting repercussions (Mei and Pearson 2014).

These gaps – and in general, local policy outcomes in China – have been characterized as the result of "fragmented authoritarianism," in which several arms of the bureaucracy compete for rule ownership, and the resulting ambiguity is resolved through bargaining and incremental reforms (Lieberthal and Oksenberg 1988). This replaces the unitary theory of the Chinese government with a decision-making structure defined at multiple levels of government, at the heart of which is the well-known phenomenon of bureaucratic politics (Allison 1969).

Targeting Technology Development and Deployment

Technology development and adoption in China, similar to local officials' political targets, are frequently guided by central government policies and incentives, orchestrated by an array of central-level committees (Zhi and Pearson 2016). These policies attempt to align incentives for firms and local governments (primarily, provincial and municipal) with central goals when making and implementing economic and industrial policy. Inevitably, however, local preferences and conditions vary, which can give rise to numerous implementation challenges. Where the technology is part of a networked system, integrating with local physical and regulatory systems can add to the complications.

The first challenge relates to how an ordering is created from the proliferation of centrally managed goals. Lower level officials' autonomy is restricted (enhanced) when central priority setting emphasizes (ignores) policy areas relevant to the region. Choosing priorities, however, is a complex process driven by the center's desire to solidify control, public demands, and external factors. The rational response would be to satisfy local constituencies in lieu of costly reforms with uncertain political benefit (Mei and Pearson 2014). The next section below illustrates this: in the provincial annual generation planning process in the electricity sector, central mandates to promote renewable energy take lower precedence than economic and employment metrics that are better satisfied by incumbent (primarily, coal) generators because of its related industries (e.g. mining) and higher tax rates.

A second challenge relates to framing the technology targets or indicators. Technology research and development (R&D) programs tend to specify the desired technologies as well as their characteristics with some precision. As shown below in the example of advanced coal-fired power, this can create a ready supply of relatively homogeneous products. Technology deployment targets are most often framed in terms of physical quantities, such as the amount of capacity deployed or money invested. This creates a demand for the new products. However, a different set of indicators may be appropriate to understand how the technologies are eventually utilized, such as annual production or savings, in what could be considered more broadly as economic or integration indicators. In the case of operational issues of China's advanced coal fleet presented below, newly built plants following large central R&D investments remain underutilized.

Targeting technology utilization is further complicated in a particular class of technological systems known as infrastructures – which can be understood as durable, immobile investments with a high degree of interaction deriving from underlying networks (Gómez-Ibáñez 2003). Predicting and assessing changes in infrastructure sectors such as electricity systems require more complex analyses that consider properties ranging from the capital intensity and competition structure to externalities and other system-wide properties (Markard 2011). For example, building a steel factory typically has a more predictable impact on the market for steel than a new generation plant has on the market for electricity. Infrastructure regulation, in particular, has a range of implications on technology choice, because of the existence of natural monopoly segments (i.e. decreasing marginal costs as companies scale) where it is generally socially beneficial not to induce direct competition (Shy 2001).

EXPANDING LOCUS OF DECISION-MAKING IN CHINA'S ELECTRICITY SECTOR

At each stage of electricity sector reform away from strict government control – opening to non-ministry actors in the 1980s, separating regulation and operations in the late 1990s, and unbundling generation from network activities in the early 2000s – the number of stakeholders with explicit decision-making roles has increased. In the presence of multiple overlapping authorities, none of which currently has the role of an independent regulator, changing incumbent institutions requires significant coordination and negotiation. As in other areas of the Chinese bureaucracy outlined above, this reduces the power of either central or local governments to unilaterally pursue a reform agenda, leading to incremental reforms.

Brief History of China's Electricity Reforms

China's electricity sector was historically planned and operated through a single ministry and its provincial bureaus. In response to electricity shortages and lack of capital to fund expansion of the sector, the generation sector was partially opened in the mid-1980s (Zhang and Heller 2007). Planning decisions were increasingly decentralized as provincial governments and some private companies became investors, representing the first important shift in the central-local political bargain.

In 1998, the ministry was split into the State Power Corporation (SPC), controlling 46 percent of the country's generating assets and most of its transmission and distribution infrastructure, and a new regulatory division under the key government planning agency, the State Economic and Trade Commission. The reorganization was precipitated, first and foremost, by broader economy-wide trends in state-owned assets reform: corporatizing production formerly handled by ministries into new SOEs, and privatizing poor-performing SOEs. Second, the Asian Financial Crisis in 1997 reduced electricity demand revealing inefficiencies in the ministry-run system, in particular inefficient and unfair production planning by provincial bureaus (Zhang and Heller 2007). Citing a fundamental economic shift from shortage to "basic supply-demand balance," the State Council laid out its goals to create a single "open, competitive and orderly electricity market" (State Council 1998).

In 2002, with pressing energy shortages following improved macroeconomic conditions, a "significant change in the electricity supply-demand conditions" had once again revealed problems in the structure, notably anti-competitive practices by the monopoly operators and insufficient inter-provincial electricity transmission (State Council 2002). The State Council split up the SPC into the current arrangement of two major grid companies – State Grid and Southern Grid – and five large generation SOEs, with regional grid companies maintaining their previous territories after divesting generation assets. Pricing was more standardized through administratively determined benchmark tariffs at the provincial level as an interim measure before competitive wholesale markets were established (Kahrl, Williams, and Hu 2013).

During the subsequent decade, many pilots introducing more economic incentives into the sector were attempted and later abandoned (Andrews-Speed 2013). Instead, mandatory measures to meet specific administratively determined targets proliferated, such as the small plant early retirement program beginning in 2005 and measures focusing on operations – annual and sub-annual generation decisions – such as "energy-efficient dispatch" (where dispatch refers to electricity production decisions) designed to prioritize high-efficiency coal plants over low-efficiency plants (Zhao and Ma 2013). Some of these, particularly related to investments and retirements, were effective in changing local government behavior and technology deployment, while others, particularly those focusing on operations, have run up against the countervailing sector priorities discussed below.

The latest round of electricity reforms was preceded by a set of high-profile decisions made by central party leaders in 2013 calling for markets to play a "decisive role" in resource allocations, envisioning an expansive set of SOE privatization reforms and price reforms in many sectors including energy (CPCCC 2013). Over the course of 2014, President Xi Jinping chaired a leading group explicitly mentioning timetables for electricity reforms, followed closely by a 2014–20 energy strategy document incorporating this language (State Council 2014b).

In 2015, the State Council Document No. 9 laid out the blueprint for electricity sector reorganization. Unlike previous rounds, the emphasis shifted away from establishing international model organization and regulation, instead focusing on a few aspects related to partial generation markets, laying out the path for revenue cap regulation of the grid companies based on allowable costs, and calling for separation of distribution and retail functions and the creation of retail markets (State Council 2015). At the same time, the National Development and Reform Commission (NDRC) and National Energy Administration (NEA) published an *Opinion* aimed at increasing utilization of renewables and promoting efficient operation of thermal plants, reiterating the same basic issues with previous reform implementations and encouraging market mechanisms to improve efficiency and flexibility of the grid (NDRC and NEA 2015a).

Local Planning and Operations Decision-Making

The basic central-local political bargain in electricity since the 1980s has been an understanding that shortages could only be addressed through decentralization. Local autonomy over the sector is seen in two important processes – planning for new investments, and operation of existing assets – whose incentive structures reveal their connections to system-wide inefficiencies outlined later.

Investment Incentives at the Local Level

Approval authority of new power plants has traded hands between central agencies and provincial governments many times over the past several decades. Until recently, there was typically a threshold capacity below which central approval was not required. For example, until 2013, only wind farms below 50MW could be approved locally without central oversight, resulting in an abundance of 49.5MW farms being built (Kahrl & Wang 2015). All coal plants can be approved directly by provincial governments, though these can be rescinded by the center (NDRC and NEA 2015b; NEA 2016d). All wind and solar projects can also be approved locally, though NEA can restrict overall expansion at a provincial level according to integration conditions (NEA 2014a).

Approvals tend to increase when authority is decentralized because local governments seeking to maximize economic output have de facto incentives to permit as much capacity as possible, potentially beyond the social optimum. Local governments see large increases in economic activity for construction, and can be relatively assured of consistent employment because the plant's economic conditions are guaranteed by the generation planning process (described below) that the provincial government also directs. State-owned generation firms are also willing to continue to invest beyond what is privately optimal because of a stronger focus on total capacity and generation rather than profit when conducting internal assessments.[1]

Annual Generation Planning

In terms of operations, the generation quota planning process has been highly resistant to reform, persisting even following introduction of multiple generation companies. The basic process is directed by provincial Economic and Information Commissions and Industrial and Information Commissions, which collect input from a range of stakeholders, create annual quotas of minimum generation for plants, and coordinate with neighboring provinces and regions on total net exports (Kahrl and Wang 2014).

Notably, while investment in both conventional and renewable energy technologies brings benefits to local governments, taxation of

---

[1] Interview with respondent in state-owned firms with a range of energy investments, November 2016. The specific process of getting generation allocation is sometimes called "grabbing generation" (抢电量), where generation companies will compete for generation with less regard for price, confirmed by respondents in other SOEs.

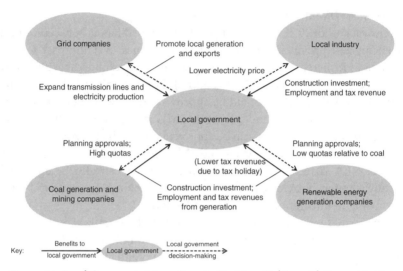

Figure 4.1 Local Government Incentives in Decision-Making with Respect to Key
Local Electricity Sector Stakeholders

these assets differs dramatically: renewable energy generators can deduct half of their value-added tax and are exempted from corporate tax the first three years and at half-rate for the subsequent three years. This ensures that annual tax revenues from wind farms lag far behind, and may never match, revenues from similar-sized coal plants (Zhao, Zhang, Zou, and Yao 2013). The resulting incentives and preferred decision-making strategies for local governments are illustrated in Figure 4.1.

Central priorities in operations introduced in recent years have had some limited success in changing this dynamic. For example, in the annual planning process, "energy-efficient dispatch" has been piloted in some provinces, which requires grid operators to give precedence to renewable energy over fossil generators and to more efficient coal generators over less efficient (Kahrl et al. 2013). However, inefficient allocation of generation quotas persists (described in the next section). The provincial grid company is evaluated primarily on how closely its dispatch decisions follow agreed generation plans, a task carried out formerly by the State Electricity Regulatory Commission (SERC), and now by the National Energy Administration (NEA 2016a). Therefore, grid companies have less autonomy with respect to dispatch, governed extensively by annual plan priorities that are subservient to other local economic factors.

OUTWARD SIGNS OF ELECTRICITY SYSTEMS INTEGRATION CHALLENGES

As can be seen from the above discussion, successful introduction of electricity technologies in China is highly dependent on a range of decisions from multiple actors with varied interests. In particular, strong provincial autonomy in electricity systems functions as well as physical constraints on electric power systems operation are key factors in determining electricity technology integration outcomes. Electricity systems must instantaneously match supply and demand within a relatively small tolerance, creating a complex production coordination problem.[2] This task is further complicated by uncertainties in demand and in the electricity generating technologies themselves which due to the mechanics of their energy conversion processes place a number of constraints on operation, such as minimum stable outputs and the times required to startup and shutdown.

The aggregate efficiency penalties of these integration difficulties can be seen in at least three negative system-wide outcomes discussed here: the under-utilization of advanced coal-fired power plants, low transmission network utilization, and high levels of renewable energy curtailment.

It is useful to have a benchmark of efficient system operations in mind when discussing these challenges. It can be shown that the most efficient dispatch is the result of an optimization that maximizes marginal welfare, or when demand is fixed as commonly assumed, minimizes the sum of marginal production costs, subject to technical and reliability constraints. Short-term "spot markets" attempt to approach this threshold through competitive bidding and system marginal prices at each time and location in the network (Schweppe, Caramanis, Tabors, and Bohn 1988). The resulting "merit order" dispatch thus prioritizes low marginal cost resources ahead of high marginal cost ones wherever possible. As renewable energy generators have no fuel costs, their marginal production costs are typically much lower than conventional plants and will be automatically prioritized under merit order dispatch. Furthermore, an electricity market operating under these marginal pricing rules is also efficient in the long-run, incentivizing the appropriate amount of investment in new generating capacity (Pérez-Arriaga and Meseguer 1997).

---

[2] Electricity storage technologies, which consume and regenerate electricity at controllable intervals with losses, can help arbitrage across time but are expensive and/or constrained by geography.

Overcapacity and Under-Utilization of Advanced Coal-Fired Power Plants

Starting in 2000 and accelerating in the 11th Five-Year Plan (FYP) (2006–10), a massive industrial upgrading mandate was rolled out to shut down small coal-fired power plants and industrial facilities and replace them with larger, more efficient units. As of 2016, the phase-out policy has resulted in roughly 100GW of coal power plant retirements. Yet, over the same time period (2005–16) approximately 690GW of new coal capacity was added to the grid (CEC 2017). The net additions to the grid coupled with slowing demand and growing non-fossil fuel capacity have led to historically low thermal fleet capacity factors,[3] falling from 64 percent to below 50 percent (see Figure 4.2).

Overcapacity was particularly pronounced following the release of approval authority to the provinces in 2014, prompting the first ever large-scale cancellation by the central government of already locally approved coal projects in 2016 (NEA 2016d). In its 13th FYP (2016–20) for electricity development, central energy agencies still plan for an additional 200GW of coal to come on line, while aiming for 20GW of retirements (NDRC and NEA 2016). Based on one analysis conducted prior to this announcement, under realistic electricity demand growth projections (4.2 percent) out to 2020, this level of growth would lead to 138GW of excess coal capacity and coal capacity factors dropping to 47.5 percent (Yuan et al. 2016).

Lists of annual small plant closures are set administratively, and large units should compensate smaller units (for up to three years), with details left to the provinces (NDRC and NELG 2007). Additional incentives include reducing the tariffs for these targeted smaller plants to encourage closure and allowing generation companies to build new capacity to replace them (Williams and Kahrl 2008). As newer plants were larger than the retired facilities, this resulted in massive expansions of new capacity, justified by overoptimistic demand growth projections.

The results of these massive investments also fell short of central expectations to increase production efficiency when several provinces were found to be dispatching their most efficient 600MW plus units less than units below 300MW (SERC 2011). Generators of the Big Five SOEs – which

---

[3] Capacity factor is defined as the ratio of actual generation to total possible generation, where possible generation on an annual basis is defined as the installed capacity multiplied by 8,760, the number of hours in the year. Some texts may also use capacity factor to refer to the loading rate of the power plant, which is the output at a given time as a fraction of total capacity.

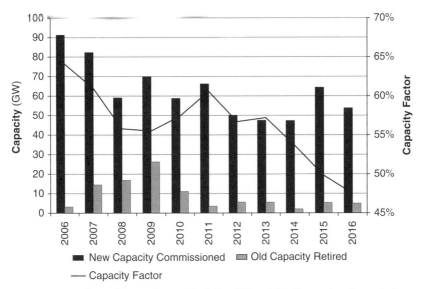

Figure 4.2 Industrial Upgrading in Coal-Fired Electricity Generation through the Small Plant Closure Program in Terms of Capacity (left) and Capacity Factor (right)
Source: Author's calculations based on CEC, NEA, and NBS data.
Note: Total coal capacities at year-end together with reported decommissioning were used to calculate additions. Only coal is reported here, in contrast to "thermal" (which includes, e.g., natural gas) as frequently used in statistical summaries. Recent years' totals were adjusted in subsequent statistics; the most recent revisions are used where available.

are in general of larger capacity – have been underutilized in comparison with local SOE and privately owned generators (Zhao and Ma 2013). Low utilization of high-efficiency generators has a double impact on efficiency as loading (the output at a given time) decreases the overall efficiency of the plant as described below.

Low and Inefficient Transmission Line Utilization

Most of China is served by two major grid companies – State Grid and Southern Grid – with regional and provincial subsidiaries whose operations are coordinated but not explicitly centralized. Strong provincial autonomy in plan setting leads to rigid dispatch procedures, with the year as the principal contracting period and sub-annual plans created to meet overall totals.

These planning processes extend naturally to cross-provincial trade. To balance supply and demand on an annual basis, most inter-provincial transmission takes place according to long-term contracts. Imbalances on shorter time scales are a small fraction of total trade, and are still resolved through a rigid negotiation process, though some recent agreements allow for informal transactions (Kahrl and Wang 2014).

The resulting utilization of the transmission network is certainly less efficient than compared to a centralized spot market, though aggregate statistics are difficult to calculate and not always reported. In one of the few early reports on trading, the former regulator[4] noted that while inter-provincial transactions are increasing, significant barriers still remain, related to the incongruence between plans and system conditions and to the inability of transmission tariffs to reflect scarcity conditions (SERC 2012b). Since then, inter-provincial trade barriers have been particularly difficult to eliminate, owing to protectionist policies benefiting local generators, differing interests of central and local governments, and a lack of basic regional market institutions (Wang 2017). The importance of regional trading has been raised specifically in the context of reducing renewable energy curtailment, discussed in the next section (NDRC and NEA 2017).

For example, according to transmission contracts between Central and North grids, hydropower is sent north during the summer months and coal electricity south during the winter. In one good rainfall year, the Central Grid sought to extend the hydropower export period – which would improve both cost and environmental performance – but instead was forced to spill hydropower while northern coal plants continued to operate (SERC 2012b). Many other lines have similar arrangements, such as the *DeBao* line connecting Central and Northwest grids, on which provinces have gone through the process of petitioning the central government to extend northbound hydropower transfers a few extra days.[5]

Inner Mongolia's export of power to North Grid is another example of suboptimal utilization of transmission infrastructure due to political considerations. Inner Mongolia has low cost coal and the best wind resources of the country, giving it cost advantages relative to its neighbor. Roughly 4GW connects the two regions, but output prior to 2011 was fixed at 3.9GW during the day and 2.1GW at night (Chen and Ma 2010). Beginning in 2011, an additional 1GW was added during night time through a special exchange to accommodate excess wind power (North

---

[4] The State Electricity Regulatory Commission (SERC), whose creation was called for in the 2002 reforms, was closed down and incorporated into the NEA in 2013, which now assumes both broad policy-making and regulatory responsibilities.

[5] Interviews with grid and regulatory officials in Northwest and Central Grids, July 2015 and November 2016.

China SERC 2013). By 2017, however, this had fallen to only 0.08GW average power (Inner Mongolia Electricity News 2017).

Prices for power from other provinces are also fixed annually, which may not be sufficiently low to incentivize trade and balance shortage and surplus conditions. This has occurred between Zhejiang and Fujian, for example, where even though Zhejiang was facing a shortage, average line utilization over a three-month period was only 25 percent (SERC 2012b). Conversely, there are examples of grids facing shortages locally while still contractually obligated to export power (Kahrl and Wang 2014).

High utilization of transmission assets, common for long-distance ultra high-voltage lines, could also reduce system efficiency if similarly inflexible (Davidson 2013). For example, most northern lines connect coal and wind power bases to demand centers in the south and east. These "coal-wind hybrid" lines are designed to operate at relatively stable levels in order to reduce coordination challenges with other system operators. However, in order to maintain this highly predictable output given the variability of wind generation, the ratio of coal to wind capacity may need to be 4:1 or even higher (Zhang, Feng, and Wang 2012). This leads to extra thermal capacity required on the sending end and potentially high wind spillage, described next.

Renewable Energy Curtailment

Integrating intermittent renewable energy – primarily, wind and solar – can lead to complications in grid operations. Inaccurate forecasts of available power or large amounts of power that suddenly become available must be managed while ensuring network security and meeting other requirements for conventional power plants (Xie et al. 2011). Coal and nuclear plants, in particular, have physical limitations and additional economic costs associated with cycling – ramping output up and down or turning on and off units – which should be co-optimized to reduce costs.

Grid operators typically respond by increasing reserve requirements, adding or improving products for flexibility such as compensating cycling capabilities, and seeking to improve coordination between regions. When these measures are insufficient, grid operators can curtail – or intentionally spill – renewable generation. Wind curtailment rates in China are the highest of any major wind power country, reaching 40 percent in some regions in 2016 (NEA 2018). Outside of China, some of the highest wind curtailment rates have been observed in Texas, where wind curtailment reached 17 percent in 2009 (see Figure 4.3), but following strengthening of

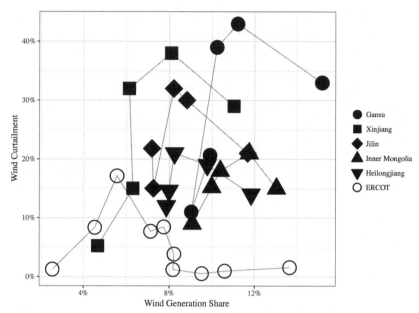

Figure 4.3 Wind Curtailment Rates by Major Wind Provinces, 2013–2017, and
ERCOT, 2007–2016
Sources: NEA (2018), Wiser and Bolinger (2017)
Note: ERCOT is the Electric Reliability Council of Texas.

a key west-east transmission line subsequently fell to near-zero levels. Other regions are consistently less than 5 percent (Bird et al. 2016; Wiser and Bolinger 2017). China is also unusual in having the grid reject large amounts of hydropower, up to 15 percent in the major hydro province of Sichuan (NEA 2015d). In other systems, curtailment of hydropower is less common, and often associated with environmental concerns (HydroWorld.com 2014).

While technical issues related to the network and inflexible conventional generators exist in China, regulatory structures are also an important determinant of curtailment. Annual generation planning, fixed inter-provincial and inter-regional transmission schedules, and out-of-merit order dispatch all present challenges to renewable integration (Davidson, Kahrl, and Karplus 2017). These institutional causes of inflexibility as well as operational parameters determined through negotiation processes are proportionally more important than technical causes for several northern regions of China (Davidson and Pérez-Arriaga 2018). In addition, related policies may have unintended and disruptive impacts, such as support for new and retrofits of must-run cogeneration plants in northern regions (Zhao, Zhang, Yang, and Wang 2012). Sichuan's hydro curtailment has been attributed to insufficient transmission capacity and utilization, low integration space between demand and conventional generation, and sub-optimal thermal operations (NEA 2015d).

This has been increasingly the subject of NEA scrutiny; its notices highlight some of these planning and administrative conflicts and have restricted expansion in areas with already high curtailment (NEA 2013, 2014a, 2015b). Mandatory and minimum purchase agreements exist, though even if they include penalties for non-compliance, enforcement is rare, as noted below.

POLICY RESPONSES TO ELECTRICITY SECTOR INTEGRATION CHALLENGES

Mandatory Requirements

As described above, the entire system is subject to substantial political intervention. Based on concerns of fairness, changes to grid operation often take the form of mandatory requirements nominally applicable to all, but each province has a lot of autonomy in whether and how these are formed. This has led to wide variation in power system operations even between neighboring provinces, which complicates inter-provincial coordination.

This process of adding bureaucratic priorities while not entirely dis-mantling the older ones is a fixture of China's policy-making. In the context of many new central edicts, provincial governments – the primary implementers of central policy – must choose which priorities to follow. We can view this selection process as a game based on the perceived repercussions of neglecting theoretically mandatory requirements and perceptions of long-term stability of central priorities (Mei and Pearson 2014). Without a strong signal, such as exists for the small plant closure program, weak implementation is commonplace.

The largest change to electricity systems operations since the 2002 restructuring has been a central-level push to change the dispatch order to give preference to energy-savings goals, such as the "energy-efficient dispatch" (EED). NEA promulgated EED rules in 2007, which were intended to guide dispatch decisions by creating a heuristic ordering, in decreasing order of importance, of uncontrollable renewables (wind, solar, etc.), controllable renewables (hydro and biomass), preferred conventional generators (nuclear and natural gas), and coal-fired units in decreasing order of efficiency (NDRC, MEP, SERC, and NELG 2007b). Must-run units such as coal-fired cogeneration for district heating were excluded. The ordering was to be used when setting annual generation quotas based on nominal efficiencies and other parameters such as water usage and pollution control equipment (Tong et al. 2011).

In practice, while some provinces report success with EED, few have actually implemented EED (Zhong, Xia, Chen, and Kang 2015). One overriding reason is the inherent conflict between assigning minimum quotas to all plants to ensure profitability while giving preference to some based on this ordering. Compensation mechanisms for less efficient plants were envisioned in central regulations, though the details were left up to the provinces (NDRC, MEP, SERC, and NELG 2007a). Some have set up price-based compensation instruments, such as generation rights trading – transfers from efficient to inefficient generators in exchange for generation quotas – but these face a number of risks that decrease their viability, described below in the section on market mechanisms. Further, because quotas and planning are done first within provincial borders, cross-provincial EED would be difficult to design.

Even less success is reported with mandatory purchase requirements for renewable energy, an additional dispatch priority instituted in 2005 and strengthened in 2009 (NPC 2009). The grid company is the target of the requirement, but provincial governments and planning agencies, not the provincial grid subsidiaries, are primarily responsible for allocating the year's thermal generation, which already pre-determines to some extent how much renewable energy can be integrated (discussed earlier with regard to annual generation planning). The grid operator's discretion – shorter-term operations – does not override the priority of annual generation planning. In addition, there is no known instance of the grid company facing fines for failure to satisfy this requirement. In 2015, more specific conditions and penalties for grid companies failing to comply were announced, though none have been levied despite rising curtailment rates (NEA 2015a). In fact, an environmental non-profit organization has sued State Grid for environmental damages due to curtailment (CEC 2018).

Ownership Diversification

In the influential 2013 communiqué on economy-wide reforms, central party leaders called for a new round of reforms in the state-owned sector, including through ownership diversification (CPCCC 2013). Specific to the energy sector, international diversification was also envisioned (NEA 2014c). While maintaining state ownership in key monopoly sectors such as transmission, current reforms call for private investment in areas such as retail and some distribution activities (State Council 2015). These indicate a strong perceived connection between efficiency and specific ownership structure.

Standard wisdom suggests that SOEs face both soft budget constraints and political interference in market decisions. Soft budget constraints artificially prop up inefficient enterprises with promises of bailouts for poor investments, which weaken the role of price signals in managerial decisions (Kornai, Maskin, and Roland 2003). Political interference also weakens the role of markets, as by nature of their ownership these enterprises serve other public goals besides a constrained profit-maximization. Both of these are widely observed in China's SOEs (Steinfeld 1998).

In the 1990s, reforms to traditional state-directed industries focused on two types of ownership and management changes: first, transform ministries involved in production activities into SOEs, and second, increase the role of the private sector by having state-owned firms either sell off certain business activities or expand ownership through publicly traded shares. The former was seen as a necessary precondition for aligning managerial incentives with efficient outcomes. Reform advocates have, perhaps implausibly, touted share issuance as sufficient to enforce these incentives. Throughout, the focus on establishing property rights instead of what the rights mean for managers – whether private or state-owned – has undermined key progress (Steinfeld 1998).

For example, there is some debate as to the extent to which China's SOE managers are beholden to government interests. The electricity sector was corporatized in 1997, but the former ministry functions were devolved to various SOEs still influenced at various levels by government. At the center, the powerful State-owned Assets Supervision and Administration Commission (SASAC) oversees all centrally owned SOEs, and the party's Organization Department appoints heads of a third of the major SOEs under SASAC jurisdiction, who in turn have a high rank in the party (Pearson 2015). On the other hand, SOEs can flout central government directions, such as some generators (including state-owned firms) refusing to increase output in 2011 during coal price surges which led to electricity shortages (Zeng et al. 2013).

Lessons from other countries demonstrate that when well-regulated markets are in place public ownership need not necessarily impede efficient operation. In Norway, the state-owned generator has 32 percent of the country's capacity and is highly competitive, benefitting from a strong independent regulatory framework (Gronli 2009). China's generation sector is over two-thirds state-owned, but the top five SOEs each have only around 10 percent (SERC 2012a). Concentrations do increase at the regional and provincial levels, which should cause some concerns of potential undue political influence – and market power if and when generation markets are created. However, it is unclear that diversifying ownership alone will have a strong impact on the inefficiency challenges in China's power sector.

Related to this are various efforts to degrade the monopoly of the grid companies. Whether to create a nationwide grid company out of the SPC or break up into multiple regional grids was a key debate during the 2002 reforms (Xu 2016). The SPC and officials aligned with the electricity sector fought to preserve large grid companies together with various affiliated businesses (Chen 2010). Current reform rounds do not alter grid companies' geographic territories. However, they do take away some of their traditional advantages, including no longer being essentially the sole seller of electricity, initiating pilots to better audit grid costs, and allowing limited private investment in distribution grids (State Council 2015).

Decentralization of Government Functions

Together with the call for more influential market forces is a trend to further decentralize certain government functions, as in the successful reforms of the 1980s and 1990s, nominally to allow greater flexibility in finding efficient allocations of resources (State Council 2014b).

The most important example is approvals of new power plants described above. Besides efficient allocation motivations, significant corruption throughout the electricity sector has likely played an important role in the recent localization. At least eight high-ranking energy officials and twenty-five energy-related state-owned firm officials were detained on questions of corruption and bribery in 2014–15 (Li and Wen 2015; Xinhua 2016). This does not preclude provincial government corruption in the energy sector – high profile cases of this exist, for example, in Shanxi's massive coal industry (China Daily 2016).

Very recently, yet another adjustment to this policy partially rolls back some autonomy by seeking to appropriately coordinate network planning (typically done on larger geographic scales, nationally for high voltages) and generation planning. Short of reclaiming project approval authority,

NEA guidelines now specify that a province's five-year electricity development plans should be guided by national plans, and should follow appropriate guidelines such as selecting the appropriate energy type and
ensuring open participation (NDRC and NEA 2015b). This includes guidelines for electricity sector investments through coordination among energy
sectors and with many related sectors (NEA 2016b), and the sector's first
FYP in fifteen years for the 2016–20 period, which reasserts central oversight to address all the integration challenges above (NDRC and NEA
2016).

Greater localization may go in the opposite direction of addressing
current electricity systems integration challenges. First, as described
above, new coal capacity additions skyrocketed in 2015 following the
reassignment of project approval authority to local governments, exacerbating existing overcapacity. Second, expansion of long-distance transmission lines and growing output of renewable energy enhance the
importance of cross-border trading mechanisms, the latter because
renewable energy projects in China cluster in a handful of provinces or
regions far from demand centers. Notably, the 13th Five-Year Electricity
Development Plan strongly prioritizes within-province integration as
a solution to existing curtailment and proposes to increase wind development in provinces with large in-province integration potential (NDRC
and NEA 2016).

Market Mechanisms

While not changing the fundamentally rigid and government-planned
nature of the system, there have been multiple experiments over the past
decade to incorporate some market mechanisms to enhance efficiency.
Even before unbundling reforms of 2002, wholesale markets were piloted
in several provinces, and the new structure of separate grid and generation
functions was supposed to allow for competition on price for the newly
created generation companies. These early pilots and subsequent experiments to create competitive generation markets were not successful and
have been abandoned since 2006 (Zhang and Heller 2007). In their place
have been a number of alternative mechanisms tested at provincial levels,
two of which – bilateral contracts and generation rights trading – are
described here. An additional market for flexibility piloted in the
Northeast is described below in the section on operational flexibility.

Since China's grid companies encapsulate transmission, distribution,
and operation, they form a "single-buyer" market for electricity: many

generators sell power to a single (regional or provincial) grid company, which in turn sells it to many consumers. Much reform discussion has centered on inefficiency of the monopolistic and monopsonistic nature of the grid companies and the need to further decentralize this intermediate role between generator and consumer. One of the alternatives pursued in earnest has been bilateral contracts, where customers can directly contract for quantities and prices of electricity from producers outside of the normal tariff structure.

Forward (i.e. long-term, such as one month or longer) bilateral contracts can be an effective method for lowering electricity prices by reducing amounts delivered in spot markets, arriving at a new equilibrium that reflects diverse risk profiles and reducing market power of vertically-integrated utilities where markets exist (Allaz and Vila 1993; Bushnell, Mansur, and Saravia 2008). In China, where there is significant overcapacity in some regions, this could be an effective and equitable method of allocating generation.

In practice, however, forward contracting is more appropriately seen as a method for local governments to reduce electricity prices to industry, getting around high central government tariffs that cross-subsidize other users (see Chapter 8). High thresholds for consumers ensure that only large enterprises can benefit. Furthermore, some generators claim that provincial governments pressure them to participate, even setting the prices in some instances (Zhang 2015). In 2014, Gansu became the first province in China to allocate its entire generation quota through bilateral contracts, which reportedly led to massive complaints by generation companies (SCEO 2015). The central government has further had to restrict supplier participation to only more efficient generators because of conflicts with the energy-efficient dispatch priorities, adding additional arbitrariness to the market. Retail competition, which has been introduced in several provinces, should be seen as a form of forward contracting that reduces the entry barriers for consumers, but does not significantly change the drivers of supply-side inefficiencies.

To compensate losing firms in the administrative EED policy without touching the quota allocation method directly, some provinces have opted to encourage generation rights trading. This converts quotas into tradable commodities while preserving the "legal rights of generating companies," which presumably refers to an obligation to give generation companies sufficient quota (SERC 2008). This in theory can provide incentives for a dispatch order based on cost, with guaranteed contract amounts of inefficient generators purchased by efficient ones.

In practice, generation rights trading is subject to two key risks: the volatile spot price of coal and politically influenced mandatory participation. In 2008, coal prices rose so high in Jiangsu that there was no price at which both parties were willing to trade (Liu 2013) – i.e., where the inefficient generator is made whole and the efficient generator has positive marginal profit. Large units may also refuse to sign contracts – which are typically annual – because of intra-year volatility in coal prices. Transaction costs for these bilateral trades seem too high to allow trading on anything less than monthly, pointing to a significant limitation in expanding trading. Regardless, the former regulator largely lauded the pilots, and the latest round of reforms highlights both bilateral contracts and generation rights trading as appropriate market mechanisms to pursue (SERC 2012b; State Council 2015).

CASE OF ADVANCED COAL-FIRED POWER GENERATION TECHNOLOGIES

In order to highlight the challenges of integrating advanced generation technologies in China, the case of high-efficiency coal-fired power is explored from early development and adoption in the 1990s through widespread deployment in the 2000s. Retiring old capacity to make way for these more efficient plants is China's most prominent energy efficiency program (PRC 2012). However, starting from the centralized top-down nature of power plant technology development and design, through to fragmentation of grid operations, significant efficiency gains have been left uncaptured.

State-of-the-Art in Coal-Fired Power Plant Technology

Coal-fired power plants are a complex collection of components, including a boiler, multiple turbines and generators, an extensive pipe network, and numerous control systems. Over the last 100 years, in order to increase temperatures and pressures of outlet steam and unit sizes – which translate to higher overall efficiencies – engineers have increased the technical complexity and sophistication of power plant components as well as the materials used to make them. The current state-of-the-art in coal-fired power generation is the USC pulverized coal-fired power plant,[6] which can

---

[6] A completely different, relatively new combustion technology, Integrated Gasification and Combustion Cycle (IGCC), is also being explored in China and elsewhere, boasting advantages in terms of by-products capture though with lower overall efficiencies.

operate continuously at extremely high pressures and at temperatures exceeding 600°C. China's USC units in 2012 achieved efficiencies[7] of 40–45 percent (mean: 42 percent) compared to 35–40 percent (mean: 38 percent) for subcritical (SUB) designs (CEC 2013). Supercritical (SC) plants operate at intermediate efficiencies, though still requiring substantial materials advances over SUB designs.

The core engineering challenge to achieve these higher efficiencies is the demand on materials to withstand the peak steam parameters and stresses as the plant varies output. Inadequate materials – in addition to improper construction and suboptimal operation – can shrink plant lifetimes and reduce efficiencies (Nicol 2013).[8] Chinese firms producing these advanced designs either have licensing agreements or joint ventures with leading international firms (Sun, Cui, Zhang, and Long 2013). In particular, these joint ventures or licensing agreements generally leave the core design tasks to the international partner (Zhai 2008).[9]

Large coal plants worldwide are typically designed to operate at high and relatively stable outputs, i.e., "base load." However, with increasing penetration of variable renewables, more uncertain demand, and competition with other cost-effective generation such as natural gas in the United States, there is renewed interest in modifying design and operations to allow for greater flexibility (Korellis 2014). This effort for greater flexibility creates challenges for existing materials and plant designs – in which China has invested heavily – to withstand faster and deeper temperature swings.

China's Development and Deployment of Advanced Coal-Fired Power Technology

China historically relied on coal for 80 percent or more of its electricity, falling only recently to roughly two-thirds. Concerns around coal supply security and economic efficiency prompted the central government to focus on increasing generation efficiency, importing China's first SC plant in 1992. China's design and deployment of SC and higher plants since then have been primarily centrally directed and focused on a narrow set of

---

[7] Efficiency of a power plant refers to the amount of available energy converted into usable electricity. Supercritical plants have a theoretical thermodynamic efficiency of 56% (IEA 2010).

[8] Developing domestic capabilities in advanced materials was considered the most important aspect of China's "863" technology programs, described below. Interview with participating researcher, November 2015.

[9] This point was reiterated in interview with a power plant technology engineer, June 2017.

objectives, in most cases to achieve certain peak steam conditions and to generate domestic manufacturing capability and intellectual property rights.

With China's massive expansion of energy-intensive industries in the early 2000s, central leaders made energy conservation a key economic priority, setting higher goals for improving the efficiency of generation in the 10th FYP and all subsequent plans. The result has been a massive turnover in the coal-fired fleet and a 23 percent decline in heat rates – coal use per kilowatt-hour (kWh) – since 2000 (see Figure 4.4). Units of 300MW and larger – which are newer and more efficient – have increased from 43 percent of capacity in 2000 to 78 percent in 2014 (CEC 2015). Further, China's best plants, such as Waigaoqiao outside Shanghai, perform better than their international counterparts (Sun et al. 2013).

Design Choices in Research and Development and Commercialization Strategy

Since China's first SC coal plant went into operation in 1992, the central government and power utility directed an effort to learn from international designs in order to create domestic manufacturing capacity, in a process sometimes referred to as "indigenization." Deploying domestic SC

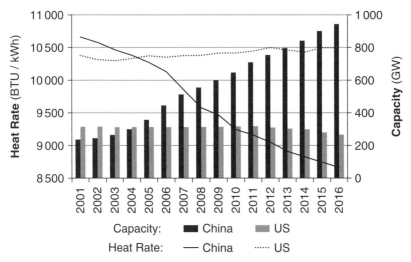

Figure 4.4 Capacity Growth and Heat Rates in Chinese and US Coal-Fired Power Sectors, 2001–2016.
Sources: CEC (2017); EIA (2017).
Note: Heat rate, equal to the energy required to generate electricity, is inversely proportional to efficiency. Generating capacity: year-end for China, summertime (June-September) for US.

technology became a key national program in the 10th FYP (2001–5), and in 2004 – just twelve years after its first import – Chinese manufactured its first SC plant (Watson, Byrne, Ockwell, and Stua 2015). This was achieved primarily through strategic licensing and joint ventures between the three major Chinese equipment manufacturers – Dongfang Electric, Shanghai Electric, and Harbin Electric – and leading international firms in the United States, Europe and Japan.

Concurrently, the newly created Ministry of Science and Technology (MOST) established a high-profile "863" program in the 10th FYP aimed at indigenizing the more advanced USC designs. Main components of this program were projects on technology selection among the available international designs in order to achieve the central goal of 45 percent efficiency (Zhang 2006). By 2007, just six years after beginning feasibility studies, China had installed its first USC plant (Watson et al. 2015).

Advanced coal technology development programs are collaborations among industry (generation companies, equipment manufacturers and materials producers), universities and research institutes, in a pattern known as *chanxueyan* (产学研) (Zhang 2006). The first phase focuses on basic science issues such as understanding materials properties, and is led by academic institutions. The second phase more closely aligns with industry and focuses on implementing projects. Since grid and generation companies were unbundled in 2002, the grid company has not had direct involvement in these research projects.[10]

Starting in the 11th FYP (2006–10) and scaled up in the 12th FYP (2011–15), coal combustion technology development plans began to explicitly consider pollution control technologies, coinciding with the adoption of nationwide sulfur dioxide and nitrous oxides reduction targets. This has added a third set of technology targets – emissions rates – to the previous targets of peak efficiency and domestic manufacturing capability. Except for integrated gasification and combustion cycle (IGCC) plants, emissions control in coal power plants emphasizes end-of-pipe measures such as installing sulfur scrubbers rather than design modifications (Tang, Snowden, McLellan, and Höök 2015). By 2020, China targets an average coal fleet-wide efficiency for 600MW plants of 300 gce/kWh (8300 BTU/kWh, or 41 percent efficiency) (State Council 2014b), and 310 gce/kWh (40 percent) for all coal plants (NDRC and NEA 2016).

---

[10] Multiple interviews with coal plant technology program participating researchers, November 2015.

Though China has domestic manufacturing capability now for both SC and USC plants, one cannot say China has 100 percent indigenized the technology as import dependencies remain in design software, high temperature materials and specialized steel (Watson et al. 2015). In particular, the three major Chinese equipment manufacturers have technology agreements with international suppliers who license specific designs. For example, Shanghai Electric buys a license for a 1000MW plant design, which includes the software for making calculations of various components. This license does not extend to an 800MW design, which would require different models of cylinders among other aspects.[11]

China's most recent manufacturing and innovation policy, "Made in China 2025," continues these efforts by including several familiar goals with respect to coal-fired power plant technology development: domestic manufacturing capabilities for high-temperature materials, design and optimization capabilities of USC plants, and 700°C materials breakthroughs (NDRC, MIIT, and NEA 2016). While "Made in China 2025" has been interpreted as a departure from previous indigenization policies because of its inclusion of traditional industries as well as specific time tables (Kennedy 2015), its approach to coal-fired power technologies is largely consistent with earlier technology programs (MOST 2012). A subsequent document lays out additional detail down to desired breakthroughs with respect to specific components by 2030 (NEA 2016c).

Operational Issues

With over 200 SC/USC units in operation, China has accumulated significant operational experience. Major materials-related issues encountered include corrosion of turbine blades leading to efficiency drops of 2–3 percentage points and leaks in boiler pipe fittings caused by thermal stresses (Sun et al. 2013). These challenges are typically framed with reference to the broader indigenization programs, whose goals include both the ability to manufacture advanced coal technologies as well as deploy them. The specific design choices and domestic manufacturing capabilities thus limit the modes of operations these coal plants are capable of achieving.

In addition to challenges when operating according to design specifications, China's advanced coal fleet also faces an operational challenge that is less emphasized in their designs. The problem stems from low loading, where plants operate at less than their rated output. If the load falls below

---

[11] Interview with a power plant technology engineer, June 2017.

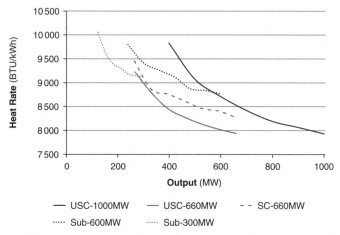

Figure 4.5 Heat Rates by Output for Sample of Chinese Ultra-Supercritical (USC), Supercritical (SC) and Subcritical (SUB) Coal Plants.
Source: Gu et al. (2016).

around 80 percent of rated capacity, USC/SC plants cannot maintain the requisite temperatures and pressures to deliver full efficiency; operations revert to the less efficient SUB mode. In a simple example, generating 500MW from a 1000MW USC plant may require more fuel than generating the same amount from a 600MW SUB plant, because at these low outputs the 1000MW plant's efficiency falls by 4–6 percentage points (see Figure 4.5). In 2013, it was estimated that less than one fifth of coal plants in China had average loadings above 80 percent, and in some provinces loadings were as low as 50 percent (Sun et al. 2013). In addition, these low loadings create the risk of exceeding hourly pollutant emissions standards (CEC 2015; Gu, Xu, Chen, Wang, and Li 2016).

Loading – the output while the unit is on – is not the same as full load hours or the capacity factor – ratio of output to total capacity, calculated over the year – described above, though the two are typically correlated. Units operating in regions with excess generating capacity will be competing for limited demand. Under these circumstances, "equal shares" dispatch – allocating generation proportionally to all units – will contribute to an overall decline in loading and performance of high-efficiency units. Low loading is likely more severe currently because of falling capacity factors in recent years (see Figure 4.2).

Larger plants also take longer to startup and shutdown in order to minimize stresses on pipes and pipe fittings. Whereas smaller plants less than 300MW could turn off and on daily to follow changes in load (known as "two-shift operation"), this is seen as uneconomical in China for larger units (Gu et al. 2016). The exact economic toll is unknown, as few compensation mechanisms exist in China for plants to operate flexibly, hence current dispatch practices typically are very conservative in terms of pushing thermal plants closer to their technical limits. For example, once scheduling a plant to turn on and begin delivering power, grid companies ensure it remains on for at least seven days (and typically much longer),[12] despite technical literature and actual operations in other countries showing that twenty-four hours or less is sufficient (Agora 2017; Cochran, Lew, and Kumar 2013).

By way of reference, if China's scheduling and dispatch practices – which consist of a number of administratively determined parameters, broad principles of equal sharing among different technology types, and a relative lack of incentives to improve efficiency – were replaced by a spot market, we would expect much of this low-loading issue to resolve itself. Neglecting startups, in the above example of dispatching 500MW, the marginal cost of the smaller unit (600MW) is lower than the larger one (1000MW), which would translate to a lower bid. When demand is low, the 600MW unit may be on the margin, and the 1000MW would not be selected to dispatch and hence shut down. When considering startups, the owner of the 1000MW unit may choose to bid below its marginal cost of production – possibly even negative – to avoid the potential costly shutdown. This creates a strong incentive to decrease costs and time between shutdowns and startups. If these types of situations were frequent and persistent over time, it would create signals against market entry of these large units.

Recent trends show that inefficiency arising from counterproductive loadings may have begun to decline, though in overcapacity situations there are still gaps with respect to an optimally run system. For example, in the Central and Eastern grids for first three quarters of 2014, average loadings of 1000MW units were 5–10 percentage points higher than 300MW units, though loadings at 600 and 300MW units were comparable (NEA 2015c). Capacity factor data, which are more readily available, generally show that larger plants are dispatched more. At the same time, however, generation at large 1000MW units fell more than all other generation size categories over 2013 to 2015, a period of slow growth in electricity demand (CEC 2016). As overcapacity continues to worsen,

[12] Interviews with multiple dispatch centers in 2015 and 2016.

this could mean continued losses from under-utilization and inefficiencies at China's newest coal plants.

Redesigning and Retrofitting for Operational Flexibility

Outside of the hydro-rich south and southwest, most regions in China rely on coal to provide not only base load but also load-following functions. In the 1980s, some small plants were explicitly designed for "two-shift operation," but as these were replaced with larger units in the 2000s, load-following has fallen on larger units that are generally not shut down, leading to some of the operational issues raised above (Gu et al. 2016). There are three decision points to improve flexibility of a coal plant: the technology R&D phase, the project design phase, and post-construction retrofits.

Optimizing for part load operations is generally preferable at the technology development stage, which would include a broader set of metrics, resulting in, e.g., different designs and material choices. In the context of China, where coal technology R&D programs are planned for at least a decade or longer (such as "Made in China 2025"), there is no indication that designers have focused on improving operational flexibility, which has only become a serious issue in the sector in the last half-decade.[13] The lack of clear economic targets and instead focusing on a single technological metric – efficiency at maximum load – has resulted in the handful of technology licenses with international partners, for which the inability to modify according to different operational characteristics represents a key barrier.

When a new plant is being proposed, it must be approved by one of various regional and provincial electric power design institutes and consulting firms separated from the grid company during the 2002 reforms (Kahrl and Wang 2015). These institutes have the power to approve or suggest changes to power plant proposals by generation companies, which could in theory include requirements for flexible operation. However, in practice, they have little incentive to go against the wishes of the generation company, since they are paid more if projects go to construction, and want to keep their clients from going to competing design institutes.[14]

Generation companies have only weak incentives to push for designs that operate better under flexible operation. Tariffs are fixed at the provincial level and not time varying. Generation quotas are largely negotiated

[13] Desired flexibility requirements are not included in "Made in China 2025" or related documents (MIIT 2016; NDRC, MIIT, and NEA 2016). Confirmed in multiple interviews with participating researchers, November 2015.
[14] Interview with design institute official, November 2015.

and not the result of direct competition. Additional revenue streams that reward flexibility – such as ancillary services – are small compared to the benchmark tariffs. In theory, a generator still benefits from increasing efficiency at low loadings, but this would likely not justify the costs of redesigning, and there is no benefit from improving startup and shutdown performance. In addition, much of China's cost reductions in power plant construction have come from indigenization coupled with a limited number of standardized designs licensed from international partners. This generally makes it more costly to customize.

Finally, some design changes to improve flexibility can be implemented as retrofits to existing plants (Korellis 2014). Due to the same issues at the design phase, there is little incentive for plants to undertake these investments, particularly at a time of falling capacity factors. In other countries that are adapting coal plants to operate more flexibly, power markets are seen as critical drivers (Agora 2017).

In the latest round of electricity reforms, a circular aimed at improving utilization of renewable energy specifically calls for more study into the flexibility of coal plants and improved compensation for various ancillary services, including "deep peaking" (low-loading) of coal plants (NDRC and NEA 2015a). These have been piloted in various regions but at very low price levels. The one exception is in the Northeast, where a "peaking ancillary service market" has been in operation since late 2014, with relatively high compensation for coal plants to go below minimum outputs (NEA 2014b). This unique market is designed to address a particular constellation of circumstances: large excess generating capacity, numerous cogeneration plants (which produce both heat and electricity, and therefore cannot be shut down during the winter months), and growing nuclear and wind fleets (Zhang and Song 2016).

Even though shorter-term markets may take several years to develop, some technology demonstration programs are piloting flexibility retrofits at plants concentrated in northern regions (NEA 2016e). The main purpose of these demonstrations is to reduce minimum outputs of coal plants to allow space for wind and solar energy (China Energy News 2016). Plants in the Northeast and other regions with "peaking markets" could potentially benefit monetarily from these retrofits.

Waigaoqiao

The case of Waigaoqiao Phase 3, a two-unit coal-fired power plant built in Shanghai's Pudong district, is instructive of the misalignment of central technology programs and operational realities. During expansion of the power plant, which is majority owned by Shanghai SOEs, its engineering team made significant changes to the design of two 1000MW USC units, as well as several retrofits following construction. Their goals were manifold – increase peak efficiency, reduce minimum stable output, decrease startup times, and decrease pollutant emissions – and according to engineers on the project were motivated by a view of the entire technology package, including design and construction through to continuous adjustments during operations.[15] The plant was able to achieve what is claimed to be the world's highest recorded coal plant efficiency, 44.5 percent, while operating at 81 percent loading in 2011 (Feng 2016; Sun et al. 2013).

Despite strong government technology initiatives during this time, Waigaoqiao did not benefit from them – no universities or outside labs were integral to the engineering work, and no funds were allocated from the 863 program – and there were uncertain market forces at the time to adopt the technology.[16] After running for some time, it slowly began to receive various ad-hoc subsidies even as large efficient generators like Waigaoqiao in Shanghai were receiving lower operating hours than smaller plants (SERC 2011). It has since received an array of ad-hoc compensation mechanisms, including designation as the first "high technology" coal power plant entitling it to reduced corporate tax rates of 15 percent compared to 25 percent for three years and tax credits for technology R&D (SAT 2009, Shanghai Morning Post 2014). In addition, they have received subsidies from the Ministry of Finance for increasing efficiency and bonuses for reducing pollutant emissions below standards from both central and Shanghai governments.[17] The experiences of Waigaoqiao have become important lessons for China, as their engineers consult on several retrofit projects in China and are in charge of designing from scratch the Pingshan plant in Anhui that will surpass Waigaoqiao's efficiency.[18]

"700°C Coalition"

Based on the successful examples of SC and USC indigenization and deployment China began scoping domestic development of "advanced ultra-supercritical" (AUSC) technology, where steam temperatures reach 700°C and with efficiencies of greater than 50 percent (Zhang 2010). This became a priority area in the 12th FYP (2011–15), focusing on all relevant

---

[15] Interviews with Waigaoqiao engineers, December 2016.   [16] Ibid.   [17] Ibid.
[18] Ibid.

componontn   boilcis, tuibinco, high temperature materials, etc. (State Council 2013). Distinct from previous efforts, however, there are no international plants to learn from, hence this has the more ambitious task of developing these new technologies domestically. In fact, other groups from Europe, the United States, Japan, and India have been pursuing similar initiatives since as early as the 1990s, though no demonstration plant has been built yet (Nicol 2013). Because of the high costs of high temperature materials for US AUSC designs, multiple estimates (including by a boiler manufacturer) show that they are not cost-competitive with USC plants without a carbon tax (Booras 2015).

Many institutes, research universities and generation companies are involved in the "700°C Coalition" initiated by the NEA. Despite the operational experiences of earlier programs, design objectives were established very early on and are the same as earlier efforts: a target pressure and temperature, translating to efficiency at maximum load. No explicit design considerations for economic performance given expected system changes, such as the demand for more flexible operation, are included.[19] Due to current thermal overcapacity and reduced demand growth in most of China, the project is not being as aggressively pursued,[20] though "Made in China 2025" does include the goal of material breakthroughs for a 700°C generator (NDRC et al. 2016). The government's long-term energy technology innovation plan targets building a demonstration plant by 2030 and to continue working toward plants achieving 60 percent efficiency by 2050 (NEA 2016c).

POLICY IMPLICATIONS

Regulatory and Policy Issues Can Truncate the Payoff to Innovation

The electricity sector is a compelling case of concerted central efforts at technological upgrading through the development of advanced generation technologies such as USC coal-fired power plants as well as transmission technologies discussed elsewhere in this volume. The pace of learning and deployment are unprecedented in the history of electricity systems.

At the same time, overcapacity and low loading of its advanced coal fleet, high and persistent renewable energy curtailment, and underutilization of the transmission network, among others, demonstrate that the full benefits of

---

[19] Interview with participating researcher, November 2015.   [20] Ibid.

these technological achievements are not materializing. While clearly incentivizing development and providing opportunities for deployment of new innovations, efforts to create markets for the fundamental commodity, electricity, are stymied by a system of policies and regulations that maintains legacy planning components with strong local autonomies. Significant fragmentation of authorities further complicates effective policy implementation.

The most recent round of electricity reforms is primarily devoted to policy and regulatory issues, calling for innovations in markets and supervision methods. This blueprint and related opinions focus on reducing the share of the plan in operations and improving priority dispatch. The documents are replete with references to improving efficiency through cost-based and emissions-based standards.

However, piloted market-based approaches seem more tailored to China's system ten years ago with stable demand growth and low levels of intermittent renewable energy, than to new and projected future demands on the grid. These approaches include contracting methods that shift production to the most efficient generators via medium-term (monthly to annual) agreements, which are ill-suited given unpredictable demand, wind and solar resources. Spot markets would create a consistent price signal that matches the true value of electricity, thus incentivizing flexibility, but are explicitly deemed "supplementary" in reform documents, and have not been included per provinces' discretion (NDRC 2015). Increased compensation for flexibility to manage these new realities could also come through strengthened ancillary services markets, as piloted in the Northeast. Ad hoc compensation, as for Waigaoqiao's improvements, generally would be a second-best solution as it does not provide predictable returns and represents yet an additional layer of incentives on top of the already complex plan and contract systems.

From the perspective of the broad class of technologies for which China has strong top-down direction in research and domestic deployment, this points to an important missing element: (primarily economic) indicators for integration potential in the broader technological system. Current and past technology development programs in electricity generating technologies establish specific targets and lay out component developments that lead to relatively homogeneous products while generating strong institutional support from a range of groups. By contrast, the future of the electricity generation sector will likely require more heterogeneous solutions to address changing demands and decarbonization objectives. Innovations such as the flexible units at Waigaoqiao have occurred in spite of this legacy technology planning approach.

Firm–Market Links Supersede Ownership Diversification Efforts

Owing to technical as well as historical reasons, the electricity sector is more complicated to diversify than simpler product sectors. It is nearly universally recognized as an essential public service, which creates substantial political obligations in managing the sector. Its delivery is also highly interdependent due to the instantaneous connections across large distances, which leads to complex market coordination challenges. Further, based on international experiences of efficient publicly owned generation companies, particularly in Europe, when properly regulated markets are in place the case for privatization is weakened.

China's market reforms will need to address a range of integration issues in the sector: under-utilization and inefficiencies in its newest plants, barriers to trading across provinces, and reducing curtailment of essentially free renewable energy. The way forward involves a shift away from reforms focused on who the owner is, to what the owner does. Encouraging private and local government investment – as in the 1980s – will not fundamentally address this issue. Some aspects of the changes to grid companies may be beneficial – particularly, in piloting better grid cost auditing. However, splitting up State Grid into independent regional monopolies, as has been proposed at times, will not aid integration issues directly.

Scale Economies Fade Without Cross-Provincial Institutional Harmonization

Since centralized generator planning decisions were relaxed in the 1980s, provincial governments have been the primary unit of analysis for electricity sector institutional reform. Annual generation plans, most day-to-day operations, and, following enhanced decentralization of project approval in 2014, many planning decisions are made at the provincial level (State Council 2014a). In varied aspects, provincial autonomy and experimentation has been a fundamental aspect of policy-making in modern China, and is also largely credited with its successful market reforms (Montinola, Qian, and Weingast 1995; Schurmann 1968).

The most recent round of electricity reforms sticks closely to this paradigm. All important new market policies are being piloted first in the provinces, with substantial autonomy given to local governments in their design and implementation. Even long-running experiments such as bilateral contracts or generation rights trading have only small-scale cross-provincial examples, likely complicated by the differing systems created to satisfy local interests. The numerous examples of difficulties with short-term inter-provincial transmission highlighted above are instructive.

Heterogeneity in provincial policies has been seen as a key engine of growth in the 1980s and 1990s, as provinces facing more intense competition experimented with ways to shore up soft budgets of local companies (Rawski 1995). However, this logic may be less applicable to electricity supply, a product that is not fungible across time periods, has strong geographic economies of scale, and requires significant coordination among jurisdictions. The benefits (and harms) of scaled-up policies may not be visible in provincial experiments. Conversely, efficient system-wide policies may not be testable on smaller geographic scales.

Local systems will continue to present integration challenges for advanced electricity generation technologies in China in the foreseeable future. Standardizing system operation through common market design and regulation is likely the only effective way of lessening the influence of local interests on overall efficiency. Given the complexity of electricity reform and establishing independent regulatory systems, China's cautious experiments over limited areas may be prudent. However, leaving much of the details up to provincial concerns could lead to a number of mutually incompatible systems, which could substantially delay effective, necessarily inter-provincial, integration.

References

Agora. 2017. *Flexibility in Thermal Power Plants*. Berlin: Agora Energiewende. p. 116.

Allaz, B. and J. -L Vila.1993. "Cournot Competition, Forward Markets and Efficiency." *Journal of Economic Theory*. 59(1). pp. 1–16. https://doi.org/10.1006/jeth .1993.1001.

Allison, G. T. 1969. "Conceptual models and the Cuban missile crisis." *American Political Science Review,*. 63(03). pp. 689–718.

Andrews-Speed, P. 2013. "Reform Postponed: The Evolution of China's Electricity Markets." In *Evolution of Global Electricity Markets: New Paradigms, New Challenges, New Approaches*. Waltham, MA: Elsevier. pp. 531–67.

Bird, L., D. Lew, M. Milligan, E. M. Carlini A., Estanqueiro, D. Flynn, and J. Miller. 2016. "Wind and solar energy curtailment: A review of international experience." *Renewable and Sustainable Energy Reviews*. 65 (Supplement C). pp. 577–86. https://doi.org/10.1016/j.rser.2016.06.082.

Booras, G. 2015. *Engineering and Economic Analysis of an Advanced Ultra-Supercritical Pulverized Coal Power Plant with and without Post-Combustion Carbon Capture*. Palo Alto, CA: Electric Power Research Institute.

Bushnell, J. B., F. T. Mansur, and C. Saravia. 2000. "Vertical Arrangements, Market Structure, and Competition An Analysis of Restructured US Electricity Markets." *American Economic Review.* 98(1). pp. 237–66.

CEC. 2018. "China's biggest grid firm faces NGO court fight for spurning renewables." April 12, 2018. https://carbon-pulse.com/50562/ (accessed April 20, 2018).

——— 2013. *National 600 MW Coal-Fired Unit Efficiency Comparison and Competition.* 《关于公示2012年度全国火电600MW级机组能效对标及竞赛数据的通知》 http://kjfw.cec.org.cn/kejifuwu/2013-04-07/99877.html (accessed May 27, 2018).

——— 2015. Status and Prospects for China's Electricity Sector. 《中国电力工业现状与展望》 www.cec.org.cn/yaowenkuaidi/2015-03-10/134972.html (accessed December 16, 2015).

——— 2016. 2015 Electricity Industry Statistical Collection. China Electricity Council. 《2015电力统计资料汇编》.

——— 2017. *Overview of Electric Power Industry (Various: 2003–2016).* Beijing: China Electricity Council.

Chen, L. 2010. "Playing the Market Reform Card: The Changing Patterns of Political Struggle in China's Electric Power Sector." *China Journal.* 64. pp. 69–95.

Chen, R. and L. Ma. 2010. "Inner Mongolia Grid Company: Promoting Wind Power Development and Contributing to Energy-Savings and Emissions Reductions." January 8, 2010. 《内蒙古电力集团:推动风电发展为节能减排作贡献》 www.china.com.cn/economic/txt/2010-01/08/content_19204130.htm (accessed March 2, 2015).

China Daily. 2016. "Ex-Shanxi official pleads guilty to bribery." August 31 2016. http://usa.chinadaily.com.cn/epaper/2016-08/31/content_26655381.htm (accessed December 12, 2016).

China Energy News. 2016, "Thermal Plant Flexibility Retrofits are Imperative." *China Energy News.* July 14, 2016. 《火电灵活性改造势在必行》 www.cec.org.cn/xinwenpingxi/2016-07-14/155591.html (accessed December 6, 2016).

Cochran, J., D. Lew, and N. Kumar 2013. *Flexible Coal: Evolution from Baseload to Peaking Plant.* Golden, CO: National Renewable Energy Laboratory.

CPCCC. 2013. Third Plenary Session Communiqué: Major Issues in Comprehensively Deepening Reform. Communist Party of China 18th Central Committee. November 12, 2013 《中共中央关于全面深化改革若干重大问题的决定》.

Davidson, M. R. 2013. "Politics of Power in China: Institutional Bottlenecks to Reducing Wind Curtailment Through Improved Transmission." *International Association for Energy Economics Energy Forum.* 4. pp. 40–2.

Davidson, M. R., F. Kahrl, and V. J. Karplus 2017. "Towards a Political Economy Framework for Wind Power: Does China Break the Mould?" In D. Arent, C. Arndt, M. Miller, F. Tarp, and O. Zinaman eds., *The Political Economy of Clean Energy Transitions.* Oxford: Oxford University Press. pp. 250–70.

Davidson, M. R. and I. Pérez-Arriaga. 2018. "Modeling Unit Commitment in Political Context: Case of China's Partially Restructured Electricity Sector."

IEEE Transactions on Power Systems. https://doi.org/10.1109/TPWRS .2018.2822480.

EIA. 2017. Electric Power Annual 2016. United States Energy Information Administration. www.eia.gov/electricity/annual/archive/2016/ (accessed May 23, 2018).

Feng, W. 2016. "Generalized Regeneration Theory and its Energy Saving and Emission Reduction Effects on Coal-Fired Power Generation." Proceedings of the ASME 2016 Power and Energy Conference. Charlotte, NC: American Society of Mechanical Engineers.

Gómez-Ibáñez, J. A. 2003. *Regulating Infrastructure: Monopoly, Contracts, and Discretion.* Cambridge, MA: Harvard University Press.

Gronli, H. 2009. "The Norwegian and Nordic Power Sectors." In G. Rothwell and T. Gómez eds., Electricity Economics. IEEE. pp. 161–86.

Gu, Y., J. Xu, D. Chen, Z. Wang, and Q. Li. 2016. "Overall review of peak shaving for coal-fired power units in China." *Renewable and Sustainable Energy Reviews.* 54. pp. 723–31. https://doi.org/10.1016/j.rser.2015.10.052

HydroWorld.com. 2014. "FERC approves formula for BPA curtailment of wind generation in favor of excess hydro." October 14, 2014. .www.hydroworld.com/articles/2014/10/ferc-approves-formula-for-bpa-curtailment-of-wind-generation-in-favor-of-excess-hydro.html (accessed December 12, 2016).

IEA. 2010. *Power Generation from Coal.* Paris: International Energy Agency.

Inner Mongolia Electricity News. 2017. Inter-Regional Exchanges – July 2017. 《2017-7-区外交易情况》. www.nmgdlxw.cn/ (accessed November 2, 2017).

Jin, H., Y. Qian, and B. R. Weingast 2005. "Regional decentralization and fiscal incentives: Federalism, Chinese style." *Journal of Public Economics.* 89. pp. 1719–42.

Kahrl, F. and X. Wang, 2014. *Integrating Renewables into Power Systems in China: A Technical Primer – Power System Operations.* Beijing: Regulatory Assistance Project.

    2015. *Integrating Renewable Energy Into Power Systems in China: A Technical Primer – Electricity Planning.* Beijing: Regulatory Assistance Project.

Kahrl, F., J. H. Williams, and J. Hu. 2013. "The political economy of electricity dispatch reform in China." *Energy Policy.* 53. pp. 361–9. https://doi.org/10.1016/j.enpol.2012 .10.062.

Kennedy, S. 2015. "Made in China 2025." June 1, 2015. www.csis.org/analysis/made-china-2025 (accessed May 26, 2018).

Korellis, S. 2014. "Coal-Fired Power Plant Heat Rate Improvement Options." November 1, 2014. www.powermag.com/coal-fired-power-plant-heat-rate-improvement-options-part-1/ (accessed December 15, 2015).

Kornai, J., E. Maskin, and G. Roland2003. "Understanding the Soft Budget Constraint." *Journal of Economic Literature.* 41(4). pp. 1095–36.

Li, W. and R. Wen, 2015."Wei Pengyuan Case Amounts to 340 million yuan." *Fazhi Wanbao.* December 29, 2015. www.fawan.com/Article/gn/2015/12/29/ 154614320054.html (accessed December 31, 2015).

Lieberthal, K. and M. Oksenberg. 1988. *Policy Making In China: Leaders, Structures, and Processes*. Princeton, NJ. Princeton University Press.

Liu, Q. 2013. "How to Implement Energy Efficient Dispatch Compensation: Jiangsu's Experience." *Power and Electricity Engineers*, 26. 《如何进行节能发电调度经济补偿－江苏省的经验和做法》.

Markard, J. 2011. "Transformation of Infrastructures: Sector Characteristics and Implications for Fundamental Change." *Journal of Infrastructure Systems*. 17(3). pp. 107–17.

Mei, C. and M. M. Pearson. 2014. "Killing a chicken to scare the monkeys? Deterrence failure and local defiance in China." *The China Journal*. (72). pp. 75–97.

Mertha, A. C. 2005. "China's 'soft' centralization: shifting tiao/kuai authority relations." *The China Quarterly*. 184. pp. 791–810.

MIIT. 2016. "Interpreting Made in China 2025: Promoting Electricity Equipment Development." Ministry of Industry and Information Technology. 《中国制造2025》解读：推动电力装备发展. www.gov.cn/zhuanti/2016–05/12/content_5072761.htm (accessed May 26, 2018).

Montinola, G., Y. Qian, and B. R. Weingast. 1995. "Federalism, Chinese style: the political basis for economic success in China." *World Politics*. 48(01). pp. 50–81.

MOST. 2012. "12th Five-Year Special Development Plan for Clean Coal Utilization Technology." Ministry of Science and Technology. 《关于印发洁净煤技术科技发展"十二五"专项规划的通知》 www.most.gov.cn/fggw/zfwj/zfwj2012/201204/t20120424_93882.htm (accessed December 16, 2015).

Naughton, B. 1995. *Growing out of the Plan: Chinese Economic Reform, 1978–1993*. New York: Cambridge University Press.

NDRC. 2015. "Implementing Opinion on Promoting the Creation of Electricity Markets." National Development and Reform Commission. 《关于推进电力市场建设的实施意见》.

NDRC, MEP, SERC, and NELG. 2007a. "Implementation Guidelines for Energy Efficient Dispatch Pilots (Provisional)." National Development and Reform Commission. 《关于印发节能发电调度试点工作方案和实施细则（试行）的通知》. www.nea.gov.cn/2011–11/22/c_131262571.htm (accessed May 3, 2015).

    2007b. "Measures for Energy Efficient Dispatch (Provisional)." National Development and Reform Commission. August, 2007. 《关于转发发展改革委等部门节能发电调度办法(试行)的通知(国办发[2007]53号)》. www.sdpc.gov.cn/zcfb/zcfbqt/200708/t20070828_156042.html (accessed May 3, 2015).

NDRC, MIIT, and NEA. 2016. "Made in China 2025: Energy Equipment Implementation Plan." National Development and Reform Commission. 《中国制造2025－能源装备实施方案》发改能源[2016]1274号. www.gov.cn/xinwen/2016–06/21/5084099/files/f64a4db485544bbdaf136fc6cbdf70ff.pdf (accessed May 26, 2018).

NDRC and NEA. 2015a. "Guiding Opinion Regarding Improving Electricity System Operational Adjustments for Increased and Complete Clean Energy Generation."

National Development and Reform Commission. 《关于改善电力运行调节促进清洁能源多发满发的指导意见(发改运行[2015]518号)》.

2015b. "Notice Regarding Electricity Planning Following Project Approval Release." National Energy Administration. 《关于做好电力项目核准权限下放后规划建设有关工作的通知》.

2016. "13th Five-Year Electricity Development Plan." National Development and Reform Commission. 《电力发展"十三五"规划》.

2017. "Implementing Plan for Solving Hydropower, Wind and Solar Curtailment." National Development and Reform Commission. 《解决弃水弃风弃光问题实施方案》.

NDRC and NELG. 2007. "Opinion Regarding Accelerating Small Thermal Power Plant Retirements." National Development and Reform Commission. 《关于加快关停小火电机组若干意见的通知》(国发[2007]2号). www.sdpc.gov.cn/zcfb/zcfbqt/200701/t20070131_115037.html (accessed March 3, 2015).

NEA. 2013. "Notice Regarding Improving the Connection and Utilization of Wind Resources in 2013." National Energy Administration. 《国家能源局关于做好2013年风电并网和消纳相关工作的通知》.

2014a. "Notice Regarding Strengthening Wind Energy Project Development Management Requirements." National Energy Administration. 《国家能源局关于加强风电项目开发建设管理有关要求的通知》.

2014b. "Summary Note on Management Rules of Northeast Electricity Peaking Market Compensation." National Energy Administration, Northeast China Energy Regulatory Bureau. 《东北电力调峰市场化补偿管理办法编制说明》.

2014c. "Xi Jinping chairs central small leading finance group." www.nea.gov.cn/2014–06/17/c_133413362.htm 《习近平主持召开中央财经领导小组会议》 (accessed December 15, 2015).

2015a. "National Energy Administration Local Bureaus List of Authorities and Responsibilities (Provisional)." National Energy Administration. 《国家能源局派出机构权力和责任清单（试行）》.http://zfxxgk.nea.gov.cn/auto81/201512/t20151216_2015.htm (accessed December 15, 2015).

2015b. "Notice Regarding 2015 Wind Integration Work." National Energy Administration. 《国家能源局关于做好2015年度风电并网消纳有关工作的通知》国能新能[2015]82号.

2015c. "Special Supervisory Report of Central and East China Grid Energy Efficient Dispatch." National Energy Administration. 《华中华东区域节能减排发电调度专项监管报告》.http://zfxxgk.nea.gov.cn/auto92/201506/t20150612_1937.htm (accessed December 15, 2015).

2015d. "Supervision Report of Sichuan Hydropower Base Hydro Curtailment Issue." National Energy Administration. 《水电基地弃水问题驻点四川监管报告》. http://gzb.nea.gov.cn/Article/1976.aspx (accessed December 15, 2015).

2016a. "2015 National Electricity Dispatch Exchange and Market Operations Supervision Report." National Energy Administration. 《能源局公布2015年全国电力调度交易与市场秩序监管报告》.

2016b, "Electricity Planning Management Rules (No. 139)." National Energy Administration. 《电力规划管理办法》国能电力[2016]139号.

2016c. "Energy Technology Innovation Action Plan (2016–2030)." National Energy Administration. 《能源技术革命创新行动计划（2016–2030年）》. www.nea.gov.cn/2016–06/01/c_135404377.htm (accessed July 14, 2016).

2016d. "Notice Regarding Cancellation of Coal Plants Without Appropriate Approval Conditions (No. 244)." National Energy Administration. 《国家能源局关于取消一批不具备核准建设条件煤电项目的通知》国能电力[2016]244号. http://zfxxgk.nea.gov.cn/auto84/201609/t20160923_2300.htm (accessed October 21, 2016).

2016e. "Notice Regarding Second Round of Thermal Power Flexibility Retrofits Demonstration Projects." National Energy Administration. 《国家能源局综合司关于下达第二批火电灵活性改造试点项目的通知》国能综电力[2016]474号. http://zfxxgk.nea.gov.cn/auto84/201608/t20160805_2285.htm (accessed December 12, 2016).

2018. "Wind Industry Development Statistics 2013–2017." National Energy Administration. 《风电并网运行情况》(2013年-2017年).

Nicol, K. 2013. *Status of Advanced Ultra-supercritical Pulverised Coal Technology.* London: IEA Clean Coal Centre.

North China SERC. 2013. "Western Inner Mongolia Off-Peak Excess Wind Electricity Exchanges Remarkably Successful." February 21, 2013. 《蒙西电网低谷富余风电消纳交易成效显著》www.cpnn.com.cn/dljg/201302/t20130220_558185.html (accessed March 2, 2015).

NPC. 2009. *Renewable Energy Law of the People's Republic of China (Amended).* Beijing: China's National People's Congress.

Oi, J. C. 1999. *Rural China Takes Off: Institutional Foundations of Economic Reform.* Berkeley: University of California Press.

Pearson, M. M. 2015. "State-Owned Business and Party-State Regulation in China's Modern Political Economy." In B. Naughton and K. S. Tsai eds., *State Capitalism, Institutional Adaptation, and the Chinese Miracle* Cambridge: Cambridge University Press. pp. 27–45.

Pérez-Arriaga, J. I. and C. Meseguer.1997. "Wholesale marginal prices in competitive generation markets." *IEEE Transactions on Power Systems.* 12(2). pp. 710–17.

PRC. 2012. "Second National Communication on Climate Change of The People's Republic of China." The People's Republic of China. http://unfccc.int/resource/docs/natc/chnnc2e.pdf (accessed December 7, 2016).

Rawski, T. G. 1995. "Implications of China's Reform Experience." *The China Quarterly.* (144). p. 1150.

SAT. 2009. "Notice Regarding Implementation Issues of High Technology Enterprise Preferential Corporate Tax Rates." State Administration of Taxation. 《关于实施高新技术企业所得税优惠有关问题的通知》. www.chinatax.gov.cn/2013/n1586/n1593/n1685/n1690/c254147/content.html (accessed December 13, 2016).

SCEO. 2015. "Intersection: Gansu Bilateral Contracts Difficulties." November 16, 2015. *Southern China Energy Observer.* 《十字路口：甘肃直购电难局》.

Schurmann, F. 1968. *Ideology and Organization In Communist China.* Berkeley, University of California Press.

Schweppe, F. C., M. C., Caramanis, R. D. Tabors, and R. E. Bohn. 1988. *Spot Pricing of Electricity.* Boston, MA: Springer.

SERC. 2008. "Temporary Measures for Regulating Generation Rights Trading." State Electricity Regulatory Commission. 《发电权交易监管暂行办法》. www .gov.cn/gongbao/content/2009/content_1205399.htm (accessed November 19, 2014).

2011. "National Electricity Exchange and Market Operations Supervision Report." State Electricity Regulatory Commission. 《全国电力交易与市场秩序监管报告》.

2012a. "2011 Annual Electricity Regulation Report." State Electricity Regulatory Commission. 《电力监管年度报告(2011)》.

2012b. "2012H1 Inter-Provincial Energy Trading and Generation Rights Trading Report." State Electricity Regulatory Commission. 《2012年上半年跨省区电能交易与发电权交易监管报告》.

Shanghai Morning Post. 2014. "World's Most Efficient Coal Power Plant at Waigaoqiao." September 2, 2014. 全球最高效煤电厂"藏"在外高桥-新闻-能源资讯-中国能源网.www.china5e.com/news/news-882463-1.html (accessed December 13, 2016).

Shy, O. 2001. The Economics of Network Industries. *Cambridge: Cambridge University Press.*

State Council. 1998. Opinion Regarding Issues Deepening Electricity Sector Reform (No. 146)." State Council. 《关于深化电力工业体制改革有关问题意见》.

2002. "Electricity Sector Reform Plan." State Council. 《电力体制改革方案》国发[2002]5号.

2013. "12th Five-Year Plan on Energy Development." State Council. 《能源发展"十二五"规划》

2014a. "Notice of Catalogue of Government Approvals for Investment Projects (2014 version)." 《国务院关于发布政府核准的投资项目目录（2014年本）》国发〔2014〕53号.

2014b, "Energy Development Strategy Action Plan (2014–2020)." State Council. 《能源发展战略行动计划（2014-2020年）》. www.gov.cn/zhengce/content/2014–11/19/content_9222.htm (accessed November 24, 2014).

2015. "Opinion Regarding Deepening Electricity Sector Reform. State Council." 《中共中央国务院关于进一步深化电力体制改革的若干意见》.

Steinfeld, E. S. 1998. *Forging Reform in China: The Fate of State-owned Industry.* Cambridge: Cambridge University Press.

Sun, R., Z. Cui, J. Zhang, and H. Long, 2013. "Summary of China's Conventional Coal-Fired Power Plant Technologies." *Power and Electricity Engineers.* 28. pp. 28–34.

Tang, X., S. Snowden, B. C. McLellan, and M. Höök. 2015. "Clean coal use in China: Challenges and policy implications." *Energy Policy.* 87. pp. 517–23. https://doi.org/10.1016/j.enpol.2015.09.041.

Tong, J., X. Zhang, J. Ren, Y. Tang, X. Xu, A. Jiang, and N. Li. 2011. "Energy-Efficient Dispatch Implementation Analysis and Policy Recommendations. Energy Foundation." 《节能发电调度实施分析和政策建议》.

Wang, P. 2017. "Breaking Inter-Provincial Trade Barriers, Government and Enterprise Jointly Promote Regional Electricity Market." June 19, 2017. 《打破省间壁垒, 政企合力加快推动区域电力市场》 http://paper.people.com.cn/zgnyb/html/2017–06/19/content_1784719.htm (accessed May 25, 2018).

Watson, J., R. Byrne, D. Ockwell, and M. Stua, 2015. "Lessons from China: building technological capabilities for low carbon technology transfer and development." *Climatic Change*. 131(3). pp. 387–99. https://doi.org/10.1007/s10584-014–1124-1.

Weber, M. 1947. *The Theory of Social and Economic Organizations*. A. M. Henderson and T. Parsons eds. and trans. New York: Free Press.

Williams, J. H. and F. Kahrl. 2008. "Electricity reform and sustainable development in China." *Environmental Research Letters*. 3(4). 044009. https://doi.org/10.1088/1748–9326/3/4/044009.

Wiser, R. and M. Bolinger. 2017. *2016 Wind Technologies Market Report*. Washington, DC: US Department of Energy.

Xie, L., P. M. S. Carvalho, L. A. F. M. Ferreira, J. Liu, B. H. Krogh, N. Popli, and M. D. Ilic. 2011. "Wind Integration in Power Systems: Operational Challenges and Possible Solutions." Proceedings of the IEEE. 99(1). pp. 214–32. https://doi.org/10.1109/JPROC.2010.2070051.

Xinhua. 2016. "China probes 64 state-owned firm officials." January 4, 2016. http://news.xinhuanet.com/english/2016–01/04/c_134977118.htm (accessed November 30, 2016).

Xu, Y. 2016. *Sinews of Power: The Politics of the State Grid Corporation of China*. Oxford: Oxford University Press.

Yuan, J., P. Li, Y. Wang, Q. Liu, X. Shen, K. Zhang, and L. Dong. 2016. "Coal power overcapacity and investment bubble in China during 2015–2020." *Energy Policy*. 97. pp. 136–44. https://doi.org/10.1016/j.enpol.2016.07.009.

Zeng, M., S. Xue, L. Y. Li, Y. J. Wang, Y. Wei, and Y. Li. 2013. "China's large-scale power shortages of 2004 and 2011 after the electricity market reforms of 2002: Explanations and differences." *Energy Policy*. 61. pp. 610–18. https://doi.org/10.1016/j.enpol.2013.06.116.

Zhai, S. 2008. "Choice of the Parameters and Main Pipe Material of 1000 MW Unit." *Huadian Technology*. 30(1). pp. 6–9. 《百万千瓦发电机组参数及主要管材的选择》.

Zhang, C. 2015. "New Electricity Reforms: Analysis of New Electricity Reform Pathways." February 13, 2015. 《新电改系列之三：新电力体制改革路径分析预测》 www.thede.cn/index.php?c=article&id=550 (accessed February 26, 2015).

Zhang, C. and T. C. Heller. 2007. "Reform of the Chinese electric power market: economics and institutions." In D. G. Victor and T. C. Heller eds., *The Political Economy of Power Sector Reform: the Experiences of Five Major Developing Countries*. Cambridge: Cambridge University Press.

Zhang, C. and W. Song. 2016. "Northeast Grid Peaking Ancillary Services Market Reform Demonstration Commences." November 23, 2016. 《东北电力辅助服务市场专项改革试点工作启动》www.cpnn.com.cn/dljg/201611/t20161122_936439.html (accessed December 7, 2016).

Zhang, Q., Y. Feng, and S. Wang 2012. "Research on UHV AC transmission of combined electricity generated from wind and thermal." *China Electric Power.* 45 (6). 《特高压交流通道风火联合送电问题研究》.

Zhang, X. 2006. "Research Summary of National 863 Ultra-Super-Critical Coal-Fired Power Plant Technology." Presented at the 2nd Annual Conference, China Ultra-Super-Critical Coal-Fired Power Technology Cooperation Network, Qingdao, China. 《国家 863 课题 "燃煤超超临界发电技术" 研究结果简述 》, 中国超超临界火电机组技术协作网第二届年会.

2010. "Thoughts on the Research Objectives of Advanced Super-Critical Coal-Fired Power Plant Technology." Presented at the China Academy of Engineering and National Energy Administration Energy Conference. 《关于先进超超临界燃煤技术未来发展目标的思考》.

Zhao, X. and Ma, C. 2013. "Deregulation, vertical unbundling and the performance of China's large coal-fired power plants." *Energy Economics.* 40. pp. 474–83. https://doi.org/10.1016/j.eneco.2013.08.003.

Zhao, X., S. Zhang, R. Yang, and M. Wang. 2012. "Constraints on the effective utilization of wind power in China: An illustration from the northeast China grid." *Renewable and Sustainable Energy Reviews.* 16(7). pp. 4508–14. https://doi.org/10.1016/j.rser.2012.04.029.

Zhao, X., S. Zhang, Y. Zou, and J. Yao, 2013. "To what extent does wind power deployment affect vested interests? A case study of the Northeast China Grid." *Energy Policy.* 63. pp. 814–22. https://doi.org/10.1016/j.enpol.2013.08.092.

Zhi, Q. and M. M. Pearson. 2016. "China's Hybrid Adaptive Bureaucracy: The Case of the 863 Program for Science and Technology." *Governance.* https://doi.org/10.1111/gove.12245.

Zhong, H., Q. Xia, Y Chen, and C. Kang. 2015. "Energy-saving generation dispatch toward a sustainable electric power industry in China." *Energy Policy.* 83. pp. 14–25. https://doi.org/10.1016/j.enpol.2015.03.016.

5

When Global Technology Meets Local Standards

Reassessing China's Communications Policy in the Age of Platform Innovation

Eric Thun and Timothy Sturgeon

INTRODUCTION

The process of industrial development is never simple or straight forward, but historically speaking, the demarcation between the global and the local was relatively clear. In the classic "late" developmental states (e.g. Japan and South Korea), domestic markets were protected, foreign technologies were licensed or reverse engineered and then incrementally improved upon, and more or less self-contained national industries developed over time. The national champions that were the focus of government largesse and discipline were then put through their paces in global markets and export assistance and import protection was gradually drawn down. Protection and import substitution policies for domestic markets were followed by export promotion and gradual and selective exposure to international competition at home. As industries matured, and domestic technological capabilities advanced, aided by national laboratories, a new class of technocrats, and politically insulated policy-makers, sectoral succession and outward investment eventually ensued sequentially in a pattern akin to "flying geese," accelerating structural transformation from agriculture, through higher levels of industrialization, and into services (Akamatsu 1961; Kojima 2000).

The orderly and sequential character of this "Late Development" model, and the sequence of policies required to see it through, with Japan and South Korea held out as emblematic cases, have long been the subject of debate and caveat, with details exposed, differences and similarities between countries and outcomes pointed out (Amsden 1989; Wade 1992; Evans 1995) and "varieties of capitalism" noted

(Schneider 2009; Nölke and Vliegenthart 2009; Carney et al. 2009). It has also been shown that countries have been able to "leapfrog" over sequential development stages by attracting foreign direct investment (FDI) in technology-intensive sectors, and "upgrade" by providing increasingly advanced intermediate goods and services according to the requirements of distant buyers (Gereffi 1994; Humphrey and Schmitz 2002; Feenstra and Hamilton 2005).

In the 2000s and beyond, global integration began to alter the character of development in new ways. As the importance of FDI has risen, and international sourcing has become more commonplace, the most dynamic segments of developing countries' economies have become integrated into industries that are both vertically and geographically fragmented in what have come to be referred to as global value chains (GVCs) (e.g. Gereffi and Sturgeon 2005; OECD 2009; World Bank 2015). With the continued spread and maturing of GVCs, Whittaker et al. (2010) observe a nearly complete breakdown of development stages. Development can be "compressed" in terms of the rate of growth, but also in terms of the spaces available for local firms and policy-makers to operate within. As a result, while industrial policy can still seek to shift costs and incentives through measures such as import taxation, local content rules, research and development (R&D) spending requirements, and export incentives, key economic actors are far less embedded in the political economy than what was envisioned by Late Development theorists. As the line separating what is global and what is local is more difficult to discern, the State's reins over the processes of industrialization loosen. The main reason is that in many industries, especially those that are technologically intensive, industry ecosystems have become global in scope, rendering it impossible to develop competitive industries within a "terrarium" of protected national industries or markets.

TELECOM AND THE CHINESE STATE

The mobile telecommunications industry in China perfectly illustrates the challenge of pursuing national objectives in the context of global-scale industry ecosystems. The information and communications technology (ICT) sector in general, and telecom in particular, have long been targets for states with developmental and security objectives. In telecom, historically, there was typically one national provider and the rents from these monopolies were used to fund R&D activities and cultivate complete value chains within national borders (Hess and Coe

2006, p. 1313) [1] While the Chinese government circa the 1990s found this formula comfortable, a combination of deregulation in the West and technological change has rendered it impossible to pursue.

In the space of only ten years (1997–2007), mobile telecommunications grew from a small, geographically fragmented industry into one of the world's largest and most globally integrated. After the 2007 introduction of the modern "smartphone," mobile handsets have been transformed from expensive novelties for making phone calls on the move to cheap, nearly ubiquitous – and essential – internet-connected devices for managing life and work. Embedded within these devices, and "riding" on top of them, are multiple "technology platform" layers, each with its own ecosystem of core technology vendors (platform leaders), third party developers, and users. The pace of innovation and change, and the competitive dynamics within this nested set of technology ecosystems places the industry far beyond the control of policy-makers.

At the same time, telecommunications networks continue to be viewed as strategic national assets. Even though it has become impossible to create a mobile telecommunications system without reliance on global technology, national operators are still common, and government scrutiny of equipment purchases for national infrastructure is the norm. In China, political sensitivities make the sector a particularly important target of state control.

In this chapter we explore the tension between the pursuit of national policy objectives and the realities of global economic integration. In the case of mobile telecom in China, the state has deployed a full arsenal of industrial policy tools – *de jure* standard setting, technology licensing and development, selection and support of specific firms as "national champions," restrictions on foreign entry, localization requirements for those firms that do enter, etc. – in an effort to support the development of domestic firms. Yet success has been elusive and very partial. We argue that state efforts to control the development of the mobile telecommunications industry have been hampered by the pace and nature of innovation in the sector. While the state was using command-and-control methods to restrict market access and subsidize the development of technologies and firms in core "interconnect" technologies, and the chipsets in which they are embedded, the advent of the smartphone shifted the locus of

---

[1] For example, citing national security concerns, the United States government effectively granted control over the radio industry to the Radio Corporation of America (RCA) with the cessation of World War I (Sturgeon 2000).

competition toward "platforms" located "downstream" in the value chain (i.e. closer to the consumer): operating systems, applications, and mobile services. As this process played out, interconnect standards and technologies have become largely generic and without the power to set the terms of competition. While Chinese vendors of smartphones and mobile services have flourished under the protection of the "Chinese Firewall," they rely extensively on the full suite of "upstream" technology platforms available in the form of interconnect solutions and other embedded technologies, semiconductor chipsets, and operating systems. Thus, a mobile handset sold anywhere by any company, including in China by Chinese brands, relies to a high degree on technologies embedded in a variety of internationally sourced and imported hardware and software components and sub-systems.

MOBILE TELECOM – HOW IT WORKS

In order to understand the interplay of policy and technological change, a short and very basic industry primer is needed. The mobile telecom industry can roughly be divided into five primary bundles of inter-related activities: network equipment design and manufacturing (e.g. cell towers, base stations, and switching equipment); handset design and manufacturing; network management and service provision (e.g. mobile operators or carriers); core components and software for both network equipment and handsets (e.g. chipsets and operating systems); and mobile applications and services (e.g. Uber, WeChat, and Facebook). In this section, we briefly discuss the evolution of two features of mobile telecom networks that span, and in many ways define, the first four segments of the industry value chain mentioned above: network interconnect standards and handset design. The fifth segment, mobile applications and services, now rides over the top of mobile networks, in large part independently of the rest of the system, the importance of which, as competition and profits migrate to this segment, will be highlighted later.

Mobile Interconnect Standards

Within a mobile network, service is divided into small cells with a reception tower and base station at the core of each cell. A call (or data transmission) originating from a handset is sent to the nearest base station using a specifically assigned radio frequency, and as the user moves between cells, the call is automatically switched from one base station to another.[2] From there the signal is sent to a central switching office, where the connection is made to broader, wired communications networks (including the Internet), and then on to the recipient. When the recipient is another mobile user, the signal is sent to a base station and cell tower near the user, and then wirelessly to the handset.

Interconnect standards play a crucial role in ensuring that connections can be made reliably. They form the basic "language" that handsets use to connect to the subscriber's network. In addition to using different "handshake" and "routing" protocols, various standards occupy different "bands," or airwave segments (electromagnetic spectrum). In the case of phone calls analog signals (e.g. the human voice) must be converted to digital signals (and vice versa) by "modems" that reside in the handset's "chipset," and because the digital signals must adhere to the interconnect standards supported by the carrier, modems/chipsets/handsets can only be used on compatible networks.

Because handsets must be compatible with the networks they connect to, and this compatibility is ensured by a specific interconnect standard, policy makers in China came to the conclusion that they could promote domestic companies by developing a unique, country-specific standard.

But China could not simply go its own way. General interconnect standards are set by the International Telecommunications Union (ITU), an international standard setting body based in Geneva. The ITU organizes study groups to produce draft recommendations on international specifications for each generation of mobile telephony (1G, 2G, 3G, 4G), and these broad standards are then approved, modified, or rejected by world telecommunications standardization conferences that include representatives from member states, industry associations, and firms. How companies propose to meet these standards is up to them, but since interoperability is needed to allow equipment such as mobile phone handsets and wireless infrastructure (towers, base stations, and network switching equipment) to interact, the strongest players, often in concert, introduce their own solutions for specific interconnect standards that meet the requirements in each general standard, and then submit these to the ITU for approval.

In each generation, the specific standards have been defined by the companies that have supplied novel and effective technical solutions, and then effectively used their market power and knowledge of the standard setting process to incorporate their patent-protected technology in a specific standard (e.g. GSM and CDMA, see Table 5.1). These specific

---

[2] If the next base station is fully occupied with active calls, the signal is "dropped."

Table 5.1 *General and Specific Interconnect Standards in Mobile Communications*

General Standard (requirements)	Specific Standard (solution)	With IP Provided Mainly by …	Deployed Mainly in …	Rough Characterization
2G (1990s)	GSM	Nokia, Siemens, Alcatel (Europe), Qualcomm (US)	Europe, Latin America, USA, etc.	2G Europe standard
	CDMA	Qualcomm, Nvidia (US)	US	2G US standard
3G (2000s)	WCDMA	Nokia, Siemens, Alcatel (Europe), Qualcomm (US), NTT, DoCoMo (Japan)	Europe	3G Europe standard
			Latin America, Japan	
	CDMA2000 (EV-DO)	5 telecommunications standards bodies: ARIB and TTC (Japan), CWTS (China), TTA (Korea) and TIA (US and Canada)	US	3G US standard
	TD-SCDMA	Siemens (Germany) Datang (China)	China	3G China standard
4G (2010s)	FDD-LTE	All incumbents	Globally	4G Global standard
	TD-LTE	China plus incumbents	Initially China, Sweden, and a few developing countries, etc.	

Source: Authors, with information drawn from various sources, including ITU and the Universal Mobile Telephone System, see: www.umtsworld.com/technology/technology.htm.

interconnect solutions can then be adopted by weaker players, who pay royalties to standard setting firms. The choices that are made are important because the technologies that underlie each standard generation tend to be path-dependent: they are built up in additive fashion over many years, and are made to be "backwardly compatible" with previous standards so older phones and network equipment are not rendered immediately and completely obsolete when newer standards arrive.

Handset Design

Early generations of mobile handsets were relatively integral products, meaning that there was little interchangeability between the subsystems of each company's products. Nokia, for instance, developed the full range of technical capabilities in both hardware (e.g. modem chipsets, circuit boards and devices, housings) and software (e.g. operating system, protocol commands, and the user interface), and maintained close, long-term relationships with suppliers. The problem was that it was extremely expensive and slow to redesign the entire system to create each new generation of phone, and the addition of new features and fierce competition between incumbent firms motivated a wave of outsourcing. As the technology matured, and the interfaces between subsystems became better codified, and handset firms were able to rely more heavily on external suppliers for core components. Nokia relied on Texas Instruments for chipsets and licensed its Symbian operating system to competitors[3], while retaining a largely integral structure for the remainder. Other firms, such as Motorola, moved to more complete modular architectures (Fine 2005).

The shift to modularity in mobile telecom made it possible for firms at multiple levels of the value chain to develop core technologies, and when these were successful and widely adapted, some, like Symbian and Qualcomm chipsets became de facto standards for large segments of the industry. The importance of interoperability in the industry drove significant network effects and allowed firms with dominant positions in core technologies significant leverage within the value chain as "platform leaders."[4]

---

[3] Symbian, originally developed by a UK-based software company and compatible only with (UK-based) ARM processors, was pushed hardest by Nokia but also used in keyboard-based "smartphones" made by Motorola and Sony-Ericsson.

[4] A platform is a modular element in a larger system that establishes a set of functional parameters for other system elements. The firm in control of a successful platform can leverage core technology to establish the de facto standards or rules through which other firms can participate by offering complementary goods or services (Gawer and Cusumano 2014, Pon et al. 2014; Van Alstyne et al. 2016).

CHINA'S MOBILE TELECOM STANDARDS GAMBIT: TD-SCDMA

Like the rest of the world, China's first large-scale deployment of mobile communications came in the 1990s, in the 2G era. The 2G network in China consisted of two standards – GSM and CDMA – and four foreign vendors (Motorola, Ericsson, Nokia, and Siemens) controlled more than 90 percent of the market (Yu 2011, p. 1082). Although efforts were made to force technology transfer to Chinese firms by tying market access to local production (either by foreign subsidiaries, joint ventures (JVs), or local firms), domestic firms only were able to produce low-end phones (Tan 2002). The maturity of 2G technologies meant that most of the significant technologies were patented and that foreign firms were much more advanced than Chinese competitors, and hence could be very selective about transferring activities to China (Vialle et al. 2012; Gao et al. 2014).

State Action

When the ITU issued a call for proposals for 3G standards in 1997, China's Ministry of Post and Telecommunication (MPT) believed that China had a significant opportunity. MPT, and its affiliate the China Academy of Telecommunications Technology (CATT), had been exploring 3G technologies since 1995 with a firm called Xinwei, a JV between CATT and two overseas Chinese engineers.[5] Another MPT study group – the "3G Transmission Technology Assessment and Coordination Group" – chose to adapt time-division duplex (TDD) technology, a transmission and reception approach that had been developed by Siemens, but not chosen for inclusion in the European 3G standard (Gao et al. 2014).[6] Based on

---

[5] The original focus of Xinwei was a "smart antennae" that was able to differentiate the direction from which it received a signal thereby reducing the amount of handset power required to reach the antennae and increasing the number of handsets that could be covered by a single base station. Because this technology was not compatible with CDMA, the company began to explore SCDMA, which in contrast to CDMA, synchronizes the transmission from handsets to the base station to reduce interference between transmissions and improve data transmission speed. These initial efforts were not intended to be the basis of a new telecom standard – the primary objective was to provide an inexpensive alternative to existing mobile and fixed line networks – but the early experiments showed promise and Zhou Huan, the Director of MPT Science and Technology Department, invested 20 million RMB in Xinwei from the "Key Technologies R&D program of the Ninth Five Year Plan" (Marukawa 2010).

[6] Because TDD allocates reception and transmission to different time slots in the same frequency band, it allows an asymmetric flow of data between transmission and reception (see www.techopedia.com/definition/27019/time-division-duplex-tdd (accessed December 17, 2018)).

thung Iechnnlngic), the China Wlreless Telecommunication Standard Group proposed TD-SCDMA to the ITU in 1998 as a candidate for a 3G standard.

Within the Chinese government, there were multiple motivations for this bid. A motivation for many policy-makers was the desire to foster technological capabilities in Chinese firms, and to do so rapidly. In China's 2G network only 8 percent of equipment (including mobile handset and base-station equipment) was sourced from local manufacturers, while 30 percent was sourced from JVs and 62 percent was imported from foreign firms (Chen et al. 2002, p. 50). Even when equipment was manufactured within China, the royalty and licensing fees that had to be made to foreign firms and associations were high (Vialle et al. 2012).[7] If Chinese firms could contribute more technology to international standards, the thinking went, they would pay less in royalties and be more profitable, and consequently have more to invest in R&D. Chinese firms would have stronger technological capabilities and hence their products would command higher prices in the marketplace. Because the standard would be global, the potential for adoption outside of China would broaden the scope of the potential market.

NDRC and the Ministry of Science and Technology (MOST) were in favor of a rapid shift toward indigenous innovation (Gao and Liu 2012, p. 538), and the Datang Group, the industrial affiliate of CATT that was charged with leading the TD-SCDMA development effort, adroitly exploited these preferences to gain support for the standard within NDRC and MOST (Gao 2014, p. 602). As one interview respondent observed, the policy-makers that hoped to promote indigenous innovation in China considered the advances achieved by firms such as Huawei in 2G (i.e. cost innovation) to be "small" innovation. They wanted "big" innovation, and believed a specific Chinese interconnect standard could deliver it (Interview, July 23, 2012).

So, nationalism was an important motivation. Royalty payments to foreign firms were opposed not only for financial reasons, but due to a feeling that it was simply not right for China to have to make payments to Western firms and industry associations that were exploiting China's promising domestic market (Chen et al. 2002; Interview, July 26, 2012). "This comes down to national pride. The government promotes

---

[7] Although official figures are not published, the royalties on 2G network equipment has been estimated at 10–13% of ex-works selling price for companies with no patents to trade (Vialle et al. 2012).

indigenous technology because it wants the Chinese to own some intellectual property," explained the director of government relations at a foreign-invested equipment maker (Hsueh 2015, p. 640).

National security concerns were an additional motivation. On top of the typical desire for levers for control over communications in case of wartime, and for tracking of international communications for national security purposes, China has especially robust peacetime efforts to monitor and quell social discussion and organizing that could lead to political unrest. For many developing countries, this sort of local control is out of reach, and foreign technology and even foreign carriers are accepted as a price of developing and maintaining a modern mobile communications system, but in China, the idea of local control was plausible given the size of the market and its high importance to the state. As Hsueh argues, the weight given to security arguments varied within the telecom sector: service provision was seen as highly strategic (i.e. ownership of the network), network equipment less so, and consumer equipment (i.e. handsets) was the lowest (Hsueh 2015).

The push for domestic control was not monolithic, however. Another set of policy-makers in China was driven by the desire to deploy the lowest cost, highest quality communications network in the shortest possible time. A good mobile communications infrastructure, for both voice and data, is increasingly important for the efficiency of all industries and activities. The main tool of these policy-makers was the promotion of an open, competitive market with free access to foreign technology and robust competition among carriers. As Gao and Liu argue, the Ministry of Information Industries (MII, which was replaced by the Ministry of Industry and Information Technology (MIIT) in 2008), was supportive of a Chinese standard, but it did not have high expectations and wanted the policy to complement rather than replace foreign technology, which had served the operators well (Gao and Liu 2012, p. 541). However, even this group drew the line at allowing foreign carriers to operate within China, as has become common in Europe, Latin America, and most developing countries with deregulation.

The ITU's acceptance of TD-SCDMA as a 3G standard in May 2000 and the Third Generation Partnership Project's (3GPP) acceptance in March 2001 began an urgent process of design, testing, and commercialization in China. The standard was far behind competing standards – Japan's NTT DoCoMo launched the first commercial WCDMA 3G network in 2001 – and the state played a key role in organizing the catch-up process.

First, the Datang Group was given key research staff necessary for this effort (Tsai and Wang 2011, p. 10). Datang became the focal point of a network of scholars, researchers, and government officials that were supportive of China's efforts to develop TD-SCDMA, and allowed the company to effectively lobby for government to support (Gao and Liu 2012; Gao 2014). Second, the TD-SCDMA Alliance was created to coordinate activities between firms and arrange for the sharing of intellectual property (IP) rights. NDRC's support for the Alliance ensured that powerful domestic firms such as Huawei and ZTE were willing to join and support the efforts of Datang. The Alliance expanded from eight members in 2002 to eighty-four in 2011 (Tsai and Wang 2011; Gao and Liu 2012). Third, MII, which had replaced MPT in 1998), NDRC, and MOST jointly invested RMB 700 million to facilitate the research activities of firms involved in the Alliance and to cover payments to Datang required by member firms for access to the company's IP (Gao and Liu 2012). State banks (ICBC, China Construction Bank, and Huaxia Bank) provided loans of approximately RMB 1.5 billion, and the China Development Bank supported the construction and testing of TD-SCDMA network equipment with loans of RMB 38 billion between 2005 and 2007 (Tsai and Wang 2011, p. 11). Finally, the government (largely NDRC), initiated the Large-Scale TD-SCDMA Network Application Trial Project, and used its administrative power to convince mobile operators to carry out pre-commercialization trials in five cities in 2006, and ten more in 2007 (Gao and Liu 2012, p. 539). Even with this support, development and implementation took a relatively long time; after much delay, China's largest mobile operator, China Mobile, launched TD-SCDMA in 2009, nearly ten years after its acceptance by the ITU.

Chinese Firm Responses

Although the objective of Chinese policy-makers was to use the development of a specific Chinese 3G telecommunications standard to promote indigenous innovation, and investments in the technology were very large, the reception of firms was mixed. Many firms in China learned a great deal by interacting closely with foreign firms with deep technological capabilities, as customers, suppliers, and licensers; and the interest of these firms was the overall financial position of the company, not just royalty costs.[8]

---

[8] In fact, we were told that royalty costs are 6% of chipset costs and 3% of handset costs; a small but significant share given the low profit margins for most handset firms.

While the Chinese mobile telecom market was poised to become the largest single country market in the world (as indeed it has), a standard deployed only in China would limit the potential of any Chinese firm with hopes to sell globally.

Carriers

The primary concern of the *mobile operators* (also known as *carriers*) was to have reliable equipment, and if they were using global standards, foreign firms would be able to offer mature technologies that had been tested and improved in multiple markets. Carriers preferred to adapt the foreign technologies that were the natural evolution for existing 2G networks (the Europe/Japan dominated WCDMA and US dominated CDMA2000) rather than build a parallel network for TD-SCDMA, and it was widely acknowledged that the standard would be a burden to the operator that had to use it (Yu 2011, p. 1084).

The choice of China Mobile as the carrier to launch TD-SCDMA was clearly designed to maximize the opportunities for the domestic standard. China Mobile was the country's largest carrier, by far, and the size of its subscriber base of over 500 million created two critical advantages. First, because telephone numbers were not portable between carriers in China at the time, and a stable number is extremely important for a highly mobile population, the existing base of 2G China Mobile subscribers gave it a critical advantage in 3G. Second, the standard would only succeed if a range of handsets, especially inexpensive models, were made available to consumers, and China Mobile had the leverage needed to persuade foreign handset makers to invest in TD-SCDMA-compatible handsets. From the perspective of foreign firms, however, the market for TD-SCDMA compatible phones was far from attractive: at the time, developing a handset for a new standard took an enormous amount of R&D, the initial market would be small, and there was only a single customer. China Mobile used carrots to entice foreign firms to develop Chinese standard handsets – a fund of RMB 650 million to subsidize the handset development process[9] – but sticks were employed as well: foreign firms recognized that China Mobile had a long memory and there would be repercussions if

---

[9] Early in 2009 there was a bidding process in which foreign and domestic handset firms needed to partner up with a chipset producer to bid. There were separate subsidies for high- and low-end phones. Winners were guaranteed volume and received R&D funding (about $20 million per bid). The funding was small change to foreign firms, but could be important to domestic firms (Interview, August 22, 2012).

they did not support its TD-SCDMA development efforts (Interview, August 22, 2012).

Without the strong arm of the state, however, it is unlikely that China Mobile would have chosen to adopt TD-SCDMA. Wang Jianzhou, the President of China Mobile, reportedly protested about the burden that was being placed on the firm, and had to be cajoled with both threats (China Mobile would not receive *any* 3G license) and inducements (the state would subsidize the expected losses that would result from launching TD-SCDMA) (Tsai and Wang 2011, p. 17).[10] As the President of a centrally controlled state firm, and with his promotion controlled by the Organization Department of the Party, Wang was unlikely to have pushed his protests too far.

Handset Firms

The domestic *mobile handset manufacturers* expected little benefit from TD-SCDMA because these firms sourced modem chipsets from global firms. Ironically, the dependence of Chinese handset firms on global technology suppliers was a result of policy initiatives motivated by the same sentiments that led to TD-SCDMA. In 1999, in an effort to trade market access for technology, the State Council imposed strict regulations on the mobile handset sector and focused on JVs with foreign firms as the primary means of technology transfer in the sector. Firms were required to have a license to produce and market mobile handsets, permission was required to add production lines, quotas were placed on imports, and minimum export ratios and local content requirements were imposed on the JVs (Imai and Shiu 2007, p. 7).[11] Under these conditions, the market share of domestic handset firms increased, but the JVs were essentially manufacturing bases for the foreign partners, and heavily reliant on imported components. The domestic handset firms that did not have JV partners sourced technology from foreign firms that were locked out of the Chinese market by the new regulations, primarily Korean and Taiwanese firms (Kimura 2009; Fan 2010; Brandt and Thun 2011). Given deep reliance on foreign technology, the introduction of TD-SCDMA gave handset firms little benefit.

---

[10] In 2005, Wang told the media "I hope China Mobile can use the most advanced technology for the 3G market," and this was widely interpreted as a preference for foreign technology (Min 2014).

[11] The new regulation was a joint proposal from MII and the State Planning Commission titled "Some propositions on promoting the development of the mobile information industry" (known commonly as "Decree No. 5") (Imai and Shiu 2007).

Equipment and Chipset Suppliers

The most likely beneficiaries of the domestic standard were *telecom equipment firms* and *chipset design firms*, which might benefit from the level playing field vis-à-vis foreign firms created by TD-SCDMA. The viewpoints of firms seem to vary according to two inter-related variables: the closeness of the firm's ties to the central government and the extent to which the firm focused on the domestic market. At one end of the spectrum was state-owned Datang, a firm whose fate was almost entirely tied to TD-SCDMA. In 2001, early in TD-SCDMA's development, Datang's market share of the 2G network equipment market in China was less than 1 percent, and the firm was behind Huawei and ZTE on almost every performance measure (Tsai and Wang 2011; Yu 2011).[12] The raison d'être of the firm was the development and commercialization of TD-SCDMA, and for this it was almost completely reliant on the state: personnel were transferred from CATT, financing came from MII and the state banks, and administrative support was needed for commercialization (e.g. network trials). As several interview respondents argued, there would be no Datang today if there were no Chinese standard (Interview, July 20, 2012a and July 20, 2012b).

Spreadtrum, a Chinese IC design firm founded by returnees from the United States in 2001, had a fate that was similarly tied to TD-SCDMA. When the firm decided to develop a 3G modem chipset in 2001, the initial plan was to focus on the more mature WCDMA market. However, as one Spreadtrum executive explained, a founder had close relationships at China Mobile, and this gave him a sense of the momentum that was gathering behind the domestic standard, and this led the firm to focus on the new TD-SCDMA standard (Fuller 2016, p. 252). Supporting the effort also made it easier to attract financing (Interview, July 27, 2012).

At the other end of the spectrum was Huawei, an equipment maker that demonstrated little early interest in investing in TD-SCDMA. While some observers attributed Huawei's lack of enthusiasm for TD-SCDMA to uncertainty as to whether and how strongly the government would support the standard (Gao 2014), this misses the crucial point: Huawei's orientation was explicitly global and the firm did not want to be distracted by a Chinese standard.[13]

---

[12] In 2001, Datang had a 1% market share for mobile switching subsystems and .2% for base station subsystems (Yu 2011). The sales revenue of Datang in 2002 was US $247 million (compared to US $2700 million for Huawei) and profits were US $36 million (compared to US $320 million at Huawei) (Tsai and Wang 2011).

[13] According to Gao (2014), the diversity of interests and preferences within the government, particularly between MII and MOST/NDRC created policy "incoherence." If the

In contrast to Datang, Huawei was not state-owned and received little state support during the firm's early years of development. When 2G networks were being installed in the 1990s, Huawei had few opportunities to sell its equipment in the domestic mobile market, and thus looked to sell abroad. China Mobile did not believe in the quality of Huawei equipment and relied on foreign suppliers for its network; China Unicom and China Telecom invested in personal handyphone systems (PHS) that allowed them to get around not being granted a mobile license, and this was not a technology that Huawei had developed (Interview, July 23, 2012).[14] So the only choice for the firm was to seek opportunities in export markets. Consequently, at the same time that Datang was leading the domestic push for TD-SCDMA, Huawei was concentrating on global expansion. In 1999, Huawei made its first major foreign sales (in Yemen and Laos); three years later international sales were 18 percent of total sales and domestic sales were declining by 21 percent a year. Five years later exports were 40 percent of total sales. By 2005, the company was providing internet and telecom switching equipment to thirty of the world's top fifty telecom operating companies (Nie et al. 2012, pp. 71–2).

This is not to say that Huawei turned its back on TD-SCDMA entirely. As the extent of the domestic support for the standard became clear, Huawei began to devote substantial resources to developing TD-SCDMA-compatible equipment. The firm joined the Industry Alliance, created a JV in Beijing with Siemens to develop, manufacture and market TD-SCDMA equipment, and invested heavily in its own R&D efforts in the technology.

The case of ZTE lies somewhere between Datang and Huawei, both with respect to the strength of its ties to the state and the extent to which it had globalized. ZTE was not as directly connected to MII as Datang, but it was a state firm (under the control of the Ministry of Aerospace Industry) with many of the characteristics of state ownership. ZTE relied on state procurement within China more heavily than Huawei, and was slower to expand abroad. At a time when half of Huawei's total sales were abroad, ZTE's foreign sales were little more than 10 percent (Fuller 2016, p. 84). ZTE took a broad approach to technologies and markets, and the firm began investing in TD-SCDMA technologies in 2005 as part of its portfolio approach. As one manager explained, the board of ZTE is composed of high-level

government had sent clearer signals to the firms, Huawei (and others) would have committed more resources to the technology earlier.

[14] A PHS system is somewhat akin to handsets that operated like a cordless phone with a range of several hundred yards. The systems were very inexpensive and popular in rural markets.

people with very good ties within the central government and they were quite certain that TD-SCDMA would be deployed and felt the firm had to be prepared (Interview, September 27, 2012).

FROM FEATURE PHONES TO SMARTPHONES

While the Chinese state faced many obstacles in its effort to use industrial policy to promote the development of domestic firms in mobile telecom, none was more important than the inability of the state to keep pace with the evolving technology of the sector and the strategic actions of firms.

Taiwan's MediaTek, Mobile Phone Reference Designs, and the Rise of the "Shanzhai"

The rise of MediaTek (MTK), a chip design company based in Taiwan, provided an early indication of how quickly state objectives could be upended by a new technology. Building on a core competency in digital signal processing (DSP) technologies gained from supplying chip sets for optical drives and DVD players (for which the market was exploding at the time), MTK first developed a "turn-key" approach to mobile phone development in 2004. The company's "reference designs" meant that small Chinese handset companies could quickly and easily develop generic "white box" phones (Shih et al. 2010). While early MediaTek reference designs included modem chips sourced from third parties, the acquisition of Analog Devices' mobile telecom division in 2007 vastly increased their capabilities and allowed them to begin to offer reference designs for all major 3G specific standards, including TD-SCDMA. A company press release (MediaTek 2007) stated:

Through this acquisition, MediaTek's wireless handset division gains: a global team of approximately 400 experienced product development and customer support professionals; an established customer base around the world; new baseband chipsets and radio transceiver products, including GSM, GPRS, EDGE, WCDMA, and TD-SCDMA chipsets to further strengthen its existing portfolio; and key patents and intellectual property to increase MediaTek's competitiveness.

MediaTek reference designs combined, or "encapsulated" modem chips with chips providing additional functions (e.g. power management and digital signal processing for multimedia) and also included user interface and application software (e.g. basic OS software, music and – later – video playback, and simple applications such as address books and alarm clocks). For small, technologically limited Chinese "shanzhai" handset companies,

MediaTek reference designs lowered costs, increased performance, reduced power requirements and, most critically, simplified the design process by eliminating tasks that previously had to be performed in-house or coordinated by handset manufacturers (Kimura 2009; Imai and Shiu 2010). Handset producers could easily customize handsets, albeit superficially (Brandt and Thun 2011), with the tradeoff of dramatically reduced R&D and design requirements. At the same time, MTK was able to benefit from the feedback it received from its customer ecosystem, and make rapid improvements. As a result, the share of handsets with MTK platform sold by Chinese firms increased from 13 percent in 2004 to 71 percent in 2005 (Kimura 2009, p. 16).

Significantly, the domestic firms that had benefited the most from the central government's tight licensing regime were not early adopters of MTK's platform. Ningbo Bird, the leading domestic handset firms at the time the MTK platform was introduced, instead worked closely with Texas Instruments (TI), the US-based chip vendor, and had invested a great deal of resources developing software that was compatible with TI chips (Interview, August 4, 2009). Bird was unwilling to switch to MTK because the technical competencies that Bird had developed in its relationship with TI were thought to be a source of competitive advantage, and adopting MTK's turnkey solution would render such competencies irrelevant. The industry leader soon found itself swamped by the superior products offered by hundreds of small scale firms, each with very limited technical capabilities of their own, but willing to rely on the MTK platform, which allowed them to be flexible and responsive to market demand (Shih et al. 2010).[15]

The Rise of the Smartphone

The emergence of the MTK platform was only a harbinger of major changes coming to the architecture of mobile phone handsets. An even more fundamental shift came with the transition to smartphones after 2007, which shifted the locus of innovation in the industry even more thoroughly from the handset's modem to its operating system (OS), downstream applications, and eventually, web-based services. The performance

---

[15] The number of unauthorized handsets produced in China by "shanzhai" handset firms increased from 37 million units in 2005 to 228 million in 2010, an increase facilitated by a relaxation of the licensing regime in 2005 (and then elimination in 2007) (Brandt and Thun 2011).

of any handset can be measured along two basic dimensions: the amount of information and speed with which the modem transmits information across the network (i.e. 1G, 2G, 3G, etc.) and the speed and capabilities of the central processing and graphics processing units (central processing unit (CPU) and graphics processing unit (GPU)), which manage applications running on the phone and the rendering of images on the screen. The capabilities of a smart phone's processors, along with the flexibility allowed by the touch screen control pioneered by Apple in 2007, which dispensed with the physical keyboard, essentially allowed the phone to become a mobile, Internet-connected computing platform.[16] As the increase in processor power made it possible to do more things with a phone, the operating system became the platform for organizing and structuring the broad ecosystem of applications and complements on the handset. After 2007, the global industry quickly became dominated by two de facto standards, with two forms of governance, Apple's iOS and Google's Android.

Apple iOS

With its iPhone handset, Apple established a platform with a partly open architecture. Third-party developers can access the platform and design tools, and sell applications (apps) on Apple's on-line store, but governance of the resulting ecosystem system is closed. Apple does not share details of its operating system and sets relatively tight rules for application designers (Van Alstyne et al. 2016). At the heart of the Apple ecosystem is the iPhone, launched in January 2007, a product with a proprietary operating system (iOS) that made it impossible for other companies easily (or legally) to produce handsets compatible with Apple's ecosystem. The iPhone was set up to easily download and play music (from iTunes), access the (real) Internet,[17] and download a host of applications (apps) developed by third parties that were carefully vetted by Apple and made available on Apple's App Store. The handset was the bottleneck: none of its functions was new, but it packaged and integrated them more elegantly than had been done previously, and Apple was the first company to find broad market success with the full screen touch interface. The flexibility and power of the iPhone

---

[16] A smart phone can run on a 2G network, but the data will be transmitted more slowly. In China, many China Mobile subscribers used iPhones even though they could not run on the 3G TD-SCDMA network. These users either relied on the 2G network or Wi-Fi networks.

[17] Apple was the first to cross the threshold of using a handset to access "real" Internet pages rather than websites with simpler content specifically stripped down for mobile users.

allowed users to take advantage of new content and applications blossoming on the Internet at the time, such as YouTube, eBay, and Facebook, without using a desktop or notebook computer. Developers were eager to make apps for the device, the blossoming ecosystem made the phone more attractive to customers, and as more customers bought the device, developers were even more eager to create apps: a classic network effect.

Google Android OS

Google launched the Android OS for mobile handsets in September 2008, partly in response to the iPhone. In contrast to iOS, Android has an open technology architecture and largely open governance. Like Microsoft's Windows OS, the Android was made available to branded hardware firms, but, in stark contrast to Windows, it was licensed for free and its "source code" published through the Android Open Source Project for all to use or modify as needed. Google imposed some rules on the ecosystem through the Android Compatibility Program, which required that handset producers follow certain hardware specification and contract terms, and exerted some (light) control over the applications available on the Google Play online app marketplace.[18] As the leading Internet search company with revenues coming mainly from on-line ad placement fees, Google was more interested in seeing more people accessing the Internet (and thus Google search) more of the time. Continued growth in the use of their search engine would create vastly more revenue than fees from Android licenses.

On the other hand, some control over the user experience was needed to protect the brand. The Compatibility Program allowed Google to reduce excessive variation across hardware devices, creating a more consistent environment for both application developers and end-users. As a Google manager explained in an interview, "If you have a seamless user experience within the ecosystem, this increases the switching cost of moving to another" (Interview, August 8, 2016). In exchange for participation, certified-compatible handset designers were allowed to use the Android logo and trademark, and were given a more robust version of the OS and access to the full suite of Google services (e.g. Gmail, Google Maps, and Google Play) (Pon et al. 2014).

The launch of a free and relatively open OS reflected the shifting power dynamics within the mobile telecom value chain. The initial obstacle to an

---

[18] In contrast to Apple, Google does not perform a manual review of apps before offering them for download in Google Play. Google also allowed users to download apps from marketplaces that it did not control (Pon et al. 2014).

open source OS were the mobile carriers in the United States, who maintained a dominant position in the early 2000s because handsets were included in mobile plans (Eadicicco 2015). The carriers determined the choice of handsets, the price, the marketing, and much of the content choices that were available to customers. Google's objective was to create a platform for distributing Google's services (and advertising) to mobile users, of course, and inevitably, this would reduce the power of the carriers.[19] When Google introduced its own proof-of-concept Android handset in 2008, very few handset OEM or carriers were interested, but the launch and instant success of the iPhone forced many within the value chain to reassess their strategy. Google worried that Apple would soon become the primary gatekeeper to mobile users, and Google search (and other apps) would be shunted aside for Apple equivalents, while mobile operators feared Apple's rapidly growing leverage within the mobile ecosystem given its exclusive deal with a single carrier – AT&T. Simply put, mobile handset firms and carriers not offering an iPhone or equivalent product faced irrelevance. Fears about an open source OS quickly seemed quaint, and both handset firms and carriers flocked to full touch screen smart phones running Android. Within just a few years, virtually the entire industry was running on either iOS or Android (see Figure 5.1). In the Chinese market, the OS market share was virtually identical to the global breakdown at the end of 2013, with the Android market share at 78.6 percent, iOS at 19 percent, and Windows at 1.1 percent.[20]

The impact of Android on the mobile telecom value chain was profound. Android made it difficult for handset firms (other than Apple) to differentiate themselves. Android gave handset makers a way to compete with Apple in the smartphone market, but, similar to MTK's reference designed for feature phones, also rendered most of the competencies associated with feature phone design and integration obsolete. Firms could use the open source version of Android, and achieve differentiation by customizing it, but this was only an option for firms with significant software development capability, since Google purposefully made the open source version far more bare bones than the proprietary version. Because consumers

---

[19] Google receives 30% of the revenue from every app sold in Google Play and the preinstalled apps included with Google Mobile Services (GMS) such as Gmail, YouTube, and browsers drive traffic to Google Search, Google's primary source of revenue.

[20] Liam Tung, "Windows Phone growth plateaus in Europe, Xiaomi beats Samsung in China," zdnet.com, January 27, 2014, www.zdnet.com/windows-phone-growth-pla teaus-in-europe-xiaomi-beats-samsung-in-china-7000025613/ (accessed December 17, 2018).

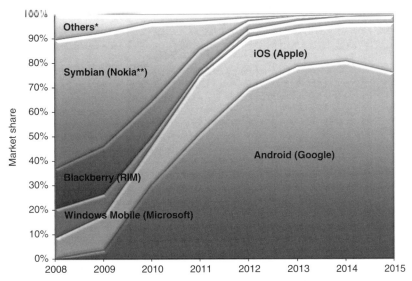

Figure 5.1 Worldwide Smartphone Operating System Market Share
Source: Authors based on Gartner Newsroom Press Releases (Various Years)
Notes: Based on unit sales to end users. * Others include Linex (open source) WebOS
(Hewlett Packard and others), and Bada (Samsung). ** Symbian, originally developed
by a UK-based software company and compatible only with (UK-based) ARM processors, was pushed the hardest Nokia but also used in keyboard-based "smartphones"
made by Motorola and Sony-Ericsson.

purchased a phone because it was on the Android platform and was part of
the Android ecosystem, the choice of handset brand was secondary.
By 2016, the profits for handset sales were almost entirely taken by two
firms, Apple (with 75 percent) and Samsung (with 25 percent) (Reisinger
2016), and as Figure 5.2 shows, the nearly complete loss of market share by
feature phone incumbents was dramatic. In fact, of all incumbent firms,
only Samsung was able to make the transition to Android successfully.

Because the Android OS required higher performance application processing chips, power in the chain reverted to those companies with deep
expertise in mobile telephony. Most important is ARM, a UK-based semiconductor design house. ARM licenses a wide variety of technology "IP
cores" to other mobile telecom chipset design companies, including Apple,
Qualcomm, MediaTek, and Huawei.[21] The strength of ARM's position is

---

[21] ARM supplies graphics processing unit (GPU) cores and central processing unit (CPU)
cores, and while ARM competes with Qualcomm and Nvidia in the market for GPUs,
both companies license ARM CPU cores for use in some of their processing chip set
products intended for mobile handsets.

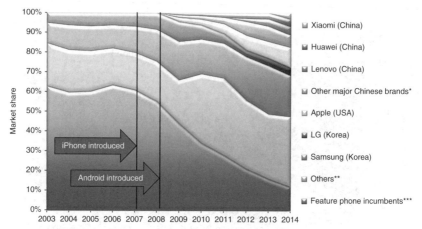

Figure 5.2 Worldwide Mobile Phone Market Share by Vendor
Source: Authors based on Gartner News room Press Releases (various years)
Notes: Based on unit sales to end users. Data are indicative only since not all firms were
identified in all years. From 2003 to 2008 only the top five firms were identified.
In subsequent years the top ten were identified.
* Unspecified Chinese brands identified in the data in various years include ZTE, TCL,
and Yulong.
** Brands identified in the data in various years include HTC (Taiwan), BenQ (Taiwan),
and RIM (Canada) are included the remainder "Others" category.
*** Feature phone incumbents include Nokia (Finland), Motorola (USA),
Sony-Ericsson (Japan-Sweden), and Siemens (Germany).

a result of significant technological and financial barriers to entry, but the
network effects of their CPU and SOC (system-on-chip combining CPUs
and GPUs) platforms is also crucial. On the supply side, ARM has about 900
"partners" producing complementary products and services; on the demand
side, about 200 semiconductor design firms licensing ARM designs. ARM
coordinates and cooperates with various platform leaders in other layers of
the value chain. It has worked with Android, for instance, to make sure that
new versions of the OS functioned smoothly with ARM's architectures, and
works with TSMC, the Taiwan-based chip contract manufacturer, or "foundry," to pre-test new versions of the CPU for manufacturability. As a result,
ARM's ready-to-manufacture verified IP cores speed up the process of chip
design for licensees and insure compatibility with other platform layers,
including Android. As a senior executive at ARM explained in an interview,
the multiple forms of coordination within the ecosystem increased barriers
to entry for competitors because breaking away from the ARM architecture,
would mean duplicating, not only the activities of ARM, but the activities of

the entire ecosystem (Interview, August 13, 2016). Most firms have found that paying the modest license fee and royalty was the easier solution, and 90 percent of the world's smartphones run on processors that contain some combination of ARM IP cores.[22]

Chinese Firm Responses

The transition to smartphones in China occurred rapidly, growing from 16 percent of the market in 2010 to nearly 90 percent in 2014 (Beijing Fuji Chimera Consulting, 2014). This reflected both the rising expectations (and incomes) of consumers and the willingness of mobile operators to subsidize smartphone sales to drive increased data usage on their networks and, for China Mobile, to help recoup its huge investment in TD-SCDMA.

The emergence of global technology platforms such as ARM technology cores, processor chips sets from Qualcomm and others offering broad functional capabilities, and the Android OS, created a double-edged sword for Chinese handset firms: they lowered the barriers to entry, but like any modular platform technology, made differentiation more difficult. The largest telecom equipment firms and personal computer firms – Huawei, ZTE, and Lenovo – used the Android platform to enter the handset business with models that had low-end specifications and could sell at much lower prices than higher-end products from Apple or Samsung. In 2014, for instance, models from these firms concentrated on the segment between RMB 1,000 and RMB 2,000, which was 30 percent of the domestic market, while Apple focused on the segment above RMB 4,000, 15 percent of the domestic market, and Samsung targeted the remaining middle market segment occupying the RMB 2,000 to RMB 4,000 range (Beijing Fuji Chimera Consulting 2014).

While telecom equipment firms (ZTE and Huawei) also benefitted from economies of scale and scope – they often bundled equipment sales to mobile operators with handsets – they also had to make significant investments in R&D. Huawei, for example, invested significant resources in chip design through its HiSilicon subsidiary, and while its chip designs are based on ARM IP cores, in-house chip design facilitates deeper and more

---

[22] The license fee is paid upfront for a customer and depends on how recent the complexity of the design; the royalty is paid on a per chip basis, and is generally 1–2% of the sales price of the chip (www.anandtech.com/show/7112/the-arm-diaries-part-1-how-arms-business-model-works/2 (accessed December 17, 2018)).

rapid customization.[23] Huawei was motivated to establish HiSilicon partly by a desire to free itself from Qualcomm licensing fees, but even more important was the need to differentiate itself from competitors: the firm would not have to follow the product cycle of its chip supplier, and could launch new models before the competition, and it would be able to optimize performance of devices more effectively. Initially, Huawei was "designing for price" but then used success in the low-end handsets to increasingly "design for performance" (e.g. processor speed and power consumption) (Interview, July 30, 2012).

Smaller handset firms that were making the transition from feature phones also adopted the new global technology platforms. However, with fewer resources than a large firm like Huawei and weaker connections to mobile operators, they found it extremely difficult to differentiate their smartphones. Tianyu, for example, was the leading domestic brand at the start of 2010, with a 7.5 percent market share from sales of feature phones (Chao 2010). When the market shifted to smartphones, the firm relied on the same suppliers as competitors: chipsets were standard models sourced from Qualcomm, Nvidia, or Spreadtrum (for TD-SCDMA phones), screens from Sharp, the Android OS, with assembly either by Foxconn or BYD (Interview, July 14, 2012). As a smaller firm, Tianyu was at a disadvantage because companies such as Google would cooperate with only a select number of larger handset firms such as Samsung, Huawei, and Taiwan-based HTC, and these firms were therefore able to optimize performance more effectively (Interview, July 18, 2011). Other than slight differences in industrial design, achieving product differentiation was extremely difficult, and Tianyu's largely futile attempt to maintain market share focused on alliances with internet companies (e.g. Alibaba) and heavy promotion in retail channels.

Xiaomi, one of the most successful of the new entrants, founded in 2010, is an example of a firm that utilizes largely standard global technology for products, and then differentiates through its knowledge of domestic consumers and an innovative business model. Xiaomi mainly relies on online sales and innovative marketing techniques that avoid retailer mark-up, and has facilitated the creation of an dynamic online ecosystem.[24] At the core

---

[23] Strategies on chip design vary. Apple acquired its processor design firm, Palo Alto (PA) Semiconductor, in 2008, which also uses ARM cores, while Samsung uses processors from Qualcomm.

[24] According to Xiaomi executives, competing handsets (e.g. Huawei, Oppo) that cost 1000 RMB to produce will sell for 2600 RMB, with 1200 going to the retail channels and 400 profit. Xiaomi is able to achieve very low-costs both by avoiding the retail channels and not taking any profit (Interview, August 11, 2016).

of the modul in a localized operating system called MIUI, which is based on the Android platform, but updated every week based on feedback from lead users and online forums. Profit from handset sales is marginal, but is supplemented with revenue from the sale of services and features such as games, custom on-screen "wallpaper" and icons, virtual gifts; applications that are sold via the Xiaomi app store; and "smart" products that can be controlled via the Xiaomi handset (e.g. air purifiers, televisions). If the firm continues to succeed with this strategy, the network of Xiaomi products will evolve into a lifestyle platform, gradually increasing switching costs for customers. If it fails, the firm will become just another producer of reasonably priced Android handsets, few of which make a profit.

The main point is that with the advent of smartphones, a nested set of global platform leaders such as ARM, Qualcomm, and Google became de facto standards in mobile handsets, driving down product differentiation and profits for mobile handset producers. The truth of this can be discerned in Appendix 5.1, which lists the technology vendors for four current model mobile phone handsets from Huawei, Samsung, Google, and Apple. The tables suggest the dominance of the Android OS (used in all of the four except the iPhone 7), Korean producers for memory products (Samsung and the Hyundai Group's SK Hynix), and the important role played by Qualcomm, not only for processor chipsets but for a wide variety of specialized functional chips as well (e.g. power management, audio encoding, and power management). Broadcom (USA) and Skyworks (USA), and NXP (Netherlands) also show up repeatedly in the Appendix tables. Apple, with its proprietary operating system and ecosystem and high price point, is one of the few companies able to generate significant profits from handset sales.

Of course, competition takes places in many arenas, and this drives handset makers, just as PC-makers have done before them, to rapidly and constantly introduce new features. The result is not always successful, as evidenced by Samsung's recall of its Galaxy Note model phones, which spontaneously caught fire due to new high-power batteries intended to create a competitive advantage though long life. So, as smartphones have largely become generic platforms for running applications and accessing the Internet, competition and profits have been shifting downstream into mobile apps and services, as just discussed in the case of Xiaomi. In China, however, this dynamic has proceeded at a great pace, and it is to this we turn the following section.

THE RISE OF CHINA'S PLATFORM INNOVATORS

Xiaomi's aspiration to become an online platform placed the firm in the company of China's most innovative companies: the internet platforms. Although the technology of the smartphone was largely global, and handsets becoming more and more generic, their capabilities unlocked new possibilities for domestic actors. Unlike much of the world, where users split on-line time between smartphones and personal computers, and where the online world quickly became dominated by hyper-scale Internet companies largely based in the United States (specifically in Silicon Valley and Seattle – Amazon, eBay, Facebook, Google, Twitter, etc.), in China most users only access the Internet via smartphone, and downstream mobile applications came to be dominated by Chinese firms. There are four reasons for this: most users skipped the PC as the main tool for accessing the Internet, the technological barriers to downstream applications and services are relatively low, success in downstream applications and services is largely determined by knowledge of the Chinese consumers and the Chinese Internet, and Chinese policy blocked the participation of powerful foreign companies, such as Google, because they could provide the population with unregulated free access to information and social networking. This last feature of the Chinese Internet has been referred to as the Great Firewall.

The Great Firewall

As was evident in the debates over TD-SCDMA, there have always been national security concerns surrounding state control over the telecom sector, but typically, the concern has been external: policy-makers fear that foreign participation in the sector might compromise the network, especially during wartime. In the case of the Chinese Internet, policy-makers also worried about internal opposition to the regime.

In order to maintain control of the Internet, policy-makers in China have designed an *intra*net that is managed in a top-down manner. First, the connections to the global Internet are strictly controlled by the six state-owned Internet operators (two of which are the major telecom operators), which allows filtering and blocking to occur at the major gateways (Feng and Guo 2013). Second, a significant bureaucracy was created to monitor and control content in China. In the 2000s, while the telecommunications bureaucracy promoted the economic benefits of expansion of the telecommunications network (e.g. MII and the telecom operators) and the science and technology bureaucracy (e.g. MOST) extolled the benefits for indigenous innovation, the propaganda bureaucracy (e.g. the Central Propaganda Department and the State Council Information Office) and public security departments focused on monitoring and control (Creemers 2016; Tsai 2016).[25]

Unlike traditional Chinese media, however, the major Internet firms in China are private, and the system relies on a significant degree of self-regulation. At an institutional level, the Internet Society of China (ISC) was created to connect firms in the sector to the Party (much like similar bodies for journalists or lawyers), and the founders of major Internet search and retailers TenCent, Alibaba, and Baidu were asked to be vice-directors. Each firm requires numerous licenses to operate, of course, so there are also strong incentives to create internal mechanisms for censorship. When Pony Ma, the founder of TenCent, was asked about internet censorship in China at a technology conference in Singapore, his response was clear: "Lots of people think they can speak out and that they can be irresponsible. I think that's wrong," Ma said. "There should be order if the development of the cyber world is to be sustainable" (Elliott 2014).

Because it is not always clear if or when specific content is politically sensitive – if the son of a high level cadre crashes a Ferrari overnight, for example, the word "Ferrari" might quickly become blocked – a firm's ability to anticipate the actions of state censors becomes a core competency.[26] The firms that are deemed "trustworthy" by the state are given more leeway to experiment, and in a sector that is often evolving more rapidly than regulatory structures, this can be a significant advantage.

The political context also leads to a reduction in foreign competition. Although in the early years of the Chinese Internet there were those who believed that it would inevitably be a force for political liberalization within China, it has become clear that the state is not only quite effective at controlling the Internet, but is seeking to use information technology as a means to more effectively exercise social control (MacKinnon 2011; Tsai 2016). In this environment, the opportunities for foreign firms that facilitate either social interaction (e.g. Facebook, Snapchat, Twitter) or access to

---

[25] In 2014, the fragmentation in information and communication technology policy-making was reduced with the creation of a Central Leading Group for Cybersecurity and Informatization chaired by Xi Jinping. This group brought together the economic, technology, security, and propaganda bodies that have an interest in cyberspace (Creemers 2016, p. 10).

[26] According to one manager at Tencent, Pony Ma frequently comments that market forces could no longer kill Tencent, but state government policy could (Interview, July 2014).

information (e.g. from Google, CNN, or the *New York Times*) are either blocked or subject to pressure that prompts the foreign company to withdraw from the Chinese market. Even when entry is allowed, the leverage of global platforms is reduced.

The case of Android is a prime example of how powerful global platforms are weakened within China. Outside of China, Google exercises significant control over the Android OS and Google Play, and as was explained above, handset makers must adhere to Google rules if they want to use the Android brand and the Google suite of services. The Google Play team "curates" the content supplied by outside developers to the app store, with the objective of attracting users to the platform, and it works with the developers to ensure that apps work well on Android. Google benefits from a 30 percent share of every app sale in Google Play, but the long-term health of the ecosystem is even more important to the company because use of the mobile Internet drives traffic to Google search.

Within China, there is a rich ecosystem of app developers, but there is no Google ecosystem.[27] Because there is no Google Play, apps are available only in a highly fragmented third-party app market (e.g. Baidu, TenCent, Xiaomi, and many others), and there is no process of developers working with Google to optimize performance. The market is highly competitive, with users often shifting between app stores, and the incentive is to maximize short-term revenue rather than ecosystem development. Because there are no Google services (search, Gmail, YouTube, maps, etc.), Google has little data on Chinese users. As a Google manager commented in an interview, the Android marketplace in China is "complete chaos" and although there are 500 million Android users in China, Google knows little about them (Interview, October 27, 2014).

WeChat

Perhaps because of this "chaos," the Android ecosystem in China seems to be in the process of being replaced by WeChat, a web-based "over the top" messaging service that has branched out to provide a full range of mobile services, from social networking to mobile payments. WeChat coordinates with app developers and commercial suppliers, and collects a tremendous amount of data from users. Introduced by TenCent as a messaging application in 2011, the initial function of the app was to allow users to send text

---

[27] In 2015, the Apple iStore paid more to app developers in China than any other country (Interview, August 13, 2016).

messages willuuul inuurring fees from mobile operators, but new functions were steadily added, including functions for meeting random people called "Shake," voice messaging, apps for sharing photos and "moments" within a user group, video calling, and group chat. Although these might not appear to be groundbreaking innovations, they were designed in such a way as to hold the attention of a Chinese user, a capability that TenCent had developed in the online gaming sector. As CEO Pony Ma explained, "if an application cannot attract a user within five to ten seconds, the user may abandon the application (Harwit 2016, p. 4)." By October 2016, WeChat had 806 million users; its average revenue per user (ARPU) was estimated at US $7, seven times the ARPU of Facebook's over-the-top messaging service WhatsApp. The extent to which WeChat pervades Chinese life is extraordinary, even in a world now used to pervasive social media platforms such as Facebook.

Building on the core competency of messaging and social media, WeChat created a platform that puts itself at the center of users' mobile internet. Central to this effort was the creation of "apps within an app" that are "lightweight" in regard to the amount of space and processing power taken up on the handset, and apps developed by third parties such as companies, media, celebrities, hospitals, pharmacies, and utilities (Chan 2015). Users are able to open WeChat, and then manage virtually their entire online experience – make a purchase, book a doctor, order dinner, hail a taxi – complete with a frictionless payment system (and over half of Weixin users link their credit card to the app) (*Economist* 2016). Of critical importance, Chinese users are far more likely to access the Internet via a mobile device than their Western counterparts and they are less fixed in their consumer behavior (e.g. credit cards are less pervasive and hence mobile payments are more popular), and TenCent adroitly built WeChat with these characteristics in mind.[28] WeChat has largely replaced email and text messages as a form of communication in China and it is the primary forum for social media (Huang and Zhang 2017; Sun 2016). Some view WeChat as a platform that facilitates every aspect of a Chinese user's life, social and non-social (Chan 2015).[29]

---

[28] As the *Economist* (2016) reported, more Chinese reach the internet via mobile phones than in the United States, Brazil, and Indonesia combined. Half of all internet sales in China are via mobile phone compared to one-third in the United States. As one venture capitalist commented, "WeChat was not a product that started as a website and then was adapted for mobile, it was . . . born into it, molded by it (Chan 2015)."

[29] Huang and Zhang (2017) analyze WeChat adoption among middle-aged urban residents; Sun (2016) examines WeChat usage in primary education in China.

Importantly for our discussion of the evolution of power in the mobile telecom value chain, WeChat can be said to be replacing the OS as the core platform that connects users to the mobile Internet. Although the rise of WeChat does not appear to be the result of direct state support – TenCent is a private firm that was not the target of industrial policy – it has certainly benefitted from of the Chinese state's control over the Internet and the exclusion of foreign competitors.

It would likely be a mistake, however, to assume that WeChat would not otherwise have succeeded. First, although WeChat was protected from foreign competition, there was no protection (or government support) within the domestic market, and the company has thrived. In 2013, Jack Ma announced Alibaba's intent to encroach on WeChat's mobile territory – "there is no goodwill to speak of when we fight in someone else's home," he said to Alibaba employees, "we smash what we must, and wreck with force" – and in six months the company made $5 billion of outside investments and acquisitions to back-up his pledge (Clover 2014). This effort did not succeed. Second, rather than use a protected market as an opportunity to imitate a Western business model, TenCent developed a new business model, becoming the first company to develop a comprehensive platform out of an app (i.e. what has been called a "super app"), an approach that is now being imitated by Silicon Valley giants such as Facebook, with limited success. The vice-president of Facebook Messenger, David Marcus, has called WeChat "inspiring" and spoke of Facebook's aspiration for transforming its Messenger function into a platform for communication and commerce (*Economist* 2016). Still, it is important to bear in mind that WeChat rides on top of the deep, and highly global mobile telecom industry ecosystem.

LESSONS FOR INDUSTRIAL POLICY

The defining feature of Chinese industrial policy in mobile telecom in general, and the effort to create a specific Chinese telecom standard in particular, has been the state's effort to separate the domestic market from the global market, exert leverage over foreign firms to transfer technology, and support the development of domestic firms. While this was not very effective in the era of the feature phone, and even less so in the smartphone era, the Chinese Firewall may have (inadvertently) opened space for indigenous innovation in the era of mobile services. Still, it is worth examining the benefits and costs of China's telecom policy in retrospect.

Reassessing the Successes and Failures of TD-SCDMA

The long delays in issuing 3G licenses within China, a result of the state's desire to give Chinese firms more time to develop, test, and commercialize the new TD-SCDMA technology, ensured that the Chinese standard would never be widely adapted outside of China, but this does not necessarily negate the value of the overall effort.

Some value chain actors benefitted more than others. The fate of Spreadtrum, the IC design firm that was targeted to be a future competitor of Qualcomm and MTK, exactly paralleled the fate of TD-SCDMA: the firm developed a TD-SCDMA chip by 2004, lost money for five years while the government delayed issuing 3G licenses, and then grew rapidly once TD-SCDMA was launched by China Mobile, with sales increasing from $100 million in 2009 to more than $1 billion in 2013 (Fuller 2016, p. 252).

China Mobile, on the other hand, paid an enormous price. The company invested an estimated RMB 188 billion in constructing a 3G network (Min 2014), but rapidly lost customers to rival operators operating 3G networks based on more mature foreign technologies and offering faster speeds, fewer dropped calls, and a wider range of compatible handsets, including the very popular iPhone.[30] In what amounted to an open acknowledgment of its weaknesses, China Mobile stopped investing in TD-SCDMA infrastructure in 2011and started re-investing in 2G GSM infrastructure with Wi-Fi hotspots in high-density areas as a means to survive until the launch of 4G. China Mobile began working with Vodafone (UK) and Verizon Wireless (USA) on the development of the 4G iteration of time division technology (TD-LTE) as early as 2008, and when 4G licenses were issued in 2013, China Mobile began to make heavy investments in both TD-SCDMA infrastructure, which could be quickly upgraded to TD-LTE, and TD-LTE (Zhao 2014). Essentially, rather than attempt to recoup the massive investment that the company had been forced to plough into TD-SCDMA, China Mobile wanted to move on as quickly as possible. "Forcing the national development of TD-SCDMA dragged down China Mobile's growth and upset the other operators' strategies," commented an equipment manufacturer executive. "They had to rush into 4G before making any money on 3G investment" (Min 2014).

Equipment manufacturers appear to be in the middle. When compared to their market share in the 2G (less than 10 percent), the rollout

---

[30] In 2011, the total mobile subscribers (in millions) for China Mobile, China Unicom, and China Telecom were 649.6, 199.6, and 126.6 respectively. In 3G for the same year, the gap had closed considerably: 51.2, 40, and 36.3 respectively (CCID presentation).

of TD-SCDMA appears to have created significant benefits. In 2010, for example, Huawei had 30.9 percent of sales to Chinese carriers for TD-SCDMA equipment, ZTE had 30.1 percent, and Datang had 16 percent (iSuppli 2011).[31] In the same year, however, Huawei had 32.4 percent of sales to Chinese carriers for WCDMA, the European standard, while ZTE had 22.6 percent and Datang had none.[32] In other words, Huawei was succeeding with both the domestic standard *and* the foreign standard, ZTE, which was closer to the government, did better with the domestic standard than foreign, while state-owned Datang would not have had any equipment sales without the domestic standard.[33] When China Mobile began to roll out the 4G TD-LTE network in 2013, the split between the three Chinese firms was roughly similar: Huawei and ZTE both had 26 percent of sales and Datang had 9 percent and was behind three foreign firms (Zhao 2014). The equipment firms were clearly able to increase their market share with the domestic standard, but given that their performance was equally strong in markets without TD-SCDMA, it is difficult to attribute this success to the domestic standard.

Given the enormous resources that were poured into the development of TD-SDMA over more than a decade, assessing the immediate outcome only within the 3G period might be shortsighted. As a foreign manager at a global IC firm commented, the TD-SCDMA experience is often seen as "a successful failure": the delays in the launch of 3G in China and the maturity of competing foreign standards limited the short-term success of TD-SCDMA in regard to commercial returns domestically or global adoption, but there would nevertheless be long-term benefits (Interview, July 13, 2014).

The strong version of this argument is that TD-SCDMA was essentially a loss leader for TD-LTE, a 4G standard that policy-makers hoped would be dominated by Chinese firms and widely adapted around the world. This is an argument that is rooted in the early era of the telecom industry, an era when standard battles were carried out by shifting coalitions of incumbent players and mediated by the ITU and competing standard-setting bodies responsible for the largest markets (the United States, Europe, and Japan).

When viewed in the context of changing technology and the rise of the smartphone, the argument weakens considerably. Chinese firms made

---

[31] The closest foreign competitor was Nokia-Siemens, with 5.8%.

[32] Ericsson had the second largest market share with 23.8%.

[33] Although Datang developed considerable IP for TD, it appears that other Chinese firms did not have to pay a licensing fee to Datang (Interview, July 20, 2012b).

important contributions to TD-LTE[54], and in contrast to TD-SCDMA, it was adopted around the world.[35] But TD-LTE is *not* a "Chinese" standard, and offers the state no leverage regarding market access and few advantages to domestic firms. While there are two versions of 4G technology, TD-LTE and FDD-LTE, they are virtually the same from a technical perspective. According to a white paper commissioned by Ericsson and Qualcomm, "LTE FDD and LTE TDD are virtually identical with the exception of a few technical characteristics that are specific to the Physical Layer (SRG 2014)."[36] This commonality, far from being an accident, was the result of operators around the world trying to avoid the fragmentation that had occurred in 3G. China Mobile, Vodafone, and Verizon collaborated on a recommendation to the 3GPP RAN Working Group urging a single optimized TDD mode. Vodafone, T-Mobile, TeliaSonera, and Telefonica also urged the group to avoid "unnecessary fragmentation" (SRG 2014).[37] The result was that distinguishing features of TD technology in 3G were largely eliminated in 4G.

Second, the companies that contributed to the two versions of LTE were largely the same. An analysis of the submissions to the 3GPP working groups that developed the standards shows that geographic representation of submissions was roughly similar for TD-LTE (Europe 28 percent, US 23 percent, China 19 percent, South Korea 17 percent, Japan 10 percent, Other 3 percent) and FDD-LTE (Europe 30 percent, US 22 percent, China 12 percent, South Korea 15 percent, Japan 16 percent, Other 5 percent), and 82.5 percent of these submissions did not distinguish between the two modes of LTE at all (SRG

---

[34] According to one respondent, ZTE has 9% of the number (*not* value) of patents in TD-LTE, Huawei has 14%, and Ericsson (Sweden) holds 16%, with the remainder highly dispersed (CCID).

[35] According to the Global Mobile Suppliers Association, 360 LTE networks have been launched in 124 countries, with 312 operators deploying FDD mode only, thirty-one operators deploying TDD mode only, and seventeen operators deploying both modes (http://gsacom.com/paper/gsa-evolution-to-lte-report-360-lte-networks-launched/ (accessed December 17, 2018)).

[36] The differences that do exist between the two standards "primarily pertain to when an action or event is done and not to why or how something is executed."

[37] In an assessment of the evolution from TD-SCDMA to TD-LTE, engineers from the Datang Group acknowledged the shift to an approach that emphasized commonalities: "several fundamental technical characteristics of TD-SCDMA are preserved for TD-LTE. However, during the process of developing LTE and LTE-Advanced specifications, the maximum commonality between TDD and FDD has been emphasized in the Third Generation Partnership Project (3GPP), and realized by achieving a good balance between the commonality of basic structures and optimization of individual characteristics (Chen 2012)."

2014).[38] China had slightly less influence in the development of FDD than FTE, but both are clearly *global* standards, as was shown in Table 5.1.

A slightly weaker version of the "successful failure" argument is that the experience of developing a domestic standard made an important contribution to the innovation ecosystem in China. First, the shift of all TD-related design activities to China on the part of handset firms, semiconductors design firms, and others supported the development of domestic engineering capabilities. Global handset firms such as Samsung, for instance, had no choice but to acquiesce to China Mobile's request for TD-SCDMA handsets, and Beijing was the natural place for this R&D and design activity to take place. Engineers at China Mobile became skilled at the process of network testing and optimization, which by necessity requires coordination with all parts of the value chain in order to make adjustments. Testing capabilities and some of the very expensive testing machines they require were created at the Chinese Academy of Telecom Research, and this allowed Chinese firms an early mover advantage at developing new technologies (Interview, July 13, 2014). Second, policy-makers and firms learned a great deal about the process of developing a global standard and the manner in which global IP is created and regulated. Although 4G LTE standards might not depend on TD-SCDMA technology – it is not an evolution in a technical sense and probably would have looked the same even if TD-SCDMA had not existed – TD-LTE has origins in China and was proposed to the ITU by China Mobile. The China Common Standards Association became an organizational partner of 3GPP and became the coordination point for the development of the TD flavor of LTE.

The weak version of the "successful failure" argument is difficult to refute; many lessons were learned from China's TD-SCDMA gambit, and the result was undoubtedly deeper capabilities within the Chinese mobile telecom ecosystem. But the tuition was extremely high. Whether similar lessons might have been learned in the absence of TD-SCDMA is difficult to assess.

Surfing the Waves of Technological Change in Mobile Telecom

The most fundamental challenge to the successful implementation of industrial policy in the Chinese mobile telecom sector was the rapid rate

---

[38] A total of 82,967 submissions made over a six-year period were examined. Submissions to the working groups were not always accepted into the published specifications, but the finding that 82.5% of the submissions do not distinguish between the two modes of LTE is consistent with the published specifications (Signals Research Group 2014, p. 26).

of technological change. This was evident in the era of feature phones, when the licensing regime and restrictions on foreign entry were made largely irrelevant by the turnkey reference design platform solution offered by MTK. When handsets were mainly used for voice communication, the interconnect standard structured the lion's share of handset design and was a key point of leverage in the value chain; it created both competitive advantage and barriers to market entry. With feature phone reference platforms and smartphones, voice communication has become simply another function among many on what is now, essentially, a mobile computing and entertainment platform. The power of modem chipsets is such that they can easily offer multiple interconnect standards on a single handset, a trend that has become even more pronounced now that the two global standards (TD-LTE and FDD-LTE) are so similar. The interconnect standards now take up only the first few layers in the handset architecture, and the handset itself acts more and more as a generic portal to on-line platforms and services.[39] Handsets are no longer the "end product" in the chain of mobile telecom, but a platform for accessing other functions and services. This nested platform structure of mobile telecom is depicted in Figure 5.3. As the figure shows, general and specific interconnect standards now make up only a small and increasingly insignificant portion of the industry's architecture. The locus of innovation, competition, and profits as shifted dramatically, and often quite suddenly and unexpectedly, downstream toward end users as new platform layers have emerged.

Tellingly, the most successful Chinese firms in mobile telecom (e.g. TenCent, and Xiaomi), are firms that did not exist (or were only just being founded) at the time when Chinese policy-makers were formulating plans for TD-SCDMA. They dominate parts of the value chain that did not exist at the time, and none of them were the explicit targets of state policy. They are all private sector firms, and while they benefitted from constraints on foreign competition, the domestic competition was intense. In almost all cases, these firms are downstream in the value chain and consumer-facing.

Several critical differences help to explain the success of these firms. First, the technological capabilities required are not very deep. Since

---

[39] Technological advances, specifically in the speed and capability of semiconductors, have also made it possible for telecommunications equipment to cover multiple standards without raising costs or diminishing the user's experience.

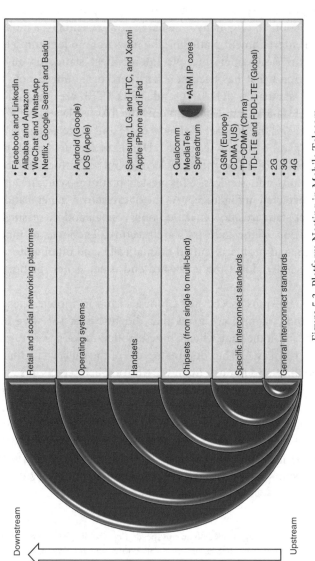

Retail and social networking platforms
- Facebook and LinkedIn
- Alibaba and Amazon
- WeChat and WhatsApp
- Netflix, Google Search and Baidu

Operating systems
- Android (Google)
- iOS (Apple)

Handsets
- Samsung, LG, and HTC, and Xaomi
- Apple iPhone and iPad

Chipsets (from single to multi-band)
- Qualcomm
- MediaTek
- Spreadtrum
- ARM IP cores

Specific interconnect standards
- GSM (Europe)
- CDMA (US)
- TD-CDMA (China)
- TD-LTE and FDD-LTE (Global)

General interconnect standards
- 2G
- 3G
- 4G

Downstream

Upstream

Figure 5.3 Platform Nesting in Mobile Telecom
Source: Authors.

downstream applications and services are built on top of global technology platforms, the technical requirements are modest, involving the design and implementation of user interfaces, web services and attendant databases. Even here, global design tools, services, and software modules (e.g. search) are readily available to help quickly build out a suite of features. In contrast, the technology and ecosystems embedded in the IP core and chipsets that were the main target of China's earlier mobile telecom policies are extremely deep and difficult to replicate or replace. Chinese smartphone and web services firms appear willing enough to build products and services based on global technology platforms.

Second, the core competency of these firms is less in developing deep competencies in core technologies and more in understanding and responding effectively to Chinese consumer behavior. At the same time, the Great Firewall creates a captive audience. Third, Chinese firms are able to draw on a rich ecosystem of application developers.[40] While the ecosystems of developers for leading upstream platforms (i.e. ARM, Qualcomm, etc.) are global in scope, and Chinese competitors are at a disadvantage, the ecosystems of developers for downstream applications do not suffer by being domestic.

In short, the downstream platforms that are controlled by Chinese firms take advantage of their superior ability (and the ability of the supporting ecosystem) to understand and navigate the local market, while fully integrating the global technologies that support this effort. The innovations that result may not be the "big" innovations that state planners often favor – services rather than semiconductors – but these firms are highly competitive, very innovative, and have tremendous leverage within the domestic value chain.

CONCLUSIONS

What we see in an era of increasing global economic integration, both in business systems characterized by global value chains and in industries governed by global standards, is that it has become more difficult for states to control the trajectory of innovation and industrial development, foster

---

[40] In the view of a senior executive in a leading Western technology firm in mobile telecom, the mobile internet ecosystem in China is more developed than in any other country (Interview, August 13, 2016).

relevant firm capabilities, and shape markets. Of course, the relevance of this observation depends on the industry. In sectors where the state or state-owned enterprises control purchasing, as in the power generation and transmission industries discussed in several chapters within this volume, where the pace of technological change is slow and products unitary, the state, often through its purchasing practices, can pick and choose technologies and define markets. But in faster moving industries with modular industry architectures and emergent global standards, such as mobile telecom, the state's control over the process of industrial development is much looser.

This is not simply a failing of the state. Many important incumbent companies, fully engaged in creating and managing the core technologies, and with dominant market shares, such as Motorola, Nokia, and Ericsson, have essentially disappeared in mobile telecom by failing to thrive in the smartphone era launched by Apple and Google. Of all the dominant incumbents, only Samsung was able to make the transition and come away stronger. If strong technology companies fail to predict and adapt to industry trends, how can policy-makers possibly cope?

APPENDIX 5.1

Technology Comparison for Four Mobile Phone Handsets

NOTES

- The tables are partial and do not include sources for all important components and subsystems, such as displays and batteries. As such they are indicative only.
- Three of the four phones use Google Android operating systems (except Apple iPhone 7).
- Three of the four phones include memory ICs from Samsung (except the Apple iPhone 7), and all four use memory ICs from Korea-based vendors.
- Three of the four phones include various functional Qualcomm ICs (except Huawei P6).
- Two of the four phones use Qualcomm processors.

Table 5.A1 *Technology Comparison: Huawei (China) P6*

Huawei (China) P6	Vendor (HQ)	Item
operating system	Google (USA)	Android Marshmallow
processor	Huawei (China)***	Kirin 955 Octa-core CPU
modem	Skyworks (USA)	WCDMA/LTE and FDD/TDD LTE modem
memory products	SK Hynix (Korea)	24 GB (3 GB) RAM
	Samsung (Korea)	32 GB eMMC flash memory (2)
various functional ICs	Texas Instruments (USA)	fast charging IC
	HiSilicon (China)	audio codec
	Broadcom (USA)**	5G Wi-Fi and Bluetooth module
	Broadcom (USA)**	GPS controller
	NXP (Netherlands)*	near field communications controller
	Vivante (USA)	graphics processor

* NXP is the former Philips semiconductor division.
** Broadcom was recently acquired by Avago Technologies (Singapore).
*** Designed by HiSilicon (China), a Huawei subsidiary, based on ARM (UK) technology: CPU: ARMv8-A; GPU: ARM Mali-T880 MP4.

Table 5.A2 *Technology Comparison: Samsung (Korea) Galaxy Note 7*

Samsung (Korea) Galaxy Note 7	Vendor (HQ)	Item
operating system	Google (USA)	Android Marshmallow
processor	Qualcomm (USA)	Snapdragon 820
modem	Qualcomm (USA)	X12 LTE modem (integrated in processor)
memory products	Samsung (Korea)	4 GB SDRAM
	Samsung (Korea)	64 GB Universal Flash Storage 2.0
various functional ICs	Broadcom (USA)	multiband multimode module
	NXP (Netherlands)*	near field communications controller
	Qorvo (USA)	high band RF fusion and diversity receive module
	Qualcomm (USA)	audio codec and DSP audio/voice processor
	Murata (Japan)	front-end module
	Samsung (Korea)**	Wi-Fi module
	Wacom (Japan)	touch control IC
	Qualcomm (USA)	power management IC
	Qualcomm (USA)	envelope tracker
	Qualcomm (USA)	RF transceiver (2)
	IDT (Japan)	wireless power receiver and power ICs

* NXP is the former Philips semiconductor division.
** Probably contains a Broadcom Wi-Fi SoC.

Table 5.A3 *Technology Comparison: Google (USA) Pixel XL*

Google (USA) Pixel XL	Vendor (HQ)	Item
operating system	Google (USA)	Android Nougat
processor	Qualcomm (USA)	quad-core, 64-bit Snapdragon 821 processor
modem	Qualcomm (USA)	LTE RF transceiver (2)
memory products	Samsung (Korea)	4 GB mobile DRAM
	Samsung (Korea)	32 GB universal flash storage
various functional ICs	Qualcomm (USA)	quick charge IC
	NXP (Netherlands)*	audio amplifier
	Qualcomm (USA)	power management IC
	Broadcom (USA)**	power amplifier
	Qualcomm (USA)	audio codec
	Skyworks (USA)	quad-band power amplifier module
	Qualcomm (USA)	dynamic antenna matching tuner (2)
	Synaptics (USA)	touch controller

* NXP is the former Philips semiconductor division.
** Broadcom was recently acquired by Avago Technologies (Singapore).

Table 5.A4 *Technology Comparison: Apple (USA) iPhone 7*

Apple (USA) iPhone 7	Vendor (HQ)	Item
operating system	Apple (USA)	iOS 10
processor	Apple (USA)	A10 Fusion SoC***
modems	Qualcomm (USA)	LTE Cat. 12 Modem
	Qualcomm (USA)	Multimode LTE Transceiver
memory products	SK Hynix (Korea)	32 GB Flash
various functional ICs	Broadcom (USA)**	power amplifier module
	Skyworks (USA)	power amplifier
	Murata (Japan)	Wi-Fi/Bluetooth Module
	NXP (Netherlands)	near field communications controller
	Dialog	power management IC
	Qualcomm (USA)	power management IC
	Qualcomm (USA)	RF Transceiver
	Bosch (Germany)	barometric pressure sensor
	Cirrus Logic (USA)	audio codec
	Cirrus Logic (USA)	audio amplifier (2)
	Lattice Semiconductor (USA)	ICE5LP4 K
	Skyworks (USA)	diversity receive module (3)

(continued)

Table 5.A4 *(continued)*

Apple (USA) iPhone 7	Vendor (HQ)	Item
	Skyworks (USA)	Skyworks 13703–21 diversity receive module
	Broadcom (USA)**	LFI626 200157 (function unknown)
	NXP (Netherlands)	610A38 (function unknown)
	TDK (Japan)	AC/DC converter****
	Texas Instruments (USA)	power management IC

* NXP is the former Philips semiconductor division.
** Broadcom was recently acquired by Avago Technologies (Singapore).
*** Integrates 2 GB RAM (memory) from Samsung (Korea).
**** Designed by EPCOS (Germany), a TDK subsidiary originally formed in a 1989 JV between Siemens and Matsushita.
Source: Ifixit teardo wn page: www.ifixit.com/Teardown.

References

Akamatsu, K. 1961. "A Theory of Unbalanced Growth in the World Economy" *Weltwirtschaftliches Archiv.* 86. pp. 196–217.

Amsden, A. 1989. *Asia's Next Giant: South Korea and Late Industrialization.* New York: Oxford University Press.

Beijing Fuji Chimera Consulting. 2014. "Market Trends of Smart Phone in China, 2014 (Report Summary)." January 24, 2014.

Brandt, L. and E. Thun, 2011. "Going Mobile in China: Shifting Value Chains and Upgrading in the Mobile Telecom Sector." *International Journal of Technological Learning, Innovation and Development.* 4 (1/2/3). pp. 148–80.

Carney, M., E. Gedajlovic, E., and X. Yang. 2009. "Varieties of Asian Capitalism: Towards an institutional theory of Asian enterprise." *Asia Pacific Journal of Management.* 26. p. 361.

Chan, C. 2015 "When one app rules them all: The case of WeChat and mobile in China." https://a16z.com/2015/08/06/wechat-china-mobile-first/ (accessed December 17, 2018).

Chao, L. 2010. "Tianyu leads rise of China's handset makers." *The Wall Street Journal.*

Chen, H.-H., and C.-X. Fan et al. 2002. "China's perspectives on 3G mobile communications and beyond: TD-SCDMA technology." *IEEE Wireless Communications.*

Chen, Shanzhi, Wang Yingmin, Ma Weiguo, and Jun Chen. 2012. "Technical Innovations Promoting Standard Evolution: From TD-SCDMA to TD-LTE and Beyond." *IEEE Wireless Communications.* 19(1). pp. 60–6.

Clover, C. 2014. "Alibaba's Ma urges climate change in war against Tencent penguin: Smartphones the battleground in ecommerce tussle." *Financial Times.*

Creemers, R. 2016. "Cyber China: Upgrading propaganda, public opinion work and social management for the twenty-first century." *Journal of Contemporary China.* Forthcoming.

Eadicicco, L. 2015. "The rise of Android: How a flailing startup became the world's biggest computing platform." *Business Insider UK.*

Economist 2016. "WeChat's world: China's WeChat shows the way to social media's future."

Elliott, D. 2014. "Tencent: The secretive, Chinese tech giant that can rival Facebook and Amazon." *Fast Company.*

Evans, P. 1995. *Embedded Autonomy: States and Industrial Transformation.* Princeton: Princeton University Press.

Fan, P. 2010. "Developing innovation-oriented strategies: lessons from Chinese mobile phone firms." *International Journal of Technology Management.* 51 (2/3/4). pp. 168–93.

Feenstra, Robert C. and Gary G. Hamilton. 2006. *Emergent Economies, Divergent Paths: Economic Organization and International Trade in South Korea and Taiwan.* Cambridge: Cambridge University Press.

Feng, G. C. and Z. S. Guo. 2013. "Tracing the route of China's internet censorship: An empirical study." *Telematics and Informatics.* 30. pp. 335–45.

Fine, C. 2005. "Are You Modular or Integral? Be Sure Your Supply Chain Knows." Strategy+Business. 39.

Fuller, D. B. 2016. *Paper Tigers, Hidden Dragons: Firms and the Political Economy of China's Technological Development.* Oxford: Oxford University Press.

Gao, P. et al. 2014. "Telecommunications Policy." *Government in standardization in the catching-up context: Case of China's mobile system.* 38. pp. 200–9.

Gao, X. 2014. "A latecomer's strategy to promote a technology standard: The case of Datang and TD-SCDMA." *Research Policy.* 43. pp. 597–607.

Gao, X. and J. Liu. 2012. "Catching up through the development of technology standard: The case of TD-SCDMA in China." *Telecommunications Policy.* 36. pp. 531–45.

Gawer, A. and M. A. Cusumano. 2014. "Industry platforms and ecosystem innovation." *Journal of Production and Innovation Management.* 31(3). pp. 417–33.

Gereffi. G. 1994. "The organization of buyer-driven global commodity chains: How U.S. retailers shape overseas production networks." In G. Gereffi and M. Korzeniewicz eds., *Commodity Chains and Global Capitalism.* Westport, CT: Praeger.

Gereffi, G., J. Humphrey, and T. Sturgeon. 2005. "The Governance of Global Value Chains." *Review of International Political Economy.* 12(1). pp. 78–104.

Harwit, E. 2016. "WeChat and political development of China's dominant messaging app." *Chinese Journal of Communication.* Forthcoming. pp. 1754–4750.

Hess, M. and N. M. Coe. 2006. "Making connections: global production networks, standards, and embeddedness in the mobile-telecommunications industry." *Environment and Planning.* 3., pp. 1205–7.

Hsueh, R. 2015. "Nations or Sectors in the Age of Globalization: China's Policy Toward Foreign Direct Investment in Telecommunications." *Review of Policy Research.* 32(6). pp. 627–48.

Huang, H. and X. Zhang. 2017. "The adoption and use of WeChat among middle-aged residents in urban China." *Chinese Journal of Communication.* 10(2). pp. 134–56.

Humphrey, J. and H. Schmitz. 2002. "How Does Insertion in Global Value Chains Affect Upgrading in Industrial Clusters?" *Regional Studies.* 36(9). pp. 1017–27.

Imai, K. and J. M. Shiu. 2007 "A divergent path of industrial upgrading: emergence and evolution of the mobile handset industry in China." *IDE Discussion Paper.*

Imai, K. and J. M. Shiu. 2010. "Value chain creation and reorganization: The growth path of China's mobile phone handset industry." In M. Kawakami and T. J. Sturgeon eds., *The Dynamics of Local Learning in Global Value Chains: Experiences from East Asia.* Houndmills: Palgrave Macmillan. pp. 43–67.

Kimura, K. 2009 "The technology gap and the growth of the firm: A case study of China's mobile-handset industry." IDE Discussion Paper.

Kojima, K. 2000. "The 'Flying Geese' Model of Asian Economic Development: Origin, theoretical extensions and regional policy implication." *Journal of Asian Economics.* 11(4). pp. 375–401.

MacKinnon, R. 2011. China's "Networked Authoritarianism." *Journal of Democracy.* 22(2). pp. 32–46.

Marukawa, Tomoo. 2010. "Chinese Innovations in Mobile Telecommunications: Third Generation vs. 'Guerrilla Handsets'." Conference on Chinese Approaches to National Innovation, University of California, San Diego La Jolla, California, June 28–29, 2010, https://web.iss.u-tokyo.ac.jp/~marukawa/Marukawa_Draft1 .pdf (accessed 17 December 2018).

MediaTEK 2007. "Mediatek Inc. to Purchase Analog Devices' Cellular Radio and Baseband Chipset Operations." Press Release, September 10, 2007. www.mediatek.com/en/ news-events/mediatek-news/mediatek-inc-to-purchase-analog-devices-cellular-radio-and-baseband-chipset-operations/ (accessed December 17, 2018).

Min, Q. 2014. "China Mobile's dead end on the 3G highway." *Caixin.*

Nie, W. et al. 2012. *In the shadow of the dragon: the global expansion of Chinese companies–how it will change business forever.* New York: American Management Association.

Nölke, A. and A. Vliegenthart. 2009. "Enlarging the Varieties of Capitalism: The Emergence of Dependent Market Economies in East Central Europe." *World Politics.* 61(4). pp. 670–702.

OECD. 2011. "Global Value Chains: Preliminary Evidence and Policy Issues" OECD Directorate for Science, Technology and Industry. Paper presented to the Committee on Industry. DSTI/IND(2011)3. Prepared by Koen De Baker. https:// unstats.un.org/unsd/trade/globalforum/publications/gvc/n%20-%20OECD%20-% 202011%20-%20GVCs%20-%20Preliminary%20Evidence%20-%20Policy% 20Issues_March%204.pdf (accessed December 17, 2018).

Pon, B. et al. 2014. "Android and the demise of operating system-based power: Firm strategy and platform control in the post-PC world." *Telecommunications Policy.* 38. pp. 979–91.

Reisinger, D. 2016. "Here's Why Only Apple and Samsung Know How to Profit Off Smartphones." *Forbes.*

Schneider, B. 2009. "Hierarchical Market Economies and Varieties of Capitalism in Latin America." *Journal of Latin American Studies.* 41(3). pp. 553–75.

Shih, W. et al. 2010 "Shanzhai! MediaTek and the 'white box' handset market." *HBS Case 9-610-081.*

Signals Research Group. 2014. "THE LTE STANDARD: Developed by a global community to support paired and unpaired spectrum deployments." http://signalsre search.com/issue/the-lte-standard-5/ (accessed December 17, 2018).

SRG 2014. "The LTE Standard." Developed by a global community to support paired and unpaired spectrum deployments S. R. Group.

Sturgeon, T. 2000. "How Silicon Valley Came to Be." In Martin Kennedy ed., *Understanding Silicon Valley: Anatomy of an Entrepreneurial Region.* Redwood: Stanford University Press. pp. 15–47.

Sun, Y. 2016. "WeChat transforms China's school days." *MIT Technology Review.* 119(3). pp. 13–14.

Tan, Z. 2002. "Product cycle theory and telecommunications industry: foreign direct investment, government policy, and indigenous manufacturing in China." *Telecommunications Policy.* 26. pp. 17–30.

Tsai, C.-J. and J.-W. Wang. 2011. "How China institutional changes influence industry development? The case of TD-SCDMA industrialization." DRUID June 15–16, 2011. Copenhagen, Denmark. pp. 1–29.

Tsai, W.-H. 2016. "How 'networked authoritarianism' was operationalized in China: methods and procedures of public control." *Journal of Contemporary China.* 25 (101). pp. 731–44.

Van Alstyne, M. W. et al. 2016. "Pipelines, Platforms, and the New Rules of Strategy." *Harvard Business Review.*

Vialle, P. et al. 2012. "Competing with dominant global standards in a catching-up context. The case of mobile standards in China." *Telecommunications Policy.* 36. pp. 832–46.

Wade, R. 1990. *Governing the Market: Economic theory and the role of government in East Asian industrialization.* Princeton: Princeton University Press.

Whittaker, D. H., T. Zhu, T. Sturgeon, M. H. Tsai, and T. Okita. 2010. "Compressed Development." *Studies in Comparative International Development.* 45. pp. 439–67.

World Bank. 2015. "Global Value Chains." Brief IBRD, IDA, July 16, www.worldbank.org/ en/topic/trade/brief/global-value-chains (accessed December 17, 2018).

Yu, J. 2011. "From 3G to 4G: technology evolution and path dynamics in China's mobile telecommunication sector." *Technology Analysis and Strategic Management Science.* 23(10). pp. 1079–93.

Zhao, H. 2014. China is ready for 4G access. *China Research*, IHS Technology.

6

The Search for High Power in China: State Grid Corporation of China

XU Yi-chong

INTRODUCTION

In 2016, a new international non-profit NGO was established: Global Energy Interconnection Development and Cooperation Organisation (Geidco).[*] Its first president was the recently retired chief executive of the State Grid Corporation of China (SGCC), Liu Zhenya, and its vice president was the Nobel Laureate, Steven Chu, former US Secretary of Energy (2009–13). Though with limited acknowledgment globally, Geidco has captured the attention of the world's largest electricity transmission companies and of international organizations, such as the International Energy Agency (IEA) and International Renewable Energy Agency (IRENA).[1] Geidco aims "to promote the establishment of a global energy interconnection (GEI) system, to meet the global demand for electricity in a clean and green way, to implement the United Nations 'Sustainable Energy for All' and climate change initiatives, and to serve the sustainable development of humanity." At the core of the GEI system is "Smart Grid + UHV Grid + Clean Energy." GEI was the brainchild of Liu Zhenya and SGCC, and brought SGCC, a state-owned corporation in China, to the global stage with its control over cutting-edge ultra-high-voltage (UHV) technologies. According to IEA, global power sector investment will be about US$20 trillion in 2015–40, averaging US$760 billion per year, and electricity networks will account for 42 percent of this investment (US$8.4 trillion). SGCC wants a piece of this action and, of course, market (IEA 2015, p. 320; IEA 2016a; IEA 2016b).

---

[*] With thanks for support from the Australian Research Council (DP120102097).
[1] See the joint IEA-SGCC workshop on "Global Energy Interconnection: Smart Grids and Beyond," 21–2 July 2015.

This chapter explains *why* and *how* the State Grid Corporation of China (SGCC) engaged in technology innovation, using the development of UHV AC and UHV DC systems as examples. SGCC's successful UHV development contradicts long held arguments that weak protection of intellectual property (IP) rights and distorted incentive structures discourage Chinese firms, especially those under state ownership, from engaging in high-risk innovation (Abrami et al 2014; Cheung et al. 2016). According to such skeptics, successful Chinese innovators, for example in industries such as telecom or renewable energy technology, tend to be private companies that benefit from state backing (Lewis 2013; Gallagher 2014; Zhou et al. 2016), with the government picking winners and pouring in resources that enable them to develop key technologies, thus confirming "the state's overwhelming power to implement innovation" (Liu and Peng 2014; Shim and Shin 2015). More often than not, however, government intervention does not lead to "innovation" but rather imitation, or what some have called, the "lower-end of the imitation-innovation with 'Chinese characteristics'" (Cheung et al. 2016). Has SGCC merely imitated its counterparts in developed countries? To what extent did it indeed engage in innovation? Why did it get involved in UHV projects in the first place? How did SGCC pursue UHV projects that were both high risk and high cost?

To address these questions, why and how, this chapter first discusses types of innovation SGCC engaged in. Transmission and distribution (T&D) business has always been considered as a natural monopoly not only because of its nature of non-exclusiveness but also because it is capital-intensive, with massive fixed investment and scale economies. The physical attributes of transmission and distribution (T&D) networks and the non-storable nature of electricity require precise coordination among generation, transmission, and distribution in real time. T&D does more than transport electricity from one location to another. It involves "a complex coordination system that integrates a large number of generating facilities dispersed over wide geographical areas to provide reliable flow of electricity to dispersed demand nodes while adhering to tight physical requirements to maintain network frequency, voltage and stability" (Joskow 1997, pp. 121–2). Given these features, for a century, the electricity industry around the world was vertically and horizontally integrated until the 1990s when electricity restructuring was pushed forward not only in developed countries but also by international financial institutions in developing countries. China first introduced the reform in the mid-1980s to lower the entry barriers to generation by allowing investments from sources other than the state. As part of the general state-owned enterprise

(SOE) reform, the electricity industry was commercialized and corporatized in the late 1990s when a vertically integrated state-owned monopoly,
the State Power Corporation of China (SPCC) was created out of the
Ministry of Electric Power in 1999.

In December 2002, the central government "unbundled" SPCC, parcelling
out its assets to five power generation companies, two grid companies and
four power services companies, all remaining state-owned under the supervision of the central government.[2] For historical reasons, SGCC was given
the responsibility of building, managing, and operating cross-region transmission networks in twenty-six of thirty provinces and regions. The rest is
covered by a smaller transmission company, China Southern Grid Corp Ltd.
SGCC inherited most transmission and distribution assets and operation in
the country from SPCC and some peak generation capacities. It was also
asked by the State Council to manage many units of SPCC pending clarification of their ownership structures. More importantly, all eleven companies
that spun off from SPCC remained state-owned under the supervision of the
central government. The 2002 electricity restructuring was much criticized
by both advocates and opponents of unbundling. Further criticism came
from international institutions, including IEA and the World Bank, which
viewed this reform as incomplete.

Even though it is among the top-tier SOEs under direct Party-state
control and supervision, SGCC, like most large corporations, is complex and diverse in terms of its management, employees and activities.
Among its 1.7–1.8 million employees, less than half worked at its
headquarters and direct subsidiaries; about a quarter were employed
by SGCC's county-level power supply companies; and one-third were
(mostly part-time) rural electricians with limited expertise. Although
SGCC was often seen as a monopoly, it owned only about 75 percent of
the transmission and distribution lines and 88 percent of the transformers in its service areas. The remainder, along with many distribution
assets were owned by local governments and other entities. Diverse
ownership of assets and jurisdictions created continuing tension among
SGCC, local governments and privately owned distribution companies.
From its creation, SGCC was expected to operate as a corporation, even
though its senior managers were appointed by the government. SGCC's

---

[2] At the time, SPCC controlled slightly over half of China's generation capacity, while the
bulk of the remaining capacity belonged to provincial and local governments. Independent
power producers with private and foreign ownership existed but were inconsequential. See
Yeh and Lewis (2004); IEA (2006); OECD (2009).

operation expanded significantly in its first decade: between 2005 and 2015, revenue nearly tripled, total assets grew by 265 percent; and profits grew by six times.

SGCC is among a very few large SOEs to receive an "A" performance ranking from the State-owned Assets Supervision and Administration Commission (SASAC). When SGCC first entered the Fortune Global 500 in 2005, it ranked 40th, with annual revenue less than one third of that of Walmart, the global leader. A decade later, SGCC is the world's largest utility and the second largest company in the Fortune Global 500 in terms of annual revenue, just behind Walmart. Its operation has expanded to overseas markets with direct investments in transmission, construction and operation in Brazil and the Philippines and equity investments in Australia, Portugal, Italy, and other countries. Investments in hundreds of transmission and distribution projects across Asia and Africa have helped transform SGCC into a truly global company.

SGCC's greatest achievement is perhaps its success in mastering the technology of constructing and operating high-voltage transmission lines (defined as anything above 500kv), and its deployment of this technology to connect China's entire population, including those living in the most remote villages in the Tibetan plateau and the Gobi desert. This chapter nonetheless focuses on SGCC's endeavor in technology innovation in constructing and operating the so-called UHV networks that deliver large electricity across long distances using high-voltage lines to reduce transmission losses.

This first section shows that SGCC's initial pursuit of UHV projects in 2004 was motivated more by self-preservation than innovation; it was also encouraged by overseas experimentation with UHV technologies. At the time, SGCC did not plan to engage in revolutionary, disruptive research and development (R&D), but rather tried to imitate and then adopt technology developed elsewhere. In the process, it changed its strategy to engage in R&D in order to succeed "in coming up with innovations that are adaptive, incremental, and appropriate to its stage of development" (Yip and McKern 2016, p. 10). Such a "fit for purpose" and "good enough" strategy, or what some call "secondary innovation" seemed to work for SGCC – "initially based on foreign technology, it goes beyond imitation and adaptation to something unique for China" (Yip and McKern 2016, p. 14).

These early efforts created a foundation for a subsequent effort to develop path-breaking transmission technology. Building on available UHV technologies, SGCC engaged in a panoply of innovative activities, from basic research, field and laboratory experiments, to equipment development and actual instalment. Worldwide absence of commercial UHV operations compelled SGCC to pursue a broad array of novel initiatives. It is important to understand why SGCC decided to take on high-risk, high-cost technology development and how it managed these risks and costs.

The second section discusses two sets of government policies – directed toward SOE reform and innovation – which provided the incentive structure within which SGCC operated. Such policies shape but do not determine the behavior of players. Some firms are willing and able to take advantage of the policies and engage in innovation, while others fail to do so. Three decades ago, Richard Nelson argued that the broad political and economic system, "certain unique attributes" of the industry, and a proprietary technology can all shape the choices of strategies and capacities of firms. Within this broad context, "discretionary firm differences within an industry exist and do matter significantly" (Nelson 1991, p. 62).

To understand the presence or absence of innovation, it is thus imperative to examine both general policies and the firm-level response. SGCC's strategies, structures, and capacities in technology innovation were not the simple consequence of its state-ownership or its status as a national champion. Indeed, SGCC's ownership and near monopoly worked as a double-edged sword as it provided SGCC with tremendous bargaining power, but also discouraged risk-taking behavior. In the transmission industry, where new technologies involve high risks, vision, leadership, and resources are much more in need than in many other sectors. Such risk factors are greater for central SOEs as their executives are not only directly accountable to SASAC, but also occasionally could be the scapegoat in the wake of accidents, disasters, or innovative failure.

The last section of this chapter explains the open-innovation strategy SGCC adopted to answer the "how" question. Instead of pursuing techno-nationalism as some have argued (Naughton and Segal 2003; Kennedy 2013), SGCC adopted what some scholars have termed "open innovation" strategy (Chesbrough 2003; Fu 2015, ch. 7), working with a range of players, universities, research institutions, suppliers and multinational corporations (MNCs), all on SGCC's terms. It was able to do so in part because of the general government policy on innovation and in part because of the entrepreneurship of its chief executive.

As the UHV projects developed, SGCC revised its objective from initial focus on self-interest and self-preservation to a more ambitious goal of reversing its position from follower to a leader in the global transmission industry by taking the commanding heights in the transition to low-carbon electricity and becoming an international standard setter. The completion of SGCC's first UHV DC project at the end of 2009 alarmed some experts and industry insiders. At the National Press Club in 2010, the then US Secretary of Energy, Steven Chu, told the audience that "China has installed the highest voltage and capacity, lowest loss HVDC (800kv) and HVAC (1000kv) lines, and plans an integrated HVDC/HVAC backbone" (Chu 2010). Secretary Chu urged the American government to "play a key role in accelerating energy innovation" to avoid the risk of losing American leadership in science and technology. The US Department of Energy listed high-voltage transmission as one of the crucial technologies where the United States must innovate to take the lead in the transition to low-carbon energy. The US National Science and Technology Council made similar suggestions.[3] Then SGCC set an even more ambitious objective – to "sell" its vision of global energy interconnection to the international community.

INNOVATION

If innovation is defined as "a process to create new knowledge in scientific development and to generate commercially sustainable breakthroughs that provide competitive economic advantage" – something new, something radical, something revolutionary and something disruptive – most Chinese firms can at best be described as partially innovative (Crooke 2012, p. 168).[4] They are known to introduce "incrementally upgraded products with unprecedented rapidity" (Steinfeld and Beltoft 2014, p. 50), by taking advantage of relatively low costs of inputs (labor as well as resources). With this cost-innovation strategy, new products may allow producers to briefly realize slightly higher margins that will quickly disappear in the absence of genuinely new knowledge (Zeng and Williamson 2007). Innovation nonetheless is not only restricted to products. It refers to a wide range of activities (processes, practices) and a wide range of result (goods, services,

---

[3] In June 2011, the Obama administration released "A Policy Framework for the 21st Century Grid: Enabling Our Secure Energy Future," accompanied by supporting studies produced by the National Science and Technology Council (Executive Office of the President 2013).

[4] The debate over what innovation entails is relevant in the following discussion because "innovation" as used here is less about invention or discovery, but more about a chain of activities from invention to commercial development, design, production, and supply of new or improved products and services in the market. Consequently, invention is only one small part of innovation. See Breznitz and Murphree (2011).

ol practices). It includes "new" as well as "significant improvement" – a "significantly improved product (good or service), or process, a new marketing method, or a new organizational method in business practices, workplace organization or external relations" (OECD 2005, p. 6).

The threat of climate change calls for revolutionising the production, distribution and utilization of electricity. Developing low-carbon sources of electricity is essential because electricity production and consumption currently contributes about 40 percent of the global greenhouse gas (GHG) emissions. Some firms have engaged in R&D in renewable energy technologies (solar, wind, geothermal, and others), some in electricity storage (e.g. battery systems), some on efficient usages by helping change consumer habits with better information (e.g. smart meters), while others focus on energy transport. Some of these efforts involve blue-sky R&D, designed to overcome "longstanding physical limits on energy conversion and storage" (Lester 2014). Examples of innovations with the potential to revolutionize entire energy systems include the efforts of US national laboratories to mimic plants by combining water and sunshine to generate energy and multilateral research on fusion under ITER (a thirty-five-country international nuclear fusion research and engineering project).

As a major transmission operator, SGCC avoided blue-sky R&D research. It built on the technologies that had been developed in other parts of the world but were not in use at the turn of the century. At that time, most R&D activities in the electricity industry focused on how to quickly develop renewable generation capacity at a cost which could be acceptable to consumers without government subsidies. Challenges facing the electricity networks as the result of an expansion of renewable sources of electricity generation were not widely appreciated until a decade later. In China, different pressures encouraged SGCC to focus on R&D in transmission technologies. In 2003–5, power shortages spread around the country, with the gap between available supply and user demand reaching 34 percent. They had an immediate economic impact. All concerned players jumped into action: generation companies, with the encouragement of provincial and local governments, quickly constructed hundreds of thermal power stations (about 95 percent of them were subcritical ones – small size, low-efficiency, and highly polluting) (IEA 2015); the coal industry expanded production with thousands of coal mines going into operation with little safety and environmental protection; the National Development and Reform Commission (NDRC), the central planner, freed coal price to encourage coal production, increased power tariffs to discourage consumption, speeded up project approval for power generation plants, adopted policies to encourage investment in renewable energy, and encouraged the adoption of energy efficiency measures; and hydro, nuclear, and renewable industries all embraced the opportunity to expand production as a solution to power shortages.

SGCC grabbed its opportunity and interpreted power shortages in its own terms. It attributed the problem to bottlenecks in China's transmission and distribution (T&D) infrastructure – that is, fragmented T&D networks meant surplus electricity in one province could not always be shared with a neighbor facing shortages. As in most countries, China's T&D system developed by connecting local power plants and supplying local end-users. It remained fragmented and disconnected at the end of the 1990s even though the number of separate grids had been reduced – from eighteen in the early 1980s to ten in 1997, and then down to six regional grids in 2002 (IEA 2006, pp. 40–1). In addition to weak interconnection, T&D management was decentralized, in part because of the different ownership of distribution companies and in part because of the large number of separate transmission grids. Fragmented networks encouraged and were reinforced by protectionist policies of local governments. This was one of the main reasons for the central government to restructure the industry.

For SGCC, electricity demand would continue to rise because of the initial low electricity consumption per capita, continuing economic growth and rapid urbanization. The way to support rising demand was to expand large-scale renewable sources of generation and to build large coal-fired thermal and hydropower power generation bases. These developments would necessitate expanded infrastructure to "wire" electricity to load centers. The uneven geographical allocation of natural resources – coal reserves are in north and northwest regions of China and hydro is in south and southwest parts of China – and location of end-users (more than three quarters are along the coast) meant that long-distance coal transportation had already clogged railways and roads in 2002–4. Investing in cross-province, cross-region interconnected networks would help solve several problems simultaneously: energy security and efficiency, congested railways and roads, and worsening environmental pollution, especially around coastal cities where population and power demand were concentrated.

SGCC needed to "sell" its diagnosis and solution for power shortages to the government officials who were besieged with proposals from many interested players. Even in China, there is no monopoly over the definition of problems, which depends on the "preferred solutions" of political players, and their interpretative maneuvres. As Cobb and Elder explained some time ago, "policy problems are not simply givens, nor are they matters of the facts of a situation; they are matters of interpretation and social definition" (Cobb and Elder 1983, p. 172). Instead of seeing the cause of power shortages as the lack of generation capacity or coal supplies, SGCC presented an alternative explanation – inadequate interconnected transmission networks. Government officials would not take a new definition of problems seriously without a proposed course of action. The management of SGCC suggested that its UHV projects could address multiple challenges facing NDRC: relieving power shortages, promoting energy security, and halting the deterioration of urban air quality. In so doing, SGCC steered the narrative in a new direction, echoing Aaron Wildavsky's observation that "If one can alter conceptions of what is problematical (not inevitable), an entire series of actions may be affected" (1979, p. 57).

GOVERNMENT POLICIES

Policies on SOE reform and on innovation provide the institutional matrix within which SGCC operates. The electricity restructuring in 2002 was part of the broader reform of SOEs, designed to rationalize the position and role of SOEs in the economy. Medium- and small-sized enterprises were "encouraged" and guided to find their way in the market through restructuring, merger and acquisition, even bankruptcy while large ones, especially in strategic sectors, such as defense, telecommunication, and energy, were placed under the supervision of the central government and encouraged to expand – a policy known as "grabbing the large and letting go of the small" (抓大放小) (Lin and Wilhaupt 2013; Naughton and Tsai 2015). SASAC was created in 2003 as the ultimate owner of 196 central SOEs, mandated to "manage the state assets" of these central SOEs and to maintain and expand the value of their assets. At the time about two-thirds of these central SOEs were loss-making entities. How to turn them around was left to SASAC to decide as there was no agreed reform strategy. SASAC took a proactive role in defining its mandates. Instead of selling off loss-making SOEs, SASAC decided to help restructure and build them into modern corporations. To achieve this objective, SASAC engineered a series of measures to encourage these SOEs to: separate and reorganize core and non-core functions; divest non-core businesses to build strong competitive firms around a few core functions; reduce the social burdens many of them had inherited from the planned economy; and encourage successful firms to acquire failing SOEs.

From the beginning, the minister of SASAC made it clear to the chief executives of these central SOEs: "We have only one objective – that is, to promote and strengthen our large SOEs and help build your global competitiveness" (Li 2004). He called on central SOEs to become the top three or top five companies in their sectors – either on their own, or by merging with or acquiring other firms. The evaluation systems of the SOE chief executives and of SOEs themselves were set in such a way to encourage them to become competitive in both domestic and global markets. Meanwhile, the SOEs were also encouraged to bring in technically adept managers and were provided greater clarity of ownership rights.

Many central SOEs quickly turned around from loss-making to profit-making corporations (Naughton 2015, p. 51). SASAC was criticized for steering cheap credit to central SOEs; enforcing rules selectively in favor of its SOEs; allowing them to monopolize key industries and increase political, social, and economic inequality with excessive managerial compensation; and, most importantly, promoting "state sector advance and private sector retreat" (国进民退), thus contributing to China's domestic imbalances with an overly rich and large state and a poor population (国富民穷) (McNally 2013, p. 51; Yang 2012; Eaton 2013). Justified or not, some SOEs responded to the incentive structure set up by SASAC while others did not. SGCC was among the successful ones. Its UHV projects were pursued in part to respond to the government policies – to build SGCC into China's GE or China's Siemens.

In early 2000s, the central government also began to formulate a new national innovation strategy. The economic reform started with the introduction of what Deng Xiaoping called, "four modernisations" in the late 1970s. One of them was science and technology (S&T) modernization. In the following two decades, the official policy was to allow and encourage foreign companies to bring technologies to China in exchange for market share. This policy represented a shift toward an outward-looking strategy designed to introduce, acquire, assimilate and improve mature technologies from advanced economies, repeat the process with a higher level of technology in the consolidation stage, and accumulate indigenous capacities to generate and commercialize new technologies. To implement this innovation strategy, the government introduced a series of major initiatives.

The National Science and Technology Development Plan (1978–85) focused on funding R&D to meet "urgent economic and social needs." The National High-Tech R&D Program (known as the 863 Program) adopted in 1986 aimed to develop high technology industries (e.g., bio-technology, new materials, lasers, energy, information, robotics, and space) and commercialize them. It introduced "the concept of peer review and a mixed method of project selection for the first time to technology plans in China" (Naughton and Segal 2003, p. 167). The Torch Program of high technology industry development (火炬计划) adopted in 1988 aimed to channel resources to support the establishment of fifty-three high- and new-tech industrial development zones. Like the previous innovation policies, the Torch Program emphasized "industrialisation and dissemina-tion of technology to generate economic growth" by focusing on commer-cialization of proven technologies (Breznitz and Murphree 2011, p. 77). The National Basic Research Program (973 Program) was launched in March 1997, again with emphasis on commercialization.

These policies changed the government's role from "direct control of resource transfer/distribution and coordination of organizations in the innovation system" to "linking R&D through a number of measures, including setting up production centres to assist firms to implement technologies originating from state R&D institutes and creating incubator centres" (Fan 2014). Yet, only a tiny minority of enterprises took advantage of the national policies to engage in serious industrial or research innova-tion as economic growth could be and was achieved by depending on abundant low-cost factors of production (land, resources, and labor) and scale of the market, rather than on technology innovation. By the early 2000s, only 0.03 percent of all enterprises were able to control their own core technologies; over 99 percent of enterprises had never applied for a patent; and 66 percent of the enterprises did not even have their own logo or brand (Bai and Wang 2015). A World Bank study shows that even in 2004–6, among 300,000 Chinese firms of all sizes, 53 percent of the large enterprises, 86 percent of the medium-sized, and 96 percent of small firms had no ongoing R&D programs. More than a third of China's international patent applications came from a single firm, while "63 percent of China's new patents for innovation were held by foreign individuals or firms, the vast majority of which were concentrated in high-tech industries" (Chen 2009, p. 129).

Many attribute low innovation activity to inadequate allocation of resources to R&D. China's R&D expenditure as a proportion of Gross Domestic Product (GDP) dropped from 0.75 percent in 1991 to a low of 0.5 percent in 1996. By then, the number of people engaging in R&D per million people in China was 10.5 percent of that in the United States and merely 9 percent of that in Japan (Yusuf et al. 2009). In addition, only a minute share (5–6 percent) of total R&D spending went to basic research (Song 2008, p. 238). During the late 1990s and early 2000s, the central government introduced a series of fiscal policy changes to encourage firms to engage in applied research and innovation by shifting funding sources. Specifically, it reduced direct budgetary allocation to research institutes; offered financial incentives for research institutes to engage in applied research and "to commercialise R&D activities" (Fan 2014, p. 732), while it steadily increased the overall budget allocation on research. In 2002–4, as the central government developed a new strategy on technology and innovation, SASAC responded by including innovation in its SOE evaluation systems. These two sets of policies – on SOE reforms and innovation – provided the incentive structure within which the newly created SGCC operated.

Ever since the "war of the currents" at the end of the 19th century, alternating current (AC) technology had been used to transport electricity from power plants to end-users because of its flexibility. As the distance between power generation and end-users expanded, utilities increased carrying capacity (voltage) to compensate for line losses, which increase with distance. By the late 20th century, most countries built power transmission networks with 220kv, 350kv, and small numbers of 500kv AC lines.

In 1955, ABB successfully built its first high voltage direct current (DC) line in Sweden. DC lines can carry electrical power over long-distance with much reduced line losses. Once electricity is transported from one end to the other, complex and expensive transformer stations then must be available to convert and transport electricity to end-users via local AC networks. Even though laboratories in several countries started researching and testing high-voltage AC transmission technologies in the late 20th century, no such line was in commercial operation by the end of the century because, unlike asynchronous DC lines, high-voltage AC lines are synchronized and therefore pose technical difficulties in maintaining operational stability and reliability.

China started late in its electricity development. It had been far behind in interconnected transmission infrastructure and in its ability to design and construct high-voltage transmission networks. It constructed its first ±500kv DC transmission system, connecting the Gezhouba hydro station in western Hubei to Shanghai, only in 1989–90, more than thirty years after the technology came into widespread use in advanced economies. This was a cross-region asynchronous parallel operating system when China's highly fragmented provincial systems were predominantly connected and supported by 200kv lines. This first 500kv system was a turnkey project from the Swiss firm BBC, which soon merged with Sweden's SAEA to form what is known as ABB. BBC provided a complete package, including design, technology, and equipment. This dependence on imported technology and supply continued when China constructed its first 750kv transmission line in the late 1990s.

Having monitored worldwide R&D in transmission technology, the technology department of the Ministry of Electrical Power (MEP) suggested to the State Planning Commission in 1999 that China should develop its own technologies for high-voltage DC (±800kv) and AC (750kv) transmission systems to meet rising demand, as traditional 220kv, 350kv, and even 500kv transmission lines were both insufficient and also incapable of carrying electricity to distant end-users without excessive line losses. No one picked up the suggestion because both the risk and the price tag would be too high for the country in need of resources for everything. In addition, no single agency fully controlled the resources for transmission construction and R&D for new technologies.

Throughout the reform period, transmission and distribution always had to fight for attention and resources with generation. Generating capacity expanded quickly as provincial governments and large enterprises were keenly aware of the disruption associated with frequent power shortages. In addition, investing in generation was much less intensive than for T&D networks – a public good with widespread benefits. In 1985–95, only 20 percent of the total power sector investment went to T&D which remained the responsibility of the central government, while investment in generation came from a range of sources. Investment in distribution in the second half of the 1990s increased significantly as the central government used it to stimulate the economy following the Asian financial crisis. On average, it remained low, less than 30 percent of the total investment in the electricity industry, well below the average level of 50 percent among OECD countries (Table 6.1).

China's electrical equipment industry also lagged far behind. The grid industry depended on imports for nearly all necessary components – from switchgears, transformers, all types of circuit-breakers and surge arresters, to a multitude of specialized devices of all designs, equipment, and technologies. These imports were not from just one country or company; all major companies were competing for the market. Imports came from ABB, from Germany's Siemens, France's Schneider, Japan's Mitsubishi, and General Electric (GE). Industry specialists compared the situation to the "united army" of major powers that extracted territorial concessions from

Table 6.1 *Average Share of Investment in Generation and in Transmission & Distribution, 2001–2005*

	USA	Britain	Japan	France	China
Generation	47%	45%	46%	31%	70%
Transmission and Distribution	53%	55%	54%	69%	30%

Source: SGCC (2006, p. 22)

China in the early 20th century – 八国联军. This international mosaic made it extremely difficult and costly for China to absorb foreign technologies and develop its own.

The formation of SGCC changed all this. For the first time, T&D had a single "spokesman" and champion. It no longer had to fight for attention and resources with its colleagues in generation and other segments of the power industry. SGCC management viewed implementation of the mandate to construct and expand cross-province, cross-region interconnected T&D infrastructure as a vital corporate objective. SGCC proposed to deploy UHV technologies (both AC and DC, and synchronized AC/DC) to create a national interconnected T&D infrastructure network. With UHV projects as a platform, SGCC in turn could build its capacity and expand too.

The SGCC management, especially its chief executive, took up a critical role as policy entrepreneur, combining vision, "love for the game," and willingness "to invest resources – time, energy, reputation, money" (Kingdon 1995, p. 179). More importantly, SGCC had the institutional capacity to support T&D initiatives with financial resources, "professionals with recognised expertise and competence in a particular domain and an authoritative claim to policy-relevant knowledge within that domain or issue area" (Haas 1992, p. 3). In addition, SGCC management responded to the flow of political events, often using existing ideas to reset policy narratives with the goal of recruiting and expanding political support. This was not only a political strategy but also "the first-order economising" of firms – adaptation (Williamson 1991). In actively pursuing policy agenda setting, SGCC behaved like all corporations, state-owned or private alike, as a political, institutional, and economic entrepreneur, trying to control its destiny.

SGCC's active policy entrepreneurship worked at a time when the central government was in the process of drafting a national innovation strategy. SGCC mobilized institutional resources to "sell" its technologies and projects to decision makers throughout 2005. It organized research teams supervised and guided by experts, including many drawn from China's prestigious academies of science and engineering, to conduct preliminary studies and report their findings to national and international conferences that SGCC organized.

To incorporate its vision, ideas, and projects into the national innovation strategy, SGCC had to compete with many demands from all corners of the society (Wessner 2011). More importantly, it had to convince key decision makers who were being lobbied by many sectors and groups, including those who opposed UHV projects.[5] The opposition came from several directions: some opposed the UHV projects on political grounds, insisting that SGCC sought to further monopolize and centralize its control over China's power sector. Some did so for economic reasons – that is, UHV projects would necessitate large increases in electricity prices, massive government subsidies, or both. Others opposed it for technical reasons, arguing that the proposed jump to frontier technology was premature for an industry that had barely finished its first 750kv line, and also that SGCC's proposed innovations in long-distance transmission could endanger the stability and reliability of China's entire electricity system.[6]

SGCC appealed for policy makers' support from two perspectives: to build SGCC into an internationally competitive technology powerhouse, and to master UHV technologies in order to take the commanding heights in global competition for the transition to low-carbon electricity. This was SGCC's key selling point – to invest in the development of UHV technologies, master them and actually utilize them would enable SGCC to reverse

---

[5] An increasing number of studies highlight the pluralization of decision making in China. The debate over the UHV projects was only one example. See the discussion on the pluralization of decision making in Mertha (2009) and Hammond (2013).

[6] Scale matters in transmission infrastructure: in general, as transmission voltages and capacities increase, carrying distance extends, line losses decline, greater scale economies accumulate, and costs decline. The voltage level of a transmission line is the key factor that determines its power-carrying capacity. Given its physical attributes, the higher the voltage of a transmission line, the more power it can carry. For instance, over the same distance, a 345kv line can carry approximately as much power as six 138kv lines; a 765kv line can carry as much power as five 345kv lines or thirty 138kv lines; and the natural transmission capacity of a 1000kv AC circuit is about four to five times that of a 500kv AC line, while a circuit ±800kv DC line has the capacity equivalent to 2.1 times that of a ±500kv DC line. High voltage transmission lines thus economize on land use: a 1000kv AC line saves 50–66% of the corridor area required by a 500kv AC line, while a ±800kv DC line saves 23% of the corridor required by a 500kv DC line in transmitting the same capacity. For the merits of these technologies, see Scherer, Jr. and Vassell (1985); Lings (2005); Huang et al. (2009); and MIT (2009).

its position as "second fiddle" depending on "technology transfers from multinational companies" (Williamson and Raman 2011, p. 110) and place a Chinese firm among world leaders in this major industry.

After a three-year drafting process, the State Council released the *Medium- to Long-Term Plan for the Development of Science and Technology, 2006–2020* in 2006 (the 2006 MLP). The 2006 MLP consisted of three specific provisions: firstly, to build strong Chinese enterprises, technology, and brands, and to reduce their dependence on foreign technology; secondly, to require government ministries and SOEs to procure at least 80 percent of their goods, when feasible, from domestic sources; and, thirdly, to encourage foreign firms doing business in China to transfer their latest and most advanced technology to Chinese partners. To help Chinese firms develop their capacity to compete, the 2006 MLP included some specific fiscal measures, such as exemption from tariffs or import-related VAT on equipment for firms engaging in technological renovation and product upgrading, and income or turnover tax relief for foreign firms or joint ventures engaging in technology transfer, and direct grants to R&D activities. The centerpiece of the 2006 MLP was a transition from encouraging imitation to pursuing innovation focusing on *indigenous innovation* (自主创新) to address China's weak record of firm-level innovative capacity for sustainable economic growth.[7]

The national priority list included energy-related technologies, among them SGCC's proposals for large-scale, large-capacity, long-distance DC technology, UHV AC technology and equipment, technologies for integrating intermittent generation sources into the grid, and grid safety and reliability. Even though in theory, both UHV AC and UHV DC were "relatively mature technologies" that several countries had tried to implement, no UHV DC or UHV AC line was in commercial operation at the turn of the century. Nor did an integrated system of UHV AC and UHV DC exist in any country. Since transmission networks in most countries primarily employed 220kv and a few 350kv lines, there was no commercial production of the equipment required for ±800kv DC and 1000kv AC lines.

SGCC's proposal to construct innovative long-distance UHV transmission networks required multiple technological breakthroughs. Innovation is

---

[7] The 2006 MLP was controversial outside China as many commentators argue it was a protectionist measure that the government put in place to assist Chinese firms in an increasingly global market. Without taking a position on the issue, this chapter highlights the point that some firms took advantage of the incentives offered by the Plan to engage in innovative activities while others failed to do so. For the debate, see Fan et al. (2009); Crooke (2012); Steinfeld and Beltoft (2014).

a quest into the unknown. It "involves uncertainty, risk taking, probing and reprobing, experimenting, and testing," and in the process, "'dry holes' and 'blind alleys' are the rule, not the exception" (Jorde and Teece 1990, p. 76). An electricity transmission system is a complex assemblage of individual elements, consisting of transmission lines, transformers, switching equipment, and a multitude of specialized devices necessary to assure the *safe* and *reliable* delivery of electric power to the consumer. Thus, UHV technologies were on the priority list of the 2016 MLP because of their spill-over effects. Their development would require technology breakthroughs in basic physics and engineering research, materials, and equipment manufacturing.

In combination with the 2006 MLP, SASAC adopted measures to encourage central SOEs to engage in R&D and develop indigenous technology. Included in the assessment criteria for central SOEs, for instance, were building global brand names, global networks, international standards and global leadership. These policies changed national narratives on technology innovation and brought a cultural shift among some large firms, public and private alike: it became well accepted that "the first class firms build standards; the second class firms build brands, and the third class firms make products" (一流企业做标准，二流企业做品牌，三流企业做产品).[8] Policies play an important role in moulding firms' strategies and actions, but they do not determine whether firms will respond, what strategies and actions they will take or how they implement their plans. "Firms have a considerable range of freedom regarding whether, or just how, they will take advantage of the opportunities the environment affords" (Nelson 1991, pp. 63–4). This is certainly the case with China's central SOEs; state ownership alone cannot explain their different strategies, organizational structures supporting such strategies and their capacities to implement their plans.

STATE GRID CORPORATION OF CHINA'S STRATEGY FOR INNOVATION

SGCC adopted a project-driven research strategy that was inclusive and collaborative, based on a technology innovation chain of education,

---

[8] A few central SOEs started investing heavily in R&D and technology innovation, nearly all around 2003–4. Therefore, it is more accurate to view the adoption of the 2006 MLP as a confirmation of practices than an initiative undertaken by the State Council. A six-episode documentary provides a good explanation of the motivation and the difficulties of these innovative efforts, especially how difficult it is for their new products to be accepted in China when foreign companies had already dominated the core technology markets. See CCTV-2 (2013).

research, application, and production (产，学，研，用结合的创新体系), with centralized resource allocation and centralized management of patent applications and intellectual property rights. It was an open innovation in the sense that SGCC created the Common Engineering Platform, a working group centered around its core experts, but including external specialists from a wide range of universities, research institutes, potential future customers, and equipment suppliers (both domestic and international). Meanwhile the question "who is in charge" was never in doubt. Collaboration was on the terms and conditions set by SGCC as its management controlled the agenda, provided financial support for research, and determined terms of cooperation.

Human capital is the key to firm-level innovation. Changing its position from being a "follower" to a "leader" in the grid industry would require SGCC develop the necessary "hardware, software, 'organisation-ware', 'human-ware' and other types of invisible assets" (Hagstrom and Chandler 1998, p. 2). As a grid operator, SGCC had limited capacity to engage in R&D in UHV technologies. Even at its research institutes, the core team of researchers was limited. SGCC needed research capacity at the Chinese Academy of Engineering and the Chinese Academy of Sciences, and at key universities. One of the first things the SGCC management did was to mobilize and assemble a team of internal and outside experts who shared its vision.

Three groups of people were identified and each played a different role in this effort. A group of older and established experts, including some retirees, was brought on board to provide intellectual leadership, supervise and mentor young researchers, ensure standards, serve on advisory committees, and offer legitimacy for the projects with their authoritative assessment on all aspects of UHV technologies. Many of these experts were members of the Academy of Sciences and Academy of Engineering, working in national research institutes or universities. The second group of experts were SGCC insiders who had not only technical expertise but also management capacity. They were put in leadership positions to assemble teams and to head the research institutes under SGCC or to lead specific research teams on core technologies for the UHV projects. This group included the chief executive and his deputy. These well-educated and highly intelligent specialists were willing to work in the harshest conditions possible, which was necessary for some of the most difficult tests and experiments. Many were industry insiders with decades of experience (Li 2008). The third group of researchers consisted of recent graduates who had risen to the top in their fields. These young researchers were selected from various parts of the SGCC as well as universities and other research institutes around the country and told by the management, "there are only two scales for your evaluation, 0–1; if UHV succeeds, you get one; otherwise, it is zero."

Individual researchers need an enabling institutional environment. The management team reorganized SGCC's research institutions to create such an environment supportive of ambitious and risk-laden research. In the mid-1990s MEP had ten research institutions, focusing on various aspects of the electricity industry. These research institutes were under a dual system: organizationally, they were part of the MEP and their research agenda and funding were decided by the MEP, while their research standards, professional licensing and promotion were under purview of the State Commission of Science and Technology (predecessor of the Ministry of Science and Technology, MOST). After reform started, these research institutes, like their counterparts in other fields, were burdened by social responsibilities for their retired employees and their families, but had few income sources to compensate for shrinking research budgets. The government encouraged research institutes to "adapt" to the market environment and conduct research with industrial applications. Few succeeded commercially and many suffered a serious brain drain as young and able researchers either went overseas or transferred to other industries and to multinational corporations. When the MEP was dissolved, these "loss making" research institutes were placed under SPCC. At the time of unbundling in 2002, the "best" part of the electricity industry, regarding technology, human capital or profits, was in generation, as 70 percent of the profit in the electricity industry was in the hands of generation companies, while 30 percent was in T&D. These research institutes were unwanted financial burdens (one indication is that these research institutes supported almost as many retirees as regular employees). The State Council placed them under SGCC for supervision until they could be restructured. A decade later, after SGCC managed to turn these research institutes around, the initial reasons for the arrangement were forgotten as critics attacked SGCC for monopolizing the industry's research capacities.

A few academy members and scientists in the industry, however, still remember the history:

Fortunately, unbundling and restructuring the electricity industry did not disperse the team of scientists and engineers, and SGCC kept them. It would have been so easy to let them go, but would be extremely difficult and costly to gather talents when you need them. I don't think we could have made the UHV projects work so quickly without this group of experts.[9]

---

[9] Interview with Liu Qiang, Tsinghua University, Beijing, 27 July 2014.

With the core research teams in place, headed by its chosen experts, the SGCC management began reorganizing these research institutes. At the time, there were fifty-five research, design, and experiment centers, 407 laboratories, and over 20,000 employees under SGCC's big umbrella. If they all worked on what they wanted, SGCC would never be able to develop its capacity and to master the design, technology and equipment for its UHVC projects. To deal with the problem of everybody trying to do everything (麻雀虽小，五脏俱全 [although small, a sparrow has everything a vulture has]), SGCC centralized its team building and funding around five major research institutes.

A department of science and technology was created at SGCC headquarters as a center of a research network system to coordinate all activities and manage allocation of funding. The SGCC management reorganized its five main research institutes, and established a specific focus for each: Electric Power Research Institute (EPRI) in Beijing would concentrate on UHV AC; Wuhan High-Voltage Research Institute was to specialize in UHV DC; Nari (Nanjing Automation Research Institute) emphasized automation, and so forth. It also established four research test bases focused on UHV AC, UHV DC, High Altitude, and UHV engineering, as well as two specialized research centers – SGCC Simulation Centre and Centre of Metrology on Current and Frequency. Each was led by a technically-qualified expert. These institute and center directors formed part of the core team for the UHV projects and were given research funding and independence in their specific fields. The reorganization was done to create a research system with a high degree of internal coordination and concentrated resources to meet the needs of SGCC.

More importantly, SGCC increased its spending on R&D and introduced an incentive structure to reward those who could innovate and transfer those who could not. In 2006 alone, its investment in R&D rose by 34 percent from the previous year's level. SGCC promised to invest a total of 30 billion yuan in R&D in 2006–10. The change from MEP to SPCC and especially to SGCC changed the sources of funding for research institutes and consequently the focus of research. This was part of the general reform of commercializing and corporatizing SOEs that were made responsible for their own finance and development. The research institutes attached to SGCC no longer received budget allocations from the government, even though they could apply for research funding under several national competitive schemes, such as Program 973, Program 863, the Torch Program, or the 1000 Young Talents program. Their main funding source is SGCC.

Table 6.2 State Grid Corporation of China's Research and
Development Spending, 2004–2017 (billion yuan and percent)

Year	Research and Development Spending	Change from Previous Year (%)
2004	3.79	
2005	4.82	27.2
2006	6.48	34.4
2007	10.2	57.4
2008	5.06	−50.4
2009	5.14	1.6
2010	6.13	19.3
2011	6.45	5.2
2012	7.94	23.1
2013	5.79	−27.1
2014	7.08	22.3
2015	7.38	4.2
2016	6.92	−6.2
2017	7.83	13.2

Source: SGCC, Corporate Social Responsibility Report, various years.

The research funding from SGCC HQ consists of two parts: their normal research programs, which are shaped by the demand from the various parts of SGCC; and resources allocated to specific projects. The advantage of enterprises doing R&D is that they have the money. For example, the funding for a government-funded research institute is normally in the tens of millions, but for a SGCC research institute, it is hundreds of millions of yuan. The research funding allocated by SGCC to the Electric Power Research Institute (EPRI) alone in 2005–9 exceeded the total funding EPRI had received from the central government in 1951–2004.[10] For the top researchers working on UHV technologies, management promised from the very beginning that they would not have to worry about funding. Table 6.2 shows how SGCC ramped up R&D spending – a critical ingredient in advancing high-risk research.

---

[10] This is not unique for research institutes under SGCC. After the corporatization of SOEs in the late 1990s, SOEs needed to support their own research activities. This development was reflected on the government spending on R&D. The country's total spending on R&D used to come from government only. By 2001, government's share reduced to 68% and down to 54% by 2005. A few large and successful companies in IT, for example, devoted a large share of their profits to R&D. SGCC significantly increased its spending on R&D in 2005–7 primarily because of its UHV projects (Gu and Huang 2009, p. 96).

COLLABORATING WITH SUPPLIERS AND MULTINATIONAL CORPORATIONS

When SGCC proposed the UHV projects to government, it promised to cover the cost of the first experimental UHV project and also to ensure that 80 percent of the technologies and equipment for this first UHV project would come from domestic sources. To achieve the objective, SGCC had to work with both multinationals and domestic equipment manufacturers.

Collaboration with multinationals was what SGCC initially wanted. Its management was conscious that it would need to work with the multi-nationals, especially those that not only had control of the technologies, but also had already penetrated the Chinese markets.[11] In 2006, SGCC sent its first team of senior managers to Siemens for a three-week training course. There were exchanges with Siemens, Mitsubishi, GE, and other major companies. Collaboration with the multinationals was not always easy, as SGCC wanted to gain control of core technologies; wanted to change itself from a technology buyer to a technology maker; and wanted to be in the driver's seat in collaboration, while the MNCs refused to surrender their control. The two sides had different views on "dependence"; SGCC consid-ered that the Chinese market and UHV projects offered multinationals a valuable opportunity, especially as no other countries were developing such infrastructure. For their part, the multinationals viewed their technol-ogies and equipment as indispensable components for attaining SGCC's UHV objectives.

In the early 21st century, several multinational giants – Siemens, ABB, Alstom, Toshiba, Mitsubishi, and GE – dominated the electric equipment industry worldwide. These corporations controlled the design, core technol-ogies, and manufacturing capacities of primary equipment of switchgears, transformers, rally GIS, circuit breakers, and automatic switchers, and of secondary devices, such as isolation control, signal, rally, and protection devices. ABB, for example, pioneered HVDC transmission technology in 1954 when it constructed the world's first HVDC line in Gotland, Sweden. In the following years, it dominated HVDC markets. These MNCs provided turnkey transmission substations by offering "one-stop" supply of power transmission products and services. They wanted SGCC to continue the

---

[11] For instance, in 2004, SGCC granted ABB a US$390 million contract to build a transmission line from the Three Gorges Hydropower Station to Shanghai, hoping some technologies could be transferred and its employees could learn from the project (Tse 2005).

practice of importing turnkey projects as it had done with its first 500kv and first 750kv projects. These MNCs were confident that they could translate their superior design and technology capabilities into continued dominance in the China market as long as the Chinese equipment producers remained "far behind the leading multinationals in terms of both scale and technology" (Nolan and Wang 1998, p. 418). Even for lower voltage transmission projects, imports occupied more than half of the technologies and equipment deployed throughout China's T&D system.

SGCC's effort to turn the situation around by working with MNCs encountered unanticipated difficulties. Negotiations surrounding core technologies quickly stalled. Converter valves, for instance, are core equipment for UHV DC lines. No one was producing devices suitable for ±800kv DC lines. To develop thyristor valves – a type of converter valve for UHV DC projects – SGCC researchers approached Siemens and ABB, both of which already had large operations in China. In the prolonged negotiation held in Beijing, it became clear neither firm wanted to invest in R&D in the new product because of the high risks and uncertain returns. In the end, one firm indicated that it was willing to modify the existing 5-inch (125-mm) thyristor valves used for 500kv high-voltage DC systems for SGCC's ±800kv UHV DC projects. The other agreed to collaborate with the Chinese to develop new converter valves for UHV, but insisted on controlling all potential patent rights. The SGCC team rejected both offers. It refused to take the modified product as SGCC never intended to build only one UHV DC line; the first experimental project was just the beginning and SGCC wanted to be able to produce proper products, not modified versions of an earlier product. Researchers at SGCC took the second suggestion as an insult. If there was collaboration, the Chinese proposed to share control of any resulting patents, as one chief researcher explained later:

Initially, we hoped to use our market to exchange for technology through research collaboration because we did not have the capacity at the time. We would have liked to have their collaboration and would have appreciated it too, but we would not be controlled on key technologies and they were not indispensable. We would do it with or without their collaboration (Wang 2014).

Researchers at SGCC took on the task in developing the equipment. Two years later, China became the only country able to produce this new product – 6-inch (150-mm) thyristor valves – on a commercial basis. This device now leads the world in current, voltage, and capacity. The first experimental UHV DC project from Xiangjiaba to Shanghai used over 6,000 such 6-inch (150-mm) thyristor valves. SGCC significantly reduced the cost when its own subsidiary, Xuji, was able to supply the product. The lead scientist later commented, "we could not starve just because they did not want to give us food, could we" (Wang 2014)?

Negotiations on collaborating with ABB on 1100kv gas-insulated switchgear (GIS) were equally difficult: they lasted over a month. The Chinese team laid down three principles: collaboration in designing, sharing intellectual property rights, and cooperation in production. The first principle was to ensure that Chinese researchers could develop their own new product. ABB agreed on this because, like many multi-nationals at the time, it did not think the Chinese could learn the core technology through such collaboration. ABB refused to share patents and intellectual property rights. "Yes, negotiation was very difficult," explained one chief negotiator. "In the end, ABB had to agree because of the promise SGCC had made and NDRC had written in its approval of the projects – 80 percent of the technology and equipment needed to come from domestic sources. If the final product was theirs, we could not use it and we would have to do it alone" (Ni 2014). Compromises resolved the issue of cooperation in production – ABB contributed some parts, while Chinese firms supplied other components. Indeed, research on both thyristor valves and H-GIS was eventually conducted in China, Sweden, and Switzerland.

Chinese firms now make nearly all equipment for both UHV AC and UHV DC systems. Even for the few core technologies that multinationals still control, they have to work with Chinese makers because no other countries produce these devices on a commercial scale. China is the only country investing in multiple varieties of UHV projects (AC, DC and AC-DC synchronized transmission lines). This has led many MNCs to locate their research in China. According to Siemens:

In the 1990s, 'Sold in China' gave way to 'Made in China' and eventually to 'Developed in China'. Today the new challenge is 'Innovated in China'. An international company that aims to be successful in the world's most populous and most dynamic country should forget the illustration of an inexpensive work-bench. Today, the entire value chain – from research to development and production – has to take place in China, which is the Chinese government's strategy. We have to speed up so that Siemens could stay ahead of growing local competition. Then as now, the main priorities of [Siemens'] 400 people, including 220 researchers and IP specialists at Corporate Technology in China, are to develop close collaboration with Chinese customers.[12]

---

[12] Siemens (2015). Studies have shown that advanced R&D activities of multinational corporations tend to be based in the home countries and even for those that do go global, they are often among the advanced economies with similar political systems, highly

If developing indigenous technology and innovation capacity is part of Chinese techno-nationalism, techno-globalism is also at work. Meanwhile, difficulties in collaboration with multinationals sparked episodes of techno-nationalism. For instance, laboratory managers at the US firm EPRI told visiting SGCC's delegates that "no data, no information, no camera, no recorder were allowed." "Years later when we had our own UHV technologies, we got our 'revenge' – we now tell our visitors, no data, no information, no camera, and no recorder is allowed." Hosts at TEPCO in Japan welcomed another team of SHCC visitors with warmth and politeness. The Japanese presented three huge transformers – "these are the transformers built specially for you; we are sure you would like to use our technology." The Japanese wanted to sell them as turnkey projects without technology transfer. When visiting an exhibition in Frankfurt, the Chinese team asked whether they could take pictures. It was told, "take as many as you want; you can even use video recorder if you want." Then the German host added, "you will never be able to make it anyway." The perceived arrogance or insults from MNCs seem to have created as much motivation as the incentives provided by the Chinese government (Gu and Huang 2009; CCTV-2 2013).

SUPPORTING OR DOMINATING THE TRANSMISSION AND DISTRIBUTION EQUIPMENT INDUSTRY

As a grid operator, SGCC initially had no capacity to produce equipment for its UHV projects. Under normal circumstances, SGCC would shop around until it found satisfactory equipment. To keep its promise that at least 80 percent of the equipment would come from domestic sources, SGCC intervened, first helping the electric equipment manufacturers develop the capacity to produce equipment of the required specifications and quality, and later, acquiring two of these manufacturers when opportunities emerged to reduce cost and to ensure quality. What SGCC did might be "normal" practice of firms: as Oliver Williamson and other leading economists have long argued, large corporations can lower the transaction costs associated with their multifarious activities by absorbing parts of the supply chain. That is, if firms had to contract with other firms to research, finance, manufacture, and market their products, the costs of forming, maintaining, and enforcing those relationships would far exceed

concentrated in Europe, Japan and the US. See, for example, Vernon (1966); Patel (1995); Doremus et al., eds. (1998); Boutellier et al. (1999).

the costs associated with independent ownership. By helping equipment manufacturers develop their capacity and then acquiring them as part of the supply chain, SGCC stirred up a political controversy even though all a long it had the support of SASAC. SGCC played a role as "systems integrator" or "organizing brain" at the apex of its supply chains. "As they consolidated their leading positions, the systems integrator firms, with enormous procurement expenditure, exerted intense pressure upon the supply chain in order to minimize costs and stimulate technical progress" (Nolan 2012, p. 17).

The process started when SGCC contracted with two top manufacturers in China – Tebian Electric Apparatus (Shenyang, 沈阳特变电器) and Tianwei Baobian (天威保变) – to make 1000kv transformers for its UHV project. Both products failed initial voltage tests, endangering the whole project. Opposition voices rose once again: "Why does SGCC insist on building this UHV line while even western developed countries would not do it" (Opposition 2011). Repeated test failures shook the confidence of many working on the transformer project, including some academy members. SGCC faced two options: help its domestic suppliers develop the technology or entrust the work to multinationals. Despite the risks and costs, SGCC management chose the former. In the following two months, with financial support from the corporate headquarters, the SGCC chief engineer leading the UHV project gathered experts from several manufacturers to check the design and recalculate all the data, assembled experts from research institutes to work with the manufacturers, involved academics from several universities to do the recalculation and theoretical analysis, and invited reputable international firms to help with the analysis. SGCC funded and supervised the entire effort. These were unusual measures because rival manufacturers would not normally cooperate or share information. In helping manufacturers work together by providing financial and human resources, SGCC took a huge risk. When the new product passed the test, the relationship between SGCC and the two manufacturers also changed.

In addition, SGCC management decided to bring some of these manufacturers under its own wing to internalize the cost. This meant building a strong internal supply chain, making its own specifications and standards, manufacturing equipment, and integrating the equipment into its own grids. SGCC took advantage of the policy of SASAC – to build large and internationally competitive Chinese corporations through merger and acquisition. The minister of SASAC repeatedly told chief executives of central SOEs: "there is only one objective for all of you – to build large and strong central SOEs and improve your international competitiveness" (Lu 2010). External developments also helped to make this possible. The global financial crisis in 2008 led to the large stimulus package from which SGCC benefited, the economic downturns put a lot of pressure on manufacturing industries that were looking for new ways out, and the central government's decision to provide financial resources in restructuring and revitalizing equipment industries.

In the summer of 2009, SGCC announced its decision to acquire two top, yet cash-strapped, electric equipment manufacturers – Xuji (许继) and Pinggao (平高). This move immediately triggered political controversy. Opponents criticized the acquisitions as SGCC's attempt to institute a vertical monopoly that would enable it to squeeze out competition from rival equipment manufacturers. The head of the National Energy Administration (NEA) did not conceal his opposition, telling the media, "No, I did not approve or support them." Yet, NDRC, SASAC and the Ministry of Industry and Information Technology (MIIT) all supported the acquisitions, each for different reasons. They also fitted the broader agenda of government policies aimed at revitalizing equipment manufacturing industry, including high-end electric equipment (State Council 2006).

Xuji, an important equipment producer for electrical generation, transmission, and distribution, has a long history. It relocated to Xuchang, Henan, from Heilongjiang in 1970 during the Sino–Soviet border crisis. In 1997, it listed on the Hong Kong stock market. Xuji specializes in high-voltage lightning protection systems, and high-voltage, large capacity, and flexible converter valve systems. It ranks among China's top ten electric equipment manufacturers and is a key enterprise for the country's "Torch Program for high-tech industry development." Yet, persistent quality problems gradually eroded Xuji's competitive advantage over rival domestic producers. Its domestic market share dropped to only 1.2 percent by 2005.[13]

---

[13] The negligible market share of both Xuji and Pinggao (1.2% and 1% respectively) in electric equipment manufacturing industry was the main reason that several government agencies did not hesitate to support SGCC's acquisitions. After the 1980s, "industrial concentration occurred in almost every sector." By the mid-1990s, over two-thirds of the global output of electrical equipment had come from three companies: Siemens, ABB and GE. This oligopolistic structure set high entry barriers and significantly pushed up prices. In responding to a global trend of industrial concentration, the Chinese government and especially SASAC encouraged a few successful large SOEs to become part of "the high value-added, high-technology and strongly branded segments of global markets" (Nolan 2012, p. 17).

By the end of 2008, Xuji's profit level was below the industry average, with a long chain of products, heavy dependence on borrowing and poor management. It suffered cash shortages in 2008, with its debt-asset ratio reaching 93.33 percent. In 2008, Xuji transferred all of its assets to Ping An Trust Ltd, a direct subsidiary of a central SOE, Ping An Insurance (平安 保险), hoping to get a cash injection. In early 2009, SGCC's subsidiary, EPRI, approached Ping An Trust to acquire Xuji. It wanted to use Xuji as a platform for its high-end electric equipment R&D. In the end, Ping An Trust transferred a 60 percent stake in Xuji to EPRI, with a promise from EPRI that it would buy the remainder of Xuji at a later date. Xuji accepted the arrangement because it needed a capital injection (Zhang Zirui 2010).

Pinggao Group emerged from the Pingdingshan High Voltage Switchgear Factory, founded in 1970. It was state-owned, under the Henan branch of SASAC. In the 1980s, supported by the central government, Pinggao imported French technology, helping it to become one of China's top producers of electric equipment. In 1989, for the first time, it exported its PG brand switchgears to Bangladesh. In 2000, it formed a joint venture with Mitsubishi, which then floated on the Shanghai Stock Exchange in 2001, raising 740 million yuan. In the following years, Pinggao achieved several technical breakthroughs, developing China's first enclosed gas-insulated switchgear for UHV ±800 DC lines and for UHV 1000kv AC lines in 2007. The Chinese Academy of Sciences, Chinese Academy of Engineering and MOST certified these PG-brand technologies and products, which provided core equipment for UHV projects. In 2009, SGCC promised Pinggao and the local government that it would invest one billion yuan in PG that year and an additional 5 billion yuan over the following three years to build a strong electric equipment-manufacturing base – not only for domestic grid construction but also for overseas expansion. The deal was too good to reject: the local branch of SASAC at Pingdingshan in Henan province agreed to transfer its entire stake in the Pinggao Group to SGCC at zero cost. The group was formally integrated into SGCC in early 2010 (SGCC Acquisitions 2014).

Meanwhile, that both Xuji and Pinggao are located in Henan province made it easier for SGCC to obtain support from the provincial government. In addition to helping two cash-poor local companies, SGCC promised to invest 35 billion yuan in Henan's T&D infrastructure, an attractive prospect at a time when GDP growth rates figured prominently in the evaluation of provincial leaders' performance. Large investment in T&D projects meant jobs and better infrastructure in the province. Pinggao and Xuji were happy to be absorbed by the largest buyer of their products. The two manufacturers received immediate cash injections from SGCC, and its UHV projects provided them with a market and opportunity to improve their products. In the following five years, 2009–13, with SGCC's injected capital, the debt–asset ratio quickly dropped from 93 percent to a manageable level of 64 percent at Xuji, and from 65.45 percent to 46.88 percent at Pinggao. In addition, SGCC injected 2.84 billion yuan into their R&D in 2009–13. Leveraging SGCC's financial support, Xuji and Pinggao were able to raise capital for their development (9.69 billion yuan for Xuji and 7.49 billion yuan for Pinggao in 2013 alone – see SGCC Acquisitions 2014).

With the UHV projects as platforms and with SGCC financial support, Xuji and Pinggao developed their own high-end products that could dominate the Chinese market. One of the senior managers at Pinggao explained in 2010:

Before, we could produce only circuit breakers for systems below 500kv, and switchgears and GIS for ≥200kv systems. GIS for ≤500kv was completely dominated by Foreign companies – ABB, Areva, Mitsubishi, and Toshiba. In less than three years, with the support in R&D, we have developed 23 new products, obtained over 30 patents, and led or participated in national standard setting for nine products. All this has given us a seat at the table and a voice in the industry, and it has become our advantage in competition (Zhang 2010, p. 10).

Xuji and Pinggao were able to transform themselves into effective international competitors when SGCC itself ventured overseas. By 2013, they were able to win international contracts independently from SGCC's projects. Pinggao won an order worth 200 million yuan from an Indian monopoly, the Power Grid Corporation of India (PGCIL), to supply equipment to its Kanpur and Guraon 765/400kv substation project in Uttar Pradesh in 2013. In 2014, Pinggao signed a contract with the Polish grid company to supply equipment for the construction and expansion of the Kozienice 400/220/110kv substation. The value of Xuji's overseas orders in 2013 was 744 percent of that in 2009 (Lu 2015; Wang 2015).

With UHV projects as a platform, SGCC became "a system integrator," helping the electric equipment manufacturing industry consolidate and build its capacity. By 2010, China's electric equipment industry had developed an oligopolistic structure dominated by five or six players competing but also supplementing each other. They include Xuji, Pinggao, Nanjing Automation Research Institute (NARI), Tianwei, Tebian Electric Apparatus Co (TBEA), and Xidian Group

(XD). Taking transformers as an example, by 2015 the market was split among TBEA (40 percent), XD (30 percent), and Tianbao (30 percent); Pinggao, XD and Northeast Electric dominated the GIS market; and Xuji and XD controlled the converter valve market, each commanding a 40 percent market share (Wang 2015). A few of these manufacturers were able to take their products overseas and even invest in overseas production.

In sum, the combination of corporate strategy and government support transformed the electric equipment industry, where a few "able" players emerged to dominate domestic markets, and, as international competitors, working side-by-side with the key MNCs, threatening "to crowd others out of the global markets" (Paulson Institute 2015, p. 2).

FROM "GOOD ENOUGH" TO "TAKING THE LEAD"

By the time when the first UHV DC project (Jindongnan-Jinmen, 640km) went into operation in January 2009, SGCC had already adjusted its initial objective of self-preservation to becoming a world leader. UHV projects that began as a platform to build SGCC into a modern corporation now became a launchpad for SGCC to "go global" and to become an international pacesetter. After its first overseas investment – the 2009 acquisition of a fifty-year license to operate the Philippines' national transmission grid, SGCC moved into Brazil, bringing its UHV projects in 2011. Meanwhile, it actively participated in IEC to ensure acceptance of its technologies as international standards.

In 2009–12, SGCC submitted fourteen standards to IEC; eleven have been adopted as international standards. In 2013, SGCC provided the secretariat for seven committees and chaired one. Its current chief executive, Yinbiao Shu, was elected as the vice president of IEC. In 2014, SGCC became a member of the Corporate Advisory Group of IEEE-Standard Association, joining 10 other global companies: Microsoft, AT&T, Qualcomm, Bright House Networks, Alcatel-Lucent, ATMicroelectronics, Ericsson, SanDisk, Cisco and Synopsys. SGCC takes all these positions seriously, as it is determined to lead the industry. As one of its senior scientists explained:

In the late 1990s and early 2000s, we were also attending international conferences organised by CIGRE and IEEE. The only thing we could do then was to sit there and listen. We could not participate in discussion and had no right to speak up simply because we had nothing to say. The field was dominated by the developed countries. Now, it is different, when we speak up, especially about our UHV AC und UHV DC technologies, people listen and they pay attention to what we have to say (Zhao 2013).

In 2011, once again, SGCC management restructured its research teams and redirected their focus toward a new objective: "strong and smart grids." This organizational shift included three key components:

- SGCC created a Smart Grid Research Institute by merging its department of science and technology with an existing research institute on smart grids under one of its subsidiaries – SG China Electric Power Equipment and Technology Co. Ltd (SGCET).[14]
- It relocated all basic research, blue-sky research, and research on its core technologies to EPRI, which would no longer engage in projects.
- It regrouped its projects and operations in the two subsidiaries – Nanjing Automation Research Institute and SGCET – and SGCET in particular focuses its work on overseas engineering, procurement, and construction projects.

The core idea was to separate basic from applied research. Headquarters would provide funding for the basic research at EPRI, and the rest would focus on applied research serving corporate objectives. Meanwhile, the two "new" organizations received additional resources to expand. The Smart Grid Research Institute pursues research on key technology and equipment for the smart grid, information and communication, new electric materials, computation and application, HVDC transmission, power electronic devices and application, intelliSense and measurement, and flexible AC transmission systems (FACTs). The Institute has about 600 employees; all its researchers are university graduates, among them over 100 with PhDs and 350 with master's degrees. SGCC sees the Smart Grid Research Institute as a "knowledge-intensive institution." Soon after its establishment, the Smart Grid Research Institute opened a North American branch at Santa Clara, California, close to many IT start-up companies, and, six months later,

---

[14] In 1983, the newly reconstituted Ministry of Hydro Resources and Electric Power (MHREP) created a company under its wing – China Electric Technology Import and Export Company – to help introduce foreign capital and technology into the electricity industry. In the following two decades, it did exactly that under MHREP, Ministry of Energy, and then MEP. The company was then passed on to SPCC after MEP was abolished, during which it started taking on overseas EPC (engineering, procurement and construction) projects such as the second stage of the Jili Long Hydro project in Cambodia. SGCC inherited this company. In 2010, the management changed the name of this subsidiary to China Electric Power Equipment and Technology Co. Ltd (SGCET).

a European branch in Berlin. The Institute looks for opportunities to conduct collaborative research for and with foreign researchers and research institutes. It is too early to tell what it can achieve.

SGCC significantly strengthened SGCET's manufacturing capacities and access to overseas markets by taking on EPC (engineering, procurement, construction) projects. It injected nine times its initial capital, from 150 million yuan to over 1.5 billion yuan, and more importantly, expanded its initial business scope to include acquisition of electric equipment manufacturers, and investment in overseas EPC projects that can absorb products from these equipment makers. According to one report, SGCET bought as many as sixteen equipment manufacturers, including Changzhou Toshiba Transformer Company Ltd that became SGCET Toshiba (Changzhou) Transformer Company Ltd in July 2011, and Shanghai Zhi Xin Electric Co. Ltd (Guo 2011). The reorganization sought to build NARI and SGCET into a chain that would ensure the development of core technology, test systems equipment manufacturing capacity, project construction, and standard setting. As each subsidiary expanded, top-down management became more difficult and complex. Yet the SGCC management continues to set expectations for these institutes: in addition to financial performance, they were required to improve their own research capacities, build brand name products, and set standards.

Less than a decade after it proposed UHV projects, SGCC turned its eye to the global market. This was in part because rapid expansion of renewable power generation increased the pressures on transmission systems in many countries. Integrating large amounts of renewables into the grid will require new and more flexible transmission networks. SGCC proposed the idea of global energy interconnection to the United Nations and other international forums. This initiative arose in part to counter domestic opponents' continued efforts to dismantle SGCC and in part to use its UHV technology to establish a leadership role in the coming global energy transition. Domestically, the interconnection proposal gained support from the government, which was struggling to curtail air pollution and establish its green credentials. SGCC's program of "replacing coal with electricity, replacing oil with electricity, and using electricity from afar" (以电代煤，以电代油，电从远方来) would help the country achieve its ambitious renewable targets. Globally, all major players in the field, from established players such as GE, Siemens, ABB, and Toshiba, to newcomers such as Tesla Motors, supported by government policies and resources, are racing to create technologies for the transition to low-carbon electricity production and consumption. As US President Barack Obama said in his 2014 State of the Union speech: "the nation that goes all-in on innovation today will own the global economy tomorrow." SGCC made its ambition clear: it will not "stand on the sidelines" in this round of international competition. Its *Global Energy Interconnection* would allow SGCC to expand worldwide.

By now, SGCC has achieved worldwide recognition as a major competitor for global market share. The ideas of global energy interconnection may be too bold for some. Many green energy advocates focus on micro-production by rooftop solar panels and small-scale wind turbines, and micro-grids for self-sustained production and consumption as seen in military bases in the United States and some university campuses, such as UC San Diego. While large-scale connections may be out of fashion because of political difficulties in winning public acceptance of rights-of-way for large transmission projects, SGCC's proposal for global energy interconnection has its supporters who argue it may offer a realistic global alternative for developing low-carbon electricity production and consumption.

CONCLUSION

In a decade, emerging from an old-style, inefficient, centrally controlled and yet decentralized and fragmented government agency, SGCC managed to transform itself into a global technology leader in long-distance, high-voltage electricity transmission. Encouraged by the broader political environment and favorable policies, SGCC acted as a policy entrepreneur and an aggressive initiator in strategies and deployed its immense financial resources in supporting an ambitious and audacious project

SGCC is now the world's largest utility; it ranks second behind Walmart in the Global Fortune 500 for 2016; its 2015 revenue of US\$329 billion surpassed the GDP of most countries. Its transmission networks absorb the world's largest amount of both renewable and conventional electricity. Its UHV transmission lines, based largely on its own design and on Chinese-made equipment, span longer distances, operate at higher voltage, and experience lower power loss than any competitor has achieved. These advances provide China with an infrastructure framework that has long-term lock-in effects on future development. In so doing, SGCC has built a global brand and helped some Chinese electric equipment manufacturers to move from import dependence to a new status as globally competitive

exporters. By mastering the UHV technologies and accumulating experience in constructing and operating UHV infrastructure, SGCC has become
a major global player in this demanding field.

These developments contradict the common vision of centrally directed
state enterprises as sluggish, debt-ridden, inefficient behemoths that act as
a drag on China's economy. Instead, the spirit of entrepreneurship propelled a bold and ambitious vision that enabled SGCC to move from
depending on imports for designs, technologies and equipment to a new
position of world leadership in long distance electricity transmission.
To accomplish this transformation, SGCC followed a conventional strategy common to innovative efforts in many large corporations: building an
internal R&D hierarchy, centralizing the allocation of resources, and
expanding horizontally and vertically in related industries.

Research and innovation on UHV projects and technologies became
a collective exercise, carefully orchestrated by the management with its
chief executive as its conductor, well-qualified senior executives leading
individual sections, and external consultants providing essential technical
expertise. The broader policy space also encouraged the management to,
firstly, turn perceived negative and burdensome institutes into
a contributing force by reorganizing them and injecting resources, and,
secondly, building a broader coalition for R&D involving research academies, university specialists and domestic and international competitors yet
with itself firmly sitting in the driver's seat. State Grid's innovation success
rested on the creation of broad R&D coalitions involving research academies, university specialists and even business rivals – a signal achievement
in an economy renowned for excessive vertical integration and narrow
pursuit of corporate self-interest. Along the way, State Grid's leaders
succeeded in welding unwanted and seemingly burdensome research
institutes, whose initial function was to generate budget-draining pension
obligations, into major cogs in what entrepreneurial leaders developed into
a formidable research combine that can claim to have beaten proud
multinationals at their own game. As one of China's elite state enterprises,
State Grid, administered and supervised by the central government, is
widely perceived as a mere instrument of the party-state. Yet, none of the
specific efforts and strategies that vaulted this company into global
leadership in UHV transmission came from top Communist Party or
government leaders. Initiative rested first with SGCC's entrepreneurial
executives. Government policies are important as in all countries for
technology innovation, as "the state has a central place in the national
system of innovation ... government organisations, government-funded

university laboratories, government procurement, government regulations, and publicly provided infrastructure have been essential to technological change and to the organisational development of firms" (Hart 2007, p. 170). Official actions shape but do not determine enterprise response. The success or failure of corporate entities, including China's centrally administered state firms, depends crucially on the vision, drive, and entrepreneurial capacity (or their absence) of their leaders.

This being said, firms, private or state-owned, are subject to government policies, which in China have not offered a stable environment. SGCC's scale and market power created envy and resentment on the part of local governments, local distribution companies, and some economic analysts. Long-standing calls for the break-up of SGCC contributed to the central government's 2014 issuance of the "Directives on Further Deepening Electric Power Institution Reforms" along with nine supporting documents, covering T&D pricing, cross-region and cross-province energy exchanges, power market construction, retail segment reform, and integration of renewable power generation. This new wave of reforms, discussed further in Chapters 4 and 8 of this book, empowers government auditors to set the grid's transmission charges, expands the scope for direct electricity sales from generation companies to large end users, and strips the grid of its monopoly over retail sales by allowing new firms to enter this segment of the electricity market.

The reform plan faces a serious challenge: by fixing uniform grid charges, the new system eliminates any commercial incentive to build grid connections to link new and often remotely located sources of wind and solar power with distant urban centers of electricity demand. Local governments, focused chiefly on short-term growth, continue pushing investment in generation (renewables included) leading to serious problems of curtailment as grid connections lag behind the expansion of power generation capacity (Feng 2016).

Recent reforms threaten to erode the incentives needed to motivate grid firms to mobilize their technical and economic capacity to hasten the interconnections required to achieve official promises regarding the growth of renewables in China's electricity mix. In China, both wind and solar generation capacity clusters in sparsely populated places far away from China's eastern coastal load centers. Rapid investment in renewable capacities without closing down dirty-thermal power generation plants exacerbated competition to get on grids. Meanwhile, debates continue as whether SGCC should continue investing heavily in interconnected T&D networks, especially UHV ones. This challenge is not unique to China: due to the "collective good" characteristics of T&D systems, private markets often fail to deliver sufficient investment this segment of electricity systems.

Internationally, SGCC's *Global Energy Interconnection* – a plan to combine interregional and even intercontinental UHV transmission grids with smart grid technologies to address a series of energy and environmental challenges – has received serious attention from the industry and even won the endorsement of the International Energy Agency (IEA 2016a). A global energy interconnection can potentially address issues surrounding energy security, energy poverty, and climate change, by transmitting clean energy, connecting large clean energy bases with distant distribution networks, and delivering clean energy to different types of end-users (Liu 2015). It creates the promise of a widespread, highly deployable, safe, reliable, green and low-carbon global energy distribution platform. This may be self-serving, but the successful operations of the UHV projects in China allow SGCC to propose an alternative to the international community, which is struggling to provide universal access to electricity while simultaneously making electricity clean, affordable, and sustainable. This proposal reflects what Richard R. Nelson emphasized: "it is organisational differences, especially differences in ability to generate and gain from innovation, rather than differences in command over particular technologies that are the source of durable, not easily imitable, differences among firms" (Nelson 1991, p. 72).

References

Abrami, Regina M., William C. Kirby, and F. Warren McFarlan. 2014. "Why Can't China Innovate." *Harvard Business Review*. 92(3). pp. 107–11.

Bai, Tianliang and Ke Wang. 2015. "Moving Forwards toward a Country with Brand Names." *People's Daily*, 16 July, p. 2 (白天亮, 王珂, 贴牌大国迈向品牌大国, 人民日报, 2015年7月16日, 02版。)

Berkhout, Frans. 2002. "Technological Regimes: path dependency and the environment." *Global Environmental Change*. 12(1). pp. 1–4.

Berg. S. V. and J. Tschirhart. 1988. *Natural Monopoly Regulation*. New York: Cambridge University Press.

Berkhout, Frans, Geert Verbong, Anna J. Wieczorek, and Rob Raven, Louis Lebel, and Xuemei Bai. 2010. "Sustainability Experiments in Asia: innovation shaping alternative development pathways?" *Environmental Science & Policy*. 13(4). pp. 261–71.

Boutellier, Roman, Oliver Gassman, and Maximilian von Zedtwits. 1999. *Managing Global Innovation*. Berlin: Springer.

Breznitz, Dan and Michael Murphree. 2011. *Run of the Red Queen*. New Haven: Yale University Press.

CCTV-2, 2010. 财经. 《大国重器》2013-11-06 – 2013-11-11, at http://tv.cntv.cn/videoset/VSET100177333141/.

Chen, Jia. 2009. "Overview of China's Enterprise Innovation." In Q. Fan. K. Li. D.Z. Zeng. Y. Dong, and R. Peng eds., *Innovation for Development and the Role of Government*. Washington, DC: The World Bank.

Chesbrough, Henry. 2003. *Open Innovation*. Cambridge, MA: Harvard Business School Press.

Cheung, Tai Ming, Thomas Mahnken, Deborah Seligsohn, Kevin Pollpeter, Eric Anderson, and Fan Yang. 2016. "Planning for Innovation." a report prepared for the US–China Economic and Security Review Commission. July 28, 2016.

Chu, Steven. 2010. "Is the Energy Race Our New "Sputnik" Movement?" Washington, DC: National Press Club.

Cobb. R. W. and C. D. Elder. 1972. *Participation in American Politics*. Baltimore: John Hopkins University Press.

Crooke, Paul Irwin. 2012. "China's New Development Model: analysing Chinese prospects in technology innovation." *China Information*. 26(2). pp. 167–84.

Doremus, Paul N. et al., eds. 1998. *The Myth of the Global Corporation*. Princeton: Princeton University Press.

Eaton, Sarah. 2013. "Political Economy of the Advancing State." *The China Journal*. 69. pp. 64–86.

Executive Office of the President, National Science and Technology Council. "A Policy Framework for the 21st Century Grid: a progress report." February, 2013.

Fan, Qimiao, Kouqing Li, Douglas Zhihua Zeng, Yang Dong, and Runzhong Peng, eds. 2009. *Innovation for Development and the Role of Government*. Washington, DC: World Bank.

Fan, Peipei. 2014. "Innovation in China." *Journal of Economic Surveys*. 28(4). pp. 725–45.

Feng Yongsheng. 2016. "China's New Round of Electricity Institution Reform." paper delivered at International Workshop on "Challenges Facing the Electricity Industry," February 21–3, 2016. Hong Kong.

Fu, Xiaolan. 2015. *China's Path to Innovation*. Cambridge: Cambridge University Press.

Gallagher, Kelly Sims. 2014. *The Globalisation of Clean Energy Technology*. Cambridge, MA: MIT Press.

Gu, Qingsheng (古清生) and Huang Quanhui (黄传会). 2009. 走进特高压：特高压工程记 [On the road to UHV – Ultra-high voltage project diary]. 北京：中国电力出版社. 2009. p. 96.

Guo Kai. 2011. "Chinese Electric Equipment Industry." *Economic Observer*. 23 July (郭开, 中电装备身世, 经济观察报, 2011-07-23).

Haas, Peter M. 1992. "Introduction: Epistemic Communities and International Policy Coordination." *International Organisation*. 46(1). pp. 1–35.

Hagstrom, Peter and Alfred D. Chandler, Jr. 1998. "Perspective on Firm Dynamics." In Alfred D. Chandler, Jr., Peter Hagstrom, and Orjan Solvell eds., *The Dynamic Firm*. New York: Oxford University Press.

Hammond, Daniel R. 2013. "Policy Entrepreneurship in China's response to Urban Policy." *Policy Studies Journal.* 41(1). pp. 119–46.

Hart, David M. 2007. "Corporate Technological Capabilities and the State." In Kenneth Lipartito and David B. Sicilia eds., *Constructing Corporate America: History, Politics, Culture.* New York: Oxford University Press.

Huang, Daochun, Yinbiao Shu, Jiangjun Ruan, and Yi Hu. 2009. "Ultra High Voltage Transmission in China: Developments, Current Status and Future Prospects." *Proceedings of the IEEE,* 2009, 97(3). pp. 555–83.

IEA. 2006. *China's Power Sector Reforms.* Paris: OECD.

2015. *World Energy Outlook 2015.* Paris: OECD.

2016a. *Large-Scale Electricity Interconnection.* Paris: OECD.

2016b. *World Energy Investment.* Paris: OECD.

Jorde, Thomas M. and David J. Teece. 1990. "Innovation and Cooperation." *Journal of Economic Perspectives.* 4(3). pp. 75–96.

Joskow, Paul L. 1997. "Restructuring, Competition and Regulatory Reform in the US Electricity Sector." *Journal of Economic Perspectives.* 11(3). pp. 119–28.

Kennedy, Andrew B. 2013. "China's Search for Renewable Energy: Pragmatic Techno-Nationalism." *Asian Survey.* 53(5). pp. 909–30.

Kingdon, John W. 1995. *Agendas, Alternatives and Public Policies.* 2nd edn. New York: Harper Collin College Publishers.

Kim, Linsu. 1997. *From Imitation to Innovation.* Boston, MA: Harvard Business Review Press.

Lester, Richard. 2014. "Energy Innovation." In Richard M. Locke and Rachel L. Wellhausen eds., *Production in the Innovation Economy.* Cambridge, MA: The MIT Press. pp.109–38.

Lewis, Joanna. 2013. *Green Innovation in China.* New York: Columbia University Press.

Li Rongrong. 2004. "Press Conferences held by the Press Office of the State Council." November 30, 2004.

Li, Cheng, ed. 2008. *China's Changing Political Landscape.* Washington, DC: Brookings Institution Press.

Lin, Li-Wen and Curtis J. Milhaupt. 2013. "We Are the (National) Champions." *Stanford Law Review.* 65(4). pp. 697–760.

Lings, Raymond. 2005. "Overview of Transmission Lines Above 700kv." *Inaugural IEEE PES 2005 Conference and Exposition in Africa.* Durban, South Africa, July 11–15, 2005. pp. 33–43.

Liu, Feng-chao, Denis Fred Simon, Yu-tao Sun, and Cong Cao. 2011. "China's Innovation Policies: evolution, institutional structure, and trajectory." *Research Policy.* 40(7). pp. 917–31.

Liu, Xielin and Cheng Peng. 2014. "National Strategy of Indigenous Innovations and its Implication to China." *Asian Journal of Innovation and Policy.* 3(1). pp. 117–39.

Liu, Zhenya. 2015. *Global Energy Interconnection.* New York: Academic Press-Elsevier.

Li Rei 鲁花. 2010. 中集融与央企七年：即在前在一人遗憾 [Li Rongrong and SOEs for Seven Years]. 新华网 [Xinhua News Agency]. September, 2, 2010.

Lu Zheng 路郑. 2015. 输配电设备企业成特高压建设最大受益者 [The Electrical Equipment Industry as the Largest Beneficiary of UHV Projects]. 中国能源报 [China Energy Report]. February 9, 2015.

McNally, Christopher A. 2013. "Refurbishing State Capitalism." *Journal of Current Chinese Affairs*. 4. pp. 45–71.

Mertha, Andrew. 2009. "'Fragmented Authoritarianism 2.0': Political Pluralisation in the Chinese Policy Process." *China Quarterly*.

MIT. 2009. *The Future of the Electric Grids*. Cambridge, MA: MIT.

Naughton, Barry. 2011. "China's Economic Policy Today." *Eurasian Geography and Economics*. 52(3). pp. 313–29.

2015. "The Transformation of the State Sector." In Barry Naughton and Kellee S. Tsai eds., *State Capitalism, Institutional Adaptation, and the Chinese Miracle*. New York: Cambridge University Press.

Naughton, Barry and Adam Segal. 2003. "China in Search of a Workable Model." In William W. Keller and Richard J. Samuels eds., *Crisis and Innovation in Asian Technology*. New York: Cambridge University Press. pp. 160–86.

Naughton, Barry and Kellee S. Tsai, eds. 2015. *State Capitalism, Institutional Adaptation, and the Chinese Miracle*. New York: Cambridge University Press.

Nelson, Richard R. 1991. "Why do Firms Differ, and How Does it Matter?" *Strategic Management Journal*. 12. pp. 61–74.

Ni Wen 倪旻. 2014. 特高压让我们站在全球设备研发最前端 [UHV Leads R&D in Equipment Manufacturing]. 国家电网 [State Grid]. No.12. pp. 84–9.

Nolan, Peter. 2012. *Is China Buying the World?* Cambridge: Polity.

Nolan, Peter and Wang Xiaoqiang. 1998. "Harbin Power Equipment Company and the Battle for the Chinese Market." *Competition and Change*. 3(4). pp. 417–48.

OECD, 2005. *Oslo Manual: Guidelines for Collecting and Interpreting Innovation Data*. 3rd edn. Paris: OECD.

2009. "Power Sector Reform." *Review of Regulatory Reform: China 2009*, Paris: OECD. pp. 229–66.

2015. *Energy Technology Perspectives 2015*. Paris: OECD.

Opposition. 2011. 专家们对特高压的反对声音 [Opposition of Experts against UHV Projects]. 财新网 . April 25, 2011. *Caixin*.

Patel, Pari. 1995. "Localised Production of Technology for Global Markets." *Cambridge Journal of Economics*. 19(1). pp. 141–53.

Paulson Institute. 2015. "Power Play: China's Ultra-High Voltage Technology and Global Standards." Chicago: Paulson Institute. April, 2015.

Scherer, Jr., Harold N. and Gregory S. Vassell. 1985. "Transmission of Electric Power at Ultra-High Voltages." *Proceedings of the IEEE*. 73(8). pp. 1252–78.

SGCC. 2006. State Grid Corporation Corporate Responsibility Report. Annual.

SGCC Acquisitions. 2014. 国家电网公司重组整合许继、平高集团纪头 [The History of SGCC's Acquisitions and Restructuring of Xuji and Pinggao]. 国家电网报 [State Grid News]. September 9, 2014.

Shim, Yongwoon and Dong-Hee Shin. 2015. "Neo-techno Nationalism." *Telecommunications Policy*. 40(2–3). pp. 197–209.

Siemens. 2015. "China's Innovation Pipeline." *Siemens Newsletter Innovation*. March 12, 2015.

Song, Jian. 2008. "Awakening: evolution of China's science and technology policies." *Technology in Society*. 30. pp. 235–41.

State Council. 2006. "Accelerating the Revitalisation of Equipment Manufacturing Industries." (国务院关于加快振兴装备制造业的若干意见, 2006).

Steinfeld, Edward S. and Troels Beltoft. 2014. "Innovation Lessons from China." *MIT Sloan Management Review*. 55(4). pp. 49–55.

Thun, Eric and Loren Brandt. 2010. "The Fight for the Middle: Upgrading, Competition, and Industrial Development in China." *World Development*. 38 (11). pp. 1555–74.

Tse, Vivian. 2005. "ABB Aims to Make China its Largest Market by 2009." Dow Jones International News. April 28, 2005.

Vernon, Raymond. 1966. "International Investment and International Trade in Product Cycle." *Quarterly Journal of Economics*. 80(2). pp. 190–207.

Wang Jing 王菁. 2015. 特高压工程释放3000亿投资点燃输配电设备市场 [Expansion of the Electrical Equipment Industry as the Result of 300 Billion Investment in UHV Projects]. 中电新闻网 [China Power News Network]. February 5, 2015.

Wang Weimin 王为民. 2014. 给世界树立一个榜样 [Set an Example for the World]. 国家电网 [State Grid], No.12, pp. 110–17).

Wessner, Charles W., ed. 2011. *Building the 21st Century: U.S.-China Cooperation on Science, Technology, and Innovation*. Washington, DC: National Academies Press.

Wildavsky, Aaron. 1979. *Speaking Truth to Power*. Boston: Little Brown.

Williamson, Oliver E. 1991. "Strategizing, Economizing, and Economic Organization." *Strategic Management Journal*. 12(S2). pp. 75–94.

Williamson, Peter J. and Anand P. Raman. 2011. "How China Reset Its Global Acquisition Agenda." *Harvard Business Review*. 89(4). pp. 109–14.

Yang, Dali L., ed. 2012. *The Global Recession and China's Political Economy*. New York: Palgrave Macmillan.

Yeh, Emily T. and Joanna I. Lewis. 2004. "State Power and the Logic of Reform in China's Electricity Sector." *Pacific Affairs*. 77(3). pp. 437–65.

Yip, George S. and Bruce McKern. 2016. *China's Next Strategic Advantage*. Cambridge, MA: The MIT Press.

Yusuf, Shahid; Shuilin Wang, and Kaoru Nabeshima. 2009. "China's Fiscal Policies for Innovation." In Qimiao Fan, Kouqing Li, Douglas Zhihua Zeng, Yang Dong, and Runzhong Peng eds., *Innovation for Development and the Role of Government*. Washington, DC: World Bank. pp. 149–80.

Zeng, Ming and Peter J. Williamson. 2007. *Dragons at Your Door*. Cambridge, MA: Harvard Business School Press.

Zhang, Zirui 张子瑞. 2010. 该谁来整合输变电设备业 [Whose Responsibility to Restructure and Reorganise the Electric Equipment Industry]. 《中国能源报》 [China Energy Report]. February 1, 2010. p. 24.

Zhao Yining. 2013. "Interview of Chen Weijiang on UHV Projects." *21st Century Economic Herald*. June 4, 2013 (赵忆宁, "特高压技术研发科学家陈维江详解为什么只有中国取得了成功."《21世纪经济报道》2013年06月04日).

Zhou, Yu, William Lazonick, and Yifei Su, eds. 2016. *China as an Innovation Nation*. New York: Oxford University Press.

7

Growth, Upgrading, and Limited Catch-Up in China's Semiconductor Industry

Douglas B. Fuller

INTRODUCTION

Semiconductors (this chapter uses the terms integrated circuits i.e. ICs, chips, and semiconductors interchangeably[1]) represent a major building block of high-tech industry. This chapter analyzes the trajectory of China's rapidly growing semiconductor sector, focusing on the interplay among global technology developments, Chinese government policy, and three groups of firms: purely domestic manufacturers, Chinese operations of multinational corporations (MNCs), and hybrid firms based in China but with largely offshore ownership and financing.

China has pursued a strategy of expansion and upgrading, aiming to build a domestic industry that can supply the needs of Chinese industry, limit dependence on foreign technology, and move toward eventual global leadership. Broader policy instruments beyond semiconductor-specific ones, such as opening China to foreign investment and outlays on technical education, have increased the semiconductor sector's financial, technological, and human resource pool. In contrast, the more focused semiconductor industry initiatives that channel investment funds, imported technology and product demand toward favored domestic firms, which are typically state-owned, have thus far fallen far short of creating the Chinese technological leadership in ICs to which the government aspires.

---

[1] To be precise, the term semiconductors often refers to the broad category of elements that have electrical conductivity somewhere between conductors and insulators, but in common discussions of the industry semiconductors and integrated circuits (ICs) are often used interchangeably. This chapter, which is focused on the narrower category of ICs, follows suit in its usage of both terms. Chips typically refer to ICs and not the broader category of semiconductors.

The rapid evolution of cutting-edge product characteristics and manufacturing processes typical of global semiconductor leaders means that large-scale investment and substantial upgrading in follower countries may fail to reduce the gap separating domestic producers from global leaders. This summarizes Chinese experience. MNCs have built production facilities in China, but generally refrained from committing to cutting-edge production and research operations, partly through concerns about protection of intellectual property (IP). Despite massive expansion and strong government backing, domestic state-owned firms have generally failed to generate the technological dynamism that official policy seeks. Among China-based semiconductor firms, only the hybrids, which, like favored state firms, see China as their technological home base, but unlike state firms, face tough financial discipline from offshore backers, have delivered substantial technological advance.

Recent policy initiatives continue to lavish resources on sluggish state-owned firms. Rival investments by central and provincial governments create further difficulties. Government influence limits the capacity of potentially more innovative hybrid and domestic private operators to expand and upgrade. Growing domestic demand has encouraged domestic output growth, for example in chipsets for smartphones in which Chinese manufacturers have recorded massive gains. Although Huawei, a leading maker of telecom equipment, shows signs of leveraging its manufacturing prowess to elevate its semiconductor design capability, domestic design and production operations cluster in lagging process technologies and mature or maturing product areas that leading MNCs are abandoning in favor of new processes and products with innovative features and potentially higher profitability.

As a result, China's semiconductor industry appears locked into a path that combines quantitative expansion with low financial returns and limited qualitative improvement. This trajectory offers little prospect for attaining China's long-term objective of propelling domestic semiconductor manufacture toward the global frontier of technology and innovation.

This chapter begins by introducing the semiconductor industry. The following section reviews industrial policies for the IC sector prior to the 2014 IC industry megaproject. It then examines the activities of hybrid firms and MNCs from 1997 to 2013. The final section evaluates the IC industry megaproject's implementation thus far. The conclusion considers the likely future result of the megaproject and related policies and situates the likely future status of Chinese producers within the context of the global IC industry.

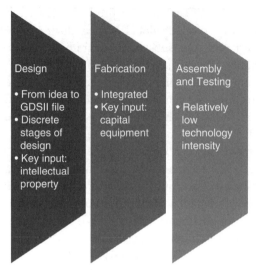

Figure 7.1 Integrated Circuit Value Chain
Source: Fuller (2016, p. 115)

INDUSTRY STRUCTURE

The semiconductor value chain includes the three large blocks of activities (in addition to marketing and distribution) displayed in Figure 7.1: design, fabrication, and assembly and testing (A&T in industry parlance). IC design is the capture of the idea for a chip in code (typically a GDSII[2] file) that then serves as the blueprint for the IC in the fabrication stage. The design stage itself consists of a number of discrete steps and relies on the use of electronic design automation (EDA) tools, which are computer programs that allow IC designers to write and test the design code. The fabrication stage follows the design code, using lithography to inscribe circuitry onto physical material (typically a type of silicon), and then treats the physical material with chemicals. The result of this fabrication process is an unpackaged IC. In the final A&T stage, the addition of packaging both protects the circuitry and permits connection to other electronic components and devices, while testing assures proper operation of the finished product.

While the IC industry value chain today is a modular one characterized by digitized interfaces between value chain segments, the amount of information exchanged at the interface between design and fabrication is

---

[2] GDSII stands for Gerber Data Stream Information Interchange.

prodigious. In order to facilitate designs that fit a particular fabrication process, the wafer foundries provide sophisticated sets of models for designers to utilize in designing to particular fabrication process and device (chip) specifications. These models allow designers to simulate the operations of circuits prior to fabrication. Successful wafer foundries have considerable expertise in making this interface user-friendly with the aid of web-based tools for easy information transfer.

Traditionally, vertically integrated firms called integrated device manufacturers (IDMs) dominated the IC industry in part because the tools to manage easy information transfer from design to fabrication did not yet exist. IDMs perform all three functions, though they often outsource A&T operations. Today, many IDMs are following a fab-light strategy utilizing less internal chip-making capacity that follows the progressive abandonment of in-house assembly and test operations. In place of IDMs, the industry has witnessed the rise of dedicated design-only firms (often called fabless design firms) and dedicated fabrication-only firms (pureplay foundries[3]) over the last twenty-five years (Hurtarte et al. 2007). There are two types of dedicated design firms: fabless design houses that design and market their own chips, and design service firms that undertake part or the whole design process for other firms.

Foundries typically have large research and development (R&D) departments that develop process technology and also capture value by improving the flexibility of fabrication operations and enhancing efficiency through focus on fabrication alone. Greater flexibility also enhances efficiency by allowing multiple processes and multiple products to share the same fabrication facilities and even the same wafer in the case of multi-product wafer (MPW) production. Leading foundries offer customers real-time data on their wafers as the fabrication process unfolds. The need for a design firm to reveal IP to foundries in order for the foundry to be able to fabricate the chips necessitates that foundries strive to protect customer IP in order to keep clients and attract new ones.[4]

---

[3] Foundries that only do dedicated fabrication for others are often called pureplay foundries in order to differentiate them from other firms that mix foundry manufacturing with their own in-house manufacturing e.g. Samsung. In this chapter, the term pureplay foundry will denote these dedicated fabrication firms; rankings of pureplay foundries will exclude firms with mixed strategies. e.g. Samsung has a large foundry business but is not included in the rankings of pureplay foundries because it is not one.

[4] The preceding three paragraphs draw on Fuller et al. (2013).

Technical Note on Industry Metrics

Before we begin the account of fabrication in China, a technical note is in order. Standard measures of the IC fabrication process technology focus on the width of lithography used to etch the circuits onto silicon. Shrinking widths reflect improved process technology that permits the installation of more complex and sophisticated circuitry onto a given surface. Improved process technology has reduced lithography widths from several microns – the industry standard during the 1990s – to nanometers, the current technology frontier.[5] Table 7.2 shows that SMIC, a prominent Chinese IC firm, lowered lithography width from 0.13 microns in 2003 to 40 nanometers, or 0.04 microns in 2012.

The size of wafers that fabrication equipment can process is another common metric for the sophistication of fabrication technology. Larger wafers can accommodate more chips, a clear productivity improvement. The newest fabs accept 300-mm (or 12-inch) wafers, a considerable advance from the previous limit of 200-mm (or 8-inch) wafers. Table 7.2 relies on both these metrics to compare China's industry to the international technology frontier over time.

However, for both design and, to a lesser extent, fabrication, these metrics and others[6] are often only useful guides to technological sophistication within product categories. The two largest and broadest categories of chips are logic chips (chips where gates within the chips create combinational logic that allows the chips to perform complicated algorithms) and memory chips, which serve to store data. Globally, foundries tend to specialize in logic chips while many of the remaining IDMs focus on memory. Correspondingly, most fabless design firms focus on logic or other niche chips, and not memory. For design particularly, comparing firms' technical prowess really requires comparing within product areas at a much finer degree of specification than a simple comparison across all logic or memory chips. The chapter makes brief comparisons at this finer degree in the discussion of particular firms and product areas.

---

[5] One micron, typically written 1 μm, equals 1,000 nanometers; household plastic wrap is 10–12 μm thick.

[6] For example, the number of gates (called gate counts) within a chip is often a good measure of a given chip's complexity, but companies are very reluctant to provide this information because they fear it can provide competitors with insight into their IP. Thus, these gate counts are not a practical way to compare widely across firms.

IC INDUSTRIAL POLICIES, 1990–2013

1990s: The 908 and 909 Projects

Although China's first integrated circuit was created in 1965, a mere seven years after the first IC was created in the United States, China's industry lagged badly behind world standards by the beginning of the China's economic reforms in the late 1970s (see Table 7.2). By the 1990s, the Chinese state decided that the time had come to rectify this situation with bold new industrial policies. The two principal industrial policies were the 908 and 909 Projects that covered the Eighth (1991–5) and Ninth Five-Year Plans (FYP) (1996–2000).[7]

In 1990, the state anointed Huajing, a state-owned enterprise (SOE) originating out of Wuxi Factory No. 742, a unit that had played a leading role in training China's first generation of IC engineers, to lead the 908 Project to be carried out over the imminent 8th FYP. Despite technology transfer from Lucent Technology and relatively modest technological ambitions to build a mature generation fab (fabrication facility or plant) with older process technology (a 150-mm fab using 1.2-micron process technology), Huajing failed. The fab did not start production until 1998, and then was confronted with a lack of suitable products to bring to the marketplace.

The only thing that saved the 908 Project from being a complete disaster was the appearance of a corporate savior, Central Semiconductor Manufacturing Corporation (CSMC), a Hong Kong-registered firm with strong links to Taiwan's Mosel-Vitelic, an established IC IDM. CSMC originally agreed to rent Huajing's 908 fab in 1998 and subsequently formed a CSMC-controlled joint venture (JV) with Huajing to take over the fab in 1999. CSMC was the first in a line of hybrid firms registered and heavily financed from outside of China but led by ethnic Chinese entrepreneurs that became active in the IC industry.

With the 908 Project clearly not going well as the 9th FYP loomed, the Chinese government created a more ambitious 909 Project. This time the state wanted a formal JV partner as a stable source of technology and chose NEC. NEC initially had a 28.6 percent stake while the Chinese state-owned partner, Huahong, had its ownership split between the then Ministry of Information Industry's (MII) China Electronics Corporation (CEC) and

---

[7] During the 1980s and 1990s, three minor joint ventures (JVs) (Shanghai Belling, ASMC, and Shougang NEC) were established, but none of these firms have become significant within the industry (compare with Fuller 2016, ch. 5).

the Shanghai government in a 60:40 split. In the 1997 initial agreement, NEC would run the fab for five years and then to turn it over to Huahong's management.

The aim for the Huahong-NEC (HHNEC) JV was to create a viable Chinese IC national champion equipped with a then-current 200-mm wafer fab and its own IP by leveraging NEC's participation. Unfortunately, NEC was careful about keeping control of technology in Japanese hands. The fab started pilot production in 1999, but Japanese engineers continued to control production in 2002 and even 2003. As one Chinese industry expert close to the company lamented in 2002 while unfavorably comparing Chinese engineers in HHNEC to the technological prowess of Taiwan's IC fabrication engineers, "The Taiwanese can build wafers; we cannot. We do not have process technology. Our engineers [in Huahong] can handle a single process but do not have integration capacity." More disappointing still, in 2003 a potential customer talked to HHNEC's Chinese staff only to discover that HHNEC's technology was further behind than its corporate marketing claimed (they could only run a 0.35-micron process not a 0.25-micron one). In addition, customers would have to go to Japan to meet with NEC's Japanese employees in order to verify that HHNEC could actually fabricate the chip. In other words, despite the fab being equipped with older technology, the Japanese were reluctant to turn over control of this mature technology to their Chinese JV partners even six years after concluding the JV agreement. Furthermore, HHNEC was deeply dependent on Chinese government procurement in the form of various types of smart cards in order to stay in business.

In addition to plans to create fabs, both the 908 and 909 Projects also aimed to foster design capabilities among a wider array of firms and organizations. 908 gave funds to a variety of firms and research centers in Beijing, Shanghai, Shenzhen, and Wuxi to do IC design research, especially electronic design automation (EDA) research. Huada in Beijing had the main role in distributing the technology to other firms and research units. 909 saw the direct distribution of funds to various local firms. Unfortunately, none of these firms emerged as viable commercial enterprises in the subsequent two decades with the small exception of SMIT.[8] In the wake of the 909 Project, the State Planning Commission[9]

---

[8] This firm was a spin-off of SSMEC (also known as Shenzhen Guowei) via a management buy-out.

[9] Interview, January 2002.

and the Ministry of Science and Technology (MOST) viewed this effort to create viable IC design firms as a failure (DYGB No. 11 2002).

2000s: New Policies, Same Poor Outcomes

Recognizing the failures of the 908 and 909 Projects, the government issued State Circular No. 18 in January 2000 to offer further support for this sector. No. 18 promised to cut China's VAT to 3 percent from 17 percent for ICs fabricated or designed in China. The policy also offered the *liang mian san jian ban* (两免三减半 two years tax-free and three years at half the tax rate) tax deduction and zero import duties for the IC and software industries.

This policy's implementation was not very effective. By mid-2004, subsidy payments amounted to only 200 million RMB, an amount equivalent to only 0.3 percent of China's total 2004 domestic IC production. Firms complained that the bureaucratic hurdles to receive the VAT breaks were so onerous and slow that it was hardly worth applying for these grants. Despite the actual weakness in implementation of this policy, the US government at the urging of the Semiconductor Industry Association (SIA) of the US sued China in World Trade Organization (WTO) court because these VAT tax breaks requiring China-based production were clearly illegal under Trade-Related Investment Measures (TRIMs). China did not contest the lawsuit and officially dropped the VAT policies.

Despite China's retreat in the face of the WTO lawsuit, industrial policy continued. The parts of No. 18 that did not conflict with WTO regulations continued and the Chinese central and local governments spent large sums of money promoting the industry, primarily through procurement, investment, and research subsidies. Estimates from industry insiders put the range of government support at 10 to 100 billion RMB, with the narrower estimates probably limited to central government subsidies and the larger estimates including a wide range of local government subsidies. The opaque nature of many of these subsidies meant they were unlikely to face challenges under WTO rules even if they may have violated the letter and/or spirit of WTO rules.

The divergent implementation of No. 18's design-related VAT policies and its under-the-radar additions after the WTO ruling demonstrate once again the bias toward policies that favor state firm insiders. The original VAT tax breaks were open to all and half of them went to foreign firms (JJGC July 19, 2004), but the onerous, even perhaps stingy implementation made this policy unimportant even before the WTO ruling. In contrast, subsequent under-the-radar funding for design firms seems to have focused on boosting state procurement, with benefits entirely directed toward state-linked firms (see Table 7.1). The scale of support rose many times above the 200 million RMB spent on the VAT tax breaks (see discussion below on procurement).

The State Council announced continued support for the IC industry in Circular No. 4 in 2011 as the No. 18 policies expired in 2010. There was much continuity with the No. 18 policies, although some tax breaks were more compelling. There were vague promises for other support for industry, although the statement that procurement would favor domestic suppliers in No. 18 was now missing in No. 4. *The 21st Century Economic Herald* speculated that this vagueness was intentional, as China wanted to pursue industrial policies without aggravating relations with trading partners (ESJJBD February 21, 2011).

In addition to these efforts, the procurement policies mentioned above continued apace and provided the main markets for most of the state-linked design firms.[10] Much of this state procurement has been through the series of Golden Projects to promote various technology-intensive goods. The most important has been the Golden Card project to promote the adoption of IC cards through state procurement. IC cards are cards with chips that carry adjustable information used for such things as telephone cards and transportation cards in China. A director of the China's most active national IC design center admitted the outsized role of state procurement when he noted that the center supported two types of products: "global products" and "completely government-guided market products," the latter a euphemism for direct government procurement (Interview, November 2008).[11] On the surface, developing "government-guided market" products seems to be offset by supporting "global products," but the reality is that the state-linked firms almost completely relied on the former as shown in Table 7.1. This phenomenon of state procurement channeled

---

[10] The following three paragraphs are slightly revised version of three paragraphs from Fuller (2016, pp. 159–61).

[11] Direct government procurement is the situation where the government buys the product or service. Indirect government procurement is the situation where a government-controlled entity (often a firm) buys products or services under the behest or guidance of the government. Given the large amounts of purchasing by SOEs and other government-controlled entities and the government's interference in many of these purchasing decisions, indirect government procurement usually is more significant than direct government procurement in China e.g. the telecommunications infrastructure equipment market consists almost entirely of indirect government procurement.

Table 7.1 Top Ten Fabless Firms and State Procurement, 2011

Company Name	Ownership	2011 Revenue (USD millions)	Role of State Procurement
1. Spreadtrum*	hybrid	663	minimal
2. RDA*	hybrid	281	minimal
3. Galaxycore	hybrid	181	minimal
4. SSMEC**	domestic state	173	military procurement
5. Leadcore	domestic state	146	most sales due to state support in the telecommunications sector (formerly part of Datang)
6. CEC Huada	domestic state	127	most sales to the various outlets of the Golden Card project
7. CR Semico	domestic state	124	most sales due to state procurement of power meters
8. Rockchip	domestic private	98	minimal
9. Datang Microelectronics	domestic state	97	most sales to Golden Card state procurement
10. Shanghai Huahong IC	domestic state	94	most sales to Golden Card state procurement

Note:
* Spreadtrum was bought out and RDA agreed to be bought out by Tsinghua Unigroup in 2013.
** SSMEC was bought out by Tongfang Guoxin, another state firm, in 2012.
Sources: Reprinted from Fuller 2016, p. 160. Original sources were PwC (2012) and Interviews. Only independent fabless firms were included.

to state-linked firms is widely understood within the industry in China. As one IC designer who had originally worked in the state sector wryly put it when giving his assessment of Huahong Beijing's ID card chips, "Not anything special – just a special relationship with the government" (Interview, October 2008). These markets are extremely large, with the bank IC card market alone estimated to be worth 30 billion RMB (almost USD 5 billion) in 2012 (Sina Tech August 10, 2012).

While Silicon Valley's commercially successful IC industry emerged from an initial reliance on US military procurement (Leslie 2000), official procurement in China has not nurtured producers capable of competing in commercial markets. After over twenty years of heavy government support, 908 and 909-supported firms, and certain state telecommunications firms, such as Datang and its spin-off Leadcore, still rely on state procurement to survive. These firms bear no resemblance to Intel or any of the other "Fairchildren" that sprang up in Silicon Valley following an initial boost from military spending and human capital exodus from the original Silicon Valley IC firms, Fairchild and Shockley.

The primary reason that state procurement in China's IC sector has worked differently from state procurement in the United States is that the Chinese state targets state-owned firms that differ greatly from their American private counterparts. Chinese state-owned firms aim to survive rather than thrive for two reasons. They do not have the performance pressure investors place on their American counterparts, while at the same time preferential access to the state banking system and state procurement make survival relatively easy without honing true capabilities to compete in the open commercial marketplace. In addition, the managers of these SOEs avoid risky activities – including technological experimentation – that could expose them to future accusations of losing or destroying state assets. If Intel's founders had limited their ambitions to the minuscule market opportunities offered by the Pentagon during the 1960s, or if Intel had enjoyed comfortable access to credit irrespective of performance, or if Intel's managers had faced potential sanctions for the failure of risky entrepreneurial or technological initiatives, then Intel would never have attained the technological and commercial success that followed its early Pentagon contracts. If the Chinese government were to open up procurement in high-tech products to real competition, its purchases could probably generate a much-expanded array of positive externalities.

Sadly, access to state procurement remains closed to most private firms. One local private firm reported that it had tried to compete with the state-linked firms in the large IC card market, but had to resort to supplying a state-linked firm with chips because it could not get into the state's procurement channels. The margins were very low since it could not sell directly to the state and it decided to try to develop alternative businesses (Interview, October 2003).

Alongside of the state's rollout of No. 18, MOST decided to sponsor seven national IC design bases. Over 2000–1, MOST selected Beijing, Chengdu, Hangzhou, Shanghai, Shenzhen, Wuxi, and Xi'an to take part. In 2008, MOST added Jinan as an eighth base. The primary aim of these bases was to offer services, such as cheap EDA tools, to local design firms. While this policy represented a sensible effort to lower financial barriers to entry, the more promising hybrid firms backed by foreign venture capital by and large avoided using the bases' services either because they had sufficient financial resources to purchase their own superior EDA tools and services or because they feared that exposure to these bases would endanger their IP. In contrast to many Chinese industrial policies where the state has spent lavishly, this design base policy appears to be one where the state invested very limited resources. This has constrained the quality and scope of the services offered. However, even in the cities where the local governments provided better funding to supplement the funding from MOST, such as Shanghai and Shenzhen, the results were not dramatically different. The quality hybrid firms in Shanghai and Shenzhen did not use the services for fear of IP leakage and instead used their financial ability courtesy of foreign venture capital to pay for their own EDA tools.

THE RISE OF THE HYBRIDS AND MULTINATIONAL CORPORATIONS' INVESTMENTS, 1997–2013

Starting in the late 1990s, various local governments attempted to entice foreign investment in IC fabrication with cheap land and subsidies. These policies led two hybrid firms, SMIC and Grace, to set up their companies in Shanghai in 2000. With the tax incentives introduced under Document No. 18 and reinforced under Document No.4, the investment inducements strengthened. Over time, Hynix invested in Wuxi, Intel in Dalian and Samsung in Xi'an.

The incentives arguably led to over-investment. The arguments made by local governments that these fab investments would spur subsequent investment in upstream design activities are highly questionable. My interviews from 2001 to 2015 with the relevant local officials in a number of jurisdictions that had lured fab investment or were trying to do so all shared this common theme i.e. the local officials emphasized that bringing in the fabs would result in attracting the entire industrial supply chain, particularly the valuable upstream design segment, to the locale. Dalian's mayor made this argument in print in regards to the Intel fab in his city (Zhongguo Dianzi Bao, October 26, 2010). In fact, thus far such upstream investments in these locales have not appeared.

Under these incentives, SMIC under Richard Chang over-expanded, and there have been persistent rumors that SMIC also committed fraud during these expansion by passing off old equipment as new or at least less depreciated than the equipment actually was. To be specific, this alleged fraud victimized the Chinese state in the sense that SMIC was falsely fulfilling its contractual investment obligations to the local government by overvaluing this old equipment. As SMIC reduced its capacity by shedding fabs, it sold its Chengdu fab to Texas Instruments in 2010 and sold off its share of the Wuhan fab in 2013 to its JV[12] partner, Wuhan government's XMC. XMC itself is now part of state-owned Yangtze Memory Technology Corporation (YMTC).

It is important to point out that local officials have incentives to lure investment, but these same incentives make them care much less about such fraud. To wit, fab investment helps local officials hit their hard economic targets for industrial investment (see Fuller 2016, ch. 2) so these incentives would perversely lead them actually to prefer SMIC to overvalue its old equipment (if SMIC were only willing to invest a set amount of old equipment) as long as no one gets caught in the process. Similarly, there are suspicions that Dalian government-backed loans essentially paid for Intel's actual investment of used equipment (Fuller 2016, p. 154). With the economic hard targets in place for local officials, such practices of loaning money to firms to make investments in the relevant locale are logical politically if not economically.

Across a number of sectors over the last decade, the phenomenon of *guo jin min tui* [国进民退 the state advances, the private (sector) retreats] has appeared and the IC industry is no exception. Shanghai's own state-owned entities arranged the takeover of the weaker of the two major hybrid foundries, Grace. Grace from the beginning had a weaker management team than SMIC, which had brought a core team from leading pureplay foundry TSMC to Shanghai. Furthermore, SMIC was able to list abroad in 2004, and this put great pressure on Grace in terms of retaining technical talent as the best technologists already perceived SMIC as the more successful firm. Grace stumbled into a vicious cycle: departure of talented personnel undermined operational efficiency and growth, delaying initial public offering (IPO) plans and encouraging further personnel defections. After delaying its IPO a third time in 2006, Grace never again announced a planned IPO date.

While Grace had always had some Shanghai state ownership through Shanghai Alliance Investment Limited (SAIL), the encroachment of Shanghai state entities was gradual. The first sign of serious state encroachment that pointed toward effective state control of Grace was the appointment of Dong Yeshun, an executive from SAIL, as acting CEO in 2004 in the interim between the original Taiwanese management team and the

---

[12] Wuhan's SOE was essentially a shell company and a very passive JV partner. The Wuhan government arranged the financing for the fab via this shell while SMIC ran the fab without any interference from this JV partner.

team of ex-Chartered executives that began to run the firm in 2005.[13] In 2009, Fu Wenbiao, who had been the director of Shanghai's Informatization Commission, became in succession chairman of Grace and then Huahong. Following this joint chairmanship, in January 2010, the two firms announced their plan to build a joint 300-mm fab.

Finally, in December 2011, the long-anticipated merger was announced. In conjunction with the merger, ownership in Huahong itself was re-organized to bring it under effective control of the Shanghai government (as opposed to the previous situation in which there was joint central and Shanghai government ownership) with certain assets given in return to central government-owned SOE, CEC, which had been a large shareholder in Huahong. The merger has not reoriented this firm toward market competition. Instead, the firm has continued to rely heavily on state procurement and to trail far behind the Big Four pureplay foundries (TSMC, Global Foundries, UMC and China's own SMIC).

The rise of hybrid IC firms combining ethnic Chinese management/ founding owners, China-based HQs and foreign finance began with the founding of IC design firm, Newave, in 1997. This Shanghai-based firm founded by a Taiwanese, a Hong Konger and a Mainland China returnee, all of whom had extensive work experience in the United States, combined foreign venture capital-backing with a strategy to utilize Chinese resources to compete in world markets. In subsequent years, there was a boom in founding pureplay foundries specializing in the fabrication of chips and fabless design firms.

The first hybrid foundry was CSMC, which took over the 908 Project's fab as discussed in the previous section. This firm served as an important entry point for experienced Taiwanese fabrication experts including Nasa Tsai (Cai Nanxiong) and Tony Liu (Liu Youhai), who after their time at CSMC ran Grace and ASMC, respectively. In 2000, two much more ambitious foundries, SMIC and Grace, were founded.

SMIC started out in an advantageous position vis-à-vis Grace because of SMIC's superior foundry management team, which included a number of high-profile TSMC executives including Richard Chang as SMIC's CEO and, arguably much more important, T.Y. Chiu, a well-respected fab operations guru. Grace lagged behind SMIC from initial ramp up of its foundries onward, and SMIC's 2004 IPO ended Grace's hopes of winning the battle for fabrication talent waged by the two foundries in their home town of Shanghai. These defeats set up Grace's acquisition by Huahong discussed in the last section.

In contrast, SMIC utilized large numbers of Chinese engineers to push China's fabrication closer to the technology frontier while at the same time expanding its fabrication capacity around China. From 2003 onward, the firm as a classic fast follower has stayed within two years of the International Technology Roadmap of Semiconductors (ITRS) for logic process technology. More importantly, SMIC has trained thousands of local engineers and set up fabs in a number of cities beyond Shanghai including Chengdu, Wuhan, Shenzhen, Beijing and Tianjin.[14] SMIC has had the largest amount of capacity of any fabrication operator in China since 2002.[15] However, as mentioned in the last section, SMIC under Richard Chang over-expanded; in 2009, a new CEO, David N. K. Wang, a Taiwanese American who had previously headed Applied Materials' China operations, instituted a rationalization that included selling off some of its fabs. The key point is that the Chinese industry lagged far behind the industry technological frontier until the advent of hybrid firms, CSMC and then SMIC, as Table 7.2 demonstrates.

For the hybrid fabless design firms, the true bonanza came when foreign venture capital investment began to pick up in the early years of this century. From 2000 to 2001, the number of fabless design firms more than doubled from 98 to 200, and then by 2002 nearly doubled again to 389. Most of the hybrid firms that grew to become major firms, such as Spreadtrum, RDA, Vimicro, and Galaxycore, were founded during 2000–3. Furthermore, the hybrids contributed more in terms of training IC designers than domestic firms and MNCs combined during 2001–11 (Fuller 2016, p. 174).[16] Hybrids accounted for most of the commercially oriented firms that did not depend on state procurement for the majority of their revenue. As late as 2012, the state procurement

---

[14] SMIC bought Motorola's small fab in Tianjin in 2003 and greatly expanded it.

[15] In certain years SK Hynix and even Intel have had more revenue from their China operations than SMIC (see PwC 2017, p. 31), but their operations include assembly and testing facilities as well as fabrication and the estimates for fabrication revenue from captive Chinese fabs of these MNCs vary widely.

[16] To be precise, the data in Fuller (2016) is from two distinct periods, 2001–5 and 2007–11.

Table 7.2 *China's Gap with Leading International Integrated Circuits Fabrication, 1979–2012*

Year	China (embedded)	Years behind
1979	25- to 30-mm wafers	16
1986	5-microns technology	14
1995	3 microns	19
1998	0.8 microns (CSMC)	10
2003	0.13-microns logic (SMIC)	1–2
2012	40-nm logic (SMIC)	1–2

Note: Data for years behind uses the International Technology Roadmap of Semiconductors (ITRS) and its predecessors. The leading technology in the ITRS is not technically the global technological frontier because Intel, and intermittently Samsung, IBM and IBM-related GlobalFoundries, have used process technologies that are ahead of the ITRS. The ITRS is useful because most major IC firms are not ahead of it and it provides continuity through-out the table as the early data is also based on ITRS predecessors.
Source: Fuller (2016, p. 122).

channels that many state firms relied upon were large enough to comprise more than half of domestic IC design revenue.[17]

Why does the state keep rewarding the same SOEs rather than creating a more competitive procurement process that rewards quality and innovation? It is possible that corruption and side payments are present in the process, and perhaps even play a role in sustaining the system. Discussions with semiconductor executives with experience in applying for grants and trying to sell into the state procurement suggest that state bias toward maintaining existing firms and, secondarily, bureaucratic incompetence in judging the technical merits of various firms play major roles. The 2005–6 scandals around new entrants, ARCA and Hanxin, that employed false claims of technological prowess to obtain generous government support also points to the role of bureaucratic incompetence. In the Hanxin scandal, an anonymous tip on a Tsinghua University bulletin board exposed the firm's fraud e.g. passing off a Freescale chip (with the

---

[17] This calculation was made as follows: the bank IC card market, one form of procurement, alone was a 30 billion RMB market in 2012 when China's total IC design revenue was US$ 9.87 billion or approximately 62.2 billion RMB at 6.3 RMB per dollar (Sina Tech, August 10, 2012; PwC 2017).

corporate logo rubbed off) as its own to government officials. In the ARCA case, the firm never tried to hide the fact that it was not meeting its contractual obligations to its sponsor, MOST, but it only became a scandal when someone leaked this information to the press. Furthermore, this state bias toward existing state-linked firms in procurement extends to other high-technology sectors.[18]

Even before the advent of the new IC megaproject, China's techno-nationalist ambitions for this sector fit uncomfortably with the existence and prominence of hybrid firms. While official reports demonstrate that Chinese bureaucrats recognized that these firms were not ordinary MNCs and had ethnic ties to the domestic economy (e.g. DYBG 2002, No. 12 on SMIC), the foreign control and perhaps the heavily Taiwanese or Taiwanese American character of SMIC's management team in particular were markers of political unreliability (Interview, June 2013). At least such fears provided ammunition for politically savvy SOEs intent on empire building in this industry.

SMIC had Shanghai Industrial Holdings (SIH), a Shanghai government-owned holding company, as a shareholder from the beginning, but SIH played a very passive role and never appeared to aspire to take over SMIC. Perhaps Shanghai's government did not treat SMIC like Grace because SMIC's large foreign shareholders and overseas listing would have made any attempted acquisition of SMIC by Shanghai's government too difficult.

The passivity of SOE shareholders in SMIC changed dramatically with the arrival of Datang as a major shareholder in December 2008. Taking advantage of the onset of the financial crisis, Datang used its deep ties to the state to procure the financing to purchase 16.57 percent of SMIC and place two representatives on its board. Speculation was rife that Datang aimed to turn SMIC into a captive foundry (ESJJBD July 4, 2011). Datang increased its shareholding to 19.12 percent in 2010 after TSMC became a major shareholder in wake of settlement of TSMC's lawsuits against SMIC.[19] When state-owned China Investment Corporation (CIC) bought shares, Datang increased its shareholding to 19.43 percent in April 2011.

---

[18] ZTE has fared as well or better than Huawei in recent large government procurement decisions despite the fact that ZTE is much less competitive than Huawei so on the merits should receive much less. Similarly, Datang continues to receive procurement orders despite its lack of capabilities. In computers, weak firms such as Founder and Tongfang still receive government procurement support and even Lenovo arguably is receiving support based on past performance (see Fuller 2016, ch. 3).

[19] TSMC launched a series of lawsuits against SMIC alleging IP theft given the number of TSMC personnel that moved to SMIC.

Datang did more than place representatives on the board. During David N. K. Wang's tenure as CEO (2009–11), Zhen Caigui, Datang's then chairman, interfered in very unhelpful and even corrupt ways in SMIC's management. Zhen allegedly blocked an investment of US$500 million by Citigroup and JP Morgan by refusing to dilute Datang's shareholding while cloaking its motives for refusing to sell shares to foreigners in patriotism. More egregiously, Zhen allegedly demanded a three percent fee from SMIC in order to get a state bank loan according to former SMIC insiders (Interviews, June 21, 2013 and July 6, 2017). These allegations are highly plausible given that Zhen was taken into custody in May of 2017, and on July 14, the State-owned Assets Supervision and Administration Commission (SASAC) announced that due to serious disciplinary infractions, Zhen was under investigation.

In late June 2011, Datang actually attempted a coup in SMIC's management. Taking advantage of the death of SMIC's chairman, Jiang Shangzhou, Datang voted against re-electing CEO David N. K. Wang, to the board. Rather than supporting this move, the other state representatives chose to abstain, suggesting that they did not see eye-to-eye with Datang's purported move to place a Mainlander, Simon Yang, as CEO. Indeed, on July 15, 2011, Jiang's protégé, Zhang Wenyi, became acting CEO and then former SMIC executive, T.Y. Chiu, was appointed CEO in August. After the appointment of Chiu, Datang's CEO-in-waiting, Yang, quit the firm. Thus, prior to the new 2014 IC policy, SMIC appeared to have avoided the fate of Grace and other firms that were gobbled up by state firms armed with cheap financing.

THE 2014 IC MEGAPROJECT

In June 2014, the Chinese government issued its outline for the new IC megaproject. The industry megaprojects (重大专项 in Chinese) originated with the 2006–10 Medium- and Long-Term Plan for Science and Technology. In October 2010, the State Council decided that these megaprojects would drive the implementation of the Strategic and Emerging Industries initiative. The IC megaproject was just one of sixteen large-scale industrial policies envisioned in the Medium- and Long-Term Plan for Science and Technology (2006–20). Thus, from the start of the Medium-and-Long-Term Plan there was a plan for an IC megaproject, but like many of the other megaprojects, it took years to formulate the policy. The key features of the megaproject outline were a central government fund of 120 billion RMB for the industry and plans for regional and local complementary funds to support the industry in their respective regions. The outline called for the achievement of scale production using 14/16 nm, world leading assembly technology and internationally competitive materials and semiconductor capital equipment sectors by 2020, and for reaching the international technology level in all major segments (design, fabrication, A&T, capital equipment and materials) of the IC industry value chain by 2030.

At least a year before the official announcement of the new IC megaproject's outline in June 2014, there were strong indications that officials and firms involved in the industry knew large-scale support was imminent or already available in advance of the official announcement, which itself trailed the drawing up of the policy by six months. For example, Jiang Shoulei, who had served as a high-level executive in Huahong and the Shanghai Semiconductor Industry Association, acknowledged that Tsinghua Unigroup (also known as Ziguang) was not acting on its own when it began acquisitions of NASDAQ-listed firms in 2013 (*Dongfang Zaobao* November 12, 2013). Contemporaneously, Xu Xiaotian of the China Semiconductor Industry Association and a former official of the Ministry of Industry and Information Technology (MIIT) indicated in November 2013 that the central government was ready to commit large sums for the IC industry that went beyond previous support (*Dongfang Zaobao*, November 12, 2013). Indeed, without state support for acquisitions in the IC industry, Unigroup would have had neither the financial wherewithal nor probably any active interest in a sector in which it had no prior experience. Thus, the actions by a number of state actors in 2013 should also be considered as results of what they understood to be a more aggressive IC industrial policy if albeit vaguely defined one.

This section will proceed as follows. First, it considers the antecedents of the policy in terms of how the state perceived the previous policies' failures and how it proposed to address these failures. It then examines the actors and initiatives involved in the new policy.

Interpreting China's IC Industry Policy Failures

While China's industry had grown through 2012 across IC design, fabrication and A&T, there still were major concerns for the state. The general issue was the perception that China was running a large trade deficit in ICs, a high-tech and strategic good. While China's chip trade deficit is exaggerated given that China's export platforms in industries such as

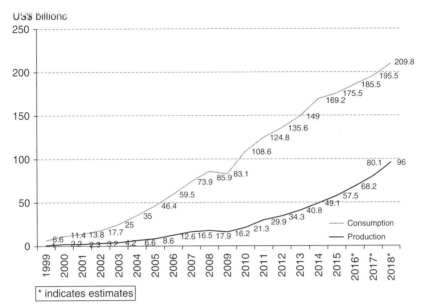

US\$ billions

Figure 7.2 Comparison of China's Integrated Circuit Consumption and Production, 1999–2018
Source: Data from PwC (2017, pp. 6, 14), for years 1999–2015, and CSIA for 2016–18.

electronics import and then export large quantities of ICs, the nominal deficit is quite large (see Figure 7.2) and foreign firms continue to dominate China's chip market as shown in Figure 7.3.

For design, as Table 7.1 above demonstrates, state backed firms did not have significant success outside of state procurement. Subsequent deployment of state funds to de-list hybrid firms from foreign exchanges shows that this very hybridity (i.e. the foreign financial ties of these China-based firms) bothered techno-nationalist bureaucrats. Finally, while IC revenue had grown substantially (see Figure 7.4 below), with the exception of Huawei, the emergence of large Chinese firms as major global corporate consumers of chips (see Table 7.3) had not made the same firms major designers or producers of such chips like Huawei's HiSilicon nor had this phenomenon spurred purely domestic (i.e. non-hybrid) chip vendors.

As for fabrication and, secondarily, A&T, the MNCs predominated in domestic production even as domestic production lagged far behind China's consumption. Similarly, even as China's consumption of chips soared to 52.5 percent of the world total (inclusive of discrete

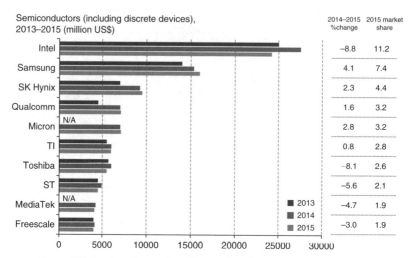

Figure 7.3 Semiconductor Suppliers to the Chinese Market, 2013–2015
Source: Recreated from data in PwC (2017, p. 11).

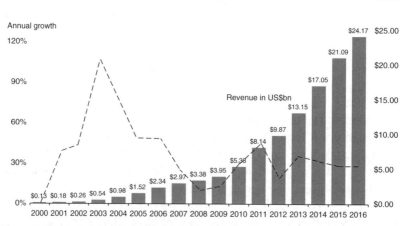

Figure 7.4 China's Integrated Circuit Design Industry Revenue and Growth, 2000–2016
Sources: Data from PwC (2017, p. 20) for years 2000–15 and CSIA for 2016.

semiconductor components), China has not created any significant suppliers of semiconductor capital equipment.

The lessons the Chinese state learned from what it viewed as a frustrating
lack of progress are as follows. First, China needs to spend even more money
than past industrial policies to expand its IC production base and strengthen

Table 7.3 *Global Top 10 Integrated Circuits Consumers in 2016*

Ranking	Company	Spending (US$ billion)	Market Share (%)
1	Samsung Electronics	31.7	9.3
2	Apple	30	8.8
3	Dell	13.3	3.9
4	*Lenovo*	12.8	3.8
5	*Huawei*	9.9	2.9
6	HP Inc.	8.5	2.5
7	Hewlett Packard Enterprises	6.2	1.8
8	Sony	6.1	1.8
9	*BBK*	5.8	1.7
10	LG Electronics	5.2	1.5
Others		210.2	61.9
Total		339.7	100

Note: Firms in italics are Chinese.
Source: EE Times.

its chosen homegrown champions.[20] Estimates for spending beyond the central government fund have ranged from one trillion (McKinsey 2014) to 1.24 trillion RMB.[21] Second, it should try to purchase advanced technology abroad either through taking hybrid firms listed abroad private and in the process under state control, or purchasing purely foreign firms in order to absorb their technology. The first objective would center on fabrication. The second would focus on both design and fabrication. Emphasizing these two areas makes sense in that these are the two most technologically intensive segments within the IC value chain. When one takes a broader view to include the capital equipment and EDA tools (the computer programs that facilitate IC design), these two additional areas are also technology intensive, but China's participants in these areas are also especially weak. Given this weakness, it makes sense that the outline for the new policy mentions them, but the policy as outlined and subsequently rolled out has not emphasized them. Indeed, recent history has shown how difficult it is to enter the capital equipment and EDA segments even for emerging IC powerhouses. Since their rise in 1980s and 1990s, Korea and Taiwan have not been able to foster

---

[20] And this is in the context where Chinese central and local governments likely spent 100 billion RMB per Five-Year Plan (FYP) for the several FYPs prior to the 13th FYP (Interview, June 21, 2013).

[21] www.chinamoneynetwork.com/2017/01/13/rise-of-trillion-rmb-government-funds-reshapes-chinas-investment-landscape/2 (accessed August 23, 2017).

large and competitive semiconductor capital equipment sectors despite state efforts to do so. As for EDA tools, American MNCs dominate this area with the exception of Siemens, which purchased Mentor Graphics.

Agents and Policy Implementation

Beyond China's past industrial policy failures, a more pressing reason to be skeptical of the likelihood of success is the continued insistence on using state-owned vehicles as the main agents for carrying out the renewed industrial policy. While China Resource Holdings (the owners of the former Huajing and CSMC) and Huahong have not played major roles in this policy, XMC (the former SMIC-Wuhan municipality JV sold back to Wuhan), Innotrong and Tsinghua Unigroup have emerged as important actors. The fact that Unigroup and its chairman, Zhao Weiguo, have no prior IC industry experience should give one pause. Innotrong as a brand new entity may have more potential upside, but this Hefei government venture shows indications of not being willing to countenance selling control to either foreign or private investors (Interview, July 6, 2017). XMC's merger in July 2016 with Unigroup-backed Yangtze Memory Corporation (YMTC) has created a YMTC management team with industry experience including Simon Yang, formerly of SMIC, but some question the team's depth and point to its lack of experience in its area of focus, memory (Interview, June 2013; EE Times, January 26, 2017).

A similar dynamic has occurred in the funds set up in the wake of the policy. Summitview is the only significant and active investment fund in the IC industry with no government links. The other major funds (Sino IC Capital, Hua Capital, JAC Capital, Canyon Bridge, UNIC, E-Town Fund, and Pudong Science and Technology) are closely tied to the government. This dynamic is important not only due to the issue of whether or not government venture funds can perform well, but also in determining the ability to acquire foreign technology. According to one source, officials at the Committee on Foreign Investment in the United States (CFIUS) actually told Summitview that they regard this private fund as quite different from the state funds that they regard with suspicion (Interview, July 5, 2017).

The state links matter because with the possible exception of private Summitview, which is run by ex-executives of Spreadtrum, Chinese funds have faced increasing obstacles in acquiring overseas assets in the IC industry. Between 2013 and 2015, Chinese funds acquired a number of foreign firms

Table 7.4 *China's Successful and Failed Major Acquisitions in the Integrated Circuits Industry*

Deals Completed	Deals Blocked or Likely to be Blocked
Tsinghua Unigroup acquired Linxens (France) July 2018	China Resources' bid for Fairchild (US)
Canyon Bridge acquired Imagination Technologies (UK) November 2017	UNIC and Xcerra (US)
ChipOne and E-Town acquired IML from Exar (US) November 2016	Canyon Bridge and Lattice (US)
JAC Capital purchases NXP (Netherlands)'s RF business in December 2015 and then with Wise Road Capital and JAC Capital acquired its Nexperia standard products division in June 2016	Fujian Grand Chip Investment and Aixtron (Germany)
Summitview/Uphill acquired ISSI (US) in June 2015	TCL and Inseego (US)
JCET acquired STATS ChipPac (Singapore) in November 2014	Unigroup and Western Digital (US)
Tianshui Huatian bought out Flipchip (US) in November 2014	Unigroup and Micron (US)
Hua Capital bought out Omnivision (US) in August 2014	Unigroup and three Taiwanese A&T firms
Pudong S&T with CEC acquired Montage (US) in August 2014	
Unigroup bought out Spreadtrum (Cayman Islands) December 2013 and RDA (Cayman Islands) July 2014	

Note: Successful acquisitions' dates are often the date of the public bid rather than the date of completion.

including hybrids, all with foreign corporate homes. Since then, foreign regulatory agencies, such as CFIUS, have blocked some deals and derailed others by delaying approvals (see Table 7.4). Indeed, only US$5.3 billion out of $43 billion of announced acquisitions actually went through in 2015.

There have been some minor differences in approaches of foreign regulatory agencies with the United States and Taiwan being relatively tough and the Europeans taking a slightly more relaxed approach.[22] Of course, ICs are not a competitive strength of the EU economies with the possible exceptions of Brexiting United Kingdom and the Netherlands so the relaxed approach may reflect the strategic weight placed on the

---

[22] Witness the 2018 approval of Tsinghua Unigroup's acquisition of France's Linxens. However, Linxens smart card technology is far from cutting edge (Interview, September 5, 2018).

industry rather than a general approach to Chinese investment. Indeed, MERICS in Berlin has called upon the German government to take a tougher approach on Chinese investment, particularly in areas of competitive strength, such as Industry 4.0-related technologies (MERICS 2016). As for Japan, the general perception is that the Japanese government has made it clear behind the scenes that Chinese investment in Toshiba's IC division would not be welcome.

In general, the successful acquisitions were firms listed in offshore tax havens, A&T firms, and/or smaller fabless design firms. The largest fabless firms acquired were Omnivision, ISSI, and Spreadtrum with the bids placed prior to 2016. Since then, the most significant acquisition has been JAC Capital's acquisition of Nexperia, NXP's former standard products division. Many proposed ambitious acquisitions of large IC industry-related businesses, such as Western Digital, Micron and Fairchild, have gone nowhere. These failures may be in part due to connections between various funds and the Chinese state receiving more attention, but the larger pools of technology these companies represent probably played a more decisive role in pushback against Chinese acquisition. After all, CFIUS in 2017 has also rejected Infineon of Germany's proposed acquisition of Cree's Wolfspeed division on the grounds of national security.[23] Similarly, CFIUS rejected TCL's acquisition of Inseego while approving Summitview's acquisition of ISSI even though both acquirers are private Chinese entities.[24] The ability to acquire A&T firms (except those in Taiwan where economic relations with China have become politically sensitive) also demonstrates this logic because specialists view A&T as the least technologically intensive segment of the IC value chain.

Recent discussions with investors involved with both state and private entities revealed various degrees of pessimism about the openness of foreign, particularly American, technology to acquisition. One interlocutor stated bluntly, "Difficult for Chinese companies to acquire any US semiconductor assets" (Interview, June 20, 2017). Another investor with links both to private and state investors when asked about foreign firms wishing to sell assets said,

---

[23] While nixing the Infineon bid for Wolfspeed occurred during the early Trump administration, the decision came so early on in the administration and after an extensive review started in the Obama administration that Trump's arrival probably had nothing to do with the decision, http://fortune.com/2017/02/11/cfius-infineon-cree-wolfspeed-secur ity/ (accessed July 19, 2017).

[24] To be precise, ISSI was acquired by a consortium called Uphill that was led by Summitview and included both private investors, such as Gigadevice, and state ones, such as E-Town.

"Lots of people still talk to us." In addition, he pointed out in reference to the Infineon bid for Wolfspeed, "CFIUS is not just against China." However, he also conceded that there are "not many deals going on" even while arguing that private investors from China have a regulatory advantage vis-à-vis state ones because "US will look at us differently" (Interview, July 5, 2017). This somewhat more optimistic interpretation of CFIUS' openness to Chinese investment should not be dismissed out of hand because this investor went to Washington to talk directly with CFIUS shortly prior to the interview. To support the interpretation that CFIUS has taken a nuanced rather than knee-jerk response to Chinese investment, we note that CFIUS and the rest of the US government did nothing to prevent Chinese firms' 2015 and 2016 acquisitions of NXP's two divisions.[25] While NXP is European so CFIUS does not strictly have jurisdiction over NXP's decision to sell various business units to Chinese investors, the US government can legally intervene in Chinese acquisition of European companies, as in the case of Fujian Grand Chip's bid for Aixtron, when the target firm has significant US-based assets.

Have the completed acquisitions succeeded in accelerating China's semiconductor technological development? In the short term, the answer on balance is that these acquisitions have done little to promote the industry. The purchase of the hybrid firms, Montage, RDA, and Spreadtrum, has made little sense because these firms already had their functional headquarters and core technology teams in Shanghai. RDA's acquisition went quite badly. Vincent Tai, RDA's CEO at the time, opposed the acquisition of RDA by Unigroup so he quit the firm and took its core technology team with him. Unigroup thus bought a mere shell of a firm aside from a few overseas patents, while Tai and his team have set up a new hybrid firm, ASR Microelectronics,[26] in Shanghai. In 2018, Leo Li, the former CEO of Spreadtrum credited with its past turnaround, abruptly left Unigroup as well. Unigroup's combination of Spreadtrum and RDA, which were respectively baseband processor[27] and radio frequency[28] (RF)

---

[25] It may not just be coincident that NXP was required to divest its radio frequency (RF) division in order to receive China's Ministry of Commerce approval of its own acquisition of Freescale and then sold this entity to a Chinese firm (EE Times, February 2, 2017).

[26] And ASR, not being a Chinese firm, was able to acquire Marvell's LTE (the main fourth generation telecommunications standard) thin-modem business, a technology Tsinghua Unigroup would have loved to acquire.

[27] Baseband processors are chips or parts of chips that manage the radio functions. They are the key processors within mobile phones.

[28] Radio frequency chips are key components in wireless products. Applying a radio frequency current to an antenna creates an electromagnetic field that can travel through space (Hurtarte et al. 2007, p. 236)

chip companies, makes sense because the combined firm can offer a more complete chip solution for smartphones. Unfortunately, with the loss of RDA's core team and no improvement in Spreadtrum's competitive position vis-à-vis the big baseband processors (e.g. Qualcomm and MediaTek), Unigroup appears to have overpaid for a mediocre baseband chip company. Pudong Science and Technology has managed to retain Howard Yang and his technology team at Montage, but there is a looming potential conflict, as the management team would like to re-list abroad, whereas the Chinese state wants these acquired firms to list in China.

Looking beyond the acquisition of these hybrids, it is too early to evaluate the potential for these assets to enhance the capabilities of Chinese firms since the acquiring firms are mostly investment funds rather than active IC producers. Perhaps JAC Capital will leverage its purchase of NXP's RF division (Ampleon) to help to bolster the new JV, JLQ, in which it has a stake, but most of the investment vehicles lack such direct links.

The JVs themselves appear to be a ploy to avoid foreign regulatory blocking of Chinese acquisition of IC industry assets. The Datang-Qualcomm JV, JLQ, with participation from state funds, JAC Capital and Wise Road Capital, may not worry the US government much since the JV appears to focus on low-end smartphone chip sets. However, the JV between AMD and Tianjin Haiguang greatly concerns the US government given that it involves microprocessor technology that serves as the brain of supercomputers.[29] Indeed, there have been repeated calls in the US for new rules to prohibit JVs that lead to sharing sensitive technology (WSJ, January 2, 2017; FT, January 17, 2017).

With routes to overseas technology acquisition blocked, Chinese firms have looked to spend copious state funds at home. The prime example of this phenomenon is Tsinghua Unigroup. After failing to complete major acquisitions abroad in the memory chip space, Unigroup has turned toward acquiring assets at home. Unigroup has directed nearly 24 billion USD into the new YMTC. With large pools of money and few outlets, Unigroup also bought five percent of SMIC in November 2016, but declined to appoint a member to its board. Unigroup also purchased a controlling 36.4 percent stake in Tongfang Guoxin, a chip design subsidiary of the Tongfang Group, which itself is under the same Tsinghua Holdings as Tsinghua Unigroup (NYT, November 5, 2015).[30]

---

[29] AMD had an earlier microprocessor JV in 2005 with Chinese partners including a Ministry of Education-owned firm and Beijing Normal University called Beijing CBE AMD Information Technology Co. Ltd. This firm did not succeed and no longer exists.

[30] One feature of this transaction is that an investment vehicle personally controlled by Tsinghua Unigroup chairman, Zhao Weiguo, also bought shares in Tongfang Guoxin.

Shanghai's fund reportedly is considering buying an old SOE called Huayue running a 5-inch fab in Shaoxing in neighboring Zhejiang Province (Interview, April 1, 2017). The fact that the fund from Shanghai, which has the biggest cluster of both design and fabrication in China, is considering to invest in a failing SOE with old technology in a neighboring province strongly suggests that investment capital has outstripped good investment opportunities.

One outcome of these investments in local firms was the end of SMIC's independence. SMIC finally succumbed to state control due to the funds available to various state entities. The central government's investment vehicle for the IC megaproject, Sino IC Capital,[31] bought 11 percent of SMIC in February 2015 and then another 6 percent in June of that year. In February 2016, Sino IC Capital appointed its second representative to SMIC's board. Since that time, state representatives including the two state bureaucrats who are now executive directors, have outnumbered directors who are not state bureaucrats. Some evidence points toward the state interfering in SMIC's management in order to pursue the state's own policy goals. For example, in May 2016 SMIC purchased a 14.3 percent stake in Jiangsu Changjiang Electronics Technology (JCET), a state-owned A&T firm, just as JCET was struggling with losses resulting from its acquisition of STATS ChipPac (SCMP, July 4, 2016). Also, in the same month, T. Y. Chiu was removed as CEO and made vice chairman.[32] Zhao Haijun replaced Chiu, initially serving as CEO, and then, in October 2017, becoming co-CEO along with Liang Moong-Sung.

Thus far, IC design has experienced little departure from its past trajectory. On the positive side, the state's take-over of a number of promising hybrid fabless design firms has not turned these firms away from their commercial orientation i.e. they have not morphed into state procurement-dependent SOEs (see Table 7.5).[33] On the negative side, the

The combined holdings of this investment vehicle and Unigroup amounts to 88% of Tongfang Guoxin's shares. What is disturbing is the mixing of Chairman Zhao's private interests with a SOE and state industrial policy, but as we can see from the problems of Zhen Caigui's interference with SMIC, SOE executives and state officials can blur the lines between private interests and public policy.

[31] Sino IC Capital is the sole management company of the central government's China IC Fund.

[32] From correspondence with industry insiders on October 26 and 27, 2017, it is still unclear if T.Y. Chiu stepped down willing or unwilling. Zhao is a Mainlander who has worked for SMIC since 2010. Liang is under a cloud for having been found guilty of stealing TSMC's IP and taking it to Samsung (EE Times, October 17, 2017).

[33] While the overall trend of retaining their commercial market orientation is true thus far, there are worrying signs that Spreadtrum is beginning to get roped into government

Table 7.5 *Integrated Circuits Design Firms and State Procurement, 2015*

Company	Ownership	2015 Revenue (US$ min)	State Procurement
HiSilicon (Huawei)	private	3518	minimal
Spreadtrum/Unigroup	state	1749	minimal
CEC Huada	state	538	Golden Card
Datang	state	439	state telecom: Golden Card
RDA/Unigroup	state	409	minimal
Focal Tech Sys	hybrid	385	minimal
Vimicro	hybrid	294	minimal
Galaxycore	hybrid	285	minimal
Guoke	state	285	minimal
CR Semico	state	206	power meters
Rockchip	private	205	minimal
Montage	state	200	minimal

Source: Interviews, EE Times and PwC (2017).

long established fabless design SOEs have failed to develop a commercial orientation and remain dependent on government procurement. Moreover, the new JVs do not appear to offer dramatic breakthroughs. The AMD-Tianjin Haiguang appears oriented toward government procurement of servers. The Qualcomm-Datang JV in contrast is commercially oriented, but focuses on low-end baseband chipsets for the smartphone market. Similarly, Xiaomi is trying to create its own smartphone chipsets. Tellingly, the two big firms that have dominated this market, Qualcomm and MediaTek, are moving to diversify away from this increasingly competitive and unprofitable product area into growth areas, such as automobile electronics. The one major domestic Chinese success is the subsidiary of Huawei, HiSilicon, but this firm remains heavily dependent on Huawei's internal consumption of these chips that would probably encounter IP licensing issues if sold on the market (Interview, November 12, 2014). Furthermore, HiSilicon's success is simply an extension of Huawei's own disciplined focus on technological development, which stands in sharp contrast to the vast majority of China's

procurement for secure smartphones (WSJ, January 27, 2015). A little of this type of production is fine, but the firm needs to be careful it does not become dependent on state procurement like many other technology sector SOEs in China.

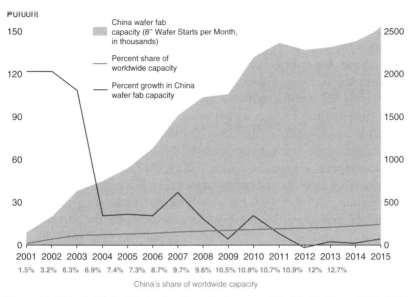

Figure 7.5 China's Wafer Fabrication Capacity Increases Worldwide Share, 2001–2015
Source: Recreated from data in PwC (2017, p. 24).

domestic technology firms (Fuller 2016), and there is no evidence of significant interactions between HiSilicon and the current IC industry megaproject.

The trend of China's increasing share of global fabrication capacity has continued (see Figure 7.5 below) even when including an absolute dip in China's capacity in 2012. As mentioned earlier, regional and local governments have had incentives to seek large-scale foreign investments. Fabrication investments fit this criterion well prior to the IC industry megaproject. The IC industry megaproject undoubtedly has served to justify the raising of regional and local funds as the 2014 Outline called for just these measures, but any acceleration in the growth of China's relative capacity is likely to appear a few years down the line for two reasons. First, fab construction takes time. Second and more critically, there is more money available than there are capable teams to lead new projects. SEMI estimates that Chinese projects account for twenty-six of sixty-two announced new fabs worldwide (EE Times, December 15, 2016); however, the history of the IC industry suggests that many fabs reportedly under construction never materialize. The CEO of China's most prominent capital equipment vendor, Gerald Yin, estimates that only half of the seventeen fabs slated to receive US$64 billion in government support by 2020 will actually be built (EE Times, January 12, 2017). In short, estimates of fab construction vary, and the actual number of new plants will probably fall far short of new project announcements.

While the IC megaproject emphasizes Chinese control of the industry, it also has emphasized import substitution i.e. increasing China-based production. Indeed, an oft-stated policy goal, although one not explicitly mentioned in the 2014 Outline, is for China to produce 70 percent of the chips it consumes by 2025. However, when it comes to choosing between techno-nationalism (i.e. foregoing projects just because they are owned or operated by MNCs) or MNC-owned production in China, regional and local governments generally have a built-in bias toward choosing the latter despite the 2014 Outline because incentives for local and regional officials still prioritize industrial investment (see Fuller 2016, ch. 2). These incentives combined with the scarcity of capable local firms, have led to the new policy encouraging many MNC investments as well as some local ones (see Table 7.6). As one IC expert, who often engaged with local officials in charge of developing the IC industry, put it:

Most of them (local officials), they don't like foreign companies investing in IC projects in China because they [the foreign companies] get all the resources and local companies get nothing, but they [the local officials] do it anyway because they want foreign investment into [sic] their cities and Chinese companies do not have these technology [sic] capabilities so that is why they like foreign companies (Interview, June 20, 2017).

The three[34] new major local fabrication companies, Innotrong, Jinhua Integrated Circuit Company (JHICC), and YMTC, sensibly focus on memory chips. Memory chips are high volume products so they can fill fabs. Also, successful new entrants in the memory chip business have relied on large amounts of patient capital to ride out the combination of vicious market cycles and large amounts of capital investment required for this sub-sector (Fuller et al. 2003). With the IC megaproject deploying copious amounts of capital, domestic producers can anticipate financial resources that are likely to be sufficient to survive steep memory market downturns.

---

[34] In addition to its subsidiary, YMTC, Tsinghua Unigroup is building a mega-fab in Nanjing, but this fab is far from complete so it is not included in this discussion nor in Table 7.6.

Table 7.6 *New Fab Investments*

Company	Total Invest (US$ billion)	2016 Invest (US$ billion)	Location	Product	Process Technology
YMTC	24	0.5	Wuhan	3D NAND	30 nm
SMIC	15	2.6	BJ, SH	Logic	28,40 nm
UMC	6.2	0.1	Xiamen	Logic	28,40,55 nm
Samsung	7.5	0.4	Xi'an	3D NAND	32 nm
Intel	5.5	0.5	Dalian	3D NAND	30 nm
SK Hynix	5.5	0.1	Wuxi	DRAM	20 nm
TSMC	3	0.5	Nanjing	Logic	16 nm
Powerchip	2–3	1	Hefei	LCD Driver	90,110,150 nm
HLMC (Huahong)	5–7	0	SH	Logic	28 nm
Innotrong	8–9	7	Hefei	DRAM	?
GloFo	10	0	Chengdu	Logic; FD-SOI	180/130 nm;22 nm
JHICC	5.65	0	Quanzhou	Specialty DRAM	?

Note: SH= Shanghai BJ= Beijing.
Source: EE Times, May 27, 2017, and Interviews.

What remains in question is whether or not China will muster the requisite human capital needed for this sector. The MNC investments from 2004 onward relied on the large numbers of engineers trained by SMIC because under Richard Chang's ambitious fab-building plans, SMIC prepared a workforce far ahead of its revenues. As revenues, capacity and workforce were brought closer into alignment, many of these engineers went to the new MNC fabs. Today, there is no large firm with the requisite workforce slack to supply others. Thus, there has been a battle for scarce human resources (EE Times, January 12, 2017; January 26, 2017; May 23, 2017).

One example of the hunt for human capital is Hefei Municipality's Innotrong (Ruili瑞力), a new dynamic access memory (DRAM) fab. Innotrong considered recruiting ex-Elpida CEO Yukio Sakamoto and a group of 1000 Taiwanese, Korean, and Japanese engineers he had assembled, but their salary demands were too high or he could not actually recruit the critical mass of engineers he claimed. Innotrong then tried to recruit a Korean team, but the Koreans wanted to have complete control over the operations and Innotrong as a SOE wanted the firm to remain in

Chinese hands. Finally, Innotrong was able to recruit former Huahong International and SMIC CEO, David N. K. Wang, to head the firm.[35] While Wang did an admirable job of rationalizing SMIC's production in order to achieve profitability, it is still unclear if he has the team in place to bring the fab to scale.

Similarly, Unigroup's YMTC faces a stiff uphill battle to try to become a major player at the cutting edge of flash memory, 3D NAND.[36] The firm has supposedly recruited 1,000 operators from Samsung's Xi'an fab, but operators are not what separate the wheat from chaff in fabrication.[37] YMTC has plans to recruit Korean flash memory engineers from Samsung and SK Hynix, but it is not clear whether the firm will succeed in doing so (EE Times, January 26, 2017). What is clear is that the current team led by Simon Yang lacks experience in flash memory and thus probably is not up to the task. Unigroup's plans to build fabs in Nanjing and Chengdu have attracted skepticism from insiders who doubt that these plans will come to fruition, especially because of hints that Unigroup may attempt the difficult task of simultaneously initiating mass production of both DRAM and flash memory[38] (Interview, July 6, 2017).

Given these issues, it is not at all surprising that local and regional governments have also turned to established MNCs to set up fabs. The three major foundries, TSMC, GlobalFoundries, and UMC, have all agreed to set up new fabs in new locations in China. GlobalFoundries is particularly interesting because this new fab is its first fab in China and is

---

[35] Information on Innotrong is from EE Times, January 26, 2017, where Sakamoto's team is referred to as Sino King, and Interview, July 6, 2017.

[36] 3D here means that there are multilayer dice stacked on top of each other with wafer-level packaging. China's National Center of Advanced Packaging (NCAP) is working on this technology with SMIC's SJ Jiangyin in Wuxi. Hybrid fabless firm, Galaxycore, is reportedly also quite strong in wafer-level packaging for CMOS image sensors, the critical chip for camera and video applications. See note 35 for further details of NAND flash. CMOS stands for complementary metal oxide semiconductor and is one of the main types of semiconductor.

[37] TSMC is considered to have the best-run fabrication operations among foundries worldwide, and TSMC's operators are generally low-skilled workers recruited from Southeast Asia. What separates TSMC from the competition is its core engineering staff.

[38] DRAM is a type of memory chip that needs power (electric charge every few milliseconds) to maintain its contents whereas flash is a "non-volatile" memory that doesn't need power to maintain its contents. The two main types of memory are DRAM and NAND flash. DRAM typically has been used as the main memory in computing and NAND flash has been used in consumer applications although mobile telephony is consuming increasing amounts of both types of memory.

niming to use sophisticated fully depleted silicon-on-insulator (FD-SOI) process technology. Taiwan's Powerchip is establishing a new fab in Hefei where Innotrong is located. Three of the four largest IDMs, SK Hynix, Intel, and Samsung, are taking advantage of the megaproject's copious funding to expand through subsidized loans their respective established Chinese bases in Wuxi, Dalian, and Xi'an. Local and regional governments like to defend the generous deals given to MNCs by arguing that these deals will propel the development of the larger industrial value chain or eco-system (see Fuller 2016, ch. 5). While there is good reason to doubt the ability of individual fabs, especially ones that are in vertically integrated IDMs, to transform local or regional economies along the lines anticipated by local boosters, the subsidization of MNC fabs will certainly promote a rapid increase in China's fabrication capacity. In the longer term, these efforts seem likely to enlarge China's pool of experienced fabrication engineers.

To try to sum up the distance of China's firms from the leading global firms, Table 7.7 takes prominent Chinese firms in major segments and compares them to the global firms. Left out of the table are major product areas where China does not yet have significant local competitors (e.g. DRAM and NAND flash) although China is trying to build such competitors right now. The area where China comes closest thus far is in the foundry business via SMIC. The firm's recent take-over by the state casts doubt on its competitive sustainability. The long-term prospects for Spreadtrum, which lags even further behind its global competitors, seem even more problematic. In contrast, Omnivision looks impressive, but this firm was an American firm until bought out in 2014 so it too may begin to decline under Chinese state control.[39]

CONCLUSION: CHINA'S PROSPECTS IN THE GLOBAL IC INDUSTRY

China's government is determined to spend its way to prominence in the global IC industry. If the goal were simply for China to grab a larger

---

[39] Omnivision had a small amount of patenting activity with lead inventors based in China from 2011 to 2015 (eleven US Patent and Trademark Office utility patents), which given the lead times needed for patent approval, represents a period prior to Omnivision's take-over by Hua Capital.

Table 7.7 *Comparisons of Chinese Firms and Leading Global Firms*

Product Area	Chinese Competitors	Leading Global Firms	Notes
Foundry	SMIC M+ Huahong L	TSMC H+ (global leader) GlobalFoundries H UMC H–	Samsung is also a major player in the foundry business but is not its main business. SMIC had 3 times Huahong's revenue in 2016, and is the fourth largest pureplay foundry globally.
Baseband chipsets	Spreadtrum M– Leadcore/Datang L– HiSilicon (Huawei) ?	Qualcomm H+ (global leader) MediaTek H–	Unclear what the quality of HiSilicon chips are because sold only in-house. Apple and Samsung also design some of their own baseband chipsets in-house.
Central Processing Units (CPUs)*	AMD-Tianjin Haiguang ? China CPU (formerly BLX) L– Suzhou Powercore L–	Intel H+ (global leader) AMD H ARM H	The Chinese vendors are not commercially oriented and have virtually no presence outside of state procurement channels.
CMOS image sensors	Omnivision (orig. US firm) M+ Galaxycore M–	Sony H (global leader) Samsung H ON Semi M+	Omnivision is the third largest image sensor firm, but this market is smaller than other three product areas in this table.

Note:

L = relatively low technology capability within the given category.

M = intermediate level of technological capability.

H = high level of technological capability within the given category.

+/– refer to a firm being slightly higher/lower than the given technology capability e.g. M– means slightly below the intermediate level of technological capability.

? indicates not enough information to assess the technological capability of the firm.

* CPUs are the microprocessors that run computer systems.

share of global IC industry production, then one could already deem the policy a success. Indeed, by 2013, China's fabrication capacity (most of it foreign-owned to be sure) had already surpassed Europe's, and had increased twenty-fold from a very low base in 2000 (Houseman et al. 2014). However, according to China's successive techno-nationalist policies' actual goals of creating competitive national champions to rival the leading global firms across the IC industry value chain, past policies and future prospects for policy success do not look good.

Certainly, the Chinese state's choice of preferred policy agents, old and new SOEs, are a hindrance, and the very choice of these agents has helped to create or at least bolster another obstacle, foreign regulatory hurdles to Chinese acquisition of foreign technology. Even if the market for foreign technology were completely open to the Chinese, the choice of policy vehicles is a good reason for pessimism. To wit, the state favors SOEs that have a track record in this industry of having relatively low absorptive capacity i.e. they very well might make little use of whatever technology they acquire. The other major obstacle is the very speed at which the Chinese state wishes to move. As one industry expert put it using the most ominous of Chinese historical analogies, "I think what they are doing in fabrication is another Great Leap Forward" (Interview, April 1, 2017). Of course, no one will starve to death in the wake of this ambitious IC industrial policy, but without adequate training of the requisite engineering workforce to fill the fabs being built, some of them may prove as useful as the infamous backyard steel factories of the Great Leap Forward.

We should not be overly gloomy about the industry's prospects. For if we look beyond the state's implicit and explicit goals, there are clear signs of industrial development. Barring a collapse in its IC consumption, China is very unlikely to fulfill 70 percent of its IC consumption needs by domestic consumption by 2025, but domestic production will increase as a share of both domestic and global consumption. Even if all the SOEs' planned fabs fail to materialize, which is unlikely, this increase in China's share should hold.

China's gain will not necessarily create severe oversupply because there are tentative signs of a "silicon super cycle" driven by rising demand in new and existing products. Artificial intelligence (AI) is likely to drive up demand for processors and memory chips alike. Smartphones are gobbling up more and more NAND and DRAM with

DRAM per smartphone likely to double by 2018. Similarly, cloud computing is likely to drive demand for flash memory. If this super cycle actually appears, then even China's inexperienced new entrants in NAND and DRAM may survive without the Chinese state having to bear a large financial burden for the patient capital it has offered. Without such a super cycle, global demand conditions may become more fraught and the longer-term costs of China's IC industrial policy will most likely outweigh the benefits even when taking into account the wider net social costs/benefits calculus.

While China's policy impact on the worldwide balance of industry supply and demand might be quite negative if China could meet its policy target of supplying 70 percent of its nominal domestic consumption in the absence of a semiconductor super cycle, this scenario is very unlikely. China would still need to almost double its already substantial operating capacity to meet the 70 percent goal even if one were unrealistically to assume an utter lack of growth in China's consumption of ICs.[40] Given the human capital constraints China is facing in the industry, this level of expansion simply is not likely to happen so quickly. Moreover, one needs to consider the industry context. Despite the IC industry's increasing maturation, even between 2000 and 2013, global fabrication capacity more than doubled without serious, long-lasting gluts (Houseman et al. 2014) so a super cycle may not be necessary to absorb the additional investment.

Furthermore, many of the MNCs that China would need to supply the human capital are very busy investing in new fabrication capacity at home. According to SEMI, the IC capital equipment association, Korea will have spent on IC capital equipment more than double the amount China is predicted to have spent during 2017–18 and China's spending

---

[40] China had US$63 billion in IC fabrication production in 2016. The 2015 figure for China's domestic consumption is US$175.5 billion. Even comparing the higher production figure of 2016 with the likely lower consumption figure of 2015, China would need to produce US$122.85 billion worth of ICs to meet 70% of domestic assumption, assuming – quite unrealistically – completely stagnant demand. And of course, this estimation assumes that the added fabrication capacity would be equally productive (measured in dollars not units) with China's current fabrication. There are two reasons to think the new capacity might actually be less productive: firstly, the greater weight of state-owned capacity in the newly added capacity and, secondly, the potential problem of facing more severe human resource constraints due to the now already large size of China's capacity.

will only surpass Taiwan's In 2018 (EE Times, June 7, 2017). These commitments will likely limit the amount of human capital Korean and Taiwanese MNCs can transfer to China to train staff and ramp up fabs in the near term. Korean and Taiwanese firms are investing in China, but not at the scale that would sustain such rapid human capital expansion. And the respective governments of Korea and Taiwan are unlikely to countenance the high level of investment in China necessary to sustain China's rapid human capital expansion in an industry vital to each country's economy.

Of course, most of the funds in China are contingent on the wider financial system remaining crisis-free. Indeed, most of these funds are simply bank loans lent on very generous terms by banks to regional/local government-owned investment vehicles[41] that pass on the financing to their IC industry partners. This local/regional financing comes with matching funds from the central government's fund.[42] For regional funds where the money has not already been spent, the promised funding could disappear instantly were the Chinese financial system to suffer a serious crisis or disappear more gradually if serious deleveraging ensues. Michael Pettis (2013) among others argues that one of these two outcomes is quite likely to happen long before 2025 or 2030. If such financial distress were to happen, the predictions above about China's tentative progress would no longer hold.

Finally, China also faces two major technology obstacles within the wider IC industry value chain, and the IC megaproject has shown little evidence of having addressed them in any substantial manner. First, EDA tools are the major repositories of the accumulation of technology over the past fifty years of the IC industry. When one runs simulations using these tools, why certain design parameters work and others do not is essentially based on this repository of knowledge. Thus, China is unlikely to build up competitors to the major existing EDA firms given their accumulated knowledge advantage. Similarly, the other deep source of technology is the capital equipment. In this area, the key to

---

[41] In WeChat correspondence on August 21, 2017 with an IC industry executive familiar with these deals, this executive confirmed that these deals were structured in this way i.e. banks lend on generous terms to these local/regional state-owned investment vehicles, which pass on the generous financial terms to their corporate partners in the IC industry-related investment.

[42] See EE Times, January 26, 2017, on the matching funds approach of the central government.

the precision of this equipment is material research, but China is quite weak in this area (Interview, June 15, 2017). With China's focus not on either of these critical technology inputs, China may very well emerge as one of or even the largest producer of ICs, but prospects for its ownership of these core technologies behind the IC industry appear to be a long way off.

What does the limited success of China's industrial policy in chips tell us about China's industrial policymaking more broadly? The experience in ICs suggests quite strong limitations on policy learning within China's government. The Chinese state continues to prefer SOEs as the main vehicles for pursuing IC industry development despite decades of failure via these agents. The SOEs have proven time and again to possess very limited absorptive capacity and limited entrepreneurial capability to discover and develop market opportunities. The continued use of state procurement irrespective of firm performance has exacerbated these deficiencies in the SOEs.

One of the few breaks with past policy was accepting new participants, but these new participants were generally still SOEs, such as Tsinghua Unigroup and state investment vehicles that purchased overseas assets. The most disturbing aspect of bringing in these new actors is that some of them are completely unqualified. The exemplar of this problem is Tsinghua Unigroup. Whether at the corporate level or the individual level, the firm does not have expertise in ICs. Tsinghua Unigroup did not have any IC business until it hopped on the bandwagon of the new IC policy. Similarly, Unigroup's leader, Zhao Weiguo, has no personal experience in this industry either.

One could argue that the scale and ambition of the new IC mega-project is a departure from past practice, but these bold moves and goals are also fraught with problems. The megaproject has garnered the financial resources necessary to increase China's IC fabrication capacity, but it has not addressed the concomitant need to increase China's human capital resources in line with the planned expansions. It is not surprising that some have compared the megaproject to the Great Leap Forward given its blind rush for quantity over any practical considerations of quality and know-how. The Chinese state appears to have overestimated China's ability to provide adequate industry-specific human capital for the task. While it is true that China has invested heavily in the educational infrastructure for electrical engineering, there is still a lack of industrial experience among the engineering staff needed to fill the planned fabs and a dearth of experienced IC industry management teams to run them.

Equally dismaying to the Chinese state's stubborn lack of learning regarding its unwise reliance on SOEs is the Chinese state's continued discrimination against non-state firms. In spite of two decades of success of hybrid firms in the absence of much state support, the Chinese state has been reluctant to embrace these or other non-state firms as central actors in or targets of the industrial policy implementation process other than spending money to convert them into politically more palatable SOEs.

The fact that hybrids and MNCs still find themselves at the center of this industry in China is in part due to what might be termed a policy accident. China has encouraged foreign direct investment (FDI) over time and one unplanned consequence of this policy was that it allowed foreign venture capital to invest in China-based hybrids. The other consequence was not unplanned, but arguably unwelcome in terms of the goals of the IC industry's industrial policy. The emphasis on hard economic targets for local cadre promotion that include industrial investment has had the effect of spurring local governments to be very open to FDI, even in instances where the policy signals from the central government indicate otherwise. The IC industry appears to be just such a case where the stated goals are to promote purely domestic firms, but the local and regional governments are more than willing to promote investment by MNCs in this industry instead due to the incentives they face. Interlocutors cited in this chapter indicate that this alternative of seeking foreign investment is considered a second-best solution and perhaps even an outright policy failure within the context of the IC megaproject. Paradoxically, the hard economic target incentives beyond the industrial policy for ICs provide the motivation for local officials to support the very "foreign" firms that actually propel IC industry development. Accidentally, the incentives beyond the megaproject and the funds within the megaproject have combined to promote those firms most capable of IC industrial development despite the political suspicion in which they are held.

Since the announcement of the IC megaproject in 2014, further major initiatives have appeared, including Made in China 2025 and the Next Generation Artificial Intelligence Development Plan. As often occurs in China, one policy or program can get rolled up into a subsequent initiative. In this case, Made in China 2025 essentially subsumed the IC megaproject as the IC sector component of this multi-sector policy. Similarly, the AI Development Plan encourages AI-related chips. However, these policy changes have not changed the basic nature of the IC megaproject, particularly the continued favoritism shown to SOEs. The 2025 plan is still supporting large SOE investments in IC fabrication. Similarly, for AI chips, a spin-off from the Chinese Academy of Sciences, Cambricon, has received support and substantial venture investment from state entities even though other non-state firms, such as Horizon Robotics, have already assembled deeper technical teams (Interview, May 31, 2018).

References

DYBG (调研报告). 2002. Reports 11 and 12. Beijing: Ministry of Science and Technology.

Fuller, Douglas B. 2016. *Paper Tigers, Hidden Dragons: Firms and the Political Economy of China's Technological Development*. Oxford: Oxford University Press.

Fuller, Douglas B., Akintunde I. Akinwande, and Charles G. Sodini. 2013. "Global Reorganization of the IT Industry and the Rise of Greater China." In Douglas B. Fuller and Murray A. Rubinstein eds., *Technology Transfer between the U.S., China and Taiwan: Moving Knowledge*. New York: Routledge.

Fuller, Douglas B., Akintunde I. Akinwande, and Charles G. Sodini. 2003. "Leading, Following or Cooked Goose: Explaining Innovation Successes and Failures in Taiwan's Electronics Industry." *Industry and Innovation*. 10(2). pp. 179–96.

Houseman, Susan N., Timothy J. Bartik, and Timothy J. Sturgeon. 2014. "Measuring Manufacturing." *Upjohn Institute Working Paper*. pp. 14–209.

Hurtarte, Jorge S., Evert A. Wolsheimer, and Lisa M. Tafoya. 2007. *Understanding Fabless IC Technology*. Oxford: Newnes.

Leslie, Stuart. 2000. "The Biggest 'Angel' of Them All: The Military and the Making of Silicon Valley." In Martin Kenney ed., *Understanding Silicon Valley: The Anatomy of an Entrepreneurial Region*. Stanford, CA: Stanford University Press.

McKinsey. 2014. "Semiconductors in China Brave New World or Same Old Story?" August, 2014.

MERICS. 2016. *Made in China 2025 Report: The Making of a High-Tech Superpower and Consequences for Industrial Countries*. Berlin: MERICS.

Pettis, Michael. 2013. *Avoiding the Fall: China's Economic Restructuring*. Washington, DC: Carnegie Endowment for International Peace.

PwC. 2017. China's Impact on the Semiconductor Industry 2016 Update. San Francisco: PwC.

2012. *Another Strong Year of Growth: China's Impact on the Semiconductor Industry 2012 Update*. San Francisco: PwC.

NEWSPAPER ABBREVIATIONS

JJGC	经济观察 *Economic Observer*
EE Times	*Electrical Engineering Times*
ESJJBD	二十一世纪经济报道 *The 21st Century Economic Herald*
FT	*Financial Times*
NYT	*New York Times*
SCMP	*South China Morning Post*
WSJ	*Wall Street Journal*

8

Growth, Upgrading, and Excess Cost in China's Electric Power Sector

Thomas G. Rawski

INTRODUCTION

Electricity is the ubiquitous facilitator of modern economic activity.* While typically taken for granted, the consequences of power outages quickly demonstrate that electricity truly is the indispensable resource.

This chapter reviews the recent trajectory of China's power sector, which has delivered an impressive combination of growth, technological upgrading, network expansion, and improved reliability during the past several decades. These advances come at high cost. Chinese and US electricity prices are similar; Chinese power providers enjoy multiple cost advantages over US electric utilities, but achieve consistently weaker financial results. This combination of prices and financial outcomes implies that the average cost of producing and delivering each unit of electricity is higher in China than in the United States.

This surprising discovery signals the presence of substantial inefficiency. Our review of the years 2005–16 identifies 30 percent as a lower bound for excess costs within China's electricity system. I conclude with a survey of recent reform initiatives, which fix prices for transmission and delivery of

* Many people have assisted my efforts to understand this complex industry. Particular thanks go to Midhu Balasubramanian, Loren Brandt, Michael Davidson, Marco diCapua, FENG Fei, Lee Hwa Gebert, GU Xiaoyun, Dan Guttman, Yi Han, John Hanson, Carsten Holz, Zixuan Huang, Fritz Kahrl, Nicholas Lardy, Lotus Liu, LIU Pei, LIU Qilin, Ravi Madhavan, Tom Nguyen, Gregory Reed, Ryan Rutkowski, Yang Song, Richard P. Suttmeier, TIAN Qingfeng, Tianni Wang, Ivy Wong, Tim Wright, Harry X. Wu, Irene Wu, Haihui Zhang, ZHANG Peili, ZHANG Wenkui, ZHENG Xinye, Xiuying Zou, and dozens of patient Chinese informants. Seminar participants at Renmin University, at the Shanghai campus of New York University, at the Hitotsubashi University Institute of Economic Research, and at a Rissho University event sponsored by the Japanese Association for Chinese Economy and Management Studies provided stimulating comments. Responsibility for errors rests with the author.

electricity, expand the scope for direct contracting between generating companies and end-users and introduce competition into retail electricity sales.

These changes have begun to exert downward pressure on electricity prices. Falling prices force producers to explore the potential for cost reductions. Prospects of lower costs cluster in the generation and delivery of coal-fired thermal electricity, the technology that has long dominated China's electricity industry. The likely outcome is an unexpected and, given China's environmental ambitions, unwelcome increase in the volume and possibly the share of coal-based electricity production.

I begin with a brief summary of features that distinguish electricity from other widely utilized products.

Electric power is a network industry with considerable scale economies and huge fixed costs. The network element means that costs shrink and benefits multiply as the number of interconnected users expands. In China, as elsewhere, the electricity sector originated with isolated power plants, each connected to multiple customers. By the 1930s, the need to ensure timely and sufficient power supplies encouraged Japanese-controlled generating firms in China's northeast (but apparently not in Shanghai) to establish rudimentary arrangements that unified the characteristics of power from multiple generating facilities and enabled big industrial users to absorb electricity from multiple sources (Manshū kaihatsu 1964, 2, pp. 536–9).

Networking is synonymous with scale economies, meaning that unit costs decline as the number of participants and the volume of power flow expands. The production process contributes to further scale economies as the size of standard generation plants rises. The share of thermal generation capacity rated at 300 MW and up rose from 17 percent in 1990 to 39 percent and then to 79 percent in 2000 and 2015 (Energy Report 1997, p. 58; Table 8.2).

Technical factors complicate electricity markets. On the supply side, high fixed costs mean that power companies incur substantial expenses regardless of sales volume. Large differences in operational flexibility as well as the varying split between fixed and variable cost across multiple power generating technologies – coal, hydro, natural gas, nuclear, wind, solar – complicate efforts to achieve high levels of operational efficiency.

The unusual combination of long lead times for expansion of generation and distribution facilities with the need for instantaneous supply response – customers expect power to flow at the flip of a switch – and wide variations in power demand according to time of day, season and economic conditions, creates a potential for mismatch between shifting user requirements and available production capabilities.

Avoiding such mismatches, which can cause temporary blackouts or more serious system disruptions, requires continuous oversight to ensure smooth matching of supply and demand throughout the power grid. "Dispatch" – assigning delivery quotas to individual power plants – is a key element of system operation.

These complexities lead to universal problems of governance and management. Historically, policymakers viewed electricity as a "natural monopoly." Customers typically had no choice of supplier, but were protected from overcharging either by public ownership or by regulatory bodies that controlled pricing and limited utility companies' charges to levels consistent with "reasonable" profits.

Beginning in the 1980s, reformers, arguing that monopoly and regulation concealed vast excess costs, initiated an agenda of "unbundling" – forcing vertically integrated utilities to divest some segments of their businesses in order to expand commercial rivalry and consumer choice. The reform agenda aimed to inject elements of market pricing in place of governmental price-setting. Implementation began in the United Kingdom and gradually spread across the globe.

Several decades later, results remain limited. Unusual features of the electricity industry, especially the combination of extreme reliability requirements, lack of viable large-scale storage for surplus power and absence of effective rationing mechanisms to resolve episodes of excess demand, make it difficult to implement economists' standard recommendation of "marginal cost pricing" that equates retail price with the cost of producing the final unit purchased. As in other capital-intensive sectors, there is an unavoidable tension between marginal cost pricing and the need to provide incentives for new investment.

Efforts to use auctions to steer production quotas toward low-cost suppliers have stumbled into frightening episodes of instability in which temporary power shortages trigger price spikes that threaten to bankrupt suppliers or to inflate retail power prices. There is some evidence that clever participants can reap windfall profits from actions that magnify or even initiate such episodes.

As a result, there is no consensus on how best to organize, administer, and govern the production and distribution of electricity. The current US structure combining elements of regulated (via officially imposed price controls) and deregulated (without price controls) electricity markets reflects this state of affairs. China's circumstances display similar ambiguity: despite the substantial impact of past and recent reform initiatives, the architecture of a fully reformed electricity sector remains unclear, as does the nature of concrete steps that could advantageously restructure this large and important industry.

CHINA'S ELECTRICITY INDUSTRY

Basic Elements of Industry Structure

Following several decades of rapid growth, China's electricity sector is now the world's largest. Notwithstanding rapid expansion of renewable technologies, especially wind farms (Mathews and Tan 2014), coal continues to dominate, with coal-fired thermal facilities accounting for 64.5 percent of 2017 production and 55.1 percent of generating capacity at year-end 2017 (Electricity Report 2017).

Industry is the largest electricity user, absorbing 69.2 percent of 2017 consumption (Electricity Summary 2017). Households occupy a relatively small share of power consumption (13.8 percent in China versus 37.4 percent in the United States during 2017), but seem likely to absorb a rising share of China's future electricity supply.[1]

Geographic imbalance is a central feature of China's energy economy. China's energy resources are concentrated in a wide arc stretching from Heilongjiang (oil) in the northeast through Inner Mongolia (coal, wind) and Shanxi (coal) in the north, Shaanxi (coal), Gansu (wind) and Xinjiang (coal, wind, sun) in the northwest and Sichuan, Chongqing, Guizhou and Yunnan (hydropower) in the southwest. Demand clusters in a diametrically opposed arc running southward along the coast from the Beijing metropolitan area through Shandong, Jiangsu, Shanghai, Zhejiang, and Guangdong.

In the absence of international trade in electricity or large-scale local power production from nuclear plants or offshore wind farms, feeding the electricity needs of this coastal belt requires some combination of large-scale domestic coal haulage and cross-regional power transmission. Recent economic expansion in central provinces like Hubei, Hunan, and Jiangxi has created new gaps between energy demand and local supply that intensify the pressure to build nuclear plants or expand long-distance shipments of coal or power (Jiang 2014; Zhu 2016).

The institutional evolution of China's power sector is well understood (Xu 2002, 2004). In the pre-reform planned economy, electricity was a state-run monopoly under the Ministry of Electric Power. Once reform

---

[1] Chinese data from Electricity Data 2017; US data from US EIA 2018, Table 5.1.

policies implemented from the late 1970s began to accelerate overall economic growth, and hence the growth of demand for electricity, severe shortages of electricity created a powerful incentive for reform.[2]

Early reform initiatives focused on decentralization: provincial and local governments were permitted to organize, manage, and finance (sometimes with foreign investments) new power plants, actions formerly reserved for the center. This accelerated the growth of production capacity, especially in regions that had suffered the biggest supply gaps. There were significant unintended results: a proliferation of small, high-cost producers as well as the emergence of substantial de facto provincial and local control over power supplies, developments that increased the potential for local authorities to oppose, obstruct or simply ignore unwelcome instructions from Beijing.

Next came a 1998 initiative aimed at commercializing the power sector by transforming the Ministry of Electric Power into the State Power Corporation. Subsequent reforms, implemented in 2002, involved "unbundling" the formerly integrated electricity sector to roll back vertical integration, expand competition, and establish a clear demarcation between commercial enterprises and the state.

The new structure eliminated the State Power Corporation, transferring its regulatory authority to a new body, the State Electricity Regulatory Commission (SERC), and assigning its generation and grid equipment to newly created companies. The reform poured massive resources into five generating companies and two immense grid management firms. These generating firms produce nearly half of China's electricity. They own and operate power plants on a nationwide scale, ensuring some degree of commercial rivalry. Two giant grid firms manage the transmission and delivery of electricity. China Southern Grid, spans five provinces in the south and southwest. The far larger State Grid Corporation, the world's largest utility enterprise, manages power networks elsewhere. The two do not compete directly, but their presence creates the potential for performance comparisons.[3]

Further reform plans produced extensive discussion, but, until recently, little action. Reform stalled through a combination of institutional resistance to unbundling, transparency, and marketization, priority for

---

[2] The author recalls touring factories by flashlight during the summer of 1982; one manufacturer of cashmere garments reported large losses from the destruction of yarn stranded in dyeing vats during repeated episodes of unexpected power outages.

[3] Smaller grid companies manage power networks in western Inner Mongolia and parts of Shaanxi.

eliminating chronic power shortages, and difficulties revealed in experimental reform pilots.

The resulting system combines elements of plan and market. Substantial competition (as well as lobbying) surrounds the construction and equipping of new generation facilities, typically involving rivalry among giant state-controlled generation, construction, and machine-building enterprises. Generating companies face single buyers – all power goes to the local grid company, which acts as a monopoly seller of electricity in its service territory, a circumstance that recent reforms, discussed below, have begun to change.

Three prices dominate the finances of these firms: the wholesale or "on-grid" tariff that generating firms receive from the grid, the retail price that the grid charges to end-users, and the price of coal, the main component of variable cost for China's predominantly coal-fired power producers. Table 8.1 lays out the trajectory of these prices since 2003.

Two of these prices, the on-grid and retail tariffs, are controlled by the National Development and Reform Commission (NDRC), which sets basic tariffs. These vary according to power source (low on-grid tariffs for hydropower and for western thermal plants, higher feed-in tariffs for thermal plants in coastal regions and for nuclear, wind, and solar power) and user (low retail prices for households and for agriculture, higher prices for industry and commerce). A blizzard of taxes, fees, and subsidies, many imposed by provincial and local governments, surrounds these reference prices, resulting in a labyrinth of charges – more than 300 in Beijing alone (Zhang Xudong 2013).

Table 8.1 includes two coal price indexes: a domestic series that tracks mine-mouth prices and a more volatile indicator reflecting Asian regional coal prices. Gradual domestic marketization and growing Chinese participation in global coal markets makes the latter index increasingly relevant to the finances of Chinese power producers; the domestic index clearly understates the volatility of coal costs during the past decade.

This combination of official price regulation, with its slow and politically charged adjustments, and an increasingly volatile coal market has created a financial roller coaster. Coal price spikes in 2008, 2011, and 2016/17 pushed up generation costs, whereupon inflexible on-grid tariffs splashed red ink over large segments of the generating sector. Falling coal prices have the opposite effect. A mechanism linking coal costs and power prices, adopted in 2004, has worked poorly, as NDRC officials have blocked prompt implementation of supposedly automatic price changes for electricity in the wake of coal price fluctuations (Huang and Yu 2014; Bie 2014).

Table 8.1 China and US Electricity Price Comparison: Economy-Wide and for Industrial Users, 2003–2016

	2003	2004	2005	2006	2007	2008	2009	2010	2011	2012	2013	2014	2015	2015
Unit Prices and Costs (RMB per MWh)														
Retail Price														
Economy-wide	434.7	455.1	485.0	499.0	508.5	532.1	530.7	571.2	583.2	625.2	635.5	647.1	643.3	614.8
Large-scale Industry	426.0	457.0	485.0	516.0	523.0	536.0	555.3	617.7	718.6	770.4	652.5	655.9	644.0	645.7
General Industry & Commerce											843.9	856.5	825.1	817.4
Average On-grid Price	308.5	312.5	318.8	330.5	336.3	360.3	382	384.6	396.5	441.20	442.8	438.9	388.3	371
T&D Cost*	126.2	142.6	166.2	168.5	172.2	171.8	148.7	186.7	186.7	184.0	192.7	208.1	216.5	215.2
Percent of Retail Price	29.0	31.3	34.3	33.8	33.9	32.3	28.0	32.7	32.0	29.4	30.3	32.2	32.2	32.2
Exchange Rate (RMB/$)														
Market	8.277	8.277	8.192	7.972	7.604	6.945	6.831	6.77	6.459	6.313	6.193	6.158	6.228	6.642
PPP	2.695	2.804	2.822	2.844	2.988	3.159	3.132	3.309	3.506	3.524	3.545	3.517	3.466	3.524
China Retail Price ($ per MWh)														
Economy-wide**	52.52	54.98	59.20	62.60	66.87	76.62	77.69	84.38	90.29	99.04	102.61	105.07	105.07	92.57
Large-scale Industry**	51.47	55.21	59.21	64.73	68.78	77.18	81.29	91.25	111.26	122.05	105.35	106.50	106.50	97.21
PPP Economy-wide	161.29	162.30	171.86	175.47	170.18	168.44	169.45	172.63	166.33	177.41	179.26	183.98	185.61	174.47
PPP Large-scale industry	158.07	162.98	171.86	181.43	175.03	169.67	177.31	186.68	204.97	218.62	184.05	186.48	185.80	183.22
US Retail Price ($ per MWh)														
Economy-wide	74.4	76.1	81.4	89.0	91.3	97.4	98.2	98.3	99.0	98.4	100.7	104.4	104.1	102.7
Industrial Users	51.1	52.5	57.3	61.6	63.9	69.6	68.3	67.7	68.2	66.7	68.9	71.0	69.1	67.6

(continued)

Table 8.1 (*continued*)

	2003	2004	2005	2006	2007	2008	2009	2010	2011	2012	2013	2014	2015	2016
China Average Price, US Same Year Price = 100														
Economy-wide	70.6	72.3	72.7	70.3	73.2	78.7	79.1	85.8	91.2	100.7	101.9	100.6	100.9	90.1
Industrial Users*	100.7	105.2	103.3	105.1	107.6	110.9	119.0	133.8	166.8	183.0	152.9	150.0	154.1	143.8
PPP Economy-wide	*216.8*	*213.3*	*211.1*	*197.2*	*186.4*	*172.9*	*172.6*	*175.6*	*168.0*	*180.3*	*178.0*	*176.2*	*178.3*	*159.9*
PPP Industrial Users***	*309.3*	*310.4*	*299.9*	*294.5*	*273.9*	*243.8*	*259.6*	*275.7*	*300.5*	*327.8*	*267.1*	*262.7*	*268.9*	*271.0*
Coal Price Indexes (2005 = 100)														
China Mine-mouth	82.5	85.6	100.0	105.0	109.0	116.5	110.2	118.8	125.9	123.7	121.4	108.0	92.2	90.6
Asian Market	58.1	115.1	100.0	89.8	134.4	235.3	125.3	167.6	199.9	167.7	144.5	123.8	101.0	111.1

Note:

* T&D cost refers to unit cost for transmission and delivery of electricity.

** Conversion to US$ uses market exchange rates.

*** Ratio of Chinese price for large industrial users to US average for industrial users.

Sources:

US data from US EIA 2012 and 2014, Table 2.7; and 2015a, Table 2.4. Chinese price data for 2003–11 from Tang 2014, for 2013–14 from State Energy Administration 2013–14.

2012: Chinese retail price and T&D cost from Chen 2015. Average on-grid price calculated as a residual.

2011/2012: price change for large-scale industry is assumed to be the same in percentage terms as the change in overall average retail prices.

2015: Chinese prices and T&D cost from Price Competition 2 2016; Price Competition 4 2016; Price Competition 5 2016; and State Energy Administration 2015.

2016: Chinese prices and T&D cost from State Energy Administration 2016a.

exchange rates: Abstract 2014, p. 143; 2016, p. 167; National Bureau of Statistics website.

coal prices: for Asian markets, from BP 2017, Table headed "Coal: Prices." See www.quandl.com/data/BP/COAL_PRICES-Coal-Prices (accessed June 19, 2017). for China, see Yearbook 2007, p. 333 (for 2003–6); Price Yearbook 2011, p. 548 (for 2007–10); Price Yearbook 2014, p. 573 (for 2010–13); information for 2014–16 from www.stats.gov.cn (accessed April 7, 2018).

source for China PPP conversions: https://data.oecd.org/conversion/purchasing-power-parities-ppp.htm (accessed April 7, 2018).

Prior to recent reforms, grid company revenues came from the spread between the on-grid tariffs paid to generation companies and the retail prices collected from end-users (Table 8.1). Until recently, the grid companies' refusal to provide detailed cost information – State Grid famously classified up to 31 percent of its costs under the opaque heading "other" (其 他 *qita*) – prevented regulators from calibrating grid charges to actual costs (Power Prices 2014; Yu 2014).

Financial volatility originating in the coal market has not spared the grid companies. In 2009, for example, NDRC raised on-grid tariffs to give generation companies some relief from higher coal prices, while imposing a slight reduction in average retail prices (Table 8.1). This resulted in an unexpected drop in the grid companies' price-cost differential that eliminated profits until subsequent adjustments restored grid company margins.

Table 8.1 uses standard currency exchange rates to convert average Chinese retail prices, as well as the prices charged to "large industrial users" (大工业) into US dollars.[4] The comparison shows that the average price of electricity in China has risen in recent years to match comparable US figures. For large industrial users, average Chinese retail tariffs consistently exceed US industrial electricity prices, with Chinese costs outrunning corresponding US prices by 50 percent or more beginning in 2011. This observation contradicts claims, for example by Haley and Haley (2013), that Chinese manufacturers enjoy cheap electricity supplies

The run-up to the 13th Five Year Plan (FYP) (2016–20) brought a push to revive electricity reform, partly to curb the power of the State Grid Corporation, which had strenuously resisted official regulatory efforts,[5] and particularly to implement the Xi Jinping administration's mandate to elevate market forces to a "dominant role" in China's mixed economy.

The current reform wave, discussed later in this chapter, focuses on three issues: cost audits leading to imposition of fixed and transparent grid charges; expansion of direct power transactions between large end-users and generating companies; and replacing the former grid company retail

---

[4] Italicized figures in Table 8.1 show trends in the purchasing-power parity (PPP) exchange rate between the Chinese and US currencies, and use this rate to calculate absolute and relative (to US figures) Chinese electricity prices in PPP terms. Further discussion is postponed until later in this chapter.

[5] When the National Energy Administration (NEA), responding to complaints that large-scale spillage of wind power was hampering efforts to raise the share of renewables in China's electricity mix, "ordered grid companies 'to plug in all renewable power sources'," State Grid's leader promptly demurred, insisting that "'the approval process for wind power and for the grid are different'" (Shepherd and Hornby 2016).

monopoly with a competitive regime that allows the entry of new retail sales companies.

DEVELOPMENT AND INNOVATION
IN CHINA'S POWER SECTOR

Growth

The central task for any electrical system is to supply customers with power on demand. With overall economic growth approaching, and annual increments to power consumption often exceeding 10 percent, fulfilling this basic function posed a huge challenge. Figure 8.1 illustrates the protracted, and finally, successful response that enabled power supply to catch up with demand.

This supply surge established China as the world's largest producer and consumer of electricity, with 2017 power consumption reaching 171 percent of the comparable US figure. In 1990, China's power use was a mere 22 percent of the US total. Figure 8.1 also demonstrates the magnitude of subsequent Chinese investment: beginning in 2005, annual increments to generating capacity consistently exceeded 57 GW, the peak annual increment to US capacity achieved in 2002. In 2010, and again in 2014–16, new Chinese generating capacity more than doubled the historic US peak.[6]

As the addition of new power plants and grid connections began to shrink the gap between power demand and available supply, China's grid operators implemented pre-announced rotating power blackouts; this reduced the costs associated with power shortages.[7] The initial decade of the current century brought a general balance between demand and

---

[6] Chinese output and capacity data for 2015–16 are from www.cec.org.cn/guihuayutongji/tongjxinxi/niandushuju/2017–01–20/164007.html (accessed March 22, 2017); data for 2014 are from China Electricity Council 2016. For earlier years, data on Chinese generation capacity are from www.cec.org.cn/guihuayutongji/tongjxinxi/niandushuju/2015–11–30/146012.html (accessed December 19, 2015); annual data on Chinese power consumption are from Fifty Years (2000, p. 279), Energy Statistics (1997–9, p. 143; 2006, pp. 110–11; 2011, pp. 124–5; 2015, pp. 122–3), and from Yearbook 2016, Table 9–6. US electricity output from various issues of US EIA Monthly, Table 7.1; US electric power industry generating capacity from US EIA 2015b. These comparisons ignore slight differences among different Chinese data sources and in the measures used to tabulate US and Chinese electricity output.

[7] During the 1990s, the fifteen-storey office building of the Chinese Academy of Social Sciences in downtown Beijing had a regular schedule of Friday power outages. In 2005, an invitation to visit a Beijing-area machine tool plant came with the proviso that power shortages limited operating hours to midnight–6am.

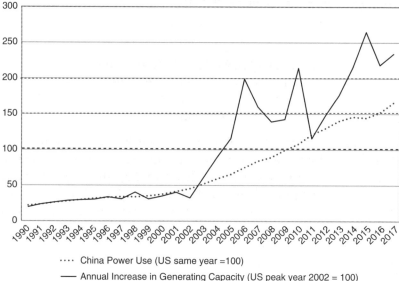

···· China Power Use (US same year =100)

—— Annual Increase in Generating Capacity (US peak year 2002 = 100)

Figure 8.1 China Power Expansion in US Perspective, 1990–2017

supply, despite the persistence of regional and seasonal shortages (State Grid 2012, pp. 32, 157).[8] Most recently, continued investment together with an unexpected fall-off in the growth of electricity demand have created a new problem: widespread excess capacity, which has sent utilization rates for generation facilities into a downward spiral: on average, thermal plants operated for only 4,165 hours during 2016, the lowest figure since 1964 (see Table 8.3 below).

Scale

Rather than replicating existing facilities, expansion of China's power industry has pursued the scale economies characteristic of electricity generation and distribution by increasing the average size of individual facilities.

Table 8.2 summarizes a massive shift toward large-scale thermal generation plants. Between 2000 and 2015, the number of generating stations with capacity of 600 MW and up rose from twenty-two to 609, and their

[8] Kahrl and Wang (2014) provide a detailed account of the "orderly electricity use" (有序用 电 *youxu yongdian*) system developed to cope with power shortages.

Table 8.2 *China Electricity – Rising Scale of Plant and Equipment, 2000–2015*

A. Thermal Power Generation Facilities (GW)

Category	Thermal Generation Facilities 2000			Thermal Generation Facilities 2015		
	Number of Units	Generating Capacity GW	Share (%)	Number of Units	Generating Capacity GW	Share (%)
Total	5235	282.9	100.0	7526	970.3	100.0
600 MW & up	22	13.2	4.7	609	416.4	42.9
300–599	291	96.8	34.2	1051	346.0	35.7
200–299	232	47.4	16.8	254	54.9	5.7
100–199	376	43.6	15.4	467	64.0	6.6
Under 100	4314	81.9	29.0	5145	89.0	9.2

B. Length of Power Transmission Lines 35 kv and Higher (1000 km)

	Transmission Lines 2000		Transmission Lines 2015	
	Length (1000 km)	Share of Total (%)	Length (1000 km)	Share of Total (%)
Total	726.2	100.0	1696.8	100.0
Under 220 kv	562.6	77.5	1087.7	64.1
220 kv and up	163.6	22.5	609.1	35.9
of which:				
1000 kv			3.1	0.2
±800 kv			10.6	0.6
750 kv			15.7	0.9
±600 kv			1.3	0.1
500 kv	26.8	3.7	169.8	10.0
330 kv	8.7	1.2	26.8	1.6
220 kv	128.1	17.6	380.1	22.4

Sources:
for 2000: China Electricity Yearbook 2001, pp. 668, 676
for 2015: China Electricity Report 2016, pp. 67, 69

share in overall capacity jumped from 5 to 43 percent. Table 8.2 also tracks a parallel, but less rapid extension of the length and voltage of power transmission lines – an essential component of China's energy economy due to the rail system's limited coal-carrying capacity as well as growing dissatisfaction with the environmental costs of coal-burning generation facilities in coastal cities.

This shift to larger facilities brings multiple benefits. Standard technical indicators increasingly resemble outcomes observed in advanced market economics. Table 8.3 documents a steady decline in coal consumption per KWh of electricity, which, thanks to large numbers of new plants, has fallen below the US average.[9] Similar conditions apply to the grid, which has achieved a steady decline in transmission losses, which now approach the US level of 5–6 percent.[10] The share of power consumed within generating facilities has also declined.

Reliability and Access

Although 2009 data show that "the number of outage hours would need to be reduced by more than half to reach current US average" levels (Kahrl et al. 2011, p. 4036), recent information demonstrates impressive levels of reliability. Average annual power outages for urban customers dropped from over sixty-six hours in 1991 to under two minutes beginning in 2012 (Wang Zhixuan 2017). Table 8.4 shows that Chinese respondents report fewer outages, and quicker response to requests for new connections than informants in Brazil, India, or the Russian Federation. The proportion of Chinese firms owning or sharing backup generators matches outcomes in Brazil and Russia and is far smaller than in India. Firms in Brazil, India, and Russia are more than ten times as likely to identify electricity as a "major constraint" than their Chinese counterparts.

Reliability is highest in major cities. A visitor to western Sichuan province reported daily power outages in May 2016 (personal communication).

China has reached a remarkable milestone by extending electricity to its entire rural populace. The electrification of isolated communities in Qinghai province completed this task in 2015 (Jia 2015a; China Electricity Yearbook 2015, p. 68). China has attained universal access at a far lower income level than in other large nations; in the US, the share of farm dwellings with electricity surpassed 50 percent only in 1946 and reached 95 percent only in 1956 (Historical Statistics 1975, series S, pp. 108–19).

Falling Construction Costs

Despite the considerable challenge of developing equipment and materials capable of withstanding the elevated temperatures and pressures associated

---

[9] "In 2007 China's average heat rate for coal-fired power plants was . . . roughly 5% higher than the US equivalent" indicating lower unit coal consumption (Williams and Kahrl 2008, p. 4). Average coal consumption in Chinese thermal generating plants declined thereafter (Table 8.3).

[10] See www.eia.gov/tools/faqs/faq.cfm?id=105&t=3 (accessed August 20, 2018).

Table 8.3 Technical Indicators for China's Electricity Sector, National Averages, 1965–2017

| Year | Generating Plants | | Transmission and Distribution Loss % | Standard Coal Consumption Grams per KWh | | Aggregate Power Use Share Shipped Across | |
| | Annual Operating Hours | | | | | (percent) | |
	All Plants	Thermal Plants	Internal Power Use All Plants %		Generated	Delivered	Provinces	Districts
1965	4920	n.a.	6.98	7.31	477	518	n.a.	n.a.
1975	5197	n.a.	6.23	10.21	450	489	n.a.	n.a.
1985	5308	n.a.	6.42	8.18	398	431	n.a.	n.a.
1995	5216	n.a.	6.78	8.77	379	412	n.a.	n.a.
2005	5425	5865	5.87	7.21	343	370	13.5	3.2
2006	5198	5612	5.93	7.04	342	367	9.1	2.9
2007	5020	5344	5.83	6.97	332	356	11.7	2.9
2008	4648	4885	5.90	6.79	322	345	12.9	3.0
2009	4546	4865	5.76	6.72	320	340	14.2	3.3
2010	4650	5031	5.43	6.53	312	333	14.0	3.6
2011	4730	5294	5.39	6.52	308	329	13.3	3.6
2012	4579	4965	5.10	6.74	305	325	14.4	4.1
2013	4521	5012	5.05	6.69	302	321	15.4	4.9
2014	4348	4739	4.83	6.64	300	319	16.4	6.0
2015	3988	4329	5.90	6.64	297	315	16.8	5.9
2016	3797	4186	5.57	6.49	294	312	16.9	6.4
2017	3790	4219	4.80	6.48	n.a.	309	17.9	6.7

Sources:

Except as noted, data for 1965–2016 are from Electricity Summary 2016; for 2017 from Electricity Summary 2017.
Thermal plant operating hours: for 2005–12 from Zhang Weirong 2014, p. 48; for 2013–2015 from Han 2016; for 2016–17 from Electricity Summary 2017.
Internal power use: for 2014 from Electricity Summary 2014; for 2015: from Price Competition 1 (2016); for 2016 from State Energy Administration 2016a.
Interregional shipments: data for 2016–17 from China Electricity Report 2017 (unpaginated online version); for 2014–15 from Electricity Databook 2015, pp. 48, 5☐.
Cross-district transfers: 2005–2013 from China Electricity Report 2014, p. 68.
Cross-province shipments: 2005 and 2007–9 from China Electricity Yearbook 2006, p. 39 and 2010, p. 34; for 2006 from Lin Boqiang 2008; for 2010–13 fro☐
Electricity Databook 2011, pp. 64–7; 2012 pp. 58–61; 2014, p. 54.

Table 8.4 *Power System Reliability and Access Compared: China, Brazil, India, Russian Federation, 2009–2014*

Category	China	Brazil	India	Russia
	2012	2009	2014	2012
Number of Outages in a Typical Month	0.1	1.6	13.8	0.3
Days to Obtain an Electrical Connection	6.9	27.7	21.9	120.4
Percent of Firms				
Owning or Sharing a Generator	8.0	7.9	46.5	8.9
Identifying Electricity Supply as a Major Constraint	1.8	46.0	21.3	23.1
Rural Electrification Rate, 2013 (percent)	100.0	97.0	74.0	100.0

Sources:
World Bank Enterprise Survey Data www.enterprisesurveys.org/data/exploreTopics/Infrastructure #all-countries–7 (accessed March 31, 2016).
Rural electrification: www.worldenergyoutlook.org/resources/energydevelopment/energyaccess database/ (accessed March 31, 2016).
Russia access: http://data.worldbank.org/indicator/EG.ELC.ACCS.ZS (accessed March 31, 2016).

with new generations of power generating equipment, the accumulation of experience in equipment manufacture and plant construction resulted in the downward trend in the unit cost of new thermal plants shown in Figure 8.2. North America and Western Europe experienced the opposite – rising costs of building new thermal plants (Samaras et al. 2011, p. 18).

The magnitude of Chinese cost reductions is surprising: between 1996 and 2004, investment cost (工程造价 *gongcheng zaojia*) per kilowatt of new thermal generating capacity declined by 38.4 percent while the economy-wide investment cost index[11] rose by 12 percent – a gap of 50 percentage points. Comparing 1996 with 2012 shows an even larger gap of 77.3 percentage points between (declining, then stable) power plant costs and the steadily rising investment cost index. Unit cost for thermal power plants declined slowly after 2012, while the overall investment cost index continued to creep upward (China Electricity Report 2014, pp. 55–6; 2015, pp. 49–50; Abstract 2016, p. 57).

The contrasting trends between unit cost of new thermal plants and the overall investment cost index indicates a remarkable combination of productivity gains and cost controls in building and equipping thermal power

---

[11] Investment cost index from http://data.stats.gov.cn/workspace/index?m=hgnd (accessed December 4, 2014); unit cost data from author's file "Thermal power construction costs.042316."

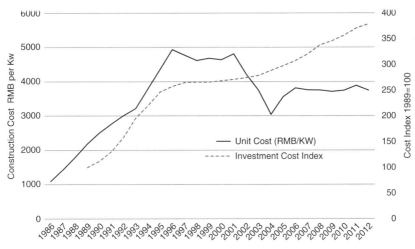

Figure 8.2 Thermal Power Plant Construction Cost per KW versus National Investment Cost Index, 1986–2012

plants. This episode recalls a 1940s phenomenon in which unexpectedly rapid productivity gains accompanied steep wartime increases in US production of cargo vessels known as "Liberty ships" (Thornton and Thompson 2001; Thompson 2001).

Technological Catch-up and Innovation

Successive international comparisons highlight the extent of technical progress in China's power sector. In 1990, the efficiency of coal-fired power generation in China, Korea, and India lagged far behind results for the United States and Western Europe. By 2011, China and Korea had closed this gap, nearly matching the US figure, while thermal efficiency in India's coal-fired plants showed little change from the 1990 level (Hussy et al. 2014, p. 66).

As the scale of China's power sector expansion created what quickly emerged as the world's biggest market for power plant equipment, major producers from Europe, North America, and Japan rushed to seize this new opportunity. As in other sectors, Chinese officials adroitly deployed market size as a bargaining tool, steering international firms into joint ventures and technology licensing agreements that enabled domestic firms, most notably China's big three power equipment makers – Dongfang Electric, Harbin Electric, and Shanghai Electric – to access advanced technology.

Although I cannot gauge the relative importance of various sources of knowledge and information, Chinese equipment-makers clearly benefited from expanded interaction with foreign partners. Chinese firms accelerated efforts to increase the scale of their equipment, while simultaneously introducing new generations of thermal technology – first "super-critical" and then "ultra-supercritical" – that employ elevated temperature and pressure in the boiler to reduce fuel requirements and boost thermal efficiency.

Chinese policymakers place heavy emphasis on import substitution, especially in sectors like electricity that officials view as central components of national economic growth. With domestic firms supplanting overseas equipment suppliers, rapid upgrading – not just for thermal generation, but, as is evident from several chapters in this book, in multiple segments of the power sector, reflects advances on the part of equipment producers as well as among generation and grid companies.

China's success in "breaking into the top ranks of global power-equipment exporters," together with growing overseas marketing of grid management services, and, most recently, of nuclear power expertise (see Chapter 10), underlines the rapidity and extent of China's catch-up. While "Chinese equipment makers face questions about quality control on their power turbines ... multinational companies that once cooperated with Chinese business groups now face them as competitors" (Areddy and Glader 2010). Similar comments apply to leading multinational suppliers of equipment for electric grids, hydroelectric facilities, wind turbines, solar assemblies, and nuclear plants.

Along with diminishing industry-wide technological and quality gaps, China's power sector has begun to approach the global technology frontier in specific areas, of which long-distance transmission of ultra-high voltage AC current provides a leading example. The chapter by Xu Yi-chong attributes China's advance in this area to an entrepreneurial campaign by leaders of State Grid Corporation, the world's largest utility company. While some commentators question the economics of long distance AC power transmission and other State Grid innovations, Chinese grid facilities now use domestically manufactured equipment to move larger volumes of electricity over longer distances and at higher voltage than in Europe or North America.

Evidence of innovative effort is readily visible in Chinese factories and trade journals. A cutting-edge coal-fired generation plant in Shanghai reports unit coal consumption of 276 grams per KWh; combined with low effluent levels, the result is "far superior to the original design ...

creating the world's best level" (Jiu 2014u). Chapter 10 shows that Chinese researchers are investigating novel approaches to nuclear power generation. Shanghai Electric is experimenting with elongated rotors that could increase the efficiency of steam turbines (Interview, May 28, 2014). Alloy U-shaped tubes from Baoyin Special Steel Co. used in nuclear plants' steam generators reportedly deliver superior resistance to pitting while matching other characteristics of imported alternatives (Baiyin 2014).

Growing Environmental Concerns

Despite reductions in unit coal consumption (Table 8.3), expansion of power output and continued dominance of thermal generation place electricity generation among the leading contributors to urban air pollution. Data for 2013 show thermal power plants accounting for over one-third of China's total emissions of sulphur dioxide, 17 percent of soot and dust, and over half of nitrous oxides (Li 2016). The combined impact of industrial emissions (with power plants contributing a considerable share) and exhaust from China's rapidly expanding fleet of motor vehicles has reversed two decades of gradual improvement (Rawski 2009) in urban air quality. Protracted episodes of haze and smog have aroused public indignation and turned urban air quality into a major political issue.

The official response has powerfully affected the electricity sector:

- Rapid expansion of renewables, especially wind power, has raised the combined share of hydro (18.6 percent), wind (4.8 percent), nuclear (3.9 percent), and solar (1.8 percent) in 2017 electricity output to 29.1 percent (Electricity Summary 2017). Although the size of China's power industry limits the pace of structural change – the share of thermal facilities in overall generating capacity declined from 73.4 to 62.2 percent between 2010 and 2017 (China Electricity Council 2016; Electricity Summary 2017), the "leading edge" of both capacity and output growth is "demonstrably getting greener" (Mathews and Tan 2014).
- Efforts to move dispatch toward prioritizing supply quota allocations for "clean" energy providers.
- Choice of technologies. Beijing has banned construction of new coal-fired generation plants in leading cities and, in some instances, required the conversion of coal-fired plants to natural gas. A nationwide campaign has sought to close small generating plants employing technologies now regarded as obsolete; modest results are visible in Table 8.2.

- Retrofitting. New policies require new coal-burning plants and incentivize older facilities to install modifications that increase combustion efficiency and/or remove harmful effluents from smokestack emissions, often with partial compensation in the form of supplements to on-grid tariffs.[12] Regulators have ramped up enforcement, imposing fines on violators (Jia 2014c).
- Subsidy elimination. Further policy initiatives have required provincial and local governments to eliminate power price discounts that had encouraged the expansion of energy-intensive industries like aluminum, steel, cement, and heavy chemicals.[13]
- Penalty pricing. NDRC has added surcharges to electricity prices charged to energy-intensive industries, particularly for firms employing older technologies. In some cases, provincial governments may increase these levies.
- Long-distance transmission. Planners appear to be considering proposals that would increase the transmission of electricity from coal-rich provinces like Shanxi and Xinjiang to power-hungry coastal regions. Alternatives include building conventional coal-fired generation facilities or converting solid coal into coal gas, which could serve as fuel for power generation. Such proposals relocate rather than reduce effluents. In addition, the associated water requirements would strain the capacity of water-scarce mining regions. Use of air-cooled generation technology economizes on water, but reduces thermal efficiency, which raises coal consumption and unwanted emissions (Jia 2014b).

Globalization

Following an initial period in which the electric power sector's global involvement focused on equipment imports and absorption of overseas technology, China's electricity sector has emerged as a growing force in global markets for electrical equipment, project management and the construction and operation of generation facilities and electrical grids.

---

[12] In December 2015, for example, NDRC joined with the Ministry of Environmental Protection and the National Energy Bureau to announce a program that awards price top-ups to coal-fired generation plants that meet "ultra-low" emission guidelines. See NDRC 2015 (reference courtesy of Fredrich Kahrl).

[13] Provincial and municipal power tariffs issued between 1980 and 2009 in Gansu and Lanzhou, for example, included concessional rates for electric furnace production of iron alloys and other enumerated industrial activities (Lanzhou 2011, pp. 265–82).

- Hydropower. Sinohydro Corporation is "the world's largest hydropower construction company with a 50% share of the international hydropower market" (www.internationalrivers.org/campaigns/sino hydro-corporation (accessed December 12, 2017).
- State Grid Corporation, the world's largest utility company, has substantial overseas investments in power generation and grid construction and management (Xu 2016).
- China's Big 3 equipment makers are major sellers of thermal power equipment, with a combined 2013 global market share slightly trailing Alstom, the third-ranking firm (behind General Electric and Siemens) (Dash 2014).
- Slowing domestic demand growth has encouraged generation and construction firms to seek international contracts (Li 2015; Chen 2016).
- China's nuclear industry has recorded major progress in raising its global profile, with recent agreements and contracts in Argentina, Romania, Pakistan, and the United Kingdom (Chapter 10).

Overseas activity is mostly, but not entirely in low- and middle-income countries: State Grid has invested in Australia, Portugal, Italy, and Greece, while China General Nuclear has joined a consortium to build the UK's Hinkley nuclear project and is pursuing approval of a proposed Chinese-designed reactor at Bradwell.

The motivation for overseas involvement combines standard trade drivers – Chinese firms offer an attractive price-quality combination – and special circumstances, including growing excess capacity and the obligation for big electricity firms, as centrally directed state-controlled enterprises (SOEs), to join the government's "Go Outward" and "One Belt One Road" campaigns.

This survey highlights China's electricity sector as the locus of dramatic achievement during the past several decades. Electricity producers and grid companies have increased supply, overcome massive power shortages, built a nationwide service network, improved reliability, absorbed new generations of technologies, and approached – in some cases, reached or even extended – global technology frontiers. These advances have transformed China's electrical industry from a weak laggard into a major force in global markets.

Despite these substantial and impressive accomplishments, discussions of China's electricity system bristle with negative evaluations. Thus "China's electricity sector continues to demonstrate a number of fundamental shortcomings in its basic institutions and functions" which lead to "intractable implementation problem[s]" (Williams and Kahrl 2008, p. 12).

SHORTCOMINGS AND DEFICIENCIES IN CHINA'S ELECTRIC POWER SECTOR

What are these "fundamental shortcomings"? How do they lead to "intractable problems"? It is immediately evident that some difficulties reflect circumstances that extend far beyond the electric power industry: thus knowledgeable observers comment that "Many of the obstacles to electricity reform in China lie outside the electricity sector" (Kahrl et al. 2011, p. 4033).

Overview

Although electricity markets in many countries display uncomfortable compromises between state control and market allocation, the imprint of the former plan system is particularly strong in China's power sector even after four decades of market-leaning reform. Documents and reports highlight details about physical quantities – of power production and consumption, coal use, equipment stocks, operating hours, and so on. Aside from information about investment spending, systematic compilations regarding prices, revenues, costs, and profits – the lifeblood of any market system – remain scarce. Rigid prices largely divorced from market pressures – another legacy of the plan era – may partly explain the tendency of official sources to omit information about values.

Preoccupation with investment reflects an emphasis on scale, a Stalinist legacy that permeates Chinese policymaking and is particularly prominent in the power sector. Even if expected financial returns are scant, investment projects that establish specific firms or industries as "key" or "backbone" elements in their regional or sectoral surroundings may achieve handsome payoffs in the form of favorable policy treatment. The emergence of massive excess capacity beginning in 2014 did not induce a major pullback in investment spending that one would anticipate in a market system. Instead, investment spending rolls on as firms "intensify investment to stake claims" (跑马圈地愈演愈烈投资 *paoma quandi yuyanyulie touzi*) to capture market share in anticipation of the official preferences routinely awarded to scale (Wang and Yu 2016; Jiao 2016).

Vertical integration and self-reliance represent further plan legacies that figure prominently in today's electricity system. While specialization intended to develop firms' "core capabilities" is a central principle of the worldwide unbundling campaign, Chinese desire to limit dependence on outsiders, to avoid unexpected price changes, and to create opportunities for resource extraction via opaque transactions among related parties motivates power companies to acquire coal mines, encourages grid firms and coal mines to invest in power generation, and inspires both generating and grid firms to acquire captive equipment producers.

Local and provincial governments, the subject of Chapter 3, pursue their own version of vertical integration through actions that reveal their preference for locally generated power and, especially under the shadow of possible electricity shortage, for avoiding commitments to transfer or purchase electricity to or from other jurisdictions.

These tendencies have major consequences. Table 8.3 (above) reveals the surprisingly modest scale of power transfers across provincial boundaries and especially between China's seven multi-province electric power districts.[14] Under the heading of "current problems facing the power industry's development," a 2001 report notes tartly that "the inter-provincial market is closed" (China Electricity Yearbook 2001, p. 16). Recent discussions emphasize the persistence of obstacles to interregional power sales. A 2015 analysis proposed "allowing cross regional transactions and creating a nationwide power market" (Fan 2015). Numerous references to "barriers" (壁垒 bilei) hampering power sales across jurisdictions indicate that this issue remains unresolved (Lu 2017; Wang Peng 2017).

Given the geographic gap between energy supply and demand, limited interregional power flow translates into larger shipments of coal and therefore greater concentration of air quality problems in coastal urban centers of electricity demand.

Similarly uncomfortable arrangements arise when central and local authorities joust for control. Provincial and local taxes, fees, and subsidies modify benchmark on-grid tariffs and retail prices, often with Beijing's assent, but sometimes in direct contradiction of central government preferences. Long lists of projects built without official authorization, invariably with the connivance of local leaders, testify to persistent incentive conflicts between different levels of China's complex administrative hierarchy (Cheng and Tsai 2009). In one particularly egregious episode,

---

[14] Specialists at the US Department of Energy report that there are no comprehensive data on interstate electricity shipments within the United States (personal communication).

Neimenggu concealed the construction of major power facilities, only to be caught out following a fatal accident. Local authorities allowed work to continue, "even after it was labeled illegal by central authorities" (Officials Penalized 2006; Oster 2006). The problem continues: commencing projects without approval appears among the offenses that can place electricity firms on a "blacklist" announced in 2018 (Blacklist 2018). Flouting of regulations may extend to the nuclear sector: 2016 draft regulations "clarify penalties for unauthorized construction or operation" of nuclear plants (NPP Siting 2016).

While the boundaries between plan and market and between central and local control remain unsettled, reform has injected intense focus on financial outcomes into every segment of the electric power system. Dispatch arrangements illustrate how the resulting combination of profit seeking with ill-defined regulatory jurisdictions, conflicting governmental incentives,[15] and dysfunctional prices[16] manufactures inefficiency.

Inefficient Dispatch

Modern power grids deliver electricity from multiple producers to thousands of users. Since the demand for electricity reflects trends in overall economic activity as well as seasonal and time-of-day variations, the continual ebb and flow of power requirements calls for careful management of deliveries to the grid. This "dispatch" function assigns annual, monthly, daily, hourly, and even minute-by-minute delivery quotas to individual power plants. Unless production falls short of demand, in which case dispatch involves nothing more than asking each plant to maximize output, effective grid operation requires the intervention of a system operator (in China, the grid company; elsewhere often an independent agency) that assigns hourly, daily etc. production quotas to specific generating facilities in order to match deliveries to shifting power demand.

In what order will the operator assign production quotas to various producers? The obvious answer: begin with the lowest-cost operator (where cost might include both environmental and financial metrics), then the next

---

[15] Shenzhen officials complain of being required to purchase expensive electricity from external suppliers while low-cost local generation facilities are limited to fractional operation (Shenzhen Grid Reform 2015). Electricity Databook (2014, pp. 468–81) confirms low operating hours for Shenzhen plants.

[16] In the Hami district of Xinjiang, where the benchmark on-grid price is RMB 0.25 per KWh, large-scale industrial users pay RMB 0.35–0.4 per KWh, the same amount charged for deliveries to Henan, 2000 km away, even though local deliveries entail no long-distance transmission costs (Zhang Shuwei 2015).

cheapest, etc. This procedure is unusual in China. Instead, continuing a practice inherited from the former planned economy, multiple operators – mostly coal-fired plants – are typically assigned similar operating hours, even though some may have lower costs and/or lower unit coal consumption (and hence fewer effluents) than others (Interview, May 17, 2012). Thus the world-leading Shanghai Waigaoqiao plant mentioned above reported a load factor of only 78 percent, evidently because regulators sacrificed some of its "clean coal" potential to allow dirtier plants their "fair share" of sales (Jia 2014a). Elsewhere, ad hoc arrangements favor specific plants: at one Shaanxi firm, foreign investors obtained a special quota enabling them to sell 40–50 percent more power to the grid than nearby rivals (Interview, June 11, 2013).

Organized trading of quotas, which would allow clean, low-cost producers to purchase quota from high-cost operators (thus reducing system costs while improving financial outcomes for all parties), although present, is not widespread. The result: unnecessarily high consumption of coal, excessive discharge of effluents, avoidable financial and maintenance costs (the latter resulting from capacity fluctuations in coal-fired plants that are designed to run near rated capacity). The current system also encourages overbuilding, because new plants expect to receive a "fair share" of future demand (Kahrl et al. 2011, p. 4034). Reform advocates propose a "truly market-oriented investment mechanism" that offers "no annual generation quota for any new coal-fired power projects" (Zhao et al. 2017, p. 9).

Chinese grid operators have begun to introduce "merit dispatch," which prioritizes generators with low variable cost, thus dispatching hydro, nuclear, wind, and solar energy ahead of power from coal-fired plants (Kahrl et al. 2013, p. 362). This approach holds the promise of limiting environmental costs, but can be problematic because the intermittent power flow from non-nuclear sources of clean energy necessitates reliance on a flexible production component to fill temporary or seasonal gaps in the availability of water, wind, or sun. Since limited resources and ill-advised policies have hindered the expansion of (relatively flexible) gas-fired power plants,[17] grid managers generally rely on coal-fired plants to fill

---

[17] Domestic production of natural gas remains small; imports of Russian gas will provide no more than a modest increase in the share of gas-fired generation. Large shale gas deposits will be difficult to develop. High domestic gas prices and low profitability limit prospects for import-fueled development. Lu Bin (2016a) emphasizes the potential of gas-fired power expansion. He (2015a, 2015b) blames "existing pricing mechanisms and policies" for the slow advance of natural gas, reports low utilization of existing facilities, and proposes a price link between gas and electricity of the sort that has functioned poorly in responding to fluctuating coal prices.

supply gaps, a policy that, as noted above, raises both financial and environmental costs.

Despite these difficulties, efforts to quantify the inefficiencies arising from current dispatch arrangements deliver surprisingly small results. As the "equal hours" system would predict, plant-level data reveal low correlation between unit coal consumption and annual operating hours: a simple regression depicting 2010 operating hours as a linear function of coal use per delivered KWh accounts for only 1.2 percent of observed variation in operating hours among 957 plants nationwide. Adding provincial fixed effects raises this figure to 8.7 percent; further inclusion of an interaction term linking coal use to interior location achieves a further increase, but only to 9.0 percent.[18] Similar analysis for Shandong province, among China's largest power users, finds differential coal use accounting for only 7.3 percent of the variation in operating hours among 149 coal-fired plants.

Underutilization of efficient plants prompts the following experiment with the 2010 data for Shanxi province: assign 6,000 operating hours (a high figure) to the most efficient coal-fired plant; then assign 6,000 hours to the next-best plant. Continue the process until the cumulative output of included plants matches the actual 2010 total. Then compare coal consumption under this hypothetical arrangement with the actual outcome. Although this procedure would result in the closure of 43 of 74 generating facilities, projected reduction in coal use is only 3 percent.

The reason: massive investment has boosted the share of large, modern thermal plants (Table 8.2). In Shanxi, the combined 2010 output share of the plants (hypothetically) assigned zero operating hours was only 10.7 percent. This outcome confirms an earlier finding using 2008–9 data for Guangxi province: "energy efficient dispatch delivers at most a modest (2–4%) coal savings" (Kahrl et al. 2013, p. 365).

The surprising finding that glaring episodes of misallocation – inefficient dispatch is one, large-scale "spillage" of wind and hydropower is another – impose only marginal increases in system-wide costs prompts a different approach focused on the analysis of costs for the entire power system.

Excess Cost – a Sector-wide Perspective

Electricity, a large, high priority sector that affects China's entire economy, offers a unique opportunity to gauge the scale of inefficiency. This industry

---

[18] Plant-level data are from Electricity Databook 2010. Following advice from Michael Davidson, I eliminated observations for which reported coal consumption per KWh of delivered electricity was below 280 or above 600 grams. Statistical analysis courtesy of Professor Yang Song.

produces a single, homogeneous product. Five enterprise groups generate nearly half of total output, and two grid firms virtually monopolize distribution and delivery. The presence of a reasonable statistical base, along with extreme concentration, enhances the prospect that analyzing power sector data can provide fresh insight into China's economic performance and prospects.

Hsieh and Klenow (2009) estimate the productivity gains achievable by limiting cross-industry efficiency variations to the level observed in US manufacturing. I follow their approach by using information about US prices and profitability to identify excess costs – the mirror image of inefficiency-related productivity shortfalls – in a single Chinese industry, the production and distribution of electricity. Since perfect efficiency is rare, reference to observable benchmarks – outcomes in the US electricity sector – avoids the exaggeration implicit in comparing actual outcomes with assumed perfection – a procedure that Demsetz (1969) ridicules as the "economics of nirvana."

Table 8.5 summarizes basic information about the Chinese and US power systems in 2011, when the two systems generated similar volumes of electricity (Figure 8.1). The two sectors are roughly comparable in terms of generating capacity and geographic expanse, but show widely divergent patterns of employment and labor productivity.

The procedure for ascertaining the rough dimensions of excess cost in China's power sector is simple and direct. A review of price and profitability shows that Chinese electricity prices are higher for industrial (but not for household or agricultural) users, and profits generally lower than in the US power sector. The combination of high prices and low profits carries an unexpected implication: the unit cost of generating, transmitting, and delivering electricity is higher in China than in the United States.

Excess costs measure the cost reductions needed to enable financial outcomes in China's electricity sector to match US results over 2005–16 under a sequence of successively more demanding circumstances: maintaining the current price regime, imposing a 40 percent reduction in prices charged to industrial users, or assuming an across-the-board reduction of 33 percent in electricity prices.

The calculations that follow are far from precise. China's utility majors mine coal and manufacture equipment; sectoral totals include outcomes from these and other non-power businesses. The US figures relate exclusively to investor-owned companies, and may also include results from non-power businesses. There is no adjustment for possible differences in Chinese and US data definitions or accounting standards. As a result, the margin of error surrounding our estimation of excess costs is large. This means that only large, decisive verdicts can be plausible.

Table 8.5 *China and US Electricity Comparison for 2011*

	Unit	U.S.	China Power Sector	
			Value	Index with US=1
Electricity Output	Bill. KWh	4,100	4,713	1.15
Power Generating Capacity	GW	1164.0	1062.5	0.91
Workers	1000s	395.7	2,589.0	6.54
Electricity Output				
per Man-year	MWh	10361	1820	0.18
per GW of Capacity	Bill. KWh	3.5	4.4	1.26
Installed Capacity per 1,000 Workers	GW	2.94	0.41	0.14
Annual Average Wage	US$	66,830	*8,763*	0.13
	RMB		56,600	
Annual Wage Bill	Bill. US$	26.4	*22.6*	0.86
	Bill. RMB		145.8	
Sales Revenue	Bill. US$	371.0	*455.5*	1.23
	Bill. RMB		2941.8	
Wages as Percent of Sales	percent	7.1	5.0	0.70

Note: Figures in italics converted at the average exchange rate for 2011: US$1=RMB 6.4588. See Abstract 2016, p. 167.
Sources: Output and installed capacity: see sources for Figure 8.1. Labor and wages: Labor Yearbook 2012, Table 3.02b; US Bureau of Labor Statistics 2011. Sales revenue: Chinese data (adjusted to avoid double counting) from Table 8.A.1; US data from US EIA (2012), Table 1.1.

Prices. Table 8.1 presents annual averages for Chinese electricity prices for all users and for "large industrial" purchasers (大工业 *dagongye*) covering 2003–16. Chinese prices are converted to US dollars at standard exchange rates for comparison with US electricity prices for all users and for industrial customers. I derive an index of Chinese prices, taking the relevant US price for each year as 100.

The economy-wide Chinese price average stood at roughly 70 percent of the comparable US figure during 2003–6, after which a combination of domestic price increases and increases in the international value of China's renminbi currency pushed Chinese prices to approximate parity with the US average beginning in 2012.

Economy-wide averages conceal major differences in the internal structure of Chinese and US electricity charges. In comparison with US rates, prices charged to Chinese households are far lower, and unit costs for Chinese businesses are much higher. Table 8.1 shows that, once converted to US dollar terms, electricity costs for Chinese large-scale industry consistently match or exceed comparable US prices, with the gap between (higher) Chinese and (lower) US rates rising from under 10 percent during 2003–7 to 50 percent or more for most years beginning in 2011. Unit costs facing manufacturers outside the scope of large-scale industry are even higher: rates for "ordinary industry and commerce" (一般工商业 *yiban gongshangye*) averaged 28.7 percent above the charges for large-scale industrial users during 2013–16 (Table 8.1).[19]

Currency exchange rates are not ideal for comparing prices and costs in economies with widely varying levels of per capita output and income. The central difficulty is the presence of activities like internal transportation and personal services that are rarely traded across national borders and therefore do not contribute to the determination of currency exchange rates. Purchasing power parity (PPP) exchange rates, calculated from price arrays that include non-traded as well as traded commodities and services, aim to overcome this weakness. Because non-traded commodities and services are often relatively inexpensive in low-income countries, multiple studies find that shifting from market to PPP exchange rates substantially raises the values of currencies of low-income countries relative to those of advanced economies.

China is no exception: Table 8.1 shows that PPP exchange rates for recent years value China's RMB currency at roughly RMB 3.5 per US dollar, far above the market price of approximately RMB 6.3 per dollar. This study uses market exchange rates to compare prices, profits and costs of electricity generation, transmission, and distribution in China and the United States. Shifting to PPP rates would sharply increase the US dollar price of Chinese electricity – as shown by the italicized rows marked PPP in Table 8.1 – which would strengthen the unexpected conclusion that the cost of generating, transmitting, and distributing each KWh of electricity is substantially higher in China than in the United States.

Profitability. Compared with US electric utilities, Chinese power firms benefit from low prices for labor, equipment, and materials as well as low construction costs for new facilities and less stringent environmental requirements.[20] Chinese power operations use newer equipment that, on average, consumes less coal and may require less maintenance than is needed at older US facilities.[21] At times, Chinese power plants have

---

[19] A comparison of "fully burdened" power costs for 2015, including all taxes and fees, found that "median electricity prices for industrial loads in the US tend to be 34–49% lower than Chinese prices" (Comerford et al. 2016, pp. 2–3).

[20] Renmin University Professor ZHENG Xinye 郑新业 emphasized the latter item in an October 2016 seminar.

[21] Chinese specialists express surprise at the age and limited capacity of equipment that they encounter in US power facilities. One informant commented that computers installed at a California dispatch facility "could not run the software that I write" for China's power system (Interview, June 3, 2013).

enjoyed access to domestic coal at prices below international market levels.

Industry-wide figures[22] summarized in Table 8.6 confound the expectation that high power prices and low costs should enable Chinese electricity firms to reap substantial profits. Table 8.6 provides two measures of returns showing annual industry-wide profits as percentages of annual sales revenue and of total assets during 2005–16.[23]

Profit margins – the ratio of profits to annual sales – are modestly higher for US investor-owned electric utilities than for Chinese electricity firms. The average and median of annual profit margins on the US side exceed comparable Chinese figures by 40 and 6 percent.

Profit margins are far more volatile on the Chinese side. During this twelve-year period, profit margins for US investor-owned utilities fluctuate between 9.97 and 13.25 percent. Annual profit margins in China's power sector fall within the range of 11.3–13.5 percent in the initial and terminal years, but decline sharply during the intervening years, reaching a low of 2.83 percent in 2008.

Figures showing the annual pre-tax return on assets display a similar contrast: ROA, the ratio of annual pre-tax profits to total assets, is substantially higher for US investor-owned electric utilities (average 3.92 percent, median 3.99 percent) than for Chinese firms (average 2.95 percent, median 2.98 percent). As with profit margins, volatility is far higher on the Chinese side. Average and median ROA values for US utilities during 2005–16 exceed comparable results for China's electricity firms by 71 and 22 percent respectively.

These observations establish low profitability in China's electricity system as a long-term rather than a cyclical phenomenon. Low profits span intervals of rising (2005–8, 2016) and declining (2012–15) coal prices, variations that massively affect costs in China's coal-dominated power sector.[24] Low profits

---

[22] Industry-wide figures come from annual industrial statistics yearbooks that omit small plants and include firms that produce heat as well as electricity; both categories are small.

[23] As explained in the Appendix, adjustments to reported sales totals eliminate double counting that would otherwise artificially reduce the profit-sales ratio.

[24] Coal purchases account for approximately 70% of variable costs for thermal plants, which in turn supply roughly two-thirds of China's electricity. Coal-fired generating plants absorbed 1.84 billion tons of coal in 2012 (Energy Statistics 2015, p. 109). Prices of thermal coal declined by RMB 150 during the course of 2013. A price decline averaging RMB 100 would have reduced 2013 production costs by RMB 184 billion, an amount equal to nearly two-thirds of the entire power industry's reported 2012 profits. See Table 8.6; also Wang 2014 and Yearbook 2014, p. 264.

Table 8.6 *Profitability of Chinese and US Electric Utilities Compared, 2005–2016*

	2005	2006	2007	2008	2009	2010	2011	2012	2013	2014	2015	2016	Average	Median
China Electric Power Sector (Billion RMB and percent)														
Sales Revenue														
Reported [S]	1774.6	2151.8	2636.8	2975.0	3331.7	4044.9	4716.5	5127.4	5593.9	5931.5	5493.1	5311.6		
Adjusted [S']	1024.3	1260.8	1597.6	1799.4	1994.4	2514.9	2948.4	3039.1	3310.4	3510.8	3396.1	3201.0		
Assets [A]	3937.5	4645.7	5348.5	6223.8	6908.7	7672.5	8382.1	9207.3	10246.8	10376.2	11934.4	12833.3		
Profit [π]	115.8	168.9	198.2	50.9	120.6	196.8	192.7	274.6	394.4	418.6	457.4	383.2		
Sales Cost [S'−π]	908.6	1091.8	1399.4	1748.6	1873.8	2318.1	2755.8	2764.5	2916.0	3092.2	2938.6	2817.8		
Profit Margin (%) = $100*\pi/S'$	11.30	13.40	12.41	2.83	6.05	7.83	6.53	9.03	11.91	11.92	13.47	11.97	9.89	11.61
Pre-tax ROA (%) $100*\pi/A$	2.94	3.64	3.71	0.82	1.75	2.57	2.30	2.98	3.85	4.03	3.83	2.99	2.95	2.98
Major US Investor-owned Electric Utility Operating Results ($ Million and Percent)														
Revenues [S]	234,909	246,736	240,864	266,124	249,303	260,119	255,573	249,166	257,718	271,832	260,121	261,047		
Costs	207,830	218,445	213,076	236,572	219,544	234,173	228,873	220,722	227,483	240,643	228,366	226,457		
Net Income (π)	27,079	28,291	27,788	29,552	29,759	25,946	26,700	28,444	30,235	31,189	31,755	34,590		
Profit Margin (%)	11.53	11.47	11.54	11.10	11.94	9.97	10.45	11.42	11.73	11.47	12.21	13.25	11.51	11.50
Pre-tax ROA (%)	3.60	4.43	5.09	5.00	4.25	4.53	4.56	3.05	3.38	3.73	3.37	2.09	3.92	3.99

(continued)

Table 8.6 (continued)

	2005	2006	2007	2008	2009	2010	2011	2012	2013	2014	2015	2016	Average	Median
Ratio: US to Chinese Annual Power Sector Financial Metrics														
Profit Margin (%)	1.02	0.86	0.93	3.93	1.97	1.27	1.60	1.26	0.98	0.96	0.91	1.11	1.40	1.06
Pretax ROA (%)	1.22	1.22	1.37	6.12	2.43	1.77	1.98	1.02	0.88	0.93	0.88	0.70	1.71	1.22

Note: Chinese data exclude "below norm" firms with annual sales less than RMB 5 million (RMB 20 million beginning in 2011) and, for some years, include firms that produce heat; both components are small.

Sources: Chinese data on sales revenue, assets and profits for 2005–11 from Industrial Economy, various issues; for 2012 and 2013, from Industrial Statistics 2013 and 2014; 2014 data from China Electricity Report 2015, p. 136 (assets), p. 137 (profits); 2014 sales revenue S calculated from 2013 figure using annual change in retail price (Table 8.1) and 4.14% rise in nationwide power consumption (China Electricity Report 2015, p. 93).

2015–2016 data for sales revenue(主营业务收入), assets, and profits (营业利润) from Industrial Statistics 2015 i: 68, 99, and 129; and 2016 i: 68, 99, and 129;
adjusted sales [S'] to eliminate double counting from Appendix Table 8.A.1.

US data: return on assets (ROA) from Appendix Table A.8.2; other data from US EIA 2017, Table 8.3.

persist through periods of rapid (2005–7, 2009–11) and slow (from 2012) demand growth.

The figures in Table 8.6, while highlighting the US power sector's superior financial results, may exaggerate the profitability of Chinese electricity firms. The difficulty involves possible underreporting of depreciation allowances, which reflect the annual costs assigned to long-lived assets (structures, machinery, vehicles, etc.). Standard sources give annual figures for "cumulative depreciation allowances" (积累折旧费 *jilei zhejiufei*); data for "current year depreciation" (本年提取折旧费 *bennian tiqu zhejiufei*) appear for some, but not all years. I approximate missing "current year" entries as the difference between cumulative depreciation totals for successive years.

Variation in the projected service lives of various assets adds unavoidable complexity. Although I cannot replicate the underlying calculations, industry-wide figures covering 2005–16, summarized in Table 8.7, reveal obvious difficulties. China's power sector invests on a massive scale, resulting in substantial net annual additions to the stock of depreciable assets.[25] With no dramatic variation in the mix of assets or in the rules governing depreciation,[26] abrupt shifts in the scale of depreciation allowances or their relation to broad measures of assets or capital stock are highly improbable.

Sudden declines in annual depreciation allowances in 2008–9, 2011–12, and 2014–15, as well as the near-stagnation of depreciation expenses in 2012–13 and the sudden leap in 2014, seem unlikely to reflect actual operating conditions. These improbable sequences appear to confirm claims that China's large power-generating conglomerates (and other listed companies) periodically reduce depreciation allowances to embellish reported profits.[27] A 2014 account quotes an industry specialist's view that China's big-five power generating firms, which reported combined 2013 profits of RMB 74 billion, would have earned little or no profit had they employed the depreciation rates in place ten years earlier (Wang 2014). Another study claims that depreciation reported by China's grid companies during 2007–11 was at least five times the permissible amount (Power Prices 2014).

The following discussion focuses on officially reported data, ignoring possible overstatement of profits.

---

[25] Net additions to the asset stock refer to newly added assets less the sum of current depreciation expenses and the undepreciated value of facilities and equipment removed from service.

[26] Successive depreciation guidelines for the power sector show no major changes since 1985 (Depreciation 1985; Depreciation 1994; Depreciation 2015).

[27] Weiying Zhang mentions widespread claims "that SOE managers often under-report fixed asset depreciation as well as other kinds of measurable costs" (2009, p. 71).

Table 8.7 *Depreciation Allowances for China Electric Power Sector, 2005–2016 (Billion RMB and Percent)*

	2005	2006	2007	2008	2009	2010	2011	2012	2013	2014	2015	2016
Accumulated Depreciation	1116.5	1324.2	1558.2	1927.9	2114.6	2517.2	2944.7	3324.0	3704.5	4284.3	4730	5309
Current Year Depreciation												
Reported	192.9	230.5	271.3									
Derived		207.7	234.0	369.7	186.7	402.6	427.5	379.3	380.5	579.8	445.6	579.2
Change from Previous Year's Depreciation (%)												
Reported		19.5	17.7									
Derived			12.7	58.0	−49.5	115.7	6.2	−11.3	0.3	52.4	−23.1	30.0
Comparison: Annual Change in Generating Capacity (%)	14.9	22.3	14.7	11.1	10.3	14.0	6.6	7.9	8.8	9.8	11.0	8.2

Note: Derived depreciation for year t is the difference between accumulated depreciation in years t and t-1.

Sources: Depreciation data for 2005–11 from annual issues of Industrial Economy; for 2012–14, from Industrial Statistics 2013, 2014 and 2015, i: 79 in each case; for 2015 and 2016 from Industrial Statistics 2016 and 2017, i: 69 in each case. Annual change in capacity computed from sources underlying Figure 8.1.

China: a high-cost electricity producer. Despite operating under a regime of high sales prices and low costs, China's power sector delivered consistently weak financial results during 2005–16. Financial results for Chinese electric utilities generally lag behind comparable measures for US power companies (Table 8.6). Domestic comparisons reinforce the impression of weak financial performance: ROA for the electricity sector trailed the average for centrally administered, state-controlled firms operating under China's State-owned Assets Supervisory and Administration Commission (SASAC) throughout 2005–16 (Table 8.6; Lardy 2014, p. 56; Finance Yearbook 2017, p. 377).

Low profitability combined with retail prices that, beginning in 2012, have matched or exceeded the US averages imply that, beginning in 2012 if not earlier, and despite multiple cost advantages, the unit cost of generating, transmitting and delivering Chinese electricity, when converted to US dollar terms, exceeds comparable costs for US electric utilities.

What is the scale of excess costs? China is the world's leading producer of electrical equipment, construction materials and many other manufactures needed to erect power plants, build grid systems, and generate and deliver electricity. The term "China price" reflects the reputation of Chinese industry for delivering serviceable products at low prices. Immense recent expansion means that the average age of equipment is far lower in China's power sector than in America's. This should translate into lower maintenance costs. Low wages provide Chinese firms with a further cost advantage (Table 8.5).

With the partial exception of coal, the chief variable cost item for China's power sector, for which domestic prices increasingly reflect international values,[28] major cost elements endow China's electricity sector with a considerable advantage over US utilities. Lean and efficient operations should translate this advantage into distinctly lower costs than the US utility system can achieve. High production costs for Chinese electricity signal the presence of substantial excess costs – expenses that attaining US levels of operational efficiency would eliminate.

These observations suggest a trio of benchmarks for appraising the magnitude of excess costs in China's power system during 2005–16:

- Excess costs [A] measure the cost reductions required to enable China's electric power sector to match the observed financial

[28] Cui and Wei (2017, p. 150) present data showing average market prices for coal exceeding the average price of thermal coal throughout 2002–10, indicating an additional cost advantage arising from access to coal supplies at low government-managed prices.

performance of US utilities without changing the electricity prices charged to Chinese end-users.

- Excess costs [B] measure the cost reductions required to enable China's electric power sector to match the observed financial performance of US utilities following an assumed 40 percent reduction in the price charged to industrial electricity users.
- Excess costs [C] measure the cost reductions required to enable China's electric power sector to match the observed financial performance of US utilities following an assumed 33 percent across-the-board reduction in Chinese electricity prices.

Each calculation determines the magnitude of cost reduction – in renminbi and as a percentage of reported sales costs (adjusted sales revenue minus profits, see Table 8.6) – needed for each year's Chinese financial outcomes to match average US performance during 2005–16.

These performance targets reflect observations in Table 8.6. The target for the profit-sales ratio is 11 percent – slightly below the 11.5 percent average and median of annual results for US utilities during 2005–16. The target ROA is 4.0 percent, which is 40 percent above the average Chinese ROA of 2.95 percent during 2005–16 and slightly above the comparable US average and median ROA of 3.92 and 3.99 percent (Table 8.6).

Version [A] calls for sufficient cost reduction to match average US financial metrics with no change to historic Chinese power prices. The results show that modest cost reductions averaging no more than 3.8 percent could have permitted actual results to match both the 11 percent profit-sales target and the 4 percent ROA benchmark during the decade ending in 2016.

Version [B], which requires cost reductions that elevate financial outcomes to the target levels in the face of a hypothetical 40 percent reduction in industrial power charges, is more demanding. Results in Table 8.8 show that meeting either benchmark would require cost reductions of in the neighborhood of one-third.

Version [C] investigates the magnitude of cost reductions needed to match recent financial outcomes for US electric utilities under the assumption of a 33 percent across-the-board reduction in Chinese electricity prices. This approach avoids excessive focus on high prices imposed on industrial users, which arise from administrative choices rather than cost considerations.

Early reports following the recent wave of electricity reforms, discussed in greater detail below, include instances in which expansion of

Table 8.8 *China Electricity Excess Cost Analysis, 2005–2016*

| | Industry | Percentage Cost Reduction Needed to Achieve | | | | | | Cost Reduction to Attain 4.0% ROA (RMB billion) | | |
| | | 11 Percent Profit/Sales Ratio | | | 4.0 percent Return on Assets | | | | | |
Year	Share in Electricity Use %	Version [A] Current Retail Prices	Version [B] 40% Price Reduction for Industry	Version [C] 33% Price Reduction for All Users	Version [A] Current Retail Prices	Version [B] 40% Price Reduction for Industry	Version [C] 33% Price Reduction for All Users	Version [A] with Current Retail Prices	Version [B] 40% Price Reduction for Industry	Version [C] 33% Price Reduction for All Users
2005	74.3	-0.3	29.5	32.8	4.6	38.1	41.8	41.7	346.0	377.8
2006	74.4	-2.8	27.8	31.1	1.5	35.9	39.7	16.9	392.1	432.9
2007	74.3	-1.6	28.6	31.9	1.1	35.0	38.8	15.7	490.2	549.9
2008	73.5	8.4	35.3	38.6	11.3	41.6	45.3	198.1	727.1	790.9
2009	72.5	5.3	32.8	36.5	8.3	39.2	43.4	155.8	734.3	811.9
2010	73.8	3.4	32.0	35.3	4.7	36.8	40.5	110.1	852.7	940.0
2011	72.7	4.8	32.5	36.2	5.2	36.3	40.5	142.6	1000.5	1115.6
2012	72.7	2.2	30.6	34.4	3.4	35.4	39.7	93.7	978.0	1096.6
2013	72.4	-1.0	28.2	32.3	0.5	33.4	38.0	15.5	973.6	1107.9
2014	70.7	-1.1	27.5	32.2	-0.1	32.0	37.4	-3.6	983.8	1149.6
2015	71.6	-2.9	26.6	31.1	0.7	33.8	38.8	19.9	992.1	1141.6
2016	70.1	-1.1	27.2	32.3	4.6	36.5	42.1	130.1	1027.8	1185.4
Average	72.7	1.1	29.9	33.7	3.8	36.2	40.5	78.0	791.5	891.4
Median	72.7	-0.7	29.0	32.5	4.0	36.1	40.1	67.7	913.2	1013.3

Sources: Calculated from data on adjusted sales S', profits π, and sales costs (= S'·π) from Table 8.6. For industry's share in electricity use, see Energy Yearbook 2011, pp. 82–3 (for 2005–10); China Electricity Report 2013, p. 79 (for 2011–12); ibid. 2014, pp. 87–8 (for 2013) Electricity Operations 2014 (for 2014); China Electricity Council 2015 (for 2015); https://chinaenergyportal.org/2016-detailed-electricity-statistics-updated (for 2016).

direct trading alone reduced prices by more than 30 percent in Guangdong, Anhui, and Yunnan (Yao Jinnan 2016; May 2016 interviews); elsewhere, direct trading has delivered smaller cost savings (e.g. Jiangsu Power Exchange 2016; Lu Zheng 2016). Wide variation in the price consequences of direct trading and the paucity of information about the likely outcome of continuing changes in grid charges and in development of new retail electricity sellers make it difficult to anticipate the eventual result. The assumed 33 percent price reduction embodied in Version [C], however, surely falls within the range of possible outcomes.

Results in Table 8.8 show that matching historic US financial performance during 2005–16 under an assumed 33 percent across-the-board price reduction in electricity prices would have required Chinese electricity firms to lower costs by approximately 35 percent.

The right-hand columns of Table 8.8 summarize the actual amount of cost reduction needed to attain an assumed ROA of 4 percent during the decade 2005–16 under alternative assumptions. Average annual cost reductions range from RMB 78 billion for Version [A] (no price change) to much higher figures of RMB 791.5 billion for Version [B] (40 percent reduction in prices for industrial users). Imposing a 33 percent across-the-board price reduction (Version [C]) would require annual cost reductions averaging RMB 891.4 billion. Beginning in 2011, attaining a 4 percent ROA following either a 40 percent reduction in industrial power prices or a 33 percent sector-wide price cut would require annual cost reductions approaching or surpassing RMB 1 trillion.

The central role of industrial electricity use, which consistently accounts for 70 percent or more of overall Chinese power consumption (Table 8.8), offers a natural focus for appraising the magnitude of possible excess costs. Firms classified in the tariff category "large-scale industry," which absorb the largest portion of industrial electricity sales, face tariffs that, when converted to US dollars, exceed prices charged to US industrial electricity users throughout 2005–16; during 2011–15, the price gap is 50 percent or higher (Table 8.1). As noted above, industrial users outside the scope of "large industry" pay even more.

US electricity prices are neither artificially reduced to benefit industrial users nor inflated to ensure outsized financial returns to electric utilities. With the benefit of multiple cost advantages, a well-managed Chinese electricity system should be capable of matching US financial outcomes if the price charged to industrial users, who absorb the bulk of Chinese electricity (Table 8.8) were the same in China as in the US.

Excess cost estimates based on Version [B], which imposes a 40 percent reduction on electricity prices charged to Chinese industrial users, provide a plausible lower bound answer to the question "What is the magnitude of cost reductions needed to enable financial outcomes in China's electricity system to match the performance benchmark represented by the US electricity system?"

Why do the excess costs associated with Version [B] provide a plausible lower bound?

The assumed 40 percent reduction in prices charged to industrial users is considerably smaller than the actual gap between Chinese and US industrial electricity prices in recent years. Table 8.1 shows that, on average, electricity prices paid by "large industry" in China exceeded average US industrial electricity prices by 50 percent during 2009–16. Higher prices charged to small and medium industrial users raise the industry-wide average: in 2014, the Chinese industry-wide average was perhaps 60 percent higher than average US industrial power prices.[29]

- Bank lending rates are far higher in China, where the average rate on one-year loans during 2005–16 was 6.23 percent, than in the US, where, on average, the banks' prime lending rate was 4.43 percent during the same period.[30] Changing the financial performance benchmark underlying Table 8.8 from matching US utilities' average ROA (3.92 percent) to matching the United States, utilities' ratio of ROA to cost of capital (3.92/4.43 or 0.88) would increase the magnitude of estimated excess costs. This is because the Chinese ratio of ROA to capital cost, 2.95/6.23 = 0.47, is only 54 percent of the US figure, whereas the Chinese ROA is 75 percent of the comparable US figure (2.95/3.92 = 0.752).

- High prices charged to Chinese industrial electricity users conceal cost-shifting intended to underwrite low prices offered to households and to agricultural power users. This sort of cross-subsidy represents a

---

[29] Based on fragmentary data for 2016 showing that "large industry" absorbed 50.3% of Hubei power sales during the first two quarters (Hubei electricity 2016) and that "ordinary industry and commerce" (一般工商业 *yiban gongshangye*) absorbed 17.8% of total first-quarter sales in Jiangsu (Jiangsu electricity 2016). If sales to industry account for 70% of the total, with 50% going to "large-scale industry" at a price 50% above the economy-wide average and 20% going to "ordinary industry and commerce" at a price 30% higher than for "large-scale industry," the combined average would be 62.8% above the US average for industrial electricity.

[30] Chinese lending rates courtesy of Nicholas R. Lardy. US rates from https://fred.stlouisfed.org/series/MPRIME (accessed August 30, 2018).

politically motivated financial transfer rather than any sort of cost overrun. These cross-subsidies, however, are far smaller than the amounts shown in the right-hand columns of Table 8.8.

Tang (2014) estimates the combined subsidy for household (RMB 49.3 billion) and for agricultural (RMB 14.1 billion) electricity users at RMB 63.4 billion for 2010.

Chinese households used 698.9 billion KWh of power in 2013 (Yearbook 2015, Table 9–12), when the average power price was RMB 0.55748 per KWh for households and RMB 0.63549 for all Chinese users (State Energy Administration 2015).

I take the US, where residential electricity prices were 18.5 percent above the overall average in July 2015 and 18.4 percent higher than the average for July 2016, as a benchmark. This allows a crude approximation of the 2013 subsidy enjoyed by Chinese households as the difference between an assumed price of RMB 0.7498 (18 percent above the 2013 economy-wide average) and the actual household unit price, multiplied by 2013 household power consumption:

$$2013 \text{ subsidy} \approx 698.9 * [(0.63549 * 1.18) - 0.55748]$$

$$= 698.9 * 0.1924 = \text{RMB } 134.5 \text{ billion}$$

Assuming no change in the ratio between subsidies for household and for agricultural power use between 2010 and 2013, our crude projection of combined 2013 subsidies for these sectors is:

$$\text{RMB } 134.5 \text{ billion} * (63.4/49.3) = \text{RMB } 173 \text{ billion}$$

Raising the assumed reduction in industrial power prices from 40 to 50 percent, a change that is entirely compatible with available information on electricity pricing, would increase the estimate of cost reduction required to attain a 4 percent ROA in 2013 by RMB 239.5 billion – far larger than the cross-subsidy amount for that year.

I conclude that the scale of cost reductions needed for China's electric power system to attain a profit/sales ratio of 11 percent or average ROA of 4.0 percent following an assumed 40 percent reduction in industrial power prices during 2005–16 does indeed provide a plausible lower-bound measure of excess costs within China's electricity sector.

The scale of cost reductions required to match US financial outcomes following a hypothetical 40 percent reduction in prices for industrial electricity shown in Table 8.8 ranges from an annual average of 29.9 percent (to attain an 11 percent profit-sales ratio) to an average of 36.2

percent (to reach an average ROA of 4.0 percent). I focus on the lower of these results, and propose 30 percent as a plausible lower bound estimate of excess costs in China's electricity industry.

There is no claim of precision. Inconsistencies within the Chinese data underlying our calculations along with conceptual differences between Chinese and US statistical compilations create the expectation of large error margins.

As noted earlier, only big conclusions retain credence in the presence of large error margins. The findings summarized in Table 8.8 represent just such an outcome. Investigation of the simple relation Cost = Revenue – Profit shows that, notwithstanding the presence of multiple favorable circumstances, the unit cost of producing, transmitting and delivering electricity is substantially higher in China than in the United States. While the exact measure of the cost gap, which I place at a minimum of 30 percent, remains uncertain, the present analysis, which builds on quantitative materials distributed by Chinese industry and official sources, leaves no room to question this conclusion.

Where Do Excess Costs Cluster?

What follows is an initial foray into the structure of Chinese electricity costs.

High rail freight and logistics expenses? Movement of goods in China is expensive. Coal, the largest single cargo in China's transport system, is no exception. The cost of shipping coal attracts vociferous complaints, which often repeat the claim that "the logistics cost of shipping coal over 1,000 km in China is 10–15 times the cost in the United States and 15–20 times that in Japan" (Coal Logistics 2015).

Following the cessation of Japanese coal mining in 2002, rail carriage of coal has all but disappeared, rendering the Japan comparison irrelevant. Rail freight costs for shipping coal are indeed higher in China than in the US. Conversion of cost figures at prevailing exchange rates shows that average rail freight cost per ton-km for Chinese coal shipments was 21–29 percent higher than comparable US costs during 2003–8. Thereafter, the cost gap increased, in part because of the increased value of China's renminbi currency. By 2015, unit rail freight costs for Chinese coal exceeded comparable US figures by 78 percent (Rawski 2015).

Commodity shipments attract numerous taxes and fees, many imposed by local authorities that resist Beijing's efforts at systematization and control. Again, coal is no exception: one survey reported 109 varieties of taxes and fees (Coal Costs 2015).

The potential for cost savings in the shipment of coal is considerable. China's power plants burned an average of 1.78 billion tons of coal annually during 2010–15 (Energy Statistics 2015, p. 109), most delivered by rail. In 2012, when power plants consumed 1.84 billion tons (ibid.), average length of haul for railway shipments of coal was 645 km and average rail fees per ton-km were RMB 0.131 (Rawski 2015). Thus, the cost of rail shipment was roughly 645 * 0.131 * 1.84 or RMB 155 billion. With fees reportedly occupying the same share of delivered coal costs as rail freight – 20 percent for each – and adding additional costs for short-haul trucking (8 percent) and port charges (5 percent) (Coal Logistics 2015), the 2012 data imply that annual costs of moving coal from the mines to China's power plants are in the neighborhood of RMB 155 billion * 49/20 or RMB 380 billion.

Chen Deming, China's Minister of Commerce, noted in 2012 that imposition of fees accounted for over half of logistics costs, and indicated that suitable reforms might halve the cost of moving goods (Yu 2012). Using 2012 figures, a 50 percent reduction in logistics costs would amount to RMB 190 billion. Even this large number, which amounts to 6.2 percent of 2012 (adjusted) sales costs for China's electricity sector (Table 8.6), would provide only a modest contribution to the cost reductions linked to Version [B] in Table 8.8.

Overbuilding? Beginning in the early 1980s, China experienced repeated episodes of severe power shortage. This stimulated a strong and eventually successful effort to accelerate supply growth and eliminate the economic damage arising from electricity-related production stoppages. Given the long history of shortage, it is hardly surprising that supply growth overshot demand, leading to growing reports of falling utilization and idle generating facilities beginning in 2013.

The ongoing response to the recent demand slowdown, which has seen the annual growth of electricity consumption plunge from double-digits as recently as 2011 to less than 1 percent in 2015 before rebounding to 5.6 and 6.6 percent in 2016 and 2017, demonstrates that excess investment is a long-term structural issue rather than a short-term adjustment problem. Building of new plants and requests for approval of additional projects continue even as utilization rates plunge dramatically (Table 8.3), estimates of excess generation capacity reach 38 percent (Lin, Liu and Ke 2016) and forecasts for future demand growth cluster in the low single digits. Lu Bin (2016d), for example, cites experts' expectations of "no quick rebound" in the pace of demand growth.

Even though operating hours declined for four consecutive years beginning with 2012/13, with 2016 figures plumbing depths last seen in the 1960s before rebounding slightly in 2016/17 (Table 8.3), data in Table 8.9

Table 8.9 *China Electricity Sector Investment and Generating Capacity, 2008–2017*

	Power Sector	Annual Investment Spending Billion RMB, Current prices			New Generating Capacity 1000 MW			Year-end Generating Capacity 1000 MW		
		Power Generation		Power Grid						
		Total	Thermal	Total	Total	Thermal	Coal	Total	Thermal	Coal
2008	630	341	168	290	92	66	n.a.	793	603	599
2009	770	380	154	390	97	66	62	874	651	592
2010	742	397	143	345	91	58	54	966	709	649
2011	761	393	113	369	94	62	58	1062	768	709
2012	739	373	100	366	83	52	48	1147	820	754
2013	773	387	102	386	102	42	34	1258	870	796
2014	780	369	145	412	104	48	35	1370	924	832
2015	858	394	116	464	132	67	54	1525	1006	900
2016	883	341	112	543	121	50	39	1650	1061	946
2017	801	270	74	531	134	46	35	1777	1106	980

Source: Except as noted:

Detailed electricity statistics for 2009, 2010, 2012, 2014, 2016 and 2017 from https://chinaenergyportal.org (accessed August 28, 2018).

n.a. indicates gaps in data.

Year-end capacity of coal plants for 2008–12 omits installations below 6 MW capacity. The 2008 figure includes plants burning coal gangue, which are excluded elsewhere.

For 2017: new coal capacity from Cao 2018; year-end coal capacity from China Electricity Report 2018.

show that investment spending on new power plants remained high, with 2015 spending approaching the 2010 peak before falling back. Stubbornly high investment in the face of declining utilization spurred attacks on generation firms and regional governments for pursuing "blind investments" (盲目投资 *mangmu touzi*) and "Great Leap Forward-style" expansion of coal-fired generation facilities – referring to a period of recklessly wasteful investment during the late 1950s (Yuan Jiahai 2016; Li Beiling 2016).

Since construction costs do not enter into the calculation of annual profits, the direct impact of overbuilding on profits is limited to increased interest costs associated with the financing of new facilities. Overbuilding, however, burdens the industry with underutilized facilities, depressing the return on assets. During 2013–16, power plants absorbed an average of 45.7 percent of annual electricity sector investment. Reducing asset accumulation during those years by 35 percent – allowing a margin for expansion of renewables – would have elevated overall return on assets above the 4 percent target during 2013–15 (but not in 2016, when high coal prices slashed profits), showing how excess capacity erodes profitability,[31] particularly for heavily indebted power generation companies. Thus a 2016 report notes double-digit declines in operating cash flow for four of China's five largest generation companies and comments that their businesses face "increasing pressure" and "increasingly urgent cash flow needs" (Working Capital 2016).

Pursuit of uneconomic technology? Field interviews raise the possibility of ill-advised outlays on upgrades that deliver only marginal efficiency gains. One plant manager reported that improvements costing RMB 260 million at two 300 MW thermal plants lowered coal consumption per KWh by about 20 grams; increasing utilization rates from 60 to 90 percent would reduce unit coal use by 11 grams and also lower internal power consumption – with zero investment expense.[32] In Chapter 4 Michael Davidson finds that underutilization hobbles the performance of China's newest, cleanest, and most fuel-efficient coal generation facilities. Detailed operational information illustrates the magnitude of losses: in 2011/12, 2013/14, and 2014/15, average hours for 1000 MW plants, China's newest and largest, declined more than in several smaller size categories. In 2014/15, plants in the two largest categories experienced declines of 7 and 9 percent,

---

[31] Nicholas Lardy alerted me to the importance of this point.

[32] Interview, June 2013. In addition to reducing coal use, the improvements enabled these plants to meet specific environmental regulations.

while hours for plants in three smaller categories declined by 5, 6 and 0.4 percent.[33] These observations point to limited economic benefit associated with China's technically impressive development of ultra-supercritical generation technology.

Similar issues arise in other segments of the power sector. Domestic critics complain that the productivity of State Grid Corporation's investment spending is low, in part because efforts to develop long-distance high-voltage AC power transmission, described in Chapter 6, have encumbered China's grid system with expensive and often underutilized facilities.[34] Others pillory efforts to build turbines for offshore wind farms as "floating white elephants" (Gao 2014). Loren Brandt and Luhang Wang find that Chinese wind turbine producers rush to produce high-capacity models while neglecting quality issues affecting smaller models that dominate market sales (Chapter 9).

Trapped power? As the share of power from intermittent sources (hydro, wind, solar) increases, the likelihood of "spillage" or "curtailment"– electricity that never enters the grid and is therefore wasted – increases. Spillage can arise from technical conflicts or from economic choices – for example if grid companies resist pressure to pay high prices or to build expensive links to absorb "clean" power. China has the unfortunate distinction of the world's highest wind curtailment rates – 17 percent in 2016 – more than double the highest reported elsewhere (Chapter 4; Bai 2017). Unexpectedly low demand growth has encouraged Guangdong and other provinces to prioritize local thermal plants (and build new ones) while limiting incoming power transfers from hydroelectric facilities in western provinces, resulting in at least one large hydro plant "commencing production with nowhere to send electricity" (quote from Clean Energy 2018; see also Fu 2015). Massive curtailment of wind, hydro, solar, and even nuclear generation (Xiao 2016; Zhu 2017) has spurred strenuous efforts to reduce spillage from renewable power sources (Dong 2018).

Too many workers? 2011 data assembled in Table 8.5 show that, compared with its US counterpart, China's electricity sector deployed slightly less installed capacity, generated 15 percent more power, and employed more than 6.5 times as many workers. Part of this employment gap arises

---

[33] Based on data compiled in the author's file Change in operating hours ... 041118 from China Electricity Yearbook 2013, pp. 25–6; Electricity Databook 2013, p. 48, and 2015, p. 36; China Electricity Report 2016, pp. 68–9.

[34] Zhou and Lu note that "around 30%" of China's "long-distance transmission lines are underutilized" (2017, p. 11). Fu 2014; He 2015b and Wang 2018 raise issues of cost and utilization.

from the need to service a far larger number of (especially household) consumers. A portion represents a sensible response to China's relatively low labor costs. Even so, rapid progress of equipment modernization and automation – for example, computerizing the monitoring of generation equipment and deploying drones to inspect power lines (Yao Haitang 2016; Lu Bin 2018a) – suggests that efficient operation of each unit of Chinese generating, transmission and distribution capacity does not require six times the number of workers associated with comparable US installations. The combination of increasing automation and declining growth of labor productivity, measured as power output per man-year, which rose steadily until 2014, but stalled thereafter (Table 8.A.1), points to substantial opportunities to pare the costs – not just wages, but equipment, vehicles, office space, and housing outlays – associated with overmanning.

Of these potentially quantifiable items, only coal transport costs and overbuilding offer potential cost reductions that can partially match the excess cost estimates associated with substantial price reductions (Table 8.8). Neither wages, which amounted to 3.1 percent of 2011 power sales (Table 8.5), nor interest payments, which absorbed 9.4 of generation companies' 2016 sales revenue and 1.2 percent for grid companies (Industrial Statistics 2016, I, pp. 99, 129) could generate savings on the scale needed to attain US-style profit/sales or ROA outcomes if electricity charges to industrial users were lowered by 40 percent (Version [B]).

System costs? Our inability to attribute China's surprisingly high electricity costs to specific, quantifiable causes directs attention to possible inefficiencies arising from the institutional matrix within which this sector operates. Three areas stand out:

- Managerial complexity. "General fragmentation of authority" in China's administrative system means that "policy-making is … characterized by an enormous amount of discussion and bargaining … " (Lieberthal 1995, 173). While this description refers to governmental processes, the multiplicity of official and corporate actors involved in decisions about siting, building, and operating power plants, the construction and operation of grid facilities, the dispatch, allocation, and pricing of power flows, and the remediation of power plant effluents ensure the expenditure of "enormous" resources in everyday decision-making surrounding China's power sector.
  - Since "discussion and bargaining" are the function of managers, rather than ordinary workers, it is not surprising to find in Table 8.10 that

managers at sixteen large Chinese power-related firms account for 17.76 percent of 2014 employment at these companies, eleven percentage points above the US figure of 6.77 percent for electricity generation and transmission.

- I apply the proportion of managers in sixteen firms, which employ 80 percent of China's electricity work force, to the entire Chinese power sector, and take the US proportion of managers as a benchmark. This implies that the unusual complexity of Chinese business arrangements may require 0.11 * 2536.9 = 279,000 additional managers, a figure equivalent to over 70 percent of the entire US electricity industry work force! This calculation vividly illustrates the potential magnitude of system costs in a major segment of China's economy.

- Institutional conflicts. Many examples can illustrate the pervasiveness of costly outcomes arising from conflicting interests within China's power system.

  - Critics excoriate the "Great Leap Forward-style" rush to build new thermal power plants even as utilization of existing coal-fired facilities plunges (Li 2016; State Energy Administration 2016b). Despite "strict and even punitive policy constraints" limiting the development of new coal plants, the "more lenient" approval process for co-generation plants that produce both heat and power (Lu Bin 2016c) attracts investment planners, who appear undeterred by a report that 70 percent of co-generation plants run by the Big Five generating companies lost money during 2013 (Yu 2015). In Shandong, supplying heat has become a "required course" (必修课 *bixiuke*) to "ensure sustainable development for every thermal power company" (Lu Bin 2018a). In Sichuan, critics call for "strictly controlling the conversion of coal plants to dual power and heating operations" to "avoid further displacement of hydro by coal" (Sichuan 2018).

  - Numerous reports (e.g. He Ying 2018) describe the construction and operation of power facilities without official approval. One account cites government estimates that "One fifth of the power plants in China are illegal" (Oster 2006). Recent expansion of self-managed coal generation facilities (燃煤自备电厂 *ranmei zibei dianchang*), many unauthorized, pushed this category to occupy 7.9 percent of overall capacity at year-end 2017. Advocates oppose a strict "one size fits all" policy, and call for measures to "normalize and legalize" the operation of rogue plants "as soon as possible" providing that they "pay relevant fees on time" (Self-managed 2018).

Table 8.10 *China and US Electricity Sectors: Employment and Proportion of Managers, 2014*

	Employment (1000s)	Of which: Managers (Percent)	Number (1000s)
China: Electric Power Sector	**2536.9**		
Total for Sixteen Large Firms	**2084.2**	**17.76**	**370.1**
Five Big Generation Firms	**589.8**	**17.95**	**105.9**
Huaneng	139.9	12.26	17.2
Datang	103.8	16.39	17.0
Huadian	104.6	22.76	23.8
Guodian	128.3	18.25	23.4
CPI	113.2	21.65	24.5
Two Major Grid Firms	**1067.3**	**15.61**	**166.6**
State Grid	785.0	17.95	140.9
Southern Grid	282.3	9.11	25.7
Regional Electricity Firms	**43.7**	**20.80**	**9.1**
Guangdong Power	13.7	27.49	3.8
Neimengu Power	17.6	11.37	2.0
Shaanxi Power	12.4	26.80	3.3
Construction Firms	**343.4**	**24.62**	**84.5**
China Electric Construction	188.5	25.30	47.7
China Energy Construction	143.5	22.74	32.6
Beijing Energy Investment	11.4	36.96	4.2
Others	**40.0**	**9.79**	**3.9**
China National Nuclear	8.9	14.24	1.3
China General Nuclear	29.8	7.69	2.3
Shenhua Energy	1.3	27.49	0.4
US: Electricity Generation and Transmission	**389.8**	**6.77**	**26.39**

Note: The share of managers in 2016 employment for the same fifteen firms is 17.77 percent (China Electricity Report 2016, p. 261).
Sources: China: sector-wide data: Industrial Statistics 2015, i: 191; firm-level data from China Electricity Report 2015, p. 273. US data: US Bureau of Labor Statistics 2014.

- Local protectionism encourages expansion of local power generation along with efforts to channel electricity demand to local producers. Thus "local governments intentionally raise the threshold for inter-provincial [electricity] transactions" (Lu Bin 2017). Guangdong, for example, not only limits "imports" of cheap hydropower to protect local thermal plants but has quintupled planned construction plans, for costly offshore wind farms (Zhang Zirui

2018), which, upon completion, will compound to the difficulty of reducing spillage from inland hydro facilities.

- Prior to recent reform initiatives, major grid companies were notorious for concealing detailed cost information. An official of the former State Electricity Regulatory Commission explained that key cost items related to grid management are "intentionally hidden from outside view" (Interview, May 17, 2012).

- Resource extraction. China's electricity system is the home of massive state-owned firms, whose politically potent leaders, labyrinthine organization, and multiple layers of subsidiaries deter external scrutiny. These firms' extensive involvement in one-off construction projects, no-bid contracts and related party transactions creates ample opportunities for leaders at all levels to secure private benefits at the expense of corporate financial outcomes.[35] One regulatory official sees these firms as "cradles for corruption" (Huang and Yu 2015). While the recent anti-corruption campaign seeks to diminish actual or potential political opposition as well as financial malpractice, continuing focus on the energy sector, including major electricity firms, leaves no doubt that resource extraction remains deeply embedded within China's electricity sector. The resulting excess costs, while not subject to even the crudest estimation, could be very large.

RETROSPECT AND PROSPECT

The experience of China's electric power sector during the past several decades is, first and foremost, a story of remarkable success. Formerly dominated by small, antiquated, fuel-gobbling generating plants and bypassing vast rural areas while scrambling to satisfy urban demand, China's power system now comprises a nationwide array of modern generation facilities linked to regional grid networks. Important metrics such as unit coal consumption, self-consumption of power by generating facilities, and transmission losses resemble the values attained in advanced nations. Theft of power and payment arrears, phenomena that destabilize

---

[35] Gezhouba Dam Group (葛洲坝集团 *Gezhouba jituan*), ranked forty-eight and thirty-six in 2012 and 2014 among China's 100+ central SOEs for "rule of law," illustrates these difficulties. During 2012–14, the firm worked to "establish contract management" and "standardized management." During 2015, "the company reviewed a total of 62,091 contracts valued at RMB 431 billion" – evidently a new development. Although "building a legal system is not easy," integrity among subsidiary enterprises "improved." See Duan (2016).

electricity operations in many low- and middle-income nations, are notably absent: State Grid reported collecting over 99.9 percent of electricity charges in 2011, in part because of "improved risk control" including legal actions aimed at recovering unpaid bills (State Grid 2012, p. 164).[36]

This impressive transformation coexists with a regime of surprisingly high costs and prices. China's unexpected combination of high electricity prices, low prices for materials, equipment and labor, and low profits signals the presence of large-scale inefficiency. A lean and efficient power system should deliver electricity to China's firms and households at substantially reduced costs.

Our finding that attaining financial outcomes similar to those achieved by US electric utilities while lowering industrial electricity charges toward the prevailing US level would require cost reductions in the neighborhood of 30 percent represents a lower-bound estimate of the potential for cost reduction within China's electricity system. Alternative calculations using PPP rather than market rates to convert Chinese electricity prices to US dollars, a plausible approach in cross-national comparisons involving economies at different levels of development, would dramatically increase our estimate of excess costs.

Since readily quantifiable sources of excess costs cannot account for more than a fraction of the savings needed to match US utilities' financial outcomes following an assumed shift of industrial power prices toward the US level, I conclude that elevated costs are deeply embedded within the structure of China's electricity system. Major reductions will not be a matter of lopping off obvious cost overruns, but seem likely to require far-ranging reform of current business structures and regulatory practices.

This diagnosis exactly matches the thinking underlying recent Chinese policy initiatives. Following a decade-long hiatus, far-ranging electricity reform reappeared on Beijing's policy horizon in 2015. This new reform push employs transparency as a lever to extend market pressures and thus reduce power costs. Beginning with Shenzhen, regulators have conducted audits of formerly concealed grid costs. In place of opaque negotiations between the grid companies and government agencies, I see the gradual emergence of a system conforming to international regulatory standards described in Chapter 2 by Irene Wu. Under the new arrangements, regulators determine authorized grid charges by adding a specified profit markup to a roster of approved costs (Shenzhen Grid Reform 2015); published accounts suggest that regulators typically allow profit margins

---

[36] Lu Bin (2016e) cites an exception – residents stealing steam from a troubled Jiangsu plant.

in the neighborhood of 8 percent above approved costs.[37] Standardization of grid charges smooths the path for rapid expansion of direct sales agreements between generating companies and large industrial users.

Although the financial impact of initial grid pricing reforms is small when compared to 2015 grid revenues of RMB 3.6 trillion (China Industrial Statistics 2016, i: 99), consequences have mounted as the reform unfolds. The Shenzhen reforms anticipated reductions in grid fees amounting to RMB 700 million during 2015–17 (Shenzhen Grid Price 2015). Price adjustments lowered 2017 revenues of provincial grid companies by RMB 48 billion (Lu Bin 2018b).

The potential impact of direct sales is substantial. Market transactions rose 45 percent in 2016/17, reaching 1.63 trillion kWh or 25.8 percent of aggregate power consumption, with price discounts amounting to RMB 60.3 billion (Lu Bin 2018b). With "general industrial and commercial" (一般工商业) power users enjoying a 10 percent price decline in early 2018 (NDRC 2018) the ongoing push toward full liberalization of industrial and of commercial power sales (Jia 2016) seems likely to promote further reductions in electricity charges.

The impact of expanded entry into retail electricity sales, the third leg of the current reform agenda, remains unclear. However with the number of power sales firms rising from "over 300" to 6,387 between March 2016 and February 2017, and with entry open to newcomers, including private firms from outside the power sector, this initiative opens the door to further reduction of electricity charges (Lu Bin 2016b; Power Sales 2017).

Except for reductions in taxes and fees, reforms that lower costs to electricity users impose identical revenue reductions on the companies that generate and deliver electricity. Opposition by representatives of generating and grid firms (Jia 2015b; Lu Binggen 2016) cannot withstand the pressure arising from China's current combination of high electricity prices, massive overbuilding of power plants, declining operating hours, and financial exigencies among power users, many suffering from the consequences of their own past investment excesses. The inevitable result: increased pressure on electricity providers that enter the latest round of reform initiatives with a history of weak financial results (Table 8.6) will magnify an already formidable array of challenges.

---

[37] Cheng (2016) cites a range of 8–10% for solar projects; Zhang Zirui (2016a) interviews an industry specialist who uses 7.38% in analyzing prospects for offshore wind projects; Pipeline (2016) cites 8% as the prospective rate of return for natural gas pipelines.

Slowing demand growth is the central reality confronting China's entire electricity supply chain: coal mining, generation and grid companies, equipment manufacturers, design institutes, and construction firms. Nationwide growth of electricity consumption, which raced ahead for decades at or near double-digit rates, has slowed. Following near-stagnation in 2015, China's National Energy Agency projects annual demand growth during 2016–20 in the range of 3.6–4.8 percent (Electricity Plan 2016). Reflecting the impact of this growth slowdown, an executive of Shanghai Electric, a leading supplier of power plant equipment, commented in 2014 that demand for thermal power equipment had dropped by 50 percent during the previous five years, and, with government officials blacklisting coal, could face a similar decline during the following five years (Mu and Shu 2014).

Interaction between the unexpected slowdown of demand expansion and massive capacity growth (Figure 8.1) has produced a steep drop-off in utilization rates (Table 8.3). Average operating hours for China's vast fleet of thermal generating plants, which typically face breakeven points (at which revenues suffice to cover loan repayments as well as operating expenses) of 5,000–5,500 annual hours, plunged to 4,165 hours in 2016, the lowest since 1964, before creeping up to 4,209 hours in 2017.

At the same time, thermal generating firms, which are major sources of airborne effluents, face escalating cost pressures arising from the government's increasingly forceful response to widespread public concern over urban air pollution. Officials have ordered power plants to retrofit effluent-reducing devices; offsetting increments to on-grid prices offer only partial compensation for the resulting cost increases; promised subsidy payments are often in arrears (Yu Chunping 2015; Zhang Zirui 2016b). Several of China's largest cities have banned new coal-fired plants – ignoring industry assurances regarding the benefits of "clean coal" (Jia 2014a, 2014b) – and forced existing plants to shut down or convert from coal to natural gas.

Three additional developments may escalate financial pressure:

- Growth of power from intermittent sources raises costs for both grid companies and for the (typically coal-based) back-up operations that supply power when wind and sun falter (Xie 2016). Kahrl and Wang (2014, p. 7) present 2011 provincial data showing a steep rise in wind curtailment once wind power exceeds 4–5 percent of provincial electricity output.
- Proposed use of demand management (e.g. Zhang, Jiao, and Chen 2017) aimed at reducing peak power requirements, for example

through the extension of time-of-day power pricing, could further reduce operating hours.

- Implementation of plans to raise deposit rates paid by China's banks could lead to higher lending rates, and thus impose fresh cost increases on the heavily indebted generating sector. The 2017 debt-asset ratios of China's Big Five power generation firms exceeded 80 percent (versus 66.6 percent for all centrally directed state-owned firms in 2016; see Lu Bin 2018b; Finance Yearbook 2017, p. 377).

These circumstances create mounting financial uncertainty, especially for the five big generating companies. Reduced cash flow (Working Capital 2016) may push cost cutting ahead of capacity expansion among the priorities of electricity executives, especially in the generation sector.

Looking Forward

The central finding of this study, summarized in Table 8.8, is that advances in technology, scale, and service provision conceal massive opportunities to reduce costs. While downward price pressure affects all segments of the industry, cost reduction of the order suggested by the results in Table 8.8 can only occur in the production and distribution of electricity from coal-fired generating facilities. Fixed costs predominate at both hydroelectric and nuclear plants; opportunities for reducing operational costs appear slight, particularly in the nuclear sector, where post-Fukushima safety measures have imposed layers of unforeseen expenses. Wind and solar, with a combined 2017 output share of 6.6 percent, have low operating costs, but are too small to deliver cost reductions that would meaningfully affect industry-wide totals.

The intensification of market forces inherent in ongoing electricity reforms will channel demand toward low-cost suppliers. Successful pursuit of cost reduction has the potential to lower the absolute and relative cost of coal-fired power. Institutional arrangements and policy structures that routinely tilt toward long-dominant coal interests (Zhang Shuwei 2016), illustrated by the November 2016 announcement of long-term contract arrangements that will provide electricity producers with thermal coal at a 25 percent discount to the current market price, reinforce this prospect (Zheng 2016).

Substantial reductions in nuclear plant operating hours (Chapter 10; Nuclear Facilities 2016) show how interaction among excess capacity, latent cost reduction potential, and market deepening could spark a slowing or even reversal of recent declines in the share of coal-fired power generation – the exact opposite of Beijing's declared policy objectives and of the international community's expectations following the 2016 Paris accord. Massive expansion of thermal power generation envisioned in the November 2016 announcement of 13th Five-Year Plan (FYP) (2016–20) targets for electricity, along with the likelihood of additional growth inherent in the repeated proviso that Beijing would "strive to limit" 2020 thermal capacity to the targeted figure, highlights the formidable resilience of China's coal interests.

Can the current revival of reform momentum overcome a tangled web of circumstances that has allowed institutional legacies, inchoate policies, ineffectual regulation and large-scale misappropriation of resources to transform this technically progressive sector's bright prospects into a latent financial nightmare? Can ongoing reform efforts limit or reduce the environmental costs associated with Chinese electricity production?

Although the obstacles to thoroughgoing reform appear formidable, so too are the capabilities available to China's electric power system. Individual segments have avoided the accumulation of excess costs that plagues the system as a whole: power output per unit of installed capacity exceeds performance in the US (Table 8.5) and the trajectory of new plant costs demonstrates an exceptional capacity for cost control (Figure 8.2). China leads the world in erecting wind and solar generation facilities, and boasts a large and rapidly growing fleet of nuclear power plants.

The threatened transformation of a crucial economic sector into a long-term fiscal burden and environmental incubus may elicit a determined effort to mobilize the resources responsible for the power sector's many achievements to create institutional systems surrounding the production and distribution of Chinese electricity that can match the system's technical excellence.

APPENDIX

Calculation of Profit-Sales Ratio

Annual yearbooks of Chinese industrial statistics provide information on sales revenue (S), assets (A), and profits (π) of the electricity industry. I use this information to calculate the ratio of profits to sales as well as the return on assets.

The yearbook figures on sales revenue, however, do not match comparable information regarding US investor-owned utilities. Chinese grid companies purchase electricity from power plants, then resell the electricity to end-users. This means that amounts paid to generating companies are counted twice in compiling data on industry-wide sales: once when the generating companies sell electricity to the grid, and a second time when the grid resells this power (less transmission losses) to end users.

Under US institutional arrangements, when separate companies generate and transmit electricity, end-users are billed separately for electric power and for transmission and delivery services, so that summing the sales of various companies counts generating company revenues only once.

Using reported data to compare the profit/sales ratio for Chinese and US electric utilities will thus exaggerate the relative profitability of US firms because total sales of generating firms will appear once in the denominator of the formula $100^* \pi/S$ for the US industry but twice in a similar calculation on the Chinese side.

To avoid this distortion, Table 8.A.1 derives adjusted sales figures for Chinese electric utilities that eliminate this double counting. The adjusted sales figures, denoted by S', are comparable with reported sales for US investor-owned electric utilities. In Table 8.A.1, adjusted revenue S', measured in billion RMB, is derived from reported sales – S – measured in billion RMB; reported power production Q – measured in billion KWh; the percentage of gross electricity output – c – consumed within generation facilities; and the average wholesale or on-grid price – P – received by the generating companies, measured in RMB per MWh.

The derivation is: $S' = S - [(.001P) * (.01Q*(1-c))]$.

I thus obtain a revised sales total by subtracting the grid's payment to generating companies for incoming power flows from reported industry-wide sales.

$.001*P$ is the wholesale electricity price expressed in RMB per KWh (1 MWh = 1000 KWh)

$.01*Q*(1-c)$ is the total of electricity supplied to the grid. Q measures gross power output, including electricity consumed within generating plants.

For example, If c = 5 percent, then (100-c) is 95 percent, $.01*95 = 0.95$, which is the share of power output that reaches the grid; more generally, $.01*Q*(1-c)$ is the actual power flow to the grid.

Return On Assets for US Electricity Firms, 2005–2016

Profit figures for China's electricity sector appear in Table 8.6; these are pre-tax figures.

Table 8.A.2 provides an estimate of the pre-tax ROA for investor-owned US utilities. John Hanson of Riverstone Advisers LLC compiled annual

Table 8.A.1 *Chinese Electricity Industry Sales Revenue Adjusted to Avoid Double Counting, 2005–2016*

Variable	Unit	2005	2006	2007	2008	2009	2010	2011	2012	2013	2014	2015	2016
Reported Sales Revenue, S	RMB Billion	1774.6	2151.8	2636.8	2975.0	3331.7	4044.9	4716.5	5127.4	5593.9	5931.5	5493.1	5311.6
Power output, Q	Bill. KWh	2,500.3	2,865.7	3,281.6	3,466.9	3,714.7	4,207.2	4,713.0	4,987.6	5,431.6	5,794.5	5,739.9	6,024.8
Self-consumption share, c	(%)	5.87	5.93	5.83	5.90	5.76	5.43	5.39	5.10	5.05	4.83	5.90	5.57
Power supplied to Grid, G	Bill. KWH	2353.5	2695.8	3090.2	3262.3	3500.9	3978.5	4459.1	4733.2	5157.1	5514.7	5401.2	5639.2
On-grid price, P	RMB per MWH	318.79	330.53	336.28	360.34	381.99	384.56	396.50	441.20	442.79	438.94	388.25	370.97
Double counting, D	RMB Billion	750.3	891.0	1039.2	1175.6	1337.3	1530.0	1768.0	2088.3	2283.5	2420.6	2097.0	2110.5
Adjusted Sales Revenue, S'	RMB Billion	1024.3	1260.8	1597.6	1799.4	1994.4	2514.9	2948.4	3039.1	3310.4	3510.8	3396.1	3201.0
Reported industry-wide profit, π	RMB Billion	115.8	168.9	198.2	50.9	120.6	196.8	192.7	274.6	394.4	418.6	457.4	383.2
Assets, A	RMB Billion	3937.5	4645.7	5348.5	6223.8	6908.7	7672.5	8382.1	9207.3	10246.8	10376.2	11934.4	12333.3
Profitability													
Profit/Adjusted Sales	%	11.30	13.40	12.41	2.83	6.05	7.83	6.53	9.03	11.91	11.92	13.47	11.97
Profit/Assets (ROA)	%	2.94	3.64	3.71	0.82	1.75	2.57	2.30	2.98	3.85	4.03	3.83	2.59
Employment	Millions	963	1106	1277	1336	1338	1526	1913	1992	1997	2260	2252	2300
Output per worker	MWH	2.60	2.59	2.57	2.59	2.78	2.76	2.46	2.50	2.72	2.56	2.55	2.62

Sources: P is the average on-grid price from Table 8.1; for S, A and π, see Table 8.6; for c, see Table 8.3. Q: Yearbook 2016, Table 13–13; for 2015, Electricity Databook 2015, p. 2; for 2016: Electricity Table 2017. Employment data: for 2006–2010, from Industrial Economy 2007, p. 67; 2008, p. 67; 2009, p. 65 and 2010, p. 56. For 2011–2012, China Electricity Report 2013, p. 119; for 2013, Industrial Statistics 2014, i: 155; for 2014, Table 8.10; for 2015, Industrial Statistics 2016, i: 129; for 2016, Industrial Statistics 2017, i: 129.

Notes: Double counting, D =.001*Q*(100-c)*P; Adjusted Sales Revenue, S' = S – D; Power Supplied to the Grid, G = .01*Q*(100-c).

Table 8.A.2 Average Return on Assets (ROA) for US Investor-Owned Electric Utilities, 2005–2016 (percent)

Symbol	Firm	2014 Sales $ Billion	2014 Revenue Share	2005	2006	2007	2008	2009	2010	2011	2012	2013	2014	2015	2016	Amounts in $ 1000s			2014 tax rate
																2014 income before tax	2014 income tax	
AEE	Ameren	6.05	0.020	3.40	2.90	3.07	2.79	2.64	0.59	2.20	-4.25	1.34	2.70	2.69	2.70	970000	377000	0.39
AEP	American Electric Power	17.02	0.058	2.30	2.70	2.78	3.24	2.91	2.46	3.79	2.36	2.67	2.82	3.33	0.98	2490000	942000	0.38
CMS	CMS Energy	7.18	0.024	-0.53	-0.50	-1.45	2.03	1.52	2.20	2.59	2.28	2.62	2.61	2.45	2.63	729000	250000	0.34
CNP	CenterPoint Energy	9.23	0.031	1.43	2.49	2.25	2.38	1.89	2.22	6.49	1.87	1.39	2.71	0.00	2.00	885000	274000	0.31
D	Dominion Resources	12.44	0.042	2.11	2.71	5.74	4.52	3.04	6.58	3.18	0.65	3.50	2.51	3.27	3.26	1780000	452000	0.25
DTE	DTE Energy	12.3	0.042	2.41	1.84	4.09	2.26	2.18	2.57	2.79	2.33	2.53	3.36	2.51	2.85	1280000	364000	0.28
DUK	Duke Energy	23.93	0.082	3.30	3.02	2.53	2.65	1.95	2.27	2.81	2.00	2.33	1.60	2.34	1.70	4130000	1670000	0.40
ED	Consolidated Edison	12.92	0.044	3.03	2.86	3.38	3.91	2.61	2.86	2.81	2.84	2.59	2.58	2.61	2.65	1660000	568000	0.34
EIX	Edison International	13.41	0.045	3.34	3.32	2.98	2.96	1.97	3.01	0.05	-0.20	2.23	3.58	2.22	2.58	1980000	443000	0.22
ES	Eversource Energy	7.74	0.026	-2.05	3.99	2.15	2.08	2.35	2.72	2.62	2.39	2.80	2.85	2.91	3.01	1300000	468300	0.36
ETR	Entergy	12.49	0.042	3.04	3.66	3.51	3.53	3.37	3.33	3.44	2.07	1.69	2.14	0.00	-1.29	1550000	589600	0.38
EXC	Exelon	27.43	0.094	2.16	3.65	6.10	5.89	5.60	5.05	4.65	1.74	2.17	1.95	2.41	1.08	2490000	666000	0.27
FE	FirstEnergy	15.05	0.051	2.74	3.98	4.12	4.08	2.97	2.15	2.16	1.57	0.78	0.59	1.11	-12.96	171000	-42000	-0.25
LNT	Alliant Energy	3.35	0.011	-0.10	4.26	5.96	3.99	1.50	3.34	3.39	3.28	3.44	3.39	3.10	2.87	440000	44300	0.10
NEE	NextEra Energy	17.02	0.058	2.94	3.72	3.46	3.86	3.46	3.86	3.49	3.14	2.85	3.43	3.35	3.38	3650000	1180000	0.32
PCG	PG&E	17.09	0.058	2.67	2.88	2.82	3.49	2.94	2.50	1.79	1.62	1.53	2.51	1.40	2.11	1800000	345000	0.19
PEG	Public Service Enterprise	10.89	0.037	2.24	2.53	4.70	4.14	5.52	5.34	5.03	4.14	3.87	4.48	4.47	2.29	2460000	938000	0.38
PNW	Pinnacle West Capital	3.49	0.011	1.66	2.87	2.72	2.13	0.58	2.87	2.66	2.88	3.02	2.86	3.04	2.85	644400	220700	0.34
PPL	PPL	11.5	0.039	3.80	4.39	6.58	4.50	1.87	3.41	3.96	3.54	2.51	3.66	1.74	4.89	2130000	690000	0.32
SCG	SCANA	4.95	0.016	3.45	3.21	3.20	3.26	3.03	3.00	2.92	2.98	3.16	3.36	2.80	3.32	786000	248000	0.32
SO	Southern	18.47	0.063	4.14	3.80	3.91	3.84	3.40	3.81	3.97	3.95	2.68	3.01	3.11	2.60	3010000	977000	0.32

(continued)

Table 8.A.2 (continued)

Symbol	Firm	2014 Sales $ Billion	2014 Revenue Share	2005	2006	2007	2008	2009	2010	2011	2012	2013	2014	2015	2016	Average 2005–2016	Amounts in $ 1000s		
SRE	Sempra Energy	11.04	0.037	3.47	4.83	3.81	4.08	4.11	2.55	4.22	2.48	2.74	3.02	3.53	3.08		1520000	300000	0.20
WEC	WEC Energy Group	5	0.017	3.08	2.93	2.94	2.95	3.02	3.54	3.91	3.88	3.98	3.97	2.18	3.16		950000	361700	0.38
XEL	Xcel Energy	11.69	0.040	2.45	2.63	2.56	2.68	2.71	2.87	2.96	2.99	2.92	2.88	2.52	2.80		1550000	523820	0.34
	SUM of 2014 Revenues	291.68	1																

Annual Average ROA (%)	2005	2006	2007	2008	2009	2010	2011	2012	2013	2014	2015	2016	Average 2005–2016		
After-tax: Unweighted	2.35	3.11	3.50	3.38	2.80	3.13	3.25	2.19	2.56	2.86	2.46	1.86	2.79		0.29
After tax: 2014 sales weights	2.59	3.19	3.67	3.60	3.06	3.26	3.28	2.19	2.43	2.69	2.43	1.50	2.82		0.28
Pre-tax ROA Assuming 28% Tax Rate	3.60	4.43	5.09	5.00	4.25	4.53	4.56	3.05	3.38	3.73	3.37	2.09	3.92		

Summary	Unweighted	Sales Weights
After-tax ROA, 24 Firms, 2005–16		
Average ROA	2.79	2.82
Median ROA	2.83	2.87
Coefficient of Variation	0.18	0.22

after-tax ROA data for twenty-five US electric utilities covering the years 2005–14. I eliminated one firm for which the data series was incomplete and calculated industry-wide ROA for each year in two versions: the unweighted average of twenty-four firm-level ROAs, and a weighted average using 2014 sales figures as weights. After-tax ROA data for 2015 are from csimarkets.com. The 2015 figure for one firm, CMS, is the average of figures for Q1 and Q4.

The right-hand columns of Table 8.A.2 derive actual 2014 income tax rates for each firm. The unweighted and sales-weighted average tax rates for that year are 29 and 28 percent respectively.

I apply the 2014 sales-weighted average tax rate of 28 percent to the entire period 2005–14 to obtain a series of estimated pre-tax ROA for the US electric utility sector. Results appear in Tables A.8.1 and Table 8.6.

The list of firms, annual ROA, 2014 sales and tax rates appear in Table 8.A.2.

References

Abstract. 2014. 中国统计摘要 2014 [China Statistical Abstract 2014]. Beijing: Zhongguo tongji chubanshe.

——. 2016. 中国统计摘要 2016 [China Statistical Abstract 2016]. Beijing: Zhongguo tongji chubanshe.

Areddy, James T. and Paul Glader. 2010. "India Deal Puts China in GE's League." *Wall Street Journal*. October 28, 2010. http://www.wsj.com/articles/SB10001424052702 304173704575579261842597870 (accessed April 3, 2016).

BP 2015. BP Statistical Review of World Energy 2015.

Bai Yanfeng 白彦锋. 2017. "弃风"怪圈如何破 [How to break the cycle of 'abandoned wind']. 中国能源报 [China Energy Report] June 28, 2017, p. 18.

Baiyin 2014. "Industrialization of 690 Alloy U-tube for Nuclear Power Plant Steam Generator." Presentation by Baiyin Special Steel Tube Co., Ltd. Conference presentation, Pudong, China. May 29, 2014.

Bie Fan 别凡. 2014. "煤价续跌 煤电价格联动被重提" [Falling coal prices highlight the link with power prices]. 中国能源报 [China Energy Report] June 23, 2014, p. 10.

Blacklist. 2018. 发改委: 建立涉电力领域市场主体"黑名单"制度 [Development and Reform Commission to establish a 'blacklist' system for market principals in the electricity sector]. www.china5e.com/news/news-1021283-1.html (accessed March 14, 2018).

Cao Yali 曹雅丽. 2018. 我国电力结构进一步优化 电力供需总体宽松 [China's power structure is further optimized]. Posted July 10, 2018. www.china5e.com/news/news-1033873-1.html (accessed July 16, 2018).

Chen, Jinqiang. 2017. "Promises of Greening China's Economy." Harvard Kennedy School Belfer Center Discussion Paper 2017–01. January, 2017.

Chen Zheng 陈峥. 2016. "中国能建动员部署加快业务转型."[Chinese Energy Builders Mobilize to Accelerate Transformation of their Business]. 中国能源报 [China Energy Report]. April 18, p. 25.

Chen Zongfa 陈宗法.2015. 新电改后电价还会涨吗？ [Can tariffs still rise after the new electricity reform?]. March 31, 2015. http://weibo.com/p/230418131f6e6ce0102vh99?from=page_100206_profile&wvr=6&mod=wenzhang mod (accessed December 21, 2015).

Cheng Sisi 成思思. 2016. 标杆电价开启光热大市场 [Benchmark price opens a big market for solar power]. 中国能源报 [China Energy Report] September 5, 2016, p. 1.

Cheng, Tun-jen and Chung-min Tsai. 2009. "Powering rent seeking in the Electricity Industry." In Tak-Wing Ngo and Yongping Wu eds., *Rent Seeking in China*. London and New York: Routledge.

China Electricity Council. 2016. 中电联发布《2016年度全国电力供需形势分析预测报告》[China Electricity Council issues 'Forecast report for 2016 national electricity supply-demand situation']. www.cec.org.cn/yaowenkuaidi/2016–02–03/148763.html (accessed March 3, 2016).

China Electricity Council. 2018. 中国电力行业年度发展报告2018 [2018 Annual development report for China's electric power industry]. Unpaginated online version of report issued June 14, 2018.

China Electricity Report. Annual. 2013–17. 中国电力行业年度发展报告[Annual Development Report of China's Electricity Industry]. Beijing: Zhongguo shichang chubanshe.

China Electricity Yearbook. Annual. 2001–15.中国电力年鉴 [China Electricity Yearbook]. Beijing: Zhongguo dianli chubanshe.

Clean Energy. 2018. 清洁能源消纳需站高望远(社评). [Editorial: High profile needed for absorbing clean energy]. 中国能源报[China Energy Report]. January 8, 2018, p. 1.

Coal Costs. 2015. 我国煤炭为何成本高？ [Why is China's cost of coal so high?} www.chinabidding.com/infoDetail/224959193-News.html (accessed March 27, 2016).

Coal Logistics. 2015. "煤炭物流成本分析报告" [Analytic report on logistics costs for coal]. www.chinawuliu.com.cn/xsyj/201503/24/299730.shtml (accessed March 27, 2015).

Comerford, Tim, Dennis Meseroll, Tracey Hyatt Bosman, and Gao Yong. 2016. "A Comparison of US & China Electricity Costs." Biggins Lacy Shapiro & Company/Tractus Asia Limited.

Cui, Herui and Pengbang Wei. 2017. "Analysis of thermal coal pricing and the coal price distortion in China from the perspective of market forces." *Energy Policy*. 106. pp. 148–54.

Dash, Parismita. 2014. "A Comparative Analysis of BHEL & Shanghai Electric Co. in reference to Power Industry of India and China." http://13jgbs-pdash.blogspot.com/ (accessed April 23, 2016).

Demsetz, Harold. 1969. Information and Efficiency: Another Viewpoint. *The Journal of Law and Economics.* 12(1). pp. 1–22.

Depreciation. 1985. 国营企业固定资产折旧试行条例一九八五年四月二十六日 [Draft Provisions on Fixed Asset Depreciation by State-operated Enterprises, April 26, 1985]. www.nxcz.gov.cn:7002/%5Cdocuments%5Clib1%5C200004030247.HTM (accessed March 22, 2016)

——— 1994. "电力工业企业固定资产年折旧率表（自一九九四年七月一日起施行). [Table of Annual Depreciation Rates for Fixed Assets of Electric Power Enterprises (effective July 1, 1994)]. www.sbgl.cn/news/news8/2010–06-05/2020.html (accessed March 22, 2016).

——— 2015. "2015固定资产折旧年限最新规" [New 2015 Regulation on Annual Depreciation Limits for Fixed Assets]. http://jskjxh.com/infoview.asp?id=601 (accessed March 22, 2016).

Dong Xin 董欣. 2018. 能源行业市场化改革持续推进 [Continued advance for energy industry marketization]. 中国能源报 [China Energy Report]. March 12, 2018. p. 2.

Duan Guiheng 段贵恒. 2016. 建设法治央企 打造法治能建 [Building rule of law in central SOEs]. 中国能源报 [China Energy Report]. August 8, 2016, p. 25.

Electricity Databook. 2010. 2010年电力工业统计资料汇编 [Electricity Industry Data Compendium 2010]. Online edition accessed through CNKI zhishi wangluo fuwu pingtai.

——— 2014. 2014年电力工业统计资料汇编 [Electricity Industry Data Compendium 2014]. N.p.: Guojia dianligongsi zhanlue guihuabu.

——— 2015. 2015年电力工业统计资料汇编 [Electricity Industry Data Compendium 2015]. N.p.: Zhongguo dianliqiye lianhehui guihuafazhanbu. 2016.

Electricity Outcome. 2016. 国家能源局关于2015年度全国电力价格情况汇总 [National Energy Agency summary regarding 2015 nationwide electricity pricing]. November 2, 2016. http://shoudian.bjx.com.cn/news/20161102/785537.shtml (accessed May 30, 2017).

Electricity Plan. 2016. 国家能源局正式发布《电力发展"十三五"规划（2016-2020 年》[National Energy Agency formally issues "Electricity Development Guidelines for the 13th Five-Year Plan Period (2016–2020)']. www.escn.com.cn/news/show-362013.html (accessed November 12, 2016).

Electricity Report. 2017. 中电联发布《2017-2018年度全国电力供需形势分析预测报告》[China Electricity Council issues "2017–2018 Analysis and Forecast Report on Electricity Supply and Demand"]. www.cec.org.cn/guihuayutongji/gongzuodongtai/2018–02-01/177584.html (accessed February 7, 2018).

Electricity Summary. Annual, 2014–17. 2017年全国电力工业统计快报一览表 [National Electricity Industry Statistical Summary Table].www.cec.org.cn/guihuayutongji/tongjixinxi/niandushuju/2018–02-05/177726.html (accessed April 3, 2018).

Energy Report. 1997. 中国能源'97白皮书 [China's Energy: 1997 White Paper]. Beijing: Zhongguo wujia chubanshe.

Electricity Table. 2017. 2017年全国电力工业统计快报数据 一览表 [Flash report on 2017 national electricity data]. Posted February 5, 2018.www.cec.org.cn/guihuayu tongji/tongjixinxi/niandushuju/2018–02-05/177726.html (accessed August 29, 2018).

Energy Statistics. Annual. 1997–2015. 中国能源统计年鉴 [China Energy Statistics Yearbook]. Beijing: Zhongguo tongji chubanshe.

Fan Ruohong. 2015. "State Council Aims to Cut Power Prices for Big Manufacturers." http://english.caixin.com/2015–12-15/100888436.html?utm_source=The+Sinocism +China+Newsletter&utm_campaign=cfe50428e6-Sinocism12_15_1512_15_2015& utm_medium=email&utm_term=0_171f237867-cfe50428e6-29602929&mc_cid=c fe50428e6&mc_eid=05464ef5ec (accessed December 18, 2015).

Fifty Years. 2000. 中国工业交通能源50年统计资料汇编 1949–1999 [Statistical Compendium: 50 Years of China's Industry, Transport and Energy]. Beijing: Zhongguo tongji chubanshe.

Finance Yearbook. 2017. 2017 中国财政年鉴 [China Finance Yearbook 2017]. Beijing: Zhongguo caizheng zazhishe.

Fu Yuewen傅玥雯. 2014. 10项典型电网工程投资成效报告发布.[Report Released on 10 Typical Power Grid Construction Projects]. 中国能源报 [China Energy Report]. June 9, 2014. p. 2.

———. 2015. 今年汛期, 再议弃水 [Again, Proposals to Abandon Hydropower During This Year's Flood Season]. 中国能源报 [China Energy Report]. August 10, 2015. p. 16.

Gao Wei 高为. 2014. 海上风电不是"水中白象" [Offshore Wind Power Generators are not 'Floating White Elephants']. 中国能源报 [China Energy Report]. May 5, 2014. p. 4.

Haley, Usha C. V. and George T. Haley. 2013. *Subsidies to Chinese Industry*. New York: Oxford University Press.

Han Xiaoping. 韩晓平. 2016. 十三五能源规划不能再搞竭泽而渔2.0 [Energy Guidelines for the 13th Five-Year Plan cannot drain the swamp again to catch fish]. July 12, 2016. www.china5e.com/energy/news-951417–1.html (accessed October 10, 2016).

He Ying 何英. 2018. 政策直击增量配电网争议问题 [Policy addresses controversy over incremental grid extension]. 中国能源报 [China Energy Report]. April 9, 2015. p. 9.

He Yongjian 何勇健. 2015a. 价格改革:如何当好能源革命的先行军 [The Path Forward for Energy Price Reform]. 中国能源报 [China Energy Report]. July 20, 2015. p. 3.

———. 2015b. "十三五"电力规划应强调系统优化. [13th Five-year Plan Should Emphasize Electric Power System Optimization]. 中国能源报 [China Energy Report]. August 3, 2015. p. 3.

Historical Statistics. 1975. *Historical Statistics of the United States, Colonial Times to 1970*. Washington, DC: Bureau of the Census. 1975.

Hsieh, Chang-tai and Peter J. Klenow. 2009. "Misallocation and Manufacturing TFP in China and India." *The Quarterly Journal of Economics*. 124 (4): 1403–48.

Huang Kaishi and Yu Ning. 2014. "Debates on Ways to Reform Power Industry Heat Up." http://english.caixin.com/2014-11-10/100749059.html (accessed December 12, 2014).

Hubei Electricity. 2016. 一季度湖北省用电量增长5.32% 增幅超全国约3个百分点 [Hubei 2016 Q1 electricity usage up 5.32%, 3 points above the national figure]. www.hubei.gov.cn/zwgk/hbyw/hbywqb/201604/t20160412_817764.shtml (accessed September 20, 2016).

Hussy, Charlotte, Erik Klaassen, Joris Koornneef, and Fabian Wigand. 2014. *International Comparison of Fossil Power Efficiency and CO2 Intensity – Update 2014*. Utrecht: Ecofys.

Industrial Economy. Annual. 2006–12. 中国工业经济统计年鉴 [Yearbook of China Industrial Economy Statistics]. Beijing: Zhongguo tongji chubanshe.

Industrial Statistics. Annual. 2013–16. 中国工业统计年鉴. [China Industrial Statistics Yearbook]. 2 vols. Beijing: Zhongguo tongji chubanshe.

Jia Kehua贾科华. 2014a. 冯伟忠：煤电完全可以建在城市 [Feng Weizhong says absolutely OK to build coal-fired power plants in our cities]. 中国能源报 [China Energy Report]. May 5, 2014. p. 15.

———. 2014b. 煤电酝酿革命性技改 [Coal-fired Power Brewing a Revolutionary Technical Transformation]. 中国能源报 [China Energy Report]. June 9, 2014. p. 15.

———. 2014c. 脱硫问题突出 14家煤电受罚 [14 power plants fined to crack the SO_2 problem]. 中国能源报 [China Energy Report],June 23, 2014. p. 15.

———. 2015a. 青海无电人口年底通电 [Qinghai's Populace will Achieve Full Access to Electricity by Yearend]. 中国能源报 [China Energy Report], March 28, 2015. p. 2.

———. 2015b. 电改时机对电企不利 [Timing of Electricity Reform Will Damage the Power Generating Companies]. 中国能源报[China Energy Report]. July 20, 2015. p. 4.

———. 2016. 电力市场建设路线图现雏形 [Electricity market roadmap taking shape]. 中国能源报[China Energy Report]. March 28, 2016. p. 2.

Jiang Lei 江镭. 2014. 内陆核电建设具备内生动力. [Inland Nuclear Power Construction Brings Endogenous Dynamics]. 中国能源报[China Energy Report]. November 17, 2014. p. 18.

Jiangsu Electricity. 2016. 江苏一般工商业及其他用电类别价格每千瓦时降低0.73分 [Jiangsu power cost falls 0.73 cents per KWh for ordinary industry and commerce and for users classified as 'other']. www.js.xinhuanet.com/2016-06/21/c_1119076806.htm (accessed September 20, 2016).

Jiangsu Power Exchange. 2016. 江苏拟年内开展电力竞价交易 [Jiangsu to open an electricity exchange with competitive bidding this year]. 中国能源报[China Energy Report] August 22, 2016. p. 10.

Jiao Yue 矫月. 2016. 电力业产能过剩堪比煤炭：分配发电量仅够维持电厂不饿死 [Power sector excess capacity comparable to coal; dispatch allocations preserve plants from starvation]. 证券日报 [Securities Daily]. April 1, 2016. www.china5e.com/news/news-938341-1.html (accessed September 1, 2016).

Kahrl, Fredrich and Xuan Wang. 2014. *Integrating Renewables into Power Systems in China: A Technical Primer – Power System Operations*. Beijing: Regulatory Assistance Project.

Kahrl, Fredrich, Jim Williams, Ding Jianhua, and Hu Junfeng. 2011. "Challenges to China's transition to a low carbon electricity system." *Energy Policy*. 39. pp. 4032–41.

Kahrl, Fredrich, James H. Williams, and Hu Junfeng. 2013. "The political economy of electricity dispatch reform in China." *Energy Policy*. 53. pp. 361–69.

Labor Yearbook. 2012. 中国劳动工资统计年鉴 2012. [China Labor and Wage Statistics Yearbook 2012]. Beijing: Laodong renshi chubanshe.

Lanzhou. 2011. 兰州供电公司志 1986–2009 [Annals of the Lanzhou Power Supply Company, 1986–2009]. Lanzhou: Gansu renmin chubanshe.

Lardy, Nicholas R. 2014. *Markets over Mao: the Rise of Private Business in China*. Washington, DC: Peterson Institute for International Economics.

Li Beiling. 李北陵. 2016. "控制火电盲目增长应成共识" [Controlling Blind Expansion of Thermal Power Should be a Consensus]. 中国能源报 [China Energy Report]. January 4, 2016. p. 5.

Li Fenglin. 李凤琳. 2015. "电企加快布局"一带一路"建设." [Power companies accelerate arrangements for construction under 'One Belt, One Road']. 中国能源报 [China Energy Report]. July 13, 2015. p. 15.

Lieberthal, Kenneth. 1995. *Governing China: from revolution through reform*. New York: W. W. Norton.

Lin Boqiang 林伯强. 2008. 中国能源发展报告 2008 [China Energy Development Report]. Beijing: Zhongguo caizheng jingji chubanshe. Unpaginated online version. https://books.google.com/books?id=3QtUDQAAQBAJ&pg=PT567& lpg=PT567&dq=2006%E5%B9%B4%E8%B7%A8%E7%9C%81%E9%80%81%E5% 87%BA%E7%94%B5%E9%87%8F&source=bl&ots=A77gSEbuC5&sig= SqqfcStimQ2dcHnW_BAuROqYME0&hl=en&sa=X&ved=2ahUKEwjt8NiV5pLdAh UJn-AKHWZ9AeUQ6AEwAnoECAgQAQ#v=onepage&q=2006%E5%B9%B4% E8%B7%A8%E7%9C%81%E9%80%81%E5%87%BA%E7%94%B5%E9%87% 8F&f=false (accessed August 29, 2018).

Lin Jiang 林江, Liu Xu 刘栩, and Ke Yizhi 柯意志. 2016. 从备用容量视角看中国电力过剩 [China's electricity surplus from the perspective of spare capacity]. 中国能源报 [China Energy Report]. July 25, 2016. p. 4.

Lu Bin 卢彬 2016a. 气电代替煤电优势明显 [Obvious advantages of replacing coal with gas-fired electric power]. 中国能源报 [China Energy Report]. March 7, 2016. p. 10.

2016b. 多元主体进军售电领域 [Multiple agents enter electricity sales]. 中国能源报 [China Energy Report]. March 21, 2016. p. 10.

2016c. "热电联产迎来新机遇."[Co-generation of Heat and Power Ushers in New Opportunities]. 中国能源报 [China Energy Report]. April 11, 2016. p. 10.

2016d. "盈利空间缩水 经营压力陡增 [Profit margins shrink amidst sharp increases in operating pressure]. 中国能源报 [China Energy Report]. September 5, 2016. p. 10.

2016e. 煤电"寒冬"迎供暖考验 [Can Coal-fired power plants meet the challenge of providing heat during a cold winter]. 中国能源报 [China Energy Report]. October 17, 2016. p. 10.

2017. 各地电力市场建设步伐加快 [Establishment of regional power markets accelerates]. 中国能源报 [China Energy Report]. March 20, 2017. p. 10.

2018a. "绿色经"让煤电厂焕发生机 ['Green Classic' rejuvenates coal power plants]. 中国能源报 [China Energy Report]. April 9, 2018. p. 11.

2018b. 电力行业三年"让利"近7000亿 [Three-year electricity reform 'dividend' approaches RMB 700 billion]. 中国能源报 [China Energy Report]. April 16, 2018. p. 2.

Lu Binggen卢炳根. 2016. 直购电尚需加快择点试行 [Accelerate Selection of Experiment Points for Direct Power Sales]. 中国能源报 [China Energy Report] April 11, 2016. p. 5. '

Lu Zheng 路郑. 2016. 江苏电力交易持续释放改革红利 [Jiangsu electricity exchange releases sustained reform bonus]. 中国能源报 [China Energy Report]. September 12, 2016. p. 21.

Manshū kaihatsu. 1964–5. 满洲开发40年史*Manshū kaihatsu yonjū nenshi* [Forty-year History of Development in Manchuria]. 3 vols. Tokyo: Manshū kaihatsu yonjū nenshi kankōkai.

Mathews, John A. and Hao Tan. 2014. "China's renewable energy revolution: what is driving it?" *The Asia-Pacific Journal*, 12 (43), No. 3. November 3.

Mu Sinan牟思南 and Shu Li 黍离. 2014. 上海电气：好辰光还要自己把握 [Shanghai Electric: Holding its own in good times]. 中国能源报 [China Energy Report]. June 9, 2014. p. 19.

NDRC. 2015. 国家发展改革委 环境保护部 国家能源局关于实行燃煤电厂超低排放电价支持政策有关问题的通知 [NDRC, Ministry of Environmental Protection, National Energy Administration, Circular of the People 's Government of the People' s Republic of China on the Issue of Ultra Low Emission Electricity Tariff Support Policies for Coal – fired Power Plants]. December 2, 2015. www.sdpc.gov.cn/gzdt/201512/t20151209_761941.html (accessed November 4, 2016).

2018. 发改委：一般工商业电价合计已降821亿元以上! [NDRC: Power price reductions for general industry and commerce already reach RMB 8.21 billion!]. August 21, 2018. www.china5e.com/news/news-1037598–1.html (accessed August 26, 2018).

NPP Siting. 2016. 两部门拟规定核电厂选址事项应征求公众意见 [Two Departments Draft Regulations Require Seeking the Public's Opinion on Siting for Nuclear Power Plants]. September 20, 2016. www.china5e.com/news/news-960847–1.html (accessed September 20, 2016)

Nuclear Facilities. 2016. "China to build more nuclear power facilities in next five years." *China Daily*. November 10, 2016. www.chinadaily.com.cn/business/2016–11/09/content_27322467.htm (accessed November 12, 2016).

"Officials penalized for accidents at unauthorized power station." 2006. http://news. xinhuanet.com/english/2006–08/17/content_4970889.htm (accessed November 6, 2016).

Oster, Shai. 2006. "Illegal Power Plants, Coal Mines In China Pose Challenge for Beijing." www.wsj.com/articles/SB116718773722060212 (accessed April 5, 2016).

Pipeline. 2016. 管输天然气定价将出新规 [New Pricing Regulations for Natural Gas Pipelines]. 中国能源报 [China Energy Report]. August 22, 2016. p. 2.

Power Equipment Review. 2017. 我国电力工业设备管理多项指标居世界领先地位 [Management of Equipment – China's Electric Power Sector leads the world in multiple dimensions]. April 1, 2017. www.china5e.com/news/news-983305–1 .html (accessed April 4, 2017)

Power Prices. 2014. "揭示上网电价矛盾真相 控诉上网电价政策违法" [Reveal the truth about contradictory on-grid power prices: true complaints of illegalities in power pricing policy]. http://bbs.bjx.com.cn/thread-1202785-1-1.html (accessed December 11, 2014).

Power Sales. 2017. 全名单 | 全国已成立6389家售电公司（截止2017-2-10）[List of enterprise names: 6389 power sales firms established as of 2-10-2017]. www .wxhaowen.com/article_b915ce59436a4fb79c295c0a88ea11b1.shtml (accessed June 29, 2017).

Power Sector Preview 2016. 中电联发布《2016年度全国电力供需形势分析预测报告》[China Electricity Council Issues Report estimating 2016 electricity supply and demand]. February 3, 2016. www.cec.org.cn/yaowenkuaidi/2016–02–03/ 148763.html (accessed March 13, 2016).

Price Competition 1. 2016. "全国电价大比拼系列1: 发电"自损指数" [National price competition series 1: power generation 'self-loss index']. http://shoudian.bjx.com. cn/news/20161123/791039.shtml (accessed June 1, 2017).

Price Competition 2. 2016. 全国电价大比拼系列2: 发电"上网卖个好价钱" [National price competition series 2: power generation 'online to sell at a good price']. http:// shoudian.bjx.com.cn/news/20161124/791369.shtml (accessed June 1, 2017).

Price Competition 4. 2016. 全国电价大比拼系列4: 电网盈利的法宝 [National price competition series 4: the magic of power grid profit]. http://shoudian.bjx.com.cn/ news/20161129/792404.shtml (accessed June 1, 2017).

Price Competition 5. 2016. 全国电价大比拼系列5: 哪旮电最贵？哪旮居民最幸福？ [National price competition series 5: Which grid charge is most expensive? Which residents are happiest?]. shoudian.bjx.com.cn/news/20161201/793150. shtml (accessed June 1, 2017).

Price Yearbook. Annual. 中国物价年鉴. [China Price Yearbook]. Beijing: Zhongguo wujia chubanshe.

Rawski, Thomas G. 2009. "Urban Air Quality in China: Historical and Comparative Perspectives." In Nazrul Islam ed., *Resurgent China: Issues for the Future*. Houndmills and New York: Palgrave-Macmillan, pp. 353–70.

2015. "China's Railways – another instance of large-scale excess costs?" Unpublished.

Samaras, Constantine, Jeffrey A. Drezner, Henry H. Willis, and Evan Bloom. 2011. *Characterizing the US Industrial Base for Coal-Powered Electricity*. Santa Monica: RAND Corporation.

Self-managed. 2018. 治理燃煤自备电厂不能搞"一刀切" [Do not adopt a 'one size fits all' approach to controlling self-managed coal-fired power plants]. Posted August 27, 2018. www.china5e.com/news/news-1037552–1.html (accessed August 27, 2018).

Shenzhen Grid Price. 2015. 深圳输配电价公布 成本测算中核减1/4资产 [Shenzhen Cost Estimates for Electricity Transmission and Distribution Remove one-fourth of Assets]. www.nandudu.com/article/14810 (accessed April 2, 2016).

Shenzhen Grid Reform. 2015. "一分钱后的博弈，算清电网糊涂帐从深圳开始" [Game on following a one cent reduction – Shenzhen begins to decipher muddled grid accounts]. www.wusuobuneng.com/archives/16489 (accessed April 2, 2016).

Shepherd, Christian and Lucy Hornby. 2016. "Beijing Wind Energy Law Tested." *Financial Times*, April 1, 2016. p. 3.

Sichuan. 2018. 四川：电力产能过剩下，大量水电仍在开工 [Despite excess power generation capacity, large-scale hydropower construction continues]. www.china5e.com/news/news-1020478–1.html (accessed March 11, 2018).

State Energy Administration. 2013–14. 2013–2014年度全国电力企业价格情况监管通报. [Supervisory report on electricity companies' price conditions during 2013–2014]. http://zfxxgk.nea.gov.cn/auto92/201509/t20150902_1959.htm (accessed December 21, 2015).

2015. 2015年度全国电力企业价格情况监管通报. [Supervisory report on electricity companies' price conditions during 2015]. www.cnenergy.org/dl/201611/t20161102_402875.html (accessed November 11, 2016).

2016a. 2016年度全国电力企业价格情况监管通报. [Supervisory report on electricity companies' price conditions during 2016]. http://m.in-en.com/21-0-2264652–1.html (accessed March 31, 2018).

2016b. "2015年全国6000千瓦及以上电厂发电设备平均利用小时情况." [2015 Average Operating Hours for Generation Equipment of 6000 kw and up]. www.cec.org.cn/yaowenkuaidi/2016-01-29/148607.html (accessed March 13, 2016).

State Grid. 2012. 国家电网公司年鉴 2012. [State Grid Corporation of China 2012 Yearbook]. Beijing: Zhongguo dianli chubanshe.

Tang Yaojia 唐要家. 2014. "电价管制刚性的政治经济学逻辑" [Political Economy Logic of Rigid Electricity Pricing] 中国地质大学学报（社会科学版）14.4 (July 2014). p. 3.

Thompson, P. 2001. "How Much did the Liberty Shipbuilders Learn." *Journal of Political Economy*. 109(1). pp. 103–37.

Thornton, R. A. and P. Thompson, "Learning from Experience and Learning from Others: An Exploration of Learning and Spillovers in Wartime Shipbuilding." *American Economic Review*. 91.5 (2001). pp. 1350–68.

US Bureau of Labor Statistics. 2011. May 2011 National Industry-Specific Occupational Employment and Wage Estimates: NAICS 221100 – Electric Power Generation, Transmission and Distribution.

2014. Occupational Employment Statistics, May 2014. www.bls.gov/oes/tables.htm (accessed February 10, 2018).

US EIA. 2012. *Electric Power Annual 2012.*

2014. *Electric Power Annual 2014.*

2015a. *Electric Power Annual 2015.*

2015b. US Energy Information Administration. "Electricity. Detailed State Data. 1990–2013 Existing Nameplate and Net Summer Capacity by Energy Source, Producer Type and State (EIA-860)." www.eia.gov/electricity/data/state/ (accessed April 18, 2016).

2018. Electric Power Monthly with Data for December 2017. February.

Monthly. *Monthly Energy Review.*

Wang Bingning 王冰凝. 2014. 电企盈利虚假繁荣 [Power Company Profits Show False Prosperity]. 华夏时报[Huaxia Times]. January 24, 2014. www.chinatimes .cc/article/40810.html (accessed March 1, 2014).

Wang Lu 王璐 and Yu Yao 于瑶. 2016. 产能过剩创纪录电企陷亏损 为抢市场仍大量投资 [Despite record excess capacity and company losses, power firms pursue big investment to capture the market]. 经济参考报 [Economic information news]. August 22, 2016. http://blog.china5e.com/jiangxiaojuzi/archives/10488 (accessed September 11, 2016).

Wang Peng 王鹏. 2017. 打破省间壁垒,政企合力加快推动区域电力市场 [Let government and enterprise join to break the barriers between provinces and accelerate the promotion of cross-regional electricity markets]. 中国能源报 [China Energy Report]. June 19, 2017. p. 4.

Wang Xuhui 王旭辉. 2018. 特高压统筹运营加速提效 [UHV Coordinates operations and improves efficiency]. 中国能源报 [China Energy Report]. April 16, 2018. p. 21.

Wang Zhixuan 王志轩. 2017. 推动能源利用方式的转变, 关键在电力 [Electricity is the key to advancing the transformation of energy use]. October 10, 2017. www .china5e.com/news/news-1005235–1.html (accessed October 11, 2017).

Williams, James H. and Fredrich Kahrl. 2008. "Electricity reform and sustainable development in China." *Environmental Research Letters*. 3(2008). 044009.

Working Capital. 2016. 发电企业密集发债 补充流动资金 [Power Generation Firms issue debt to replenish liquidity]. 中国能源报 [China Energy Report]. September 19, 2016. p. 10.

Xiao Qiang 肖蔷. 2016. 国家建立风电投资监测预警机制 [Government establishes monitoring and warning systems for wind power]. 中国能源报[China Energy Report]. July 25, 2016. p. 1.

Xie Guohui 谢国辉. 2016. 大规模风电并网成本上升不容忽视 [Do not ignore large-scale cost increases from integrating wind power into the grid]. 中国能源报 [China Energy Report]. March 7, 216. p. 22.

Xu, Yi-chong. 2002. *Powering China: Reforming the Electric Power Industry in China.* Aldershot, Hants.: Ashgate.

2004. *Electricity Reform in China, India and Russia: the World Bank Template and the Politics of Power.* Cheltenham and Northampton: Edward Elgar.

2016. *Sinews of Power: The Politics of the State Grid Corporation of China.* Oxford and New York: Oxford University Press.

Yao Haitang 姚海棠. 2016. "不断破解无人机"成长"的密码 [Continue to Crack the Code for Expanded Use of Drones]. 中国能源报 [China Energy Report]. April 18, 2016. p. 24.

Yao Jinnan. 姚金楠. 2016. "发改委：配电价改革试点初见成效"[NDRC: Preliminary View of Results from Pilot Reforms to Pricing of Electricity Transmission and Distribution]. 中国能源报 [China Energy Report]. April 4, 2016. p. 2.

Yearbook. Annual. 2007–16. 中国统计年鉴 [China Statistical Yearbook]. Beijing: Zhongguo tongji chubanshe.

Yu Chunping 余春平. 2015."正视煤电科学发展面临的挑战 [Recognize the Challenges Facing the Science of Coal-fired Electricity]. 中国能源报 [China Energy Report]. January 12, 2015. p. 15.

Yu Menglin 于孟林. 2012. 煤炭物流高成本有望缓解 [High Cost of Shipping Coal May Ease]. 中国能源报 [China Energy Report]. April 2, 2012. p. 17.

Yu Ning于宁. 2014. "电改十二年为何理不清输配电价？"[Why This Disarray in Electricity Transmission and Distribution Price after 12 Years of Reform?]. www.tgpcanada.org/news.aspx?vid=962 (accessed January 25, 2016).

Yuan Jiahai 袁家海. 2016. 中国燃煤发电项目经济性研究 [Economic analysis of China's coal-fired thermal power generation projects]. Beijing: Greenpeace.

Zhang Shuwei 张树伟. 2015. 能源管理"量价分离"亟需改变 [Separation of Quantity and Price in energy management requires reform]. 中国能源报 [China Energy Report]. January 5, 2015. p. 4.

2016. "十三五"如何改善弃风限电? [How can we deal with abandoned wind power under the 13th Five-Year Plan?] 中国能源报 [China Energy Report]. October 10, 2016. p. 1.

Zhang, Sufang, Yiqian Jiao, and Wenjun Chen. 2017. "Demand-side management (DSM) in the context of China's on-going power sector reform." *Energy Policy* 100, pp. 1–8.

Zhang Weirong 张维荣. 2014. 中国火电产业发展概论 [Introduction to the development of China's thermal power industry]. Beijing: China Electric Power Press.

Zhang, Weiying. 2009. "Is State Ownership Consistent with a Market Economy? The Chinese Experience." In Janos Kornai and Yingyi Qian eds., *Market and Socialism: in the light of the experiences of China and Vietnam.* Houndmills: Palgrave Macmillan. pp. 66–109.

Zhang Xudong. 张旭东. 2013. "电价"迷宫"：一地300多种销售电价"[Electricity Price Labyrinth: One Locality, 300+ Prices]. 第一财经日报 [First Economic Daily] May 14, 2013. http://finance.people.com.cn/n/2013/0514/c1004-21469980-2.html (accessed August 30, 2018).

Zhang Zirui 张子瑞. 2016a. 缺乏适宜国产机组掣肘海上风电 [Lack of suitable domestic equipment constrains offshore wind power]. 中国能源报 [China Energy Report]. March 7, 2016. p. 12.

2016b. "十三五"风电如何破茧重生 [How can wind power break out of the cocoon under the 13th Five Year Plan]. 中国能源报 [China Energy Report]. June 19, 2016. p. 18.

2018. 广东加码海上风电 [Guangdong steps up offshore wind farms]. 中国能源报 [China Energy Report]. April 16, 2018. p. 18.

Zhao, Changhong, Weirong Zhang, Yang Wang, Qilin Liu, Jingsheng Guo, Minpeng Xiong, and Jiahai Yuan. 2017. "The Economics of Coal Power Generation in China." *Energy Policy*. 105. pp. 1–9.

Zheng Xin. 2016. "Coal mines, utilities ink long-term price deal." *China Daily*. November 10, 2016. www.chinadaily.com.cn/business/2016–11/10/content_27329554.htm (accessed November 12, 2016).

Zhou, Yiyi and Sophie Lu. 2017. *China's Renewables Curtailment and Coal Assets Risk Map: research findings and map user guide*. N.p: Bloomberg New Energy Finance.

Zhu Xuehui朱学蕊. 2016. "内陆核电：静候发令 蓄势待跑" [Inland nuclear power: when the order is issued, be ready to run]. 中国能源报 [China Energy Report]. September 5, 2016. p. 18.

2017. 核电"消纳症"仍待解 [Nuclear power absorption issue still awaits resolution]. 中国能源报 [China Energy Report]. February 13, 2017. p. 12.

9

China's Development of Wind and Solar Power

Loren Brandt and Luhang Wang

INTRODUCTION

Since the early 2000s, two issues have heavily shaped policy making in China: first, the desire to maintain high rates of economic growth, and second, the environment.[*]

Concerned that China was soon to exhaust the returns to an earlier growth model based on low-cost labor, high rates of investment, and exports, a new focus emerged centered on accelerating innovation and the shift into higher value-added activities and sectors.[1] At the same time, growing public awareness of the escalating economic and social costs of environmental degradation helped to increase the weight on environmental outcomes in the policy choices of the Chinese government.[2]

Over the last two decades, an aggressive strategy has evolved to promote the development of new domestic industries and Chinese firms in them – that not only fosters upgrading, innovation, and economic growth, but also helps address environmental issues.[3] Rapid growth of China's solar and wind turbine sectors, especially during the last ten years, is a clear reflection of these efforts.

---

[*] We would like to thank Yijun Gai, Guenther Lomas, and Jialiang Wang for excellent research assistance on this project.

[1] A key document here is "The National Medium- and Long-Term Plan for the Development of Science and Technology (2006–2020)." The MLP called for using *zizhu chuangxin*, or "indigenous innovation," as a guiding principle to leapfrog China into a leadership role in science-based industry by the year 2020.

[2] Policy pronouncements during the recent 19th Party Congress suggest more weight on the environment.

[3] Two key documents are the Renewable Energy Law (2005) and Long-Term Development Plan for Renewable Energy in China (2006). The Energy Law introduced nationwide renewable energy targets, a feed-in tariff system for wind energy, an obligatory purchase and connection policy, and a fund for renewable energy development.

Overall, assessments of policy effectiveness in the renewable sector have been highly favorable (Lewis 2013), and as of the end of 2016, China's solar and wind turbine manufacturing sectors were the largest globally. The role of both forms of energy has also increased considerably in China's overall energy mix, and in 2016, the two were the source of slightly more than 5 percent of total electricity generated in China.

The rapid rise of China's renewable energy sector parallels impressive growth in China's manufacturing sectors, an expansion in which exports and a rapidly growing domestic market both figure prominently (Brandt and Thun 2010). Within the manufacturing sector however we observe considerable heterogeneity in how well individual sectors have performed in terms of productivity, profitability, and international competitiveness. In general, the sectors that have performed best are those that have been most open to competition – domestic as well as international – and relatively free from the visible hand of the state (Brandt 2016; Brandt et al. 2017a). The same may also be true in the case of solar and wind.

In this chapter, we examine the two sectors in turn, with an eye to linking critical differences in outcomes at the firm and industry level to government policy, technology choices, and the market environment in which Chinese firms compete. Table 9.1 provides a summary comparison of the two sectors in dimensions that figure prominently in our analysis including barriers to entry, technology choice, sources of market demand (domestic versus exports), the role of state-owned firms, etc. By most outcome measures – productivity growth, rates of learning, export penetration – solar has outperformed wind. The solar sector however has not been totally immune from the distorting effects of government policy, especially more recently as the domestic market has become more important for solar panel firms. China's renewable energy sector continues to be handicapped by the limited reform on the regulatory side of China's power sector. Our analysis of the experience of solar and wind suggests perhaps a much more cautionary tale for renewables than often told with important lessons moving forward for Chinese industry in terms of how best to promote firm and industry upgrading and international competitiveness, and for environmental policy.

CHINA'S SOLAR (PHOTOVOLTAIC) INDUSTRY
IN HISTORICAL CONTEXT

The origins of China's solar sector date back to the 1960s. Through the late 1990s the photovoltaic (PV) sector was dominated by SOEs, very small in

Table 9.1 *Comparisons of Solar and Wind*

	Solar	Wind Turbines
Barriers to Entry	Relatively low, but significant capital investments required for silicon and cell production.	Overall, relatively low, with existing domestic capabilities in key components, e.g. gearboxes and generators. Weak domestic capabilities in design and control systems overcome through technology transfer.
Form of Technology Transfer	Returning Chinese with experience in sector; much of technology embodied in equipment.	Licensing of designs from leading international firms.
Major Market	Overseas, but more recently, increase in domestic sales. Highly standardized product for overseas market. Growth in the domestic market has been largely to solar farms developed by state-owned firms, but residential and commercial use expanding.	Domestic to wind farm developers, most of whom are now state-owned.
Ownership	Largely private, especially further down the value added chain. Role of foreign invested enterprises in the sector has been modest from the beginning. With designation as a strategic sector, State-owned enterprises (SOEs) moving in.	Largely SOEs, but several prominent private firms (Mingyang and Yuanjing, which are currently ranked 3rd and 4th).
Industry Concentration	Medium, but higher upstream in silicon.	High.
Government Support	Local government support. Central government support in the form of feed-in tariffs (FIT) and subsidies. Research and development (R&D) support for 2nd and 3rd generation technologies. Export financing.	Central government support for firms in the sector. FITs. Government-imposed barriers on FIEs and local content requirements. R&D support for offshore and larger onshore turbines.

size, served only the domestic market, and it was beset with a long list of problems. (See, for example, Energy Research Institute 2000; Song et al. 2015; and Zhang and White 2016.)[4] Beginning in the late 1990s and early 2000s, however, barriers to entry and other restrictions on private firms began to recede, much as was occurring in other sectors of the economy.[5] New private solar firms were established by returning Chinese with advanced degrees and deep experience and connections in the industry (Gallagher 2014), as well as by local entrepreneurs who wanted to take advantage of emerging opportunities. Notable examples include: Trina (1997), Yingli (1998), and Suntech (2001), and a few years later in a second wave of solar start-ups, JA Solar (2005), LDK (2005), and Jinko (2006).[6]

With new entry and the expansion of existing firms, growth in China's solar sector accelerated. Listings on the New York Stock Exchange (NYSE) and Nasdaq by leading domestic firms helped to provide the capital for unprecedented rates of expansion.[7] From producing less than 100 MW in 2000, a decade of nearly triple-digit annual growth catapulted domestic panel production in 2010 to 10.8 GW, and a global market share for Chinese producers to more than half. Five years later, China's production exceeded 40 GW, and the local industry commanded a global market share of nearly two-thirds (see Figure 9.1). Quantitatively, the rapid growth in solar production in China explains much of the expansion of the global solar sector.[8]

Several features of solar technology and the market for panels and modules are critical to explaining China's solar success including: a relatively mature first generation solar technology; the prominent role of external demand in advanced economies; and the ability of firms to

---

[4] The report by the Energy Research Institute under the National Development and Reform Commission (NDRC) put the total number of firms in the late 1990s at thirty-three, seventeen of which were involved in PV module manufacturing, and sixteen of which were component suppliers. With the exception of a US–China joint venture (JV), all of these firms were SOEs. Technical bottlenecks resulted in production levels well below capacity. Panels, on the other hand, suffered from low levels of efficiency, and problems of degradation.

[5] Included here are rights to export directly (rather than through state-owned trading companies), to retain and use foreign exchange earnings from exporting, and to access finance, especially through international IPOs. For an excellent discussion on restrictions facing private firms in these often newly emerging sectors, see Huang (2003).

[6] For a brief summary on these entrepreneurs and firms, see Zhang and White (2016), Table 1.

[7] Leading firms listed on the New York stock market include JA (2007), Canadian Solar (2006), Yingli (2007), Trina (2010), CSUN (2007), and Suntech (2005).

[8] Globally, the annual rate of growth in the industry rose from 16% between 1990 and 1998, to 85% between 1998 and 2005, and 45% from 2005 to 2015.

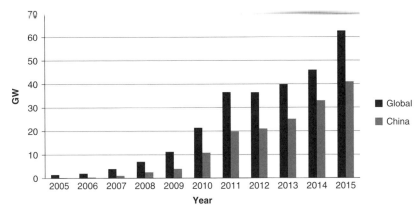

Figure 9.1 Solar Panel Production
Source: China Renewable Energy Industry Development Report, miscellaneous years.

organize exports through the processing trade. Together, these factors helped to lower the barriers to entry for Chinese firms, facilitated rapid localization in the supply chain, and enforced high quality thresholds on producers. We examine each of these in turn.

SOLAR TECHNOLOGY AND VALUE CHAIN

A PV is a device that transforms light energy into electric energy. Certain features of solar technology, including its value chain, are important to explaining how the industry evolved in China. We define a value chain here to be the set of value-adding activities that need to be undertaken for a product to be made or a service provided. Currently, solar panel manufacturers have access to three generations of technologies that differ in terms of their production processes, value chains, and costs. For first generation solar technology – the technology that today remains most widely in use – manufacturing entails four highly discrete activities that can be carried out independently: the production of silicon, the manufacture of ingots and cutting of wafers, the production of cells, and finally the assembly of modules.[9] In 2015, mono- and multi-silicon cell versions of

---

[9] In addition to the panels, other components of the value chain for solar power include a solar inverter to convert the electric current from DC to AC, and mounting, cabling and other electrical accessories to set up a working system. Solar tracking systems and an integrated battery solutions are also part of some systems. By 2016, and reflecting the exponential fall in solar panel prices, panels represented less than half of the total cost of the system.

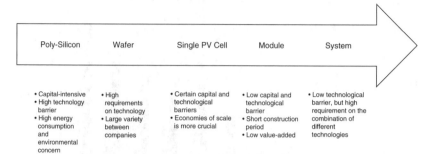

Figure 9.2 The Value Chain for Solar

first generation technologies represented 95 percent of all solar panels manufactured globally in terms of gigawatt hours (GWh).

Figure 9.2 lays out important features of each stage of the first-generation technology, including capital and technology requirements, and barriers to entry. Moving downstream in the value chain from silicon to panels for first-generation silicon wafer-based technology, the barriers to entry fall appreciably in terms of capital requirements and technical knowhow, with manufacturing becoming much more labor intensive. Although technical and engineering knowledge of downstream manufacturing processes was required, much of the technology was embodied in the equipment itself (de la Tour et al. 2010; and Interviews, 2014 and 2016). Entry was further facilitated by the ability to import turnkey equipment for key stages of the value chain from leading international suppliers (Zhi et al. 2014). In line with their comparative advantage in labor-intensive assembly, Chinese firms initially concentrated in the downstream stages, e.g. panels and modules, sourcing key intermediate components and materials globally, but subsequently entered and came to occupy prominent positions in all segments of the value chain, including the production of silicon. Technological complementarities throughout the value chain with other sectors in China facilitated this localization. In short, features of the technology enabled entrants to focus initially on the less demanding, more downstream segments, and over time ultimately come to dominate the sector.

To help put the solar industry in perspective, barriers to entry for panel manufacturers using first-generation technologies in the sector are slightly higher than in LED lighting but much lower than in semiconductors, two industries that are also tied to silicon.[10] On the other hand, the value chain

---

[10] The purity of the silicon required for wafers and solar cells is also lower than in semiconductors (Interviews).

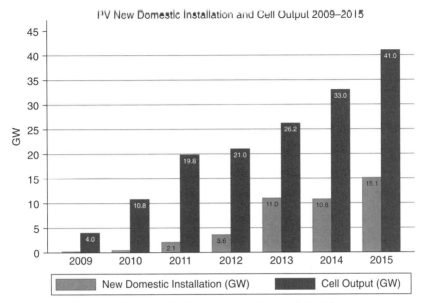

Figure 9.3 Domestic Production versus Domestic Installation
Source: China Renewable Energy Industry Development Report, select years.

for second-generation thin film solar cells is much shorter but also more demanding in terms of manufacturing knowhow. Modules are manufactured in a single step from raw silicon and other compounds by depositing the PV material and other chemicals on glass or plastic.[11]

THE ROLE OF EXTERNAL DEMAND AND QUALITY THRESHOLDS

Rapid growth in overseas demand has been a key driver of growth in China's solar industry. Figure 9.3 provides information on the breakdown between total cell production in China and domestic installation of solar panels (both measured in terms of GW) over the period between 2005 and 2015. The difference between the two represents Chinese exports. Even as late as 2011 more than 90 percent of solar panel sales were overseas, with less than 10 percent going to the domestic economy. In value terms, the percentage was even higher. Table 9.2 breaks down solar exports by

[11] Second-generation technologies have lower efficiency than first-generation, but they are also cheaper to produce, making them serious competitors to first generation technologies. In contrast, third-generation technology offers the promise of efficiencies that are double that of first-generation technologies.

Table 9.2 *Solar Panel Destination Countries for Major Chinese Exporters*

	2006		2008		2010		2012		2014	
	Country	Share	Country	Share	Country	Share	Country	Share	Country	Share
	Germany	37.7	Spain	37.5	Germany	31.2	Netherlands	34.7	Japan	40.7
	Spain	22.8	Germany	26.4	Italy	20.0	United States	13.2	United States	16.2
	Japan	8.7	Italy	10.0	Netherlands	17.5	Germany	9.2	Netherlands	9.3
	Belgium	7.3	Netherlands	6.0	United States	7.3	Belgium	8.7	Britain	6.7
	United States	6.8	Belgium	4.3	Belgium	3.4	Japan	8.5	India	3.2
% Top Three		69.1		73.9		68.7		57.1		66.2
% Top Five		83.3		84.2		79.4		74.3		76.2
% H Income		99.3		99.7		99.2		96.0		90.4
% Low Income		0.7		0.3		0.8		4.0		9.6

Source: Computed by authors using China Customs trade transaction data.

destination countries, highlighting the prominent role of Europe and the United States. Central to the rapid expansion in both cases were high FITs and government support for the renewable sector.[12] In Europe, the primary customers were utility companies, and demand was for a highly standard product, 72-inch panels. This put a priority on cost (as opposed to product) innovation, which fit in well with the capabilities of China's emerging manufacturing system, notably, mass production and localization (Nahm and Steinfeld 2014).

Firms wanting to export to these destinations faced high quality standards – measured here in terms of solar cell efficiency and panel life – both of which are important determinants of the returns to investment in solar energy. Twenty-five-year warranties on panels, for example, have been the norm in the industry since the late 1990s.[13] For overseas solar projects, strict quality audits of Chinese panel manufacturers by third-party companies have been essential to maintaining high product standards. Audits extend not only to the panels, but entail regular monitoring and auditing of the entire value chain—often on a 24/7 basis – to ensure that no shortcuts are taken in the manufacturing process (Interviews, 2014, 2016. See also, *PV Modular Reliability Scorecard Report* 2016). Only certified suppliers can be used on solar projects. These requirements consistently imposed a high "quality threshold" on Chinese solar manufacturers, and their supply chain. Local sourcing in China could only increase as long as quality levels could be maintained, suggesting at least in this setting no room for a "race to the bottom" (Steinfeld 2004).

More recently, as a result of anti-dumping and countervailing duties imposed on Chinese sales to the United States and Europe, exports to both of these destinations fell off. This setback for the industry has been offset by Chinese central government policies to expand the role of solar power in China's energy mix, and by additional support for export expansion to lower income countries.[14] By 2015, domestic solar panel sales constituted over 30 percent of total domestic production. Exports to low-income countries, on the one hand, rose from less than one percent in 2006 to almost 10 percent by 2014 (see Table 9.2). With the shift in the market, quality issues have surfaced, an issue to which we return below.

---

[12] For a discussion of policy support for solar and renewable energy in Germany, see Hoopman et al. (2015).

[13] In the late 1990s, Siemens Solar increased their warranty from ten to twenty-five years. Warranties of this sort allow for some product degradation, typically on the order of 1% per annum.

[14] For a review of these policies and those that proceeded it, see Zhi et al. (2014).

Processing versus Ordinary Trade

There are two primary forms of trade in China, processing and ordinary. Processing trade is officially defined as "business activities in which the operating enterprise imports all or part of the raw or ancillary materials, spare parts, components, and packaging materials, and re-exports finished products after processing or assembling these materials/parts" (Law of the People's Republic of China 2004).[15] The primary advantage for firms of organizing export production through the processing trade is that firms do not have to pay duties on imported materials used in the manufacturing process.[16] These same firms face restrictions in selling their products on the domestic market however, and legally must set up segregated production lines (facilities) if they desire to do so. This requirement helps to prevent the "leakage" of tariff-free imports into the domestic economy. For firms exporting through ordinary trade, it is the reverse: they must pay tariffs on imported raw materials and inter-mediates, but can sell freely to the domestic market. In the context of high domestic tariffs on imported goods to protect local manufacturers, the rationale for the processing regime was to allow firms to better leverage China's "cheap" labor in labor-intensive assembly for exports using imported intermediates. Generally speaking, this was much easier for industries with technologies that allowed manufacturing processes to be easily disassembled, or were modular in nature. Up through 2007, the processing trade was upwards of 60 percent of the total value of China's foreign trade, but has declined more recently (Lemoine and Unal 2017).

Drawing on China's trade transaction data, Table 9.3 provides detailed information on solar exports between 2000 and 2014, with a focus on the roles of processing and ordinary exports. Our analysis is slightly handicapped by data limitations. Prior to 2009, solar cells and panels were not a separate line item in the Harmonized Commodity Code and Classification System (HS), and were grouped with LED lighting in a single six-digit code. In 2009 cells and panels dominate the category however, and were two times larger in value terms than those for LED lighting. Data reported at the six-digit level (second column) suggest that for solar the role of the processing trade was in the vicinity of 90 percent in 2000, and 75 percent by 2005. In 2009, the first year for which we can calculate the role of the processing trade separately for

---

[15] www.asianlii.org/cn/legis/cen/laws/motcotprocotsoptg947/ (Article 3, accessed June 20, 2016).

[16] On the factors underlying the organization of China's trade, see Manova and Yu (2016); and Brandt and Morrow (2017).

Table 9.3 *China's Solar Exports, 2000–2014*

	HS Code 85414000		HS Code 85414020, Solar Cells			
Year	Total Value	Share Processing Exports	Total Value	Total Quantity	Share Processing Exports	Unit Price
	Billion $US	%	Billion $US	Million	%	$US
2000	0.15	90.2				
2001	0.14	86.6				
2002	0.20	82.2				
2003	0.30	80.1				
2004	0.64	81.7				
2005	1.26	75.9				
2006	2.46	73.1				
2007	5.25	73.9				
2008	11.75	55.9				
2009	10.72	64.2	7.11	169.3	58.7	42.02
2010	25.18	59.7	20.19	242.6	56.6	83.23
2011	27.95	NA	22.78	339.1	NA	67.18
2012	24.70	NA	18.70	365.4	NA	51.17
2013	21.14	NA	14.35	587.9	NA	24.40
2014	19.39	51.8	12.32	690.8	49.2	17.83

Note: Incomplete data on trade regime prevent the estimate of the role of processing in 2011, 2012, and 2013.
Source: Computed by authors using China Customs trade transaction data.

solar, it is 60 percent, and by 2014, it falls below one-half. Table 9.4 provides comparable estimates for a group of leading solar panel exporters, including Trina, Yingli, and JA Solar.[17] For these firms, the role of processing in their total exports is even higher – nearer to 70 percent – but also shows a marked decline over time in line with our estimates for the entire sector.

Deepening in the Supply Chain – Local Sourcing of Intermediates and Equipment

The high-quality threshold in overseas markets combined with limited sourcing opportunities in the domestic market initially necessitated the use of imported intermediates. In Table 9.4, we provide estimates for leading panel exporters on the role of imported intermediates, reported in two ways: first, as a percentage of their solar exports, and second, as a share of total manufactured intermediates (imports plus those domestically sourced) used in production.[18,19] In 2006, imported intermediates were one-half of total exports, and upwards of 90 percent of the estimated total intermediates used by these firms.

Severe downward pressure on solar prices because of competitive pressures from new firm entry and industry expansion encouraged Chinese solar firms to look for ways to lower costs without compromising quality levels. Development of local suppliers and import substitution were important channels, as they had been in other industries such as autos and heavy construction (Brandt and Thun 2010). Rapid expansion in demand also provided incentives for Chinese firms and subsidiaries of multinationals to enter throughout the supply chain. These forces contributed to a deepening

[17] Beginning in 2009, we identify the top twenty solar panel exporters in each year. We then track the exports of these firms for earlier years. Since nearly all of these firms' exports after 2009 were for panels, we are reasonably confident that our estimates for earlier years are also largely for cells and panels.

[18] Prior to 2009, exports also included LED lighting. By focusing on leading exporters between 2009 and 2014 for whom solar exports were 99% of their total exports, we are reasonably assured that imported intermediates for earlier years were also used in the manufacture of solar panels.

[19] We do not have information on the total expenditure on intermediate goods by these firms. We obtain an estimate using a value-added share for total output for the sector of 30%, and assume that 80% (20%) of intermediates came from the manufacturing (service) sector. A lower value-added share implies a larger expenditure on total intermediates, and thus a smaller role for imported intermediates. Because we do not have information on domestic sales at the firm level, we use total exports for output. The rise in the role of the domestic market after 2010 implies an even larger reduction in the share of imported intermediates.

Table 9.4 *Panel Exports and Imports of Intermediates by China's Leading Exporters*

Year	Number of Exporting Firms	Total Value of Exports	% of Total Exports	Share of Processing Exports	Total Value of Imported Intermediates	Silicon	Cells	Key Chemicals	Imported Intermediates as % of Total Exports	Imported Intermediates as % of Total Intermediates Used
		Billion $US	%	%	Billion $US	%	%	%	%	%
2006	13	0.82	33	89.5	0.41	51	27	6	50.2	89.7
2007	16	2.28	43	84.4	0.85	39	33	6	37.2	66.5
2008	22	5.08	43	61.0	1.54	44	26	9	30.3	54.2
2009	26	4.77	67	69.6	1.49	26	42	18	31.1	55.6
2010	32	12.64	63	75.6	3.29	25	45	22	26.0	46.5
2011	31	14.20	62	NA	3.58	37	27	26	25.2	45.1
2012	35	8.15	64	NA	1.77	28	46	23	21.7	38.8
2013	35	6.86	68	NA	1.93	14	65	18	28.1	50.2
2014	36	8.39	68	62.8	2.05	17	68	14	24.4	43.7

Source: Computed by authors using China Customs trade transaction data.
Note: Incomplete data on trade regime prevent the estimate of the role of processing in 2011, 2012, and 2013.

in capabilities throughout the domestic supply chain that enabled firms to source locally key intermediates inputs such as silicon, wafers, and glass.[20] Estimates reported in Table 9.4 show that the role of imported intermediates declined sharply over the next six years, and in 2012 was below 40 percent. Sourcing requirements imposed on exports to the United States as part of anti-dumping rulings slightly reversed this trend after 2012.

Initially, silicon used to make wafers was the most important imported intermediate – a half or so of the total – followed by cells and then a variety of chemical products and materials used in the manufacturing process. New Chinese firms such as LDK and GLC entered the more demanding and capital-intensive upstream stages of the value chain, usually with government financial support, and as they did, demand for imports of silicon and wafers softened.[21] By 2015, Chinese silicon firms selling exclusively into the domestic market were the source of a third of global silicon production, and were supplying in upwards of half of the silicon used in China.[22]

Localization also occurred through vertical integration. New manufacturers of silicon and wafers moved downstream while early entrants that initially focused only on cells and panels extended their operations upstream. A major motivation was the desire to eliminate supply uncertainty and achieve cost reductions (Zhang and Gallagher 2016). Significant differences in vertical integration strategies emerged among major domestic players, some of which are captured by Figure 9.4.

Localization was not limited to intermediates. Equally important were local capabilities in the manufacture of the capital goods (machinery and equipment) used throughout the value chain. Table 9.5 provides information from the vantage point of 2014 on the number of equipment suppliers by stage of the value chain, including those with turnkey solutions, and of these firms, the number that are "domestic" (Chinese-owned). In cells and panels, for example, Chinese equipment suppliers were providing turnkey solutions by the late 2000s, and in 2014, there were three and twenty-one firms with these capabilities in cells and crystalline panels, respectively.[23] Chinese firms were not offering turnkey solutions in wafers and silicon

---

[20] A leading panel glass manufacturer in Zhejiang, for example, had formerly been involved in the manufacturing of residential and commercial windows.

[21] Capital costs for a thousand-ton poly-silicon plant are estimated to be in the vicinity of $US 100 million.

[22] The imposition of tariffs by China on silicon imports in retaliation for the anti-dumping duties also shifted local demand toward domestic silicon manufacturers, thereby increasing their domestic market share.

[23] In addition, there were five Chinese firms that had developed turnkey solutions for the manufacture of thin film panels, the second-generation technology.

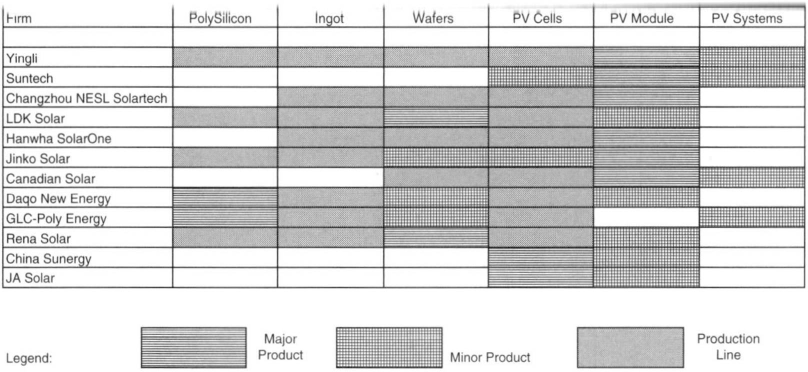

Firm	PolySilicon	Ingot	Wafers	PV Cells	PV Module	PV Systems
Yingli						
Suntech						
Changzhou NESL Solartech						
LDK Solar						
Hanwha SolarOne						
Jinko Solar						
Canadian Solar						
Daqo New Energy						
GLC-Poly Energy						
Rena Solar						
China Sunergy						
JA Solar						

Legend: Major Product — Minor Product — Production Line

Figure 9.4 Vertical Integration of Leading Photovoltaic Manufacturers in the Solar Value Chain

Source: Junfeng Li, Presentation at the Photon Poly Silicon conference, Berlin, April 12, 2011, cited in National Survey Report of PV Power in China, 2011, p.16

manufacturing, but they were capable of producing some of the key equipment required, including that for crystalline ingot growing; cutting, polishing and grinding; and testing of wafers.[24] Estimates suggest that the costs of locally sourced equipment and machinery were on the order of 30 percent of that for imports, but enjoyed 90 percent of the efficiency.[25] The ability to source domestically also put downward pressure on import prices. In the context of an industry in which capital's share of costs was more than half, reductions in the price of machinery and equipment represent a major component of the reduction in per unit production costs. By helping to lower initial investment costs, falling equipment prices also encouraged new entry into the sector, as well as expansion by existing firms.[26]

INVESTMENT IN RESEARCH AND DEVELOPMENT AND INCREMENTAL PRODUCT UPGRADING

Increases in production scale and localization in the sector contributed significantly to sharply falling costs. Both played to the strengths of China's

[24] The same was true before the late 2000s for key pieces of equipment used in the manufacture of cell and panels.

[25] An important reason for the lower efficiency is tooling stability, which in this context refers to the ability of the production line to produce consistently high-quality products.

[26] New entrants were also an important early source of demand for local equipment manufacturers, a dynamic that is frequently ignored.

Table 9.5 *Summary of Solar Production Equipment Manufacturers, 2014*

Ingot/Block	Number of Suppliers		Wafer	Number of Suppliers		Cell	Number of Suppliers		Crystalline Panel	Number of Suppliers	
	Total	Chinese		Total	Chinese		Total	Chinese		Total	Chinese
Turn-Key System	1	0	**Turn-Key System**	11	0	**Turn-Key System**	20	2	**Turn-Key System**	63	21
Installation Year							2008			2006	
Equipment			**Equipment**			**Equipment**			**Equipment**		
Crystalline Ingot Growing	58	38	Cutting	60	26	Etching	84	32	Cleaning	52	20
Cutting and Grinding	35	19	Cleaning	87	68	Diffusion Furnace	62	23	Tabbing and Stringing	50	50
Inspection & Testing	28	9	Polishing and Grinding	18	5	Screen Printing	96	23	Laminating	100	56
			Inspection & Testing	100	21	Coating	50	12	Cutting and Scribing	68	32
						Other Furnace	62	29	Framing	79	55
						Inspection & Testing	100	34	Inspection & Testing	100	41

Source: www.enfsolar.com/directory/equipment.

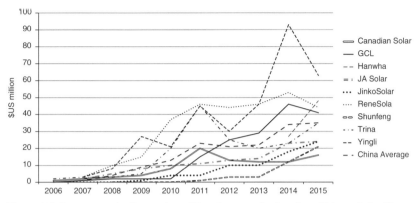

Figure 9.5 Investment in Research and Development by Leading Chinese Solar Firms
Source: Ball et al. (2017, p. 105). The original numbers were taken from Bloomberg.

manufacturing sector (Naim and Steinfeld 2014). Over time, we also observe rising investments by leading firms in R&D and product upgrading. Figure 9.5 shows R&D spending reported in millions of $US by leading Chinese firms for the period between 2006 and 2015. In 2006 R&D was less than one $US million per firm, or 0.5 percent of sales. By 2015, each of these firms was spending on average $US 35 million (235 million RMB), or slightly less than 2 percent of their sales revenues, however there were significant differences among firms.[27] Much of the investment in R&D appears to have been in the context of first-generation solar technologies, and in the form of incremental improvements in the efficiency of solar cells over time.

Figure 9.6 shows the evolution of "maximum laboratory efficiency" for solar cells by technology generation. Solar cell efficiency here refers to the portion of energy in the form of sunlight that can be converted via photovoltaics into electricity.[28] In addition to the mono- and multi-crystalline silicon first-generation cells, Figure 9.6 also includes second-generation thin film such as copper indium gallium selenide (CIGS) and cadmium telluride (CdTe), multi-junction concentrated PV, and organic and perovskite third-generation technologies, which have not been commercialized. For first-generation solar cells, labeled mono- and multi-crystalline

[27] There is debate over how much of this R&D was financed out of these firms' resources or by government subsidies and grants. Differences in the items included in R&D spending also make comparison with other countries difficult.

[28] Improvements in cell efficiency are also reflected in the watts of a panel, and a reduction in the surface area of the panels needed to generate the desired level of electricity.

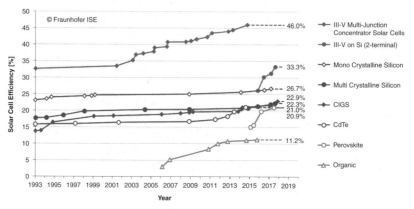

Figure 9.6 Laboratory Solar Cell Efficiency
Source: Fraunhofer (2018, p. 27).

silicon in the figure, maximum lab cell efficiencies in 2015 were 26 and 21 percent, respectively, nearly identical to their level twenty years earlier.

Incremental innovations in manufacturing processes have helped to raise the efficiency of manufactured panels to levels achieved in the lab. Recent innovations in the context of first-generation solar technologies include the use of "light-reflective" ribbons as well as the introduction of the Passive Emitted Real Cell (PERC) technology. First developed in the 1980s, this technology adds an extra layer to the rear side of the solar cell, which boosts cell efficiency.[29] Interviews with firms and industry analysts in China suggest that these improvements are well known, and that the current process of technological improvement is "very transparent." Much of the expenditure on R&D by Chinese solar firms has been in these areas (Wu and Matthews 2012), and more recently possibly at odds with the priorities of the Chinese government for solar.[30]

Figure 9.7 shows cell efficiency in 2017 by type of solar cell and manufacturer. For first generation, silicon-based technologies, the range is

[29] For a description of this technology, see www.solarpowerworldonline.com/2016/07/what-is-perc-why-should-you-care/ (accessed July 27, 2016).
[30] The priority for the government has been on "emerging" technologies in contrast to firms who are more interested in technologies with immediate commercial use. A recent examination of lapse rates of Chinese patents suggests much higher rates in the case of these emerging technologies (Sun 2016). As the study suggests, this may reflect a preference on the part of firms for "near-term" technologies rather than emerging ones. It may also reflect differences between firms and government in their estimates of the returns to the "emerging" technologies that the government is supporting.

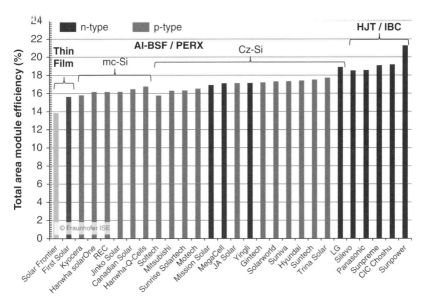

Figure 9.7 Manufacturer Efficiency by Solar Cell Type
Source: Fraunhofer (2018, p. 28).

between 16 percent and 20 percent.[31] Chinese firms are in the middle of the pack, with efficiency levels one to two percentage points lower than international leaders. A related measure of efficiency of the panels is in terms of wattage. Five years ago, 72-inch panels were at 280 watts. Today Hanwha-Solar One, a leading Korean firm, is at 340–5, with leading Chinese firms slightly behind at 310–15. Over this period, Chinese firms have narrowed the gap at the rate of 5 watts per year.

Learning by Doing and Productivity Growth

Underlying the ability of Chinese firms to capture a rising share of the rapidly expanding global market were improvements at the firm and industry level, which helped to lower costs. Over time, we expect production costs to fall with industry expansion through *learning by doing*, a phenomenon that has been well documented for other industries (Levitt et al. 2013). Several channels of cost reduction are important in this context:

---

[31] These technologies include both the czochralski-silicon (Cz-Si) and multi-crystalline (Mc-Si) varieties.

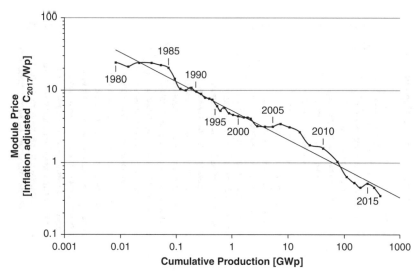

Figure 9.8 Solar Module Price as a Function of Cumulative Production
Source: Fraunhofer (2018, p. 43).

first, improvements made by upstream suppliers that result in lower input costs; second, modifications in the production process for the end product; and third, product improvements, for example, in cell efficiency, that effectively reduce costs to the end-user. These channels should not be viewed as mutually exclusive and often occur simultaneously (Rubin et al. 2015). The relationship between cumulative production and costs should also not be viewed as causal.

Module prices per watt of electricity provide a comprehensive measure of cost reductions coming through these channels.[32] Figure 9.8 shows the behavior of module prices per watt of electricity between 1980 and 2015 as a function of cumulative output in the industry. Estimates suggest that each doubling of global panel output, much of it because of increases in output in China, resulted in a 23 percent reduction in solar panel prices. Estimates of Chen et al. (2014) using real cost data for Chinese firms for silicon panels show similar rates of learning. Rapidly falling solar prices allowed for a reduction in FITs and thus a reduction in implicit subsidies for solar energy, as solar became increasingly competitive with other energy sources.

---

[32] Prices may also fall because of reductions in market power, which are reflected in profitability of firms in the industry, a point to which we return below.

Table 9.6 *Breakdown in Module Costs, $ per W*

	Total Costs			Contribution to Cost Reduction			Reasons for Reduction
	2006	2011	2017	2006–11 %	2011–17 %	2006–17 %	
Total	4.25	0.90	0.36	100.0	100.0	100.0	
Module	1.05	0.23	0.12	24.5	20.4	23.9	Lower capital costs; redesign of modules; improved efficiency
Cell	1.3	0.18	0.08	33.4	18.5	31.4	Reduced material costs; improved cell efficiency
Ingot/ Wafer	1.12	0.16	0.09	28.7	13.0	26.5	Use of thinner wafers and reduced material costs.
Silicon	0.78	0.32	0.07	13.7	46.3	18.3	Localization of Production

Sources:
For 2006: Zhang and Gallagher (2016).
For 2011: www.greentechmedia.com/articles/read/top-chinese-manufacturers-will-produce-solar-panels-for-42-cents-a-wat.
For 2017: www.greentechmedia.com/articles/read/solar-cost-reduction-drivers-in-2017.

For the period between 2006 and 2017, Table 9.6 breaks down the cost reductions by stage in the production chain for "best in class" vertically integrated solar module manufacturers in China. It also identifies major sources of the cost reductions. Over this eleven-year period, costs of solar modules per watt of capacity fell from $US 4.25 to $US 0.36. Significant cost reductions are observed in every stage of the value chain, with the largest in absolute terms coming in cells, followed by those in the costs of ingots and wafers.

Profits were also affected. Estimates of profit rates (profits over sales) compiled by Zhang and Gallagher (2016) are noteworthy in two respects. First, in manufacturing, profit rates fell throughout the production chain, but most sharply upstream, i.e. silicon and wafers, where barriers to entry, e.g. knowhow and capital and firm mark-ups were initially much higher. For a fully integrated manufacturer, profit rates fell from 46 percent in 2006 to only 6.7 percent in 2012. Second, as solar modules became more of a commodity, profits shifted downstream into deployment, prompting firms such as Yingli and Canadian Solar to expand their business model to

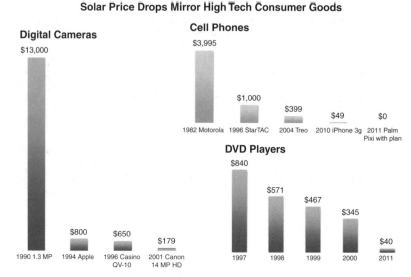

Figure 9.9 Price Drop in High Tech Consumer Goods

include renewable energy project development (Zhang and Gallagher 2016, Table 5).

In key respects, the rapid expansion observed in the solar sector has parallels with related industries in the electronics sector in which innovation, automation of production processes and scale are important. Figure 9.9 shows the long-run trends in prices for other leading electronic products including digital cameras, DVD machines, and cell phones, all of which have been primarily manufactured in China. In key respects, the rate of decline in prices in these products, and thus the rate of learning, has been very similar.

An important source of the cost reductions in the solar sector was productivity improvements in the sector. Data from China's National Bureau of Statistics (NBS) annual firm level survey for industry for the period between 1998 and 2013 allow for estimates of total factor productivity (TFP) growth at the four-digit industry level. Productivity is defined here as output per unit "bundle" of inputs, where inputs include labor, capital, e.g. equipment and machinery, and intermediate goods. Full details regarding the estimation are spelled out in Brandt et al. (2017b) and here we only highlight a few things. First, production function parameters estimated separately for each sector are used to obtain estimates of firm-level productivity in each sector. Second, firm-level productivity in each year is "aggregated" up to the industry level using as weights each firm's share of total output in that year. Finally, productivity growth at the industry level is obtained from the difference in productivity between any pair of years and converted to annual rates.

There are several limitations in our calculations: first, the sectors in China's industrial classification system do not map exactly into solar (and wind power). Solar firms fall into primarily two "sectors" and wind turbine firms are a subset of manufacturers of electricity generating equipment. Second, up through 2010, only firms with annual sales larger than 5 million RMB per year were included in the survey; after 2010, the minimum size threshold increased to 20 million RMB. Firms below these thresholds represent relatively small and declining percentages of total industry sales, and thus our estimates capture productivity growth in most of the industry. We address these issues by using information on each firm's main product to better identify firms in the solar and wind sector. In solar, we separately identify firms producing silicon, and cells and panels.

Over the period between 1998 and 2013, real output, i.e. nominal output adjusted for price changes, in the solar sector for the firms in the sample grew at an annual rate upwards of 40 percent. Productivity gains were experienced over the entire period by firms in both the production of silicon-related products and cells and modules. A weighted average for the two sectors implies annual productivity growth of slightly less than one percent for the full period. These estimates conceal an important reversal in productivity growth for the period after 2008, during which productivity growth was actually negative. In the next section, we discuss some of the factors underlying this sharp decline. For the period between 1998 and 2008, productivity growth in the solar sector averaged a highly respectable 3 percent per annum, and suggests a contribution of productivity growth to learning curve cost reductions on the order of a quarter to a third.

The growth in productivity can be decomposed into several components including: improvements by incumbent firms; the entry of new more productive firms; the reallocation of resources to more productive firms; and the exit of less efficient firms (see Table 9.7). In general, much of the growth in productivity over the period between 1998 and 2013 in the solar sector occurred through the entry of new firms, followed by improvements in productivity of incumbent firms already established in 1998. For the period after 2008, a decline in the productivity of existing firms, as well as entry of new firms at levels of productivity below incumbents is the source of most of the sharply falling productivity. This is reinforced by the reallocation of resources to less efficient firms in the sector. The sole source of productivity gains is the exit of less efficient firms.

Table 9.7 *Productivity Growth and Decomposition*

| | | | Sources of Productivity Change (% of Total) | | | |
Sector	Period	Annual Productivity Growth	Incumbents	Between	Entry	Exit
Wind-Generation Equipment	2003–2008	0.39%	375%	−340%	−136%	0%
	2008–2013	−4.54%	6%	−20%	−84%	−2%
Solar, Total	1998–2013	1.3%	8.1%	−8.3%	99.5%	0.8%
Silicon-related		1.7%	6.8%	−4.6%	99.6%	−1.8%
Cells, Panels, and Modules		0.9%	11.4%	−18.4%	99.3%	7.7%
Solar, Total	1998–2008	3.00%	13%	−12%	97%	1%
Silicon-related		3.74%	12%	−11%	96%	3%
Cells, Panels, and Modules		1.71%	18%	−12%	100%	−5%
Solar, Total	2008–2013	−1.6%	−53.7%	−7.7%	−66.3%	27.7%
Silicon-related		−3.6%	−42.2%	−6.0%	−69.9%	18.2%
Cells, Panels, and Modules		−1.0%	−67.2%	−9.6%	−62.0%	38.8%

ISSUES NOW FACING CHINA'S SOLAR SECTOR

Our analysis highlights the contribution of robust external demand, relatively modest initial technological barriers to entry, links with international networks and Chinese entrepreneurship to the solar sector's impressive growth. The sector, however, has not been immune from difficulties, especially more recently. These issues surface elsewhere in the economy, including wind, and likely have common roots.

Problems Related to Expanding Role of the Domestic Market

With Chinese panel manufacturers finding markets in the United States and Europe more difficult to access because of anti-dumping and counter-vailing duties, the domestic market has become more important.[33] Chinese

---

[33] These measures have also forced Chinese manufacturers to move more of their production offshore. Estimates suggest that much of the recent expansion in capacity by these firms has occurred elsewhere in Asia, including Malaysia, Taiwan and the Philippines.

policymakers have used a combination of rising targets for renewables in the national energy plan and expanding subsidies for panel users to promote domestic sales and use. Local government support also figures prominently here. Within a period of only five years, and in the context of continued rapid growth in production by local manufacturers, the percentage of panels produced in China that were sold domestically rose from only a few percent in 2010 to 30 percent in 2015 (see Figure 9.2).

The expansion in domestic sales has been accompanied by a number of problems that have important implications for both solar operators and solar panel manufacturers. First, generating capacity has expanded at a rate far outstripping the capacity of the power system to absorb it. New solar farms experience difficulty in connecting to the grid, while existing installations face issues of curtailment. Estimates suggest that upwards of 10 percent of China's solar capacity remained unused in 2015, and in 2016 solar curtailment reportedly rose by an additional 50 percent because of grid congestion.[34,35] These problems are most severe in the western provinces of Xinjiang and Gansu, where China's best solar resources are located, and energy demand is more limited. The losses to the industry in 2016 were estimated to be $US 3.5 billion.

Ultra-high voltage transmission lines connecting the region with demand centers in the coastal provinces will help bridge this gap (Xu, Chapter 6, this volume), but this new technology presents a new set of difficulties, and should not be viewed as an immediate panacea. Because of the need to maintain even higher voltage within the grid, local integration between renewables and conventional power sources such as coal becomes even more challenging for the power system.[36] In addition, capacity in all power sources continues to expand in coastal provinces.

Second, in sharp contrast to the experience for exports, panels sold domestically are facing quality issues. Product audits reveal that a significant portion of panels used in utility-scale projects suffer from quality issues that surface within only a year or two of installation and entail significantly lower panel efficiency because of product degradation.[37] The

---

[34] www.forbes.com/sites/greatspeculations/2015/11/10/the-opportunities-and-challenges-in-the-chinese-solar-market/#3e99cbe6637f (accessed August 1, 2017).

[35] http://energydesk.greenpeace.org/2017/04/19/china-wind-solar-renewable-curtailment-energy-wasted/ (accessed August 1, 2017).

[36] www.chinapower.com.cn/informationhyfx/20160823/49100.html (accessed August 15, 2017).

[37] In some solar farms, between 30 and 70% of panels have hot spots and cracks; see, www.bloomberg.com/news/articles/2015–01–20/defective-panels-threatening-profit-at-china-solar-farms-energy (accessed January 29, 2015).

reduction in power generation also causes a decline in investment returns and losses for solar farms. Similar problems have been identified in panels sold for distributed generation.

Informational asymmetries in the domestic market between buyers and sellers of the sort that third-party audits have helped to minimize in the context of exports to advanced countries are one source of the problem. Independently, domestic solar farm operators appear to be putting a high priority on low solar panel prices and project costs in awarding contracts to the neglect of quality and long-run returns. Kayser (2016) points out that under the current regulatory environment " . . . market participants are not compensated for quality and so choose the lowest cost materials and contractors regardless of quality."[38]

To help address these concerns, new government regulations have been designed to restrict who can bid on projects – limiting participation, for example, to firms whose panels either pass quality audits or satisfy other requirements – but the certification process has its own set of difficulties (Interviews, 2017). In addition, state-owned enterprises such as China General Nuclear Power Group and United Photovoltaics Group Limited, the latter controlled by China Merchants Group, dominate the downstream solar energy sector, with limited room for private sector competition.[39]

Expansion, Excess Capacity, and Rising Debt Ratios in the Industry

Rapid expansion of the solar sector has occurred through the entry of new firms, as well as investment in additional capacity by incumbents. One factor motivating this behavior is perceptions of new market opportunities. Expansion, however has been accompanied by persistent problems of excess capacity in nearly every segment of the value chain, including silicon, wafers, and cells. In this regard, solar appears similar to other sectors such as steel, cement, glass, shipbuilding, autos etc., in which excess capacity has been the norm and not the exception (Stewart 2016; *Economist*, September 9, 2017).

The root of these problems likely lies in China's political economy, and the often-distorted incentives facing individual firms and local governments to expand, but not contract and exit. Firms often compete

---

[38] Kayser goes on to argue that in the absence of strict and transparent quality requirements, the focus on cost minimization to win concession tenders is the fundamental difference between Chinese and European/US project development.

[39] http://guangfu.bjx.com.cn/news/20140411/502982-2.shtml (accessed June 16, 2014).

with each other on the basis of quantity. Easier access to finance and subsidies as a result of government promotion policy encourages this behavior on the part of firms; local governments and cadres have their own incentives to promote local champions and economic growth, especially in sectors that national leaders and policymakers identify as strategic such as solar (designated in 2006). Soft budget constraints and weak exit mechanisms for poorly performing firms likely compound the problems, and also help explain why firm exit and the reallocation of resources to more productive firms do not contribute to productivity growth in the sector. These mechanisms have been thwarted.

Information on excess capacity in the sector at the firm level is lacking, but the combination of a high debt-asset ratio and low profitability among industry leaders is a likely reflection of this behavior. Several major firms already have gone bankrupt (LDK in the fall of 2016, and Suntech, which was taken over by a holding company of the Wuxi Municipal Government in 2013).[40] Four leading firms in the sector currently have debt-asset ratios of 80 percent or higher, with that for Yingli, which has been championed by the Hebei provincial government, in the vicinity of 120 percent. In June of 2018, Yingli was forced to de-list from the New York Stock Exchange as its market capitalization fell below the minimum $US 50 million. Many small- and medium-size firms reportedly have similar problems. The list of companies facing difficulties includes both those that became more vertically integrated, such as Yingli and LDK, and those that specialized in downstream operations (Suntech, Tianwei).

Some encouragement can be taken from the recent examples of bankruptcy. The effect on total capacity in the sector, however, appears small – both LDK and Suntech, for example, were taken over by local SOEs, and remain in operation. In addition, reductions in capacity throughout the value chain are often the product of top-down decisions, in which case connections and ownership are often more important than efficiency. At least through 2017, it is difficult to find much in the way of market-driven consolidation, as reflected, for example, in the share of leading firms in China's solar exports.

Through 2021, continued pressure on prices and firm profitability is predicted.[41] Better firms in the sector pay for these excesses, both through

---

[40] On the bankruptcy of LDK, see: http://english.caixin.com/2016–10-11/100995606.html (accessed October 30, 2016).

[41] "Solar Manufacturing in China," IBISWorld, May 2016 (accessed online June 20, 2016; no longer available).

the effect of excess capacity in the sector on panel prices and profitability, but also through added pressures they face to expand capacity in order to maintain market share. Ultimately, this leaves firms with fewer resources to direct to R&D and innovation, which may help to explain relatively modest levels of R&D expenditure in the sector (Ball et al. 2017).

DEVELOPMENT OF CHINA'S WIND TURBINE SECTOR

In comparison with solar, China's wind turbine industry's evolution is noteworthy in several respects: the prominent role of the domestic and not the international market as the key source of industry demand; the prevalence of SOEs throughout the entire value chain (component suppliers, manufacturers of the wind turbines, and wind farms); and the influence of state policy on technology choice, localization, and vertical integration.

Rapid growth the last decade and a half has elevated China's wind turbine sector to the world's largest. There are clear signs of product upgrading, most notably, in the form of larger wind turbines and turbines used offshore. However, the sector continues to be mired in excess capacity, very low (if not negative) productivity growth at the firm and industry level, and quality issues. The latter help to explain the sector's lack of success in penetrating the international market. These difficulties can be linked to explicit policy choices and their effect on local actors and the domestic market. System-wide problems related to integrating wind energy into the electricity grid – similar to those facing solar – compound these difficulties and are likely having dynamic consequences. We examine these issues below.

Quantitative Expansion of China's Wind Turbine Sector

China's early clean energy bet was on wind and not on solar, largely reflecting the belief that wind power offered the best prospect of much lower energy costs. As a result, growth in domestic market opportunities for local wind turbine manufacturers far outstripped those for their solar counterparts up until only a few years ago. Expansion of the Chinese wind turbine sector has been predicated almost exclusively on the domestic market, with the role of exports negligible to this point. Between 2001 and 2010, installed wind capacity in China expanded nearly ten-fold, from only .4 GW to 44 GW (See Table 9.8.). It increased an additional four-fold over the next six years, and by 2016, installed capacity totaled nearly 170 GW, or slightly more than a third of world total installed wind capacity. Reflecting the geography of China's wind resources, installed capacity is highly

Table 9.8 *New and Cumulative Installed Wind Capacity*

Year	New	Total	Growth
	MW	MW	%
2001		404	
2002	66	470	16.3
2003	98	568	20.9
2004	197	765	34.7
2005	485	1,250	63.4
2006	1,349	2,599	107.9
2007	3,311	5,910	127.4
2008	6,110	12,020	103.4
2009	13,785	25,805	114.7
2010	18,928	44,733	73.4
2011	17,631	62,364	39.4
2012	12,960	75,324	20.8
2013	16,089	91,413	21.4
2014	23,196	114,609	25.4
2015	30,753	145,362	26.8
2016	23,370	168,732	16.1

Source: China Renewable Energy Association, 中国风电装机容量统计 (various years).

concentrated in the north, northeast, and northwest, with capacity in the three remote provinces of Xinjiang, Gansu, and Inner Mongolia alone exceeding 35 percent of the total in 2015 (See Figure 9.10.). Located far from the major sources of electricity demand in the east, this feature of the industry has posed a unique set of issues for China's wind sector.

The early growth of the sector has been well documented (Lewis 2013). Up through the mid-2000s, much of the growth in the demand for wind turbines was met through the local production of wholly owned subsidiaries of leading global wind turbine manufacturers such as Gamesa, Vestas, Nordex, and GE. Estimates put the market share of these firms in China's wind turbine market upwards of 75 percent as late as 2005, and even higher in earlier years. The rest of the market was served by either SOEs, or JVs between SOEs and smaller international wind-turbine companies who provided key technology through licensing arrangements.

China's New Energy Law in 2005 provided an important catalyst for the development of the local, i.e. Chinese-owned, wind industry. Subsequently, a series of central government policies covering local content requirements for wind turbines, VAT rebates for domestic manufacturers, and subsidies to

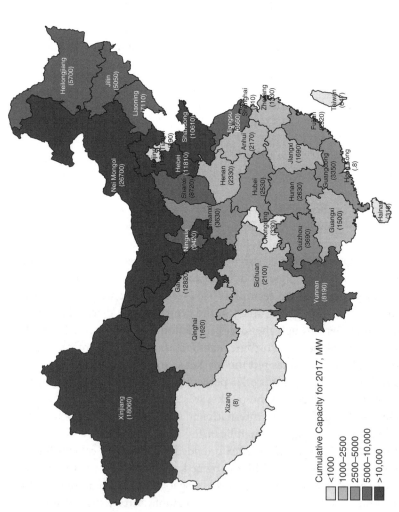

Figure 9.10 Wind Capacity by Province in China, 2017
Source: Chinese Wind Energy Association Annual Report, 2017.

eligible domestic wind turbine manufacturers (and their suppliers) quickly tilted the playing field heavily in favor of local, i.e. Chinese-owned, firms (Yuan 2015). These effects were reinforced by procurement biases of state-owned wind farm developers and local governments that typically favored Chinese wind turbine manufacturers over the multinationals.[42]

Huge increases in wind turbine capacity and production followed as a result of new firm entry and expansion by incumbents. Estimates put the peak number of wind turbine manufacturers at nearly a hundred. By 2010 more than 90 percent of the market was captured by domestic firms that were usually either SOEs, or SOEs with controlling interests in JVs with foreign firms. From the perspective of multinationals, it became increasingly difficult to win bids to supply turbines for local wind farm projects (Interview, 2014).

Table 9.9 provides a breakdown of the top ten firms for select years (2006, 2011, and 2016), and captures the growing marginalization of leading international firms in the domestic industry. Market concentration initially fell with the rapid expansion, but by comparison with other industries in China, concentration remains fairly high – the top five firms enjoy upwards of 60 percent of the domestic market, and the top ten have more than 85 percent. Several non-state firms, most notably, Ming Yang and Envision, have also emerged recently as major players in the domestic industry.[43]

Estimates put annual wind turbine production capacity in China in 2011 in the vicinity of 30 GW, and newly installed capacity at only 16 GW. By 2016 production capacity had expanded an additional third to 40 GW, however "planned" annual expansion in installed capacity in China between 2015 and 2020 is only 20 GW.[44] Low rates of capacity utilization by Chinese wind turbine manufacturers as well as their suppliers look to be the norm.

Technology and the Value Chain

Power generated by a wind turbine is determined by four key factors: the size or capacity of the turbine, the height of the turbine, the diameter of the

---

[42] These biases help explain the modest impact of the revocation of local content rules in 2009 on the share of the multinationals in the domestic market.

[43] Also notable is the decline in Sinovel, which was sued for IP theft by its US partner, ASMC, in courts in both the US and China (as well as Austria).

[44] See www.eco-business.com/press-releases/competition-in-chinas-wind-power-sector-shifting-to-export-market/ (accessed March 11, 2015), citing a report by the marketing company CCM.

Table 9.9 *Leading Firms and Market Concentration, Wind Turbine Manufacturers*

	2006			2011			2016		
Firm	Output*	Share	Firm	Output*	Share	Firm	Output*	Share
Goldwind	445	33.3	Goldwind	3600	20.4	Goldwind	6343	27.1
Vestas	312	23.3	Sinovel	2939	16.7	Envision	2003	8.6
Gamesa	213	15.9	United Power	2847	16.1	Ming Yang	1959	8.4
GE	170	12.7	Ming Yang	1178	6.7	United Power	1908	8.2
Sinovel	75	5.6	Dongfang Electric	946	5.4	CSIC Haizhuang	1827	7.8
CASC-Acciona	50	3.7	XEMC	713	4.0	Shanghai Electric	1727	7.4
Nordex	27	2.0	Shanghai Electric	708	4.0	XEMC	1236	5.3
Windey	20	1.5	Vestas	662	3.8	Dongfang Electric	1227	5.3
Suzlon	13	0.9	Huachuang	623	3.5	Windey	724	3.1
Dongfang Electric	9	0.7	CSR Zhuzhou Locomotive	451	2.6	Huachuang	715	3.1
Others	4	0.3	Others	2964	16.8	Others	3701	15.8
Total	1335	100.0	Total	17631	100.0	Total	23370	100.0
Share, Top 3 (%)	72.6		Share, Top 3 (%)	53.2		Share, Top 3 (%)	44.1	
Share, Top 5 (%)	90.9		Share, Top 5 (%)	65.3		Share, Top 5 (%)	60.1	

Source: China Renewable Energy Association, 中国风电装机容量统计 (various years).

*Output is expressed in numbers of wind turbines.

rotors (blades), and wind speed.[45] Over time, wind turbines increased significantly in each of the first three dimensions, which has helped to make them more efficient.[46] Other elements of design also matter for turbine efficiency, including the methods used to control the power output from the blades (pitch versus stall control), and the use of "fixed" versus "variable" speed generators. The electronic control system, which monitors and controls turbine parameters such as rotor speed and blade pitch, also exerts a significant effect on power generation and the durability and operational life of the wind turbine.

Chinese firms initially licensed designs from leading international wind turbine companies such as Aerodyn (Germany), AMSC (United States), Repower (Germany), Gerrard Hassan (United Kingdom), Vensys (Germany), and Darwind (Netherlands). Subsequently, Vensys was acquired by Goldwind (2008), and Darwind by XEMC (2009). Co-development has also become slightly more common as capabilities in Chinese firms deepened, but licensing continues and remains important. Currently, domestic wind turbine manufacturers are focusing much of their product R&D efforts on producing larger onshore wind turbines, and those used offshore, which are even larger in size, and technically more complicated. Table 9.10, which provides product portfolio information for leading Chinese and international turbine companies for 2012, is highly suggestive. The differences between the two groups of firms appear to be marginal.

The economic rationale for developing larger turbines is that they are more cost effective, i.e. lower costs per watt of capacity, but Chinese government policy has also aggressively encouraged "leap-frogging" by Chinese firms in terms of size and offshore capabilities. First mover advantages are believed to be important in terms of future success. Competition among leading Chinese firms to be the "first" to introduce new models intensified. Yuan (2015), for example, cites the competition between Sinovel, Shanghai Electric, and XEMC with respect to offshore turbines. Between 2007 and 2015, the average size of newly installed turbines in China increased from slightly more than 1 MW per turbine to nearly 2 MW; moreover, in 2015, more than 15 percent of newly installed capacity was in turbines larger than 2 MW.

---

[45] For a brief introduction to wind power technologies, see IRENA, "Wind Power." Renewable Energy Technologies: Cost Series Analysis. Volume 1: Power Sector, Issue 5/5 (2012).

[46] Outside of China, the average size of onshore wind turbines is 2.5–3 MW, and two times that for offshore turbines.

Table 9.10 *Major Wind Turbine Manufacturers' Product Portfolio, 2012*

Wind Turbine Size (MW)	0.60	0.85	1.00	1.25	1.50	1.60	1.65	1.80	1.85	2.00	2.10	2.40	2.50	2.60	2.75	2.85	3.00	3.20	3.30	3.60	4.10	4.50	5.00	5.50	6.00	6.50	8.00
Chinese Companies																											
GoldWind					1								1				1								2		
Sinovel					1					1							1						1		1		
Guodian United Power					1					1							1						1		1		
Ming Yang Wind Power					1					1			1		1		1				1				2	1	
Dongfang Turbine			1		1					1			1				1						2	2			
XEMC Wind Power										1							2						1				
Shanghai Electric				1						1										1			2				
China Creative Energy					1					1							1			1			1				
CSR Zhuzhou					1		1			1			1										1		2		
CSIC Haizhuang WindPower		1								1			1										1				
Foreign Companies																											
Vestas								1		1				1			1		1								1
GE		1							1				1		1	1*		1			2						
Gamesa		1		1						1			1									1	1				
Suzlon*	1			1	1						1								1								
Nordex***	1				1					1		1	1						1								

Note:

* Suzlon bought Germany's Repower which has more wind turbine sizes that are not listed here.

** Nordex planned to develop 6 MW offshore in 2011, but terminated the plan at the end of 2012.

Source: Company reports (various years). 1 = currently selling 2 = have prototype

Much less focus has been put on improvement in slightly more mature models through better design and software that would raise efficiency, for example, by enabling them to better fit local wind conditions, and increase durability. Interviews with one leading Chinese firm suggested that returns on these margins remain high especially as project development extends to regions with less abundant wind resources.

Chinese wind turbine companies have also become much more vertically integrated over time, especially in the supply of key components such as blades, generators, gearboxes, the yaw system, convertors and control systems (see Table 9.11). These components make up upwards of half of total costs, with the tower and the nacelle (the housing for the turbine) an additional 25 percent.[47] Components such as generators and gearboxes, which have wide use in other industries and in which Chinese firms such as NGC Gears already had capabilities, were originally out sourced, but have often moved in-house. Chinese wind turbine companies also appear to be more vertically integrated than leading international companies.[48]

This tendency toward higher degrees of vertical integration mirrors that in other Chinese industries identified as strategic and pillar.[49] Policy also figures prominently. Motivated by a desire to advance domestic market consolidation and international technological leadership in wind turbines, in 2015 the central government began to limit bidding on domestic jobs to Chinese firms with the capability to produce turbines over certain size thresholds, and who had access to a complete supply chain. Several firms in the industry have resisted these pressures, choosing to direct more resources toward turbine design and development of critical components such as the control systems, and to invest much less in production capacity.

A final important link in the wind energy value chain is the wind farm operators. Top wind farm developers are usually state-owned and include the leading power generating companies such Guodian, Datang, Huaneng, Huadian, and Guohua, which combined have developed more than half of China's wind-connected capacity.[50] Other state-owned companies make up much of the rest. A number of the leading power generators have also

---

[47] Megawind, "Strategy for Wind Turbine Components and Subsystems," 2012, p. 17.

[48] A compilation of information on the top seven international firms shows that all of them have developed and use their own control systems and manufacture their own blades, however gearboxes and generators are often out-sourced.

[49] Fan et al. (2017) find that in the 2000s Chinese firms were more vertically integrated than those in the United States in the 1990s.

[50] Estimate for 2011 for new capacity and cumulative grid-connected capacity from China Wind Power Development Outlook 2012, p. 39.

Table 9.11 *Vertical Integration among Leading Wind Turbine Firms*

Component	Rotor Blades	Rotor Hub	Rotor Bearings	Gearbox	Generator	Power Converter	Control System**	Nacelle Housing	Tower
Cost Share (%)*	22.2	1.37	1.22	12.91	3.44	5.01	3.91	1.35	26.3
Goldwind					■	■	■		
CSIC Haizhuang	■			■	■	■	■		
XEMC			■		■	■			
Newunited					■		■		■
United Power					■	■	■		
Dongfang Electric		■			■		■		■
Mingyang							■		
Sanyi				■	■		■		
Sinovel							■		
Zhejiang Windey							■		
Shanghai Electric					■	■	■		
CSR Wind Power	■			■	■	■	■	■	
China Creative Winder Energy	■						■		
Baoding Tianwei	■						■		■
Vestas				■			■		
Gamesa							■		

Note:

* Information on cost shares for key components is taken from www.wind-science.org/iresen/page/wind-turbine-manufacturing.html (accessed July 15, 2017).

** The control system generally includes the power control, pitch control, yaw control, and auxiliary equipment control.

acquired wind turbine companies, including China Creative Wind Energy by Datang in 2011, and United Power, ranked now among the top five domestic wind turbine companies, by Guodian in 2007. After both acquisitions, wind farms developed by these two leading generating companies sourced wind turbines heavily from their own subsidiaries. More recently, leading wind turbine companies such as Goldwind and Mingyang have moved downstream into wind farm development, presumably to better ensure outlets for their own turbines.

MEASURING IMPROVEMENT AMONG CHINA'S WIND TURBINE MANUFACTURERS

We documented the rapid expansion of wind turbine production in China at the firm and industry level. As in the case of solar, increases in scale have been identified as an important source of the advantage enjoyed by Chinese industry (Naim and Seinfeld 2014) and should have contributed to lower wind turbine costs per KWh of energy. Over the same period, average wind turbine size has increased, and Chinese firms have developed capabilities in turbines designed for offshore use. Both have been widely cited in the literature as indicators of rapid upgrading by Chinese firms.

Measuring per unit costs, or its dual in the form of productivity, is inherently difficult however. As we did for solar, we examine several measures of industry performance including rates of learning, industry productivity, and wind turbine quality. Despite differences in methodology, a fairly consistent picture emerges: At best, only modest improvements in performance have accompanied the huge quantitative expansion in the wind turbine industry.

Learning by Doing

Several recent studies (Qiu and Anadon 2011; Yao et al. 2015; and Lam et al. 2017) utilize cost data for China's onshore wind farm projects collected by the United Nations as part of the Clean Development Mechanism (CDM) to estimate the learning rate for the wind turbine sector between 2004 and 2012.[51] The learning rate here is the relative

---

[51] The CDM provided a mechanism through which developing countries can earn "saleable" certified emission reduction credits (CERs) by building projects that would reduce greenhouse gases. Industrialized countries are the customers, and use these credits to help meet their emission reduction targets. As part of the CDM, detailed information on these projects was collected.

cost reduction achieved per doubling of cumulative installed capacity.[52] Over this period, cumulative installed wind capacity increased a hundred-fold. Since nearly all wind projects in China up through 2012 participated in the CDM, the estimates are comprehensive.[53] For onshore projects, turbine costs typically represent upwards of two-thirds of total project costs, and thus are the key driver of learning rates through the several channels identified above.

Estimation details differ slightly between these studies, but in general the results are highly robust: Over the period in question, and controlling for important changes in raw material prices, the learning rate for wind turbines was conservatively placed in the vicinity of 4 percent. This implies that costs per KWh fell by 4 percent with each doubling of production, and suggests a total reduction in costs per KWh since 2005 through learning by doing of between 25 percent and 30 percent.

How do these estimates for learning compare? There are two obvious comparisons. First, estimates for Denmark and Germany over comparable periods in the development of their wind sectors are between 8 percent and 12 percent, or two and three times larger than those estimated for China. A "meta" analysis of wind turbine costs by Lindman and Söderholm (2012) also puts learning rates for China at the low end of the distribution for the industry.[54] Second, estimates cited earlier for China's solar sector over the same period imply learning rates for panels and modules of over 20 percent, or rates of learning that are five times larger. The rates of learning for solar are also in line with those estimated for other key electronic goods such as digital cameras, DVD machines, and televisions.

Measures of Productivity Growth

Over the period between 2003 and 2013, real output, i.e. nominal output adjusted for price changes, in the wind turbine sector grew at an annual rate upwards of 40 percent, or similar to that we measured for solar.

---

[52] More complicated two-factor models incorporate the "knowledge stock" as captured by the cumulative public and private investment in R&D into the analysis, as well as the price of key inputs such as steel. In general, estimation results are very robust to incorporating these additional factors.

[53] After 2012, the sharp reduction in the price of carbon in the European market eliminated the incentives or Chinese firms to participate.

[54] For a review of other electricity supply technologies, see Edward S. Rubin, M. L. Inês, Paulina Jaramillo Azevedo, and Sonia Yeh (2015).

Estimates of productivity for the sector reported in Table 9.7 are much smaller than those for solar, especially for the period after 2008 as new firms enter to try to take advantage of expanded government support for the industry. For the period between 2003 and 2008, improvements by existing firms were more than offset by the disproportionate flow of resources to less efficient firms, and the lower productivity of entrants. Productivity growth between 2003 and 2008 averaged only 0.39 percent. Overall, these estimates for productivity growth line up reasonably well with those for learning by doing for the two sectors, which arguably are more comprehensive and include cost reductions coming through any improvements in the supply chain not captured in estimates of productivity of the wind turbine manufacturers.

Wind Turbine Quality

Measuring product "quality" is difficult. For a product like wind turbines, there are two key dimensions: the ability of the turbines to convert the available supply of wind into electricity, and durability and lifetime of the turbines. For both of these dimensions, wind turbine design, the control system and its interfaces with the hardware, and the quality of key mechanical components, either self-supplied or sourced from other companies, are important. Comparisons of wind turbines over extended periods of time that control for differences in size, wind conditions and operating environments, etc. and thus allow for estimates of quality, are limited. The Chinese press is replete however with articles highlighting quality issues in China's wind turbine sector arising from poor design, component failure, etc., problems that occasionally spill over in the form of grid disruption.[55]

Motivated by the observation that China generates significantly less electricity from wind than the United States despite having two-thirds more installed capacity, a recent comparison of the wind power sector in the two countries for 2012 by Lu et al. (2017) provides useful numbers. Differences in wind resources, as well as problems of non-connection and curtailment need to be controlled for when trying to estimate the role of quality. With information on these factors, the authors are able to decompose differences in power generated by wind farms in the two countries into those resulting from differences in capacity, connection rates,

---

[55] See, for example, Xiao (2016), p. 2.

curtailment, wind resources, and finally, quality.[56] With domestic turbines the source of more than 90 percent of installed capacity in China, the estimated measure of quality is primarily that of Chinese manufacturers. A small portion of the difference in "quality" can be attributed to the lower average size of turbines in China, but these differences have been narrowing rapidly and the largest portion is related to how well turbines of any given size perform.

In 2012, capacity in China was 67.7 percent larger than in the United States. This was partially offset by inferior wind resources, the relative contribution of which was negative 17.9 percent. Far more important was lower generation arising from system-wide issues of low connection rates (negative 50.3 percent), and curtailment (negative 49.3 percent). Quality differences, our focus here, were found to be as important as curtailment and delayed connection to the grid and are an additional negative 50.2 percent.[57]

The authors also estimate the "loss" in electricity associated with each factor. Electricity output from China's wind turbine sector would have been an additional 20 TWh (or 20 percent higher) if quality levels were the same as those of the studies' benchmark US turbines. Similar gains would come from resolving issues of curtailment and non-connection. To put a monetary value on the loss, the average price of electricity in China in 2012 was approximately $US 0.08/Kwh, implying a cost of $US 1.6 billion from each of the three sources, and a total cost of $US 5 billion.[58]

SYSTEM WIDE ISSUES: PROBLEMS OF CURTAILMENT AND CONNECTION RATES

Our focus to this point has been on measuring improvements in the wind turbine sector at the firm and industry level. There are equally important issues related to wind's integration with the entire power sector. In principle, similar issues face solar, but with a much smaller percentage of solar production going to serve the domestic market, these issues are currently

---

[56] As the authors point out, quality here is a composite that primarily reflects turbine quality, but also reflects technical limits on the operation of the wind farms relating to the micro-siting of the project.

[57] The reduction in output from these sources adds up to more than 100% because of the offsetting effect of the positive contribution from more installed capacity in China. In total, the sum of all factors is 100.

[58] Electricity prices are taken from: www.theenergycollective.com/lindsay-wilson/279126/ average-electricity-prices-around-world-kwh (accessed August 1, 2018).

much less serious. As the role of solar in the domestic energy mix increases however, this will change.

As we described above, China has not been able to leverage fully its huge investment in wind turbine capacity because of issues of non-connection and curtailment. Non-connection is self-explanatory: Wind farms are built but do not get connected to the grid, and therefore are not able to supply power the grid. Curtailment entails the generation of electricity that goes unused. Of the two, curtailment is the slightly more complicated issue, and is tied to the ability to balance power generated by wind with that from other sources in light of demand.[59] Output of the wind turbines is variable and intermittent, and is often greatest at night, while peak demand occurs during the morning and early evening. For any given level of demand, an increase in the power generated by wind must be offset by a reduction from other sources such as coal.

Limited transmission capacity between the location of the turbines and the major load centers prevents power balancing at a wider geographic scale. Thus, accommodation of the variable and intermittent output of the turbines has to occur locally through reduction of the power from other generating sources. In most locations of China, coal burning powered plants are the other major source of power, but they must typically operate at capacity utilization rates of 50 percent or higher. On paper, this seems like a relatively low bar, but the huge expansion in coal power generating capacity combined with the slow growth of demand have exacerbated the problem.

Figure 9.11 provides estimates of the rejection rate (curtailment plus non-connection) for wind for the period between 2010 and 2017. The behavior is cyclical, and the rate first rises, then falls, and rises again through 2016. Preliminary estimates for 2017 put the rejection rate at 12 percent. On average, rejection rates are two-and-a-half to three times higher than in the United States and Europe. There is also a huge regional dimension to the problem, with the problem especially severe in the north and northwest.

CONCLUSION

China has invested heavily in its renewable energy sector during the last decade and a half. Benefits have flowed from these investments, but a case can be made that these investments have not been fully leveraged as a result of

---

[59] Some of the non-connection is also related to the current problems of balancing supply and demand.

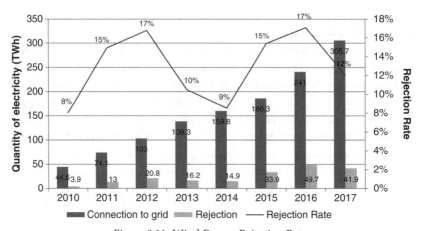

Figure 9.11 Wind Energy Rejection Rates
Sources: Data for 2010–15 are from Zhang et al. (2016). Data for 2016 and 2017 are from
Global Wind Report, 2017, p. 40.

the economic, political, and regulatory environment in which these firms operate domestically. There are important lessons to be learned from the experience of the two sectors.

Above all, sectors in which firms are most open to competition and foreign participation and enjoy freedom over sourcing decisions and technology, and customers have choices in the market, have been the most successful in developing and upgrading their capabilities in line with China's evolving comparative advantage. China's solar sector was extremely successful under these terms over a significant portion of the period we examine – expanding market penetration in advanced countries, increasing the role of local sourcing, and narrowing the gap with firms from advanced countries in the use of more mature technologies.

In sharp contrast, policy choices have made China's wind turbine sector much less open over time to foreign involvement, all but eliminating these pro-competitive pressures on local firms. In nearly all advanced manufacturing sectors, the world's leading firms keep their innovative edge by working collaboratively with top-tier suppliers. Chinese mercantilist industrial policy discourages this sort of cooperation, thereby limiting the flows of knowledge and skilled personnel between these firms. These problems have been compounded by government priorities favoring bigger turbines (and those used offshore), which have misdirected R&D efforts and raised costs; by incentives for firms to vertically integrate; a near monopoly of downstream activity by state and state-connected firms; and a regulatory environment that has muted the role of the market at every level.

Unique features of the electricity market present an additional layer of complication, as solar and wind must compete with traditional power sources, as well as alternatives such as hydro and nuclear for the right to supply power to the grid. These problems have intensified as capacity continues to expand, but growth in demand for electricity has slowed considerably.

Recent policy pronouncements point to huge investments in electricity storage technology, long distance transmission, and smart grid technology. It remains to be seen, however, how far these new investments in technology go to alleviating the inefficiencies and costs tied to earlier policy choices and the environment in which generators of electricity as well as manufacturers of solar panels and wind turbines actually compete.

References

Ball, J., D. Reicher, X. Sun, and C. Pollock. 2017. *China's Evolving Solar Industry And Its Implications for Competitive Solar Power In the United States and the World.* Stanford: Steyer-Taylor Center for Energy and Finance.

Brandt, Loren. 2016. "Policy Perspectives from the Bottom Up: What Do Firm Level Data Tell Us China Needs to Do." In Reuven Glick and Mark M. Spiegel eds., *Policy Challenges in a Diverging Global Economy.* San Francisco: Federal Bank of San Francisco. pp. 281–302.

Brandt, L. and P. M. Morrow. 2017. "Tariffs and the organization of trade in China." *Journal of International Economics.* 104. pp. 85–103.

Brandt, Loren and Eric Thun. 2010. "The Fight for the Middle: Upgrading Competition, and Industrial Development in China." *World Development.* 38(11). pp. 1555–74.

Brandt, Loren, Johannes Van Biesebroeck, Luhang Wang. and Yifan Zhang. 2017. "WTO Accession and Performance of Chinese Manufacturing Firms." *American Economic Review.* 107(9). pp. 2784–820.

Brandt, Loren, Luhang Wang, and Yifan Zhang. 2017. "Productivity in Chinese Industry: 1998–2013." Background report prepared for Development Research Centre-World Bank project on "China's New Drivers of Economic Growth."

Carbon Trust. 2012. "Detailed appraisal of offshore wind in China."

Chen Y., Z. Feng, and P. Verlinden. 2014. "Assessment of module efficiency and manufacturing cost for industrial crystalline silicon and thin film technologies 6th World Conference on Photovoltaic Energy Conversion." www.researchgate .net/publication/269393369_assessment_of_module_efficiency_and_manufactur ing_cost_for_industrial_crystalline_silicon_and_thin_film_technologies (accessed December 28, 2018).

de la Tour, Arnaud, Matthieu Glachant, and Yann Meniere.2010. "Innovation and International Technology Transfer." CERNA Working Paper Series, Working Paper. 2010–12.

Economist. 2017. "Created Destruction: Making sense of capacity cuts in China." September 7, 2017.

Energy Research Institute. 2000. "Commercialization of Solar PV systems in China." Center for Renewable Energy Development, National Development and Reform Commission, Beijing, China.

Fan, Joseph P. H., Jun Huang, Randall Morck, and Bernard Yeung. 2017. "Institutional determinants of vertical integration in China." *Journal of Corporate Finance.* 44. pp. 524–39.

Fraunhofer Institute for Solar Energy Systems, ISE. 2018. Photovoltaics Reports. November 17, 2016 (original date).

Gallagher, Kelly S. 2014. *The Global Diffusion of Clean Energy Technology: Lessons from China.* Cambridge, MA: MIT Press.

Hoppmann, Joern, Joern Huenteler, and Bastien Girod. 2015. "Compulsive policy-making—The evolution of the German feed-in tariff system for solar photovoltaic." *Research Policy.* 43.8. pp. 1422–41.

Huang, Y. 2003. *Selling China: Foreign direct investment during the reform era.* Cambridge: Cambridge University Press.

IRENA. 2012. "Wind Power," Renewable Energy Technologies: Cost Series Analysis, Volume 1: Power Sector, Issue 5/5

Kayser, Dirk. 2016. "Solar photovoltaic projects in China: High investment risks and the need for institutional response." *Applied Energy.* 174(C). pp. 144–52.

Lam, L., L. Branstetter, and I. Azevedo. 2017. "China's wind industry: Leading in deployment, lagging in innovation." *Energy Policy.* 106. pp. 588–99.

Law of the People's Republic of China. 2014. "Measures of the Customs of the People's Republic of China on the Supervision of Processing Trade Goods." www.asianlii .org/cn/legis/cen/laws/motcotprocotsoptg947/ (accessed June 20, 2016).

Lemoine, F. and D. Unal. 2017. "China's Foreign Trade: A "New Normal." *China and World Economy.* 25: 1–21.

Levitt, S. D., J. A. List., and C. Syverson. 2013. "Toward an understanding of learning by doing: Evidence from an automobile assembly plant." *Journal of Political Economy.* 121(4). pp. 643–81.

Lewis, Johanna. 2013. *Green Innovation in China: China's Wind Power and the Global Transition to a Low-Carbon Economy.* New York: Columbia University Press.

Li Jungfeng et al., eds. 2012. 中国风电发展报告. [China Wind Power Development Outlook 2012]. Beijing: China Environmental Science Press.

Lindman Å, and P. Söderholm. 2012. "Wind power learning rates: A conceptual review and meta-analysis." *Energy Economics.* 34(3). pp. 754–61.

Lu, X., M. B. McElroy, W. Peng, S. Liu, C. P. Nielsen, and H. Wang. 2016. "Challenges faced by China compared with the US in developing wind power." *Nature Energy.* 1. p. 16061.

Manova, K. and Z. Yu. 2016. "How firms export: Processing vs. ordinary trade with financial frictions." *Journal of International Economics.* 100. pp. 120–37.

McDonald, Alan and Leo Schrattenholzer. 2001. "Learning rates for energy technologies." *Energy Policy.* 29. pp. 255–61.

Megawind. 2012. Strategy for Wind Turbine Components and Subsystems.

Meydray, J. and F. Dross. 2016. PV Module Reliability Scoreboard.

Nahm, J. and E. S. Steinfeld. 2014. "Scale-up nation: China's specialization in innovative manufacturing." *World Development.* 54. pp. 288–300.

Qiang, Zhi, Sun Hongzhang, Li Yanxi, Xu Yurui, and Su Jun. 2014. "China's Solar Photovoltaic Policy: An Analysis Based on Policy Instruments." *Applied Energy.* 129. pp. 308–19.

Qiu Y. and L. D. Anadon. 2011. "The price of wind power in China during its expansion: Technology adoption, learning-by-doing, economies of scale, and manufacturing localization. *Energy Economics.* 34(3). pp. 772–85.

Rubin, Edward S., M. L. Inês, Paulina Jaramillo Azevedo, and Sonia Yeh. 2015. "A review of learning rates for electricity supply technologies." *Energy Policy.* 86. pp. 198–218.

Song, D., H. Jiao, and C. T. Fan. 2015. "Overview of the photovoltaic technology status and perspective in China." *Renewable and Sustainable Energy Reviews,.* 48. pp. 848–56.

Steinfeld, E. S. 2004. "China's Shallow Integration: Networked Production and the New Challenges for Late Industrialization." *World Development.* 32(11). pp. 1971–87.

2010. *Playing Our Game: Why China's Rise Doesn't Threaten the West.* Oxford: Oxford University Press.

Stewart, Terrence P. 2016. Testimony Before the United States-China Economic and Security Review Commission. China's Shifting Economic Realities Panel III: Overcapacity and Global Markets.

Sun, Xiaojing. 2016. "The Role of Policy and Markets in the Development of the Solar Photovoltaic Industry: Evidence from China." PhD Dissertation. Georgia Institute of Technology.

Wu, C. Y. and J. A. Mathews. 2012. "Catching-up of Technological Innovation Capabilities: the solar photovoltaic industries in Taiwan, China, and Korea." Unpublished.

Xiao Qiang 肖蔷. 2016. "十三五"风电发展将更重质量 将建立公正的质量评价体系与名单制度，加快形成优胜劣汰市场机制，" 中国能源报 [Wind Power Development in 13th Five Year Plan to Emphasize Quality: A Fair and Impartial Quality Evaluation and Blacklist System to be established to accelerate formation of market based system based on survival of fittest]. August 4, 2016.

Xu, H., C. Dou, S. Wang and F. Lv. 2011. National Survey Report of PV Power Applications in China. August 15, 2012.

Yao, X., Y. Liu, and S. Qu et. al. 2015. "When will wind energy achieve grid parity in China? – Connecting technological learning and climate finance." *Applied Energy.* 160(C). pp. 697–704.

Yuan, Jiahai, 2015. "Wind Turbine Manufacturing in China: A Review." *Renewable and Sustainable Energy Reviews.* 51. pp. 1235–44.

Zhang, Fang and Kelly Sims Gallagher. 2016. "Innovations and technology transfer through global value chains: Evidence from China's PV Industry." *Energy Policy.* 94. pp. 191–203.

Zhang, Wei and Steven White. 2016. "Overcoming the liability of newness: Entrepreneurial action and the emergence of private solar photovoltaic firms." *Research Policy.* 45. pp. 604–17.

Zhang, Yuning, Ningning Tang, Yuguang Niu, and Xiaoze Du. 2016. "Wind energy rejection in China: Current status, reasons and perspectives." *Renewable and Sustainable Energy Reviews.* 66. pp. 322–44.

10

Capability Upgrading and Catch-Up in Civil Nuclear Power: The Case of China

Ravi Madhavan, Thomas G. Rawski, and Qingfeng Tian

INTRODUCTION

On some northerly approaches into Pittsburgh's international airport, aircraft fly past Shippingport, PA, where the Western world's first commercial nuclear reactor was connected to the electrical grid in 1957.[*] Although that plant ceased operations in 1982, a dominant proportion of the world's 453 operating reactors continue to use designs based on, or inspired by, technology developed by the Pittsburgh-based Westinghouse Electric Company. However, the very first reactor based on Westinghouse's latest design, the AP1000, began generating electricity in the summer of 2018 not in the United States, but 7,000 miles away in Sanmen, China. Following Westinghouse's 2017 bankruptcy filing and subsequent reorganization, the outlook for AP1000 construction projects in the United States remains uncertain. These developments powerfully illustrate the nuclear industry's shifting center of gravity toward China. Of the fifty-eight nuclear power reactors under construction in mid-2018, China accounts for eighteen, by far the largest share.[1]

This chapter analyzes China's improbable progression from pygmy to emerging giant in civilian nuclear power. The Qinshan (Zhejiang) nuclear facility, a domestically developed plant rated at 298 MW, was connected to

[*] All three authors have received financial support from their home institutions. We are particularly grateful to Jean-Patrick Ducruet for penetrating comments and to Qilin Liu, Xiaoyun Gu, and Peiyuan Huang for their assistance and advice with fieldwork, data analysis and manuscript preparation. Many industry participants in China, the United States and Japan gave generously of their time and insights; this study would not have been possible without their input and guidance. The authors assume sole responsibility for what follows.
[1] See www.iaea.org/pris/worldstatistics/underconstructionreactorsbycountry.aspx (accessed May 7, 2018).

the grid in 1991. Twenty-five years later, the People's Republic not only operates a fleet of thirty-eight nuclear plants and hosts more than one-third of global nuclear construction projects, but also boasts an extensive nuclear supply chain, stands on the brink of commercializing its own *Hualong 1* (Dragon 1) reactor design, and is riding a wave of momentum in the global nuclear market. This chapter describes this dramatic shift and considers its potential implications for China and for the global nuclear power industry. In the process, we highlight the role of industrial policy, regulation, and enterprise initiative as drivers of catch-up and innovation.

We expect industrial policy and regulation to exert major influence in an industry that faces significant safety risks and shares technology with the military. However, our analysis produces the surprising insight that the state-owned entities that constitute the Chinese nuclear power plant (NPP) sector also engage in robust competition and entrepreneurial action to shape those policies to their own ends. Thus, our case study presents industrial policy, regulation, and enterprise initiative as complementary forces driving catch-up and innovation.

Systems Integration

Figure 10.1 illustrates the array of steps underlying the design, construction, equipping, testing, and operation of nuclear plants. Individual components require the organization of sprawling networks of collaboration: plans for *Hualong 1* involved 300 projects covering seventy specialties, which fed information into an online design platform shared among more than twenty institutes (Lu Bin 2016). Changes in the dimensions or physical properties of a single component reverberate throughout the supply chain. The need for "traceability" – which allows managers to track defects to their source – necessitates the creation and constant updating of vast archives that specify the exact origin – date, batch, machine, material – of every item or component.[2]

Accordingly, successful design, fabrication, and operation of nuclear power plants requires substantial expertise in systems integration, an amalgam of skills that evolve over time and with the accumulation of experience. Hobday, Davies, and Prencipe (2005, p. 1110) define systems

---

[2] To illustrate: after discovering "hairline cracks ... in the ... structure connecting the car body and the framework for the wheels" of train cars shipped to Singapore, CSR Qingdao Sifang Locomotive found that the defects were "due to impurities in the aluminum material used for the car" bodies caused by "an aluminum alloy used in manufacturing processes" (Vasagar 2016).

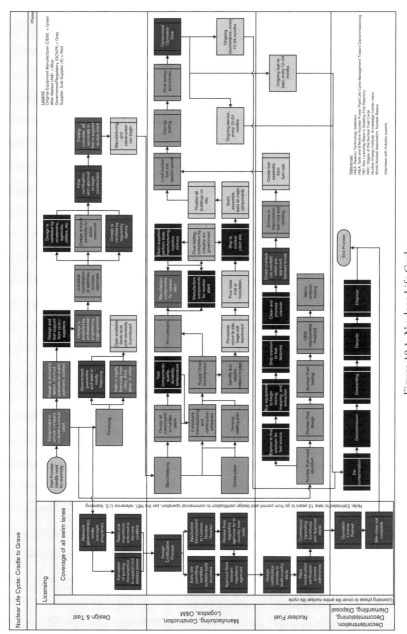

Figure 10.1 Nuclear Life Cycle
Source: Reproduced with permission from Oyler (2014)

integration as the process of combining high-technology components, sub-systems, software, skills, knowledge, engineers, managers, and technicians to produce a product in competition with rival suppliers. The more complex, technically advanced, and costly the product, the more significant systems integration becomes to the firm's success. The NPP business is a complex, multi-technology endeavor that is both capital- and management-intensive, with challenges concentrated in three areas: policy development, infrastructure, and project implementation. NPP projects require long cycles, typically taking six to seven years from the awarding of contracts to grid connection – even longer for "First of a Kind" projects that involve new reactor designs, such as the initial AP1000 reactor in Sanmen, China.

Systems integration capabilities cluster in advanced economies, particularly in networks of private companies (e.g. Westinghouse, Boeing, Toyota, Siemens) and in public agencies (e.g. NASA) that specialize in extremely complex design and production processes. China and other "follower nations" typically have comparatively limited capacity in this area. Latecomer suppliers of complex capital goods face multiple barriers: less developed national innovation systems, limited participation in international networks of suppliers and users, underdeveloped local supply chains, lack of experience in coordinating networks of suppliers, and lack of trust among industry actors (Kiamehr, Hobday, and Kermanshah 2014).

Plan-era legacies represent a further potential obstacle for China. Gholz (2007, p. 634, citing Brooks 2005) links Soviet decline to failures of systems integration: "design bureaus were poorly integrated with manufacturing plants, so they rarely considered the challenges of actually building their high-end products, and the rigidity of the plan often prevented simple substitution of components or materials ... with equivalents (or even better inputs) from another domestic supplier." China's planned economy displayed similar shortcomings; Chinese experts continue to criticize the tendency of manufacturers to put quantity, speed, and cost considerations ahead of quality control – an unfortunate legacy of the socialist past. Political rivalry and bureaucratic infighting among the (state-owned) firms and official agencies responsible for nuclear operations, as well as reported capability gaps in IT, instrumentation, and controls indicate that Chinese nuclear efforts may encounter similar difficulties.

Notwithstanding such challenges, China's nuclear sector demonstrates a growing mastery of complex products and rapid expansion of both domestic and transnational supply chains. Comparable recent advances in civil aviation and in the manufacture and operation of high-speed trains, activities that also require substantial systems integration capabilities, indicate that China may be uniquely positioned to overcome the systems integration deficit confronting follower nations.

DRIVERS OF NUCLEAR POWER PLANT INNOVATION

Although a nuclear weapons state since the 1960s, China is a relative newcomer to commercial-scale nuclear power. However, driven by the rising demand for clean power, as well as by the ambition to master advanced industries, China is now investing heavily in nuclear energy. Realization of current plans will equip China with the world's largest NPP fleet. Innovation in this context is best viewed as a composite of capability formation and catch-up rate (vis-à-vis OECD rivals), as well as the creation of new-to-the-world technology. Despite delays and occasional setbacks, China's nuclear program has advanced steadily, particularly in the areas of construction and operational experience and the development of domestic equipment manufacture.

The Chinese NPP fleet deploys multiple technologies with Russian, French, and American roots (Figure 10.2), but there is also evidence of progress in domestic research and development (R&D), especially with

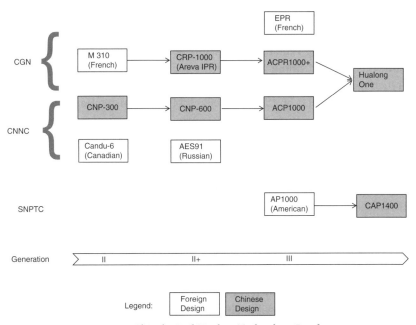

Figure 10.2 China's Civil Nuclear Technology Roadmap

regard to future generations of reactors. The policy drivers of innovation include a massive and unprecedented "new build" program; a strong localization imperative; the trend toward a dominant platform strategy (first the adoption of the Westinghouse AP1000 and later the indigenous design of the *Hualong 1*, both pressurized water reactors); proactive industrial organization moves such as domestic mergers and joint ventures with foreign technology suppliers; systematic, well-resourced pursuit of international markets; and R&D aimed at modification or extension of foreign designs as well as frontier technologies where rivals have no incumbency advantage.

Given the risk characteristics of nuclear energy, capability expansion, and sustained innovation depend on effective regulatory institutions. Evidence of regulatory progress is subdued, but unmistakable: significant cooperation with, and learning from, the International Atomic Energy Agency (IAEA) and regulatory counterparts in other countries; initial steps toward a multi-layered legal framework; and a slow but gradual strengthening of domestic regulators' technical expertise and enforcement capacity.

Along with industrial policy and regulation, we see enterprise initiative as a third driver of innovation amid continuing struggles among bureaucratic and corporate actors. Three major state-owned enterprises (SOEs) dominate China's NPP industry. They have distinct sets of capabilities, compete robustly against each other, and lobby strongly to slant national policy to their advantage. Thus while the 2007 decision to adopt Westinghouse's AP1000 technology was heavily contested, with one company pushing for home-grown technology and another for that of its French partner (Xu 2010, p. 138), rival firms routinely hold shares in each other's projects and join forces to lobby for pro-nuclear policies.

In concert, these three factors have propelled significant capability formation not only in construction and operation but also in design, manufacturing and R&D. Constraints do exist, in the form of soft factors such as safety culture and human resources, as well as fuel availability. Overall, however, the evidence points to considerable momentum for China in this advanced industry of great economic and strategic importance.

The following section briefly reviews the evolution of China's nuclear power sector. We then focus on the key sources of China's growing nuclear capabilities: government policy, official regulation, and enterprise initiative. Next, we examine how these factors have shaped developments in various segments of the nuclear industry. Finally, we turn to the substantial opportunities and formidable obstacles that jointly define China's future prospects in civilian nuclear power.

EVOLUTION OF CHINA'S NUCLEAR POWER PLANT SECTOR

Figure 10.3 highlights milestones in the development of Chinese nuclear power. This section briefly reviews the chronology and scale of China's nuclear development, then focuses on the organization of China's nuclear industry, its transition from isolation to international engagement, the development of China's domestic nuclear supply chain, and China's recent emergence as a major participant in global nuclear markets.

Chronology

Nuclear power is typically an offshoot of military programs – e.g. the Shippingport reactor was repurposed for commercial use following the cancellation of plans for a nuclear-powered aircraft carrier (Weinberg 1992). China is no different; its nuclear history began with a military program initiated in 1954 with Soviet technical support. Following the termination of Soviet assistance in 1959, Chinese scientists continued the effort, led by the Second Ministry of Machine-Building, culminating in a 1964 atomic test, a thermonuclear test three years later and a nuclear submarine in 1974 (Lewis and Xue 1988; Zhou et al. 2011). Subsequently, a Ministry of Nuclear Industry was carved out of the Second Ministry of Machine-Building in 1982. In 1989, this Ministry was reorganized as China National Nuclear Corporation (CNNC), a vertically integrated SOE active in all stages of nuclear energy (Zhou et al. 2011).

The first stage of China's civil nuclear effort began in the 1970s and lasted until 2005. The shift toward a more market-driven economy initiated during the late 1970s gradually spilled over into the nuclear industry. The 1982 creation (through renaming) of the Ministry of Nuclear Industry reflected a policy shift from "military uses first" to "combining military and civilian uses" (Zhou et al. 2011). Progress was slow. Nuclear power was not a key element of national energy policy, CNNC was ill-prepared to operate in a market-oriented context, resources were scarce, and an inconsistent technology strategy hampered the sector (Zhou et al. 2011). In 1994, a second nuclear company, China Guangdong Nuclear Power Corporation (CGN, subsequently renamed China General Nuclear Corporation) was set up.

By the 2000s, the imperative of balancing energy security and pollution control had become urgent: growing awareness of the economic and human costs of environmental pollution led to the widespread acceptance of an expanded role for nuclear power in the nation's energy mix (Xu 2010,

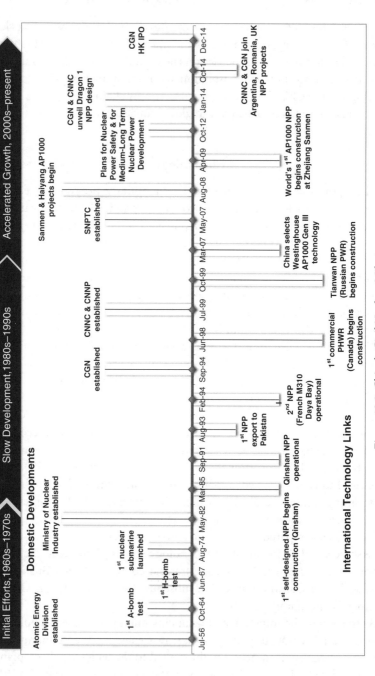

Figure 10.3 China's Civil Nuclear Milestones

p. 195). Foreshadowing the new emphasis, the State Council established State Nuclear Power Technology Corporation (SNPTC) in 2004 to select a foreign technology as the basis for a new cohort of reactors.

Development of the "Medium- and Long-Term Nuclear Power Development Plan (2005–2020)," formally approved by the State Council in November 2007, initiated a new phase of nuclear expansion (Nuclear Plan 2007). In 2007 a decision was made to adopt Westinghouse's AP1000 reactor, a Generation III+ design with advanced passive safety features, as the main vehicle for China's nuclear expansion. It was widely reported that the key consideration behind the AP1000 choice was Westinghouse's willingness to fully transfer the underlying technology.

Several big power generation companies sought avenues to enter the rapidly growing nuclear field. At the same time, SNPTC, eager to extend its operations after fulfilling its initial objective of introducing advanced NPP technology into the domestic economy, pursued a succession of merger options. These efforts came to fruition with the 2015 merger uniting China Power Investment Corporation (CPI), one of China's five power generating giants, with SNPTC. The resulting entity, State Power Investment Corporation (SPI) joins CNNC and CGN to form a triumvirate of nuclear firms, each capable of designing, building, and operating nuclear power plants.

Scale

The migration of Chinese policy from "moderate development" of nuclear power to "positive development" in 2004, and further to "steady development with safety" in 2011–12 following the 2011 Fukushima disaster (World Nuclear Association 2016) dramatically expanded the scale of nuclear operations, construction, and future plans. Table 10.1 lays out the unprecedented scale of the "new build" program. China's National Energy Administration (NEA) reports, and nuclear equipment specialists confirm, that Chinese manufacturers can deliver six to eight full sets of reactor equipment per year (World Nuclear Association 2016).[3]

Completion of plants now in process will bring China's nuclear capacity to fifty-eight reactors by 2020, an increase of twenty over the current base

---

[3] A Chinese nuclear equipment specialist commented that it would be "no problem" for domestic producers to deliver eight sets of nuclear plant equipment annually (Interview, May 2016). Li Ye, an official at the National Energy Agency, sets annual production capacity at eight to ten sets of equipment (2017).

Table 10.1 *The Evolution of China's Nuclear Power Plant Fleet: Present and Future*

Current Status	Number of Reactors	Gross Capacity (GWe)
Operating*	38	36.647
Under construction*	20	21.546
Planned**	41	48.500
Proposed**	98	111.800
Contemplated (less definite)**	79	90.770
Total	276	307.263

Notes: Capacity measured in terms of Gigawatts (1 GW = 1,000 megawatts; 1 MW = 1 million Kilowatts KW).

In addition to eighteen commercial NPP projects mentioned in the text, this compilation includes two experimental projects now under construction – a 60 MWe floating nuclear reactor and a 600 MWe demonstration fast reactor.

Sources:

* International Atomic Energy Agency, Power Reactor Information System (PRIS) in China, www .iaea.org/PRIS/CountryStatistics/CountryDetails.aspx?current=CN (accessed May 7, 2018).

** World Nuclear Association (2017), "Nuclear power in China (updated April 2018)," www .world-nuclear.org/information-library/country-profiles/countries-a-f/china-nuclear-power .aspx (accessed May 7, 2018).

of thirty-eight operating reactors. Completion of the longer-term plans summarized in Table 10.1 would expand China's nuclear fleet to 276 reactors – in comparison, the May 2018 global total of "operable reactors" is 449 reactors, of which the United States and France, the nations with the largest fleets, operate ninety-nine and fifty-eight reactors respectively.[4] (See subsequent section "Potential Difficulties for Chinese Nuclear Power" for some factors that suggest the actual number of reactors eventually built may be substantially smaller than planned.)

From Isolation to International Engagement

China's nuclear program developed in isolation for two decades following the Soviet withdrawal in 1959. Following the resumption of US–China diplomatic ties (1972) and the associated relaxation of US-led economic sanctions, China's nuclear establishment began to pursue overseas links, particularly with the United States, in order to explore options for acquisition of civilian nuclear technology (Xu 2010, pp. 41–3).

---

[4] www.world-nuclear.org/information-library/facts-and-figures/world-nuclear-power-reac tors-and-uranium-requireme.aspx (accessed May 7, 2018).

Beginning in the 1980s, Chinese nuclear organizations cultivated increasingly deep ties with overseas vendors of nuclear technology, with the vendors' governments, and with national and international entities dedicated to nuclear regulation, information-sharing and safety. China's nuclear establishment is an enthusiastic participant in multiple venues for international cooperation, including IAEA and the World Association of Nuclear Operators (WANO). China has also forged surprisingly robust links with the US Nuclear Regulatory Commission involving frequent interaction among Chinese and US nuclear specialists. China's nuclear establishment includes growing numbers of individuals with overseas experience of academic study, work, or short-term training. One source reports that "so many scientists from [the US nuclear installation at] Los Alamos have returned to Chinese universities and research institutes that people have dubbed them the 'Los Alamos club' (Chen 2017).

Chinese nuclear operators and suppliers also engage in active cooperation and information exchange with non-government agencies such as the American Society of Mechanical Engineers (ASME), which both propagates technical standards and, through interaction between its professional staff and global (including Chinese) members, works to resolve emerging issues relating to manufacturing standards.

China's "Go Outward" (走出去 (*zouchuqu*)) policy encourages, indeed virtually requires major state-controlled entities like the three nuclear giants and their big SOE equipment suppliers, to aggressively pursue overseas marketing opportunities. For two decades, Pakistan was China's lone overseas nuclear client – a partnership that resembles foreign aid rather than commercial exchange. Beginning in 2014, China exploded onto the global nuclear scene, scoring a succession of agreements with Argentina, Romania, Iran and, most remarkably, the United Kingdom, with extensive cooperation arrangements creating prospects for future contracts in other countries, including South Africa, Turkey, and Saudi Arabia.

Dual Technology Path and Growing Domestic Supply Chain

Ongoing debate between advocates of self-reliance and proponents of importing advanced technology to jump-start domestic upgrading resulted in simultaneous efforts along both paths, with CNNC pursuing rapid transition from imports to domestic versions of design and equipment, while CGN opted for "importing foreign [primarily French] equipment and technology to minimize the time needed to master" advanced systems (Xu 2010, p. 138).

With two and, following SNPTC's emergence as the champion of Westinghouse Electric's AP1000 design and the 2015 creation of SPI, now three major firms following largely autonomous technological development paths, China's nuclear industry encompasses a bewildering array of United States, French, Russian, and Canadian reactor designs along with domestic variants of the American and French blueprints.

Given China's emergence as the world's largest producer of industrial equipment and the government's determined promotion of near-universal import replacement in technology-bearing industries, the development of an extensive domestic production network for nuclear equipment and components comes as no surprise. The scale of China's domestic nuclear supply chain is evident from a 2014 reference to "over 5,400" nuclear-linked manufacturers and from the growth of nuclear supply clusters in Shanghai and Sichuan as well as in localities adjacent to nuclear power plants in Guangdong, Jiangsu, Liaoning, Shandong, and Guangdong (Localization 2014; Ma Zhe 2013; Clusters 2015).

The following section seeks to understand how China's nuclear industry developed the capabilities that have enabled this astonishingly rapid transformation.

BUILDING NUCLEAR CAPABILITIES

Following separate discussions of government policy, official regulation, and enterprise initiative, we consider how their interaction affected each segment of the nuclear power business: design, construction, materials, equipment, operation, fuel cycle, and decommissioning.

Key Components

Government Policy
Government's central contribution is its determination that China should develop a complete array of expertise in the field of civil nuclear power that encompasses the current "state of the art" while simultaneously pursuing the global technological frontier. This policy stance has generated a long-term push to establish an extensive network of nuclear-related organizations and institutions as well as generally strong financial support for nuclear education, supply chain enhancement and R&D efforts directed toward both catch-up and cutting-edge innovations.[5] The same motivation

---

[5] Xu (2010, pp. 75, 167–9) notes a partial withdrawal of support under the administration of Premier Zhu Rongji, who used a shortened time horizon and thus wanted to shut down unprofitable operations.

encouraged energetic expansion of international ties – with national gov
ernments, international organizations, and multinational firms – in the
civil nuclear field.

Bureaucratic conflicts and corruption limit the impact of official support. Xu (2010, ch. 4) emphasizes the depth and severity of rivalry among
nuclear-related agencies and firms. These conflicts have prevented the
resolution of major issues, such as the organization of China's nuclear
sector – vertical integration versus specialization and the choice between
domestic technology development and cooperation with overseas
multinationals.

The nuclear sector has not escaped the episodes of corruption that have
rocked China's energy establishment. In 2009, a bid-rigging scandal led to
the removal of CNNC's top leader. In 2015, CNNC and China Nuclear
Engineering Corporation were among six major SOEs "scolded publicly
for bribery, nepotism and management loopholes which led to loss of state
assets" (SOE Corruption 2015).

Regulation

Regulation poses difficulties everywhere. Successful systems typically
evolve over decades, with major advance often following horrific failure.
China's nuclear regulation fits this mold, but with an unusual twist: the
disaster responsible for a major safety overhaul occurred in Japan.

The 2011 Fukushima catastrophe highlighted long-standing concerns
about the safety of China's nuclear program. In a 2009 speech, Li Ganjie,
head of the National Nuclear Safety Administration, warned that "over-
rapid expansion . . . [could] threaten construction quality and operation
safety of nuclear power plants." At the same time, an official of the
Vienna-based IAEA asked "whether China would have enough nuclear
inspectors with adequate training." Just two months before the
Fukushima meltdown, Fan Bi (2011), a deputy director at the State
Council Research Office, warned of excessive speed and inadequacies
associated with expertise, equipment, and oversight, concluding that "if
too many nuclear power projects are started too quickly, it could jeopar-
dize the healthy, long-term development of nuclear power" (Patel and
Haas 2014).

Subsequent interviews with Chinese nuclear personnel reveal widespread concern about the pace of pre-Fukushima nuclear expansion. One
specialist described CGN's rapid promotion of inexperienced personnel
members as "very dangerous" (Interview, May 2016). In a discussion
involving visiting academics and staff members at a major nuclear

equipment manufacturer, one of the factory personnel commented that the Fukushima disaster had diverted China's nuclear program from a path of "blind development" (盲目发展 (*mangmu fazhan*); Interview, June 2015). Further interviews as well as conversations reported by international nuclear specialists confirm widespread concern: one informant writes of encountering fears that "development at breakneck speed" had left China's nuclear program "heading towards catastrophic failure" and of finding Chinese colleagues "relieved when China's nuclear development finally slowed down" following Fukushima (private communication).

The Fukushima episode shocked both the Chinese nuclear industry and the general public. Domestic nuclear critics were quick to respond: Wang Yi, a prominent researcher with the Chinese Academy of Sciences, spoke of "neglected nuclear security risks" and raised the possibility that the government might have "concealed nuclear safety hazards" (2011).

China's leadership responded forcefully, ordering system-wide safety inspections and imposing a temporary suspension on new project approvals. The National Nuclear Safety Agency (NNSA) received a big budget increase as its staff jumped from 300 to over 1,000 (Nakano 2013). Project approvals resumed in October 2012, but only for projects located in coastal regions, a restriction that continues as this is written.[6]

Domestic and external observers agree that post-Fukushima initiatives have markedly improved China's nuclear safety arrangements. Safety issues were among the topics addressed at a May 2014 conference of qualified suppliers for China's AP1000 nuclear power projects now in operation at Sanmen (Zhejiang) and Haiyang (Shandong).[7] Two regulators – one based at NNSA's head office, the other associated with its North China division, addressed the conference, attended by representatives, including many top executives, from China's leading nuclear agencies and largest nuclear equipment suppliers.

The tone of their discussion was entirely different from the ritualized and formalistic discussion of intellectual property rights. The regulators' comments included direct threats against violators of safety protocols, with specific reference to treating offenders "without leniency," enforcing

---

[6] At a June 2014 meeting "of the Central Leading Group for Financial and Economic Affairs ... President Xi Jinping said ... 'By adopting top international standards and ensuring safety, China should lose no time in *constructing nuclear power projects in eastern coastal regions.*" *Sinocism* June 17, 2014, quoting Xinhuanet, with emphasis added.

[7] GEN III NP AP/CAP Qualified Suppliers Symposium, Dongjiao State Guest Hotel, Pudong. See www.snptc.com.cn/en/index.php?optionid=922&auto_id=16004 (accessed August 15, 2014).

penalties, including possible "lifetime sanctions," "without delay," and ousting "unfit participants" from the nuclear supply chain.

The regulators also offered realistic appraisals of quality challenges, warning against passive approaches to quality and safety issues in which enterprise leaders issue brochures, sponsor presentations and respond to lapses rather than aggressively pursuing quality objectives. They insisted on the need to reform incentive structures that encourage managers to overlook quality issues in order to meet production timetables, while discouraging workers from flagging actual or potential safety lapses.

Reinforcing this image of muscular oversight was the news, widely circulated among Chinese nuclear specialists and foreign business executives, that nuclear safety authorities had issued a "stop work" order to a unit of Dongfang Electric (东方电气(DEC)), one of China's largest electrical equipment manufacturers, in early 2014 following discovery of an attempt to conceal defective welding on a nuclear-related project.[8] In a 2015 interview, a senior NNSA official mentioned two episodes in which quality problems led to the removal of nuclear manufacturing licenses from the offending firms. Publication of a critical report directed at Shanghai Electric, another leading nuclear equipment supplier, further demonstrates NNSA's capacity to discipline powerful SOEs whose top executives may outrank NNSA's leaders within China's bureaucratic hierarchy (Shanghai Electric 2014). The 2016 nuclear valve quality scandal, discussed below, reinforces this observation (NPP Valve 2016a, 2016b).

Presentations by leaders of major equipment manufacturers at the 2014 conference demonstrated substantial executive "buy-in" to the analysis and concerns expressed by the regulators and by speakers from Westinghouse Electric and other international partners. The Chairman of Harbin Electric (哈尔滨电气 (HEC)), echoing comments by Westinghouse Electric's Tim Collier, emphasized that development of quality and safety is not a natural process, but can advance only with sustained attention from enterprise leaders. He then explained how his firm had restructured reporting arrangements to isolate the division responsible for quality assurance, which now evaluates its own personnel, and is no longer subordinate to executives in charge of production scheduling. If quality problems delay or halt production, it falls to the General Manager to resolve any consequences for production timetables.

---

[8] We learned of this episode from a journalist, and subsequently received confirmation from an industry insider. We obtained no details about the location, the identity of the DEC unit involved, or the specific project.

The General Manager of the nuclear pump subsidiary of Shenyang Blower Group (沈阳鼓风机集团核电泵业有限公司) reported that employees initially rejected the idea that nuclear production required them to move away from "traditional company culture." Only when EMD, the firm's overseas joint venture partner, became dissatisfied with lax operations and halted production on two separate occasions, did the Chinese workers begin to appreciate the importance of nuclear safety culture. Several years later, circumstances are much improved. People are more aware of nuclear safety requirements, better prepared to accept individual responsibility for maintaining high standards, and willing to stop production when problems arise.

The Deputy General Manager of Yantai Taihai Manuer Nuclear Equipment Company (烟台台海玛努尔核电设备股份有限公司) reported on his firm's use of internal audit procedures to identify "deviations from best practice," noting that a recent review revealed over 219 such gaps, for example the start of pipe manufacturing prior to completing an audit of bending tools. The speaker emphasized the importance of transparency, which he defined as verifying that documents circulated within the firm exactly match information shared with customers and partners.

The same speaker emphasized that his firm's effort to promote safety culture extended "all along the value chain." This is a key element. Effective pursuit of comprehensive quality assurance demands that a firm's suppliers commit to the same goals. Without extending quality assurance programs throughout the supply chain, efforts to improve outcomes can fail if materials, equipment, components or services purchased from outside suppliers overlook the quality requirements that the receiving firm is struggling to implement.

The unexpected outcome of our inquiry is that, in contrast to general weakness of Chinese regulatory efforts, a combination of strong motivation, aggressive official behavior, and responsive corporate leadership has delivered substantial progress toward China's goal of developing an effective regime to assure quality and safety in nuclear design, equipment, and operations.

This is not to say that all is well. NNSA semi-annual reports initiated in 2015, part of an industry-wide effort to increase transparency in the face of public skepticism[9] about nuclear safety, recount a litany of lapses: welding defects, valve malfunctions, non-standard operations, and much else that

---

[9] A Chinese nuclear specialist advised us that 70% of online postings oppose further expansion of nuclear power plants (Interview, May 19, 2014).

the inspectors attribute to insufficient skills, design flaws, and shortcomings in systems for managing assembly and construction work (NNSA Briefing 2015, 2016). The reports also make ominous reference to "fraud" (弄虚作假 (*nongxu zuojia*)) and "operational violations" (违规操作(*weigui caozuo*)).[10]

Although the institutional framework surrounding nuclear operations continues to develop – as illustrated by the 2016 announcement of a national plan for meeting nuclear emergencies (State Council Information Office 2016) – the structure is far from complete. Two episodes during 2014, brief disappearance of radioactive material at a Nanjing facility and discovery of an unlicensed radiation center associated with Yangzhou (Jiangsu) University, illustrate the limitations of current arrangements. Keenly aware of such difficulties, regulators describe 2015 as "the first year of strictly implementing new regulatory requirements according to law" for nuclear safety (Nuclear Safety 2015).

Legal developments illustrate both the progress and the slow pace of institution building. Amid a growing body of laws and regulations (Nuclear Laws 2009, also www.lawinfochina.com/SearchList.aspx (accessed July 10, 2018), more than thirty years were required to complete China's first nuclear safety law, which took effect at the start of 2018.[11] In 2010, a visiting team of IAEA experts advised that "nuclear safety-related legislation and policies should be further enhanced for all nuclear activities" (IAEA Team 2010). Plans to "accelerate" the legislative process in 2011 fizzled. A 2014 report attributed the logjam to bureaucratic jousting among multiple agencies responsible for science, energy, environment, land, and weapons: once a draft is completed, "various departments experience difficulty in reaching a consensus" (Zhu Xuerui 2014). Nuclear legislation returned to the agenda for 2016 (Nuclear Safety Law 2016), reportedly at the personal request of President Xi Jinping (Interview, June 2015). A visiting IAEA delegation pushed for "adopting the draft Nuclear Safety Act, making pointed reference to the need to "ensure the independence of . . . NNSA as a regulatory body" (IAEA Visit 2016).

Despite increased staffing, larger budgets, development of in-house research operations, and extensive interaction with the international

---

[10] A US-based nuclear engineer remarked that the deficiencies described in these reports recalled circumstances in the US nuclear sector prior to the 1979 meltdown at the US Three Mile Island plant.

[11] For the text of this law, see www.npc.gov.cn/npc/xinwen/2017-09/01/content_2027930 .html (accessed July 8, 2018).

nuclear community, questions persist about NNSA's capacity to manage its rapidly expanding responsibilities:

- *Insufficient manpower.* Despite expanding to over 1,000 employees (Nakano 2013), NNSA may lack sufficient personnel to effectively execute its mandate. Zhou (2013) reports that the average number of regulatory staff per reactor in China is only 8.3, versus 33.5 in the United States. Philippe Jamet, one of five governing commissioners of France's Autorité de Sûreté Nucléaire, testified before the French parliament in February 2014 that "the Chinese safety authorities lack means. They are overwhelmed" (Patel and Haas 2014).
- *Restless regulatory staff.* Many NNSA personnel are former or potential employees of nuclear companies that offer far higher pay scales. A high-ranking NNSA official noted that NNSA sometimes loses both experienced officials and fresh graduates to higher-paying nuclear companies. The same individual also indicated that CGN employees with the same rank earned five times his/her own salary (Interview, June 2015). To increase the attractiveness of NNSA employment, the State Council has placed substantial numbers of coveted residential permits (编制(*bianzhi*)) at the disposal of NNSA's headquarters, its Beijing research campus, and its regional offices (Interview, June 2015).
- *Too many reactor designs.* The presence of multiple technologies (French, US, Russian, domestic) within China's nuclear power portfolio complicates NNSA's work: Zhou and Zhang (2010, p. 4285) note that the presence of multiple technologies "constitutes a great challenge ... as more work is required to ensure nuclear safety." This complexity seems likely to increase as domestic firms – China National Nuclear (CNNC), China General Nuclear (CGN), and State Power Investment (SPI) – pursue domestic projects incorporating their own proprietary designs alongside new projects based on technology supplied by US, French, and Russian partners. One reason for Beijing's insistence that CNNC and CGN combine their separate Dragon 1 efforts into a single common design was NNSA's concern that limited resources would hinder its effort to conduct a thorough and comprehensive review of the new reactor design (Interview, May 2016).

These actual and potential weaknesses have not prevented China's nuclear programs from compiling a considerable record of achievement. China's growing fleet of nuclear plants continues to extend its three-decade long record of successful operation, experiencing no incidents above Level 1 (anomaly) on the International Nuclear and Radiological Events Scale maintained by the World Association of Nuclear Operators (WANO), which classifies major episodes such as Chernobyl and Fukushima as Level 7.[12] CGN, China's biggest nuclear operator, achieves consistently excellent ratings from WANO and in cross-national competitions among plants using designs originating with Électricité de France (EDF) (Zhu Xuerui 2016c – summarizing the firm's 2015 corporate social responsibility report).

China's gradually deepening and surprisingly effective system of nuclear regulation certainly shares credit for these and other accomplishments in the nuclear power industry. Whether ongoing improvements can keep pace with the regulatory burden associated with rapid nuclear expansion – including domestic and overseas operations and a large and growing domestic supply chain – remains an open question.

Enterprise Initiative

Broad official support for nuclear power masks internal struggles that have not only slowed the passage of nuclear legislation, but have prevented definitive responses to a series of controversial issues:

- The degree and timing of cooperation with foreign firms and of reliance on imported technology and equipment.
- Whether or not to focus on a "master" or "core" reactor design.
- Industrial organization of the nuclear sector.
- Location of nuclear installations.

The inability of top policy-makers to resolve such issues has opened the door to policy entrepreneurship on the part of China's nuclear companies. Agencies and leaders fail to settle major policy issues, but have repeatedly agreed to specific proposals regarding individual nuclear projects, domestic corporate mergers, and cooperative links with specific foreign firms. As a result, the developmental trajectory of China's seemingly top-down

---

[12] For details about the event scale, see https://en.wikipedia.org/wiki/International_Nuclear_Event_Scale. Nakano's statement that "China has not had nuclear events that exceed Level 2 on the INES" (2013, p. 6) appears incorrect, apparently reflecting a Chinese linguistic ambiguity in which "no nuclear occurrence above Level 2 (没有发生2级以上核电事件)" can mean either "no occurrence *above Level 2*" or "no occurrence *at or above Level 2*." For precise statements confirming the absence of incidents "at or above Level 2" see Liu Jia (2014) and Zhang Tinke (2018). Thanks to Yi Han for clarifying this matter.

system in reality reflects the joint outcome of official policy and of initiatives originating in major nuclear enterprises, which, as noted above, operate in an environment that blends fierce competition with cooperative endeavor.

Cooperation versus indigenous development. What is the quickest and most efficient path toward China's objective of developing a full range of nuclear capabilities, from reactor design and equipment manufacture to construction and operation of nuclear plants and refining, storage and disposal of nuclear fuel and waste, all based on Chinese intellectual property? One approach, illustrated by Soviet/Russian experience, emphasizes independent effort from the start, with minimal involvement of foreign expertise or technology. The Korean example, which used initial reliance on foreign tutelage to develop knowledge and experience that propelled a rapid transition to independent effort, provides a plausible alternative.

Beijing-based CNNC, which resembles Russia's ROSATOM in combining civil and military operations into a complete package of nuclear capabilities, has consistently promoted a domestic development strategy with minimal involvement of overseas technology, foreign firms or imported equipment. CNNC's lobbying efforts, however, were not successful. Its initial nuclear monopoly crumbled as first China General Nuclear (CGN, formerly China Guangdong Nuclear) and then State Power Investment (SPI formed by the 2015 merger of technology specialist SNPTC and electricity giant CPI) entered the nuclear power business, each fortified with technology acquired from foreign partners. CGN, China's leading NPP operator, has developed a succession of projects in cooperation with French firms Électricité de France and Areva. SNPTC, now part of State Power Investment, initially focused on absorbing Westinghouse Electric's AP1000 reactor technology.

Unplanned enterprise initiative has provided the motive force for shifting China's nuclear development strategy from its initially self-reliant approach to what now more closely resembles the Korean model of using imports and foreign cooperation as a springboard for enlarging domestic capabilities. This is particularly evident in the recent merger involving SNPTC, which pursued several potential partners in an effort to extend its corporate life after completing its initial task of transferring the AP1000 technology to domestic operating companies.

Reactor design. Figure 10.2, which traces the lineage of Chinese reactor designs, highlights the importance of enterprise initiative in choosing technologies for successive projects. The 2007 agreement with Westinghouse Electric for the complete transfer of AP1000 technology and design information seemed to herald the arrival of a uniform standard, with domestic accounts reporting that "China has officially adopted AP1000 nuclear power technology" and citing an industry expert's reference to "confirmation of a technology base" for nuclear power (Li Qiyan 2008).

Subsequent developments quickly shattered any prospect of standardization. In October 2007, an SNPTC official emphasized China's continued openness to French and Russian technology (China Open 2007). "Before the ink was dry" on the AP1000 agreement, CGN won approval for its plan to build two reactors at Taishan (Guangdong) using Generation III+ technology from the French firm Areva (Wang Lu 2012; Areva 2007).

Recent years have seen independent efforts by CNNC, CGN, and SNPTC to develop and market proprietary reactor designs both at home and abroad. SNPTC, now part of post-merger SPI, champions its CAP1400 design, a modified and enlarged version of the Westinghouse AP1000. CNNC and CGN developed similar but competing designs, each boasting the patriotic title of "China Dragon 1" (*Hualong 1*). The two rivals grudgingly agreed to pool resources to produce a common Dragon 1 design only after the central government, fearing possible loss of future export revenues as well as the escalating costs of supervising multiple reactor models, threatened to exclude both companies from domestic and foreign project competitions. Even then, both firms vowed to pursue their independent proprietary design efforts.

Industrial Organization. Long-standing absence of clear policy regarding the choice between vertical integration, in which individual firms span multiple segments of the industry, and concentration of specific functions within specialized independent entities, provides further insight into the importance of enterprise initiative in mapping out China's nuclear trajectory. The shifting organization of the reactor sector illustrates the point:

- SNPTC began as a technology and design specialist in 2004, tasked with absorbing and then, through its design division, modifying the AP1000 technology licensed from Westinghouse Electric to develop the enlarged CAP1400 reactor being built at Shidaowan (Shandong) and the still larger CAP1700, now in the preliminary design stage (Zhu Xuerui 2017e).
- SNPTC's 2015 merger with CPI, one of China's largest power generation firms, represented a move toward vertical integration. Interviews with industry participants suggest that Wang Binghua, the chairman first of SNPTC and subsequently of SPI, was the prime mover behind

this deal, which positions SNPTC to compete directly with CNNC and CGN now that it can operate as well as design nuclear plants.

- Following the imposition of Beijing's demand that they produce an integrated version of their rival Dragon 1 designs, CNNC and CGN jointly established a Hualong Design Institute, with the two firms each contributing half of the necessary staff and funds. This perhaps marks a shift toward concentration of reactor design efforts in a specialized entity.

Location of nuclear installations. While China's current reactor fleet is confined to coastal provinces, pre-Fukushima plans called for nationwide construction of nuclear facilities: documents posted at the World Nuclear Association's website identify several dozen projected inland nuclear sites spanning nearly every province. When project approval resumed in 2013 following the post-Fukushima review, consideration was restricted to nuclear proposals in coastal regions.

Not surprisingly, Fukushima has strengthened domestic opposition to nuclear expansion. Anti-nuclear sentiment has coalesced around the coast-inland divide, even though the United States and France, countries with the largest NPP fleets, operate numerous inland reactors. Well-informed skeptics, including some with extensive nuclear expertise, focus on limiting the pace of nuclear growth and the risk of depleting or contaminating freshwater supplies in regions where water is both scarce and heavily used for agriculture. Other opponents stoke public fears, highlighting potential nuclear risks while ignoring more immediate dangers associated with coal mines and thermal power plants – the main alternative to nuclear power.

Faced with strenuous public opposition, China's nuclear establishment has responded with tactics that might be expected from their counterparts in democracies like France or the United States:

- *Publicity.* Transparency has become the order of the day in China's nuclear industry, with major companies hosting open houses, holding press conferences, and issuing corporate social responsibility reports replete with the fashionable jargon of western political correctness.
- *Lobbying.* Local and provincial governments have joined with nuclear firms to plead their case for approving projects that promise to stimulate local economies and provide local administrations with increased levels of much-valued energy independence. Hunan even dispatched a delegation to visit the US headquarters of Westinghouse Electric, presumably in the hope of prodding Beijing to hasten approval of the proposed nuclear facility at Taohuajiang.

- *Begin work in anticipation of eventual project approval.* Pre-approval work on infrastructure: site preparation, roads, bridges, power lines etc. is standard practice. In addition, at least one major supplier has signed contracts to deliver large pieces of NPP equipment to sites in three inland provinces. Although none of these projects has received official approval, this firm had acquired materials and begun manufacturing operations in connection with these agreements (Interview, June 2015).

In each case, our evidence confirms Yi-chong Xu's characterization of China's nuclear policies as "inconsistent, contested and fragmented" (2010, p. 8), a circumstance that has opened the door to multiple instances of successful policy entrepreneurship on the part of individual nuclear companies.

We conclude that the industrial policy drivers of innovation, such as the initiation of a massive and unprecedented "new build" program and a strong localization imperative, combine with unmistakable progress in regulatory capacity and resolve to provide a firm basis for catch-up and innovation. However, our analysis reveals enterprise initiative as a critical third driver of innovation. Robust competition among corporate actors and policy entrepreneurship by enterprise leaders shape policy in directions that have helped to advance the capability frontier. In concert, these three factors have propelled significant catch-up not only in construction and operation but also in design, manufacturing and R&D.

CATCH-UP AND INNOVATION IN CHINA'S NUCLEAR POWER PLANT SECTOR

In 1990 China was simultaneously scrambling to cobble together its initial Qinshan NPP operation and foraging across the international landscape for opportunities to acquire advanced nuclear technology from the likes of Framatom, Siemens, General Electric, and Westinghouse. A quarter-century later, China debouches onto the global scene as a nuclear power-house, claiming the capacity to design, erect, equip, finance, and operate nuclear plants embodying major elements of the most advanced commercial technology, and replacing its former subordinate relationship with major multinational firms with a combination of cooperation and rivalry. To understand the processes that contributed to this transformation, we focus on successive segments of the nuclear supply chain.

Design

The decision to license Westinghouse's AP1000 design followed "a major struggle between . . . CNNC . . . pushing for indigenous technology and the small but well-connected . . . SNPTC . . . favoring imported technology."[13] Together with CGN's partnership with Areva to construct French-designed reactors in South China, this has launched China's nuclear sector on a path similar to the prior experience of France, Japan, and Korea, which used imported technology as a springboard to develop independent reactor designs.

After decades of work, efforts to build Chinese-designed nuclear plants appear close to fruition. Chinese firms have begun to offer the CAP1000, a homegrown modification of the AP1000 system, as well as the CAP1400, a scaled-up version of the same system, to prospective domestic and overseas buyers. Construction of a CAP1400 demonstration reactor is underway at Shidaowan, Shandong.[14]

In late 2014, China officially approved a separate reactor design, the Dragon 1 (*Hualong 1*) developed jointly by CNNC and CGN (Hualong-1 Review 2014). This combination originated in official concern that overseas competition among the two Chinese nuclear giants – both developing proprietary reactor systems – would reduce potential export revenues by allowing foreign buyers to bargain for lower prices. Following official instructions to produce a unified design for international markets, the two firms engaged in what informants describe as lengthy and acrimonious negotiations that resulted in an improbable design partnership: Hualong International Nuclear Power Technology, a fifty/fifty joint venture inaugurated in March 2016.[15]

Information Systems

Designing, constructing, and operating nuclear power plants is an enormously complex activity that requires libraries of technical, legal and regulatory materials. Interdependencies abound – a single alteration

---

[13] See www.world-nuclear.org/information-library/country-profiles/countries-a-f/china
-nuclear-power.aspx (accessed September 13, 2016).

[14] See www.world-nuclear.org/information-library/country-profiles/countries-a-f/china
-nuclear-power.aspx (accessed September 13, 2016).

[15] See www.world-nuclear-news.org/C-Hualong-One-joint-venture-officially-launched
-1703164.html (accessed September 14, 2016).

might require changes in thousands of documents. Navigation of these complexities requires sophisticated management information systems. Their absence invites errors. A 2015 report attributes wiring defects at the Hongyanhe nuclear facility to management's failure to control the distribution of design documents. The result: working with outdated information, installers made mistakes that control systems failed to detect, resulting in a cascade of difficulties (NNSA Briefing 2015).

A pair of December 2015 announcements highlights efforts to attack these issues. CNNC trumpeted the completion of Nestor, a package incorporating "68 pieces of software that. . ... covers the design, manufacturing, installation, testing and operation of a nuclear power project based on our Hualong One design." This software "will pave the way for China to export entire nuclear power projects and technologies" (Nestor 2015). At the same time, a subdivision of the rival SPI unveiled its COSINE product: "China's first set of nuclear power design and safety analysis software. . ... integrating research & development, engineering design, equipment manufacture, project management, nuclear power plant operation and operational services" (COSINE 2015).

In 2016, China Nuclear Power Engineering Co. Ltd, a CNNC affiliate, released its ProMIS system, a "digitized virtual factory . . . in real-time simulation . . . covering nuclear and conventional islands, BOP [balance of plant] environment, involving the fuel system, the overall geology, building, structure, water, electrical, instrumentation and control, radiation protection, safety analysis, engineering construction, commissioning and other special areas." Unlike previous arrangements, which included separate and unconnected information systems for "design, procurement, construction and commissioning," ProMIS combines these segments within an integrated "digital library" that will provide "the latest and most accurate information," thus "greatly reducing the communication barriers . . . [as well as] management costs including time, manpower and resources" (Zhu and Kong 2016).

Construction

The nuclear sector has benefited from the huge expansion of domestic construction activity that accompanied China's overall economic boom. Declining costs for building thermal power plants, discussed by Thomas Rawski in Chapter 8, point to the presence of strong competitive pressures in construction. Skills and experience accumulated in building hundreds of power plants as well as dams, airports, railways, highways, bridges, and other infrastructure projects surely accelerate progress toward mastery of the exacting construction requirements for nuclear installations.

Industry sources report that AP1000 projects at Vogtle GA and Summer SC adopted welding techniques developed at China's AP1000 projects in Sanmen and Haiyang (http://chronicle.augusta.com/news-metro-latest-news/2013-02-10/chinas-nuclear-project-offers-lessons-vogtle-expansion (accessed August 18, 2017)).

The rapidity of China's nuclear build-out allows construction specialists to hone their skills from a succession of nuclear projects. Modular construction, for example, reportedly shortened civil construction for the nuclear island at Fuqing Unit 5 by seventy days (Lu Bin 2016). Not surprisingly, a veteran US nuclear specialist expressed a desire to learn more about Chinese firms' building techniques (Interview, August 2013).

A Chinese nuclear specialist contrasted local circumstances with conditions in Europe, where companies with no nuclear experience can bid for NPP construction contracts (Interview, June 2015). Recognizing the value of experience accumulated in China's world-leading nuclear expansion program, the IAEA chose China as the site for the world's first international center for training in nuclear construction, and a Chinese firm, China Nuclear Industry 23 Construction Co. Ltd, to operate this new agency (Construction Training 2011).

Materials

Independent nuclear capability includes domestic manufacture of a wide array of specialized materials. A 2014 report identifies specific annual requirements – including 70,000 tons of specialty steel, 1,200 tons of nuclear grade zirconium, and 2,000 tons of zirconium and zirconium alloy ingot, lists suppliers tasked with delivering these products and emphasizes the importance of accelerating the development of specialty metals (Cheng Sisi 2014). Progress in manufacturing zirconium and special steel can illuminate this process.

Zirconium is a key ingredient in the cladding that surrounds the reactor's fissile core, assuring containment of radioactive material and insulating the reactor's coolant from contact with uranium fuel. Following an eight-year effort that included the procurement and installation of over 200 sets of key equipment and the absorption of 16,000 sets of technical documents, a Baoji, Shaanxi manufacturer of nuclear-grade zirconium products obtained certification from both Westinghouse and Chinese agencies in 2016. Its initial output contributed to fuel assemblies at the Haiyang AP1000 installation (Zhu and Jia 2016).

Steel is equally important. Formidable requirements for purity, chemical composition, dimensions, durability, and resistance to corrosion, heat and pressure pose major challenges despite China's status as the world's largest steel producer. A 2014 report announcing the achievement of Taiyuan Iron & Steel Group in delivering "the first batch" of "high-end stainless steel materials" for manufacturing nuclear equipment emphasized China's limited capacity to satisfy the metallurgical requirements for Generation III reactors, which impose more demanding requirements than Generation II and II+ devices – systems for which steel supplies are "basically localized." While applauding Taiyuan's achievement, the report flagged problem areas, among them steel smelting, limited product variety, and incomplete technical standards. The result: major reliance on imported steel for the AP1000 reactors at Sanmen and Haiyang (Cheng Sisi 2014).

Progress in manufacturing duplex stainless steel plates reveals both the difficulties surrounding upgrading and the potential for breakthroughs. S32101 is a steel variety developed by a Swedish firm in 2002. Taiyuan Steel began experimental production of S32101 sheets in 2007, the year after this item's acceptance within US. standards. In 2009, the firm successfully poured "several heats" of duplex stainless billet. By 2013, the firm had delivered over 2,000 tons of S32101 sheets, most destined for AP1000 fuel pool construction (Li Jun 2013; Xu Honglin and Fang Xudong 2010). Next came an interlude during which domestic producers successfully turned out sheets as wide as 2.6 meters, enabling in a 50 percent reduction from the import price of RMB 100,000 per tonne, but failed to produce satisfactory output in the 2.6–3.1-meter range – the reigning international standard. After unsuccessful efforts to produce sheets with a width of 3.2 meters – output deteriorated at high temperatures and failed to meet other standards, a 2016 report announced that "well-known domestic steel mills" successfully developed S32101 stainless steel sheets with a width of 3.5 meters – extending the previous global frontier of 3.1 meters. If confirmed, this represents a substantial advance. Substituting the wider plates for 2.6-meter materials can eliminate 300 meters of welding in a single NPP project, reducing the manufacturing cycle for structural modules by "nearly two months" (Zhu Xuerui 2016b).

Equipment

China is the world's largest equipment manufacturer. Recent years have brought growing recognition that successful Chinese firms match global leaders in a growing array of products, including construction equipment, mining machinery, and telecom gear, and are rapidly closing long-standing technical gaps in other sectors (Digging 2013; Chazan and Wilson 2014; Brandt and Thun 2010, 2016). The same pattern of growing capability and competitiveness applies to Chinese makers of conventional power plant equipment, for which leading Chinese firms like Dongfang Electric, Harbin Electric, and Shanghai Electric have joined the ranks of the world's largest producers.

To close the initial technology gaps, Chinese entrants have relied on varying combinations of licensing, joint ventures, reverse engineering, in-house R&D and unauthorized appropriation of intellectual property rights, the last a common feature in the industrialization of follower nations including the United States and Japan, to improve the quality and competitiveness of their products (Brandt, Rawski, and Sutton 2008). In China, as in Japan and Korea, producing and marketing products that combine adequate quality with low price has been a key component of this upgrading process.

Two features differentiate nuclear equipment from the machinery used for thermal or wind-powered generating devices, telecoms, construction sites, and other segments in which Chinese firms have rapidly approached global frontiers. Construction and operation of nuclear power facilities require layers of extreme quality requirements that affect every segment of the supply process: design, materials, fabrication, installation, and operation. As a result, buyers may refuse to sacrifice quality – especially if this increases the risk of nuclear accidents, undermines reliability, or threatens to shorten the reactor's service life – in order to lower costs.

These characteristics limit the opportunity for new entrants to "cut their teeth" and gain experience by selling inferior goods to price-conscious buyers. Nuclear-related goods demand an immediate transition to extreme requirements for materials composition, durability, machining tolerances etc. Rapid expansion of nuclear plant construction coupled with ongoing import replacement requires large numbers of entrants to rapidly master demanding standards for quality, precision, and reliability.

Despite these obstacles, import substitution has progressed swiftly. Numerous reports indicate rising localization rates, which measure either the proportion of components or the (typically smaller) share of component costs contributed by domestic products: at the Ling Ao complex in Guangdong, for example, this measure (presumably the former version) rose from 55 percent to 73 percent between the first and second stages of construction (Tan Gan 2012, p. 43).

Chinese firms have begun to produce the most complex and exacting components, initially in collaboration with overseas partners. The evolution of work on reactor pressure vessels illustrates this process. Beginning in 2007, China First Heavy Industries (CHFI) participated in the manufacture of pressure vessels for the first AP1000 units at Sanmen and Haiyang. Working "under the supervision of" domestic authorities as well as Westinghouse and Doosan, CHFI sent "some forgings" to the main production site at Doosan's Korean works. Seven years later, the pressure vessel for the second unit at Sanmen, now supplied by CFHI, "successfully passed a pressure test." Shanghai Electric Group will manufacture the pressure vessel for the second unit at Haiyang (First AP1000 vessel 2014).

Table 10.2, which identifies the manufacturers of key components for the Sanmen and Haiyang projects, shows that this process of import replacement now encompasses the entire array of major components. For the second stage construction at both sites, Chinese firms participate in the manufacture of all key components, working jointly with overseas firms to produce squib valves and reactor coolant pumps – evidently the most difficult items – and taking the lead role elsewhere.

Information from publications and interviews offers mixed views of Chinese equipment quality. A Japanese nuclear specialist asserts that engineers regard components manufactured by Harbin Electric (in joint ventures (JVs) and under technical licenses) as indistinguishable from original Toshiba products (Interview, 2014). Others are less sanguine: Liu Baohua, the head of the National Energy Agency's Nuclear Office, commented in 2014 that "key technology and equipment being deployed as [China] shifts towards advanced nuclear reactors were 'still not completely up to standard'" (Reuters 2014). A US executive described conversations with a Chinese nuclear manager who declined an invitation to purchase surplus nuclear components, saying that comparable devices were available more cheaply from Chinese suppliers even if they required several attempts to produce a satisfactory item (Interview, July 2014). Documentary sources occasionally mention remanufacturing to meet product standards (Mou Sinan and Hu Qing 2016b).

Labor

Operation and oversight of nuclear plants requires skilled and experienced personnel. China's slowdown in nuclear power development during the 1990s led to the closure of some nuclear engineering programs

Table 10.2 *Growing Chinese Capacity for Domestic Production of Nuclear Power Plant Components as Seen from Four Projects Implementing Westinghouse's AP-1000 Design*

Component	Nuclear Project:				Chinese Term
	Sanmen 1	Haiyang 1	Sanmen 2	Haiyang 2	
Project Started	2009	2009	2009	2009	
Planned Completion	2016	2015	2016	2016	
Reactor Coolant Pump	EMD (US)	EMD (US)	EMD (US)	EMD/*SHENYANG BLOWER WORKS*	屏蔽电机主泵
Squib Valve	SPX (UK)	SPX (UK)	SPX (UK)	*SPX/JIANGSU VALVE*	爆管阀
Steam Generator	Doosan (Korea)	Doosan (Korea)	*SHANGHAI NUC./* ENSA (Spain)	*SHANGHAI NUCLEAR*	蒸汽发生器
Reactor Pressure Vessel	Doosan (Korea)	Doosan (Korea)	*#1 HEAVY INDUSTRY*	*SHANGHAI NUCLEAR*	反应堆压力容器
Reactor Vessel Internals	Doosan (Korea)	Newington (US)	*SHANGHAI #1 MACHINE TOOL*	*SHANGHAI #1 MACHINE TOOL*	堆内构件
Control Rod Drive Mechanism	Newington (US)	Newington (US)	*SHANGHAI #1 MACHINE TOOL*	*SHANGHAI #1 MACHINE TOOL*	控制棒驱动机构
Heat Exchanger	Mangiarotti (Italy)	*DONGFANG HEAVY EQUIPMENT*	*HARBIN HEAVY ELECTRICAL*	*DONGFANG HEAVY EQUIPMENT*	非能动余热排出热交换器
Fuel Handling Machine	Westinghouse Electric (US)	*DALIAN CRANE*	*SHANGHAI CRANE*	*DALIAN CRANE*	装卸料器
Polar Crane	PaR Nuclear (US)	*TAIYUAN HEAVY INDUSTRY*	*DALIAN CRANE*	*TAIYUAN HEAVY INDUSTRY*	环行吊车
Containment Vessel	Westinghouse/ *SHANDONG NUCLEAR*	*SHANDONG NUCLEAR EQUIP.*	*SHANDONG NUCLEAR EQUIP.*	*SHANDONG NUCLEAR EQUIP.*	钢制安全壳

(continued)

Main Piping	*BOHAI HEAVY INDUSTRY*	*#2 HEAVY INDUSTRY*	*#2 HEAVY INDUSTRY*	*BOHAI HEAVY INDUSTRY*	主管道
Pressurizer	*SHANGHAI NUCLEAR*	*DONGFANG HEAVY EQUIPMENT*	*SHANGHAI NUCLEAR*	*DONGFANG HEAVY EQUIPMENT*	稳压器
Core Makeup Tank	*SHANGHAI NUCLEAR*	*HARBIN HEAVY ELECTRICAL*	*SHANGHAI NUCLEAR*	*HARBIN HEAVY ELECTRICAL*	堆芯补水箱
Accumulator	*SHANGHAI ELECTRIC*	*SHANGHAI ELECTRIC*	*SHANGHAI ELECTRIC*	*SHANGHAI ELECTRIC*	安注箱

Note: Chinese firms are identified in capital letters with boldface italics. The heavy dotted line separates domestically manufactured components (below the line) from components that are imported or, as in the case of the containment vessel for Sanmen 1 and several other items, produced by partnerships involving Chinese and international firms.

Sources: Adapted from presentation by Sun Wenke of China State Nuclear Engineering at the GEN III NP AP/CAP QUALIFIED SUPPLIERS SYMPOSIUM Pudong, China, May 29, 2014. Timetable information for Sanmen and Haiyang projects from http://www.world-nuclear.org/info/Country-Profiles/Countries-A-F/China-Nuclear-Power/ (accessed October 19, 2014).

and to the departure of specialized personnel from the nuclear industry (Nakano 2013). Subsequent acceleration of nuclear construction raises the possibility of manpower shortages in plant operation as well as regulatory oversight.

A 2014 interview with Lu Qizhou, the head of China Power International (CPI), underscores the possibility of future manpower shortages. After describing CPI's current strategy as developing coastal nuclear sites and "protecting inland sites while waiting for opportunities to ripen," Lu comments that "the current period [of limited post-Fukushima expansion] enables us to rectify a long-standing problem of human capital lagging behind the pace of development by accumulating nuclear talent" (Caijing 2014).

Two circumstances act to alleviate any possible manpower shortfall. Rapid expansion of university-level programs in nuclear engineering as well as electrical engineering and other related fields promises a large and growing supply of potential recruits. Complementing university-level programs, corporate training programs are also being contemplated – in the summer of 2018, we were told of plans for a "CNNC University" to train reactor operators and support staff.

In addition, the accumulation of operational experience has revealed opportunities to reduce labor requirements. Between 2005 and 2010, CGN, China's largest NPP operator, reduced the size of work teams assigned to initiate operation of new nuclear plants from 104 at Ling Ao #2 to 34 at Yinjiang and then to twenty-one at Fangchengwan; performance improved even as the workforce declined (Zhu Jiaqi 2014).

CGN management has also restructured operations to capitalize on opportunities for specialization. Beginning in 2002, CGN developed plans to establish regional operating companies to manage routine operations at its fleet of nuclear plants. When this initiative ran afoul of legal and regulatory conflicts, CGN reassigned 3,500 workers at its Daya Bay complex to a new entity, the Daya Bay Nuclear Operations Management Company, which took charge of day-to-day operations at Daya Bay's six nuclear units. Then in 2012, 1,500 workers from that unit were transferred to another new body, CGN Nuclear Power Operations Ltd, to implement specialization, intensification (集约化 *jiyuehua*) and standardization throughout CGN's nuclear fleet (Zhu Jiaqi 2014).

CGN's experience indicates that current staffing arrangements may conceal opportunities to shift considerable numbers of experienced personnel to new plants, which would alleviate concerns over possible shortages of experienced operational staff as China's nuclear fleet continues to expand.

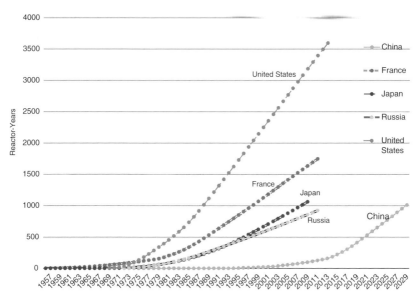

Figure 10.4 Cumulative Nuclear Plant Operating Experience in Reactor-Years, 1957–2030: China, France, Japan, Russia

Operation

Figure 10.4 compares Chinese operating experience, projected to 2030 by assuming continued operation of plants currently in service or under construction, with the nuclear history of the United States, France, Japan, and Russia – all measured in cumulative reactor-years.[16] These data identify the United States and France as global leaders in nuclear operating experience. Recent expansion of China's nuclear program puts the People's Republic on track to match the current cumulative experience of Japan and Russia, today's second echelon nuclear operators, by 2030.

As noted above, international bodies award high marks to Chinese NPPs for operational safety of the current fleet of (mostly Generation II and II+) reactors. In addition, the US Nuclear Regulatory Commission has begun to incorporate trial results from initial operations at China's Sanmen and Haiyang AP1000 installations as part of its certification

---

[16] Cumulative reactor years R(t) = R(t-1) + [N(t) + C(t) – O(t)], where N, C, and O are annual numbers of reactors Newly commissioned and in their first full year of operation, Continuing in service, or taken Out of service.

process for US plants of similar design.[17] This situates Chinese plants at the forefront of operational experience for the world's first Generation III+ nuclear plants.

Fuel Cycle

Fuel cycle choice is a critical factor in the design and operation of nuclear systems. The process of energy production from uranium (U) in NPPs encompasses many stages.[18,19,20,21] First, uranium ore is mined and concentrated (or milled) to produce "yellowcake." Yellowcake is then converted into uranium hexafluoride (UF6), which is then enriched to increase the concentration of uranium-235. The enriched UF6 is then fabricated into reactor fuel.

There are two options for dealing with the spent fuel that is removed from NPPs. In the "open" or "once through" fuel cycle employed in the United States and Canada, spent fuel is stored indefinitely in storage pools or casks until it can be disposed of safely in an underground geological repository such as the much-delayed Yucca Mountain project in Nevada.

China has followed France, Japan, and Russia in implementing the "closed" cycle approach, which involves the development of special facilities that separate spent nuclear fuel into its various components, some of which (uranium, plutonium) are then fabricated into oxide fuel or mixed oxide fuel (MOX) for reuse in conventional nuclear reactors. Further, new types of reactors have the capacity to transform spent fuel extracted from conventional NPPs into new reactor fuel. Unlike conventional reactors, the new systems use coolants (e.g. sodium) that do not moderate the fission process; some fast reactors, named breeder reactors, are designed to produce more fuel than they consume.[22]

Open and closed fuel cycles involve different tradeoffs.[23] The open cycle has a cost advantage, because reprocessing is costly and complex. Further,

---

[17] See http://chronicle.augusta.com/news-metro-latest-news/2013-02-10/chinas-nuclear-project-offers-lessons-vogtle-expansion (accessed August 18, 2017).

[18] www.nrc.gov/materials/fuel-cycle-fac/stages-fuel-cycle.html (accessed May 15, 2016).

[19] www.nrc.gov/waste/spent-fuel-storage.html (accessed August 23, 2016).

[20] www.nrc.gov/waste/hlw-disposal.html (accessed August 23, 2016).

[21] http://web.mit.edu/nuclearpower/pdf/nuclearpower-ch4-9.pdf (accessed May 15, 2016).

[22] Karam 2006, www.scientificamerican.com/article/how-do-fast-breeder-react/ (accessed August 23, 2016).

[23] http://web.mit.edu/nuclearpower/pdf/nuclearpower-ch4-9.pdf (accessed May 15, 2016).

the open cycle offers "proliferation resistance"[24] since reprocessing operations produce plutonium, the primary ingredient for nuclear bombs. The closed cycle is more expensive, but offers fuller resource utilization (because more of the uranium is converted into energy) and reduces (but does not eliminate) the need for long-term waste disposal.

China declared its commitment to the closed fuel cycle as early as 1987.[25] As Xu (2007, p. 129) puts it, "From the thermal reactor to the fast reactor and then to the fusion reactor; this is the three-step strategy that has been decided for a sustainable nuclear energy supply in China." Given the scale of China's new build program, dealing with the anticipated spent fuel quantity poses a significant challenge. A 2030 operating level of 80 GWe – certainly feasible under current plans summarized in Table 10.1, would produce an annual spent fuel discharge of 2,000 metric tons.[26] Current estimates indicate a 2030 used fuel stock totaling 23,500 metric tons, of which 15,000 metric tons will be in dry cask storage. CNNC is responsible for the back-end processing of China's nuclear fuel, with most operations located in Gansu province. A subsidiary company, CNNC Ruining Technology Co Ltd, was set up in 2011 to handle industrial-scale reprocessing and MOX fuel production – a critical step in the closed cycle. CNNC Ruining has partnered with Areva to develop a Sino–French nuclear recycling project.[27]

Commitment to the closed fuel cycle encouraged China to pursue the development of Generation IV designs and concepts, such as fast breeders and the use of molten salt fuels, which are covered in a subsequent section on China's Gen IV initiatives.

CHINA'S NUCLEAR POWER OPPORTUNITIES

Going Global

China views nuclear power as "a nexus of clean energy, economic incentives, and international prestige."[28] In 2014, National Energy

---

[24] http://web.mit.edu/nuclearpower/pdf/nuclearpower-ch4-9.pdf (accessed May 15, 2016).

[25] www.world-nuclear.org/information-library/country-profiles/countries-a-f/china-nuclear-fuel-cycle.aspx (accessed May 15, 2016).

[26] www.world-nuclear.org/information-library/country-profiles/countries-a-f/china-nuclear-fuel-cycle.aspx (accessed May 15, 2016).

[27] www.world-nuclear.org/information-library/country-profiles/countries-a-f/china-nuclear-fuel-cycle.aspx (accessed May 15, 2016).

[28] *The Diplomat* 2014.

Administration director Wu Xinxiong (吴新雄) announced China's intent to become a world leader in nuclear power (South China Morning Post 2014). Energy investment, including nuclear power, is a major component of China's twin global initiatives, "Go Outward" and "One Belt One Road" (一带一路 *yidai yilu*).

China's path into overseas nuclear markets builds on its strong international presence in markets for conventional power systems and equipment. China's emergence as the world's largest producer and consumer of electric power and of power-related equipment, coupled with Beijing's "Go Outward" campaign promoting overseas direct investment on the part of (especially state-controlled) Chinese companies has prompted rapid expansion of Chinese presence in global markets related to conventional electricity. Chinese equipment manufacturers have become a major force in world markets. Annual exports of steam generating boilers, for example, exceeded US$1.5 billion throughout 2009–2013, years in which no other country's exports reached that figure; indeed, only South Korea's annual exports reached US$1 billion, and then only in 2011 and 2012 (Ueno, Yanagi and Nakano 2014, Figure 1). Sinohydro has become "the world's dominant dam builder," occupying "50 percent of the global market for hydropower contracts" (Brosshard 2014). State Grid Corporation, the subject of Xu Yi-chong's chapter, has major overseas investments, including operations in Australia, Brazil, and the Philippines.

The importance of nuclear technology as a potential "Chinese calling card" in the nation's quest for global technology leadership prompted organizational efforts that extend far beyond commercial marketing. In February 2014, China's three major nuclear companies, along with nuclear equipment manufacturers, power generating firms and banks – all state-controlled entities, established the China Nuclear Energy International Development Alliance (中国核电技术装备"走出去"产业联盟 *Zhongguo hedian jishu zhuangbei zouchuqu chanye lianmeng*). This association, which has subsequently expanded to include leading universities, operates with "the support of relevant government departments" (国家相关部门的支持下*guojia xiangguan bumen zhichixia*), which participate in the Alliance's annual meetings (China Electricity Council 2014; Annual Meeting 2014; Jian 2015b). The group's objectives include "strengthening information sharing and industry self-discipline" – the latter presumably including ensuring that participants respect the global spheres of influence assigned to individual firms in order to avoid price competition between rival Chinese firms (Annual Meeting 2014).

Table 10.3 *Chinese Nuclear Power Plants – Export Performance to Date*

Country	Location	Type	Estimated Cost	Company	2018 Status
Pakistan	Chasma 1–4	CNP-300	$2.7 billion for units 3–4, 82% financed by China	CNNC	operating
	Karachi 1 & 2	Hualong 1	$9.6 billion, likely 82% financed by China	CNNC	under construction
Romania	Cernavoda 3 & 4	Candu 6	€7.7 billion, Chinese financing	CGN	planned; project is to complete partially built units
Argentina	Atucha 3	Candu 6	$5.8 billion, of which $2 billion is Chinese investment	CNNC	planned; 2018 reports of possible cancellation
	5th Argentine reactor	Hualong 1	$7 billion	CNNC	planned
United Kingdom	Bradwell	Hualong 1		CGN	promised future opportunity
Iran	Makran coast	2 x 100 MWe		CNNC	agreement July 2015
Turkey	Igneada	AP1000 & CAP1400		SNPTC	exclusive negotiations involving Westinghouse following 2014 agreement
South Africa	Thyspunt	CAP1400		SNPTC	bid preparation
Kenya		Hualong 1		CGN	memorandum of understanding July 2015
Egypt		Hualong 1		CNNC	memorandum of understanding May 2015
Sudan		ACP600?		CNNC	framework agreement May 2016
Armenia	Metsamor	Undetermined		CNNC	discussion under way
Undetermined		HTR600		CNEC	export intention
Kazakhstan		Fuel JV		CGN	agreement December 2015

Note: CNEC is China Nuclear Engineering & Construction Group, a CNNC affiliate.
Source: Data derived from World Nuclear Association (2017), "Nuclear power in China (updated April 2018)," www.world-nuclear.org/information-library/country-profiles/countries-a-f/china-nuclear-power.aspx (accessed July 9, 2018).

Table 10.3 summarizes current information about China's nuclear export efforts and initial successes. Following a lengthy period in which China's overseas nuclear involvement was limited to Pakistan (CNNC), China's nuclear export ambitions received a major boost from a flurry of activity beginning in 2014. Multiple successes involving all three nuclear firms include firm agreements for Chinese involvement in Romanian (CGN), and Argentinian (CNNC) projects, and CGN's financial participation in the United Kingdom's Hinkley Point development (plus possible follow-on construction of a *Hualong 1* plant at Bradwell). In addition, cooperation agreements, technical exchanges, training programs and ongoing negotiations with Iran, Turkey, South Africa, and numerous other prospective partners hold the prospect of future major project opportunities.

CGN's entry into the UK market provides a particularly valuable endorsement of China's global nuclear standing. The Chinese press sees an "eye-catching ... agreement for China to partly finance a UK nuclear power plant," the Hinkley Point NPP, which constitutes "the first major Chinese investment in a Western nuclear facility." Even more important is the proposed lead role for CGN and for Chinese technology in the subsequent Bradwell project, which press accounts trumpet as "China's first showcase for its nuclear technology" (Wu and Zhang 2015).

The financial struggles of three multinational nuclear incumbents – Westinghouse's bankruptcy and subsequent sale, Toshiba's implosion and Areva's stumbling into the arms of EDF – all in 2017, will surely expand China's global nuclear sales prospects. And the missteps that contributed to these corporate disasters – long delays, technical holdups and cost overruns at the AP1000 projects, failure of due diligence and governance lapses at Toshiba, manufacturing problems in Areva's supply chain – all encourage the idea that the Chinese can do better.

Disruption in the Global Nuclear Power Plant Market

John Sutton sees producers as facing "windows" of market opportunity: combinations of price, characteristics, and quality that buyers are willing to accept. For technologically complex and potentially dangerous products like large-scale passenger aircraft and nuclear power plants, we anticipate exceptionally narrow windows located at the upper extremity of the quality space (Sutton 1998). Historically, the global market for nuclear power has behaved in this exact fashion. After absorbing and then developing their own adaptations of technology originally imported from the United States,

French, Japanese, and Korean firms have emerged as full fledged global competitors, but only after lengthy periods of maturation during which their firms' skill and experience gradually came to match that of Westinghouse and other original innovators.

Clay Christensen's disruptive innovation theory (Christensen 1997; Christensen, Anthony, and Roth 2004) provides a quite different framework for analyzing possible shifts in the wake of growing Chinese prominence in the global civil nuclear industry. Disruptive innovation theory focuses on situations in which new entrants use relatively simple, low-cost innovations to create growth and potentially unseat incumbents.

China's arrival as a major force in the global NPP market combines elements of both approaches. Once Chinese firms gain access to world-class nuclear technologies, there is a period of absorption and maturation, as Sutton's analysis would anticipate. But, as Christensen might predict, this focus on internal capability growth is surprisingly brief. We now see a campaign of aggressive export promotion based on the expectation that Chinese firms can design, build, and operate advanced nuclear systems at lower cost than incumbent global leaders. If realized, these expectations will create an outcome more akin to Christensen's vision of industrial dynamics than to Sutton's: the emergence of a two-tiered market for nuclear power plants, with American, French, and South Korean firms occupying the upper and Chinese (and possibly Russian) rivals populating the lower tier of a global price-quality ladder.

Although this differentiated (i.e. two-tiered) market remains in its infancy, the characteristics of the second, lower tier are already visible. They include:

- *Acceptably high ("good enough") levels of quality, longevity and durability.* Success in winning nuclear business (especially its role in the UK Hinkley/Bradwell agreement) and in obtaining certification (AP1000 start-up data accepted by US Nuclear Regulatory Commission; a joint venture between Westinghouse and SNPTC seeking to prepare Chinese equipment firms to qualify as global suppliers for AP and CAP type reactor projects) from national authorities in advanced countries with stringent safety requirements is crucial to China's overseas nuclear ambitions. It is these accomplishments that will persuade decision-makers in countries like South Africa that China's nuclear companies can be trusted to build (and in some cases operate) nuclear installations with the highest level of reliability.

- *Low cost.* Nuclear facilities embody hugely expensive safety systems – for example protection against a direct hit from a large-scale passenger aircraft. If Chinese alternatives are perceived as safe and reliable, potential buyers, especially in low- and middle-income countries, will welcome any cost advantage available from Chinese equipment-makers and construction specialists.

Chinese expertise in construction and equipment manufacture creates the prospect of substantial cost savings. Chinese firms lead the world in every dimension of civil construction, including nuclear power, where a Chinese engineer proudly reports "30 consecutive years of construction experience in nuclear electricity" (Jian 2015a). Rawski finds stable or declining construction costs for Chinese thermal power plants during a period of substantially rising costs for similar plants in Europe and North America (Chapter 8). There is good reason to anticipate that Chinese firms can complete the construction component of NPP projects at lower cost than overseas rivals.

Equipment represents the largest cost component for nuclear projects: 55 percent for current Chinese NPP projects (Nuclear Issues 2017), a figure that closely resembles results of an earlier OECD study (2000, p. 29) using data from European and North American projects. A Chinese nuclear specialist advises that, except for materials-intensive devices, Chinese firms can typically undercut the costs of international vendors of nuclear-related equipment by approximately one-third (Interview, May 2014). However, an executive at a Western nuclear company expressed skepticism about the claimed cost advantage, citing his experience working on a joint NPP bid for a European project in which efforts to reduce costs by enlisting Chinese equipment suppliers failed (Interview, 2015). The multiplicity of nuclear designs currently under construction burdens Chinese equipment manufacturers with excess costs that standardization could eliminate (Yu 2017). More broadly, industry participants suggest that high domestic transport charges and re-work stemming from inadequate manufacturing processes may reduce or even nullify possible Chinese cost advantages for NPP equipment.

Limited experience with overseas nuclear construction and with the Hualong design means that future Hualong projects may run afoul of the design changes, manufacturing defects, construction delays and cost overruns that have bedeviled Generation III projects built with US and French designs. Initial evidence from the first wave of China's global "wins" suggests limited cost advantage: the US$7 billion price tag attached to the Argentinian *Hualong 1* matches the original budget for the AP1000 Vogtle projects under construction in Georgia.[29]

- *Chinese project financing.* The daunting cost of nuclear facilities creates problems even for buyers in advanced countries. This gives a big advantage to vendors whose tenders incorporate offers of financial backing from their home governments. China's "Go Outward" and "One Belt One Road" initiatives include generous financing for large-scale overseas infrastructure projects,[30] along with support for technical training and preparatory cooperation[31] that increases the prospects for future reactor sales. Financing can be crucial to buyer decisions: Japanese nuclear firms have warned Japan's government that their industry's viability is critically dependent upon Tokyo's willingness to finance overseas nuclear projects (Interview, May 2014). China's most potent business weapon might well be its ability to provide vendor financing to customer nations that might otherwise be unable to afford a nuclear power plant.
- *Political and regulatory flexibility.* The size of nuclear projects and the involvement of materials and technologies with military applications mean that negotiations surrounding international nuclear projects involve official as well as commercial participants. We expect Chinese government agencies and regulatory bodies to show greater willingness to deal with nations that might face difficulty obtaining regulatory approvals for the export of sensitive US, French, or Japanese technologies. In combination, deep pockets and regulatory flexibility may well work to make China's reactors particularly appealing to prior non-consumers such as emerging nations in Asia, Africa and South America.

If our analysis of China's new-market disruption is accurate, Chinese nuclear companies can anticipate excellent overseas market opportunities in the next decade. The reason: potential growth areas in the global civil nuclear market cluster in regions that are likely to find the Chinese business model appealing. The US International Trade Administration locates

---

[29] For Argentina, see www.world-nuclear-news.org/NN-Argentina-China-talks-on-new-nuclear-plants-08051501.html (accessed May 19, 2018); for the Vogtle project, see Merchant 2017.

[30] Ueno, Yanagi and Nakano (2014) discuss Chinese financing for exports of conventional power equipment.

[31] Under a 2014 agreement, for example, CNNC offered a two-year training program to 300 staff members of the South African Nuclear Energy Corporation (South Africa 2014).

the most promising new build opportunities in newly emerging markets such as Vietnam and the Middle East (International Trade Administration 2015; see Table 10.3 above). Also promising are existing markets considering fleet expansion, such as the United Kingdom, India, and Brazil. In contrast, mature NPP markets such as Canada or Spain provide only service or decommissioning opportunities. Given China's unmistakable and well-resourced intention to go global and this alignment of capabilities and growth opportunities, China's nuclear ambitions are anything but unrealistic, *provided the anticipated projects move forward.*

Innovation

While building capabilities to shrink the technology, quality and safety gaps separating domestic firms from global leaders is the main agenda for China's nuclear industry, we already encounter claims that Chinese firms are approaching, reaching or even surpassing current international frontiers of best practice. China occupies a leading position in the construction and operation of AP1000 reactors. We have mentioned Chinese manufacture of large duplex steel plates. We note two further claims of frontier innovation even though the present authors lack the technical expertise to evaluate their significance:

- At the 2014 Pudong conference mentioned previously, a representative of the Baoyin (宝银) Special Tube Ltd. reported that 690 alloy produced for U-tubes to be installed in AP1000 and CAP1400 reactors exceeded the performance of imported alternatives in resisting pitting while delivering comparable results in other categories.[32]
- Visitors touring a Shanghai Electric workshop in 2014 were advised that this facility had succeeded in producing turbine blades measuring 1.17 meters (versus the industry standard of 1 meter) and was experimenting with increasing blade length to 1.9 meters (Interview, May 2014). In 2017, Dongfang Electric reported successful completion of "high-speed dynamic balance" testing for the "world's largest half-speed nuclear turbine rotor" measuring 1.828 meters (Mou Sinan 2017).

---

[32] This firm was cited in 2017 as a national leader among energy equipment producers; its achievements include the development of twenty-four import-replacing new products over a twenty-year period, of which six have reached the "world advanced level" (Baoyin 2017).

Generation IV Technologies

"China's R&D in nuclear technologies is second to none in the world, particularly in high-temperature gas-cooled and molten salt-cooled reactors," goes an assessment by the World Nuclear Association (World Nuclear 2016). China has been a member of the thirteen-nation Generation IV International Forum (GIF) since 2006. Gen IV technologies are all in the development stage, with 2030 being the earliest anticipated entry into service, with many technical barriers remaining. Gen IV reactor technology consists broadly of six designs currently receiving investment: High Temperature Gas-cooled Reactor (HTGR), molten-salt reactors, sodium-cooled fast reactors, supercritical water-cooled reactors, gas-cooled fast reactors, and lead-cooled fast reactors (GIF 2014). As an example, TerraPower's (the Seattle nuclear technology startup backed by Bill Gates) Traveling Wave Reactor is a 1150 MWe liquid sodium-cooled fast reactor that uses depleted uranium as fuel. Similarly, the pebble bed reactor is a type of gas reactor. Across the various technologies, Gen IV reactors are designed for life-cycle economic advantage (e.g. they tend to be smaller, which reduces construction time), enhanced safety (e.g. by eliminating possible core meltdowns), minimal waste (e.g. by using depleted fuel), and proliferation resistance (GIF 2014).

Worldwide, Gen IV initiatives have progressed in fits and starts. In the United States, for example, despite the Energy Policy Act of 2005 mandating the construction and operation of an HTGR by 2021, there are as yet no plans to build a demonstration plant (Kadak 2016). China's nuclear establishments, in contrast, display considerable Gen IV R&D momentum. For example, the pressure vessel was put in place for an HTGR at the Huaneng Shidao Bay nuclear power plant in March 2016 (*China Daily* 2016) and the pressure vessel head was installed in December 2017 (*World Nuclear News*, January 4, 2018).

Chinese enthusiasm for pursuing multiple Gen IV approaches has attracted substantial overseas cooperation (Experimental Reactors 2017). Chinese nuclear companies have also signed memoranda of understanding (MOUs) with Saudi Arabia and the UAE for the co-construction of HTGR nuclear power plants (China Daily 2016).

Further, China is one of only five countries actively investing in fast breeder reactors, along with France, India, Japan, and Russia (Pandza 2013). The China Experimental Fast Reactor (CEFR), at the China Institute of Atomic Energy achieved first criticality in 2010 and completed a full-power test run in 2014 (*World Nuclear News*, December 19, 2014, www.world-nuclear-news.org/NN-Chinese-fast-reactor-completes-full-power-test-run-1912144.html (accessed January 23, 2015)). In partnership with the US Department of Energy's Oak Ridge Labs, the Shanghai Institute of Applied Physics is also developing a molten-salt reactor, applying technology invented in the US but subsequently all but moth-balled there (Martin 2016). Similarly, TerraPower signed a 2015 agreement with CNNC to further develop and build a traveling wave reactor in China. In addition to investing in the conventional Gen IV technologies, Chinese nuclear companies are also developing new formats, such as CGN's reported demonstration project of a floating reactor (*New York Times*, 2016).

Since Gen IV technologies differ radically from previous reactor designs in approach and scale, they represent a competitive domain in which existing players have little incumbency advantage. This increases their attractiveness as investment targets for recent entrants like China.

POTENTIAL DIFFICULTIES FOR CHINESE NUCLEAR POWER

Looking to the future, potential difficulties cluster in two areas: rapid deterioration of the financial outlook for China's domestic nuclear indus-try and risks associated with efforts to accelerate import replacement within the nuclear supply chain. We examine each in turn.

Diminishing Financial Prospects

China's development of nuclear power coincided with an extended period of excess demand for electricity. The key task for producers was to expand generation and grid capacity to match the needs of (mostly industrial) customers. Grid companies assigned nuclear plants to continuous "baseload" operation, with pauses only for maintenance and refueling. On-grid prices for NPP electricity were fixed in the vicinity of RMB 0.43/KWh, approximating the prices paid to coal-fired thermal power plants in the provinces where NPPs operate. With thermal producers receiving seven price increases between 2004 and 2011 (Fagaiwei 2015), there was little reason to consider possible threats to the competitive position of China's growing NPP fleet.

Recent developments have upset this comfortable equilibrium. The 2008 global crisis and ensuing recession halted double-digit growth in electricity consumption. Annual demand growth plunged from 14 percent during 2003–7 to 6 percent during 2008 and 2009. After rebounding to 14.8 and 12 percent during 2009/10 and 2010/11, annual demand growth dropped to

5.6, 7.2 and 4.5 percent during 2012–14, then vanished in 2015. Despite a modest subsequent revival, industry specialists now anticipate future demand growth in the low single digits; none predicts a return to the former double-digit advance.

The fall-off in demand growth coincided with a surge in new generating capacity. Annual additions to capacity in 2014–17 surpassed figures for all prior years. This investment binge in the face of sagging demand growth attracted fierce criticism: Zhou Dadi, a respected energy specialist, asks "How can we curb excessive investment, especially irrational excesses in energy structure?" (Du 2018). Less restrained critics decry "blind expansion" and pillory the "Great Leap Forward-style" expansion of coal-fired generation facilities (Li Beiling 2016).

Excess capacity is the inevitable result. When average operating hours for thermal plants, the workhorses of China's power system, dropped below 5,000 hours in 2008, an annual summary described the situation as remaining "within a reasonable range" reflecting "basic supply-demand balance" (Power Yearbook 2009, p. 58). After fluctuating between 4,865 and 5,305 during 2008–13, average operating hours for thermal plants plunged to 4,706 in 2014 – the lowest since 1978, 4,329 in 2015 – the lowest since 1969, and 4,165 in 2016 – a fifty-year low, before rising slightly in 2017 (annual data from Chapter 8, Table 8.3). NPP operating hours also declined. After fluctuating between 7,679 and 7,874 between 2006 and 2013, average annual hours for China's nuclear fleet dropped to 7,489 in 2014, to 7,350 in 2015 and to 6,987 (according to the China Nuclear Energy Association) or 7,042 (according to the China Electricity Council) in 2016 before rebounding to 7,108 in 2017 (China Electricity Council 2017; Ouyang 2017; Zhou 2017).

Even as interest rate reductions and a temporary decline in coal prices stoked short-term profits for conventional operators, the downward march of operating hours sounded a financial alarm that spurred the revival of long-delayed reform plans. From the nuclear perspective, the key component of the new reforms, described more fully by Irene Wu (Chapter 2) and Thomas Rawski (Chapter 8) is the establishment of fixed charges for transmitting electricity between generators and end-users. This change spurred rapid expansion of direct power sales, which now threaten the commercial viability of China's nuclear power industry.

Both thermal and nuclear plants face massive fixed costs – loan repayments and other expenses that arise regardless of output volume. A 2016 study by RAP, a well-regarded NGO, shows fixed costs accounting for roughly one quarter of total costs for coal generators and over 70 percent for nuclear plants.[33] High fixed costs mean that falling hours, which reduce output and sales, increase unit costs, even with stable power prices. Price reductions intensify financial pressures. This exact combination of reduced hours and falling prices has tipped China's nuclear industry into a cauldron of financial uncertainty. Nuclear operators see no escape from the risky path of offering price reductions to maintain operating hours.

Electricity is a homogeneous commodity. Under market arrangements, "since cost is the only difference [between alternative power sources] ... it is the sole criterion" (Guo Feng 2016). Fixed grid charges facilitate bilateral deals between generating companies and large users. As buyers respond to price discounts for thermal power, demand for nuclear electricity begins to erode, causing grid companies to strip nuclear plants of their former status as providers of baseline power. During 2016, "power distribution issues" caused the operation of one new reactor to be "delayed by months"; in the new world of excess supply, some nuclear units "operate at full output only at times of peak demand," while others are "temporarily shut for extended periods" because of "coal units getting preference over nuclear stations" (Hua Wen 2016a).

Beginning in 2016, top nuclear executives find themselves obliged to use the annual March meetings of China's National People's Congress for lobbying to preserve the status of nuclear plants as baseline operators, ameliorate pricing anomalies, facilitate inter-provincial power transmission, and override unwelcome interventions by grid companies and provincial governments (Ouyang 2017; Zhu Xuerui 2017a, 2017c; Zhang Zirui 2017; Zhong and Qu 2017). In 2018, China Nuclear Construction Group Board Chairman and Party Secretary Wang Shoujun (王寿君) appeared to concede the commercial weakness of nuclear electricity, noting that nuclear costs are low only "after the loan period expires," so that the "Qinshan and Daya Bay nuclear plants put into production in the 1990s are now fully able to withstand relatively low electricity prices" (Lu and Dong 2018). The unspoken implication: newer nuclear facilities cannot withstand market competition.

Available data illuminate the realities informing Chairman Wang's pessimism. CGN Group Party Secretary He Yu (贺禹) states that nuclear plants need 7,000 working hours to earn the returns needed to repay outstanding loans. "If hours are limited," he explains, "there is no means of assuring economic returns" (如果限电, 经济效益便无法保障, Zhong et al. 2017).

---

[33] RAP 2016, pp. 71–2. For thermal plants, the importance of fixed costs fluctuates with coal prices – high coal prices reduce the share of fixed costs, and vice versa.

The struggle to maintain hours is reflected in a comment that Fujian's agreement to supply 6.334 billion KWh of power, half from nuclear plants, to Jiangsu during the fourth quarter of 2017 "adds 430 hours to the operations of Fujian's nuclear plants" (Li Mingguang 2017).

With fleetwide average hours hovering close to 7,000 hours, equivalent to 80 percent of capacity (100*7000/[365*24] = 79.91 percent), nuclear finances depend crucially on the sellers' capacity to maintain a substantial gap between average sales prices and unit costs. But with market pressures forcing price concessions, sales prices are creeping downward. The average wholesale or on-grid price paid to nuclear producers in 2016 was RMB 0.42089 per KWh, 3.41 percent less than in 2015 (Price Notification 2017).[34] Benchmark prices announced during 2017 for individual facilities within CGN's nuclear fleet averaged RMB 0.4207, with only one exceeding the 2016 fleet-wide average (Ten Cent 2018). The 2016 share of nuclear power sales to end-users more than doubled from the 2015 figure of 7.5 percent.[35] Reported prices for these transactions cluster in the neighborhood of RMB 0.35.

There is an evident link between low operating hours, large shares of marketed output and big price discounts. Fangchenggang (Guangxi province), with market sales amounting to 60 percent of output, sold power for as little as RMB 0.264 during 2016; Hongyanhe (Liaoning province) the facility with the lowest utilization rate, has concluded a heat supply contract at the remarkably low rate of RMB 0.18/KWh (Gen III Overview 2017).

Specifying the average cost of generating nuclear power is difficult. Costs vary across facilities and with changes in operating rates for individual plants. Estimates compiled during 2015/2016 place the average cost of generating nuclear power at RMB 0.2978 (RAP 2016, p. 72) or RMB 0.31 (for Generation II+) and 0.34 (for Generation III plants, see CICC 2015, p. 29). The RAP calculation uses improbably low investment costs of RMB 11,500 per KW, far below available figures for the newly completed Generation III plants – recent figures collected by the World Nuclear Association project unit investment costs for *Hualong 1*, the least expensive design that Chinese specialists classify as Generation III, at

---

[34] Professor Yuan Jiahai advises us that average price figures include direct sales to end users as well as sales to the grid. For confirmation, see First Half Power Market 2017, with thanks to Michael Davidson.

[35] For 2016, see Ouyang 2017. Market sales in 2017 for China's two major nuclear operators 2017 amounted to 21% for CNNC and 14% for CGN (CNNC Report 2018; CGN Dividend Report 2018).

$3,500 or RMB 21,000 per KW of capacity.[36] In addition, both estimates assume annual operating hours (7,200 for RAP, 7,500 for CIIC) well above recent outcomes. Another 2016 study offers cost estimates of RMB 0.29 and 0.33 per KWh for two plants: Ling Ao #1 and Daiya Bay.

We speculate that the average 2017 cost of generating each KWh of nuclear electricity fell in the RMB 0.31–0.34 range specified in the 2016 study cited above. The shift to Generation III plants has increased initial investments; construction delays and cost overruns further inflate the cost of the newest cohort of nuclear facilities. With multiple plants approaching completion – 2018 plans call for production start-ups at five facilities – average costs face an upward trajectory.

We lack sufficient information to estimate the markup needed to enable nuclear plants to meet their loan obligations. Available information does show, however, that Chinese nuclear plants face similar challenges to those confronting their American counterparts. In the United States, cheap natural gas has eroded the commercial logic of nuclear electricity. In China, the deteriorating price picture undermining the commercial viability of Chinese nuclear power is evident in Figure 10.5, with the competitive danger coming from coal, rather than natural gas.

Average 2015 on-grid prices for coal power were lower than average prices for nuclear power in three of five provinces with nuclear plants: Liaoning, Jiangsu, and Fujian. In 2016, the relative price of coal power declined in all five provinces, with Zhejiang joining the roster of provinces with cheaper average prices for coal power. 2016 also saw two provinces, Guangxi and Hainan, added to China's provincial nuclear club.

Even though coal prices spiked upward during 2016, with high prices persisting into 2018, thermal power prices continued along a downward path. On-grid prices for coal power sold by large generating companies during the first half of 2017 averaged RMB 0.347 per KWh, 4.2 percent below the 2016 national average for coal power (Price Notification 2017; First Half Power Market 2018). Initial entry of CGN's Guangdong-based nuclear plants into competitive power markets during 2018, with

---

[36] See www.world-nuclear.org/information-library/nuclear-fuel-cycle/nuclear-power-reac tors/advanced-nuclear-power-reactors.aspx (accessed May 14, 2018), with thanks to Professor Daniel Cole. Perhaps reflecting the impact of construction delays affecting Generation III projects, veteran nuclear official Zhao Chengkun reports unit investment costs of RMB 36,000–42,000 for AP1000 (Westinghouse technology) and EPR (French technology) and RMB 24,000 for VVER (Russian technology; see Lu Yinling 2018). We convert dollar figures to RMB at RMB6 = US$1.

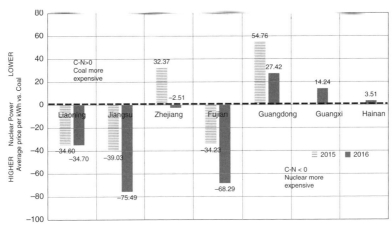

Figure 10.5 Average Gap C-N between Average Wholesale Prices for Coal (C) and Nuclear (N) Electricity (RMB per MWh), Provinces with Nuclear Plants, 2015–2016

agreements offering price discounts that exceeded the average discount for 2017 (Guangdong Contracts 2017), reflects the ongoing encroachment of market forces and the escalation of associated financial pressures.

Newly commissioned nuclear plants entering production in 2018 will face market pressures from the start, as they are located in provinces where average nuclear prices exceed average coal prices (Jiangsu, Zhejiang), where competitive pressures have forced existing plants to pursue market sales (Guangdong), and in Shandong, where average coal power prices are below RMB 0.40 (Power Market 2018).

National policy trends offer scant relief from the financial shoals surrounding China's nuclear operators. Regulations issued in 2013 specify that benchmark on-grid prices for new nuclear plants will not exceed benchmark prices for local coal-fired plants (Zheng and Chen 2016), which have declined in recent years. Anticipated expansion of electricity marketing will continue to push average prices below the benchmark prices governing non-market transactions. A 10 percent price reduction for users of "general industrial and commercial" electricity in 2018 intensifies pressures for cost reduction; efforts to streamline China's expensive transport and logistics systems promise benefits to users of coal, the leading cargo (Cost Reduction 2018). Proposed growth of electricity transmission networks promises both benefits (through enlarged cross-provincial sales of nuclear power) and risks (increased competition from western sources of hydro, wind, solar, and thermal power in the home markets of coastal nuclear plants).

The competitive strength of conventional and renewable electricity suppliers is growing. Removal of institutional barriers limiting inflows of cheap western hydropower may enlarge long-distance sales to Guangdong. Loren Brandt and Luhang Wang show that wind and solar power have achieved large cost reductions (Chapter 9), a trend that seems likely to continue. Rawski finds China's thermal power sector riddled with excess costs (Chapter 8). Ongoing market pressures and institutional reforms seem poised to extend the recent downward trend in thermal costs and prices.

Producers of nuclear power, by contrast, have little scope for cost reduction.[37] Fixed costs are large and inflexible; both the shift to Generation III designs and enhanced safety requirements are pushing them upward (Interview, May 2016). Despite the possibility of lower initial costs associated with the rising share of domestically produced components and initiatives to lower some operational expenses (discussed above), post-Fukushima upgrades to quality and safety requirements seem certain to drive ongoing increases in variable costs. In the words of a nuclear construction executive:

"Main manufacturing work is increasingly complex; rising standards for materials and rising safety and redundancy requirements have pushed up the costs of equipping, building and operating nuclear plants. All this poses an increasingly difficult challenge for the market prospects of nuclear power. Based on economic projects for newly built nuclear plants, nuclear power is losing cost competitiveness vs. conventional energy" (Zhu Xuerui 2017d).

This loss of cost competitiveness undergirds CNNC Chairman Wang Shoujun's 2018 observation that "absorption of nuclear power mainly depends on the relevant government departments" (Lu and Dong 2018). Without state intervention to impose a stiff carbon price, to compel grid companies to give special preference to nuclear electricity or to raise effluent fees on coal combustion, the commercial viability of China's nuclear power industry is very much in doubt.

The combined effect of the above-mentioned factors is to reduce the number of NPPs that can be built and operated economically. During our Summer 2018 field work, we heard more realistic estimates of the eventual size of China's reactor fleet: possibly a maximum of 100–120 reactors over

[37] Westinghouse officials, acknowledging that the premature start to constructing the AP1000 projects at Sanmen and Haiyang eliminated anticipated cost savings from the reactor's unique modular design, anticipate that future AP1000 projects will demonstrate the importance of these benefits. However, as this is written in mid-2018, prospects for future China-based AP1000 projects appear remote.

the next thirty years. Indeed, one well-informed industry participant stated that China might not build as many reactors as the United States (which has ninety-nine operating reactors in 2018). Clearly, the emerging realities of the domestic electricity market have tempered the exuberance of initial plans. Paradoxically, though, this implies that export pressure will be even stronger: if industry capacity is six to eight equipment sets per year but only one or two reactors are built domestically each year, the incentive grows to capture more of the possible global reactor bids.

Risks Associated with Aggressive Import Replacement

Developing a complete nuclear supply chain makes sense for a nation that is both the world's largest arena for nuclear construction and the largest producer of machinery, including both conventional generation and grid equipment. There is also an ideological agenda visible in frequent complaints about limits on Chinese nuclear ambitions arising from the "stranglehold" of foreign "monopolies" on advanced technology. Thus, Sui Yongbin, a prominent machine industry leader, insists that "Without localization, the foreigners will choke us" (Localization 2014). Zero-sum thinking reinforces this perspective, equating foreign firms' profits with Chinese losses – depredations that enlarge the historic tally of suffering and indignity that serves as a staple of popular nationalism.

The combination of calculation and emotion underpinning China's push to "domesticate" (国产化 *guochanhua*) every segment of the nuclear supply chain risks costly and potentially dangerous missteps. China's push to demonstrate independent innovative excellence by implementing the domestically created *Hualong 1* reactor design illustrates such risks. As of August 2017, a *Hualong 1* reactor is under construction in Karachi (Siddiqui 2017), while demonstration reactors are taking shape at CNNC's Fuqing installation in Fujian and at CGN's Fangchenggang site in Guangxi (Reuters 2017a). Argentina has agreed to begin building a *Hualong* 1 reactor in 2020 (Argentina 2017) and domestic supporters are proposing to "speed up batch construction of Hualong reactors" (Zhong and Qu 2017).

Despite this activity, the design remains incomplete. A June 2016 "standard system project table" included 1,023 items, but issued only 743. A subsequent commentary noted these materials offered "complete coverage" (全面覆盖 *quanmian fugai*) for Generation II+ technology (for which China no longer permits new construction) but only "basic coverage" (基本覆盖 *jiben fugai*) for Generation III design – including *Hualong 1*. The commentary quotes unnamed experts who warn that "absence of a complete set of standards will greatly hinder overseas sales of nuclear technology and equipment" and stress the need to "create a complete set of standards as rapidly as possible" (Zhu Xuerui 2017b).

The 2016 quality scandal arising from premature replacement of imported nuclear valves (核电泵阀 *hedian bengfa*) provides a concrete instance of difficulties linked to premature replacement of nuclear equipment imports. A 2013 report, noting the prevalence of imported valves for both the nuclear and conventional islands in nuclear power plants, touted domestic valve production as having "great prospects" (Ma Zhe 2013). Ironically, the same account warned against "blind development," which is exactly what ensued. The localization rate reached 85 percent in 2013 but plunged to 35 percent in 2016 following a rash of quality problems that machinery specialist Shen Liechu associated with the industry's reputation for delivering equipment that is "not quite reliable" (不太可靠 *butai kekao*) because of "small defects" (小毛病 *xiao maobing*); see Hu Qing 2016).

NNSA reports on quality issues in nuclear plant construction and commissioning during 2015 bristle with references to valve issues involving both foreign and domestic suppliers. Multiple plants experienced single or recurrent episodes of frozen or jammed valves, including a December 2015 incident that led to a reactor shutdown at the Yangjiang facility's #3 unit (NNSA Briefing 2015, 2016).

Further details emerged from unusual publicity surrounding a June 2016 forum on nuclear power valve quality attended by the "principal leaders" of twenty-six valve manufacturers (NPP Valves 2016a, 2016b). Along with lectures invoking platitudes about the need to "attach great importance to quality problems" and to "protect the reputation of China's nuclear equipment manufacturing," enterprise leaders were obliged to affix their personal signatures and corporate seals to documents that pledged future allegiance to strict quality requirements and promised to avoid specific offenses – presumably reflecting recent lapses. These documents were then published in China Energy Report (中国能源报 *Zhongguo nengyuanbao*), a widely circulated trade journal.

Shanghai Apollo Machinery Ltd, for example, promised to "gradually lower the repeat rate for . . . nonconformance reports," to halt "the return of products to the plant for quality issues" and to prevent "inattentive management and neglect of responsibility from causing frequent quality distortions and safety issues."

Shanghai Electric's KSB Nuclear Pump Valve Ltd. Undertook to "ensure full rights and independence to departments and personnel engaged in supervision, audits, inspection and testing."

Jiangsu Shuangda Pump Group Company Ltd pledged to "follow reporting requirements on major quality issues and to submit timely reports to the National Nuclear Safety Agency." Chongqing Pump Works and three others pledged to avoid "falsification" (弄虚作假 *nongxu zuojia*) and "operational violations" (违规操作 *weigui caozuo*).[38]

Quality issues extend beyond valve production. A 2016 paper by an employee of CFHI (中国第一重型机械公司), a major nuclear equipment supplier, reeled off a litany of quality problems affecting nuclear equipment: purchasing materials with erroneous technical specifications, unauthorized product alterations, low and stagnant levels of quality management, and widespread (普遍) procedural violations (Shao 2016). More generally, Chinese specialists report problems with components, testing equipment, and quality control management affecting broad segments of equipment manufacture (Equipment Report 2016).

Hard-hitting reports and public shaming – as in the nuclear valve episode – may have a beneficial impact on quality outcomes. However, the willingness of Sui Yongbin to cite valve localization in connection with claims about the "flying advance" of China's nuclear equipment industry less than three months after presiding over the June 2016 exposé of quality issues affecting nuclear valve producers illustrates an unfortunate tendency toward emphasizing gains and downplaying shortcomings (Xie Wenquan 2016; Localization 2016).

The gains, however, are very real. Enterprise and government agencies organize R&D consortia to attack specific issues, as when Shanghai Baosteel's special steel unit convened a 2016 session at which representatives of fifty-eight units discussed means of accelerating the localization of steel varieties and other nuclear-related materials, with the hosts offering to "make joint efforts with all parties" in pursuit of this objective (Baosteel 2016).

In an effort that recalls Toyota's close ties with its suppliers, China General Nuclear (CGN) stations "large numbers of supervisory and quality assurance personnel with major nuclear equipment manufacturers to fully

---

[38] One of these firms, CNNC Sufa Technology Co. Ltd (中核苏阀科技实业股份有限公司), won recognition in 2017 as a "China energy equipment leader" for pioneering domestic production of several types of valves (Leaders 2017).

extend quality assurance ... to help the manufacturers develop nuclear safety culture and technical capacity among the workers ... and to ensure that equipment quality satisfies design requirements" (Localization 2014).

Dalian Heavy Industries, citing its own experience of delivering polar cranes that avoided defects encountered with imported materials and equipment, has launched a campaign to extend stringent quality practices beyond the boundaries of the nuclear sector. Their argument: establishing supply chains that "begin with strict screening of suppliers, followed by imposition of strict procurement documents and strict implementation of quality requirements," while perhaps damaging to short-term profit margins, will deliver long-term benefits (Mou Sinan and Hu Qing 2016a).

Rapid expansion of domestic equipment procurement for the initial AP1000 installations at Sanmen and Haiyang summarized in Table 10.2 provides an excellent index of China's growing capacity to deliver nuclear-related materials and devices that meet extreme standards of precision and durability. Ongoing accumulation of experience and expertise will continue the process of extending and deepening China's nuclear-related capabilities. Government funding, guidance and encouragement can accelerate this process, but only if official agencies, including provincial and local as well as national authorities, avoid repeating the excesses that have pushed elements of China's nuclear development in the direction of frantic excesses both before and after the 2011 Fukushima disaster.

CONCLUSION

The evolution of China's nuclear industry shows how industrial policy, regulation, and enterprise initiative have shaped the direction and scale of investment and capability building in this technically demanding field. In concert, these three factors have propelled significant catch-up not only in construction and operation but also in design, manufacturing, and R&D for civil nuclear activity. Despite the post-Fukushima pause and continuing controversy over the proposed construction of nuclear plants in inland locations, China's nuclear industry has advanced from obscurity to growing global prominence during the course of a few short decades. China now appears on track to join the United States, France, Russia, and Japan as a global leader in the NPP sector.

Chinese nuclear policy has proven controversial from the start, with frequent clashes between proponents of self-reliance and advocates of absorbing and then building on the best available technologies. While policy choices have generally favored the internationalists by choosing foreign designs and welcoming the participation of Areva, Westinghouse, and other overseas firms, strong and consistent official emphasis on import substitution has steadily expanded Chinese capabilities in designing, constructing, equipping, and operating nuclear plants.

In the nuclear field, as in other sectors, a key link in the transfer of technology and experience from overseas firms is the skillful bargaining that has enabled Chinese officials to trade market entry (for foreign companies) for access to the technology and experience of foreign firms in both formal (blueprints, licenses) and informal (personal interaction, on-the-job training) dimensions. At the enterprise level, Chinese managers, engineers, technicians, and workers have converted exposure to foreign technology and experience into enlarged personal and organizational capabilities. Effective micro-level responses to new prospects arising from official initiatives have transformed joint ventures and cooperative arrangements into transmission belts supporting rapid and extensive upgrading of China's entire nuclear supply chain. Interaction between scale economies linked to China's world-leading nuclear construction program and learning has driven rapid expansion of capabilities. Proximity to areas of established Chinese leadership in construction and equipment manufacture has facilitated this upgrading process.

Reflecting official preferences, China's nuclear sector revolves around an unusual blend of rivalry and cooperation among vertically integrated enterprise groups. This structure encourages beneficial competition in multiple spheres, especially technical innovation and project execution. The recent completion of the *Hualong 1* design as a joint product of China's two leading nuclear groups illustrates the capacity of central coordination to limit wasteful duplication.

Nuclear safety may constitute an exception to the general weakness of Chinese regulatory systems. Regulatory learning, particularly through links with Western regulatory agencies, appears to be providing a basis for growth with safety. Despite persistent questions about regulatory independence, we find substantial evidence of increasing regulatory "teeth" in China's nuclear industry.

Recent success of Chinese nuclear companies in joining overseas NPP projects represents the leading edge of what promises to develop into a major push to establish Chinese designs, equipment and services as a major force in the global nuclear market. Strong backing from China's government and banks will strengthen this export drive. China's entry into world markets seems likely to promote market segmentation, allowing China to focus on customers for whom incumbent technologies come with advanced features and political demands that make them too expensive both financially and politically. This emerging segment, unable to justify the expense of purchasing the most advanced technology and with limited capacity for local nuclear manufacturing, may well be China's natural market in the coming decades.

China, along with Russia and the United States, continues to develop possible paths to a fourth generation of nuclear power technology. If these efforts yield commercially viable outcomes, it is likely that the Chinese, who already occupy the operational forefront of Generation III, will share in global leadership of a future Generation IV nuclear technology.

Our review of China's nuclear sector illustrates the potential for effective policy intervention, in conjunction with effective corporate management and high levels of absorptive capacity at the enterprise level, to promote quantitative and qualitative upgrading in a technically demanding industry. Decades of safe nuclear operation, successful absorption of a wide array of design, engineering, and operational systems, rising capabilities throughout a growing domestic supply chain, ongoing experimentation with new technologies, and, most recently, a flurry of successful overseas project agreements, including one in the United Kingdom, all testify to China's emergence as a major player in global nuclear power.

Despite this lengthy and impressive list of accomplishments, China's nuclear future is by no means risk-free.

The ongoing development of safety culture and other "soft" skills involves long-term processes that can run astray. Concerns about possible shortages of qualified operational and regulatory staff seem especially plausible if China's leaders decide to accelerate nuclear construction under the 14th Five-Year Plan (FYP) beginning in 2020.

In the absence of carbon taxes or other policy initiatives that offset the emerging cost advantage of thermal and renewable generating technologies, falling electricity prices expose China's nuclear plants to a growing risk of commercial failure as producers of thermal and renewable power explore cost reduction options that are simply not available to nuclear operators. As the share of electricity sales transacted at negotiated market prices continues to increase, "economics has become the soft underbelly of nuclear electricity" (Zhu Xuerui 2017d).

The nuclear sector is not exempt from economy-wide patterns of inefficiency that seem particularly acute in industries dominated by state-controlled enterprises like CNNC, CGN, and SPI. The current ᴏᴦɢᴀɴɪᴢᴀᴛɪᴏɴᴀl ᴎᴛʀᴜᴄᴛᴜʀᴇ ᴄᴜffᴇʀꜱ from the rigidities associated with the inefficiency and corruption that pervade state-controlled industry, and from the Chinese system's inherent bias against new, small-scale and privately owned firms.

Limited experience with the best design tools and lack of tooling innovations represent possible obstacles to incremental improvements and especially to frontier innovation prospects. China's promising foray into overseas nuclear markets could stumble into negative "Country of Origin" effects (the extent to which buyer perceptions and purchasing decisions are influenced by broader perceptions about the seller's home country) or encounter obstacles associated with the complex intergovernmental relationships that lubricate commercial nuclear transactions. Integration of local labor and locally produced components into nuclear projects, an area in which firms like Westinghouse and Areva have accumulated vast experience, may pose unforeseen difficulties for Chinese nuclear firms.

Finally, and perhaps most worrisome, is the continued prominence in China of the exact circumstances responsible for recent nuclear mishaps in Japan and Korea: intimate and opaque government-business ties, limited media pressure for disclosure of unwelcome realities, and considerable levels of corruption. Adding the further ingredient of intense official pressure to achieve ambitious import replacement targets creates a potentially explosive combination that could quickly derail China's promising nuclear prospects.

References

Note: Authors of Chinese-language materials are named in the Chinese fashion, with the surname capitalized – thus CHEN Yinying.

Annual Meeting. 2014. 中国核电技术装备产业联盟在京召开2014年年会 [China Nuclear Energy International Development Alliance Holds 2014 Annual Meeting in Beijing]. April 8, 2014. www.gov.cn/xinwen/2014–04/08/con tent_2654683.htm (accessed May 19, 2018).

Areva 2007. "China: AREVA and CGNPC sign the biggest contract ever in the history of nuclear power and enter into a long-term commitment. AREVA and CNNC strengthen their links." www.areva.com/EN/news-6508/china-areva-and-cgnpc-sign-the-biggest-contract-ever-in-the-history-of-nuclear-power-and-enter-into-a-longterm-commitment-areva-and-cnnc-strengthen-their-links.html (accessed July 12, 2016).

Argentina. 2017. "Argentina and China sign contract for two reactors." *World Nuclear News.* May 18, 2017.

Baosteel. 2016. "国内五十八家涉核单位共聚一堂为实现中国核电"走出去"建言献策" [Fifty-eight domestic nuclear-related units gather to suggest ways to facilitate implementation of overseas ventures in nuclear power]. June 2, 2016. www.cnlc .org.cn/site951/nypd/2016–06-02/823896.shtml (accessed August 2, 2016).

Baoyin 2017. 第五届（2017）中国能源装备领军企业 [Fifth selection of China's pace-setting energy equipment enterprises]. 中国能源报 [China Energy Report]. September 25, 2017. p. 9.

Brandt, Loren, Thomas G. Rawski, and John Sutton. 2008. "China's Industrial Development." In Loren Brandt and Thomas G. Rawski eds., *China's Great Economic Transformation*. Cambridge and New York: Cambridge University Press. pp. 569–632.

Brandt, Loren and Eric Thun. 2010. "The Fight for the Middle: Upgrading, Competition, and Industrial Development in China." *World Development*. 38(11). pp. 1555–74.

——— 2016. "Constructing a Ladder for Growth: Policy, Markets and Industrial Upgrading in China." *World Development*. 80. pp. 78–95.

Brooks, S. G. 2005. *Producing Security: Multinational Corporations, Globalization, and the Changing Calculus of Conflict*. Princeton: Princeton University Press.

Brosshard, P. 2014. "China's global dam builder at a crossroads." December 15, 2014. www.internationalrivers.org/blogs/227/china%E2%80%99s-global-dam-builder-at-a-crossroads (accessed September 12, 2016).

Caijing. 2014. "你们什么都可以问"——专访中电投总经理陆启洲 ["You can ask anything" – special interview with China Power Investment Corp. General Manager Lu Qizhou]. 财经 [Finance and Economics] June 16, 2014. http://maga zine.caijing.com.cn/20140616/3570343.shtml (accessed August 29, 2017).

CGN Dividend Report. 2018. 业绩会直击：中广核电力接近4%的股息率，未来还会继续增长 [Performance will strike: CGN's dividend approaches 4%, future increases will continue]. March 12, 2018. http://cj.sina.com.cn/articles/view/ 5115326071/130e5ae77020004esb?cre=tianyi&mod=pcpager_fin&loc=16&r=9& doct=0&rfunc=100&tj=none™9 (accessed May 14, 2018).

Chaudhury, Dipanjan Roy. 2017. "India, Russia Sign 3 Contracts on Kundankulam." *The Economic Times*. August 1, 2017. http://economictimes.indiatimes.com/indus try/energy/power/india-russia-sign-3-contracts-on-kundankulam/articleshow/ 59867215.cms (accessed August 26, 2017).

Chazan, Guy and James Wilson. 2014. "Shell to buy more shale kit from China to cut US costs." *Financial Times*. April 5–6, 2014. p. 9.

Chen, Stephen. 2017. "America's Hidden Role in Chinese Weapons Research." *South China Morning Post*. March 29, 2017. www.scmp.com/news/china/diplomacy-defence/article/2082738/americas-hidden-role-chinese-weapons-research (accessed March 29, 2017).

CHEN Yinying 陈吟颖. 2016. 煤电上网标杆电价下调影响几何 [Geometry of Impact from Reducing the Benchmark Price for Coal-fired Thermal Power]. 中国能源报 [China Energy Report]. April 18, 2016. p. 5.

CHENG Sisi 成思思. 2014. 高端核电用钢需加快国产化步伐 [Accelerate the Localization of High-end Steel for the Nuclear Power Sector]. 中国能源报 [China Energy Report]. September 22, 2014. p. 20.

China Daily. 2016. "China's new nuclear power plant installs key component." www
.chinadaily.com.cn/bizchina/2016–03/21/content_23992392.htm (accessed
September 25, 2016).

China Electricity Council. 2014. 中国核电技术装备"走出去"产业联盟成立 [China
Nuclear Energy International Development Alliance established]. February 7, 2014.
www.cec.org.cn/yaowenkuaidi/2014–02-07/116390.html (accessed May 19, 2018).

China Electricity Council. 2016. 中电联发布《2016年度全国电力供需形势分析预
测报告》[China Electricity Council issues report analyzing projected 2016
nationwide electricity supply and demand]. February 3, 2016. www.cec.org.cn/
yaowenkuaidi/2016–02-03/148763.html (accessed March 13, 2016).

——— 2017. 中电联发布《2016-2017年度全国电力供需形势分析预测报告》 [China
Electricity Council report analyzing 2016–2017 nationwide electricity supply
and demand]. January 25, 2017. www.cec.org.cn/yaowenkuaidi/2017–01-25/
164285.html (accessed February 19, 2017).

China Open. 2007. "SNPTC: China still open to French, Russian 3rd-generation N-
power technologies." Xinhua English. October 28, 2007. http://english.sina.com/
china/1/2007/1028/129750.html (accessed July 12, 2016).

Christensen, Clayton M. 1997. *The Innovator's Dilemma: When New Technologies
Cause Great Firms to Fail*. Boston, MA: Harvard Business School Press.

Christensen, Clayton M., Scott D. Anthony, and Erik A. Roth. 2004. *Seeing What's Next:
Using the Theories of Innovation to Predict Industry Change*. Boston, MA: Harvard
Business School Press.

CICC. 2015. 中金公司 [CICC Capital]. 中广核电力 [Security research report: China
General Nuclear Electricity]. January 21, 2015.

Clusters. 2015. 核电产业集群发展正处上升期 [Development of Nuclear Industry
Clusters on the Rise]. Posted March 23, 2015. www.ns.org.cn/c/cn/news/2015–
03/23/news_1781.html (accessed September 6, 2016).

CNNC Report. 2018. 中国核电年报及一季报点评 [China National Nuclear annual
report and first quarter update]. May 8, 2018. http://power.in-en.com/html/
power-2289756.shtml (accessed May 10, 2018).

COSINE. 2015. "China's First Set of Nuclear Power Design and Safety Analysis
Software with Fully Independent IPRs Released." December 22, 2015. www
.snptc.com.cn/en/xwzx/hdyw/201512/t20151222_3406.html (accessed August 29,
2017).

Construction Training. 2011. "The World's First International Construction Training
Center on Nuclear Power Established in CNEC." www.cni23.com/eng/show.asp?
cataid=A00470001&id=851 (accessed August 28, 2016)

Cost Reduction. 2018. 关于做好2018年降成本重点工作的通知 [Notice on important
provisions for cost reduction in 2018]. NDRC item 634. April 28, 2018. www.ndrc
.gov.cn/zcfb/zcfbtz/201805/t20180509_885791.html (accessed May 15, 2018).

Diplomat. 2014. "Why China Will Go All-In on Nuclear Power." http://thediplomat
.com/2014/10/why-china-will-go-all-in-on-nuclear-power/ (accessed September
25, 2017).

DU Mingli 杜明例. 2018. 周人地回应：如何看待政府工作报告中的"大力化解煤电过剩产能"？[How to view to the Government Work Report's call to "vigorously resolve excess coal power capacity"? Zhou Dadi's response]. 中国电力新闻网 March 6, 2018. www.china5e.com/news/news-1022415–1.html (accessed March 12, 2018).

Economist 2013. "Digging for Victory." December 21, 2013. p. 110.

Equipment Report. 2016. 中国装备制造业发展报告2016 [2016 Development Report on Equipment Manufacturing]. Beijing: Shehui kexue wenxian chubanshe.

Experimental Reactors. 2017. "Experts head to Beijing to test experimental nuclear reactors." *Bloomberg News*. September 24, 2017.

Fagaiwei. 2015. 发改委：降低燃煤发电上网电价和工商业销售电价 [National Development and Reform Commission to Lower On-grid Price for Coal-fired Thermal Electricity as well as Retail Prices for Industrial and Commercial Power Users]. December 30, 2015. http://china.huanqiu.com/article/2015-12/8286837 .html (accessed January 22, 2016).

FAN Bi 范必. 2011. "合理把握核电发展的规模和节奏" [Reasonably grasp the scale and pace of nuclear power development]. Originally published in 瞭望新闻周刊. January 2011. http://news.sina.com.cn/c/sd/2011–01–10/092421789094.shtml (accessed August 26, 2016).

First AP1000 Vessel. 2014. "China Produces First AP1000 vessel." World Nuclear News. June 11, 2014.

First Half Power Market. 2018. 2017年上半年全国电力市场交易数据 [National electricity market transaction data for the first half of 2017]. August 30, 2018. www .chinapower.com.cn/bigdataNew/20170830/89142.html (accessed May 14, 2018).

Gen III Overview. 2017. 第三代核技术AP1000 入华十年 [Ten years of Gen III AP1000 technology in China]. August 21, 2017. www.china5e.com/news/news-999225–1.html (accessed August 21, 2017).

Generation IV International Forum (GIF). 2014. Technology Roadmap Update for Generation IV Nuclear Energy Systems. www.gen-4.org/gif/upload/docs/applica tion/pdf/2014–03/gif-tru2014.pdf (accessed September 25, 2017).

Gesheng. 2015. 各省电价调整表 [Provincial Electricity Price Adjustment Table]. April 22, 2015. http://news.bjx.com.cn/html/20150422/610893.shtml (accessed June 9, 2016).

Gholz, Eugene. 2007. "Globalization, Systems Integration, and the Future of Great Power War." *Security Studies*. 16(4). pp. 615–36.

GUO Feng 郭丰. 2016. 绿色电力投资≠绿色电力消费 [Green energy investment does not mean green energy consumption]. 中国能源报 [China Energy Report]. August 1, 2016. p. 4.

Guangdong Contracts. 2017. 核电广东首战, 长协降价7分：这是核电最聪明的选择 [Guangdong's first nuclear power battle: long-term agreements cut prices by RMB .07 – the smartest choice for nuclear producers]. November 4, 2017. www.in-en .com/article/html/energy-2263713.shtml (accessed May 9, 2018).

Hobday, Michael, Andrew Davies, and Andrea Prencipe. 2005. "Systems Integration: a Core Capability Of The Modern Corporation." *Industrial and Corporate Change.* 14(6). pp. 1109–43.

HU Qing 胡清. 2016. 国产装备如何杜绝质量瑕疵 [How to eliminate quality defects in Chinese-made equipment]. 中国能源报 [China Energy Report]. July 11, 2016. p. 20.

Hua, Wen. 2016a. "China parliament delegates call for baseload operation of nuclear power." *Platt's Nucleonics Week.* 57(11). p. 1.

2016b. "China nuclear firms' profit growth to slow: brokers." *Platt's Nucleonics Week.* 57(23). p. 1.

Hualong-1 Review. 2014. "Independent Gen-III Hualong-1 reactor technology passes national review." August 22, 2014. http://en.cgnpc.com.cn/n1305391/n1305404/c1028119/content.html (accessed August 26, 2017).

IAEA Team. 2010. "IAEA team reviews Chinese regulatory system." *World Nuclear News.* August 2, 2010. www.world-nuclear-news.org/RS-IAEA_team_reviews_Chinese_regulatory_system-0208104.html (accessed August 26, 2017).

IAEA Visit. 2016. "Chinese regulatory system must keep up with growth, says IAEA." September 8, 2016. www.world-nuclear-news.org/RS-Chinese-regulatory-system-must-keep-up-with-growth-says-IAEA-0809164.html (accessed September 13, 2016).

International Trade Administration. 2015. "2015 top markets report: Civil nuclear." http://trade.gov/topmarkets/pdf/Civil_Nuclear_Top_Markets_Report.pdf (accessed April 26, 2016).

Jian Jingwen 简靖文. 2015a. "Preparation and Progress of China Nuclear Power Mid- and Long-term Development Plan." Presentation at International Nuclear Atlantic Conference. www.aben.com.br/Arquivos/403/403.pdf (accessed May 19, 2018).

Jian Jingwen 简靖文. 2015b. "Nuclear Power Industry Cooperation." Presentation slides. October 6, 2015. www.aben.com.br/Arquivos/363/363.pdf (accessed May 19, 2018).

Kadak. (Undated). "Nuclear power: "Made in China." http://web.mit.edu/pebble-bed/papers1_files/Made%20in%20China.pdf (accessed April 26, 2016).

Kiamehr, Mehdi, Michael Hobday, and Ali Kermanshah. 2014. "Latecomer systems integration capability in complex capital goods: the case of Iran's electricity generation systems." *Industrial and Corporate Change.* 23(3). pp. 689–716.

Leaders. 2017. 第五届（2017）中国能源装备领军企业 [The Fifth Cohort of China's Energy Equipment Leaders]. 中国能源报 [China Energy Report]. September 25, 2017. p. 9

Lewis, John W. and Litai Xue. 1988. *China Builds the Bomb.* Stanford, CA: Stanford University Press.

Li Beiling 李北陵. 2016. 控制火电盲目增长应成共识 [We need a Consensus to Control Blind Increases in Thermal Power Investment]. 中国能源报 [China Energy Report]. January 4, 2016. p. 5.

LI Jun 李俊. 2013. 双相小锈钢S32101生产工艺研究 [Research on S32101 Duplex Stainless Steel production technique]. 山西冶金 [Shanxi Metallurgy]. No. 146. www.doczj.com/doc/9dba4cf1b9d528ea80c77963.html (accessed September 15, 2016).

LI Mingguang 李明光。2017. 福建第一批53家售电公司公示 核电大省售电市场怎么样? [Fujian's first batch of fifty-three power sales companies explain how a big nuclear province markets its electricity]. December 19, 2017. http://mp.163.com/v2/article/detail/D610N2VO0511E624.html (accessed May 9, 2018).

Li, Qiyan. 2008. "U.S. Technology Picked for Nuclear Plants." September 11, 2008. http://english.caijing.com.cn/2008–09-11/110011665.html (accessed August 30, 2016).

LI Ye 李冶. 2017. 能源技术装备发展是改革的重要内容 [Developing technology for energy equipment is a major element of the revolution]. 中国能源报 [China Energy Report]. September 25, 2017. p. 4.

LIU Jia 刘佳. 2014. 中国从未发生过2级及以上核事件 [China has never had a nuclear occurrence at or above Level 2. 南方都市报 [Southern City News], October 28, 2014. http://epaper.oeeee.com/epaper/A/html/2014–10/28/content_3334221.htm?div=-1 (accessed February 12, 2017).

Localization. 2014. "中国核电自主化装备制造完成'十年 生聚'" [China's localization of equipment manufacture for nuclear power completes a decade of "joint study"]. 瞭望新闻周刊 [Outlook Weekly]. December 26, 2014. www.legaldaily.com.cn/Civil-military-integration/content/2014–12/26/content_5903562.htm (accessed July 31, 2016).

2016. 政府行业协会高度重视国产化 [Government and Industry Association Attach Great Importance to Localization]. 中国能源报 [China Energy Report]. July 11, 2016. p. 8.

LU Bin 卢彬. 2016. 华龙一号：创新打造强国重器 [Dragon 1: Innovation to Build National Power]. 中国能源报 [China Energy Report]. June 6, 2016. p. 12.

2018. 电力行业三年"让利"近7000亿 [Three years' yield in the electricity industry: nearly RMB 700 billion]. 中国能源报 [China Energy Report]. April 16, 2018. p. 2.

LU Qixiu 卢奇秀 and DONG Xin 董欣. 2018. 希望国家尽快核准核电新项目（代表委员面对面）– 访全国政协委员、中核集团董事长王寿君 [Hoping for rapid state approval of new nuclear power projects – interview with CNNC Board Chairman and member of the Chinese People's Political Consultative Conference Wang Shoujun]. 中国能源报 [China Energy Report]. March 12, 2018. p. 5.

LU Yinling 吕银玲. 2018. 抢抓机遇加快三代核电发展 [Seize opportunities to develop Generation III nuclear power]. 中国能源报 [China Energy Report]. April 9, 2018. p. 12.

MA Zhe 马喆. 2013. 核电产业链升级正当时 [Now is the Time to Upgrade the Supply Chain for Nuclear Power]. 中国能源报 [China Energy Report]. April 29, 2013. p. 21.

Martin, Richard. 2016. "Fail-safe nuclear power." MIT Technology Review. www.technologyreview.com/s/602051/fail-safe-nuclear-power/ (accessed September 25, 2017).

Merchant, Emma Foehringer. 2017. "Georgia Power CEO: Completing Vogtle Reactors Is the 'Best Economic Choice'." November 7, 2017. www.greentechmedia.com/articles/read/georgia-power-vogtle-nuclear-plant-hearings#gs.LaDSnQs (accessed May 19, 2018).

MOU Sinan 牟思南. 2017. [CAP1400国核示范项目汽轮机取得重大突破 [Major turbine breakthrough for CAP1400 demonstration project]. 中国能源报 [China Energy Report]. July 10, 2017. p. 20.

MOU Sinan 牟思南 and HU Qing 胡清. 2016a. 产品质量 提升中国品牌 [Product Quality Raises the China Brand]. 中国能源报 [China Energy Report]. August 1, 2016. p. 20.

2016b. 中国功夫锻造核电大动脉 [China's Effort to Forge the Aorta of Nuclear Power Plants]. 中国能源报 [China Energy Report]. September 12, 2016. p. 20.

Nakano, Jane. 2013. "The United States and China: Making Nuclear Energy Safer." Washington, DC: Brookings.

NESTOR. 2015. "China unveils software for independent nuclear power technology." http://news.xinhuanet.com/english/2015–12/17/c_134927721.htm (accessed August 29, 2017).

New York Times. 2016. "U.S. acts to spur development of high-tech reactors." www.nytimes.com/2016/01/20/science/advanced-nuclear-reactors-department-of-energy.html?_r=0 (accessed September 25, 2017).

NDRC. 2015. 国家发展改革委关于降低燃煤发电上网电价和一般工商业用电价格的通知 [National Development and Reform Commission Notice on lowering the on-grid electricity price for coal-fired generation and lowering the user price for general industry and commerce]. December 27, 2015. www.ndrc.gov.cn/zwfwzx/zfdj/jggg/201512/t20151230_769630.html (accessed October 9, 2017).

2018. 发改委：推进电价市场化改革 2017年全年降低企业用电成本约1000亿元！ [NDRC says that 2017 advances in reforms to marketize electricity prices lowered enterprises power bills by RMB 100 billion!]. April 25, 2018. http://power.in-en.com/html/power-2289329.shtml (accessed May 8, 2018).

Nguyen, Tom and Ivy Wong. 2013. "China's nuclear industry." Informal presentation, University of Pittsburgh. August 15, 2013.

NNSA Briefing. 2015. 关于2015年度上半年核电厂建造和调试质量事件与问题的通报 [Briefing on quality events and problems in the construction and commissioning of nuclear power plants during the first half of 2015]. August 16, 2015. http://nnsa.mep.gov.cn/ywdh/ywjyfk/201508/t20150814_308166.html (accessed July 31, 2016).

2016. 关于2015年度下半年核电厂建造和调试质量事件与问题的通报 [Briefing on quality events and problems in the construction and commissioning of nuclear power plants during the second half of 2015]. April 25, 2016. http://nnsa.mep.gov.cn/ywdh/ywjyfk/201604/t20160425_336694.html (accessed July 31, 2016).

NPP Valves. 2016a. 核电泵阀制造企业质量承诺书（原文）[Nuclear valve manufacturers' original quality commitment documents]. 中国能源报 [China Energy Report]. July 11, 2016. p. 8.

2016b. 核电泵阀主要企业庄严承诺 [Solemn commitments of the major nuclear valve manufacturers]. 中国能源报 [China Energy Report]. July 11, 2016. p. 9.

Nuclear Issues. 2017. 核电消纳难题仍待解 设备利用率跌破 80% [Nuclear power absorption issue awaits resolution; operating rates drop below 80%]. February 24, 2017. www.china5e.com/news/news-979164–1.html (accessed February 26, 2017).

Nuclear Laws. 2009. 核电相关法律法规汇编 [Compendium of Laws and Regulations Related to Nuclear Electricity]. 2 vols. Beijing: Falv chubanshe.

Nuclear Plan. 2007. 核电中长期发展规划(2005–2020年) [Medium- and Long-Term Nuclear Power Development Plan (2005–2020)]. www.chinanews.com/gn/news/2007/11–04/1067944.shtml (accessed July 12, 2016).

Nuclear Safety. 2015. [Undated document evidently posted in 2015]. 优化监管体系 开创核与辐射安全监管新局 [Improve the regulatory system to create a new situation in nuclear and radiation safety supervision]. www.shhdb.gov.cn/hdaq/656019.htm (accessed August 2, 2016).

Nuclear Safety Law. 2016. "China drafts nuclear safety law." January 27, 2016. http://news.xinhuanet.com/english/2016–01/27/c_135049500.htm (accessed July 16, 2016).

OECD Nuclear Energy Agency. 2000. *Reduction of Capital Costs of Nuclear Power Plants*. Paris: OECD.

OUYANG Kai 欧阳凯. 2017. 三大核电董事长再联名提案：建设跨区电网通道消纳核电 [Board Chairmen of 3 big nuclear companies jointly propose construction of trans-regional power links to distribute nuclear electricity]. March 8, 2017. www.nbd.com.cn/articles/2017–03-08/1082581.html (accessed August 27, 2017).

Oyler, Stephen. 2014. "Nuclear Skills and Resources." MBA Study Report, University of Pittsburgh.

Pandza, Jasper. 2013. "China's nuclear power cycle and proliferation risks." *Survival*. 55 (4). pp. 177–90.

Patel, Tara and Benjamin Haas. 2014. "Nuclear Regulators 'Overwhelmed' as China Races to Launch World's Most Powerful Reactor." June 19, 2014. www.bloomberg.com/news/2014–06-18/french-nuclear-regulator-says-china-cooperation-lacking.html?utm_source=The+Sinocism+China+Newsletter&utm_campaign=72043d04cc-Sinocism06_20_14&utm_medium=email&utm_term=0_171f237867-72043d04cc-29602929&mc_cid=72043d04cc&mc_eid=05464ef5ec (accessed June 25, 2014).

PING Fan 平凡. 2015. 发改委：降低燃煤发电上网电价和工商业销售电价 [National Development and Reform Commission: Reduce the on-grid price for coal-fired power and lower the retail price for industry and commerce]. December 30, 2015. http://news.sohu.com/20151230/n433011774.shtml (accessed June 14, 2016).

Power Market. 2018. 苏、粤、鲁三大电力市场较量 [Sales volume in 3 big power markets: Jiangsu, Guangdong and Shandong]. May 17, 2018. www.china5e.com/news/news-1029238–1.html (accessed May 18, 2018).

Power Yearbook. 2009. 中国电力年鉴 2009. [China Electric Power Yearbook 2009]. Beijing: Zhongguo dianli chubanshe.

Price Notification. 2017. 2016年度全国电力价格情况监管通报 [National electricity price regulatory notification for 2016]. December 29, 2017. http://m.in-en.com/21-0-2264652–1.html# (accessed March 31, 2018).

RAP. 2016. The Regulatory Assistance Project 中国上网电价机制改革研究 [Research on reforming China's system of on-grid electricity pricing]. Beijing: Author.

Reuters. 2014. "China's new nuclear technology not yet fully up to standard, energy official says." December 5, 2014. www.scmp.com/news/china/article/1655799/new-nuclear-tech-not-yet-fully-standard-china-energy-official-says?utm_source=The+Sinocism+China+Newsletter&utm_campaign=4dbc7fb73a-Sinocism12_05_1412_5_2014&utm_medium=email&utm_term=0_171f237867-4dbc7fb73a-29602929&mc_cid=4dbc7fb73a&mc_eid=05464ef5ec (accessed December 4, 2014).

2017a. "China nuclear firm urges more homegrown reactors to cut costs." April 27, 2017. www.reuters.com/article/china-nuclear-idUSL4N1HZ7V3 (accessed August 28, 2017).

2017b. "South Africa to sign new nuclear power pacts after court ruling." May 13, 2017. www.reuters.com/article/us-safrica-nuclearpower-idUSKBN18906I (accessed August 28, 2017)

SASAC. 2016. 国资委研究局称半数央企平均资产负债率超过 65% [SASAC Research Office Reports Half of Central State Enterprises With Debt-Asset Ratios Above 65%]. June 24, 2016. http://gggs.yqylf.com/bqlz/17296.html (accessed July 30, 2016).

Shanghai Electric. 2014. 关于印发《上海电气核电设备有限公司核安全机械设备制造活动专项检查报告》的通知 2014–10–27 [October 27 announcement regarding issuance of 'Investigation report on nuclear safety in equipment production operations at Shanghai Electric Nuclear Equipment Company']. http://nro.mep.gov.cn/haq/jxjd/201410/t20141027_290726.htm (accessed July 31, 2016).

SHAO Yong 邵勇. 2016. 国内核电设备制造业质量管理分析与对策 [Analysis and countermeasures regarding quality control in domestic nuclear equipment manufacturers]. 质量探索 [Quality Dialogue]. No. 3. pp. 55–6.

Siddiqui, Sabena. 2017. "Third-gen Chinese nuclear technology arrives in Karachi." *Asia Times*. June 23, 2017. www.atimes.com/third-gen-chinese-nuclear-technology-arrives-karachi/ (accessed August 29, 2017).

SOE Corruption. 2015. "China's top graft-buster warns of corruption in state enterprises." July 14, 2015. http://news.xinhuanet.com/english/2015–07/14/c_134411175.htm (accessed August 28, 2017).

South Africa. 2014. 国家核电与南非核能集团、中国工商银行、南非标准银行签合作协议 [Cooperation agreement signed by CNNC, South African Nuclear Energy Corporation, Industrial & Commercial Bank of China and South Africa's Standard Bank Group]. December 5, 2014. http://news.xinhuanet.com/energy/2014–12/05/c_127280786.htm (accessed December 13, 2014)

South China Morning Post. 2014. "China plans to be world leader in nuclear power by 2020." www.scmp.com/news/china/article/1591984/china-plans-be-world-leader-nuclear-power-2020 (accessed April 27, 2016).

State Council Information Office. 2016. China's Nuclear Emergency Preparedness (English language text). January 27, 2016. http://english.cri.cn/12394/2016/01/27/4201s914768.htm (accessed February 2, 2016).

Sutton, John. 1998. *Technology and Market Structure: Theory and History*. Cambridge MA: MIT Press

TAN Gan 覃乾 2012. 国产核电安全几何？[How safe is China-made nuclear power?] 中国新时代 [*Zhongguo xinshidai*] #174 (August).

Ueno, T., M. Yanagi, and J. Nakano. 2014. "Quantifying Chinese public financing for foreign coal power plants." University of Tokyo Graduate School of Public Policy Discussion Paper GraSPP-DP-E-14–003.

Vasagar, Jeevan. 2016. "China train maker 'deeply saddened' by order defects." *Financial Times*. July 9–10, 2016. p. 11.

WNA World Nuclear Association. 2017. "Nuclear Power in Russia." www.world-nuclear.org/information-library/country-profiles/countries-o-s/russia-nuclear-power.aspx (accessed August 26, 2017).

WANG Lu 王璐. 2012. 中国创造"的自主化核电技术路线图 [Made in China maps the route to domestication of nuclear power technology]. www.sasac.gov.cn/n1180/n1271/n20515/n2697190/14685810.html (accessed March 10, 2014).

WANG Yi 王毅. 2011. 核电发展要具前瞻性 核安全的监管需要独立性 [Nuclear power development forward-looking with independent safety regulation]. http://finance.jrj.com.cn/people/2011/03/1501179447316.shtml (accessed January 1, 2015).

WANG Zhiming 王志明, MA Peifeng 马培锋, and MA Xiaoyu 马小瑜. 2012. 核电设备供应商评价体系的研究与应用. [Research and application of evaluation system for suppliers of nuclear power equipment]. 价值工程 [Value Engineering] #27. p. 15.

Weinberg, Alvin M. 1992. *Nuclear Reactions: Science and Trans-science*. New York: American Institute of Physics.

World Nuclear Association. 2016. "Nuclear power in China." www.world-nuclear.org/information-library/country-profiles/countries-a-f/china-nuclear-power.aspx (accessed April 26, 2016).

Wu, Jiao and Chunyan Zhang. 2015. "China, UK, sign landmark deals." October 22, 2015. www.chinadaily.com.cn/world/2015xivisituk/2015–10/22/content_22249027.htm (accessed April 27, 2016).

XIAO Jianwei 肖健维. 2015. "十三五"期间核电电价趋势分析" [Analysis of Price Trends for Nuclear Power under the 13th Five Year Plan]. 新经济 [New Economy], No 2. p. 43.

XIE Wenquan 谢文川. 2016. 我国自主核电技术推升核电装备水平 [Chinese Nuclear Technology Raises the Level of Nuclear Power Equipment]. September 5, 2016.

XU Honglin 徐鸿麟 and FANG Xudong 方旭东. 2010. 太钢双不锈钢坯的试制 [Taiyuan Steel Trial Production of Stainless Steel Billets]. 轧钢 [Steel Rolling] 27.5: 68. www.wendangku.net/doc/2305b5667fd5360cba1adbbe.html (accessed September 15, 2016).

Xu, Mi. 2007. "PWR-FBR with closed fuel cycle for a sustainable nuclear energy supply in China." Frontiers of Energy and Power Engineering in China 1.2: 129–134. http://link.springer.com/article/10.1007/s11708-007-0016-8?no-access=true (accessed May 15, 2016).

Xu, Yi-chong. 2010. *The Politics of Nuclear Energy in China.* Houndmills, Basingstoke, and New York: Palgrave Macmillan.

YU Chunping 余春平. 2015. 正视煤电科学发展面临的挑战 [Facing the challenge of scientific development for coal-fired thermal power]. 中国能源报 [China Energy Report]. January 12, 2015. p. 15.

YU Haijiang. 于海江. 2017. 我国三代核电装备制造能力成熟 [China's capacity to manufacture Gen III nuclear power equipment has matured]. June 8, 2017. www.china5e.com/news/news-990595-1.html (accessed June 13, 2017).

YU Menglin 于孟林. 2012. 煤炭物流高成本有望缓解 [High Cost of Shipping Coal May Ease]. 中国能源报 [China Energy Report]. April 2, 2012. p. 17.

ZHANG Tingke 张廷克. 2018. 抢抓机遇加快三代核电发展 [Seize opportunities to accelerate the development of third-generation nuclear power]. 中国能源报 [China Energy Report]. April 4, 2018. p. 4.

ZHANG Zirui 张子瑞. 2017. 问计清洁能源消纳难 [Problems in absorbing clean energy]. 中国能源报 [China Energy Report]. March 13, 2017. p. 2.

ZHENG Yuhui 郑玉辉 and CHEN Rong 陈荣. 2016. 中国核电经济竞争力遇挑战 [China's nuclear power faces the challenge of economic competitiveness]. 中国能源报 [China Energy Report]. March 21, 2016. p. 12.

ZHONG Yinyan 钟银燕 and QU Peiran 渠沛然. 2017 尽快启动华龙机组批量建设 [Speed up batch construction of Hualong reactors]. 中国能源报 [China Energy Report]. March 13, 2017. p. 4.

ZHONG Yinyan 钟银燕, QU Peiran 渠沛然, and ZHANG Zirui 张子瑞. 2017. 我们采访了四位核电行业的政协委员, 问了所有你关心的核电问题 [We interview four China People's Political Consultative Congress members from the nuclear sector and ask them about core issues regarding nuclear electricity]. March 15, 2017. www.sohu.com/a/128961463_468637 (accessed May 13, 2018).

ZHOU Dadi 周大地. 2017. 克服市场失效是推动能源革命的关键 [Resolving market failures is the key to promoting the energy revolution]. 中国能源报 [China Energy Report]. September 9, 2017. p. 5.

Zhou, Sheng and Xiliang Zhang. 2010. "Nuclear energy development in China: a study of opportunities and challenges." *Energy.* 35. pp. 4282–8.

Zhou, Yun, Christhian Rengifo, Peipei Chen, and Jonathan Hinze. 2011. "Is China ready for its nuclear expansion?" *Energy Policy.* 39. pp. 771–81.

Zhou, Zhanggui. 2013. "China's nuclear power safety regulations outlook." http://esi
.nus.edu.sg/docs/default-source/event/presentation-6_zhou-zhanggui.pdf?
sfvrsn=2 (accessed April 30, 2016).

ZHU Jiaqi 朱嘉琪. 2014. 大亚湾核电二十年专业化运营之路 [20 Years on the road to
specialization at Daiya Bay nuclear plant]. 中国能源报 [China Energy Report].
May 5, 2014. p. 16.

ZHU Xuerui 朱学蕊. 2014. 《原子能法》立法进程或将提速 [Accelerate the drafting
and submission of the Nuclear Energy Law]. 中国能源报 [China Energy Report].
May 5, 2014. p. 2.

2016a. 一季度三省核电遇消纳问题 [Nuclear Plants in 3 Provinces Face Demand
Problems During the First Quarter]. 中国能源报 [China Energy Report]. April 11,
2016. p. 12.

2016b. 我国成功研制世界最宽幅双相不锈钢板 [China Successfully Develops the
World's Widest Duplex Stainless Steel Sheets]. 中国能源报 [China Energy
Report]. May 2, 2016. p. 12.

2016c. 宁德核电一期：八年交出优异答卷 [Ningde Nuclear Plant Phase 1: 8 Years
of Excellence]. 中国能源报 [China Energy Report]. September 12, 2016. p. 12.

2017a. 核电"消纳症"仍待解[Nuclear power "absorption issue" still awaits resolu-
tion]. 中国能源报 [China Energy Report]. February 13, 2017. p. 12.

2017b. "华龙一号"核电标准体系加快建立 [Speed up the establishment of a system
of standards for the Hualong-1 nuclear power]. 中国能源报 [China Energy
Report]. March 13, 2017. p. 12.

2017c. 中广核：挺起腰杆 "闯"世界 [China General Nuclear: Standing up and
venturing into the world]. 中国能源报 [China Energy Report]. May 15, 2017.
p. 11.

2017d. 经济型已成核电软肋 [Economics has become the soft underbelly of nuclear
electricity]. 中国能源报 [China Energy Report]. July 10, 2017. p. 2.

2017e. 力争2020年清洁能源发电占比50% [Strive to push the share of clean electricity to 50% by 2020]. 中国能源报 [China Energy Report]. July 10, 2017. p. 12.

ZHU Xuerui 朱学蕊 and JIA Yunde 贺云德. 2016. AP1000三代核电核级锆材投料生
产 [Production of Nuclear-grade Zirconium Feedstock for Generation III Nuclear
Plants]. 中国能源报 [China Energy Report]. April 25, 2016. p. 12.

ZHU Xuerui 朱学蕊 and KONG Meirong 孔美荣. 2016.核电项目管理"直面"信息化
革命 [Nuclear project management faces the information revolution]. 中国能源
报 [China Energy Report]. August 8, 2016. p. 12.

Index